PAST INTO PRESENT

An Anthology of British and American Literature

Roger Gower

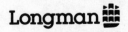

Longman Group UK Limited,
Longman House, Burnt Mill, Harlow,
Essex CM20 2JE, England
and Associated Companies throughout the world.

First published 1990

Set in Linotype Palatino

Printed in Italy
by G. Canale & C S.P.A. Turin

ISBN 0582 00992–8

British Library Cataloguing in Publication data
Gower, Roger
Past into present: readings for the classroom in
British and American literature.
1. English literature Critical studies – For schools
I. Title
820.9

Author's Acknowledgements

I am very grateful to the following for their assistance:
Giorgio De Giorgi for his comments on the material and
Ann Jennison for her suggestions about which extracts to
choose.

I would also like to acknowledge my debt to the following
books: *The Oxford Companion to English Literature*
(ed Drabble, Oxford 1985); *English Literature Made Simple*
by H. Coombes (Heinemann 1977); *The Norton Anthology
of English Literature* by W.H. Allen (W.W. Norton and
Co 1979) and in particular to the excellent *Longman
Companion to English Literature* by Christopher Gillie
(Longman 1972).

Roger Gower

Contents

UNIT 8 **Modern times**

Introduction

Texts   *Past Into Present* contains a range of literary texts in roughly chronological order from the Anglo-Saxon period to the present day. The texts come from both Britain and North America and have been chosen not only in order to illustrate some aspect of a writer's work or a trend in literary history, but also on the basis of their potential interest to foreign learners. They have occasionally been abridged (where indicated) but they have never been simplified.

Assumptions   This book is intended for readers whose reading skills are of an intermediate or advanced level of English, although sufficient help has been given in the glossaries for readers of a slightly lower level. The assumption is that users will not only be learning *about* British and American literature but will be expected to read, understand and enjoy actual texts.

Past into Present, then, is mainly intended for those classes studying literature, although many language teachers may wish to integrate the material into their lessons and provide supplementary language exercises.

It is expected that all teachers will feel free to select exercises that are suitable for their teaching situation, reject others and supplement where necessary.

Support   Integrated into each unit is support for learners in the form of language glossaries, occasional 'translations' of obscure or archaic texts, biographical information, descriptions of literary trends, definitions of technical literary terms and a general history of the period. In addition to the eight main units there is a Prologue to introduce the reading of literature and an extensive supplementary section with background information and questions, so that additional texts can be included according to the needs and interests of learners and teachers. A tape also accompanies the book containing some of the poems and extracts read by professional actors. A separate Answer Key is available for teachers who are using the book with their classes.

Methodology   Overall, the exercises aim to help learners to understand the text and can be used in a variety of circumstances: for example, in large or small classes where the teacher is the focus, in classes where much of the work is done cooperatively in pairs or groups, and in situations where learners are working by themselves.

Methodological support has been provided in the form of warm-up exercises, critical and creative writing tasks, 'learner training' exercises and games, all of which are **optional** and should only be used if teachers find them helpful. Some quite difficult literary-critical work can also be found for those classes who need it.

Teachers who wish to re-order the material thematically have available a topic map and index to assist them.

To the teacher

The Prologue The Prologue is intended to give your class a way into the reading of a foreign literature before they start work on the main part of the book. Of course, it is not necessary to use all (or indeed any) of the sections if they are not suitable, or if there is too little; however, you may find many of the exercises will help your students become more aware of the purpose of the kind of work they will be expected to do later on.

Part A (the way we read in a foreign language): This could be a discussion activity. How does reading a foreign literature differ from the way we read in our own language?

Part B (different types of comprehension): Notice that the questions on the text are in this order: immediate personal response/understanding of the gist (possibly achieved by skimming the text)/scanning for specific detail/intensive reading with work on inference and the understanding of individual words in context/looking at style/giving a more considered response/reflection on the whole procedure. By the end of this section learners should be more sensitive to the differences between their immediate response to a text and their response after careful study; between getting the general idea of a text and searching it for specific information; between understanding what is stated and understanding what is suggested indirectly.

Part C (appreciating how a writer's effects are created): This section contains an introduction to imagery and rhythm, the use of hyperbole and the effect of certain sounds in poetry. Learners are also encouraged to express preferences, giving reasons.

Part D (interpreting a dramatic text): Interpretation is shown to depend on what the dramatist suggests about character and on the use of language.

Classroom activities

1. Warm-up These activities are suggestions only. They are designed to help motivate learners by getting them involved in the theme of the text before they read it. They may be ignored or substituted by other more appropriate tasks. Remember, though, that if learners are to be expected to work with a difficult text, it is easier and more enjoyable for them if they already have some interest in its subject matter. Indeed, you may wish to think up your own tasks for *all* the texts you use in the classroom.

2. Reading the text It is often better if learners listen to a text either before they read it or at the same time. Some of the poems and extracts from plays in this book are on the accompanying tape but don't feel inhibited about reading them aloud yourself. Your voice can help towards a general understanding and encourage your students not to get bogged down in detail or language difficulties.

With the prose passages you may prefer to let the class read silently. In most circumstances, though, it is probably better not to get learners to read aloud themselves (at least not without rehearsal time): it can be boring for the rest of the class and unnecessarily difficult for the reader.

On a first reading, learners should be encouraged to get a sense of the whole. They should therefore ignore the glossary and not look up words in their dictionaries. In order to ensure that this reading is uninterrupted, you may need to reassure them that you do not expect complete understanding at this stage. It helps enormously if learners are relaxed. Some easy general comprehension work may be done afterwards but it shouldn't be too detailed or threatening.

On a second reading learners should be encouraged towards a greater understanding. Perhaps they could be expected to help each other with the difficult parts rather than ask you or look up words in a dictionary. You might also be able to help them infer (or guess) what something means by getting them to look at the context. In time, this will reduce dependence on the glossaries and make your students better readers. More detailed comprehension work may also be done.

Any further study should obviously be more detailed, making full use of glossaries and dictionaries as and when necessary. If possible, learners should be allowed to listen to or read the text as often as they like.

Overall, a fine balance has to be achieved between doing sufficient work on a text for learners' responses to be based on clear understanding, and doing so much work on it that its power and interest are lost.

3. Understanding and interpretation

Under this heading fall a variety of exercises which serve to assist comprehension both of what is stated and what is suggested. You need to decide how the answers should be completed: either orally or in writing; either as a whole class or in pairs or groups. Many make good exercises for learners to do on their own at home. You may choose to get written work which has been done by individual students checked by other students before it is referred to you.

While all the comprehension exercises could be regarded as exercises which *test* comprehension, they have been designed to *assist* comprehension and are best done when learners have access to the text. Not allowing them to refer to the text while answering questions can be threatening and demotivating.

In the main, I have assumed that comprehension work will in the first instance focus on the general (unless you are asking learners to search for specific detail) and get more intensive with subsequent readings.

To supplement the exercises in the book you may wish to encourage your students to write down their own questions when they are reading and later seek answers from other students. If so, you will need to make it clear whether these are to be genuine questions they want to know the answers to or whether they are to be ones they *do* know the answers to – in which case they could be used as a checking device for others in the class.

If possible, try to guide learners towards their own understanding of the text rather than allow yourself too often to interpret it for them.

4. Language and style

These exercises are more detailed and relate to the language used by the writer and how it achieves its effects on the reader. They focus on the more obvious features of a text so you may wish to supplement them with other exercises.

5. Appreciation

These relate closely to (and sometimes overlap with) the 'Language and style' exercises. They aim to be of assistance to those classes engaged in literary-critical study. They are often quite difficult and should be used with care.

6. Language	These exercises are intended to focus on language for language's sake, and are more useful to language classes.
7. Writing	The extended writing activities fall into two categories – creative or critical – and should be chosen according to the needs and interests of the class. Obviously, they may be set for homework and marked by the teacher. They may also be done in pairs or groups. An interesting procedure is as follows: ask learners to draft out their piece of writing and show it to other learners, who will then make suggestions as to how it might be improved. A final re-drafted version is then handed in.
8. Background	Background and biographical information is integrated into the book. Learners needing to search for help should be directed to the indexes. More biographical information is given about some writers than others; some periods of literary history are also dealt with more extensively. To make the work interesting for learners the information is sometimes included in a language exercise. (Note that the separate key available from the publishers has suggested answers.) At the end of each unit there is a section entitled Chronology containing an outline history of the period. This usually includes an exercise which might best be done in pairs or groups. It can be extended or cut out according to the needs of the class. If possible, background work should be brought to life more than is possible in a book of this sort. This can be done by, for example, class projects where learners build up a visual picture of the times or by the teacher providing a pictorial montage of a writer's life.
9. Games	These come at the end of the unit and are intended as nothing more than light relief. Don't use them if they're not appropriate. You may wish to think up your own or get your students to suggest some.

Other features

1. Glossaries	These have been constructed on the assumption that the learners' reading level in English is at an intermediate to upper-intermediate level. The definitions relate to the context and are there solely as a resource.
2. Literary terminology	All the main terms are explained and exemplified as they occur and there is an index of terms which directs readers to the appropriate place. There is also a revision exercise at the end of Unit 8.
3. Topic index	This is intended to assist those teachers who prefer to work through themes rather than in chronological sequence. Obviously, a text can have several themes and the ones selected here are suggestions only.
4. Supplement	The supplementary section consists mainly of the works of writers who do not appear in the main units, although in some cases (for example, Shakespeare and Keats) there are further examples of the work of a writer who has already been studied. The assumption is that you will integrate the material into your course if and when necessary.

Prologue

Part A: First encounters

These are the covers of some works of literature. Which ones have you heard of?
Which ones interest you?

You would like to read a good novel. Imagine you are in a bookshop and have only the following three books to choose from. You must choose one. Read the opening page of each and decide. Which one would you buy? Why?

A

chapter 1

At supper that night, as many times before, his father said, "Well, spose we go to the picture show."

"Oh, Jay!" his mother said. "That horrid little man!"

"What's wrong with him?" his father asked, not because he didn't know what she would say, but so she would say it.

"He's so *nasty!*" she said, as she always did. "So *vulgar!* With his nasty little cane; hooking up skirts and things, and that nasty little walk!"

His father laughed, as he always did, and Rufus felt that it had become rather an empty joke; but as always the laughter also cheered him; he felt that the laughter enclosed him with his father.

They walked downtown in the light of mother-of-pearl, to the Majestic, and found their way to seats by the light of the screen, in the exhilarating smell of stale tobacco, rank sweat, perfume and dirty drawers, while the piano played fast music and galloping horses raised a grandiose flag of dust. And there was William S. Hart with both guns blazing and his long, horse face and his long, hard lip, and the great country rode away behind him as wide as the world. Then he made a bashful face at a girl and his horse raised its upper lip and everybody laughed, and then the screen was filled with a city and with the sidewalk of a side street of a city, a long line of palms and there was Charlie; everyone laughed the minute they saw him squattily walking with his toes out and his knees wide apart, as if he were chafed; Rufus' father laughed, and Rufus laughed too. This time Charlie stole a whole bag of eggs and when a cop came along he hid them in the seat of his pants. Then he caught

with the
naking of

OHNSON.

I

Aᴌᴛʜᴏᴜɢʜ I am an old man, night is generally my time for walking. In the summer I often leave home early in the morning, and roam about the fields and lanes all day, or even escape for days or weeks together; but, saving in the country, I seldom go out until after dark, though, Heaven be thanked, I love its light and feel the cheerfulness it sheds upon the earth as much as any creature living.

I have fallen insensibly into this habit, both because it favours my infirmity, and because it affords me greater opportunity of speculating on the characters and occupations of those who fill the streets. The glare and hurry of broad noon are not adapted to idle pursuits like mine; a glimpse of passing faces caught by the light of a street lamp, or a shop window, is often better for my purpose than their full revelation in the daylight; and, if I must add the truth, night is kinder in this respect than day, which too often destroys an air-built castle at the moment of its completion, without the least ceremony or remorse.

That constant pacing to and fro, that never-ending restlessness, that incessant tread of feet wearing the rough stones smooth and glossy—is it not a wonder how the dwellers in narrow ways can bear to hear it! Think of a sick man, in such a place as St. Martin's Court, listening to the footsteps, and, in the midst of pain and weariness, obliged, despite himself (as though it were a task he must perform), to detect the child's step from the man's, the slipshod beggar from the booted exquisite, the lounging from the busy, the dull heel of the sauntering outcast from the quick tread of an expectant pleasure-seeker—think of the hum and noise being always present to his senses, and of the stream of life that will not stop, pouring on, on, on, through all his restless dreams, as if he were condemned to lie, dead but conscious, in a noisy churchyard, and had no hope of rest for centuries to come !

Then, the crowds for ever passing and repassing on the bridges (on those which are free of toll at least), where many stop on fine evenings looking listlessly down upon the water, with some vague idea that by and by it runs between green banks which grow wider and wider until at last it joins the broad vast sea; where some halt to rest from heavy loads, and think, as they look over the parapet, that to smoke and lounge away one's life, and lie sleeping in the sun upon a hot tarpaulin, in a dull, slow, sluggish barge,

He woke to find the room full of sunlight.

A dull pain throbbed between his eyes. His face was covered with sweat.

When he turned on his side he saw that Kay was still asleep, her face sunk down in the pillows, almost hidden.

The children, presumably, had been in to open the curtains. He could hear them crashing about in their room at the front of the house. The alarm hadn't rung yet. It was almost seven o'clock.

When he went down to the kitchen his eldest daughter, Susan, appeared on the stairs. 'Are you making some tea?' she said.

'I hope to,' he said.

Her bare feet pattered down behind him.

'Did you come in and open the curtains?' he said.

'Yes,' she said. 'I heard you call.'

'Call?'

She stood by the stove, watching him light the kettle. Her head was little higher than the ring.

'You must have been asleep,' she said.

'Yes,' he said, and added, 'What was I calling?'

'I don't know,' she said. 'I didn't hear.'

'Well,' he said, 'next time you'd better listen.'

'Yes,' she said and smiled.

He went through from the kitchen, at the back of the house, to the hall and opened the front door.

3

Think back. Ask yourself some of the following questions about your reading of the three passages:

- What were your strongest feelings? Curiosity? Excitement? Panic? Can you say why?
- Did you read slowly or quickly? Was it the same for all three passages?
- Did everything interest you? Did you read the more interesting parts more carefully?
- How much did you re-read? Every phrase?
- What did you translate into your own language?
- Did you read to get the general idea of what the extract was about or did you try to understand everything?
- What did you want to do when you came across an unfamiliar word? Ignore it? Look it up in a dictionary?
- Overall, do you read English in much the same way as you read your own language?
- Are you curious about what will happen next in the novels? Can you guess?

The novels were:

A *A Death in the Family* by James Agee (1938)
B *The Old Curiosity Shop* by Charles Dickens (1840–1841)
C *Pasmore* by David Storey (1972)

Part B: Reading and understanding

What do these pictures suggest to you? Security? Love? Danger? What can we guess about the relationship between mother and child?

The sun was going down. Every open evening, the hills of Derbyshire were blazed over with red sunset. Mrs Morel watched the sun sink from the glistening sky, leaving a soft flower-blue overhead, while the western space went red, as if all the fire had swum down there, leaving the bell cast flawless blue. The mountain-ash berries across the field stood fierily out from the dark leaves, for a moment. A few shocks of corn in a corner of the fallow stood up as if alive; she imagined them bowing; perhaps her son would be a Joseph. In the east, a mirrored sunset floated pink opposite the west's scarlet. The big haystacks on the hillside, that butted into the glare, went cold.

With Mrs Morel it was one of those still moments when the small frets vanish, and the beauty of things stands out, and she had the peace and the strength to see herself. Now and again, a swallow cut close to her. Now and again, Annie came up with a handful of alder-currants. The baby was restless on his mother's knee, clambering with his hands at the light.

Mrs Morel looked down at him. She had dreaded this baby like a catastrophe, because of her feeling for her husband. And now she felt strangely towards the infant. Her heart was heavy because of the child, almost as if it were unhealthy, or malformed. Yet it seemed quite well. But she noticed the peculiar knitting of the baby's brows, and the peculiar heaviness of its eyes, as if it were trying to understand something that was pain. She felt, when she looked at her child's dark, brooding pupils, as if a burden were on her heart.

'He looks as if he was thinking about something – quite sorrowful,' said Mrs Kirk.

Suddenly, looking at him, the heavy feeling at the mother's heart melted into passionate grief. She bowed over him, and a few tears shook swiftly out of her very heart. The baby lifted his fingers.

'My lamb!' she cried softly.

And at that moment she felt, in some far inner place of her soul, that she and her husband were guilty.

The baby was looking up at her. It had blue eyes like her own, but its look was heavy, steady, as if it had realised something that had stunned some point of its soul.

In her arms lay the delicate baby. Its deep blue eyes, always looking up at her unblinking, seemed to draw her innermost thoughts out of her. She no longer loved her husband; she had not wanted this child to come, and there it lay in her arms and pulled at her heart. She felt as if the navel string that had connected its frail little body with hers had not been broken. A wave of hot love went over her to the infant. She held it close to her face and breast. With all her force, with all her soul she would make up to it for having brought it into the world unloved. She would love it all the more now it was here; carry it in her love. Its clear, knowing eyes gave her pain and fear. Did it know all about her? When it lay under her heart, had it been listening then? Was there a reproach in the look? She felt the marrow melt in her bones, with fear and pain. 50

Once more she was aware of the sun lying red on the rim of the hill opposite. She suddenly held up the child in her hands.

'Look!' she said. 'Look, my pretty!'

She thrust the infant forward to the crimson, throbbing sun, almost with relief. She saw him lift his little fist. Then she put him 55 to her bosom again, ashamed almost of her impulse to give him back again whence he came.

'If he lives,' she thought to herself, 'what will become of him – what will he be?'

Her heart was anxious. 60

'I will call him Paul,' she said suddenly; she knew not why.

After a while she went home. A fine shadow was flung over the deep green meadow, darkening all.

(from *Sons and Lovers* by D.H. Lawrence)

i) What feelings does this scene arouse in you? Does it remind you of any incident in your own life? Is the relationship between Mrs Morel and her baby a simple one?
ii) Make sentences from the following groups of words:
   a) incident – early evening
   b) passage – description – love – baby
   c) climax – offering – sun

Searching for detail

Look through the passage again. Write down as many words/phrases as you can for each of these together with their line number in the text:

a) *colours* – say what they describe (for example, 'soft flower-blue' – 'sky' l.3)
b) *words related to light, dark, heat and cold* (for example, 'glistening' l.3)
c) *Paul: physical characteristics/feelings* (for example, 'deep blue eyes' l.38). Which also suggest a quality or a feeling (for example, 'peculiar heaviness of its eyes', l.23)?
d) *Mrs Morel's feelings described directly* (for example, 'felt strangely towards the infant' l.20)

Reading more carefully

Read the passage again, this time more carefully. These notes may help you:

In the Bible, the young Joseph, a future governor of Egypt, has a dream which is taken as a sign that he will be a king. He dreams that he and his brothers are tying up 'shocks of wheat' in a field when *his* shock stands up straight and his brothers' shocks form a circle round it and bow down.

Annie is Mrs Morel's daughter and Mrs Kirk is a neighbour.

i) What can you deduce about:
   a) Mr and Mrs Morel's relationship?
   b) the significance of the baby to Mrs Morel?
   c) Paul's character?
   d) the influence of the natural environment on Mrs Morel's feelings?

Find evidence in the text.

ii) Match the words in the left-hand column with the definitions on the right according to their meaning in the passage.

fallow (l.7)	small bird with pointed wings and double-pointed tail
glare (l.11)	expression of disapproval
dreaded (l.18)	weak
swallow (l.14)	ploughed land left unplanted
stunned (l.37)	strong light
frail (l.42)	greatly feared
reproach (l.49)	shocked

iii) What do the following words mean in context? If you don't know, can you guess?

'blazed over' (l.2)   'flawless' (l.5)   'fierily' (l.6)
'frets' (l.13)   'clambering' (l.16)   'rim' (l.51)

What helped you make your guesses? Did you consider what 'word class' the words belonged to – for example, nouns, verbs, adjectives, adverbs? Was there a word in the same sentence with a similar meaning? Was there any indication that the word had a positive or a negative connotation? Did the word associate with another word – one that you knew – and give you some idea? Was it just a question of logic?

iv) Make a list of any other word you would like to know the meaning of. Does anyone else in the class know? If not, ask your teacher or look it up in a dictionary, preferably a monolingual dictionary.

v) Figurative language is any expression used in an imaginative, non-literal way to make a picture or a comparison in the mind of the reader. What do the following expressions suggest in context: 'as if all the fire had swum down there' (l.4); 'the bell cast' (l.5); 'A wave of hot love' (l.43)?

vi) You were asked to look at the passage three times. Can you compare each experience?

The passage comes from the first of the important novels of D.H. Lawrence (1885–1930), called *Sons and Lovers* (1913). It is based on Lawrence's own early life in the Midland coal-mining village of Eastwood and on the relationship with his mother and with his father, who was a mineworker. Paul is the character who corresponds most closely to Lawrence himself and the novel is often seen as Lawrence's attempt to release himself from the problems of his own early development.

Part C: Critical appreciation

Warm-up   *Either:*
Say which of the following words have a link in meaning (for example, fire—passion).

old	gently	confession	silence
passion	cold	dreaming	apart
separate	fire	chastity	time
shadows	touching		

Or:
Sit in pairs or groups. One/some of you write ten words/phrases you associate with **'loneliness'** (for example, 'sadness', 'parks'). The other(s) write ten words/

phrases you associate with '**love**' (for example, 'promises'). Exchange lists. How would your list be different? Discuss.

Prediction   The title of the first poem is 'One Flesh' and it contains all the words above. Can you guess what it is about?

One Flesh

Lying apart now, each in a separate bed,   1
He with a book, keeping the light on late,
She like a girl dreaming of childhood,
All men elsewhere – it is as if they wait
Some new event: the book he holds unread,   5
Her eyes fixed on the shadows overhead.

Tossed up like flotsam from a former passion,
How cool they lie. They hardly ever touch,
Or if they do it is like a confession
Of having little feeling – or too much.   10
Chastity faces them, a destination
For which their whole lives were a preparation.

Strangely apart, yet strangely close together,
Silence between them like a thread to hold
And not wind in. And time itself's a feather   15
Touching them gently. Do they know they're old,
These two who are my father and my mother
Whose fire from which I came, has now grown cold?

GLOSSARY

flotsam (l.7): pieces or goods from a wrecked ship floating in the sea

---

Do you find the poem sad? Realistic? Is it more about old age or about loneliness?

Understanding and interpretation

i) Complete the following sentence:
   The narrator describes how her parents ....

ii) Which word in each stanza most relates to the theme of that stanza? (A stanza is a unit of several lines of verse.)

iii) In 1.4, what does the phrase 'All men elsewhere' suggest? Who does 'they' refer to in the same line?

iv) Which of the following is the most accurate paraphrase for the lines 'Silence (1.14) ... in' (1.15)?
   a) They can't get closer to each other because of the silence.
   b) The silence keeps them separate but connected.

Language and style

i) There are many images in the poem. 'Similes' are figures of speech – images – in which one thing is said to be like another using 'as' or 'like'. 'Metaphors' are figures of speech in which unlike objects are identified with each other (without using 'as' or 'like'). In the poem, which image most suggests
   a) useless waste? b) a fragile relationship?

ii) Do any of the ends of lines rhyme with each other? Is there a pattern?

iii) Look at each of the first two lines of the second stanza. How many syllables are there? Which words carry most stress?

iv) The poem is partly built on a series of contrasts (for example, 'he' and 'she'). Find others. Choose one and say what effect it has.

9

Listen to the second poem.

A Red, Red Rose

O My Luve's like a red, red rose,   1
   That's newly sprung in June;
O My Luve's like the melodie
   That's sweetly played in tune.

As fair art thou, my bonnie lass,   5
   So deep in luve am I;
And I will luve thee still, my dear,
   Till a' the seas gang dry.

Till a' the seas gang dry, my dear,
   And the rocks melt wi' the sun: 10
O I will love thee still, my dear,
   While the sands o' life shall run.

And fare thee weel, my only luve,
   And fare thee weel awhile!
And I will come again, my luve,   15
   Though it were ten thousand mile.

GLOSSARY

fair art thou (l.5): beautiful you are (*archaic*)

bonnie lass (l.5): pretty young lady (*Scottish expression*)

a' (l.8): all

gang (l.8): go (*Scottish*)

sands (l.12): (the sand in an hourglass which measures time)

fare thee weel (l.13): goodbye (*archaic*)

fare thee weel awhile (l.14): take care of yourself for a short time (*archaic*)

Though it were (l.16): even if I were going

What do you notice about the tone and attitude in contrast with the previous poem?

Understanding and interpretation

Match the following descriptions with stanzas in the poem:

a) The narrator says his lady is beautiful, declares his love and says it will last for ever.

b) He departs but says he will return.

c) He says his love is fresh, full and pleasing to his senses.

d) He promises to love her for ever.

Language and style

i) Which of these are suggested by the two similes in the first stanza?

   harmony   pleasure   freshness   growth   colour   energy   youth
   fullness

ii) An 'hyperbole' is a form of exaggeration in extreme language usually used to emphasise something and/or achieve intensity. What is the effect of the hyperboles related to the 'seas' and the 'rocks' in the third stanza? Are they sincere? Comic? Cynical? Is there a hint of sadness, suggesting that the narrator knows that love of that sort never lasts forever?

iii) Do you think the narrator ever will return? What does the phrase 'sands o' life' (l.12) suggest? What do the images tell you of the narrator's background?

iv) Notice that the poem is made up of many short vowel sounds in words like 'Luve', 'red', 'lass', 'deep', which help give a feeling of directness and confidence. What do you notice about the rhythm of the verse? Is it flat or bouncy? What do you notice about the rhymes?

v) Can you find a line where the word order is not the same as that of normal conversation? Does it help make the rhythm and the rhyme more musical?

10

vi) Apart from the rhythm, how is the energy of the poem conveyed? Look at the vocabulary and the imagery.

Appreciation

i) Complete the following sentences:
The first poem is .... whereas the second poem ....
I prefer the .... poem because ....

ii) Discuss any of the following that interest you. You may strongly disagree with the statements! Try to support your arguments with reference to the text.

The first poem
- The narrator makes herself sound superior to her parents.
- The language is both very clear and imprecise at the same time.

Do you think the private, depressing atmosphere is typical of our times?

The second poem
- The narrator is both good-hearted and dishonest.
- The language is simple-minded and lacking in force and originality.
- A young man couldn't write a poem like this today.

The first poem was written by the English poet Elizabeth Jennings (born in 1926). Her collected poems were published in 1967. The second poem was written by the Scottish poet Robert Burns (1759–1796) (see page 375). It was written as a song and incorporates elements from several folk songs of the day.

Part D: Character and word play

The scene is Padua, in Italy. Katharina is noisy and bad-tempered and known as 'The Shrew'. Petruchio, a gentleman from Verona, tries to win her love.

Warm-up

i) Make guesses about these characters. For example:
How will Katharina react to Petruchio's advances?
What sort of character is Petruchio?

A pun is a humorous play on a) words which have similar sounds, or b) on a word with more than one meaning.

ii) The following sentences are from the extract you are going to hear. One meaning is given. Can you think of another?

a) You are called plain Kate: *You are just called Kate*
b) For dainties are all cates: *For delicacies are always called 'cates'*

Extract 1

Katharina and Petruchio meet for the first time. Katharina does not like her name to be shortened to Kate.

GLOSSARY

morrow (l.1): morning (*archaic*)
heard (l.2): (probably pronounced 'hard')
in faith (l.4): I believe (*archaic*)

KATHARINA ***enters***

PETRUCHIO: **Good morrow, Kate – for that's your name, I hear.**
KATHARINA: **Well have you heard, but something hard of hearing;**
They call me Katharine that do talk of me.
PETRUCHIO: **You lie, in faith, for you are called plain Kate,**

bonny (l.5): handsome (possible pun on 'bony')

curst (l.5): cursed; damned

Christendom (l.6): the Christian part of the world

of Kate Hall (l.7): (from a good family)

super-dainty (l.7): very pretty and delicate

of my consolation (l.9): my comforter

sounded (l.11): celebrated; measured the depth of

so deeply (l.12): as much

in good . . . hence (l.14-15): that's quick! let the person who brought you here take you away

And bonny Kate, and sometimes Kate the curst: 5
But Kate, the prettiest Kate in Christendom,
Kate of Kate Hall, my super-dainty Kate,
For dainties are all cates, and therefore, Kate,
Take this of me, Kate of my consolation –
Hearing thy mildness praised in every town,   10
Thy virtues spoke of, and thy beauty sounded,
Yet not so deeply as to thee belongs,
Myself am moved to woo thee for my wife.
   KATHARINA: Moved! in good time! let him that moved you hither,
Remove you hence . . .   15

i) Petruchio has insulted Katharina by praising her in a false and exaggerated way. Find at least one example.

ii) Explain the pun on 'move' (l.13 -1.15). Do you find puns humorous?

Extract 2

GLOSSARY

crab (l.2): wild, sour appled (bad-tempered person)

glass (l.6): mirror (*archaic*)

by S. George (l.10): (mild oath) (*archaic*)

withered (l.11): old and dry (like an over-ripe crab apple); wrinkled

In sooth . . . so (l.15): Really, you can't escape like that

I chafe . . . tarry (l.17): I'll irritate you if I stay here any longer

a whit (l.19): a bit

passing (l.19): exceedingly (*archaic*)

coy (l.20): quiet and distant (*archaic*)

report a very liar (l.21): the rumour is untrue

gamesome (l.22): merry

askance (l.24): with a disapproving side glance

wenches (l.25): servant girls

PETRUCHIO: Nay, come, Kate, you must not look so sour.   1
KATHARINA: It is my fashion, when I see a crab.
PETRUCHIO: Why, here's no crab, and therefore look not sour.
KATHARINA: There is, there is.
PETRUCHIO: Then show it me.   5
KATHARINA: Had I a glass, I would.
PETRUCHIO: What, you mean my face?
KATHARINA: Well aimed of such a young one.
                               [*she struggles*]
PETRUCHIO: Now, by S. George, I am too young for you.   10
KATHARINA: Yet you are withered.
                        [*touches his forehead*]
PETRUCHIO [*kisses her hand*]:   'Tis with cares.
KATHARINA [*she slips from him*]:   I care not!
PETRUCHIO: Nay, hear you, Kate. In sooth, you scape not so.   15
                 [*he catches her once more*]
KATHARINA: I chafe you, if I tarry. Let me go!
    [*she struggles again, biting and scratching as he speaks*]
PETRUCHIO: No, not a whit – I find you passing gentle:
'Twas told me you were rough and coy and sullen,   20
And now I find report a very liar;
For thou art pleasant, gamesome, passing courteous,
But slow in speech; yet sweet as spring-time flowers.
Thou canst not frown, thou canst not look askance,
Nor bite the lip, as angry wenches will,   25

conference (l.28): conversation

limp (l.30): walk slowly and with difficulty

hazel-twig (l.31): small, thin branch of a type of tree bearing nuts

kernels (l.33): seeds of the nut which can be eaten

halt (l.34): walk with difficulty

whom . . . command (l.35): tell your servants what to do

Nor hast thou pleasure to be cross in talk;
But thou with mildness entertain'st thy wooers,
With gentle conference, soft and affable . . .

[he releases her]

Why does the world report that Kate doth limp?   30
O sland'rous world! Kate like the hazel-twig
Is straight and slender, and as brown in hue
As hazel-nuts and sweeter than the kernels . . .
O, let me see thee walk: thou dost not halt.
KATHARINA: Go, fool, and whom thou keep'st command.   35

(from *The Taming of the Shrew* by William Shakespeare)

What do you think of this exchange? Is it funny?

Character

i) Which of these words best describe Petruchio?

aggressive   jolly   mocking   flirtatious   insensitive   insincere

ii) Where does Katharina defend herself well? Who do you have most sympathy for in the scene?

Language and style

Find at least one example of:

a) Petruchio's irony – where he says one thing but means something else;

b) Petruchio using the words of others to insult Katharina, while pretending to praise her.

The Taming of the Shrew – 1

The extracts were from *The Taming of the Shrew* (written ?1592) by William Shakespeare (1564–1616). Hortensio, Petruchio's friend, is prevented from marrying Bianca, Katharina's sister, until a husband has been found for Katharina. As well as trying to help his friend, Petruchio is also interested in Katharina's dowry – the money and goods that will come with her on her wedding day.

Katharina eventually agrees to marry Petruchio but he continues to humiliate her until she is 'tamed'. Bianca eventually marries someone else and Hortensio marries a rich widow. Both the widow and Bianca are contemptuous of Katharina's final obedience, which is greater than their own towards their husbands.

Understanding and interpretation

The play has been interpreted in different ways. For example:

i) Petruchio is a foolish male, an exaggerated character with no moral doubts. Katharina, on the other hand, is a vital loving character, made 'shrewish' by the fools about her.

ii) Petruchio and Katharina are a vigorous couple who fall in love and join forces against their world. Their final harmonious, mutually respectful relationship contrasts with the lack of confidence the other couples have in each other.

iii) The play is a primitive, brutal farce – a play with absurd situations which are meant to make us laugh. It reveals Shakespeare's deep male prejudices and is offensive to women.

iv) The play is a comedy – an entertaining play with a happy ending. It expresses, in a genuine and exciting way, the need to express true feeling. It shows contempt for typical male attitudes and respect for women.

How do you think the play was interpreted in these productions?

The Taming of the Shrew is one of Shakespeare's early plays, although it was not published until the 1623 First Folio edition (the first collected edition of Shakespeare's plays) after his death. It was based on George Gascoigne's comedy *The Supposes* (1566), itself a translation from the Italian of Ludovico Ariosto's *Gli Suppositi* (1509).

Getting ready

Close your eyes. Imagine it is a snowy evening in New Hampshire (northeast USA) in the 1920s. You are riding through the woods in your horse and trap. You decide to stop.

Stopping by Woods on a Snowy Evening

Whose woods these are I think I know. 1
His house is in the village though;
He will not see me stopping here
To watch his woods fill up with snow.

My little horse must think it queer 5
To stop without a farmhouse near
Between the woods and frozen lake
The darkest evening of the year.

He gives his harness bells a shake
To ask if there is some mistake. 10
The only other sound's the sweep
Of easy wind and downy flake.

The woods are lovely, dark and deep,
But I have promises to keep,
And miles to go before I sleep, 15
And miles to go before I sleep.

(Robert Frost)

Do you feel ready for what literature has to offer to you?

UNIT 1

From the beginning

1.1 Old English

Warm-up

i) *Either:*

Select one of the following or write a similar statement which is true for yourself. Explain your reasons.

– I would like to have been a soldier in the days when men fought with spears and swords.
– I am a pacifist.
– In war, I think women should fight alongside men.

Or:

Discuss the following:

– Military heroism is not possible in the modern age.
– Man is by nature a warrior.

ii) How does the battle in this picture differ from a modern war?

1.1.1
Battle of Maldon
(?AD 1000)

Battle of Maldon has been called the greatest battle poem in English. It is an Anglo-Saxon (Old English) poem by an unknown poet. It describes a battle between the English and Viking warriors from Denmark in AD 991 at Maldon in Essex on the River Blackwater, then called the River Pantan.

The Danish invaders are on the island of Northey at the mouth of the river waiting for the tide to go out. Byrhtnoth, the earl of Essex, is at the head of the English warriors on the mainland. A messenger from the Danes offers peace if they pay a sum of money. Byrhtnoth, however, rejects the offer. Then the tide begins to go out and Byrhtnoth, far too confident, is tricked into letting the enemy cross to the mainland.

● Read a modern English verse translation. Then look at the first part again in the original Anglo-Saxon.

GLOSSARY

bore (l.3): carried

linden-shields (l.4): wooden shields

fast (l.7): firm

foes (l.8): enemies

perish (l.10): die

ravens wheeled (l.11): large black birds flew in circles

carrion (l.12): food (dead flesh)

uproar (l.12): loud, confused noise

file-hard (l.13): hard as a steel tool

Grimly-ground (l.14): made cruelly sharp

onslaught (l.15): fierce attack

chamberlain (l.25): chief officer

stout-hearted (l.26): brave

the slaughtered (l.30): those that were killed

steadfast (l.31): firm

stirred them on (l.31): encouraged them to fight

Bade (l.32): ordered (to)

renown (l.33): fame

The wolves of war advanced, the viking troop,   1
Unmoved by water, westward over Pante,
Over the gleaming water bore their shields.
The seamen brought their linden-shields to land.
There Byrhtnoth and his warriors stood ready   5
To meet their enemies. He told his troops
To make a shield-wall and to hold it fast
Against their foes. So battle with its glory
Drew near. The time had come for fated men
To perish in that place. A cry went up.   10
The ravens wheeled above, the fateful eagle
Keen for his carrion. On earth was uproar.
They let the file-hard spears fly from their fists,
Grimly-ground darts; and bows were busy too.
Shield received spear-point; savage was the onslaught.   15
Fighters fell dead, young men on either side.
Wulfmar was wounded. Byrhtnoth's sister's son
Chose death in battle, he was utterly
Cut down by swords. But there at once was vengeance
Paid to the vikings, for I heard that Edward   20
Struck one of them so fiercely with his sword,
Restraining not the stroke, that at his feet
The fated warrior fell to the earth.
For this his prince, as soon as he had time,
Gave grateful thanks to his bold chamberlain.   25
So the stout-hearted warriors stood firm
In battle, and the young men eagerly
Competed who might first with point of spear
Deprive a fated soldier of his life;
And all around the slaughtered fell to earth.   30
Steadfast they stood, as Byrhtnoth stirred them on
Bade every soldier concentrate on war
Who wished to win renown against the Danes.

A warlike viking soldier then advanced,
His weapon raised, his shield up in defence,
And strode towards the earl, who in return   35
Marched resolutely forth to meet the churl.
They each intended evil to the other.
The seaman hurled a Frankish javelin
So that the leader of the troops was wounded.   40
He thrust out with his shield so that the shaft
Was shattered and the spear sprang back again.
Enraged, the hero seized his spear and stabbed
The proud, rash viking who had wounded him.
No novice was the earl, he made his spear   45
Pass through the young man's neck, guided his hand
So that he pierced the pirate fatally.

(from *Battle of Maldon*)

churl (l.37): evil person (archaic)
Frankish (l.39): German
shaft was shattered (l.41): long part was completely broken
rash (l.44): without caution
novice (l.45): beginner

Anglo-Saxon (Old English)

Wōdon þa wælwulfas,   for wætere ne murnon,   1
wīcinga werod   west ofer Pantan,
ofer scīr wæter   scyldas wēgon.
lidmen tō lande   linde bǣron.
þǣr ongēan gramum   gearowe stōdon   5
Byrhtnōð mid beornum;   hē mid bordum hēt
wyrcan þone wīhagan,   and þæt werod healdan
fæste wið fēondum.   þā wæs feohte nēh,
tīr æt getohte.   Wæs sēo tīd cumen
þæt þǣr fǣge men   feallan sceoldon.   10
þǣr wearð hrēam āhafen;   hremmas wundon,
earn æses georn;   wæs on eorþan cyrm.
Hī lēton þā of folman   fēolhearde speru,
grimme gegrundene   gāras flēogan....

Byrhtnoth dies and many of his men run away. A brave few continue the fight until they too are defeated. The second half of the poem is a powerful expression of their loyalty and determination to avenge their leader's death.

Obviously, nowadays, Anglo-Saxon is a foreign language even to native English speakers. You can hear on the tape the first few lines of this extract in the original Anglo-Saxon.

● Did you like the poem? Did you find it too violent?

<table>
<tr><td>Understanding and
interpretation</td><td>i) Indicate where on this map the English warriors and the Vikings are before the battle:</td></tr>
</table>

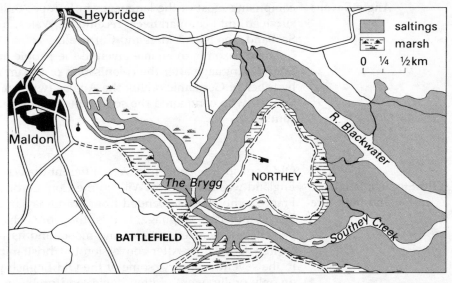

ii) Write out the following sentences, completing the gaps with as many words as you like (in some cases the first letter of a word is given)

a) The Viking seamen c.......... the water and the battle b.......... . Many

men .... Byrhtnoth .... his men to ....

b) They attacked each other with s.......... and s.......... and defended

themselves with s.......... .

c) A hostile Viking .... Byrhtnoth .... but in revenge ....

iii) The passage can be divided into five sections. Put these headings in the right order. Which lines do they refer to?

a) Avenging the death of the son of Byrhtnoth's sister
b) Battle
c) The wounding of Byrhtnoth and his revenge
d) Getting ready for battle
e) Byrhtnoth's men stand firm

iv) Which lines in particular show Byrhtnoth's qualities as a leader?

Language and style   i) What do you notice about the way the Anglo-Saxon original is laid out on the page?
ii) Can you find examples of alliteration in the Anglo-Saxon (where the same consonant sound is repeated in words close to each other)?

The original manuscript of *Battle of Maldon* (which seemed to have a few lines missing at the beginning and end) was destroyed in a fire in the eighteenth century and survives only in transcript. Nowadays, the poem is often thought of as a traditional piece of heroic propaganda in praise of ancient standards of military conduct and courage. This view, however, rather undervalues the quality of the fine verse, which is both simple and direct. In fact, it is much less ornate than other Old English poems in existence. Its movement is swift and firm and manages to convey the sense of the whole battle through a series of speeches and individual actions.

1.1.2
Celts and
Anglo-Saxons

The Celts migrated to Britain from central and western Europe about 1000 BC. Their language, belonging to the Indo-European family comprising most of the languages in Europe, India and southwest Asia, survived until comparatively recently in Wales, Ireland, northwest Scotland, the Isle of Man and Cornwall.

Anglo-Saxon is the name given to the people and sometimes the Old English language after the colonisation of Britain in the fifth century AD by tribes of Germanic origin: the Angles (who conquered the north), the Saxons (who conquered the south) and the Jutes (who conquered the southeast).

1.1.3
Old English: language
and literature

Old English was spoken in very different dialects until 1066, when England was invaded by William the Conqueror and the Normans from France, who were descended from Scandinavian adventurers. It was a heavily inflected language, that is, the words changed form to indicate person, number, tense, case, and mood, and its vocabulary was almost entirely Germanic. After conversion to Christianity became more general in the seventh century, some of the Old English poems, until then passed on only orally, were written down, and probably modified, by monks. Only about thirty thousand lines of these poems have survived.

For about five hundred years, almost all Old English verse had the following characteristics:

– each line was made up of two half-lines, separated by a caesura (a pause) and joined by alliteration;
– each half-line consisted of two 'feet' (a 'foot' contains a number of unstressed syllables and a stressed syllable);
– the alliteration linking the two half-lines fell on the stressed syllables (at least one of the main stresses in the first half-line began with the same consonant sound as the first main stress in the second half-line);
– words beginning with the same consonant had the same sound and therefore alliterated (unlike in modern English);
– a word beginning with a vowel was regarded as 'alliterating' with any other word beginning with a vowel even if that vowel sound was not the same.

Battle of Maldon, with its strong, swift verse movement, is slightly less rigid in its employment of this scheme than much other Old English verse.

● Try out the above scheme on one or two lines of either *Battle of Maldon* or *Beowulf* (see Supplement 1). Does it 'work'?

Although the metrical style of Old English was later replaced by the rhyming poetic forms brought in by the Normans, alliterative verse, in a modified style, continued to be written until the fifteenth century.

1.1.4
The Vikings

● Look at this map showing some of the Viking voyages of discovery. Can you complete the gaps with the modern place-names?

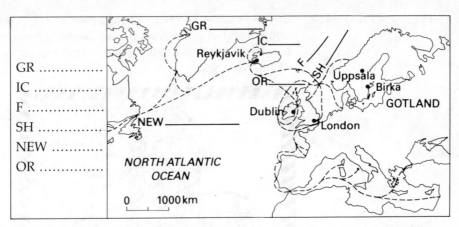

GR ....

IC ....

F ....

SH ....

NEW ....

OR ....

NORTH ATLANTIC OCEAN

0   1000 km

- What do you know about the Vikings? (See page 33 for important events of the period.)

1.2 Middle English

**1.2.1
Geoffrey Chaucer
(?1343–1400) and *The
Canterbury Tales***

Geoffrey Chaucer's great skill was as a teller of tales. He drew on the moral, religious and philosophical beliefs of the day and yet created poetry from the spoken language. His writing was full of comedy blended with tragedy as well as wonderfully realistic descriptions of characters and nature.

The Canterbury Tales, begun in 1386, consists of stories told by some of the thirty pilgrims who set off from the Tabard Inn in Southwark, London, to visit the shrine of St. Thomas à Becket, the Archbishop of Canterbury murdered in his own cathedral in 1170. The aim was to tell four stories each: two on the way, two on the way back. The teller of the best story would be given a free dinner by the cheerful host of the Tabard. In fact, the collection is incomplete and only twenty-four stories are told (including two by Chaucer) – see also Supplement 1.

Warm-up   Does this picture remind you of a story?

The Nun's Priest's Tale   The tale told by the Nun's Priest (one of the priests who accompany the female head of a religious house) begins: 'A povre wydwe, somdeel stape in age'. In modern English, this 'translates' as 'A poor widow, somewhat advanced in years'.

The Nun's Priest

Extract 1   Even though the language is probably unfamiliar, try to make some sense of the passage.

>   A povre wydwe, somdeel stape in age   1
> Was whilom dwellyng in a narwe cotage,
> Biside a grove, stondynge in a dale.
> This wydwe, of which I telle yow my tale,
> Syn thilke day that she was last a wyf,   5
> In pacience ladde a ful symple lyf,
> For litel was hir catel and hir rente.
> By housbondrie of swich as God hire sente
> She foond hirself and eek hir doghtren two.
> Thre large sowes hadde she, and namo,   10
> Three keen, and eek a sheep that highte Malle.

● i) What impression do you have of the widow?

ii) Read this modern English prose 'translation':

> Once upon a time there was a poor widow quite advanced in years, who lived in a small cottage beside a small wood situated in a valley. Since that day when she was last a wife, this widow about whom my story is concerned had patiently lived a simple life, for her property and income were small. By means of careful management of the things God sent her, she provided for herself and her two daughters. All she owned were three large female pigs, three cows and also a sheep called Molly.

Notice that in the original, Chaucer helps us feel the roughness and simplicity of her life (the rhythm of the verse is rough and inelegant, the sounds of words like 'stape', 'hogges', 'sowes', 'catel' are hard). What is lost in the 'translation'?

iii) Can you work out the modern English words for the following:

'whilom' (1.2)   'thilke' (1.5)   'catel' (1.7)   'keen' (1.11)   'eek' (1.11)

22

Extract 2   The widow keeps a fine-looking cock called Chauntecleer, whose merry, virtuoso crowing has no equal anywhere.

● Try to get the general idea. How many 'wives' does Chauntecleer have? Who was Pertelote?

GLOSSARY

governaunce (l.1): control

sustres (l.3): sisters

paramours (l.3): lovers

wonder lyk to (l.4): amazingly like

faireste hewed on hir throte (l.5): one with the brightest feathers on her throat

cleped (l.6): called

damoysele (l.6): damsel (young unmarried woman of noble birth)

Curteys (l.7): courteous; gentle

bar . . . faire (l.8): believed herself so well

Syn thilke day that (l.9): ever since

loken in every lith (l.11): locked in her every limb

wel was hym therwith (l.12): he was very pleased with himself

gan to sprynge (l.14): began to rise

lief is faren in londe (l.15): love is far away

briddes (l.17): birds

This gentil cok hadde in his governaunce   1
Sevene hennes for to doon al his plesaunce,
Whiche were his sustres and his paramours,
And wonder lyk to hym, as of colours;
Of whiche the faireste hewed on hir throte   5
Was cleped faire damoysele Pertelote,
Curteys she was, discreet, and debonaire,
And compaignable, and bar hyrself so faire
Syn thilke day that she was seven nyght oold,
That trewely she hath the herte in hoold   10
Of Chauntecleer, loken in every lith;
He loved hire so that wel was hym therwith.
But swich a joye was it to here hem synge,
Whan that the brighte sonne gan to sprynge,
In sweete accord, 'My lief is faren in londe!'   15
For thilke tyme, as I have understonde,
Beestes and briddes koude speke and synge.

● i) How would you describe the relationship between Chauntecleer and the hens?
ii) Which words/phrases describe Pertelote?
iii) What impression do you get of Chauntecleer? Is he proud or self-satisfied?
iv) How do the hens contrast with the 'povre wydwe'?
v) Do you get any impression of the narrator in the last two lines?
vi) What do you think will happen?

Extract 3   One sunny morning, Chauntecleer begins his song as usual. His heart is full of joy. However, today there is a fox hiding among the vegetables. At first he cries out in terror but the clever fox flatters him by saying that he has only come to listen to the cock's wonderful singing. He encourages him to put on a display but when Chauntecleer begins the fox attacks his throat, throws him on his back and takes him off to the woods.

GLOSSARY

sely (l.1): poor

maken wo (l.2): make sorrowful noises

This sely wydwe and eek hir doghtres two   1
Herden thise hennes crie and maken wo,
And out at dores stirten they anon,
And syen the fox toward the grove gon,

stirten they anon (l.3): they rushed out at once

syen (l.4): saw

harrow! weylaway! (l.6): help! oh, dear!

staves (l.8): sticks

dystaf (l.10): stick used for winding wool

hogges (l.11): male pigs

fered for (l.12): frightened by

yolleden . . . helle (l.15): yelled like devils in hell

dokes . . . quelle (l.16): ducks called out as though men were killing them

benedicitee (l.19): bless the lord!

Certes (l.20): certainly

Jakke Straw and his meynee (l.20): (famous rebel leader and his followers)

shrille (l.21): high and sharp

Flemyng (l.22): person from Flanders

bemes (l.24): trumpets

box (l.24): box-wood

boon (l.25): bone

powped (l.25): hooted

shriked and howped (l.26): made high, loud shouts

herkneth (l.28): listen

drede (l.32): fear

cherles (l.35): peasants

pestilence (l.36): disaster; plague

Maugree youre heed (l.38): no matter what you do

ete (l.39): eat

delyverly (l.42): quickly and cleverly

fleigh (l.43): flew

ydoon trespas (l.46): done wrong

aferd (l.47): afraid

hente (l.48): caught

wikke entente (l.49): wicked intention

sooth (l.51): truth

shrewe us bothe two (l.52): curse the two of us

bigyle . . . ones (l.54): cheat me more than once

synge and wynke with myn ye (l.56): sing and close my eyes

And bar upon his bak the cok away, 5

And cryden, 'Out! harrow! and weylaway!

Ha! ha! the fox!' and after hym they ran,

And eek with staves many another man.

Ran Colle oure dogge, and Talbot and Gerland,

And Malkyn, with a dystaf in hir hand; 10

Ran cow and calf, and eek the verray hogges,

So fered for the berkyng of the dogges

And shoutyng of the men and wommen eeke,

They ronne so hem thoughte hir herte breeke.

They yolleden as feendes doon in helle; 15

The dokes cryden as men wolde hem quelle;

The gees for feere flowen over the trees;

Out of the hyve cam the swarm of bees.

So hydous was the noyse, a *benedicitee*!

Certes, he Jakke Straw and his meynee 20

Ne made nevere shoutes half so shrille

Whan that they wolden any Flemyng kille,

As thilke day was maad upon the fox.

Of bras they broghten bemes, and of box.

Of horn, of boon, in whiche they blewe and powped. 25

And therwithal they skriked and they howped.

It semed as that hevene sholde falle.

Now, goode men, I prey yow herkneth alle:

Lo, how Fortune turneth sodeynly

The hope and pryde eek of hir enemy! 30

This cok, that lay upon the foxes bak,

In al his drede unto the fox he spak,

And seyde, 'Sire, if that I were as ye,

Yet sholde I seyn, as wys God helpe me,

'Turneth agayn, ye proude cherles alle! 35

A verray pestilence upon yow falle!

Now am I come unto the wodes syde;

Maugree youre heed, the cok shal heere abyde.

I wol hym ete, in feith, and that anon!''

The fox answerde, 'In feith, it shal be don.' 40

And as he spak that word, al sodeynly

This cok brak from his mouth delyverly,

And heighe upon a tree he fleigh anon.

And whan the fox saugh that the cok was gon,

'Allas!' quod he, 'O Chauntecleer, allas! 45

I have to yow,' quod he, 'ydoon trespas,

In as muche as I maked yow aferd

Whan I yow hente and broghte out of the yerd.

But, sire; I dide it in no wikke entente.

Com doun, and I shal telle yow what I mente; 50

I shal seye sooth to yow, God help me so!'

'Nay thanne,' quod he, 'I shrewe us bothe two.

And first I shrewe myself, bothe blood and bones.

If thou bigyle me ofter than ones.
Thou shalt namoore, thurgh thy flaterye,   55
Do me to synge and wynke with myn ye;
For he that wynketh, whan he sholde see,
Al wilfully. God lat him nevere thee!'
'Nay,' quod the fox, 'but God yeve hym meschaunce,
That is so undiscreet of governaunce   60
That jangleth whan he sholde holde his pees.'

(from *The Nun's Priest's Tale*)

i) Are you glad Chauntecleer escaped?

ii) The tale is sometimes described as very high-spirited and very human. Do you agree?

Understanding and interpretation

i) Which of the following summaries is most nearly correct?

a) The widow and her daughters tried to chase after the fox but only succeeded in disturbing the animals in the yard. The cock, realising how stupid he had been, shouted at the fox. The fox shouted back angrily, only to lose the cock as he did so. The cock flew into a tree and despite the efforts of the widow to flatter him he was not to be persuaded down.

b) The widow, her daughters and many others chased after the fox as he ran towards the wood with the cock on his back. It was a scene of noisy confusion. The cock cleverly deceived the fox by encouraging him to shout back defiantly at his pursuers. As soon as he opened his mouth to agree, the cock escaped. Realising his mistake, the fox tried to persuade the cock to come down from a tree, saying he had meant no harm, but the cock was not to be cheated by flattery twice.

c) The widow and her daughters chased after the fox and created a great deal of noise and confusion. The animals in the farmyard went everywhere and the fox panicked, dropping the cock. Quickly picking him up, the cock told the fox to shout back at his pursuers, which he did, only to lose the cock a second time. Realising his mistake, he tried to persuade the cock down from a tree, telling him that he wanted to hear him sing. The cock, though, was not to be fooled twice.

ii) Choose the best heading for each section:

a) Section 1: 'This sely . . . sholde falle.' (l.1–l.27): *The widow/The chase/The fox's cunning*

b) Section 2: 'Now, goode men . . . that anon!' (l.28–l.39): *The wheel of fortune/Chauntecleer's good luck/Chauntecleer's challenge*

c) Section 3: 'The fox . . . anon' (l.40–l.43): *Chauntecleer escapes/The fox's promise*

d) Section 4: 'And whan the fox . . . his pees.' (l.44–l.61): *The fox's despair/The fox tries to get Chauntecleer back/Chauntecleer's cleverness*

iii) What lesson does Chauntecleer seem to have learned?

Language and style

Discuss at least one of the following:

a) Which lines best show the speed and confusion of the chase? How does the movement and rhythm of these lines contrast with the opening lines of the tale ('A povre wydwe . . .')?

b) Select a humorous extract. What makes it comic?

c) What do you notice about the rhyme at the end of the lines? How many beats (main stressed syllables) does each line seem to have? Say at least one way in which the form of the verse differs from Anglo-Saxon verse.

Geoffrey Chaucer	As in most of Europe, the social structure of Chaucer's England was feudal. Roughly speaking this meant that power radiated from the king, through his noblemen to his subjects. The land was divided into large agricultural estates, owned by the king and the nobility, providing the Crown with money, material and men when it had wars to fight. Each level of society had its rights and privileges, each its duties and obligations. The system was broadly accepted as right and proper.

● i) How has European society changed?

ii) Choose from these prepositions to fill the gaps:

in   during   to   of   between   with   on

Chaucer spent much .... his life .... close association .... the ruling nobility. It was the Age .... Chivalry. He served, possibly as a squire .... a nobleman, ... France .... the Hundred Years War, and was captured .... 1359. Later, ... 1368 and 1387, he was sent .... several diplomatic missions .... Italy. He was also a senior customs official .... England. It is probable that as a page .... the royal household he learned to play and sing and to read poetry.

Chaucer's main works	*The Book of the Duchess* (?1370), an elegy (a poem written to show sorrow for the dead) for the beautiful first wife of his patron, John of Gaunt. *The House of Fame* (written sometime in the 1370s), a lighthearted dream–vision, suggested by Dante's *Paradiso*, in which the poet is carried off by an eagle to learn whether those in the service of love are happy or not. In the poem, Chaucer parodies the conventions of medieval courtly love. *The Parliament of Fowls* (written sometime between 1375 and 1385). a delightful Bird and Beast poem in celebration of St Valentine's Day. *Troilus and Criseyde* (?1385), a long love narrative, based on Boccaccio's *Il Filostrato*, full of humour and poetic beauty. *The Canterbury Tales* (probably begun in 1386). For more extracts see Supplement 1 (page 322). Chaucer was much influenced, particularly at the beginning of his literary career, by the literature of France. He translated the *Roman de la Rose*, almost a 'manual' for courtly love. He also found inspiration from the Italian writers Petrarch, Boccaccio and Dante as well as the Latin writers Vergil and Ovid.

Geoffrey Chaucer

1.2.2 **Middle English:** **language and literature**	Middle English is a term used to describe the language that came into being in the century or so after the Norman Conquest (1066) and lasted until about 1500. During those years, the inflectional system of Old English

was weakened and a large number of words were introduced from France. At that time the language consisted of a number of regional dialects, rather than a standardised language, each with its own peculiarities of sound and spelling. The Midland dialect was the dialect of the educated classes of London and of Chaucer, and the ancestor of our own standard speech. It differed greatly from dialect spoken in the west of England (the original dialect of *Piers Plowman* by William Langland – ?1330–?1386) and that of the northwest (as in *Sir Gawain and the Green Knight* by an unknown writer – ?1375). (See Supplement 1.)

The literary conventions associated both with Old English verse and Latin literature were very remote from the vernacular of common speech. Middle English literature had greater immediacy, and its characters were more human and sympathetic than the idealised heroes of Old English.

Much of Middle English poetry was written in rhyming verse in which stressed syllables alternated with unstressed syllables, adapted from the French, or, like *Piers Plowman* and *Sir Gawain and the Green Knight*, in alliterative verse descended from Old English. *The Canterbury Tales* were written mainly in rhyming couplets (pairs of lines which rhyme), each line containing five main stressed syllables (a metre known as 'iambic pentameter'). Before Chaucer, the number of main stressed syllables in a line was more often four.

1.3 Fifteenth-century prose

**1.3.1
Sir Thomas Malory
and *Le Morte d'Arthur***

Although Sir Thomas Malory (?1405–1471) had become a Member of Parliament in 1445, he was a man of violent temperament and was later charged with many crimes including theft and attempted murder. In 1468 he was put in prison for taking part in a military revolt.

Between 1468 and 1470, in prison, Malory wrote *Le Morte D'Arthur*, a prose collection of versions of the legends of King Arthur, translated from the French.

Extract 1

The heroic warrior, King Arthur, has been in France, in a half-hearted attempt to punish his friend Sir Launcelot for being the lover of his wife (Queen Guinevere). Hearing that his bastard son, Mordred, has seized his kingdom in his absence, Arthur returns but is attacked by Mordred's soldiers on landing in England. Sir Gawain, Arthur's nephew, is killed.

Before the final battle, King Arthur has a dream.

So uppon Trynyté Sunday at nyght kynge Arthure dremed a 1
wondirfull dreme, and in hys dreme hym semed that he saw uppon
a chafflet a chayre, and the chayre was faste to a whele, and there-
uppon sate kynge Arthure in the rychest clothe of golde that myght
be made. And the kynge thought there was undir hym, farre from 5
hym, an hydeous depe blak watir, and therein was all maner of
serpentis and wormes and wylde bestis fowle and orryble. And
suddeynly the kynge thought that the whyle turned up-so-downe,
and he felle amonge the serpentis, and every beste toke hym by a
lymme. And than the kynge cryed as he lay in hys bed, 10

'Helpe! helpe!'

And than knyghtes, squyars and yomen awaked the kynge, and than he was so amased that he wyste nat where he was. And than so he awaked untylle hit was nyghe day, and than he felle on slumberynge agayne, nat slepynge nor thorowly wakynge. So the kyng semed verryly that there cam sir Gawayne unto hym with a numbir of fayre ladyes wyth hym.

15

Here is the same passage with modern spelling and punctuation added:

GLOSSARY

Trinity Sunday (l.1): the eighth Sunday after Easter; the Sunday after Christ had appeared to his disciples

him seemed (l.2): it seemed to him

chafflet (l.2): wooden platform (*archaic*)

fast (l.3): firmly fixed

yeomen (l.11): men who owned the land they farm

wist (l.12): knew (*archaic*)

awaked (l.13): lay awake

nigh (l.13): nearly (*poetic*)

the King seemed verily (l.14): it really seemed to the king (*verily = archaic*)

So upon Trinity Sunday at night King Arthur dreamed a wonderful dream, and in his dream him seemed that he saw upon a chafflet a chair, and the chair was fast to a wheel, and thereupon sat King Arthur in the richest cloth of gold that might be made. And the King thought there was under him, far from him, an hideous deep black water, and therein was all manner of serpents, and worms, and wild beasts, foul and horrible. And suddenly the King thought that the wheel turned upside down, and he fell among the serpents, and every beast took him by a limb. And then the King cried as he lay in his bed. 'Help, help!'

And then knights, squires, and yeomen awaked the King, and then he was so amazed that he wist not where he was. And then so he awaked until it was nigh day, and then he fell on slumbering again, not sleeping nor thoroughly waking. So the King seemed verily that there came Sir Gawain unto him with a number of fair ladies with him.

1

5

10

15

What does the dream tell us about King Arthur's state of mind?

Extract 2

Sir Gawain, accompanied by the ladies he fought over when he was alive, has come to warn the king.

GLOSSARY

anone (l.1): soon (*archaic*)

wyghtly (l.3): quickly (*archaic*)

avision (l.5): dream (*archaic*)

slayne (l.6): killed

Than sir Gawayne and all the ladyes vanysshed, and anone the kynge called uppon hys knyghtes, squyars, and yomen, and charged them wyghtly to fecche hys noble lordis and wyse bysshoppis unto hym. And whan they were com the kynge tolde hem of hys avision, that sir Gawayne had tolde hym and warned hym that and he fought on the morn, he sholde be slayne.

1

5

● Rewrite the passage using modern English spelling and punctuation, 'translating' into modern English any phrases you wish.

Extract 3

Nevertheless, King Arthur goes into battle once again. By night there are a hundred thousand dead and only two of King Arthur's knights can be seen: Sir Lucan and his brother Sir Bedivere, both of whom have been wounded. After King Arthur has won the battle, he sees Sir Mordred leaning on his sword 'among a great heap of dead men'. In spite of Sir Lucan's warnings, he kills Sir Mordred. In turn King Arthur is wounded on the side of the head. Sir Lucan and Sir Bedivere are both weak but manage to take their king to a small chapel near the sea. On the battlefield the dead are being robbed and the wounded killed by greedy thieves. While trying – unsuccessfully – to get the king away from the chapel, Sir Lucan dies.

● Arthur has a sword called Excalibur. Before he dies he must return it to the Lady in the Lake, the mysterious half-supernatural creature who had given it to him. Can you guess which five of the following words will appear in the passage?

water	waves	threw		heavy
prayer	jewel	barge (a wide-bottomed boat)		rowed

'Therefore,' said King Arthur unto Sir Bedivere, 'take thou here   1
Excalibur my good sword and go with it to yonder water's side; and
when thou comest there I charge thee throw my sword in that water
and come again and tell me what thou sawest there.'

'My lord,' said Sir Bedivere, 'your commandment shall be done,   5
and [I shall] lightly bring you word again.'

So Sir Bedivere departed. And by the way he beheld that noble
sword, that the pommel and the haft was all precious stones. And
then he said to himself, 'If I throw this rich sword in the water,
thereof shall never come good, but harm and loss.' And then Sir   10
Bedivere hid Excalibur under a tree. And so, as soon as he might,
he came again unto the King and said he had been at the water and
had thrown the sword into the water.

'What saw thou there?' said the King.

'Sir,' he said, 'I saw nothing but waves and winds.'   15

'That is untruly said of thee,' said the King. 'And therefore go
thou lightly again and do my commandment; as thou art to me lief
and dear, spare not, but throw it in.'

Then Sir Bedivere returned again and took the sword in his hand.
And yet him thought sin and shame to throw away that noble   20
sword. And so eft he hid the sword and returned again and told the

King that he had been at the water and done his commandment.

'What sawest thou there?' said the King.

'Sir,' he said, 'I saw nothing but waters wap and waves wan.'

'Ah, traitor unto me and untrue,' said King Arthur, 'now hast   25
thou betrayed me twice. Who would have weened that thou that
hast been to me so lief and dear, and thou art named a noble knight
and would betray me for the riches of this sword. But now go again
lightly, for thy long tarrying putteth me in great jeopardy of my
life, for I have taken cold. And but if thou do now as I bid thee, if   30
ever I may see thee I shall slay thee mine own hands, for thou
wouldest for my rich sword see me dead.'

Then Sir Bedivere departed and went to the sword and lightly
took it up, and so he went to the water's side; and there he bound
the girdle about the hilts, and threw the sword as far into the water   35
as he might. And there came an arm and an hand above the water
and took it and clutched it, and shook it thrice and brandished; and
then vanished away the hand with the sword into the water. So Sir
Bedivere came again to the King and told him what he saw.

'Alas,' said the King, 'help me hence, for I dread me I have   40
tarried overlong.'

Then Sir Bedivere took the King upon his back and so went with
him to that water's side. And when they were at the water's side,
even fast by the bank hoved a little barge with many fair ladies in
it; and among them all was a queen; and all they had black hoods,   45
and all they wept and shrieked when they saw King Arthur.

'Now put me into that barge,' said the King; and so he did softly.
And there received him three ladies with great mourning, and so
they set them down. And in one of their laps King Arthur laid his
head, and then the queen said, 'Ah, my dear brother, why have ye   50
tarried so long from me? Alas, this wound on your head hath
caught overmuch cold.' And anon they rowed fromward the land.

From *Le Morte d'Arthur*

GLOSSARY

yonder (l.2): over there
lightly (l.6): quickly
beheld (l.7): looked at
pommel and the haft (l.8):
   handle and the
   rounded knob on top
That is ... thee (l.16): You
   are not telling me the
   truth
lief (l.17): beloved (*archaic*)
him thought (l.20): it
   seemed to him
eft (l.21): again (*archaic*)
waters wap and waves wan
   (l.24): waters wash the
   shore and waves grow
   dark (*archaic*)
weened (l.26): imagined
   (*archaic*)
tarrying (l.29): delay
mine (l.31): with my
girdle (l.35): sword belt
hilts (l.35): handles
brandished (l.37): waved
hence (l.40): from here
fast (l.44): close
hoved (l.44): waited
set them down (l.49):
   sat down

● i) Were your guesses correct? Do you like the story? Why/Why not?

ii) Help each other to understand any words/phrases you do not understand.

Understanding and   i) *Either:*
interpretation   Write line numbers next to each of the following. The first one has been done
for you.

a) King Arthur tells Sir Bedivere for the first time to throw the sword into the
   water. 1.1–1.4

b) Sir Bedivere hides it under a tree. ....

c) King Arthur knows he is lying and tells him to try again. ....

d) Sir Bedivere tries to deceive the king a second time. ....

e) The king is not fooled. ....

f) He accuses Sir Bedivere of greed. ....

g) The third time Bedivere does as he is told. ....

h) King Arthur is satisfied and is rowed away from the land by some
   beautiful ladies waiting in a barge. ....

Or:

Mime the narrative of the passage. Add as many expressive gestures as you wish.

ii) Why do you think Sir Bedivere at first disobeyed King Arthur? What does the final image of King Arthur in the boat suggest?

Critical response Read these views of *Le Morte D'Arthur*.

a) ... it is curious that, as we move towards the modern period, with its new spirit of enquiry, its sense of a bigger world than the Middle Ages could provide, our first important printed work in prose should evoke that misty ancient world of myth, should look to pre-history rather than to the future. (Anthony Burgess in *English Literature*, Longman 1958)

b) His book is attractive ... not only because it is the best and most complete treatment of the story of Arthur and his knights, but also because it is one of the greatest pieces of prose in English. Malory was the first English writer to make prose as sensitive an instrument of narrative as English poetry had always been. ... He is in particular a master of naturalistic dialogue ... And both he and the majority of his characters are masters of understatement who express themselves, in moments of great emotional tension, with a bare minimum of words. The result is highly provocative to the reader's imagination ... (Adapted from the introduction to the *Norton Anthology*, Vol 1, W.W. Norton 1962)

c) ... the charm of the prose is a remote charm; the imagery is without immediacy; there is a lifelessness ... about the prose for all its (in a limited sense) loveliness ... The material fascinates the reader in spite of Malory's 'magical' style, which seems to shadow and obscure rather than illuminate it. ... The recurrent appearance of the corpse or corpse-like figure on a barge and the weeping women – fragments of an ancient mythology though they are – become in Malory merely tedious after a number of repetitions, and the final effect is one of somewhat morbid sensationalism rather than of mystical vision. (Adapted from John Speirs in *The Pelican Guide to English Literature*, Penguin 1954)

From your reading of the extracts, do you think that the writing is strongly imaginative or only fantasy?

A very different story based on the King Arthur legends, *Sir Gawain and the Green Knight*, can be found in Supplement 1.

Malory's literary sources Although there was probably a British King Arthur who resisted the Anglo-Saxon invasions in the sixth century, the legend – an accumulation of narratives originating from various people at different times – has become much more important than the historical reality.

In earlier versions, Sir Gawain is the owner of the sword Excalibur and, like Sir Perceval in French and German versions, the most important knight of the Round Table (the table, devised by King Arthur, at which the knights sat as equals during a banquet). He is also the hero of the quest for the mysterious Holy Grail (the cup used by Jesus Christ during the Last Supper before his death). In Malory's story, Sir Launcelot is the most important, although it is Sir Galahad who finds the Holy Grail.

Malory was influenced more by the Christianised versions of the legend, with their taste for the tragic passions of courtly love, than by pagan nature myths (unlike the author of *Sir Gawain and the Green Knight* in Supplement 1).

● i) Are there any similar myths and legends in your own country?
ii) Punctuate the following. Add capital letters where necessary:

Malory drew from many sources he had obviously read *Le Morte Arthur* a late fourteenth-century poem from the northwest midlands which he used as a source for the death of Arthur and the english poem *Morte Arthure* the story of Arthurs victorious campaign against the emperor of rome also written in the fourteenth century however his own prose version was undoubtedly influenced by the french romances of the thirteenth century including *Suite du Merlin* the french latin *Mort Artu Tristan de Leonois* and the prose *Lancelot* Malory seemed to see the story as an example of loyalty to a great cause and a record of Englands heroic past

Malory's influence To a lesser extent, the Arthurian legend resurfaces in Spenser's *Faerie Queene* (1589–1596). However, the person Malory most notably influenced was Tennyson in his *Idylls of the King* (published 1859). The grail as a pagan symbol was used by T.S. Eliot in *The Waste Land* (1922).

1.3.2
The Wars of the Roses
Malory's book was written during the Wars of the Roses, a traumatic period in English history in which Shakespeare set many of his 'history' plays.

● Listen to a brief lecture on the period (or refer to the Key at the back of the book) and complete the chart below:

> Dates of the Wars: ....
>
> Fought between: ....
>
> Brought to an end by: ....
>
> One cause: ....
>
> ....
>
> One result: ....
>
> ....

1.4 Modern English

As London was the most important city in England and the seat of the royal court, and as William Caxton established a printing press there in 1476, the east Midland dialect quickly became what it has been ever since: standard modern English. Since then the English language has not undergone major structural changes; in fact differences of speech between social classes have been of greater importance than regional differences. However, until recent times, in northwest Scotland, Wales and above all Ireland, the Celtic languages were predominant.

As a result of the various historical influences, English vocabulary is basically Germanic, although it contains a large number of Latin words, often in their French form. After the Norman Conquest and before the fourteenth century, the aristocracy were basically French-speaking, and Latin, in the earlier Middle Ages, was both the living language of the literate classes and the language of the Church. Since then, English has also borrowed extensively from other languages: in particular, in the sixteenth century, from Ancient Greek, due to the influence of classical scholarship.

1.5 Chronology

Complete the right-hand side of the chart with information from this unit.

British history		Literature
55 BC	Invasion by Julius Caesar. Britain becomes a trading outpost of the Roman Empire.	
AD 43	Under Emperor Claudius, Britain comes under full Roman political and military domination.	
410	Roman forces withdrawn.	
449	Angles, Saxons and Jutes descend on Britain.	
597	St Augustine brings Roman Christianity to Britain.	
793	Norwegian sea-raiders sack the monastery at Lindisfarne.	
?800–?1000	Danish raids.	
871–899	Reign of King Alfred the Great.	
1066	Britain conquered by the Normans.	

Norman monarchs

1066–1087	William I.	
1087–1100	William II.	
1100–1135	Henry I.	
1135–1154	Stephen.	

Plantagenet (Anjou) monarchs

1154–1189	Henry II. Efficient ruler who carried out much legal reform. Conquest of Ireland. Thomas à Becket, Archbishop of Canterbury, assassinated by king's knights (1170).	
1189–1199	Richard I.	
1199–1216	John. Forced to sign the Magna Carta (1215) guaranteeing such rights as freedom from arbitrary imprisonment.	
1216–1272	Henry III. Rebellion by Simon de Montfort led to establishment of Great Council, from which Parliament later developed.	
1272–1307	Edward I. Conquest of Wales.	
1307–1327	Edward II. Defeated by Scots (1314).	
1327–1377	Edward III. Hundred Years War with France began (1338). Black Death struck England (1348–1349), reducing the population by between one-third and a half.	
1377–1399	Richard II. Neglect of war with France. Period of disorder. Peasants' revolt, led by Wat Tyler (1381).	

The House of Lancaster

1399–1413	Henry IV.	
1413–1422	Henry V. After great victory over French at Agincourt (1415), recognised as heir to the throne of France. Great national hero.	
1422–1461	Henry VI. Defeat in France to end Hundred Years War (1453). Wars of Roses began (1455).	

The House of York

1461–1483   Edward IV. William Caxton set up first printing press in London (1476).

1483   Edward V. Boy-king deposed by his uncle (Richard III). Imprisoned – probably murdered – in Tower of London.

1483–1485   Richard III. Defeated at Battle of Bosworth (1485) by Henry VII.

Tudor monarchs

1485–1509   Henry VII. National unity and order restored. Colombus sailed to America (1492).

1.6 Activities

Creative writing   i) Look at these pictures of different heroes at different times in history. What do they have in common? How are they different?

Samson

Robin Hood

Ulysses

Superman

ii) *Either*:
Write the word HERO vertically on the page:

H
E
R
O

Write a poem, making each line begin with one of the letters. So the first line might be:
Having someone to admire

Or:
Write a letter to a friend about your memories of a person you thought of as a hero.

Quiz   Ask each other the following questions. Answers can be found in the unit.

Student A:
  i) What was the name of King Arthur's sword?
 ii) What is a 'foot' in a line of poetry?
iii) In *The Canterbury Tales*, what was the name of the inn the pilgrims set off from?
 iv) How was the original manuscript of *Battle of Maldon* destroyed?
  v) What year was the Norman Conquest of England?

Student B:
  i) What are the first names of Chaucer and Malory?
 ii) Which Italian writer did Chaucer base his *Troilus and Criseyde* on?
iii) When did the Battle of Maldon take place?
 iv) What did Sir Mordred do when King Arthur was in France?
  v) Who were the Jutes?

UNIT 2

The English Renaissance

2.1 Poetry

Two common themes in sixteenth-century poetry were the relationship between men and women, and the treachery and hypocrisy of courtly life.

2.1.1 Sir Thomas Wyatt (?1503–1542)

Sir Thomas Wyatt was a popular member of the court of Henry VIII (1509–1547) and was often sent on diplomatic missions overseas. However, he was twice arrested, once in 1536 with the fall of Anne Boleyn, Henry's second queen, and again in 1541 with the fall of his patron, Thomas Cromwell. Perhaps his first arrest was because he had been Anne's lover before her marriage to the king. Whatever the reasons, he was fortunate to regain the king's favour. On the second occasion he was charged with treason and imprisoned in the Tower of London. Wyatt's verse, essentially English but much influenced by Italian verse forms, was written to be passed – and sometimes sung – among friends at court.

Warm-up

Either:

Write the word 'prison' at the top of a blank piece of paper. Underneath write all the words/phrases you associate with it (for example, 'loneliness').

Or:

Stand in groups. Imagine you are in prison. It is morning. You wake up and are given food. You later read a book and write letters. You are bored and frustrated as well as angry with your friends for not getting you out. Mime the scene. Be as expressive as you can. Afterwards, in your groups, discuss your feelings at the different stages.

'They Flee from Me'

- The narrator of the following poem is in prison.
- Listen and try to answer these questions:

– Who could 'they' be? (Friends at court? Women?)
– Who do you think 'she' could be? (His wife? A mistress? A symbol for 'friends'?)

GLOSSARY

flee (l.1): run away
stalking (l.2): walking slowly and carefully as when hunting an animal
meek (l.3): submissive
range (l.6): move freely without control

They Flee from Me

They flee from me, that sometime did me seek,   1
With naked foot stalking in my chamber.
I have seen them, gentle, tame, and meek,
That now are wild, and do not remember
That sometime they put themselves in danger   5
To take bread at my hand; and now they range,
Busily seeking with a continual change.

---

hath (l.8): (archaic form of 'have' used with 'he', 'she' or 'it') *array (l.10):* fine dress *guise (l.10):* style of clothing *small (l.12):* slim *Therewithall (l.13):* immediately after that *thorough (l.16):* through; because of *(archaic)* *strange . . . forsaking (l.17):* new and unusual kind of desertion *leave (l.18):* permission *newfangleness (l.19):* absence of loyalty in love; always changing *kindely (l.20):* naturally (with an ironic suggestion of 'unkindly' in a modern sense) *I fain would (l.21):* I would like to *(archaic)*	Thanked be fortune it hath been otherwise, Twenty times better; but once in special, In thin array, after a pleasant guise, 10 When her loose gown from her shoulders did fall, And she me caught in her arms long and small, Therewithall sweetly did me kiss And softly said, 'Dear heart, how like you this?' It was no dream, I lay broad waking. 15 But all is turned, thorough my gentleness, Into a strange fashion of forsaking; And I have leave to go, of her goodness, And she also to use newfangleness. But since that I so kindely am served, 20 I fain would know what she hath deserved.

Understanding and interpretation	i) Explain in your own words the line 'They flee from me, that sometime did me seek'. (It summarises the main theme of the poem.)
	
	ii) In which lines does Wyatt
	
	   a) seem to compare 'them' with half-domesticated pets, possibly falcons?
	   b) remember a loving encounter?
	   c) suggest that his own kindness is to blame for his being alone?
	
	iii) What are the narrator's feelings for 'her' in lines 9–14? What are they in lines 18–21? What is the difference? Is there any irony?
	
	iv) Which lines contain verbs in the present tense? What do you imagine the narrator's life to be like now?
	
	v) How would you describe the tone of the poem? Melancholic? Self pitying?

Language and style	The complaints of a forsaken lover were conventional in the Italian poetry that influenced Wyatt. However, Wyatt's poems sound direct and personal as though the 'voice' of the poem was not only that of a 'dramatic persona' (a character in a fictional work) but of Wyatt himself. In 1557 Richard Tottel published a poetic anthology which included Wyatt's chief works (none of which had been printed before). However, the editors made alterations to Wyatt's rhythms to make them smoother. For example, line 3 became: 'Once have I seen them gentle, tame and meek.' 'I have seen them' probably sounded too abrupt to the editors; the original line only had nine syllables instead of ten.

● Modern critics argue that Wyatt's rhythms are deliberately rough: they give the poems dramatic impact. Does the style appeal to you? Can you say why?

2.1.2 **Sir Philip Sidney** **(1554–1586)**	Sir Philip Sidney served a later court, that of Elizabeth I (1558–1603). As well as a poet, he was an aristocratic soldier and statesman. To the Elizabethans he was the ideal courtier, able to excel in all that was regarded as fitting for a nobleman. When he lay mortally wounded after a battle in Flanders (aged only thirty-two) he is reputed to have passed a cup of water to a dying soldier with the words: 'Thy need is greater than mine.'

Warm-up	A tournament (or 'tourney') was a public contest between armed horsemen in imitation of real battle, based on ideas of chivalry and accompanied by much pageantry. The field was enclosed by barriers, with pavilions at the side for notable people. In this picture, the men on horseback are using lances. What seems to be happening?
Astrophel and Stella	A sonnet is a fourteen-line poem, usually with five beats a line and a definite rhyme scheme. The following sonnet by Sidney refers to an actual tournament held in 1581. It comes from the sequence *Astrophel and Stella* (published 1591), which later influenced Shakespeare's own sonnet sequence. 'Astrophel' is the Greek for 'star-lover'; 'Stella' the latin for star. For a time, Sidney was engaged to Penelope Devereux – the daughter of the earl of Essex – who eventually had a rather unhappy marriage to Lord Rich. She is sometimes identified as Stella, although she is said to have been rather less virtuous than Stella. In the sequence, Sidney harmonises his personal tone of voice with both myth and narrative.

GLOSSARY *advance (l.5)*: speak well of *daintier (l.6)*: more careful	Having this day my horse, my hand, my lance 1 Guided so well that I obtained the prize, Both by the judgment of the English eyes And of some sent from that sweet enemy, France, Horsemen my skill in horsemanship advance, 5 Town-folks my strength; a daintier judge applies

sleight (l.7): skill

good use (l.7): experience

impute it but (l.8): only consider it

of both sides (l.9): my ancestors on both sides

did excel in this (l.10): (were distinguished in the skills needed at a tournament)

shoot awry (l.12): get it wrong

race (l.14): life

His praise to sleight which from good use doth rise;
Some lucky wits impute it but to chance;
Others, because of both sides I do take
My blood from them who did excel in this,   10
Think nature me a man-at-arms did make.
How far they shoot awry! The true cause is,
Stella looked on, and from her heavenly face
Sent forth the beams which made so fair my race.

(from *Astrophel and Stella*)

i) Which of the following were given by other people as reasons for the narrator's success?

He was good at looking after horses/he was good at riding and managing horses/he had good skill because he practised a lot/he was strong/he was handsome/he was lucky/he had inherited his ability

What reason does the narrator give?

ii) When the narrator calls France a 'sweet enemy' (l.4), we get a sense of chivalrous feelings. Where do we get a sense of the practical and realistic? Where is the narrator idealistic?

iii) Unlike Wyatt, Sidney was not aiming at the expression of strong personal emotion but at something more exalted and more confident. Which do you prefer? Why? Give an example of where Sidney's verse is smoother than Wyatt's.

2.1.3
Extension

Either:
Read the definition of a sonnet or page 38 and the Wyatt sonnet in Supplement 2 (page 332). Compare the style and content of Wyatt's sonnet with Sidney's sonnet in this unit.

Or:
Find a sonnet by Petrarch and compare it with a sonnet by either Wyatt or Sidney.

2.1.4
Creative writing

Either:
Think of a person you admire. Write a love letter (or a poem) to that person. You may use your own voice or that of a character in a book you have read.

Or:
The three great narrative influences on Elizabethan poetry were Virgil, and through him Homer, the Bible and Ovid's *Metamorphoses*.
Write to a friend summarising your impressions of English sixteenth-century poetry. If possible, add a comparison with the literature of your own country at that time.

2.2 Drama: William Shakespeare (1546–1616)

2.2.1
Hamlet
(1600–1601)

The scene is Elsinore in Denmark. Prince Hamlet is the son of the late king. Hamlet's uncle Claudius is now on the throne. To Hamlet's disgust, his mother, Gertrude, has married Claudius only a month after the death of his father. Later, Hamlet discovers from his father's ghost that he had been murdered by Claudius.

● You are Hamlet. Your father's ghost has just told you about the murder. What are your first thoughts and reactions?

Oddly, the noble Prince Hamlet fails to take immediate revenge, a situation which fills him with guilt:

GLOSSARY	

To be ... be (l.1): (i) should I endure my sorrows or take the king's life – and so inevitably lose mine? ii) should I kill myself?

slings and arrows (l.3): (all the things that attack us)

No (l.6): nothing

to say (l.6): if it is true

flesh is heir to (l.8): we are born to suffer

consummation (l.8): perfect conclusion

devoutly (l.9): sincerely

perchance (l.10): perhaps (poetic)

Ay, there's the rub (l.10): Yes, that's where the problem is

shuffled off ... coil (l.12): shaken off the turmoil of our present life

give us pause (l.13): make us hesitate

respect (l.13): consideration

makes ... life (l.14): makes disaster last so long (or that makes such a long life disastrous?)

whips and scorns of time (l.15): insults of this world

contumely (l.16): humiliating behaviour

pangs ... love (l.17): pain when love is not valued

law's delay (l.17): delays caused by legal processes

HAMLET:
To be, or not to be – that is the question.   1
Whether 'tis nobler in the mind to suffer
The slings and arrows of outrageous fortune,
Or to take arms against a sea of troubles,
And by opposing end them? – To die – to sleep –   5
No more; and by a sleep to say we end
The heart-ache, and the thousand natural shocks
That flesh is heir to; 'tis a consummation
Devoutly to be wished. To die – to sleep –
To sleep! perchance to dream. Ay, there's the rub,   10
For in that sleep of death what dreams may come,
When we have shuffled off this mortal coil,
Must give us pause. There's the respect
That makes calamity of so long life.
For who would bear the whips and scorns of time,   15
The oppressor's wrong, the proud man's contumely,
The pangs of déspised love, the law's delay,
The insolence of office, and the spurns
That patient merit of the unworthy takes,
When he himself might his quietus make   20
With a bare bodkin? Who would fardels bear,
To grunt and sweat under a weary life,
But that the dread of something after death –
The undiscovered country from whose bourn
No traveller returns – puzzles the will,   25
And makes us rather bear those ills we have
Than fly to others that we know not of?
Thus conscience does make cowards of us all,
And thus the native hue of resolution
Is sicklied o'er with the pale cast of thought;   30
And enterprises of great pitch and moment,
With this regard, their currents turn awry,
And lose the name of action.

(from *Hamlet*)

40

insolence of office (l.18): rudeness shown by those in positions of authority

spurns ... takes (l.18–19): insults which good and quiet people take from those who are unworthy

his quietus make (l.20): settle his account (release him from life)

bare bodkin (l.21): only a dagger

fardels (l.21): burdens (*archaic*)

But that the dread ... puzzles the will (l.23–25): if the fear ... didn't make us uncertain

bourn (l.24): boundary (*archaic*)

conscience (l.28): being aware

native hue (l.29): natural colour

sicklied o'er with (l.30): weakened by

cast (l.30): colour

pitch and moment (l.31): importance

With ... awry (l.32): when considered like this their forward movement is diverted

Understanding and interpretation	i) Read the lines 'To be ... end them' (l.1–5). How could you summarise Hamlet's problem?
	ii) Explain what you think Hamlet could be referring to in a) 'No more' (l.6); b) ''tis a consummation' (l.8).
	iii) Read the lines 'To sleep! ... so long life' (l.10–14) and complete the following: The problem is not dying but ....
	iv) Read the lines 'For who ... bare bodkin' (l.15–21) and rewrite Hamlet's list in the gap, using either your own words or the words from the glossary: Who would put up with .... when he can put an end to it all by killing himself?
	v) Read the lines 'Who would fardels ... name of action' (l.21–33). What does Hamlet mean by 'Thus conscience does make cowards of us all'?
Language and style	Underline some of the metaphors in the extract. Select at least two and say what they illustrate.

At the end of the play Hamlet kills Claudius and his mother Gertrude accidentally drinks from a poisoned cup. Hamlet and Laertes (the brother of Ophelia, whom he has loved) kill each other in a duel. Fortinbras, prince of Norway, appears and gives Hamlet a military funeral.

● Do you know any other important scenes from the play? Who is this? What has happened?

Copy the following paragraph, adding capital letters and punctuation where necessary.

william shakespeare englands greatest writer was born in 1564 to a stratford-upon-avon glove merchant john shakespeare who played a prominent part in local affairs until his fortunes declined william received a good education at the local grammar school and in 1582 he married anne hathaway with whom he had three children suzanna hamnet and judith from that point on very little is known about his life other than that by 1592 he was already a successful dramatist and may also have been an actor if only of small parts in the winter of 1594 he was a leading member of the Lord Chamberlains company of actors with whom he stayed for the rest of his life when it came under royal patronage in 1603 it became known as the Kings Men shakespeare died in 1616

Scripts of only half of Shakespeare's plays appeared in print in his lifetime, in a quarto edition (where the standard size paper has been folded twice). There are very few records of performances and so it is difficult to establish their order of composition; the sequence below can be disputed in parts. A first folio edition (where the stantard size paper has been folded only once) was published in 1623, after Shakespeare's death, but it did not print the plays in the order in which they were written.

Phase 1

1590–1591 *Henry VI Parts 2 and 3*
1591–1592 *Henry VI Part I*
1592–1593 *Richard III*
The Comedy of Errors
1593–1594 *Titus Andronicus*
The Taming of the Shrew
1594–1595 *Two Gentlemen of Verona*
Love's Labour's Lost
Romeo and Juliet

These plays were characterised by: a variety of different modes (histories, different types of comedies and tragedies); end-stopped blank verse (where the line ends at the end of a sentence or at a strongly marked pause); quite a lot of rhymed lines; no great complexity of imagery.

Phase 2

1595–1596 *Richard II*
A Midsummer Night's Dream
1596–1597 *King John*
The Merchant of Venice
1597–1598 *Henry IV Parts 1 and 2*
1598–1599 *Much Ado about Nothing*
Henry V
1599–1600 *Julius Caesar*
The Merry Wives of Windsor
As You Like It
Twelfth Night

This phase is noted for: its more mature style with more flexible syntax and rhythm; more concentrated imagery; more forceful characterisation; a mixture of comedies and 'history' plays.

Phase 3

1600–1601 *Hamlet*
1601–1602 *Troilus and Cressida*
1602–1603 *All's Well that Ends Well*
1604–1605 *Measure for Measure*

The so-called 'problem' plays (a term used by late nineteenth-century critics who found it difficult to detect Shakespeare's intentions); difficult to interpret; sombre in tone.

Phase 4

1604–1605 *Othello*
1605–1606 *Macbeth*
          King Lear
1606–1607 *Antony and Cleopatra*
1607–1608 *Coriolanus*
          Timon of Athens

The great tragedies, showing a mode of thought quite unlike Greek tragedy or earlier English tragedy; a fully developed style.

Phase 5

1608–1609 *Pericles*
1609–1610 *Cymbeline*
1610–1611 *The Winter's Tale*
1611–1612 *The Tempest*

The romances or 'reconciliation' plays; little of the partial realism of the tragedies; tragedy transformed into reconciliation of the opposing elements.

2.2.5
Antony and Cleopatra
(1606–1607)

Do you know what *Antony and Cleopatra* is about? Can you guess?
Read this summary of the plot.

The great and noble soldier Mark Antony, with Octavius Caesar and Lepidus, is one of the 'triumvirate' which rules Rome and its empire (43–31 BC). However, Antony is also the lover of the beautiful Cleopatra, queen of Egypt. To the disgust of his officers, his passion leads him to neglect Rome and his political and military duties. On the death of his wife, Fulvia, however – and because of political developments – Antony tears himself away from Alexandria (in Egypt) and returns to Rome, where he marries Caesar's sister Octavia. The event temporarily mends his relationship with Caesar but it also provokes the intense jealousy of Cleopatra. Antony soon abandons Octavia and returns to Egypt. Caesar is enraged, and is in any case anxious to secure sole power over the empire. War breaks out between them and, largely owing to Cleopatra's attempt to participate in the war personally, Antony is defeated at the sea battle of Actium. Antony retreats to Alexandria, pursued by Caesar. There, after a momentary success, Antony is finally defeated. After receiving a false report of Cleopatra's death, he kills himself. He is carried to Cleopatra's mausoleum where he dies in her arms. She tries to challenge the power Caesar now has over her, but realising she has failed and determined not to give Caesar a greater sense of triumph, she takes her own life.

- i) Why is Antony resented by his officers?
  ii) Why does war break out between Antony and Caesar? Who wins?
  iii) What causes Cleopatra's death?

Match these descriptions with the extracts which follow.

a) A description of Cleopatra
b) Cleopatra cross-examines a messenger from Rome about Octavia
c) Antony's death
d) Cleopatra imagines Antony in his absence

Extract 1

GLOSSARY

Do bravely (l.5): carry
  yourself proudly
  (*archaic*)

wot'st thou (l.5): you know
  (*archaic*)

demi-Atlas (l.6): (in Greek
  mythology the heavens
  were supported by the
  Titan Atlas; *demi =*
  half, so Antony bears
  up half the world)

the arm . . . men (l.6–7):
  without equal in attack
  or defence

poison (l.10): (thoughts
  about Antony which
  are so bad for me)

*with Phoebus . . . black
  (l.11):* burnt dark with
  the sun's rays

Broad-fronted (l.12): with a
  broad forehead

morsel (l.14): tempting
  delicacy

Pompey (l.14): (Gnaeus,
  son of Pompey the
  Great)

make . . . brow (l.15): open
  his eyes wide in wonder
  at the sight of my face

anchor his aspect (l.16): stare

on his life (l.17): at what
  gave him vitality

CLEOPATRA: O Charmian!   1
Where think'st thou he is now? Stands he, or sits he?
Or does he walk? Or is he on his horse?
O happy horse, to bear the weight of Antony!
Do bravely, horse, for wot'st thou whom thou mov'st,   5
The demi-Atlas of this earth, the arm
And burgonet of men. He's speaking now,
Or murmuring, 'Where's my serpent of old Nile?'
For so he calls me. Now I feed myself
With most delicious poison. Think on me,   10
That am with Phoebus' amorous pinches black,
And wrinkled deep in time. Broad-fronted Caesar,
When thou wast here above the ground, I was
A morsel for a monarch: and great Pompey
Would stand and make his eyes grow in my brow;   15
There would he anchor his aspect, and die
With looking on his life.

                                    (Act 1 Scene 5)

Extract 2

ENOBARBUS: I will tell you.   1
The barge she sat in, like a burnished throne
Burned on the water: the poop was beaten gold;
Purple the sails, and so perfumèd that
The winds were love-sick with them; the oars were silver,   5
Which to the tune of flutes kept stroke, and made
The water which they beat to follow faster,
As amorous of their strokes. For her own person,
It beggared all description: she did lie

44

In her pavilion, cloth of gold, of tissue,   10
O'er-picturing that Venus where we see
The fancy outwork nature. On each side her
Stood pretty dimpled boys, like smiling Cupids,
With divers-coloured fans, whose wind did seem
To glow the delicate cheeks which they did cool,   15
And what they undid did.

(Act 2 Scene 2)

Extract 3

MESSENGER: Most gracious Majesty.   1

CLEOPATRA: Didst thou behold
Octavia?

MESSENGER: Ay, dread queen.

CLEOPATRA: Where?   5

MESSENGER: Madam, in Rome.
I looked her in the face, and saw her led
Between her brother and Mark Antony.

CLEOPATRA: Is she as tall as me?

MESSENGER: She is not, madam.   10

CLEOPATRA: Didst hear her speak? Is she shrill-tongued or low?

MESSENGER: Madam, I heard her speak; she is low-voiced.

CLEOPATRA: That's not so good. He cannot like her long.

CHARMIAN: Like her? O Isis! 'Tis impossible.

CLEOPATRA: I think so, Charmian. Dull of tongue and dwarfish.   15
What majesty is in her gait? Remember,
If e'er thou look'dst on majesty.

MESSENGER: She creeps:
Her motion and her station are as one.
She shows a body rather than a life,   20
A statue than a breather.

CLEOPATRA: Is this certain?

MESSENGER: Or I have no observance.

CHARMIAN: Three in Egypt
Cannot make better note.   25

(Act 3 Scene 3)

Extract 4 (abridged)

GLOSSARY

Burn ... in (l.2): bring eternal darkness.

Darkling ... world (l.2–3): may the changing shores of the world remain in darkness (may the universe go in mourning for Antony)

Iras (l.4): (another of Cleopatra's attendants)

hither (l.5): to this place

woe 'tis so (l.10): how sad it should be so

importune ... awhile (l.12): beg death to wait for a while

woo't (l.17): will you (archaic)

Hast ... me (l.18): do you not care for me?

abide (l.18): stay behind (archaic)

sty (l.20): a filthy place to live in

crown o' th' (l.21): greatest man on

withered ... garland (l.23): the victory band of flowers is dead

pole (l.24): maypole around which people danced; pole star (north star); flagpole around which soldiers came together

Are ... gone (l.25): the distinction between large and small no longer exists

remarkable (l.26): to be wondered at

the visiting moon (l.27): the moon which comes and goes

CLEOPATRA: O sun,   1
Burn the great sphere thou mov'st in! Darkling stand
The varying shore o' th' world! O Antony,
Antony, Antony! Help, Charmian, help, Iras, help:
Help, friends below; let's draw him hither.   5

ANTONY: Peace!
Not Caesar's valour hath o'erthrown Antony,
But Antony's hath triumphed on itself.

CLEOPATRA: So it should be, that none but Antony
Should conquer Antony, but woe 'tis so.   10

ANTONY: I am dying, Egypt, dying; only
I here importune death awhile, until
Of many thousand kisses, the poor last
I lay upon thy lips.
...
                    Now my spirit is going,   15
I can no more.

CLEOPATRA: Noblest of men, woo't die?
Hast thou no care of me? Shall I abide
In this dull world, which in thy absence is
No better than a sty? O, see, my women,   20
The crown o' th'earth doth melt. My lord!
                                        [ANTONY *dies*]
O, withered is the garland of the war,
The soldier's pole is fall'n: young boys and girls
Are level now with men. The odds is gone,   25
And there is nothing left remarkable
Beneath the visiting moon.

CHARMIAN: O quietness, lady.
                              [CLEOPATRA *faints*]

                              (Act 4 Scene 15)

                         (from *Antony and Cleopatra*)

Understanding and interpretation

i) Select lines or phrases to support each of the following statements. Then answer the questions.

Extract 1 a) Cleopatra imagines Antony's superhuman powers. b) She assumes he is missing her.
Can you find an example of Cleopatra's sensuous language?

Extract 2 Enobarbus tries to create the impression that Cleopatra's love is magical. In what way is the description unrealistic?

Extract 3 a) Cleopatra is eager to hear about Octavia's inferior qualities. b) The messenger speaks ill of Octavia.
What does the scene show us about Cleopatra's character?

Extract 4 a) Antony expresses gratitude that he has killed himself rather than let anyone else kill him. b) Cleopatra feels that greatness has died with Antony.

What does the question 'Hast thou no care of me?' (l.18) show?

ii) What impression do you get from these extracts of Antony and Cleopatra and their love affair?

iii) Can you find out how Antony and Cleopatra killed themselves?

Appreciation   i) Sometimes, but not always, Shakespeare's lines contain five 'feet', each foot consisting of a weak stress followed by a strong stress. These lines are called 'iambic pentameter'. Verse following an iambic pattern where there is no rhyme at the end is called 'blank verse'.

Can you find an example of 'iambic pentameter'? Look, for example, at Extract 2.

ii) Rhythm is the pattern of strong and weak syllables. In Shakespeare's dramatic verse, rhythm is very important and stress is frequently used for dramatic effect. In Extract 3, Shakespeare places the word 'Octavia' (l.3) at the beginning of the line, giving it powerful emphasis – to give a sense of importance to Cleopatra's question, to show the focus of her attention and to show her anxiety about the answer.

Answer the following questions:

a) In Extract 2 what effect does the word 'Burned' (l.3) have coming at the beginning of a line?

b) What effect does the series of short questions and short exchanges in Extract 3 have?

iii) Find examples of the following literary effects in the extract mentioned.

a) hyperbole – Extract 4
b) the rhythm of the verse conveying the impression of what is being described – Extract 2
c) simile – Extract 2
d) metaphor – Extract 1
e) assonance (where stressed vowel sounds in words next to each other correspond, or nearly correspond) – Extract 4
f) enjambment (where the sentence continues into the next line of verse without any punctuation) – Extract 4

iv) Read these two contrasting views of the play:

Critical response

This is a very noble play. ... It presents a fine picture of Roman pride and Eastern magnificence: and the struggle between the two ... The characters breathe, move, and live. Shakespeare does not stand reasoning on what his characters would do or say, but at once *becomes* them, and speaks and acts for them. ... The character of Cleopatra is a master-piece. ... The Egyptian is voluptuous, ostentatious, conscious, boastful of her charms, haughty, tyrannical, fickle. ... She has great and unpardonable faults, but the   1

   5

beauty of her death almost redeems them. She learns from the
depth of despair the strength of her affections. She keeps her
queen-like state in the last disgrace, and her sense of the pleasurable
in the last moments of her life. She tastes a luxury in death. (William
Hazlitt, *Characters of Shakespeare's Plays*, 1817)

10

tyrannical (l.7): unjustly
cruel

fickle (l.8): changes
suddenly, without
reason

unpardonable (l.8): that
can't be forgiven

redeems (l.9): makes
them seem less bad

thrive on (l.17): be at its
best as the result of

Shakespeare makes it impossible for us not to question the nature
and conditions of that very energy that the lovers release in each
other ... Looking back, we can recall how often this love has
seemed to thrive on emotional stimulants. They were necessary for
much the same reason as the feasts and wine. For the continued
references to feasting ... serve to bring out the element of repetition
and monotony in a passion which, centring on itself, is self-
consuming ... (L.C. Knights, '*King Lear* and the Great Tragedies',
1955)

15

20

2.2.6 Shakespeare's plays were popular not only with aristocrats, intellectuals
and monarchs but also with ordinary people. These was in them
something for everyone.

Although their plots were often drawn from British and European
history – sometimes they were reworkings of earlier plays – they were
essentially of their time. How is it then that a playwright who was very
much an Elizabethan has had such a powerful appeal to subsequent
generations and is still popular today? The answer normally given is that
Shakespeare understood human affairs in their essential aspects and
explored them in a way which was both individual and universal at one
and the same time.

● Read this account of his achievement:

GLOSSARY

in toto (l.1): as a whole
(Latin)

epithet (l.7): descriptive
phrase

myriad-minded (l.7): with
many sides to his
mind

exalted (l.11): high-
sounding

mock-heroic (l.12): (style
which makes fun of
heroic action and
character)

fumblings (l.14): awkward
speech

allusions (l.14): indirect
references

seethe (l.16): confused
excitement

[Shakespeare's works] *in toto* exhibit a range of imaginative
sympathy and a power of varied expression unmatched in English
(and perhaps in any language). He showed, more than anyone, that
through language could be conveyed in all their strength and their
subtle manifestations the passions and thoughts, the emotional
and moral and spiritual concerns of mankind. ...

Coleridge's epithet 'myriad-minded' is appropriate in several
ways: there is the immense variety of characters from all stations
and modes of life ... and the corresponding variety of objects and
environmental references in their language; there is the variety of
styles, from ceremonial eloquence and exalted lyricism and profound affirmation and statement to the mock-heroic and everyday
realism and colloquialisms and the word-brief utterances of the
fumblings of the near dumb. ... There are the allusions to law,
medicine, travel and foreign places, music, sports, the kitchen,
trades ... And in the middle, as it were, of the seethe of life
observed and felt with such strength and keenness, Shakespeare
maintained the power of judgement. ...

1

5

10

15

keenness (l.17): sharpness
sybaritic (l.19): who like to indulge in sensual pleasures
mingled yarn (l.22): different types of thread, mixed together

Are Antony and his Cleopatra sybaritic fools, or are they noble and heroic? The only proper answer is – is it not? – that Shakespeare is here once again offering us illustration in vital and vivid form of one of his favourite thoughts: 'The web of our life is of a mingled yarn, good and ill together.' (H. Coombes, *English Literature Made Simple*, Heinemann 1977) 20

There are other extracts from Shakespeare's plays in the Prologue (pages 11–13) and Supplement 2 (pages 336–340).

2.3 The Elizabethan period

2.3.1
Elizabeth I

Elizabeth I (1558–1603), the last monarch of the House of Tudor, was a Protestant (a term used for those who broke away from the Roman Catholic Church). Her predecessor, Mary I (on the throne 1553–1558), had been a repressive Catholic, married to the most fanatically Catholic sovereign in Europe, Philip II of Spain. Although Elizabeth cut the ties with Rome, her tolerance and her ability to compromise won her the loyalty of both Catholics and Puritans (Protestant reformers who insisted on simplicity in religious forms). In 1588 Philip's attempt to conquer England led to the defeat of the great Spanish fleet known as the Armada. Sir Francis Drake (?1540–1596), a national hero, was one of the commanders of the English fleet. This victory was a great triumph for Elizabeth and through her the nation.

- i) Where necessary, add 'a', 'an' or 'the' in the gaps:
  Looking back, ... Elizabethan period was .... period when .... English national spirit triumphed, ... period between .... restraints of .... medievalism and .... rise of .... Puritanism. It was .... immensely creative period: .... flowering of .... English Renaissance, which finally reached .... people through .... court. In .... England, ... Renaissance was largely .... literary achievement, with its poetic drama, songs, lyrics and .... ballads. It was also .... period of .... great seamanship and .... time when .... wealthy upper classes built immense country .... houses all over .... land. .... queen herself, ... cautious politician, was both highly cultivated and able to rise to .... heroic demands made upon her.

- ii) What else do you know about this period in Europe?

49

2.3.2
Ideas

The Tudors inherited much of the medieval view of the world which consisted of numberless but linked 'degrees' of being, from the four physical elements (air, fire, earth and water) up to the pure intelligence of angels. Also, the whole universe was governed by divine will; Nature was God's instrument, the social hierarchy a product of Nature. Everyone had their natural place in the unity of the whole: both within the family and the state (which, it was believed, should be governed by a single head). At the same time, this order, which was founded on Nature, existed for man's benefit, and man was an integral part of it. His godlike qualities had, unfortunately, been ruined by the Fall (as described in the Bible) and he was constantly troubled by such things as wars and plagues. Nevertheless, provided that he treated this world as preparation for the next, and, with the help of human reason, he kept his body subject to his soul, he had it within his powers to enjoy civilised happiness.

2.3.3
The Elizabethan theatre

i) Make sentences from the following phrases:

a) of literary-minded noblemen / often / Actors and playwrights / had the patronage / as well as travellers and entertainers

b) in London / called The Theatre / in 1576 / was built / The first permanent theatre / by James Burbage

c) of inns and great halls / Plays / in the courtyards / were often enacted

d) in 1599 / was built / where Shakespeare's plays were performed / from the material of Burbage's Theatre / The Globe Theatre

e) took place / Performances / in the daytime

f) pageants, humour, wit, songs / Plays / and of course poetry / were full of

g) in particular those by Seneca / was initially much influenced by / English tragedy / classical plays in Latin

h) Christopher Marlowe (1564–1593) /Ben Jonson (?1573–1637) / and / Apart from Shakespeare / Thomas Kyd (1558–1594) / included / the great dramatists

ii) Here are some of the features of the Globe Theatre. Make each set of notes into no more than two complete sentences:

a) made of wood – open in the centre – structure derived from that of typical courtyards

b) galleries – looked down on yard where poorer spectators stood – theatre held about 1200 spectators

c) stage jutted out into audience – divided into three parts: front, middle and rear – no curtains at front – actors surrounded on three sides

d) upper stage – used for, for example, the walls of a town

e) inner stage – for example, used for bedroom scenes – upper-inner stage – balcony scenes – both normally had curtains in front

f) no scenery – lavish costumes – women's roles played by boy actors

What effect do you think any of these features had on the plays that were written?

2.3.4 Write captions for the following pictures. One has been done for you.

Sir Francis Drake

2.4 Prose: The humanists

The word 'humanist' was first used by Italian scholars to refer to a teacher of the *studia humanitatis* – the language and literature of Ancient Rome and Ancient Greece. The aim of such teachers was to bridge the gap between the 'classical' period and their own. Through education, they would make the religious, philosophical and moral beliefs of the day healthier, and strengthen their country in the arts of defence and peace. The movement has its origins in the Italian poet and scholar Petrarch (1304–1374) but didn't reach England until the sixteenth century. In the twentieth century, humanists assert the capacity of humans for fulfilment through a life based on reason and in so doing assume that man's command of scientific knowledge has made religion redundant. Sixteenth-century humanists were Christians, even though their critical spirit eventually brought them into conflict with the Church. The greatest of the European humanists were the Dutchman Erasmus (1466–1536) and his English friend Sir Thomas More (1478–1535).

Warm-up   Choose one of these exercises:

i) Latin and Ancient Greek are 'dead' languages in that they are no longer actively used. However, until very recently, in Europe at least, they were both widely studied. Discuss either of the following questions:
   – In some places Latin and Ancient Greek are still studied. What are arguments for and against studying them in the twentieth century?
   – Why do you think the study of them is in decline?

ii) What are the pros and cons of the following methods of learning a foreign language?
   – translation
   – working through grammar books
   – listening to native speakers talking
   – practising phrases from a phrase book
   – reading novels with the help of a dictionary

iii) Do you think children should be forced or encouraged to do their schoolwork? What should a teacher do if they refuse?

**2.4.1
Roger Ascham
(1515–1568)**

Roger Ascham, an enlightened humanist, was a tutor in Latin and Greek to Elizabeth I.

In his book *The Schoolmaster* (1570), Ascham describes his view of the best way to teach children to write good Latin using the letters of Marcus Tullius Cicero (106–43 BC) as a model. (The original spelling and punctuation have been modernised.):

Extract 1

First, let him [the schoolmaster] teach the child cheerfully and plainly the cause and matter of the letter; then, let him construe it into English so oft, as the child may easily carry away the understanding of it; lastly, parse it over perfectly. This done thus, let the child, by and by, both construe and parse it over again; so that it may appear, that the child doubteth in nothing that his master taught him before. After this, the child must take a paper book, 5 and sitting in some place, where no man shall prompt him, by himself, let him translate into English his former lesson. Then showing it to his master, let the master take from him his Latin book, and pausing an hour at the least then let the child translate his own English into Latin again in another paper book. When the child bringeth it turned into Latin, the master must compare it with Tully's book, and lay them both together; and where the child doth well, either in choosing or true placing of Tully's words, let the master praise him, and say, 'Here ye do well.' For I assure you, there is no such whetstone to sharpen a good wit, and encourage a will to learning, as is praise.

But if the child miss, either in forgetting a word, or in changing a good with a worse, or misordering the sentence, I would not have the master either frown or chide with him, if the child have done his diligence, and used no truantship therein. For I know by good experience, that a child shall take more profit of two faults gently warned of, than of four things rightly hit: for then the master shall have good occasion to say unto him; 'N., Tully would have used such a word, not this: Tully would have placed this word here, not there; would have used this case, this number, this person, this degree, this gender: he would have used this mood, this tense, this simple, rather than this compound; this adverb here, not there: he would have ended the sentence with this verb, not with that noun or participle,' etc.

Tully's (l.14): (Cicero's)
whetstone (l.17): stone used for sharpening cutting tools
chide (l.21): scold
done his diligence (l.21): given his attention and energy
used ... therein (l.22): didn't fail to do all the work he should have done (because he was lazy)
N. (l.25): Nomen (Latin; meaning [the child's] name)
case ... participle (l.27-31): (the nouns are all grammatical terms)

Understanding

i) Divide Ascham's procedure into seven stages using the words in parentheses. Stage 1 and Stage 7 have been done for you.
Stage 1: Tell the child what the letter is about.
Stage 2: (English)
Stage 3: (grammatically)
Stage 4: (again)
Stage 5: (previous letter)
Stage 6: (Latin)
Stage 7: Compare with the original.
ii) What do you think of the procedure as a way of learning to read and write a foreign language? How does it compare with your experience?

Interpretation

i) Which of these words indicate Ascham's view of what the teacher's attitude should be? 'cheerfully' (l.1); 'praise' (l.16); 'frown' (l.21); 'chide' (l.21); 'gently' (l.23)
ii) Do these have more of a positive or negative connotation in context? 'parse it over perfectly' (l.4); 'will to learning' (l.18)

Extract 2   In this extract, too, Ascham gives his views on teaching.

GLOSSARY

And, therefore ... pleasure (l.1-3): (from *Republic* by Plato, ?428–?348 BC.)
fond (l.3): foolish (archaic)

Hear what Socrates ... doth ... say: 'And therefore, my dear friend, bring not up your children in learning by compulsion and fear, but by playing and pleasure.' ... Fond schoolmasters neither can understand, nor will follow this good counsel of

Socrates; but wise riders in their office can and will do both; which is the only cause that commonly the young gentlemen of England go so unwillingly to school, and run so fast to the stable. For in very deed, fond schoolmasters, by fear, do beat into them the hatred of learning; and wise riders, by gentle allurements, do breed up in them the love of riding. They find fear and bondage in schools, they feel liberty and freedom in stables; which causeth them utterly to abhor the one, and most gladly to haunt the other. ... Therefore, if to the goodness of nature be joined the wisdom of the teacher, in leading young wits into a right and plain way of learning; surely children, kept up in God's fear, and governed by his grace, may most easily be brought well to serve God and their country, both by virtue and wisdom. ... Before I went into Germany, I came to Broadgate in Leicestershire, to take my leave of that noble lady Jane Grey, to whom I was exceeding much beholding. Her parents, the Duke and Duchess, with all the household, gentlemen and gentle-women, were hunting in the park. I found her in her chamber, reading *Phædo Platonis* in Greek, and that with as much delight as some gentlemen would read a merry tale in Boccace. After salutation, and duty done, with some other talk, I asked her, why she would lose such pastime in the park? Smiling, she answered me; 'I wiss, all their sport in the park is but a shadow to that pleasure that I find in Plato. Alas! good folk, they never felt what true pleasure meant.' 'And how came you, madam,' quoth I, 'to this deep knowledge of pleasure? and what did chiefly allure you unto it, seeing not many women, but very few men, have attained thereunto?' 'I will tell you,' quoth she, 'and tell you a truth, which perchance ye will marvel at. One of the greatest benefits that ever God gave me, is, that he sent me so sharp and severe parents, and so gentle a schoolmaster. For when I am in presence either of father or mother; whether I speak, keep silence, sit, stand, or go, eat, drink, be merry, or sad, be sewing, playing, dancing, or doing any thing else; I must do it, as it were, in such weight, measure, and number, even so perfectly, as God made the world; or else I am so sharply taunted, so cruelly threatened, yea presently sometimes with pinches, nips, and bobs, and other ways (which I will not name for the honour I bear them) so without measure misordered, that I think myself in hell, till time come that I must go to Mr Elmer; who teacheth me so gently, so pleasantly, with such fair allure-ments to learning, that I think all the time nothing whiles I am with him. And when I am called from him, I fall on weeping, because whatsoever I do else but learning, is full of grief, trouble, fear, and whole misliking unto me. And thus my book hath been so much my pleasure, and bringeth daily to me more pleasure and more, that in respect of it, all other pleasures, in very deed, be but trifles and troubles unto me.'

in their office (l.5): when they're carrying out their duties

allurements (l.10): attractions

bondage (l.11): slavery

abhor (l.12): hate

haunt (l.13): often go to

take my leave (l.19): say goodbye

Jane Grey (l.19): (1537–1554, Queen of England for nine days, was beheaded on a charge of treason; at fifteen she could write Latin, Greek, French and German and she had begun to study Hebrew)

was ... beholding (l.20): owed a lot to

Phaedo Platonis (l.23): by Plato; a dialogue concerning the nature of the soul

Boccace (l.24): Giovanni Boccaccio (?1313–1375), author of the *Decameron*

duty done (l.25): (i.e. a proper exchange of courtesies)

I wiss (l.27): certainly (*archaic*)

Quoth (l.30): said (*archaic*)

perchance (l.33): perhaps (*poetic*)

taunted (l.41): mocked

yea presently (l.41): indeed, before long (*archaic*)

pinches, nips and bobs (l.42): (a variety of little physical assaults; bobs = taps)

which ... them (l.42-43): which I won't tell you about out of respect for my parents

misordered (l.43): badly treated

Mr Elmer (l.44): John Aylmer (1521–1594), a noted Latin and Greek scholar, later Bishop of London

trifles (l.52): things of little importance

> I remember this talk gladly, both because it is so worthy of memory, and because also it was the last talk that ever I had, and the last time that ever I saw that noble and worthy lady.   55

(from *The Schoolmaster*)

Appreciation

i) To make his point of view about learning more vivid, Ascham makes a series of contrasts. For example, 'school' (l.7) is contrasted with 'stables' (l.8). What are the following contrasted with
'compulsion and fear' (l.2-3); 'fond schoolmasters' (l.3); 'beat' (l.8); 'hatred of learning' (l.9); 'fear and bondage' (l.11); 'abhor' (l.12) *'Phaedo Platonis'* (l.23); 'sport in the park' (l.27); 'sharp and severe parents' (l.35); 'so cruelly threatened' (l.41)

ii) How does the Jane Grey story illustrate Ascham's principles?

iii) Ascham was regarded as a kindly man, full of both learning and practical common sense. Where can you find these qualities illustrated?

iv) Ascham's prose served to strengthen and enrich the English language so that it rivalled the other European languages as a literary language. The following phrases have been used to describe his style:

> 'eloquent but plain'
> 'strong everyday idiom'
> 'relaxed and personal'
> 'direct'
> 'carefully framed and neat'.

Can you find examples of any of these?

Discussion

i) 'Learning teacheth more in one year than experience in twenty: and learning teacheth safely, when experience maketh more miserable than wise.' (Ascham) What are your views of the relative merits of learning and experience?

ii) What do you think of Jane Grey?

2.5 Elizabethan prose

Later influential prose works included Sir Thomas North's translation of Plutarch's *Lives of the Noble Grecians and Romans* (1579), which Shakespeare drew on for *Julius Caesar, Coriolanus* and *Antony and Cleopatra*; Richard Hakluyt's collection *The Principal Navigations, Voyages and Discoveries of the English Nation* (1589) and early prose romances such as John Lyly's *Euphues* (1578), Thomas Lodge's *Rosalynde* (1590), Thomas Nashe's *Unfortunate Traveller* (1594) and Robert Greene's *Pandosto* (1588) which Shakespeare used as a source for *The Winter's Tale*. However, the prose works which have probably had the most lasting influence are Francis Bacon's, in, for example, his *Essays* (1597) (see page 340).

● What impressions do you gain of Elizabethan England from some of these titles?

2.6 Chronology

Complete the right-hand side of the chart with information from this unit.

British history	Literature
Tudor monarchs	
1509–1547: Henry VIII. Powerful and talented. Notorious for having had six wives, with two executed, two divorced. Exerted power through Parliament. Act of Supremacy (1534) established king as head of Church in England, replacing sovereignty of Pope. Dissolution of all monasteries in England (1539). War against France (1543–1546). Mary Stuart became queen of Scotland in 1542, a few days after her birth.	
1547–1553: Edward VI. Boy-king. Act of Uniformity (1549) to secure religious unity led to *Book of Common Prayer* in English (and not Latin). Mary Stuart, a Catholic, became betrothed to the heir to the French throne at five years of age and was sent to France.	
1553–1558: Mary I. Repeal of anti-papal legislation (1555). Mary married Philip II of Spain. Wars with France led to loss of Calais (1558). Severe repression of Protestants.	
1558–1603: Elizabeth I. Restored Church of England's independence from Rome, under Acts of Supremacy and Uniformity (1559). Tolerance of Catholics. *Book of Common Prayer* required for church worship. Mary Stuart driven from Scotland (1567) but eventually executed in England (1587) for threat she posed to English throne. Francis Drake sailed round the world (1577–1581). Philip of Spain's attempted invasion defeated (1588). East India Company given a monopoly of Eastern Trade (1600). James Stuart ruled over Scotland (1566–1603) as James VI became James I of England when Elizabeth died childless.	

2.7 Activities

Creative writing

Either:

Sit in groups. Each person should take a piece of paper and write an adjective and noun combination of two words on the theme of study (for example, 'hard work' or 'modern school'). Pass the paper to the person on your left and add another combination to the paper you receive. Continue round the group. When you receive your original piece of paper back, try to make the collection of words on your paper into a poem, changing what you like. Show each other your poems.

Or:

Write a review of a film, novel or play with a teacher in it.

Discussion

Discuss your work with this book. Do you prefer to listen to the texts or read them? Why? Do you like to discuss the exercises with other students? Why?/Why not?

Crossword

Complete the crossword. The answers can be found in this unit.

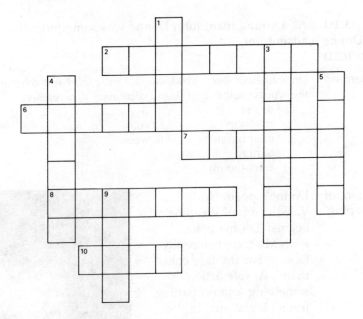

Clues

1) 'When her loose .... from her shoulders did fall'
2) Wyatt's patron
3) One of the triumvirate which ruled Rome
4) Publisher of poetic anthology in 1557
5) .... of Athens
6) ENBLOY (anagram) – a queen
7) Where Antony was defeated in a sea battle
8) Dutch humanist
9) 'How far they shoot ....!'
10) Lived 1537–1554

UNIT 3

The first half of the seventeenth century

3.1 The Metaphysical Poets

The Metaphysical Poets were a succession of poets who wrote at the beginning of the seventeenth century. Their poetry was marked by such things as: intense feeling combined with ingenious thought; elaborate, witty images; an interest in mathematics, science and geography; an overriding interest in the soul; and direct, colloquial expression even in sonnets and lyrics.

3.1.1
John Donne
(1572–1631)

As a young man, John Donne was something of a courtier and an adventurer.

Warm-up

Draw lines to show which words in the left-hand column can be associated with the words on the right. Use a dictionary if necessary.

to sigh
to stamp
grief (noun)   to coin
to mint   to weep
tears (noun)

'A Valediction: of
Weeping'

Donne's poem 'A Valediction: of Weeping' begins: 'Let me pour forth/My tears before thy face ... For thy face coins them'. A 'valediction' is something said on parting from a loved one. In the poem Donne expresses to a woman his powerful but mixed feelings on leaving her to travel overseas.

John Donne

58

A Valediction: of Weeping

Let me pour forth   1
My tears before thy face, whilst I stay here,
For thy face coins them, and thy stamp they bear,
And by this Mintage they are something worth,
For thus they be   5
Pregnant of thee;
Fruits of much grief they are, emblems of more;
When a tear falls, that thou falls which it bore,
So thou and I are nothing then, when on a divers shore.

On a round ball   10
A workman that hath copies by, can lay
An Europe, Afric, and an Asia,
And quickly make that, which was nothing, *All*,
So doth each tear,
Which thee doth wear,   15
A globe, yea world by that impression grow,
Till thy tears mixt with mine do overflow
This world, by waters sent from thee, my heaven dissolved so

O more than Moon,
Draw not up seas to drown me in thy sphere,   20
Weep me not dead, in thine arms, but forbear
To teach the sea, what it may do too soon;
Let not the wind
Example find,
To do me more harm, than it purposeth;   25
Since thou and I sigh one another's breath,
Whoe'er sighs most, is cruellest, and hastes the other's death,

GLOSSARY

forth (l.1): out (*archaic*)

Mintage (l.4): process of making coins

Pregnant (l.6): full; born (possibly also a reference to the old superstition that lovers could 'look babies' in one another's eyes)

emblems (l.7): signs

that thou . . . (l.8): since you

divers (l.9): different; foreign (*archaic*)

more than Moon (l.19): (a reference to the pull of the moon on the tides; the moon was also a traditional symbol of unchangingness and chastity)

sphere (l.20): globe; influence

forbear (l.21): hold back

wind (l.23): (suggesting; her sighs; and the wind in a storm that causes shipwrecks)

purposeth (l.25): intends

hastes (l.27): speeds up (*archaic*)

Understanding and interpretation

i) Although the poem has many layers of possible meaning, which of the following alternatives do you think get closest to the main argument of the poem? Can you improve the paraphrase?

Stanza 1:

a) Lines 1–6 ('Let me . . . of thee')
Allow me to be foolish enough to let my tears flow *in front of you before I leave/all over your face while I'm here,* since your appearance causes me sorrow and encourages tears from me with your picture on them, like coins and their picture of a queen. Since the tears are caused by you and contain you they *have no value/have value.*

b) Lines 7–9 ('Fruits . . . shore')
My tears are the products of unhappiness and signs of more unhappiness to come after we have separated. When one of my tears falls like a piece of fruit and with it the reflection of you who caused it, it seems as though we *will mean nothing to each other/will have no money* when I am away from you in a foreign land.

59

Stanza 2:

a) Lines 10–13 ('On a . . . nothing, All')
On a blank globe a workman can draw whole continents from copies he has next to him and quickly *make a world out of nothing/destroy that which was everything.*

b) Lines 14–18 ('So doth . . . dissolved so')
In the same way each of *your/my* tears, having an image of *you/me* on it, grows into a world. Then our tears will mix and flood this world with water which both comes from you and is caused by you. *And so this world of ours which is a heaven to me is destroyed/The heavens open and you are drowned.*

Stanza 3:

a) Lines 19–22 ('O more . . . soon')
O, you who are *not only a moon/more powerful and more valuable than the moon,* don't be the cause of my tears which together with your tears will drown me as we embrace. Instead, stop crying and don't give a lesson to the sea which may kill me soon enough on my journey anyway.

b) Lines 23–28 ('Let . . . death')
Don't let the wind find an example in your sighs and do me more damage than it already intends to when I'm on the sea. Since *you and I breathe less easily when we see the other sighing/we are so much part of each other* whoever sighs the most is the cruellest because it encourages more tears and speeds up the death of the other so why don't we cheer up?

ii) The following interpretations have been made by different critics. Can you find evidence in the text for at least one of them?
a) Donne is frightened he is going to be killed.
b) Donne suspects the woman might be unfaithful to him in his absence.
c) Donne's emotion is so great he can't express himself logically.
d) Donne might be enjoying his sorrow.

iii) Do you find the poem sad? Amusing? Intellectual?

Language and style Answer at least one of the following questions about the poem:
i) What can you say about
– the rhyme scheme?
– the rhythm?
Is the verse conversational? How has it been given poetic effect?

ii) What links are there between the following images a) tear, coin, globe, moon?
b) tear, fruit, pregnant?

iii) Where does Donne suggest that the woman's tears are like jewels?

iv) Explain the effect of any of the following images: coins (1.3); world (1.16); moon (1.19).

John Donne In 1596 Donne sailed with the earl of Essex to sack Cadiz and in 1597 went with Raleigh to hunt Spanish treasure ships off the Azores. Although he was elected a member of Parliament in 1601 and was secretary to Sir Thomas Egerton, a minister of the queen, he lost favour – and was briefly imprisoned – when he secretly married Lady Egerton's niece, Ann More. (She died in 1617 after giving birth to their twelfth child, of which only seven survived.) Having rejected the Catholic religion in which he was brought up, in 1615 he entered the Church of England and in 1621 became the Dean of St Paul's Cathedral. He was to become one of the most fashionable and dedicated preachers of the age.

● Put the verbs in the correct form:

Donne's poems (collect) .... by his son John and (publish) .... in 1633. His *Satires and Elegies* (write) .... in the 1590s, his love lyrics (his *Songs and Sonnets*) (write) .... at various times and his *Holy Sonnets*, (begin) .... about 1610, but mostly (finish) .... after 1621. While his career (can see) .... as (divide) .... into two halves – Jack Donne, the lover of ladies and the theatre, and Dr John Donne, the great preacher – there is nevertheless remarkable consistency in the style of his poems and prose. Not only physically vigorous and intellectually complex, his writing (have) .... considerable dramatic force and contains a wide variety of moods. Thomas Carew (1595–1640), a friend and fellow poet, (describe) .... him as 'a king that ruled as he thought fit/The universal monarchy of wit'. Frequently nowadays, Donne's prose – in the incredibly powerful sermons and *Devotions* – (use) .... to exemplify the strength of the 'unified sensibility' of English writing before rational prose objectives (become) .... separated from imaginative poetic ones.

'Batter my heart, three-personed God'

In the following sonnet, Donne addresses God. He tells Him to 'batter' – beat – his heart to make it 'admit' Him. Unfortunately, although he loves God, he is 'betrothed' to God's enemy, the Devil. In his struggle towards goodness, he seems to tell God that he can only belong to Him if He 'imprisons' him and 'ravishes' him.

GLOSSARY

three-personed (l.1): (in the Christian religion the Trinity is the unity of: God, the Father; Jesus Christ, the Son; and the Holy Spirit)

You (l.1): (the poet is addressing God. The personal pronouns 'Him' and 'You' usually begin with a capital letter when they refer to God)

usurped (l.5): seized and possessed by force

O (l.6): both 'Oh!' and 'nothing'

viceroy (l.7): governor of a state, representing a sovereign

fain (l.9): happily (archaic)

Except You enthrall me (l.13): unless you make me a slave

ravish (l.14): take me with violence (rape)

'Batter my heart, three-personed God'

Batter my heart, three-personed God; for You   1
As yet but knock, breathe, shine, and seek to mend;
That I may rise and stand, o'erthrow me, and bend
Your force to break, blow, burn, and make me new.
I, like an usurped town, to another due,   5
Labor to admit You, but O, to no end;
Reason, Your viceroy in me, me should defend,
But is captived, and proves weak or untrue.
Yet dearly I love You, and would be loved fain,
But am betrothed unto Your enemy.   10
Divorce me, untie or break that knot again;
Take me to You, imprison me, for I,
Except You enthrall me, never shall be free,
Nor ever chaste, except You ravish me.

● In what way has God been successful so far? Do you think Donne is resigned to 'losing' to the Devil? Do you find the poem shocking? If so, why?

Language and style Write out and complete the following chart with words/phrases from the poem. (One example is given.)

Instructions to God	*Batter my heart . . .*
Military images	
Images of God as a blacksmith	
Images of marriage	

3.1.2
Metaphysical poetry

One characteristic of Metaphysical Poetry is the use of the 'metaphysical conceit', an image which unites very different experiences in a single impact on the imagination:

> '. . . her pure and eloquent blood
> Spoke in her cheeks, and so distinctly wrought,
> That one might almost say, her body thought.' (John Donne in
'The Second Anniversary').

This is a conceit because bodies are not normally thought of as being able to think!

Over the years, attitudes towards the Metaphysical Poets have changed. As can be seen from the following extracts, both Dryden and Johnson (who was the first to suggest the category Metaphysical Poets) were uneasy about them. They preferred instead the assurance, clarity, restraint and shapeliness of the great Augustan poets of ancient Rome. However, in the twentieth century, the Metaphysicals have been greatly admired by both critics and poets.

GLOSSARY

affects (l.1): shows a liking for
perplexes (l.2): confuses
nice (l.3): fine and delicate
endeavour (l.9): effort
sensibility (l.10): ability to respond to experience
devour (l.11): possess

Donne affects the metaphysics not only in his satires, but in his amorous verses, where nature only should reign; and perplexes the mind of the fair sex with nice speculations of philosophy, when he should engage their hearts, and entertain them with the softness of love. (John Dryden, 1693) [1]

[5]

. . . about the beginning of the seventeenth century appeared a race of writers that may be termed the metaphysical poets . . . (they) were men of learning, and to show their learning was their whole endeavour. (Samuel Johnson in the *Lives of the Poets*, 1779–1781)

(They) . . . possessed a mechanism of sensibility which could devour any kind of experience. They are simple, artificial, difficult, or fantastic . . . (They) were . . . engaged in the task of trying to find the verbal equivalent for states of feeling. And this means both that they are more mature, and that they wear better, than later poets of certainly not less literary ability. (T.S. Eliot, 1921) [10]

[15]

Apart from John Donne, other Metaphysical Poets include Henry King (1591–1669), George Herbert (1593–1633), Richard Crashaw (?1612–1649), Abraham Cowley (1618–1667), Andrew Marvell (1621–1678) and Henry Vaughan (1622–1695).

3.1.3
George Herbert
(1593–1633)

George Herbert's poetic wit and diction are usually simpler than Donne's, drawing on images from nature and common everyday life. His poetry is sensitive and moving, combining simple directness with courtly grace.

'Peace' The following poem begins with Herbert, an ordained priest, expressing a sense of unrest. The opening phrase is 'Sweet Peace, where dost thou dwell?'.

● Can you guess what his purpose is?

Peace

Sweet Peace, where dost thou dwell? I humbly crave, 1
    Let me once know.
  I sought thee in a secret cave,
    And ask'd, if Peace were there.
A hollow winde did seem to answer, No: 5
    Go seek elsewhere.

I did; and going did a rainbow note:
    Surely, thought I,
  This is the lace of Peace's coat:
    I will search out the matter. 10
But while I lookt, the clouds immediately
    Did break and scatter.

Then went I to a garden, and did spy
    A gallant flower,
  The Crown Imperiall: Sure, said I, 15
    Peace at the root must dwell.
But when I digg'd, I saw a worm devoure
    What show'd so well.

At length I met a rev'rend good old man,
    Whom when for Peace 20
  I did demand, he thus began:
    There was a Prince of old
At Salem dwelt, who liv'd with good increase
    Of flock and fold.

He sweetly liv'd; yet sweetnesse did not save 25
    His life from foes.
  But after death out of his grave
    There sprang twelve stalks of wheat:
Which many wondring at, got some of those
    To plant and set. 30

It prosper'd strangely, and did soon disperse
    Through all the earth:
  For they that taste it do rehearse,
    That vertue lies therein,
A secret vertue bringing peace and mirth 35
    By flight of sinne.

GLOSSARY

humbly crave (l.1): ask respectfully

sought (l.3): looked for

scatter (l.12): go in all directions

spy (l.13): observe

gallant (l.14): showy in appearance (*archaic*)

Crown Imperiall (l.15): tall plant with orange bell-shaped flowers of the lily family

rev'rend (l.19): worthy of respect

Salem (l.23): Jerusalem (the Prince of Salem suggests Jesus Christ)

flock and fold (l.24): sheep? followers? family? Suggests Abraham – founder of the Hebrew people who was succeeded by the twelve tribes of Israel

foes (l.26): enemies

set (l.30): lay out (for planting)

rehearse (l.33): say

mirth (l.35): happiness and laughter

> **Take of this grain, which in my garden grows,**
> **And grows for you;**
> **Make bread of it: and that repose**
> **And peace, which ev'ry where**
> **With so much earnestnesse you do pursue,**
> **Is onely there.**

40

earnestnesse (l.41):
seriousness

Understanding and interpretation

i) 'Peace' is divided into seven stanzas. In which stanza:
 a) does the old man begin his story?
 b) does the poet suggest he had looked for Peace at the court?
 c) does the poet indicate that the life of a hermit would not allow him to find Peace?
 d) does the old man give the poet a symbolic grain to plant?

ii) Which of these more accurately describes the overall meaning of the old man's story?
 a) Accept God's love or you will be damned.
 b) You will find in Christ's love the peace you are foolishly searching the world for.

iii) Which words/phrases suggest:
 a) corruption?
 b) splendour and display?
 c) positive human strengths?
 d) the old man thinks the poet's behaviour has been ridiculous?

iv) Who or what do the following refer to?
 'thee' (l.3) 'This' (l.9) 'What' (l.18) 'His' (l.26) 'those' (l.29) 'therein' (l.34) 'you' (l.41)

v) Which of these in context has a negative connotation?
 'peace' (l.1); 'gallant flower' (l.14). Find another word/phrase with a negative connotation.

vi) Can you find an example of where symbolism and practical everyday reality seem to meet?

George Herbert

George Herbert had a distinguished university career at Trinity College, Cambridge. Although he was a favourite at the court of James I, he courageously gave up his worldly ambitions to become, in 1624, a member of the Christian ministry, probably with the encouragement of his friend, John Donne, then Dean of St Paul's. In 1630 he was appointed rector of a small parish near Salisbury called Bemerton, and was ordained the following September. Although he was only a short time in office, dying of consumption just before his fortieth birthday, he nevertheless gained a reputation for charity, energy and humility as well as for being an accomplished musician. All his poetry is deeply religious.

3.2 Biography

Although biographies had been written in Latin in the Middle Ages to glorify the lives of the saints and to justify secular rulers, it wasn't until the Renaissance, with its emphasis on the human, that biography in

England became more detailed, more anecdotal and more prepared to be critical. In 1579, Sir Thomas North's translation of Plutarch's *Parallel Lives* (first century AD) was published. It contained the biographies of the great men of Greece and Rome, illustrating their moral character through a series of anecdotes. Not only did it serve as a source book for Shakespeare's Roman plays, it later encouraged, in the seventeenth century, the biographer to see himself as an artist. In the eighteenth century, with the growth of a scientific and historical interest in many kinds of people, biographies were to become common and influence the development of the novel. (For example, *Robinson Crusoe* (1719) by Daniel Defoe (1660–1731) and *Gulliver's Travels* (1726) by Jonathan Swift (1667–1745) are both fiction disguised as autobiography.)

In 1662, two years after the end of the Civil War and the Restoration of the monarchy, the Royal Society of London was founded to explore the whole field of natural knowledge. From a philosophical base (notably expressed by Francis Bacon in 1605) the scientific spirit developed rapidly. One consequence of this was that the virtue of intellectual lucidity in the writing of prose was encouraged, and the passionate, complex prose of the beginning of the century began to disappear. Styles became plainer and more urbane, and attitudes were more tolerant.

3.2.1
Izaak Walton
(1593–1683)

Izaak Walton was the first Englishman to write biographical portraits in the modern sense.

Warm-up

This is the monument, still in St Paul's Cathedral in London, that John Donne had made before he died. How does it contrast with the picture on page 58?

● How would you like to be remembered?

Life of Dr John Donne   This is an extract from Walton's *Life of Dr John Donne* (1640).

It is observed that a desire of glory or commendation is rooted in the very nature of man and that those of the severest and most mortified lives, though they may become so humble as to banish self-flattery and such weeds as naturally grow there, yet they have not been able to kill this desire of glory, but that, like our radical heat, it will both live and die with us; and many think it should be so; and we want not sacred examples to justify the desire of having our memory to outlive our lives. Which I mention, because Dr Donne, by the persuasion of Dr Fox, easily yielded at this very time to have a monument made for him; but Dr Fox undertook not to persuade him how or what monument it should be; that was left to Dr Donne himself.

A monument being resolved upon, Dr Donne sent for a carver to make for him in wood the figure of an urn, giving him directions for the compass and height of it, and to bring with it a board of the just height of his body. These being got, then without delay a choice painter was got to be in a readiness to draw his picture, which was taken as followeth: Several charcoal fires being first made in his large study, he brought with him into that place his winding-sheet in his hand and, having put off all his clothes, had this sheet put on him and so tied with knots at his head and feet and his hands so placed as dead bodies are usually fitted to be shrouded and put into their coffin or grave. Upon this urn he thus stood with his eyes shut and with so much of the sheet turned aside as might show his lean, pale, and death-like face, which was purposely turned toward the East, from whence he expected the second coming of his and our Saviour, Jesus. In this posture he was drawn at his just height; and when the picture was fully finished, he caused it to be set by his bed-side, where it continued and became his hourly object till his death and was then given to his dearest friend and executor, Doctor Henry King, then chief residenciary of St Paul's, who caused him to be thus carved in one entire piece of white marble, as it now stands in that church ...

1

5

10

15

20

25

30

(from *Life of Dr John Donne*)

Understanding and interpretation

i) Give each of the two paragraphs a title.

ii) Complete the sentences and answer the questions:

Paragraph 1:

Walton feels that it is natural ....

Does he excuse or condemn Donne?

Paragraph 2:

First, Donne requested that a woodcarver ....

Then a painter was asked ....

As he was only going to be wearing a 'winding-sheet' ....

It was tied in such a way that ....

He stood on the urn, his eyes shut, facing the east because ....

The size of the picture was ....

He kept it .... until his death.

After Donne died, Dr King ....

What impression of Donne's state of mind do you get from this passage? What image did Donne seem to want to create?

Language and style

i) What is the effect of the following?
   a) the length of the sentence beginning 'It is observed ...' (l.1)
   b) the phrases

   'It is observed ...' (l.1) (instead of 'Some people say')
   'Dr Donne' (l.8) (instead of 'John Doone')
   'A monument being resolved upon' (l.13) (instead of 'Having decided on a monument')

ii) Find at least two phrases/sentences that suggest that Walton was a very religious man.

Life of Mr George Herbert

Do the following exercise by reading extracts from Walton's *Life of Mr George Herbert* (1670):

i) *Height*: Which is correct?
   a) George Herbert was quite tall/very tall. b) He was quite thin/thin/very thin.

ii) *Manner*: Find a word which means:
   a) happy and lively b) gentle c) willing and eager to help

iii) *Speech*: Which is more accurate?
   a) He spoke like a gentleman (but he wasn't a gentleman). b) He spoke as a gentleman (because he was a gentleman).

iv) What did he do that showed he liked and was good at music?

GLOSSARY

stature (l.1): height

encumbered (l.2): weighed down

aspect (l.3): facial expression

bespeak (l.8): ask in advance

sanctity (l.9): purity and goodness

eloquence (l.11): skilful use of language, appealing to the feelings

St Chrysostom (l.12): ?347–407. Doctor of the Church; greatest of the Greek fathers; admired for eloquence, an ascetic life and charity

piety (l.14): devotion to God

anthems (l.18): hymns of praise

lute, viol (l.18): types of stringed musical instruments

He was for his person of a stature inclining towards tallness, his body was very straight, and so far from being encumbered with too much flesh, that he was lean to an extremity. His aspect was cheerful, and his speech and motion did both declare him a gentleman; for they were all so meek and obliging that they purchased love and respect from all that knew him ...

I have now brought him to the parsonage of Bemerton, and to the thirty-sixth year of his age, and must stop here and bespeak the reader to prepare for an almost incredible story of the great sanctity of the short remainder of his holy life; a life so full of charity, humility, and all Christian virtues, that it deserves the eloquence of St Chrysostom to commend and declare it; a life, that if it were related by a pen like his, there would then be no need for this age to look back into times past for the examples of primitive piety; for they might be all found in the life of George Herbert ...

His chiefest recreation was music, in which heavenly art he was a most excellent master, and did himself compose many divine hymns and anthems, which he set and sung to his lute or viol; and though he was a lover of retiredness, yet his love to music was such, that he went usually twice every week on certain appointed days to the cathedral church in Salisbury; and at his return would say, 'That his time spent in prayer and cathedral music elevated his soul, and was his heaven upon earth.' But before his return thence to Bemerton, he would usually sing and play his part at an appointed

private music-meeting; and, to justify this practice, he would often 25
say, 'Religion does not banish mirth, but only moderates and sets
rules to it.'

And as his desire to enjoy his heaven upon earth drew him twice
every week to Salisbury, so his walks thither were the occasion
of many happy accidents to others, of which I will mention some 30
few ...

In another walk to Salisbury he saw a poor man with a poorer
horse, that was fallen under his load; they were both in distress,
and needed present help, which Mr Herbert perceiving, put off his
canonical coat, and helped the poor man to unload, and after, to 35
load his horse. The poor man blessed him for it, and he blessed the
poor man, and was so like the good Samaritan, that he gave him
money to refresh both himself and his horse, and told him, 'That if
he loved himself, he should be merciful to his beast.' Thus he left
the poor man, and at his coming to his musical friends at Salisbury, 40
they began to wonder that Mr George Herbert, who used to be so
trim and clean, came into that company so soiled and discomposed;
but he told them the occasion; and when one of the company told
him 'he had disparaged himself by so dirty an employment,' his
answer was, 'That the thought of what he had done would prove 45
music to him at midnight, and that the omission of it would have
upbraided and made discord in his conscience whensoever he
should pass by that place ...'

(from Life of Mr George Herbert)

retiredness (l.19): being alone, cut off from the world

banish (l.26): get rid of

thither (l.29): to that place (*formal*)

canonical coat (l.35): worn by Christian priests connected to the Cathedral

good Samaritan (l.37): person in the Bible who helped a man in trouble

trim (l.42): neat

soiled and discomposed (l.42): dirty and untidy

disparaged himself (l.44): put himself to shame

upbraided (l.47): scolded

● What effect did Herbert's good deed have on a) one of his musical friends in Salisbury and b) himself?

Izaak Walton

Walton was a devout Anglican and all his work was done when the English Church was under attack from the Puritans or struggling to re-establish itself after the Civil War and the Restoration of the monarchy. His portraits of eminent men humble enough to lead ordinary lives have been criticised for being inaccurate in details (some of the less holy aspects of their lives being conveniently forgotten out of a desire to present them as moral examples), but they are simple, clear, warm-hearted and full of interesting insights.

Walton also wrote a famous discourse on the sport of fishing called *The Compleat Angler, or the Contemplative Man's Recreation* (1653). Written at a time of violence and Civil War, it contains, among other things, direct, fresh descriptions of the English countryside.

3.2.2
John Aubrey
(1626–1697)

By comparison, John Aubrey – in his collection of short biographies *Brief Lives* – was more gossipy, more informal and, since he was less respectful of his subjects, frequently more entertaining. Despite the fact that he was a founder member of the Royal Society and a keen student of antiquities, his 'Lives' contained quite a few inaccuracies and were not very methodically constructed ('I now set things down ... as if tumbled out of a Sack'). Some of the early ones were written as notes for Anthony

Wood's history of Oxford – a debt Wood hardly acknowledged. As a collection, Aubrey's 'Lives' were not published in his lifetime.

This is an extract from Aubrey's life of Francis Bacon (see pages 340–341):

GLOSSARY

Mr Hobbes (l.1): his friend Thomas Hobbes (1588–1679), author of the *Leviathan* (1651), who served as a secretary to Bacon

viz (l.2): that is to say

Highgate (l.4): (in those days a village near London; now a district of London)

alighted out (l.7): stepped out

exenterate it (l.9): cut the bowels out of it

chilled him (l.10): made him cold

Gray's Inn (l.12): a building owned by one of the law societies in London

Mr Hobbes told me that the cause of his Lordship's death was trying an experiment: viz, as he was taking the air in a coach with Dr Witherborne, a Scotchman, physician to the King, towards Highgate, snow lay on the ground, and it came into my Lord's thoughts, why flesh might not be preserved in snow as in salt. They were resolved they would try the experiment presently. They alighted out of the coach and went into a poor woman's house at the bottom of Highgate Hill and bought a hen and made the woman exenterate it, and then stuffed the body with snow, and my Lord did help to do it himself. The snow so chilled him that he immediately fell so extremely ill that he could not return to his lodgings (I suppose then at Gray's Inn) but went to the Earl of Arundel's house at Highgate, where they put him into a good bed warmed with a pan, but it was a damp bed that had not been lain in about a year before, which gave him such a cold that in 2 or 3 days, as I remember he [Hobbes] told me, he died of suffocation.

(from *Brief Lives*)

● i) In what way did the experiment go wrong?
ii) Such lively verbs as 'exenterate', 'stuffed' and 'chilled' would not be found so closely together in Walton. What do they tell us about Aubrey?

The following extracts are from Aubrey's life of John Milton (1608–1674).

GLOSSARY

From his brother (l.2): according to his brother

a clock (l.4): o'clock

might ... age (l.6–7): (an activity more suited to an older person? which could have been written by an older person?)

hard (l.7): hard-working

with very good applause (l.8): and received a lot of praise

Salmasius (l.10): Claude de Saumaise (1588–1653), French scholar commissioned by Charles II to defend Charles's father and attack the English government; Milton was ordered to reply and in 1651 issued his *Pro Populo Anglicano Defensio* in Latin

He was several years beyond sea and returned to England just upon the breaking out of the civil wars. From his brother, Christopher Milton: – when he went to school, when he was very young, he studied very hard and sat up very late, commonly till 12 or 1 a clock at night, and his father ordered the maid to sit up for him, and in those years (10) composed many copies of verses which might well become a riper age. And was a very hard student in the university and performed all his exercises there with very good applause.

His sight began to fail him at first upon his writing against Salmasius, and before 'twas fully completed one eye absolutely failed. Upon the writing of other books after that, his other eye decayed. His eyesight was decaying about 20 years before his death; *quære*, when stark blind? His father read without spectacles at 84. His mother had very weak eyes and used spectacles presently after she was thirty years old.

He was a spare man. He was scarce so tall as I am – *quære*, *qot* feet I am high: *resp.*, of middle stature. He had auburn hair. His complexion exceedingly fair – he was so fair that they called him *the lady of Christ's College*. Oval face. His eye a dark grey. He had a delicate tuneable voice and had good skill. His father instructed him. He had an organ in his house; he played on that most. Of a very cheerful humour. – He would be cheerful even in his gout fits, and sing. He was very healthy and free from all diseases; seldom took any physic (only sometimes he took manna); only towards his latter end he was visited with the gout spring and fall. He had a very good memory; but I believe that his excellent method of thinking and disposing did much to help his memory. 25

His exercise was chiefly walking. He was an early riser (*scil.* at 4 a clock *mané*); yea, after he lost his sight. He had a man read to him. The first thing he read was the Hebrew Bible, and that was at 4 h. *mané* ½h. +. Then he contemplated. At 7 his man came to him again and then read to him again, and wrote till dinner: the writing was as much as the reading. 30

After dinner he used to walk 3 or 4 hours at a time – he always had a garden where he lived; went to bed about 9. Temperate man, rarely drank between meals. Extreme pleasant in his conversation, and at dinner, supper, etc; but satirical. 35

He was visited much by learned; more than he did desire. He was mightily importuned to go into France and Italy. Foreigners came much to see him and much admired him and offered him great preferments to come over to them; and the only inducement of several foreigners that came over into England was chiefly to see Oliver Protector and Mr John Milton; and would see the house and chamber where he was born. He was much more admired abroad than at home. 40

45

(from *Brief Lives*)

Understanding and interpretation

Look through the passage again. Describe in your own words Milton's physical characteristics and his behaviour. Use the cues below:

Physical Characteristics

height	face
build	eyesight
hair	health

Behaviour

study
music
manner
exercise
time of going to bed/getting up
drink

John Milton

Language and style	Find an example of

Language and style Find an example of
a) a sentence without a verb
b) a sentence containing note-like phrases

Appreciation i) Do you agree with these statements? Illustrate from the text.
   a) The descriptions are very bitty.
   b) Aubrey's enthusiasm can be seen in his prose.
ii) Whose style do you prefer, Walton's or Aubrey's? Why?

3.2.3
Creative writing Choose one:
– someone else in the class
– a friend
– a relative
– a famous person

Makes notes about their age, physical characteristics, character, habits and life history.

Either:
Write a short biography without mentioning the name of your subject. Don't make the identity too obvious. Read the biographies written by others in your class and try to guess who they describe.

Or:
Interview your subject to find out what you don't know (in the case of 'a famous person' look up necessary information). Write a short, personal biography, making it as interesting as possible.

3.3 The Civil War: Milton, Marvell and the Cavalier Poets

3.3.1
John Milton
(1608–1674)

From 1641 John Milton abandoned poetry in favour of prose propaganda for the Parliamentary and Puritan causes (see pages 74–76). In 1643, however, he married the daughter of a Royalist family and was almost immediately abandoned by her. This led to the first of his pamphlets in favour of divorce and, in 1644, to the *Areopagitica*, an appeal for freedom of expression. In 1649 he was appointed Latin Secretary to the Commonwealth and was expected to correspond with foreign governments. He held the post, despite his increasing blindness, until the Restoration of the monarchy in 1660, at which time he was only asked to pay a small fine for having worked for the Parliamentary cause. He was then left in peace to produce his most major poetry: *Paradise Lost*: started in 1658 and finished in 1663; *Paradise Regained* and *Samson Agonistes*, published together in 1671.

Warm-up Here are some pictures of Satan (the lord of evil) by different Christian artists:

What impression is each artist trying to convey? Which is the most effective? How would you represent Satan?

The following extract is from *Paradise Lost*, a long poem in twelve books, written to 'justify the ways of God to men'. It concerns both the Fall of the Angels and the Fall of Man (the story of Adam and Eve in the Garden of Eden). Satan lies in Hell in the burning lake, having been cast down from Heaven after the failure of his war with God. Around him are the fallen angels who have shared in his defeat. Beelzebub, second only to Satan, has just spoken:

GLOSSARY

the superior Fiend (l.1): Satan

ponderous (l.2): large and heavy

Ethereal temper (l.3): (which had the qualities of ether and therefore couldn't decay)

massy (l.3): heavy (*formal*)

cast (l.4): placed (on his back)

broad circumference (l.4): shield

orb (l.5): ball-shape

optic . . . Valdarno (l.6–8): the telescope the Italian astronomer Galileo – the 'Tuscan artist' – used for observation from Fiesole (outside Florence) or in the Arno valley

descry (l.8): discover

Hewn (l.11): cut down

mast . . . ammiral (l.11–12): the main mast on an admiral's flagship, the biggest ship in a fleet

wand (l.12): small stick

marle (l.14): soil

azure (l.15): unclouded sky (*poetic*)

torrid . . . fire (l.15–16): very hot air, surrounded by fire, also painfully beat against him

Nathless (l.17): nevertheless (*archaic*)

inflamed (l.18): flaming and fevered

entranced (l.19): unconscious

strow the brooks (l.20): cover the streams

Vallombrosa (l.21): (shady, woody valley near Florence, in 'Etruria', Tuscany)

embower (l.22): form a roof

sedge (l.22): plants that grow in water

Orion (l.23): a group of stars associated with autumnal storms

vexed (l.24): troubled

Red Sea (l.24): the sea, between Arabia and northeast Africa, where after a storm there is a lot of floating seaweed

Busiris . . . chivalry (l.25): the Egyptian Pharaoh and his horsemen

perfidious (l.26): treacherous

sojourners of Goshen (l.27): the Israelites, who passed through the Red Sea after escaping from Egypt

carcases (l.28): dead bodies

bestrown (l.29): lying all over the place

Abject (l.30): hopeless and degraded

He scarce had ceased when the superior Fiend   1
Was moving toward the shore; his ponderous shield,
Ethereal temper, massy, large, and round,
Behind him cast. The broad circumference
Hung on his shoulders like the moon, whose orb   5
Through optic glass the Tuscan artist views
At evening, from the top of Fesolè,
Or in Valdarno, to descry new lands,
Rivers, or mountains, in her spotty globe.
His spear, to equal which the tallest pine   10
Hewn on Norwegian hills, to be the mast
Of some great ammiral, were but a wand,
He walked with, to support uneasy steps
Over the burning marle, not like those steps
On Heaven's azure; and the torrid clime   15
Smote on him sore besides, vaulted with fire.
Nathless he so endured, till on the beach
Of that inflamed sea he stood, and called
His legions, Angel forms, who lay entranced
Thick as autumnal leaves that strow the brooks   20
In Vallombrosa, where th' Etrurian shades
High over-arched embower; or scattered sedge
Afloat, when with fierce winds Orion armed
Hath vexed the Red-Sea coast, whose waves o'erthrew
Busiris and his Memphian chivalry,   25
While with perfidious hatred they pursued
The sojourners of Goshen, who beheld
From the safe shore their floating carcases
And broken chariot-wheels. So thick bestrown,
Abject and lost, lay these, covering the flood,   30
Under amazement of their hideous change.

(from *Paradise Lost* [Book 1])

73

Understanding and interpretation	i) Describe each of the following in a single sentence, using your own words as far as possible:

i) Describe each of the following in a single sentence, using your own words as far as possible:

a) Satan's shield
b) his spear
c) his angels

What is each compared with?

ii) To whom or what do the following refer?
'his' (l.2); 'him' (l.4); 'whose' (l.5); 'her' (l.9); 'His' (l.10); 'him' (l.16); 'whose' (l.24); 'they' (l.26); 'their' (l.28); 'these' (l.30); 'their' (l.31)

Style and tone

i) The verse is unrhymed iambic pentameter. What does that mean?

ii) Find examples of some of the following:

- where Milton appears to be enjoying the beauty of proper names
- a sentence construction where the verb comes at the end (as in Latin)
- a long simile (as in Homer)
- a word with more than three syllables
- an adjectival phrase where *one* adjective precedes the noun
- an adjectival phrase where *two* adjectives precede the noun
- enjambment

iii) Discuss whether you agree with these statements:
From the extract it appears that

- Milton's grand style lacks immediacy and reality; it is too ornamental, too artificial and too heavy;
- there is no variety or subtlety in the verse;
- Milton's language is very unlike spoken English;
- he is more concerned with conveying a sense of space and grandeur than anything lively and human.

How could you defend Milton as a poet?

John Milton

Milton's main poetic influence was Spenser (see page 333). Until the twentieth century, his impressive verse was so admired that he was considered second only to Shakespeare, although Joseph Addison (1627–1719) felt that 'our language sank under him' and William Blake (1757–1827) said that Milton was '. . . of the Devil's party without knowing it'. In the twentieth century, T.S. Eliot (1888–1965) felt Milton was 'withered by book-learning' and wrote English 'like a dead language'. Like the critic F.R. Leavis (1895–1978), he claimed that Milton's poetry 'could only be an influence for the worse'. However, Milton still has many admirers, who claim that his verse is not only powerful but subtle and suggestive.

3.3.2
The Civil War

i) Write numbers next to these sentences to indicate their correct order:
- It finished with Parliamentary victories at Naseby in 1645 and at Oxford – the Royalist capital at the time – in 1646.
- Charles was beheaded in 1649 and England became a republic until 1660.
- The Civil War (also known as the Great Rebellion) was fought between King Charles I, whose supporters were known as Cavaliers (a term which suggests knights and horsemen) and Parliament, whose Puritan supporters were known as Roundheads because they cut their hair short.
- The chief commander of the Parliamentary forces was Oliver Cromwell.

Charles I   *Oliver Cromwell*

- The second stage of the Civil War, caused by the king's escape in 1647, ended in 1651 with a Parliamentary victory over the Scots, who had been the allies of Parliament in the first part of the Civil War but supported the king at the start of the second.
- The first stage of the Civil War began in 1642.

ii) Categorise each of the causes of the war given below under the following headings: **Political Economic Social Religious Geographic**. Some belong under more than one heading.

a) The urban middle class (the businessmen and merchants) were attracted to the austerity of the Puritan movement.

b) The economic interests of the Crown were closely linked to the Anglican Church.

c) There was a suspicion that since Charles I's wife was a Catholic, the court was a centre of Catholicism, and the Puritans saw themselves as the protectors of true religious belief.

d) Charles I tried to raise taxes for government without the consent of Parliament; MPs wanted to have control over how taxes were spent.

e) Since the fifteenth century, Parliamentary power was more with the House of Commons (which had a Puritan majority) than with the House of Lords (which mainly supported the Crown).

f) Charles I burst into the House of Commons with several hundred men and tried to arrest its leaders, but they had already escaped.

g) The south and east of England were more developed economically and supported the Parliamentary movement; the north and west (including Wales) were poorer, more conservative, and supported the king.

Puritans

3.3.3
The Puritan movement

i) The following notes describe the Puritan movement at its most fanatical. Try to think of one word/phrase which summarises its spirit.

dressed very simply – wanted to purify the Church of England of all Roman Catholic influence – closed the theatres – rejected any spiritual authority except that of the Bible, which was thought to be the pure word of God – said that the voice of God spoke in each person's conscience and no priest could come between – considered all images and ritual to be superstition – banned organs in churches

ii) What do these add to your understanding of the movement?
a) Many Puritans often took pleasure in sport and in the arts. Cromwell, for example, loved hunting and music.
b) Under James I Puritans were often put in prison and killed.
c) Some Puritans decided to leave England to find freedom in a new land. These 'Pilgrim Fathers', as they were called, sailed from Plymouth in 1620 in a ship called the *Mayflower* and started a new life in America.

3.3.4
The republican Commonwealth

From 1649–1660 England was a semi-democratic republic. Until 1653 it was under the rule of the House of Commons, many of whose members had been removed when they had opposed the trial of Charles I. From then until 1658, Oliver Cromwell was Lord Protector of the Realm in place of a king and rather like a modern president.

As a result of England's military strength and the confirmation of the power of the middle classes, England's international prestige increased. As a body, though, Parliament was too awkward an institution to carry out policy and Cromwell failed to rule adequately. On his death in 1658 Oliver Cromwell was succeeded by his son Richard. The country, however, decided that if it was to live under a hereditary protectorship it might as well be a king. Charles II was brought back from exile and the monarchy restored. Nevertheless, Parliament remained strong.

3.3.5
Andrew Marvell
(1621–1678)

In 1653 Andrew Marvell stayed at Eton with a Puritan friend, John Oxenbridge. Oxenbridge had earlier suffered religious persecution at the hands of Archbishop Laud and in 1635 had made a journey to the Bermudas, a group of islands in the West Atlantic.

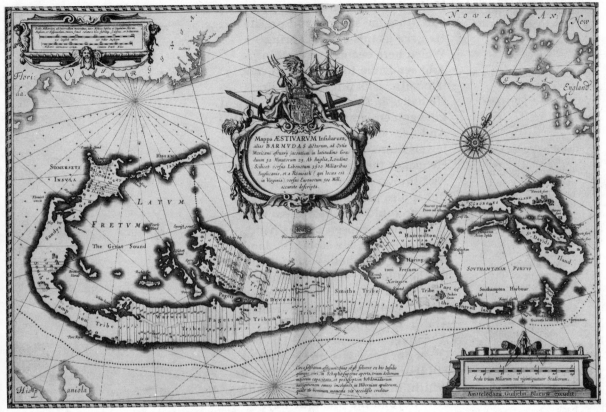

Seventeenth-century map of the Caribbean showing the Bermuda Islands

In this poem, the first four lines and the last four lines set the scene for a song of praise.

● What is the mood of those in the boat?

Bermudas

GLOSSARY

unespied (l.2): unnoticed
watery maze (l.6):
    complicated pattern of
    currents
wracks (l.9): destroys
the deep (l.10): the sea
prelate's rage (l.12): wild
    anger of bishops

> Where the remote Bermudas ride, 1
> In th' ocean's bosom unespied,
> From a small boat that rowed along,
> The listening winds received this song:
>
> 'What should we do but sing His praise, 5
> That led us through the watery maze

Unto an isle so long unknown,
And yet far kinder than our own?
Where He the huge sea monsters wracks,
That lift the deep upon their backs;   10
He lands us on a grassy stage,
Safe from the storms, and prelate's rage.
He gave us this eternal spring
Which here enamels everything,
And sends the fowls to us in care,   15
On daily visits through the air;
He hangs in shades the orange bright,
Like golden lamps in a green night,
And does in the pomegranates close
Jewels more rich than Ormus shows;   20
He makes the figs our mouths to meet,
And throws the melons at our feet;
But apples plants of such a price,
No tree could ever bear them twice;
With cedars, chosen by His hand,   25
From Lebanon, He stores the land;
And makes the hollow seas, that roar,
Proclaim the ambergris on shore;
He cast (of which we rather boast)
The Gospel's pearl upon our coast,   30
And in these rocks for us did frame
A temple, where to sound His name.
O! let our voice His praise exalt,
Till it arrive at heaven's vault,
Which, thence (perhaps) rebounding, may   35
Echo beyond the Mexique Bay.'

     Thus sung they in the English boat,
An holy and a cheerful note;
And all the way, to guide their chime,
With falling oars they kept the time.   40

enamels (l.14): decorates and makes smooth

fowls (l.15): birds (*archaic*)

pomegranates (l.19): round fruit with juicy red flesh containing many seeds

close (l.19): enclose

Ormus (l.20): ancient jewel-trading centre in the Persian Gulf

apples (l.23): pineapples

stores (l.26): supplies

Proclaim the ambergris (l.28): announce their wealth ('ambergris' is an expensive soapy substance found in sperm whales and used in the manufacture of perfumes)

cast ... coast (l.29–l.30): reference to the biblical image of casting pearls before swine – the image is ironic here in that the 'pearl' the travellers have discovered is the freedom to promote their faith in God

His praise exalt (l.33): praise God highly

vault (l.34): arched roof

thence (l.35): from that place (*formal*)

rebounding (l.35): flying back

the Mexique Bay (l.36): the Gulf of Mexico

chime (l.39): harmonious movements together (the word has a musical suggestion)

Understanding and interpretation

i) Which of these ideas are not indicated in the poem?

  a) The land of the islands is very fertile.
  b) Faith is difficult so far from home.
  c) Nature is generous.

ii) Who (or what) is the subject of these verbs?

  'led' (l.6); 'lift' (l.10); 'enamels' (l.14); 'throws' (l.22); 'exalt' (l.33); 'echo' (l.36)

iii) What do these lines suggest?
    'And yet far kinder than our own' (l.8)
    'Safe from the storms, and prelate's rage' (l.12)

iv) What do these words have in common?

'enamels' (l.14); 'golden lamps' (l.18); 'jewels' (l.20); 'ambergris' (l.28)

v) What do these suggest in context?
'bosom unespied' (l.2); 'eternal spring' (l.13); '(perhaps)' (l.35)

Language and style
i) Find an example of the following:

a) sensuous language
b) onomatopoeia (where the words sound like the noise they describe)
c) where the rhythm of the verse suggests the movement of what is being described (for example, the oars or the waves against the boat)

ii) What is the effect in context of the forceful verbs 'makes' and 'throws' in l.21–22?

iii) Which lines in particular suggest:
a) strong spiritual feeling?
b) a sense of discovery and new life?
c) an atmosphere of mystery?

Andrew Marvell
Marvell, the son of a clergyman with Puritan views, had until 1651 moderate political sympathies. He even acknowledged the 'Divine Right' of the Royalists, although he came to accept Cromwell's power, believing his 'Cause was too good to have been fought for' – in other words, he regarded Parliamentary success as an historical necessity. In 1657 he became Milton's assistant in the Latin Secretaryship. (It is said that Marvell's influence in Parliament protected Milton at the time of the Restoration of the Monarchy.) Marvell's sympathies, though, remained varied and he distanced himself from sectarian intolerance and the type of severe self-righteousness typical of Milton. Valuing good government more than political causes for their own sake, he welcomed the Restoration, although he was to grow disillusioned with the disorder of the new court.

Marvell's integrity, born of delicate feeling and careful judgement, is seen both in his life as an MP (1659–1678) and in his poetry, which manages to combine the intellectual subtlety of the Metaphysicals with a kind of sensuous immediacy. For T.S. Eliot Marvell's wit had a 'tough reasonableness beneath the slight lyric grace' which, playing over 'the great traditional commonplaces of European literature', renews them. His best-known poems are 'To his Coy Mistress' and 'An Horatian Ode upon Cromwell's Return from Ireland', often described as the greatest political poem in English.

3.3.6
The Cavalier Poets
The Cavalier Poets, such as Thomas Carew (1595–1640), Sir John Suckling (1609–1642) and Richard Lovelace (1618–1658), were supporters of Charles I. Influenced by Ben Jonson and, to a lesser extent, by John Donne, their verse is characterised by short firm lines, lively diction and graceful wit.

3.3.7
Richard Lovelace
Lovelace died a poor man, having spent all his money in support of the king. In 1642 he was imprisoned by Parliament after having presented a petition to free the king. In prison he wrote this defiant lyric to his mistress:

To Althea, from Prison

When Love with unconfined wings   1
Hovers within my gates,
And my divine Althea brings
To whisper at the grates;
When I lie tangled in her hair   5
And fettered to her eye,
The gods that wanton in the air
Know no such liberty.

When flowing cups run swiftly round,
With no allaying Thames,   10
Our careless heads with roses bound,
Our hearts with loyal flames;
When thirsty grief in wine we steep,
When healths and draughts go free,
Fishes, that tipple in the deep,   15
Know no such liberty.

When, like committed linnets, I
With shriller throat shall sing
The sweetness, mercy, majesty,
And glories of my King;   20
When I shall voice aloud how good
He is, how great should be,
Enlarged winds, that curl the flood,
Know no such liberty.

Stone walls do not a prison make,   25
Nor iron bars a cage;
Minds innocent and quiet take
That for an hermitage.
If I have freedom in my love,
And in my soul am free,   30
Angels alone, that soar above,
Enjoy such liberty.

GLOSSARY

with . . . wings (l.1): free

Hovers . . . gates (l.2): waits behind the prison bars

grates (l.4): iron bars

tangled (l.5): caught up

fettered (l.6): chained

wanton (l.7): play as they please, without restraint (*archaic*)

flowing . . . Thames (l.9–10): wine is passed round with no water in it

loyal flames (l.12): passionate love

steep (l.13): soak

healths and draughts (l.14): drinks

tipple (l.15): drink

committed linnets (l.17): caged birds

shriller (l.18): more high-pitched

voice (l.21): say

Enlarged winds (l.23): gales

curl (l.23): turn into waves

hermitage (l.28): a quiet and private retreat

soar (l.31): fly high

- i) Which is more important for the poet: freedom of conscience or physical freedom?

 ii) What images from nature are the following contrasted with?
 – the freedom of the wine drinkers
 – imprisonment

 iii) What does the poet say he has got in common with the angels?

 iv) Where in the poem is there a 'metaphysical conceit' (for a definition see page 62)?

 v) What makes the third stanza courageous?

 vi) Is the poem as a whole serious or frivolous?

3.4 Chronology

Copy out the dates below on a piece of paper. Make a chart with plenty of space. Fill it out with some of the information from this unit.

British history	Literature
Stuart monarchs	
1603–1625: James I. Ruled over whole British Isles. Literature of this period known as Jacobean.	
1625–1649: Charles I. Limited intellectual ability. Court of taste and refinement. War against France (1627–1629). Parliament dissolved (1629). Charles I executed (1649).	
1649–1660: No king. Republic. War against Holland (1652–1654).	

3.5 Activities

Creative writing   Imagine you were in the crowd at Charles I's execution. Describe the event *either* as a newspaper article in a twentieth-century style *or* as an imaginary letter from Oliver Cromwell to his son.

The execution of Charles I

Critical writing Choose one of the poems from this unit. Make notes for a critical assessment using the following guidelines:

Paragraph 1: General theme
Paragraph 2: Poetic structure (for example, sonnet), rhythm and rhyme
Paragraph 3: Each stanza/part in more detail (for example: what it is about)
Paragraph 4: General evaluation of strengths and weaknesses

Write a composition of not more than 750 words.

Word search There are seventeen literary terms hidden below. The words are written in a straight line but in any direction, including backwards! How many can you find? (One has been done for you.)

```
F  E  L  O  B  R  E  P  Y  H  L  K  U  N
Q  S  Z  X  A  L  L  E  G  O  R  Y  O  W
H  R  J  E  O  M  S  P  C  R  D  I  M  Y
C  E  W  H  V  S  B  V  G  M  T  Y  Z  E
M  V  R  U  A  S  S  O  N  A  N  C  E  N
E  R  H  Y  T  H  M  K  R  M  G  U  D  J
T  T  E  N  N  O  S  E  L  E  G  Y  B  A
A  S  Z  P  K  J  T  W  Y  P  Q  O  W  M
P  Y  N  O  R  I  S  I  M  I  L  E  R  B
H  X  W  L  L  O  E  I  Y  C  G  U  P  M
O  X  R  L  Y  R  I  C  V  F  L  J  W  E
R  F  A  B  L  E  C  O  U  P  L  E  T  N
S  W  B  Y  I  L  F  O  W  Q  H  E  I  T
```

UNIT 4

After the Restoration

4.1 Diaries

Writers in the late seventeenth century were more ready to assume that personal experience may be of general interest. Like biographies, diaries became a form of literature. Some were consciously written as a record of the times.

Warm-up
i) Do you know anything about this event? What impression do you get from the picture?

LONDONS fier began September the second 1666.

ii) Read the following information:
   – In the previous year the Great Plague killed more than 70,000 of the total population of London (460,000).
   – In the fire over 13,000 houses, 87 churches and the old St Paul's Cathedral were destroyed, and two-thirds of the population were made homeless.

83

- The fire lasted five days.
- There was a widespread belief that both the plague and the fire were the work of a God angered by rebellion and the killing of a king; there was also a belief that the fire was started by Catholics.
- The fire helped to bring an end to the plague (which was already in decline).

iii) Imagine you are part of a family of four in a house by the river. You are in the path of the fire. It is expected to reach you in two hours, but you have no boat. Decide:
- How you would try to escape.
- Which three possessions you would take with you.

4.1.1 Read the following extracts from two different diaries. The first extract is from the diaries of Samuel Pepys (1633–1703). The other is from the diaries of John Evelyn (1620–1706). Try to find on the map the places mentioned.

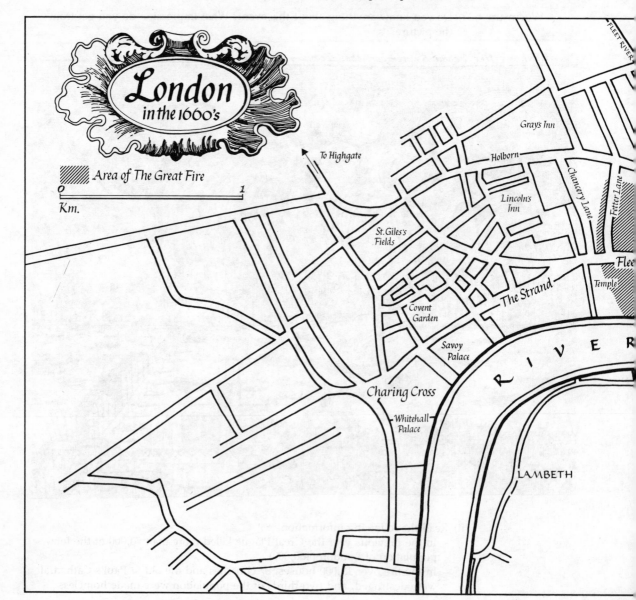

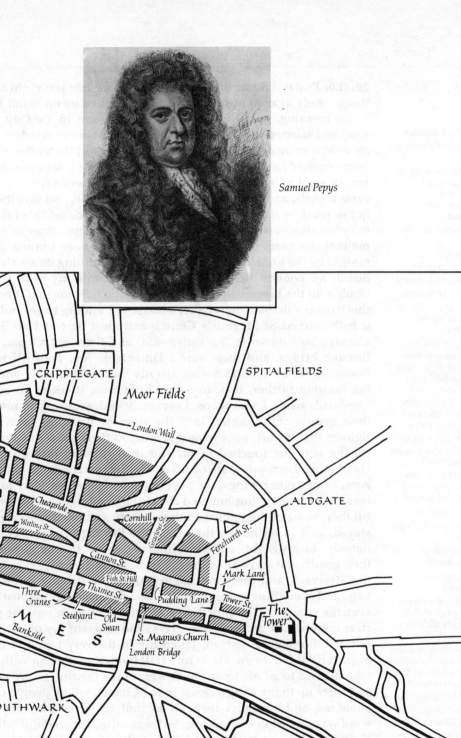

Samuel Pepys

KENWELL

CRIPPLEGATE

SPITALFIELDS

Moor Fields

Smith Field

London Wall

St. Bartholomew

St. Paul's

Cheapside

ALDGATE

Watling St.

Cornhill

Gracious St.

Fenchurch St.

Cannon St.

Mark Lane

Baynard's Castle

Fish St. Hill

Three Cranes

Thames St.

Pudding Lane

Tower St.

Steelyard

Old Swan

The Tower

Bankside

St. Magnus's Church

T H A M E S

London Bridge

SOUTHWARK

George's Fields

BERMONDSEY

Extract 1

2d. (Lord's day.) Some of our maids sitting up late last night to get things ready against our feast today, Jane called us up about three in the morning, to tell us of a great fire they saw in the City. So I rose, and slipped on my night-gown and went to her window, and thought it to be on the back side of Mark Lane at the farthest; but, being unused to such fires as followed, I thought it far enough off, and so went to bed again, and to sleep. About seven rose again to dress myself, and there looked out at the window, and saw the fire not so much as it was, and further off. So to my closet to set things to rights after yesterday's cleaning. By and by Jane comes and tells me that she hears that above 300 houses have been burned down tonight by the fire we saw, and that it is now burning down all Fish Street, by London Bridge...... So I down, with my heart full of trouble, to the Lieutenant of the Tower, who tells me that it begun this morning iñ the King's baker's house in Pudding Lane, and that it hath burned St Magnus's Church and most part of Fish Street already. So I down to the water-side, and there got a boat, and through bridge, and there saw a lamentable fire. Poor Michell's house, as far as the Old Swan, already burned that way, and the fire running further, that, in a very little time, it got as far as the Steelyard, while I was there. Everybody endeavouring to remove their goods, and flinging into the river or bringing them into lighters that lay off; poor people staying in their houses as long as till the very fire touched them, and then running into boats, or clambering from one pair of stairs by the waterside to another. And, among other things, the poor pigeons, I perceive, were loth to leave their houses, but hovered about the windows and balconies, till they, some of them, burned their wings, and fell down. Having stayed, and in an hour's time seen the fire rage every way, and nobody, to my sight, endeavouring to quench it, but to remove their goods, and leave all to the fire; and, having seen it get as far as the Steelyard, and the wind mighty high, and driving it into the City; and everything, after so long a drought, proving combustible, even the very stones of churches; and, among other things, the poor steeple by which pretty Mrs — lives, and whereof my old school-fellow Elborough is parson, taken fire in the very top, and there burned till it fell down; I to White Hall (with a gentleman with me, who desired to go off from the Tower, to see the fire, in my boat); and there up to the King's closet in the Chapel, where people came about me, and I did give them an account dismayed them all, and word was carried in to the King. So I was called for, and did tell the King and Duke of York what I saw; and that, unless His Majesty did command houses to be pulled down, nothing could stop the fire. They seemed much troubled, and the King commanded me to go to my Lord Mayor from him, and command him to spare no houses, but to pull down before the fire every way. The Duke of York bid me tell him that if he would have any more soldiers, he

shall; and so did my Lord Arlington afterwards, as a great secret. Here meeting with Captain Cocke, I in his coach, which he lent me, and Creed with me to Paul's; and there walked along Watling Street, as well as I could, every creature coming away loaden with goods to save, and, here and there, sick people carried away in beds. Extraordinary good goods carried in carts and on backs. At last met my Lord Mayor in Cannon Street, like a man spent, with a handkercher about his neck. To the King's message, he cried, like a fainting woman, 'Lord! what can I do? I am spent: people will not obey me. I have been pulling down houses, but the fire overtakes us faster than we can do it.' That he needed no more soldiers; and that, for himself, he must go and refresh himself, having been up all night. So he left me, and I him, and walked home; seeing people all almost distracted, and no manner of means used to quench the fire .... By this time, it was about twelve o'clock; and so home, there find my guests, who were Mr Wood and his wife Barbary Shelden, and also Mr Moone: she mighty fine, and her husband, for aught I see, a likely man. But Mr Moone's design and mine, which was to look over my closet and please him with the sight thereof, which he hath long desired, was wholly disappointed; for we were in great trouble and disturbance at this fire, not knowing what to think of it. However, we had an extraordinary good dinner, and as merry as at this time we could be.

(from *The Diary of Samuel Pepys*)

Extract 2

2nd September. This fatal night, about ten, began the deplorable fire, near Fish-street, in London.

3rd. I had public prayers at home. The fire continuing, after dinner, I took coach with my wife and son, and went to the Bankside in Southwark, where we beheld that dismal spectacle, the whole city in dreadful flames near the waterside; all the houses from the Bridge, all Thames-street, and upwards towards Cheapside, down to the Three Cranes, were now consumed; and so returned, exceeding astonished what would become of the rest.

The fire having continued all this night (if I may call that night which was light as day for ten miles round about, after a dreadful manner), when conspiring with a fierce eastern wind in a very dry season, I went on foot to the same place; and saw the whole south part of the City burning from Cheapside to the Thames, and all along Cornhill (for it likewise kindled back against the wind as well as forward), Tower-street, Fenchurch-street, Gracious-street, and so along to Baynard's Castle, and was now taking hold of St. Paul's church, to which the scaffolds contributed exceedingly. The conflagration was so universal .... it burned both in breadth and length, the churches, public halls, Exchange, hospitals, monuments, and ornaments; leaping after a prodigious manner, from house to house, and street to street, at great distances one from the other. For the heat, with a long set of fair and warm weather, had even ignited the air, and prepared the materials to conceive the fire, which devoured, after an incredible manner, houses, furniture, and every thing. Here, we saw the Thames covered with goods floating, all the barges and boats laden with what some had time and courage to save, as, on the other side, the carts, &c., carrying out to the fields, which for many miles were strewed with moveables of all sorts, and tents erecting to shelter both people and what goods they could get away. Oh, the miserable and calamitous spectacle! such as haply the world had not seen since the foundation of it, nor can be outdone till the universal conflagration thereof. All the sky was of a fiery aspect, like the top of a burning oven, and the light seen above forty miles roundabout for many nights. God grant mine eyes may never behold the like, who now saw above 10,000 houses all in one flame! The noise and cracking and thunder of the impetuous flames, the shrieking of women and children, the hurry of people, the fall of towers, houses, and churches, was like a hideous storm; and the air all about so hot and inflamed, that at the last one was not able to approach it, so that they were forced to stand still, and let the flames burn on, which they did, for near two miles in length and one in breadth. The clouds also of smoke were dismal, and reached, upon computation, near fifty miles in length. Thus, I left it this afternoon burning, a resemblance of Sodom, or the last day. It forcibly called to my mind that passage – *non enim hic habemus stabilem civitatem*: the ruins resembling the picture of Troy. London was, but is no more! Thus, I returned ....

4th September .... the stones of Paul's flew like grenados, the melting lead running down the streets in a stream, and the very pavaments glowing with fiery redness, so as no horse, nor man, was able to tread on them, and the demolition had stopped all the passages, so that no help could be applied. The eastern wind still more impetuously driving the flames forward. Nothing but the Almighty power of God was able to stop them; for vain was the help of man.

5th. It crossed towards Whitehall; but oh! the confusion there was then at that Court! It pleased his Majesty to command me, among the rest, to look after the quenching of Fetter-lane end, to preserve (if possible) that part of Holborn, whilst the rest of the gentlemen took their several posts, some at one part, and some at another (for now they began to bestir themselves, and not till now, who hitherto had stood as men intoxicated, with their hands across), and began to consider that nothing was likely to put a stop but the blowing up of so many houses as might make a wider gap than any had yet been made by the ordinary method of pulling

Exchange (l.20): Royal Exchange – traditional meeting place where international merchants conducted their business

prodigious (l.21): enormous; extraordinary

ignited (l.24): set fire to

were strewed with (l.29): had lying all over the place

calamitous (l.31): disastrous

haply (l.32): fortunately

outdone (l.33): surpassed

thereof (l.33): (of the world)

fiery (l.34): flaming

aspect (l.34): appearance

God grant ... behold (l.35): I strongly hope god will never allow my eyes to see

impetuous (l.38): forceful and violent

hideous (l.40): terrible

upon computation (l.44): I calculate

Sodom (l.45): place in Palestine destroyed by God for its wickedness

the last day (l.46): Judgement Day

non ... civitatem (l.46–47): 'We do not have a stable city here' (*Latin*)

Paul's (l.49): St Paul's Cathedral

grenados (l.49): grenades (small explosive missiles)

lead (l.50): (from the many buildings on fire)

bestir themselves (l.62): move into action

intoxicated (l.63): drunk

engines (l.67): mechanical appliances

stout (l.67): brave and strong

them down with engines. This some stout seamen proposed early enough to have saved near the whole City, but this some tenacious and avaricious men, aldermen, &c., would not permit, because their houses must have been of the first. It was, therefore, now commended to be practised .... It now pleased God, by abating the wind, and by the industry of the people, when almost all was lost infusing a new spirit into them, that the fury of it began sensibly to abate about noon, so as it came no farther than the Temple westward, nor than the entrance of Smithfield, north: but continued all this day and night so impetuous towards Cripplegate and the Tower, as made us all despair.

The poor inhabitants were dispersed about St. George's Fields, and Moorfields, as far as Highgate, and several miles in circle, some under tents, some under misreable huts and hovels, many without a rag, or any necessary utensils, bed or board, who from delicateness, riches, and easy accommodations in stately and well-furnished houses, were now reduced to extremest misery and poverty.

In this calamitous condition, I returned with a sad heart to my house, blessing and adoring the distinguishing mercy of God to me and mine, who, in the midst of all this ruin, was like Lot, in my little Zoar, safe and sound ....

7th September. The people, who now walked about the ruins, appeared like men in some dismal desert, or rather, in some great city laid waste by a cruel enemy; to which was added the stench that came from some poor creatures' bodies, beds, and other combustible goods .... the ground and air, smoke and fiery vapour, continued so intense, that my hair was almost singed, and my feet unsufferably surbated. The bye-lanes and narrow streets were quite filled up with rubbish; nor could one have possibly known where he was, but by the ruins of some Church, or Hall, that had some remarkable tower or pinnacle remaining .

I then went towards Islington and Highgate, where one might have seen 200,000 people of all ranks and degrees dispersed, and lying along by their heaps of what they could save from the fire, deploring their loss; and, though ready to perish for hunger and destitution, yet not asking one penny for relief, which to me appeared a stranger sight than any I had yet beheld .... In the midst of all this calamity and confusion, there was, I know not how, an alarm begun that the French and Dutch, with whom we were now in hostility, were not only landed, but even entering the City. There was, in truth, some days before, great suspicion of those two nations joining; and now that they had been the occasion of firing the town. This report did so terrify, that on a sudden there was such an uproar and tumult that they run from their goods, and, taking what weapons they could come at, they could not be stopped from falling on some of those nations whom they casually met, without sense or reason. The clamour and peril grew so excessive,

tenacious and avaricious (l.68): greedily determined (to hold on to their possessions)

aldermen (l.69): senior members of the City council

commended (l.71): recommended

abating (l.71): reducing

infusing (l.73): filling

Temple (l.74): residence for the legal profession

Smithfield (l.75): London's largest meat market

hovels (l.80): small, dirty dwellings

Lot ... Zoar (l.86–87): (Lot, a nephew of Abraham, left Sodom for Zoar before it was destroyed)

singed (l.93): burned

surbated (l.94): sore

peril (l.113): danger
appease (l.115): calm down

that it made the whole Court amazed, and they did with infinite pains and great difficulty, reduce and appease the people, sending troops of soldiers and guards, to cause them to retire into the fields again, where they were watched all this night. I left them pretty quiet, and came home sufficiently weary and broken.

(from *The Diary of John Evelyn*)

Understanding and interpretation

i) Write out and complete a chart with the following headings:

The weather:
How the fire spread:
Reaction of the people:
Attempts to halt the fire (methods/problems):

ii) Write one line next to each of the following times to summarise Pepys's actions

2nd September
3.00 a.m.
7.00 a.m.
12.00

iii) How would you summarise the mood of the people on 7th September?

Making comparisons

i) How similar/different do the writers seem to be in their reaction to what they saw and the role they played in events? Who seems to feel the horror more deeply? Are they similar in their attitude towards the king?

ii) How would you compare their style of writing? Write P (Pepys), E (Evelyn), B (both) or N (neither) next to each:

a) light and gossipy
b) emotional
c) seems to be reacting immediately
d) detailed and personal
e) seems to use important-sounding phrases for effect

iii) What do the following phrases tell you about the writers:

Pepys
'the poor pigeons' (l.26)
'by which pretty Mrs — lives' (l.35)
'Extraordinary good goods' (l.53)
'we had an extraordinary good dinner, and as merry as at this time we could be' (l.69)

Evelyn
'I had public prayers at home' (l.3)
'Nothing but the Almighty power of God was able to stop them; for vain was the help of man' (l.54)
'I returned with a sad heart to my house' (l.84)

iv) Compare the style of a few lines from each writer. For example, whose prose is more conversational and seems to move more quickly? Why is this so?

v) Which of the two writers do you prefer? Why?

Samuel Pepys	Samuel Pepys began his diary in 1660 when he was very poor. After appointment as Clerk of the King's Ships, he rose to become an important member of the Navy Board. He finished his diary in 1669, the year his wife died. In 1673 he was appointed Secretary of the Admiralty and became a Member of Parliament. Apart from a six-week spell of imprisonment in the Tower on a false charge of complicity in the 'Popish Plot' (see page 122), he worked hard to provide the country with an efficient fleet. Pepys's diary, probably intended for his eye alone, was all written in cipher (a type of shorthand recently invented and not widely known) and was not deciphered until 1825. According to his friend Evelyn, Pepys was a 'very worthy, industrious and curious person . . . universally beloved, hospitable, generous, learned in many things, skilled in music, a very great cherisher of learned men'.
John Evelyn	John Evelyn was a secretary of the Royal Society, a Royalist in sympathy, and a man of varied interests, including horticulture. In his lifetime he published various translations of Greek, Latin and French authors and in 1664 he wrote *Sylva*, a practical book on tree cultivation. His diary was first published in 1818. Unlike Pepys, Evelyn appears not to have composed regularly each day; on occasions he wrote his entry some time after the event and even added to it at a later date. He opens the volume called *Kalendarium* with an announcement of his birth 'about twenty minutes past two in the morning'.

4.2 Satire in verse (1)

The reigns of William III and Queen Anne (see pages 122–123) were called the 'Augustan Age' by the poet Oliver Goldsmith (1730–1774) to indicate admiration for the values of balanced judgement, refinement, clarity and elegance associated with Roman literature during the reign of the Emperor Augustus (27 BC–AD 14). It was the 'Age of Reason' and in general writers were more guided by social purpose than by the need to express personal feeling.

It was also the age of satire – a form of literature attacking folly and vice by making them appear ridiculous. In the sixteenth, seventeenth and eighteenth centuries the satires of the Roman poets Horace (65–8 BC) – urbane, witty and genial – and Juvenal (AD ?60–?130) – sombre, dignified and self-consciously moral – were much translated and imitated. A tradition of verse satire runs through John Donne's poems and Ben Jonson's 'Comedies of Humours' (see page 344) but the art of satire is now more associated with the period 1660–1750, when it was frequently more social and personally-directed in its attacks.

4.2.1
John Dryden
(1631–1700)

Although a dramatist and a major critic and translator, John Dryden is nowadays noted for his verse satires, in particular *Absalom and Achitophel* (1681–1682) and *Mac Flecknoe* (written in 1678 and published in 1682). An extraordinarily prolific talent, Dryden influenced many of the great writers of the eighteenth century.

91

John Dryden

Thomas Shadwell

Mac Flecknoe　*Mac Flecknoe* is an attack on the poet and playwright Thomas Shadwell (1640–1692) on the occasion of the death of the notoriously bad Irish poet Richard Flecknoe in 1678. Shadwell and Dryden used to be on good terms but they conducted a public quarrel on the merits of Ben Jonson's comedies, which Shadwell thought Dryden undervalued. 'Mac' means 'son' in Scottish, and Shadwell saw himself as one of Jonson's 'sons' (successors). However, Dryden represents Shadwell as the 'son' of Flecknoe, governor of the kingdom of poetic dullness.

This is how the poem opens:

GLOSSARY

Augustus (l.3): Octavius Caesar-became the first Roman Emperor in 31 BC at the age of thirty-two; he assumed the title of Augustus four years later and ruled for forty-five years

own'd (l.5): owned, claimed to be

issue…increase (l.8): having produced a lot: writing? children?

resolv'd (l.13): resolved, decided

All human things are subject to decay,　　　　1
And when fate summons, monarchs must obey.
This Flecknoe found, who, like Augustus, young
Was call'd to empire, and had govern'd long;
In prose and verse, was own'd, without dispute,　5
Thro' all the realms of *Nonsense*, absolute.
This aged prince, now flourishing in peace,
And blest with issue of a large increase;
Worn out with business, did at length debate
To settle the succession of the State;　　　　10
And, pond'ring which of all his sons was fit
To reign, and wage immortal war with wit,
Cried: " 'T is resolv'd; for nature pleads, that he
Should only rule, who most resembles me.

(from *Mac Flecknoe*)

make pretense (l.19): try to give the appearance of	Sh—— alone my perfect image bears, 15
deviates into sense (l.20): changes from his usual habit in order to make sense	Mature in dullness from his tender years; Sh—— alone, of all my sons, is he Who stands confirm'd in full stupidity.
lucid (l.22): clear, full of light.	The rest to some faint meaning make pretense, But Sh—— never deviates into sense. 20
prevail upon (l.24): triumph over	Some beams of wit on other souls may fall, Strike thro', and make a lucid interval;
his goodly fabric (l.25): his body (Shadwell was very fat)	But Sh——'s genuine night admits no ray, His rising fogs prevail upon the day.
Thoughtless (l.27): i) carefree ii) mindless	Besides, his goodly fabric fills the eye, 25 And seems design'd for thoughtless majesty;
monarch (l.27): king-like	Thoughtless as monarch oaks that shade the plain,
supinely (l.28): lazily; on his back	And, spread in solemn state, supinely reign...."

- What do you think Shadwell's reaction might have been on reading this?

Understanding and interpretation

i) Who or what do the following refer to? 'fate' (l.2); 'This' (l.3); 'This aged prince' (l.7); 'he' (l.13); 'me' (l.14); 'His' (l.24).

ii) Dryden attacks Shadwell for being like Flecknoe. What 'qualities' do they have in common?

iii) In your own words, explain the meaning of l.2 'And when fate summons...' and l.24 'His rising fogs....'

iv) Find a word in the passage which means:
  a) orders someone to do something
  b) thinking over carefully
  c) clear
  d) made

v) Normally, words like 'flourishing' (l.7) and 'perfect' (l.15) have a positive connotation. Comment on their use in this poem.

Language and style Look at the definition of irony on page 13.

i) Which is the first *obviously* ironic line? What makes it ironic?

ii) Are we suspicious that the passage might be ironic before that phrase? If so, why?

iii) Dryden pretends to praise what he is criticising. Find an example and rewrite it to make it a statement which is more obviously praise (so 'realms of Nonsense' in l.6 would become 'realms of sense').

iv) The poem is written in 'heroic couplets' (lines of iambic pentameter rhymed in pairs). Its style is known as 'mock-heroic', which means that what Dryden regards as trivial and stupid is inflated in a grand and lofty way and treated with solemnity so that the disparity between subject and style makes us laugh. Find phrases which give an impression of largeness and the elemental, like 'when fate summons' in l.2. Find phrases which relate to the idea of ruling. What is their effect?

John Dryden Dryden's personal sympathies during the Civil War were with the Puritans although he welcomed the Restoration as the only political solution after Cromwell's death. He was made Poet Laureate in 1668, and became the first Poet Laureate to be made a paid member of the royal household in 1670. On the accession of the Roman Catholic James II in 1685, Dryden became a Catholic and kept his faith when James was deposed by the

Protestant William III in 1688. As a consequence he lost all his royal appointments but he was generally respected as the chief poet of his age until his death.

4.3 Literary criticism

In broad terms, literary criticism (the word 'criticism' comes from the Greek word for 'judgement') can be regarded as thought *about* literature. It expresses ideas about the nature of literature (and its relation to human experience) and it describes and assesses individual works.

The first important critical essay in English was Sir Philip Sidney's *Apology for Poetry* (published posthumously in 1595), a lively and persuasive defence – in the face of Puritan attack – of the value of literature to humanity. Criticism, however, did not become a recognised profession until after 1660, when there was a large audience for printed books and professional writers became more public in tone. After Dryden the greatest of the critics was Samuel Johnson (1709–1784).

● Discuss either some of the statements from Group A or some of the questions in Group B.

Group A:

– Imaginative writers are critics in that they must have ideas about the function and value of literature.
– All significant ideas are shaped by the philosophical and religious beliefs of the day.
– Literature is criticism and criticism literature.
– Through criticism imaginative writers can influence the public and, in Wordsworth's phrase, 'create the taste by which they are appreciated'.
– Criticism inevitably assesses the character and quality of contemporary civilisation and the contribution that the past has made to the present.

Group B

– How far are we able to separate writers from the times in which they live?
– What do *you* think is the value of literature? Is it a pleasurable form of instruction, as many eighteenth-century critics believed?
– What do *you* think the function of literary criticism is?

4.4 Satire in verse (2)

4.4.1
Alexander Pope
(1688–1744) and
The Rape of the Lock

The Rape of the Lock (1712–1714) was written as an attempt to end a quarrel between two fashionable Roman Catholic families. It started when Lord Petre cut off a lock of hair, which he wished to 'possess', from the head of Miss Arabella Fermor, the lady to whom he was engaged.

Alexander Pope wrote the poem in mock-epic style in imitation of Homer, to 'make a jest' of the incident and to 'laugh them (the two families) together'. However, Lord Petre married someone else two months before the first version of the poem was published and the poem soon outgrew the occasion. In the revised version of 1714 Pope included what he called 'machinery' (supernatural agents), a term which comes from the Greek use of theatrical machinery to suspend gods over the stage. Pope, though, turned Homer's Olympian deities into sylphs (tiny, light fairies, free to do what they like) and gnomes (representing the repressed mentality of the too-easily shocked) both of which have the spiritual nature of fashionable London society.

Extract 1   In this extract Belinda (Arabella) wakes up and gets ready to put on her make-up, having been warned by her guardian angel, Ariel, that disaster is near:

And now, unveil'd, the toilet stands display'd   1
Each silver vase in mystic order laid.
First, robed in white, the nymph intent adores,
With head uncover'd, the cosmetic powers.
A heav'nly image in the glass appears,   5
To that she bends, to that her eye she rears;
Th' inferior priestess, at her altar's side,
Trembling, begins the sacred rites of pride.
Unnumber'd treasures ope at once, and here
The various offerings of the world appear;   10
From each she nicely culls with curious toil,
And decks the goddess with the glitt'ring spoil.
This casket India's glowing gems unlocks,
And all Arabia breathes from yonder box.
The tortoise here and elephant unite,   15
Transform'd to combs, the speckled and the white.
Here files of pins extend their shining rows,
Puffs, powders, patches, Bibles, billet-doux.
Now awful beauty puts on all its arms;
The fair each moment rises in her charms,   20
Repairs her smiles, awakens every grace,
And calls forth all the wonders of her face:
Sees by degrees a purer blush arise,
And keener lightnings quicken in her eyes.
The busy sylphs surround their darling care,   25
These set the head, and those divide the hair,
Some fold the sleeve, while others plait the gown;
And Betty's praised for labours not her own.

GLOSSARY

unveil'd (l.1): revealed

toilet (l.1): dressing table

mystic order (l.2): (like the furniture of an altar)

robed in white (l.3): in a white gown (suggesting a priestess's clothes)

nymph ... adores (l.3): (Belinda is adoring her own image – the Goddess – in the mirror)

cosmetic (l.4): (usually one talks of cosmic powers!)

inferior priestess (l.7): (her maid, Betty; Belinda is the high priestess)

ope (l.9): open (*archaic*)

nicely ... toil (l.11): delicately chooses things

casket (l.13): jewellery box

Arabia (l.14): (where perfumes come from)

speckled ... white (l.16): (tortoise-shell and ivory)

files (l.17): rows (like soldiers on parade)

Puffs (l.18): balls of soft material for putting powder on the face

patches (l.18): tiny pieces of black silk pasted on the face to enhance the skin's whiteness.

billet-doux (l.18): love-letters

awful ... arms (l.19): (awe-inspiring, parody of arming an epic hero)

purer blush (l.23): more even redness (the result of cheek colouring)

lightnings (l.24): (caused by drops of belladonna – a poisonous plant – used to make the eyes sparkle)

Extract 2 In the afternoon, after the 'long labours of the toilet cease', Belinda 'burns to encounter two adventurous knights' – the Baron (Lord Petre) and another love-sick admirer – in a game of ombre (a type of card game related to whist and modern bridge). Belinda's eventual victory on the 'velvet plain' (the card table) is described as though it were an epic military victory in Homer! Coffee is then taken, and the Baron is offered a pair of scissors by one of the ladies:

GLOSSARY

engine (l.4): instrument (the scissors, but can refer to large military object)

steams (l.6): (of the coffee)

sprites repair (l.7): fairies go

Thrice (l.10): three times

foe (l.10): enemy

nosegay (l.13): small bouquet of flowers worn on the dress

peer (l.19): (the Baron)

forfex (l.19): pair of scissors (archaic)

wretched (l.22): unfortunate

fondly (l.22): foolishly (archaic use: a reference to the angel in the Bible who puts by the spear which Saul throws at David)

shears (l.23): scissors (large)

So ladies, in romance, assist their knight, 1
Present the spear, and arm him for the fight.
He takes the gift with reverence and extends
The little engine on his fingers' ends;
This just behind Belinda's neck he spread, 5
As o'er the fragrant steams she bends her head.
Swift to the lock a thousand sprites repair,
A thousand wings, by turns, blow back the hair;
And thrice they twitch'd the diamond in her ear;
Thrice she look'd back, and thrice the foe drew near. 10
Just in that instant, anxious Ariel sought
The close recesses of the virgin's thought:
As on the nosegay in her breast reclin'd,
He watch'd th' ideas rising in her mind,
Sudden he view'd, in spite of all her art, 15
An earthly lover lurking at her heart.
Amazed, confused, he found his power expired,
Resign'd to fate, and with a sigh retired.
The peer now spreads the glitt'ring forfex wide,
T' inclose the lock; now joins it, to divide. 20
Ev'n then, before the fatal engine closed,
A wretched sylph too fondly interposed;
Fate urged the shears, and cut the sylph in twain,

GLOSSARY

twain (l.23): two

soon unites (l.24): (a reference to *Paradise Lost*: 'the ethereal substance closed/Not longer divisible')

dissever (l.25): separate (*formal*)

Then flashed . . . eyes (l.27): Belinda gave quick and powerful angry looks

rend the affrighted (l.28): pierce the terrified ('affrighted' is *archaic*)

lap-dogs (l.30): small, easily-manageable dogs; also used for people excessively devoted to someone else

(But airy substance soon unites again)
The meeting points the sacred hair dissever   25
From the fair head, for ever, and for ever!
  Then flash'd the living lightning from her eyes,
And screams of horror rend th' affrighted skies.
Not louder shrieks to pitying Heaven are cast,
When husbands or when lap-dogs breathe their last;   30
Or when rich China vessels, fall'n from high,
In glitt'ring dust and painted fragments lie!

Extract 3   There follows a huge row:

GLOSSARY

To arms (l.1): it's war

virago (l.1): strong, warlike woman (*archaic*); (Belinda's friend, Thalestris)

All . . . parties (l.3): they all take sides

Fans (l.4): objects for cooling the face

whalebones (l.4): used for stiffening corsets and collars

press (l.9): crowd

beau (l.11): man too concerned with his appearance

witling (l.11): someone who would like to be witty

throng (l.11): crowd

Dapperwit, Sir Fopling (l.14): (typical names for false wits and dandies in Restoration comedy)

Those . . . killing (l.16): (the words of a song in the popular opera *Camilla*)

Mæander's . . . swan (l.17): the swan on the banks of the wandering river, Mæander, sings sweetly as he dies.

'To arms, to arms!' the fierce virago cries,   1
And swift as lightning to the combat flies.
All side in parties, and begin th' attack:
Fans clap, silks rustle, and tough whalebones crack;
Heroes' and heroines' shouts confusedly rise,   5
And bass and treble voices strike the skies.
No common weapons in their hands are found,
Like Gods they fight, nor dread a mortal wound . . . .

While through the press enraged Thalestris flies,
And scatters death around from both her eyes,   10
A beau and witling perish'd in the throng,
One died in metaphor, and one in song.
'O cruel nymph! a living death I bear,'
Cried Dapperwit, and sunk beside his chair.
A mournful glance Sir Fopling upwards cast,   15
'Those eyes are made so killing,'—was his last.
Thus on Mæander's flowery margin lies
Th' expiring swan, and as he sings he dies.

(from *The Rape of the Lock*)

i) Complete the following sentences:
   a) With the help of the 'cosmetic powers' and the sylphs ....
   b) Ariel is suddenly helpless when ....
   c) After the theft of the lock there is great ....

ii) Which of these do you think describe Belinda?
   a) deliberately provocative
   b) beautiful and charming
   c) dedicated to the decoration and worship of her own beauty
   d) like a spoilt child
   e) dignified
   f) vain
   g) divine

iii) Find phrases which suggest that Belinda's make-up ceremony is like a) a religious ritual for her and b) a preparation for battle.

The lock is never found and Pope finishes the poem by advising Belinda – tenderly – to 'cease ... to mourn thy ravished hair'.

Match the statements with the quotations below (for example, 1 – f). Can any be matched with more than one quotation?

1 The line contains a 'caesura' (a main pause about the middle of the line, at the end of a verse foot, related to a pause in the syntax).
2 A word suggesting something trivial is put next to a word suggesting something serious; it makes us realise that the character does not take the serious object seriously.
3 There is a suggestion that fashionable society uses up the natural resources of the world.
4 Suggestions of epic battles both dignify the present action and make us realise how trivial it is by comparison.
5 The use of high-sounding words to describe trivial objects is a form of mockery.
6 Pope's mockery is directed towards the men just as much as the women.

a) 'The tortoise here and elephant unite,
   Transform'd to combs ...' (Extract 1 l.15–16)
b) 'Bibles, billet-doux' (Extract 1 l.18)
c) 'So ladies ... assist their knight
   Present the spear, and arm him for the fight.' (Extract 2 l.1–2)
d) 'glittering forfex' (Extract 2 l.19)
e) 'when husbands or when lap-dogs breathe their last' (Extract 2 l.30)
f) 'One died in metaphor, and one in song' (Extract 3 l.12)

Discuss at least one of the following:

i) In what way is Pope's satire both funny and serious?
ii) It has been suggested that Pope felt at home in the aristocratic world he mocked; that he was both attracted to it and critical of it on moral grounds. Can you see any signs of this in these extracts? If so, where?
iii) How would you describe the role of the 'machinery'?
iv) This painting is entitled *The Countess's Morning Levee* by William Hogarth (1697–1764), from the sequence *Marriage à la Mode* 1743–1745). A fashionable lady, recently made a countess on the death of her father-in-law, is receiving morning guests while her hair is being dressed. The painting, satirising the arrogance and greed of the richer classes, is full of comic and erotic detail.

How is the atmosphere similar to that of *The Rape of the Lock?*

vi) Is beauty made or natural? Compare twentieth century attitudes towards fashion with those in the poem.

Alexander Pope

i) Put the verbs in parentheses in the correct form:

As his parents were Catholic, Pope (suffer) .... the penalty of (be) .... in a country which (easily, alarm) .... by the threat of Catholic intrigue and invasion. Like all Catholics he (deny) .... admission to a university or public office and (have to) .... pay double taxes. Nor (his enemies, let) .... him (forget) .... his dwarf-like stature or his crooked body, (misshape) .... by adolescent tuberculosis.

ii) Which parts of Extract 1 of *The Rape of the Lock* suggest Pope's Catholic background?

Pope was one of the very few friends of the satirist, Jonathan Swift (1667–1745). He was also a great poet with an extraordinarily rich and rapid play of mind. He translated both Homer's *Iliad* and *Odyssey* (1715–1726) and wrote one of the most imaginative and profound verse satires of all time, The *Dunciad* (not complete until 1742 and inspired by Dryden's *Mac Flecknoe*), in which bad writers are elevated for the honour of the goddess Dullness.

4.5 Satire in prose

4.5.1 Jonathan Swift (1667–1745)

The following pamphlet, written by the Irish writer Jonathan Swift in 1729, attacked the way the English used the Irish for profit, leaving them poor and hungry.

Warm up

i) Title: *A Modest Proposal*

What do you understand by the word 'modest'? Can you guess what the essay is going to be about? Do you expect the proposal to be modest?

ii) The sub-heading says that the 'modest proposal' is 'For Preventing the Children of Poor People in Ireland from Being a Burden to Their Parents or Country, and for Making Them Beneficial to the Public'. Is there anything in this which worries you?

Irish peasants

Extract 1   This is the opening paragraph of the pamphlet:

GLOSSARY

great town (l.1): Dublin, in Ireland

importuning (l.4): begging

an alms (l.5): money

sustenance (l.7): money and food

Pretender (l.9): (Many Irish Catholics joined James Stuart (1688–1766), son of James II, in exile on the Continent to fight for his restoration to the throne)

Barbadoes (l.10): (Many of the Irish poor emigrated to the West Indies, often working as semi-slaves to the planters)

It is a melancholy object to those who walk through this great town or travel in the country, when they see the streets, the roads, and cabin doors, crowded with beggars of the female sex, followed by three, four, or six children, all in rags and importuning every passenger for an alms. These mothers, instead of being able to work for their honest livelihood, are forced to employ all their time in strolling to beg sustenance for their helpless infants, who, as they grow up, either turn thieves for want of work, or leave their dear native country to fight for the Pretender in Spain, or sell themselves to the Barbadoes.

1

5

10

- How would you describe the narrator's tone? Reasonable or unreasonable? Intelligent or naive? Are we meant to feel sympathetic? Does he sound concerned and humane?

Extract 2   We are led gently into the argument:

> I think it is agreed by all parties that this prodigious number of children in the arms, or on the backs, or at the heels of their mothers, and frequently of their fathers, is in the present deplorable state of the kingdom a very great additional grievance; and therefore whoever could find out a fair, cheap, and easy method of making these children sound, useful members of the commonwealth would deserve so well of the public as to have his statue set up for a preserver of the nation.

(lines 1, 5)

- Do we feel sympathetic?

Extract 3   The narrator widens the range of who he is talking about:

> But my intention is very far from being confined to provide only for the children of professed beggars; it is of a much greater extent, and shall take in the whole number of infants at a certain age who are born of parents in effect as little able to support them as those who demand our charity in the streets.

(lines 1, 5)

Extract 4   The build-up of the argument is slow:

> As to my own part, having turned my thoughts for many years upon this important subject, and maturely weighed the several schemes of other projectors, I have always found them grossly mistaken in their computation. It is true, a child just dropped from its dam may be supported by her milk for a solar year, with little other nourishment; at most not above the value of two shillings, which the mother may certainly get, or the value in scraps, by her lawful occupation of begging; and it is exactly at one year old that I propose to provide for them in such a manner as instead of being a charge upon their parents or the parish, or wanting food and raiment for the rest of their lives, they shall on the contrary contribute to the feeding, and partly to the clothing, of many thousands.

(lines 1, 5, 10)

- Are there any disturbing phrases here? Do they suggest that the writer's 'persona' (his narrator) is perhaps not really so humane?

Extract 5   To convince us of the humanity of his scheme he makes his case forcibly:

> There is likewise another great advantage in my scheme, that it   1
> will prevent those voluntary abortions, and that horrid practice
> of women murdering their bastard children, alas, too frequent
> among us, sacrificing the poor innocent babes, I doubt, more to
> avoid the expense than the shame, which would move tears and   5
> pity in the most savage and inhuman breast.

Extract 6   But before he will tell us his 'proposal' we must read some economic
calculations:

GLOSSARY

this kingdom (l.1): (Ireland)

miscarry (l.8): give birth too early, so that the baby dies

handicraft (l.15): activities using the hands

pick ... livelihood (l.16): earn a living

where ... parts (l.17–18): when they are dutiful children

rudiments (l.18): first steps

only ... probationers (l.20): only be regarded as learning the trade

principal (l.20): very important

Cavan (l.21): one of the poorest districts of Ireland

salable commodity (l.26): article which can be sold

on the Exchange (l.28): in the marketplace

turn to account (l.28): be made into a profit

nutriment and rags (l.29): food and (poor) clothes

The number of souls in this kingdom being usually reckoned one   1
million and a half, of these I calculate there may be about two
hundred thousand couple whose wives are breeders; from which
number I subtract thirty thousand couples who are able to maintain
their own children, although I apprehend there cannot be so many   5
under the present distresses of the kingdom; but this being granted,
there will remain an hundred and seventy thousand breeders. I
again subtract fifty thousand for those women who miscarry, or
whose children die by accident or disease within the year. There
only remain an hundred and twenty thousand children of poor   10
parents annually born. The question therefore is, how this number
shall be reared and provided for, which, as I have already said,
under the present situation of affairs, is utterly impossible by all
the methods hitherto proposed. For we can neither employ them in
handicraft or agriculture; we neither build houses (I mean in the   15
country) nor cultivate land. They can very seldom pick up a livelihood by stealing till they arrive at six years old, except where they
are of towardly parts; although I confess they learn the rudiments
much earlier, during which time they can however be looked upon
only as probationers, as I have been informed by a principal gentle-   20
man in the county of Cavan, who protested to me that he never
knew above one or two instances under the age of six, even in a
part of the kingdom so renowned for the quickest proficiency in
that art.

I am assured by our merchants that a boy or a girl before twelve   25
years old is no salable commodity; and even when they come to
this age they will not yield above three pounds, or three pounds
and half a crown at most on the Exchange; which cannot turn to
account either to the parents or the kingdom, the charge of nutriment and rags having been at least four times that value.   30

● What is your view now of the narrator's attitude towards human beings? Has it
changed?

Extract 7   Here is the argument. Beware the charm of the opening sentence!

I shall now therefore humbly propose my own thoughts, which I [1]
hope will not be liable to the least objection.

I have been assured by a very knowing American of my acquaintance in London, that a young healthy child well nursed is at a year
old a most delicious, nourishing, and wholesome food, whether [5]
stewed, roasted, baked, or boiled; and I make no doubt that it will
equally serve in a fricassee or a ragout.

I do therefore humbly offer it to public consideration that of the
hundred and twenty thousand children, already computed, twenty
thousand may be reserved for breed, whereof only one fourth part [10]
to be males, which is more than we allow to sheep, black cattle, or
swine; and my reason is that these children are seldom the fruits of
marriage, a circumstance not much regarded by our savages, therefore one male will be sufficient to serve four females. That the
remaining hundred thousand may at a year old be offered in sale to [15]
the persons of quality and fortune through the kingdom, always
advising the mother to let them suck plentifully in the last month,
so as to render them plump and fat for a good table. A child will
make two dishes at an entertainment for friends, and when the
family dines alone, the fore or hind quarter will make a reasonable [20]
dish; and seasoned with a little pepper or salt will be very good
boiled on the fourth day, especially in winter.

GLOSSARY
wholesome (l.5): good for
the health
fricassee/ragout (l.7):
fashionable French
stews
swine (l.12): pigs
render ... plump (l.18):
make them big
enough
fore ... quarter (l.20): front
or back part

● What is your immediate reaction?

Extract 8   In the next few paragraphs Swift's narrator goes on to explain his scheme
Here is one example:

GLOSSARY
esteem (l.2): respect
discoursing (l.2):
expressing his ideas
offer ... scheme (l.3):
suggest a way of
improving my plan
want (l.5): lack
venison (l.5): flesh of deer
deference (l.10): respect for
patriot (l.11): lover of his/
her country
*cannot ... sentiments
(l.11–12)*: cannot
completely agree with
him
*with humble submission
(l.16)*: if I may say so
scrupulous (l.19): with
moral integrity and
delicate feeling

A very worthy person, a true lover of his country, and whose vir- [1]
tues I highly esteem, was lately pleased in discoursing on this
matter to offer a refinement upon my scheme. He said that many
gentlemen of this kingdom, having of late destroyed their deer, he
conceived that the want of venison might be well supplied by the [5]
bodies of young lads and maidens, not exceeding fourteen years of
age nor under twelve, so great a number of both sexes in every
county being now ready to starve for want of work and service; and
these to be disposed of by their parents, if alive, or otherwise by
their nearest relations. But with due deference to so excellent a [10]
friend and so deserving a patriot, I cannot be altogether in his
sentiments; for as to the males, my American acquaintance assured
me from frequent experience that their flesh was generally tough
and lean, like that of our schoolboys, by continual exercise, and
their taste disagreeable; and to fatten them would not answer the [15]
charge. Then as to the females, it would, I think with humble
submission, be a loss to the public, because they soon would
become breeders themselves: and besides, it is not improbable that

some scrupulous people might be apt to censure such a practice (although indeed very unjustly) as a little bordering upon cruelty; which, I confess, hath always been with me the strongest objection against any project, how well soever intended. 20

● How would you describe the narrator's tone of voice now? Calm and logical? Superior? Can you guess what Swift's purpose in this essay is?

Extract 9   The narrator argues that there are a lot of advantages in his scheme. For example:

GLOSSARY

Papists ... overrun (l.1–2): (the fear of Catholics and their custom of having large families was often used for propaganda purposes by Protestants)
the nation (l.2): Ireland
inducement (l.5): encouragement
emulation (l.10): competition
mares (l.14): female horses
sows (l.14): fully grown female pigs
in foal/in calf/farrow (l.14): giving birth

... it would greatly lessen the number of Papists, with whom we are yearly overrun, being the principal breeders of the nation as well as our most dangerous enemies; and who stay at home on purpose to deliver the kingdom to the Pretender ... 1

... it would be a great inducement to marriage, which all wise nations have either encouraged by rewards or enforced by laws and penalties. It would increase the care and tenderness of mothers toward their children, when they were sure of a settlement for life to the poor babes, provided in some sort by the public, to their annual profit instead of expense. We should see an honest emulation among the married women, which of them could bring the fattest child to the market. Men would become as fond of their wives during the time of their pregnancy as they are now of their mares in foal, their cows in calf, or sows when they are ready to farrow; nor offer to beat or kick them (as is too frequent a practice) for fear of a miscarriage. 5 10 15

● What are the targets of Swift's mockery here?

Extract 10   In saying that nobody could object to his proposal, the narrator dismisses what we assume are Swift's more genuine proposals:

GLOSSARY

own (l.3): admit
design (l.4): purpose
expedients (l.8): practical solutions (those which he dismisses show how much the English exploited Ireland and how much the Irish were to blame themselves)
absentees (l.8): the English landlords who owned a lot of land and property in Ireland
gaming (l.12): gambling

I can think of no one objection that will possibly be raised against this proposal, unless it should be urged that the number of people will be thereby much lessened in the kingdom. This I freely own, and it was indeed one principal design in offering it to the world. I desire the reader will observe, that I calculate my remedy for this one individual kingdom of Ireland and for no other that ever was, is, or I think ever can be upon earth. Therefore let no man talk to me of other expedients: of taxing our absentees at five shillings a pound: of using neither clothes nor household furniture except what is of our own growth and manufacture: of utterly rejecting the materials and instruments that promote foreign luxury: of curing the expensiveness of pride, vanity, idleness, and gaming in our women: of introducing a vein of parsimony, prudence, and temperance: of learning to love our country, in the want of which we 1 5 10

differ even from Laplanders and the inhabitants of Topinamboo, 15
of quitting our animosities and factions, nor acting any longer like
the Jews, who were murdering one another at the very moment
their city was taken: of being a little cautious not to sell our country
and conscience for nothing: of teaching landlords to have at least
one degree of mercy toward their tenants: lastly, of putting a spirit 20
of honesty, industry, and skill into our shopkeepers ...

Therefore I repeat, let no man talk to me of these and the like expedients, till he hath at least some glimpse of hope that there will
ever be some hearty and sincere attempt to put them in practice.

But as to myself, having been wearied out for many years with 25
offering vain, idle, visionary thoughts, and at length utterly despairing of success, I fortunately fell upon this proposal, which, as
it is wholly new, so it hath something solid and real, of no expense
and little trouble, full in our own power, and whereby we can incur
no danger in disobliging England. For this kind of commodity will 30
not bear exportation, the flesh being of too tender a consistence to
admit a long continuance in salt, although perhaps I could name a
country which would be glad to eat up our whole nation without
it. . . .

I profess, in the sincerity of my heart, that I have not the least 35
personal interest in endeavoring to promote this necessary work,
having no other motive than the public good of my country, by
advancing our trade, providing for infants, relieving the poor and
giving some pleasure to the rich. I have no children by which I can
propose to get a single penny; the youngest being nine years old, 40
and my wife past childbearing.

(from *A Modest Proposal*)

vein of parsimony (l.13): element of care with money

temperence (l.13): moderation (in drink?)

Topinamboo (l.15): a wild region of Brazil; (even they love their country more than the Irish love Ireland)

animosities and factions (l.16): hostile arguments between political parties

Jews (l.17): (When Jerusalem fell, possibly to Nebuchadnezzar or to the Roman Emperor Titus)

as to myself (l.25): (Swift himself had published his genuine proposals in various pamphlets)

visionary (l.26) impractical

disobliging (l.30): offending

a country (l.33): (England)

without it (l.33): without it being kept in salt (an ironic reference to the English attitude of taking everything they want from the Irish without hesitating)

profess (l.35): declare (openly and freely)

i) What is humorous about the last sentence?

ii) Re-order these words to make a sentence summarising the narrator's argument.

the children/the rich/for/to feed/It/fattened/of the poor/humane/to be/ would be

Appreciation

i) Below are some of the targets of Swift's satire. Select one and illustrate from the text.
  a) *England's exploitation of Ireland.* Ireland was used as a source of cheap food and materials and forbidden to trade on its own; its absentee English landlords kept the too numerous Catholic peasants hungry and oppressed.
  b) *The Irish.* Swift regarded them as too passive and disgraced by the treatment they received.
  c) *The benevolent humanitarian.* A typical figure who sometimes tries to correct a social evil by a logically-conceived, theoretical plan without respect for reality and individual feeling and with rather more concern for his or her own status and glory.

ii) Explain the irony in at least one of the following phrases:

  a) 'sound, useful members of the commonwealth' (Extract 2, l.6)
  b) 'sacrificing the poor innocent babes' (Extract 5, l.4)
  c) 'most savage and inhuman breast' (Extract 5, l.6)

105

iii) Discuss at least one of the following:

At the beginning of the essay, the reader goes along with the logic of the narrator's argument without realising the implications.

The reader's shock is made greater by the narrator's apparent naivety and calm tone of voice.

As a result of the shocking proposals, we are encouraged to support Swift's genuine proposals.

Although the narrator doesn't represent the writer's real point of view, Swift nevertheless enjoys shocking us, making the overall effect of the essay more negative than positive.

Jonathan Swift   One/some of you take Part 1, the other(s) Part 2. Expand these notes either orally or in written form to tell each other the story of Swift's life.

Part 1

Born 1667 in Dublin, of English parents – future playwright Congreve as a schoolfriend – educated at Trinity College, Dublin – left for England after James II's abdication and subsequent invasion of Ireland – 1689–1699 secretary to Sir William Temple, retired diplomat, writer, friend of King William – rather reluctantly took orders as priest in Church of England in 1694 – 1702–1714 large part in literary/political life of London – divided time between London/Ireland – contributed to journals *The Tatler* and *The Spectator* – with Pope founded Scriblerus Club to ridicule 'all false tastes in learning' – first worked for Whig party (see page 122) – changed to Tories, 1710 – became Dean of St Patrick's Cathedral, Dublin 1713.

Part 2

1720–1730 wrote number of pamphlets in support of oppressed Irish – *Gulliver's Travels* (1729) a satirical fable superficially resembling *Robinson Crusoe* – Swift became popular – difficult relationships with two women who loved him: Esther Johnson ('Stella' in *Journal to Stella*, 1710–1713) and Esther Vanhomrigh ('Vanessa' in *Cadenus and Vanessa*, 1713) – lived conscientiously as Dean – gave away his wealth to charity – seriously ill – from 1742, faculties decayed – considered mad, although modern biographers say he wasn't – died 1745.

4.6 The development of the novel

A novel may be defined as a work of narrative fiction, usually in prose. As a distinct literary form, the novel came into being in Britain in the eighteenth century.

These are some of the factors which are said to have influenced its development:

A: Literary influences
i) *Journalism*: Early journalism aimed to record the facts of daily living, paying attention to detail, easy readability and immediacy of interest. In the eighteenth century journalism set out more to *enlighten* than entertain its readers. One of the most important early undertakings of English journalism was a periodical called *The Tatler* (started in 1709).

ii) *Parallel art forms*: Biography (see pages 64–65), diaries (see pages 83–91) and personal memoirs were very fashionable in the eighteenth century.

iii) *Letter writing*: With improved communications, letter writing was cultivated as an art. Letters were composed with care and at length.

iv) *Travel literature*: With the steady growth of overseas trade, books such as *New Voyage Round the World* (1697), by the navigator and explorer Captain William Dampier, were widely read. They were written in a lively, straightforward style and contained precise scientific observation.

v) *The Restoration Comedies of Manners*: Between 1660 and 1710 elegant comic plays were performed with characters drawn mainly from the London aristocracy. Plots contained love intrigues, witty sexual suggestiveness and sparkling conversational repartee. They were noted for their humour, their realism and their satire of the social surface of life.

vi) *The picaresque convention*: This convention was a form of prose fiction originating in Spain in the sixteenth century, dealing with the adventures of rogues – mischievous, dishonest people who were fond of playing tricks. In English fiction the term 'picaresque' refers to a series of episodes where the often daring hero is forced to seek his fortune outside of stable society. An early example is Thomas Nashe's *Unfortunate Traveller* (1594).

vii) *The mock romance* of knight errantry (such as *Don Quixote de la Mancha*, 1605–1615, by the Spanish writer Miguel de Cervantes) where, in comic vein, wandering knights try to put injustices to right.

B: Other influences
i) *Puritanism*: This had always encouraged:

a) a practical attitude to world affairs. When Christianity lost some of its spiritual and emotional force, practical principles began to dominate religious thought. Writers were expected to inform, to be 'useful' and to urge moral behaviour.

b) a belief in the individual conscience. Puritans followed the 'inner light', the voice of God.

c) a spirit of self-enquiry. The spirit of Puritanism encouraged the development of the 'spiritual autobiography', such as John Bunyan's *Grace Abounding* (1666).

d) a love of truth. Stricter Puritans, however, opposed the theatre, not only because they considered it a centre of immoral behaviour and disorder but because it put on works of fiction, which they equated with lies. Later Puritans, known as Dissenters, saw art as irrelevant to the serious business of living.

ii) *The rise of the middle class*: The movement had begun in Chaucer's time but the big increase in the seventeenth century, as the interests of gentry in the countryside and the money-making middle classes in the towns grew closer together, provided a new and large reading public in the eighteenth century. As a result:

a) education was available to more people and was less exclusively 'classical' than the education available to the upper classes;

b) there was more leisure time available, particularly for women;

c) there was greater individualism – a belief that one must earn a living by one's own efforts;

d) there was a growing desire to be opened up to new worlds outside one's immediate existence;

e) there was greater spiritual and social alienation and a belief that human destiny was uncertain.

iii) *Scientific philosophy*: The optimistic philosophy of 'natural philosophers', such as John Locke (1632–1704), was consistent with, and helped lead to, a greater belief in reason at the expense of the imagination. After the Restoration, moderation and religious tolerance replaced passionate religious conviction, and attention was more focused on the social destiny of the individual and the facts and circumstances of the social world.

● Read the following notes about five eighteenth-century novels. For Number 1 and at least two others indicate which of the above influences seem to apply.

1 *The Life and strange surprising Adventures of Robinson Crusoe* (1719).

By Daniel Defoe (?1660–1731), a journalist and pamphleteer with a tradesman's preoccupation with the details of life. Often thought of as the first English novel. About a man wrecked on a desert island for twenty years (Defoe identified with the hero but had never visited a desert island himself). A description of the industrious, sensible, methodical way in which he struggles to build up a life for himself. Sees people in terms of their economic, rather than their emotional or moral virtues. Describes people according to what John Locke called their 'primary qualities' (those which can be measured objectively, such as size, weight, number and shape) rather than their 'secondary qualities' (such as smell, colour and beauty which depend more on our subjective perceptions). Regards God as the Senior Partner in his commercial enterprises, a Power that provides, though a comfort when ill. Written as a personal memoir in a series of episodes. Plain style.

2 *Gulliver's Travels* (1726)

By Jonathan Swift (see pages 100–106). A fable (a story that teaches a lesson, with people who have never actually existed or animals who behave like human beings). A series of episodes about the travels of a surgeon on a merchant ship. Shipwrecked on Lilliput, where the inhabitants are six inches high making their self-importance seem ridiculous; shipwrecked on Brobdingnag, where the inhabitants are as tall as church steeples and Gulliver, an eighteenth-century man who believes in the power of reason, is made to feel petty; shipwrecked on the flying island of Laputa, where the inhabitants are absorbed in ridiculous forms of scientific enquiry and philosophical speculation; shipwrecked on the island of the Houyhnhnms, where horses endowed with reason contrast with the dirty and brutal Yahoos, beasts in human shape. The book appeals to all ages but the darker satire is usually ignored by the young. Swift believed that man would destroy himself without divine aid. Precise, sober style used for ironic effect.

3 *Pamela* (1740–1741)

By Samuel Richardson (1689–1761), the son of a humble middle-class furniture maker. Sometimes called the first true modern novel because of a sustained and realistic representation of the day-to-day behaviour and psychology of the main characters. Written in epistolary form (as a series of letters), with Richardson pretending to be the 'editor'. There are six correspondents, each with their own particular style and point of view. Part I: Pamela, a servant, resists attempts by her employer to seduce and rape her. However, she eventually marries him! Part II is about their married life together. Richardson wished to instruct readers 'how to think and act justly and prudently in the common concerns of human life'. The book was a great popular success; parodied by Henry Fielding, in *Apology for the life of Mrs Shamela Andrews* (1741), because it also pretended to be a book of moral instruction when Pamela seemed to use her virtue to obtain social advancement (the subtitle of Richardson's novel was *Virtue Rewarded*).

4 Tom Jones (1749)

By Henry Fielding (1707–1754), a magistrate of aristocratic birth and classical education, with no false delicacy in sexual matters. Disliked what he saw as Richardson's self-satisfaction and hypocrisy. The book is a vigorous and entertaining 'comic epic' (a panoramic narrative of manners and behaviour), containing mock-heroism and many classical allusions. Written as a series of events rather than around a plot. Many direct 'intrusions' by the author. Characters: social types presented as characteristic human types, with basic human motives. In contrast with Richardson, they are seen externally. About the life of a foundling (a baby of unknown parentage), discovered by an enlightened landowner, Squire Allworthy. Tom is a generous, handsome young man with an inclination to fleshly lusts. Falls in love with Squire Western's daughter, Sophie, intended for the treacherous Blifil. Disgraced by his enemies and his own behaviour, Tom is disowned by Squire Allworthy. After a series of adventures on the road, he is eventually united with Sophie and they are married.

5 The Life and Opinions of Tristram Shandy (1760–1767)

By Laurence Sterne (1713–1768), the son of an impoverished army officer. Became Anglican priest. However, he understood human instinct. Highly 'subjective' novel full of sexual humour, emotion and fantasy, controlled by cool, ironic wit. Anticipates 'stream of consciousness' novels of twentieth century. Narrator pretends he can't really begin. Nominal hero, Tristram, not born till Vol IV! The circumstances preceding and during birth dealt with in elaborate detail. Full of talk of immediate relatives and neighbours. Sounds like a conventional biography but full of digressions, jokes played on the reader, and questioning of philosophical assumptions about Time and the association of ideas. Many reservations expressed about the novel by Sterne's contemporaries on both literary and moral grounds.

4.6.1

Robinson Crusoe (1719)

Read the following extract from *Robinson Crusoe*. Where can you see the influence of Puritanism?

Robinson Crusoe

I have mentioned that I saved the skins of all the creatures that I killed – I mean four-footed ones – and I had them hung up, stretched out with sticks, in the sun, by which means some of them were so dry and hard that they were fit for little; but others, it seems, were very useful. The first thing I made of these was a great cap for my head, with the hair on the outside, to shoot off the rain; and this I performed so well that, after, I made me a suit wholly of those skins – that is to say, a waistcoat, and breeches open at the knees, and both loose; for they were rather wanting to keep me cool than to keep me warm. I must not omit to acknowledge that they were wretchedly made; for if I was a bad carpenter, I was a worse tailor. However, they were such as I made a very good shift with, and when I was abroad, if it happened to rain, the hair of the waistcoat and cap being outermost, I was kept very dry.

After this, I spent a great deal of time and pains to make an umbrella. I was indeed in great want of one, and had a great mind to make one. I had seen them made in the Brazils, where they are very useful in the great heats which are there, and I felt the heat every jot as great here, and greater too, being nearer the equinox; besides, as I was obliged to be much abroad, it was a most useful thing to me, as well for the rains as the heats. I took a world of pains at it, and was a great while before I could make anything likely to hold; nay, after I thought I had hit the way, I spoiled two or three before I made one to my mind. But at last I made one that answered indifferently well; the main difficulty I found was to make it to let down. I could make it spread, but if it did not let down too, and draw in, it would not be portable for me any way but just over my head, which would not do. However, at last, as I said, I made one to answer. I covered it with skins, the hair upwards, so that it cast off the rain like a pent-house, and kept off the sun so effectually that I could walk out in the hottest of the weather with greater advantage than I could before in the coolest, and when I had no need for it, I could close it, and carry it under my arm.

Thus I lived mightily comfortable, my mind being entirely composed by resigning to the will of God, and throwing myself wholly upon the disposal of His providence. This made my life better than sociable, for when I began to regret the want of conversation, I would ask myself, whether thus conversing mutually with my own thoughts, and (as I hope I might say) with even my Maker, by ejaculations and petitions, was not better than the utmost enjoyment of human society in the world?

I cannot say that, after this, for five years, any extraordinary thing happened to me, but I lived on in the same course, in the same posture and place, just as before. The chief thing I was employed in, besides my yearly labour of planting my barley and rice, and curing my raisins – of both which I always kept up just enough to have sufficient stock of the year's provisions beforehand – I say, besides this yearly labour, and my daily labour of going out with my gun, I had one labour, to make me a canal, which at last I

creek (l.51): narrow inlet of water coming from the sea

finished; so that, by digging a canal to it of six feet wide and four feet deep, I brought it into the creek, almost half a mile. 50

(from *Robinson Crusoe*)

● Look at the paragraph beginning 'After this . . .' (l.15). Underline the adjectives. What conclusions can you draw about Defoe's style?

4.6.2
Tom Jones (1749)

Extract 1 Tom is refused a bed by the landlord of a tavern, who suspects him of being a thief, and is forced to spend the night on a chair. However, the tavern is disturbed by a company of soldiers, described as 'gentlemen in red coats' (red was the colour of army uniforms in the eighteenth and nineteenth centuries):

The landlord was now forced from his post to furnish his numerous guests with beer, which they called for with great eagerness; and upon his second or third return from the cellar, he saw Mr Jones standing before the fire in the midst of the soldiers; for it may easily be believed, that the arrival of so much good company should put an end to any sleep, unless that from which we are to be awakened only by the last trumpet. 1 ... 5

The company having now pretty well satisfied their thirst, nothing remained but to pay the reckoning, a circumstance often productive of much mischief and discontent among the inferior rank of gentry; who are apt to find great difficulty in assessing the sum, with exact regard to distributive justice, which directs, that every man shall pay according to the quantity which he drinks. This difficulty occurred upon the present occasion; and it was the greater, as some gentlemen had, in their extreme hurry, marched off, after their first draught, and had entirely forgot to contribute anything towards the said reckoning. 10 ... 15

A violent dispute now arose, in which every word may be said to have been deposed upon oath; for the oaths were at least equal to all the other words spoken. In this controversy, the whole company spoke together, and every man seemed wholly bent to extenuate the sum which fell to his share; so that the most probable conclusion which could be foreseen, was, that a large portion of the reckoning would fall to the landlord's share to pay, or (what is much the same thing) would remain unpaid. 20 ... 25

All this while Mr Jones was engaged in conversation with the serjeant; for that officer was entirely unconcerned in the present dispute, being privileged, by immemorial custom, from all contribution.

The dispute now grew so warm, that it seemed to draw towards a military decision, when Jones stepping forward, silenced all their clamours at once, by declaring that he would pay the whole reckoning, which indeed amounted to no more than three shillings and four-pence. 30

GLOSSARY

furnish (l.1): supply

the last trumpet (l.7): the trumpet which will blow at the end of the world to wake the dead

reckoning (l.9): bill

gentry (l.11): aristocracy

apt (l.11): likely

draught (l.16): drink

deposed . . . oath (l.19): a solemn promise (a pun on the word 'oath', which also means a swear word)

extenuate (l.21): cut down

serjeant (l.27): an army officer

privileged (l.28): freed

immemorial (l.28): from the beginning of time

procured (l.34): earned

the guide (l.38): the person showing Tom the way to Bristol

Duke of Cumberland (l.41): (the rebellion by Bonnie Prince Charlie – Prince Charles Edward – in support of James II's return to the throne in 1745 was put down by 'Butcher' Cumberland; Fielding was on the side of the Protestant George II)

banditti (l.44): rebels

into England (l.44): (from Scotland)

the metropolis (l.46): London

composition (l.47): character

This declaration procured Jones the thanks and applause of the whole company. The terms honourable, noble, and worthy gentleman, resounded through the room; nay, my landlord himself began to have a better opinion of him, and almost to disbelieve the account which the guide had given.

The serjeant had informed Mr Jones, that they were marching against the rebels, and expected to be commanded by the glorious Duke of Cumberland. By which the reader may perceive (a circumstance which we have not thought necessary to communicate before) that this was the very time when the late rebellion was at the highest; and indeed the banditti were now marched into England, intending, as it was thought, to fight the king's forces, and to attempt pushing forward to the metropolis.

Jones had some heroic ingredients in his composition, and was a hearty well-wisher to the glorious cause of liberty, and of the Protestant religion. It is no wonder, therefore, that in circumstances which would have warranted a much more romantic and wild undertaking, it should occur to him to serve as a volunteer in this expedition.

35

40

45

50

● i) What effect did the soldiers' arrival have on the tavern?
ii) If Tom hadn't paid for the beer, what do you think would have happened?
iii) What impression do you think the 'guide' had given the landlord (l.36–38)?

Extract 2   On their way to London, Tom and his companion Partridge rescue the Man of the Hill from robbers and then hear his life story (one of the novel's many digressions and told like a Spanish picaresque narrative). In this episode, Tom and the Man of the Hill go for a walk:

Aurora now first opened her casement, *Anglicè*, the day began to break, when Jones walked forth in company with the stranger, and mounted Mazard Hill; of which they had no sooner gained the summit, than one of the most noble prospects in the world presented itself to their view, and which we would likewise present to the reader; but for two reasons. *First*, we despair of making those who have seen this prospect, admire our description. *Secondly*, we very much doubt whether those, who have not seen it, would understand it.

Jones stood for some minutes fixed in one posture, and directing his eyes towards the south; upon which the old gentleman asked, what he was looking at with so much attention? 'Alas, sir,' answered he, with a sigh, 'I was endeavouring to trace out my own journey hither. Good heavens! what a distance is Gloucester from us! What a vast tract of land must be between me and my own home.' 'Ay, ay, young gentleman,' cries the other, 'and, by your sighing, from what you love better than your own home, or I am mistaken. I perceive now the object of your contemplation is not within your sight, and yet I fancy you have a pleasure in looking that way.' Jones answered with a smile, 'I find, old friend, you have not yet forgot the sensations of your youth. – I own my thoughts were employed as you have guessed.'

They now walked to that part of the hill which looks to the north-west, and which hangs over a vast and extensive wood. Here they were no sooner arrived, than they heard at a distance the most violent screams of a woman, proceeding from the wood below them. Jones listened a moment, and then, without saying a word to his companion (for indeed the occasion seemed sufficiently pressing) ran, or rather slid, down the hill, and without the least apprehension or concern for his own safety, made directly to the thicket whence the sound had issued.

He had not entered far into the wood before he beheld a most shocking sight indeed, a woman stript half naked, under the hands of a ruffian, who had put his garter round her neck, and was endeavouring to draw her up to a tree. Jones asked no questions at this interval; but fell instantly upon the villain, and made such good use of his trusty oaken stick, that he laid him sprawling on the ground, before he could defend himself, indeed, almost before he knew he was attacked; nor did he cease the prosecution of his blows, till the woman herself begged him to forbear, saying, she believed he had sufficiently done his business.

The poor wretch fell upon her knees to Jones, and gave him a thousand thanks for her deliverance: he presently lifted her up, and told her he was highly pleased with the extraordinary accident which had sent him thither for her relief, where it was so improbable she should find any; adding that Heaven seemed to have designed him as the happy instrument of her protection. 'Nay,' answered she, 'I could almost conceive you to be some good angel; and to say the truth, you look more like an angel than a man, in my

GLOSSARY

Aurora (l.1): dawn

casement (l.1): window (*poetic*)

Anglicè (l.1): (an Italian word used to mean 'or as they say in ordinary English')

prospects (l.4): views

Gloucester (l.14): a town in southwest England; Tom has come from Somerset, a county further west

tract (l.15): stretch

thicket (l.31): mass of trees

ruffian (l.34): violent man

garter (l.34): band of elastic used to keep up his stockings

interval (l.36): moment (*archaic*)

villain (l.36): bad man

trusty oaken stick (l.37): worthy piece of wood made from oak

sprawling (l.37): flat out

prosecution (l.39): continuing

forbear (l.40): hold back

deliverance (l.43): rescue

presently (l.43): immediately (*archaic*)

eye.' Indeed he was a charming figure, and if a very fine person, 50
and a most comely set of features, adorned with youth, health,
strength, freshness, spirit, and good nature, can make a man
resemble an angel, he certainly had that resemblance.

The redeemed captive had not altogether so much of the human-
angelic species: she seemed to be, at least, of the middle age, nor 55
had her face much appearance of beauty; but her cloaths being torn
from all the upper part of her body, her breasts, which were well
formed, and extremely white, attracted the eyes of her deliverer,
and for a few moments they stood silent, and gazing at each other;
till the ruffian on the ground beginning to move, Jones took the 60
garter which had been intended for another purpose, and bound
both his hands behind him. . . .

Jones offered her his coat; but, I know not for what reason, she
absolutely refused the most earnest solicitations to accept it. He
then begged her to forget both the causes of her confusion. 'With 65
regard to the former,' says he, 'I have done no more than my duty
in protecting you; and as for the latter, I will entirely remove it, by
walking before you all the way; for I would not have my eyes offend
you, and I could not answer for my power of resisting the attractive
charms of so much beauty.' 70

Thus our hero and the redeemed lady walked in the same manner as Orpheus and Eurydice marched heretofore: but tho' I cannot
believe that Jones was designedly tempted by his fair one to look
behind him, yet as she frequently wanted his assistance to help her
over stiles, and had besides many trips and other accidents, he was 75
often obliged to turn about.

(from *Tom Jones*)

comely (l.51): handsome
redeemed (l.54): set free
earnest solicitations (l.64):
    determind pleas
*Orpheus and Eurydice
(l.72):* (in Greek myth
    Orpheus was allowed
    to rescue his wife,
    Eurydice, from hell on
    condition he didn't
    look back – but he did,
    and lost her)

- i) What do you imagine Tom's 'object of contemplation' might have been (l.18)?
- ii) What does Tom assume are 'the causes of her confusion' (l.65)? Does the woman *seem* 'confused'?
- iii) How would you describe Tom? Do you think he is idealised?

4.6.3
The Life and Opinions of Tristram Shandy

Extract 1   Chapter 1 in its entirety:

GLOSSARY
begot (l.3): conceived
temperature (l.6): mixture
    of different physical
    qualities (*archaic*)
aught (l.7): all
house (l.8): family

I wish either my father or my mother, or indeed both of them, as 1
they were in duty both equally bound to it, had minded what they
were about when they begot me; had they duly consider'd how
much depended upon what they were then doing; – that not only
the production of a rational Being was concerned in it, but that 5
possibly the happy formation and temperature of his body, perhaps
his genius and the very cast of his mind; – and, for aught they knew
to the contrary, even the fortunes of his whole house might take

humours and dispositions (l.9): (there were believed to be four main 'humours' in the body – phlegm, blood, choler and black bile. If any dominated it would make the character: phlegmatic – slow and lazy; sanguine – cheerful; choleric – bad-tempered; melancholic – depressed)
animal spirits (l.15): (it was believed that feelings, thoughts, movements and sensations depended on tiny particles – animal spirits – which passed from any sense organ to the brain)
transfused (l.15): transferred
&c (l.16): etc
miscarriages (l.18): failures
tracts and trains (l.19–20): systems in the body
cluttering ... mad (l.22): making a disturbance
quoth (l.26): said (*archaic*)

their turn from the humours and dispositions which were then uppermost;——Had they duly weighed and considered all this, and proceeded accordingly,——I am verily persuaded I should have made a quite different figure in the world, from that in which the reader is likely to see me. – Believe me, good folks, this is not so inconsiderable a thing as many of you may think it; – you have all, I dare say, heard of the animal spirits, as how they are transfused from father to son, &c. &c. – and a great deal to that purpose: – Well, you may take my word, that nine parts in ten of a man's sense or his nonsense, his successes and miscarriages in this world, depend upon their motions and activity, and the different tracts and trains you put them into, so that when they are once set a-going, whether right or wrong, 'tis not a half-penny matter, – away they go cluttering like hey-go mad; and by treading the same steps over and over again, they presently make a road of it, as plain and as smooth as a garden-walk, which, when they are once used to, the Devil himself sometimes shall not be able to drive them off it.

***Pray, my Dear,* quoth my mother, *have you not forgot to wind up the clock?* ——*Good G—!* cried my father, making an exclamation, but taking care to moderate his voice at the same time,——*Did ever woman, since the creation of the world, interrupt a man with such a silly question?* Pray, what was your father saying?——Nothing.**

- i) Do you think the narrator believes he has had a fortunate or an unfortunate life? What was the cause?
  ii) Who does 'they' refer to in the lines 'I wish ... proceeded accordingly' (l.1–11) and who (or what) does 'they' refer to in the lines 'Believe me ... drive them off it' (l.13–25)?

Extract 2 Chapter 6 – again in its entirety:

GLOSSARY
relish (l.10): liking
betwixt (l.11): between
O diem prœclarum (l.13): O glorious day (*Latin*)
trifling (l.14): of little importance
sparing (l.16): uneventful

In the beginning of the last chapter, I informed you exactly *when* I was born; but I did not inform you *how. No,* that particular was reserved entirely for a chapter by itself; – besides, Sir, as you and I are in a manner perfect strangers to each other, it would not have been proper to have let you into too many circumstances relating to myself all at once. – You must have a little patience. I have undertaken, you see, to write not only my life, but my opinions also; hoping and expecting that your knowledge of my character, and of what kind of a mortal I am, by the one, would give you a better relish for the other: As you proceed farther with me, the slight acquaintance, which is now beginning betwixt us, will grow into familiarity; and that, unless one of us is in fault, will terminate in friendship. – *O diem prœclarum!* – then nothing which has touched me will be thought trifling in its nature, or tedious in its telling. Therefore, my dear friend and companion, if you should think me somewhat sparing of my narrative on my first setting out – bear

trifle (l.18): play games;
talk jokingly

fool's cap (l.19): part of
the traditional uniform
for the court jester;
(Charles I was the last
monarch to have a
jester to keep him
amused)

jog on (l.22): go on slowly

with me, – and let me go on, and tell my story my own way: – Or, if
I should seem now and then to trifle upon the road, – or should
sometimes put on a fool's cap with a bell to it, for a moment or two
as we pass along, – don't fly off, – but rather courteously give me
credit for a little more wisdom than appears upon my outside; –
and as we jog on, either laugh with me, or at me, or in short, do any
thing, – only keep your temper.

20

(from *Tristram Shandy*)

- i) Reread the summary on page 109. Would you like to read the rest of the
  novel? Why/Why not?
- ii) Do you find this style of writing amusing or frustrating? What has it got in
  common with *Tom Jones*? How is it different?

Appreciation   Where you agree, write TJ (*Tom Jones*), TS (*Tristram Shandy*) or both next to these
sentences. Give an example from the text for at least one sentence from each
section.

i) *The narrator*
  a) The narrator is the main character.
  b) He tells his story in the first person singular ('I').
  c) He tries to establish a personal relationship with the reader.
  d) He teases the reader.
  e) He gives his personal feelings about what is happening.
  f) He tries to involve us in the process of novel writing.

ii) *Humour*
  a) The humour comes partly from the narrator's apparent innocence about
     what is really happening; we laugh at what we imagine is happening
     rather than what is being described.
  b) The events would not be out of place in a theatrical farce.
  c) The humour comes partly from the grand-sounding, roundabout style.
  d) Classical allusions give a humorous dignity to what is happening.

iii) *Style*
  a) There are many broken up and incomplete sentences, as in conversation.
  b) The sentences are often long and elaborate.

iv) *Tone*
  a) The writing is very energetic and high-spirited.
  b) The tone is sometimes ironic.

4.7 The comedy of manners

During the Interregnum (as the period between the reigns of Charles I
and Charles II is sometimes called) Puritans closed the theatres and
theatrical performances only took place in secret. When the theatres
reopened in 1660:

- the audience consisted mainly of the court, the wealthy and the
  fashionable (although even in Charles I's time audiences had been more
  'exclusive' than Elizabethan audiences);

- women appeared on the stage for the first time;
- most of the plays were performed in fashionable contemporary dress;
- a 'picture-frame' stage (one surrounded by a proscenium arch, as in the conventional theatre today) replaced the 'apron' stage (the kind of stage that comes forward towards where the public sit).

Restoration Comedy at the Garrick Theatre, London

Plays showed a reaction against the strict rule of Puritanism and frequently consisted of complicated plots about adultery, sexual intrigue and money.

Restoration comedies – unlike the classically-inspired but rather dull tragedies of the time – were high-spirited and cynical, uninhibited and farcical. They were full of surface brilliance, their aim being, according to Dryden, that 'Gentlemen will be entertained with the follies of each other.' In contrast with Ben Jonson's plays, which took a more consciously moral approach to fundamental human appetites, these 'Comedies of Manners', as the critic Charles Lamb (1775–1834) called them, exaggerated and laughed at the affectations and faults of those who offended less against nature than against polite, civilised behaviour. At the same time the hero was usually an attractive young man, a 'gallant' as he was called, who was frequently idealised, a figure for the males in the audience to identify with.

117

William Congreve was the master of Restoration Comedy. His witty plays give us a clear impression of the manners of the age.

Warm-up

Discuss the following:
  i) How are these words linked in meaning?
     loan   credit   bailiff   arrears   debt
     (Look up any you don't know in a dictionary)
  ii) If you needed to borrow a lot of money, who would you try: your family? friends? a bank? a credit company?
  iii) What would happen if you didn't pay the money back?!
  iv) Do you think it is a good thing to laugh at foolishness?

Love for Love (1695)

Love for Love, Congreve's prose-play written thirty-five years after the Restoration, was meant for a slightly wider circle than the court, to include the wits of the coffee houses. Valentine, a rather less flatteringly portrayed 'gallant' than was usual, is out of favour with his father, Sir Sampson Legend, because of his expensive way of living. He is visited by Trapland, a scrivener (a person who often arranged loans) and two 'officers'. Valentine is assisted by Jeremy, his servant, and his friend, the free-speaking Scandal.

Enter TRAPLAND *and* JEREMY   1

VALENTINE: O Mr Trapland! My old friend! Welcome! Jeremy, a chair, quickly. A bottle of sack and a toast – fly! – a chair first.

TRAPLAND: A good morning to you Mr Valentine, and to you Mr Scandal.   5

SCANDAL: The morning's a very good morning, if you don't spoil it.

VALENTINE: Come, sit you down; you know his way.

TRAPLAND [*sits*]: There is a debt, Mr Valentine, of £1,500, of pretty long standing –

VALENTINE: I cannot talk about business with a thirsty palate. [*to*   10
JEREMY] Sirrah, the sack.

TRAPLAND: And I desire to know what course you have taken for the payment.

VALENTINE: Faith and troth, I am heartily glad to see you. My service to you. Fill, fill, to honest Mr Trapland, fuller.   15

TRAPLAND: Hold, sweetheart. This is not to our business. My service to you, Mr Scandal – [*drinks*] – I have forborne as long –

VALENTINE: T' other glass, and then we'll talk. Fill, Jeremy.

TRAPLAND: No more, in truth. I have forborne, I say –

VALENTINE: Sirrah, fill when I bid you. And how does your hand-   20
some daughter? Come, a good husband to her. [*Drinks*]

TRAPLAND: Thank you; I have been out of this money –

VALENTINE: Drink first. Scandal, why do you not drink? [*They drink*]

TRAPLAND: And in short, I can be put off no longer.

VALENTINE: I was much obliged to you for your supply. It did me   25
signal service in my necessity. But you delight in doing good. – Scandal, drink to me, my friend Trapland's health. An honester man lives not, nor one more ready to serve his friend in distress, tho' I say it to his face. Come, fill each man his glass.

SCANDAL: What! I know Trapland has been a whoremaster, and   30

GLOSSARY

sack (l.3): dry white wine
fly (l.3): be quick
Sirrah (l.11): (a form of address to someone of lower status – *archaic*)
Faith and troth (l.14): on my word
forborne (l.19): restrained myself
did ... service (l.25–26): was very useful to me

loves a wench still. You never knew a whoremaster that was not an honest fellow.

TRAPLAND: Fie, Mr Scandal, you never knew –

SCANDAL: What don't I know? I know the buxom black widow in the Poultry – £800 a year jointure, and £20,000 in money. Ahah! Old Trap! 35

VALENTINE: Say you so, i'faith. Come, we'll remember the widow. I know whereabouts you are. Come, to the widow –

TRAPLAND: No more indeed.

VALENTINE: What, the widow's health! Give it him – off with it. 40 [*They drink*] A lovely girl, i'faith; black sparkling eyes, soft pouting ruby lips! Better sealing there than a bond for a million, hah?

TRAPLAND: No, no, there's no such thing. We'd better mind our business. You're a wag. 45

VALENTINE: No faith, we'll mind the widow's business, fill again. Pretty round heaving breasts, a Barbary shape, and a jut with her bum, would stir an anchoret. And the prettiest foot! Oh, if a man could but fasten his eyes to her feet as they steal in and out and play at Bo-peep under her petticoats, ah, Mr Trapland? 50

TRAPLAND: Verily, give me a glass – you're a wag – and here's to the widow. [*Drinks*]

SCANDAL [*to VALENTINE*]: He begins to chuckle. Ply him close, or he'll relapse into a dun.

Enter OFFICER 55

OFFICER: By your leave, gentlemen. Mr Trapland, if we must do our office, tell us. We have half a dozen gentlemen to arrest in Pall Mall and Covent-Garden, and if we don't make haste the chair-men will be abroad and block up the chocolate-houses, and then our labour's lost. 60

TRAPLAND: Udso, that's true. Mr Valentine, I love mirth, but busi-ness must be done. Are you ready to –

JEREMY: Sir, your father's steward says he comes to make proposals concerning your debts.

VALENTINE: Bid him come in. Mr Trapland, send away your officer. 65 You shall have an answer presently.

TRAPLAND: Mr Snap, stay within call.

Exit OFFICER
Enter STEWARD and whispers to VALENTINE

SCANDAL: Here's a dog now, a traitor in his wine. [*to TRAPLAND*] 70 Sirrah, refund the sack: Jeremy, fetch him some warm water, or I'll rip up his stomach, and go the shortest way to his conscience.

TRAPLAND: Mr Scandal, you are uncivil. I did not value your sack, but you cannot expect it again, when I have drunk it.

SCANDAL: And how do you expect to have your money again, when 75 a gentleman has spent it?

VALENTINE [*to STEWARD*]: You need say no more, I understand the conditions. They are very hard, but my necessity is very pressing. I agree to 'em. Take Mr Trapland with you, and let him draw the

---

whoremaster (l.30): one who goes with prostitutes

wench (l.31): prostitute (archaic)

Fie (l.33): shame on you (archaic)

buxom (l.34): with large breasts

Poultry (l.35): street near Cheapside in London

jointure (l.35): (the value of the property she was left by her husband)

pouting ... lips (l.42): with lips pushed out provocatively

sealing ... million (l.42): they are more able to secure what they attach themselves to than a promise to pay back a million pounds!

wag (l.45): joker

heaving (l.47): which rise and fall

Barbary (l.47): (elegant, like an Arab mare)

a jut ... anchoret (l.47–48): a bottom which sticks out enough to stimulate the interest of a hermit

play ... Bo-peep (l.50): (refers to a game played with babies; the adult first hides behind his or her hands, then suddenly appears to surprise the baby. Valentine means he would like to look under the woman's petticoats)

Ply ... close (l.53): give him plenty to drink

relapse ... dun (l.54): go back to being a debt-collector

Pall Mall, Covent Garden (l.57–58): other places in London

chair-men (l.58): people who carry sedan chairs (closed chairs on two poles)

abroad (l.59): out and about

chocolate-houses (l.59): fashionable meeting places, where chocolate was drunk

Udso (l.61): quite right! (archaic)

writing. – Mr Trapland, you know this man. He shall satisfy 80
you.

TRAPLAND: Sincerely, I am loth to be thus pressing, but my necessity –

VALENTINE: No apology, good Mr Scrivener, you shall be paid,

TRAPLAND: I hope you forgive me. My business requires –

Exeunt STEWARD, TRAPLAND *and* JEREMY 85

SCANDAL: He begs pardon like a hangman at an execution.

VALENTINE: But I have got a reprieve.

SCANDAL: I am surprised. What, does your father relent?

VALENTINE: No; he has sent me the hardest conditions in the world.
You have heard of a booby brother of mine that was sent to sea 90
three years ago? This brother, my father hears, is landed; whereupon he very affectionately sends me word, if I will make a deed
of conveyance of my right to his estate after his death to my
younger brother, he will immediately furnish me with four
thousand pound to pay my debts and make my fortune. This was 95
once proposed before, and I refused it; but the present impatience
of my creditors for their money, and my own impatience of
confinement and absence from Angelica, force me to consent.

SCANDAL: A very desperate demonstration of your love to Angelica;
and I think she has never given you any assurance of hers. 100

VALENTINE: You know her temper; she never gave me any great
reason either for hope or despair.

SCANDAL: Women of her airy temper, as they seldom think before
they act, so they rarely give us any light to guess at what they
mean. But you have little reason to believe that a woman of this 105
age, who has had an indifference for you in your prosperity, will
fall in love with your ill fortune; besides, Angelica has a great
fortune of her own, and great fortunes either expect another great
fortune or a fool.

(from *Love for Love*)

steward (l.63): the person who looks after his financial affairs

presently (l.66): immediately (*archaic*)

loth ... pressing (l.82): don't like being so insistent

reprieve (l.87): delay in my punishment

booby (l.90): foolish

deed of conveyance (l.92): legal document for the transfer of property rights

• Do you feel more sympathy for Trapland or Valentine? Which parts of the extract (if any) did you find funny?

Understanding and interpretation

i) Choose the best alternative:

a) Trapland sat down and $\left\{\begin{array}{l}\text{told Valentine his debt was now £1,500}\\\text{tried to remind Valentine of his debt}\end{array}\right\}$

but Valentine $\left\{\begin{array}{l}\text{tried to distract him by offering him a drink.}\\\text{was too drunk to care.}\end{array}\right\}$

b) Scandal's strategy was to

$\left\{\begin{array}{l}\text{embarrass Trapland by mentioning his visits to prostitutes.}\\\text{encourage Trapland to go with a prostitute.}\end{array}\right\}$

c) Valentine $\left\{\begin{array}{l}\text{could}\\\text{couldn't}\end{array}\right\}$ pay back his debt

$\left\{\begin{array}{l}\text{because his brother had offered to buy all his property from him when their father died.}\\\text{because he finally accepted his father's offer.}\end{array}\right\}$

ii) What do you deduce about Valentine's relationship with Angelica?

iii) Imagine you are producing the play. What advice would you give the actors to help them interpret the characters? How would you direct the scene?

William Congreve   Congreve was born in England but lived in Ireland until he was eighteen. Although he enrolled as a law student, he never applied any real discipline to his legal studies and instead became a playwright. After the production of his third comedy, *The Way of the World* in 1700, he gave up the stage. In his own day the tragedy *The Mourning Bride* (1697) was much admired.

4.8 Chronology

The late seventeenth century   These pictures illustrate important events/developments in the period. Try to give each a caption, using the information on pages 122–124.

The American …

The…rebellion

Titus…: The…Plot

William and…

121

The House of Stuart

1660–1685

The reign of Charles II – the 'Merry Monarch' as he is now sometimes called. Determined to stay in power. The House of Lords was restored but the king was forced to govern in partnership with Parliament. Puritans driven out of public life by laws passed in 1661 and 1665. Central/local government in hands of Royalist landowners and merchants.

Charles himself politically unscrupulous. His own behaviour encouraged low personal morals at court; nevertheless it was the last court in England to be a centre of cultural vitality. King's most famous mistress was Nell Gwyn, both actress and orange-seller in the theatre. Although the queen was a Catholic, Charles managed to hide his own Catholicism from a suspicious public until his death.

1660: Slave trade in America established to support plantations in Virginia.

1664: Founding of New York – named after the Duke of York, the future king, James II.

1664–1665: The Great Plague in London.

1666: The Great Fire of London. London rebuilt by classically-inspired architect Christopher Wren.

1673: Charles issued Declaration of Indulgence for Roman Catholics and Dissenters; Parliament passed Test Act to stop it and to prevent Catholics from holding office.

1673–1674: War with Holland.

1678: Popish Plot: Titus Oates, son of Puritan preacher, for personal gain pretended to uncover Catholic conspiracy. Two political parties emerged: Petitioners (later called Whigs) who attempted to petition king not to dissolve Parliament, and Abhorrers (later called Tories) who expressed abhorrence (disgust) at the Petitioners.

1681–1685: Charles ruled without Parliament. Reign of terror against Whigs and Dissenters. Charles defeated attempts to prevent succession of his Catholic brother, James, and to replace him with his illegitimate Protestant son, the Duke of Monmouth.

1685–1688

The reign of James II (James VII of Scotland). It was a smooth succession to the throne owing to the financial and political strength of Charles and the Tory landowners.

1686–1687: The king ordered a suspension of laws against Catholics and Dissenters. Poor timing. It was a reassertion of royal power. The Anglicans were insulted and the Church of England felt threatened; Dissenters realised the measures were designed to benefit only Catholics. Most of the country was against the king. He was replaced by his Protestant daughter, Mary, and her Dutch husband, William of Orange, when William landed in England with a small army. James fled abroad. Known as the 'Glorious Revolution' or the 'Bloodless Revolution'. The hereditary principle had been laid aside.

1689–1702

The reign of Mary II (until 1694) and William III. The power of Parliament increased so that sovereigns ruled by Parliamentary consent. Passionate religious and political arguments lessened. Spirit of reasonable debate and tolerant enquiry. The seventeenth century was a time of great wealth for Britain. Its empire expanded. William was the leader of the European opposition to the absolutist

Catholic French monarch King Louis XIV (who had once had a secret agreement with Charles II). However, he was very reserved and not much liked.

1697: One war with France ended and the following year a new war started.

1702–1714

The reign of Anne, second daughter of James II. Liked but not very clever. As all her seventeen children died young, Anne's named heir was – to her disgust – George of Hanover. There were fears of the claims of the Scottish House of Stuart and the possible succession of the Catholic great-grandson of James I.

1707: Union of Scotland and England.

The House of Hanover

1714–1727

The reign of George I, the German son of James I's daughter's daughter. Spoke little English and didn't like England.

1714: British Jacobites (supporters of House of Stuart) conspired to restore the House of Stuart.

1715: A rebellion, which had Scottish support, was defeated.

1721–1742: Sir Robert Walpole, more of a prime minister in the modern sense, held power based on the House of Commons. He pursued peace abroad and quietly encouraged trade. He was a Whig. The Tories were out of favour with the monarchy because of their association with the Jacobites.

1727–1760

The reign of George II. Born in Germany. George was methodical and quietly capable. He was the last English king to lead his troops into battle (1743).

1739: War with Spain to force Spain to allow access to Spanish Caribbean.

1745: Failure of the second Jacobite rebellion. The event became a romantic legend because of Charles Stuart, the handsome grandson of James II, known as 'Bonnie Prince Charlie' to his supporters and the 'Young Pretender' to his opponents.

1756–1763: War with France for control over Canada and India, controlled by the brilliant statesman William Pitt the Elder, 1708–1778.

1760

Beginning of the long reign of George III, grandson of George II. Born in England. George took an interest in science and farming methods. (Gained the nickname of 'Farmer George') Bought Buckingham House (1762), later remodelled into Buckingham Palace. Tried unsuccessfully to reassert royal power. Enormously popular in middle life. Towards the end of his reign, periods of apparent insanity (caused by physical illness). The Industrial Revolution accelerated, changing Britain from a rural agricultural community to a predominantly urban/manufacturing one. Increasing emphasis on the practical.

1769: Steam engine invented by James Watt.

1770: Growth of trade and colonialism. Australia was taken for the British Crown by Captain Cook in 1770. From 1788 it was used as a place to imprison British criminals.

1773: Boston Tea Party, where tea from the powerful East India Company was thrown into Boston harbour, partly as a protest against British government taxes.

1775:	War between America and Britain.
July 4th, 1776:	American Declaration of Independence.
1781:	British army defeated.
1782:	Lord North, the prime minister, resigned.
1783:	American independence was finally acknowledged by Britain.
1783:	Stability returned to the political scene when William Pitt, the Younger, was asked to form a ministry. Although only twenty-four, he was highly respected for his strict integrity.

4.9 Activities

Creative writing   Choose one of the following:

i) Write a short story on one of the following:
a) a fire
b) a battle
c) a romantic adventure

You may use actual people and events for inspiration but the story must be imaginary.

ii) Choose one of the following:

an important day in
– the history of your country
– the life of one of the writers in this book
– your early life

Compose a diary entry describing that day. Decide whether you wish the diary to be private or public and write in the appropriate style.

iii) Write at least one paragraph for *Tom Jones* and one paragraph for *Tristram Shandy* summarising the role of the narrator and commenting on the humour and style.

iv) Select one of the works from Supplement 4. Write a critical assessment to include a description of your personal feelings about it.

Noughts and crosses   Decide which of you is a nought/zero (0) and which a cross (X).
Aim: To be the first to make a line of three of the same marks either vertically, horizontally or diagonally.
Instructions: 1. Toss a coin to decide who is to begin.
2. Student A asks the first question. Student B answers without looking at the book. If the answer is correct (refer back to previous pages to find the answers) Student B can put his or her mark anywhere in the grid.
3. Student A must then answer a question and, if the answer is correct, put his or her mark in the grid.
4. Take turns asking and answering questions. Each student should try to position his or her marks to build a line of three, at the same time trying to prevent the other student from getting a line.
5. The game continues until one student makes a straight line of three marks (vertically, horizontally or diagonally).

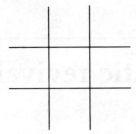

- How do you spell Pepys's first name?
- What year was the Great Fire of London?
- How was the fire put out?
- Who used the phrase 'Augustan Age' to describe the reigns of Queen Anne and William III?
- Did Dryden die a Catholic or a Protestant?
- What did Pope mean by the term 'machinery'?
- What is an 'heroic couplet'?
- How did Belinda lose a lock of hair?
- In which city was Swift dean of a cathedral?
- Give the name of a 'natural philosopher'.
- What is a picaresque novel?
- What is the name of one of the Squires in *Tom Jones*?
- Who first used the phrase 'Comedy of Manners'?
- What was the name of Valentine's servant?
- Was Congreve born in Ireland?
- Name two bodily 'humours'.
- What were the Petitioners later called?
- Who was the Young Pretender?

UNIT 5

The Romantic revival

5.1 Poetry (1)

Towards the end of the eighteenth century, there came into circulation new notions of individuality, of freedom and liberty and the power of the imagination. The libertarian writings of the French–Swiss thinker Jean–Jacques Rousseau (1712–1778), in praise of the essential goodness of nature and natural impulses and in protest against the corruption of society, helped lead to the American War of Independence (1775–1783) and the French Revolution (1789). In England, the enclosing of common village land with hedges in the interest of big landowners and farmers produced unrest in the countryside. Also, the beginnings of the Industrial Revolution were changing a predominantly rural and agricultural country into a predominantly urban and manufacturing one. A number of poets reflected these profound changes.

Warm-up Which of the following do you associate with cities? Which do you associate with living in the country?

factories
seeing lots of people
sheep farming
night clubs
walking by yourself
living alone in a cottage
going to the theatre

Which do you prefer, big cities or the country? Why?

5.1.1 William Blake (1757–1827) William Blake had no systematic education and set up a print shop in London, engraving his poems in a pictorial setting to display their themes in visual terms. In his own day, however, he was virtually unread.

Blake felt that England was beginning to rebel against the effects of the Industrial Revolution, after witnessing the burning of Newgate Prison in the Gordon riots of 1780. He was acutely aware of the injustice and oppression involved in the use of cheap female and child labour in the new factories and was a strong supporter of the French Revolution.

In the following poem, 'London', the narrator is wandering through the streets of the city.

GLOSSARY

charter'd (l.1): free to conduct its own affairs (also: possessed and hired out)

mark (l.3): notice (v); stain (n)

woe (l.4): great unhappiness

ban (l.7): curse, prohibition (possibly: excommunication; marriage proclamation)

forg'd (l.8): shaped (by heating and hammering)

manacles (l.8): iron rings used in chaining a prisoner

appalls (l.10): fills with fear and disgust (also: makes pale)

hapless (l.11): fated; unlucky

Harlot's curse (l.14): prostitute's bad language ('curse' also suggests misfortune; being damned; infection)

Blasts (l.15): curses (also: explodes)

tear (l.15): (implying prenatal blindness caused by mother's venereal disease)

blights (l.16): infects with disease

hearse (l.16): decorated framework over a coffin (also: triangular candlestick used in certain church services; vehicle for transporting dead body)

London

I wander thro' each charter'd street,   1
Near where the charter'd Thames does flow,
And mark in every face I meet
Marks of weakness, marks of woe.

In every cry of every Man,   5
In every Infant's cry of fear,
In every voice, in every ban
The mind-forg'd manacles I hear.

How the Chimney-sweeper's cry
Every black'ning Church appalls;   10
And the hapless Soldier's sigh
Runs in blood down Palace walls.

But most thro' midnight streets I hear
How the youthful Harlot's curse
Blasts the new born Infant's tear,   15
And blights with plagues the Marriage hearse.

● Does the poem sound angry to you? Do you find it depressing? Why/Why not?

Understanding and interpretation

i) Which of these does the poet seem to have most sympathy with?

'every Infant' (l.6); 'the Chimney-sweeper' (l.9); 'Church' (l.10); 'Soldier' (l.11); 'Palace' (l.12); 'Harlot' (l.14); 'new born Infant' (l.15); 'Marriage' (l.16)

How do you know?

127

ii) What does Blake seem to be in favour of? What is he against?

iii) Which word or phrase best suggests that individual people are victims?

Language and style   The word 'charter'd' (l.1) can suggest liberty. It can also suggest lack of real freedom. So instead of strong, happy people in the 'charter'd streets' we see 'marks of weakness, marks of woe'.

The word 'black'ning' (l.10) can suggest both what happens to the church as a building and what the Church does as an institution. Can you explain both meanings?

Appreciation   i) Find an example of at least one of the following:
   a) the use of rhythm to reinforce the meaning
   b) the use of repetition (what does it suggest?)
   c) the use of contrast (what is its purpose?)

ii) Where and how does Blake use visual detail to make a social point?

William Blake   Apart from his highly individual illustrations and engravings, Blake is nowadays mainly admired for the apparently simple and mysteriously beautiful *Songs of Innocence* (1789) and the more forceful and intensely questioning *Songs of Experience* (1794) (see Supplement 5), although he wrote a number of complex and often obscure prophetic allegories such as *Tiriel* (1788–9) and *The Book of Urizen* (1794). Looking back on literary history, we can see that Blake's originality of thought and his visionary and symbolic mode of expression was a courageous break with the neo-classical tradition. It is, perhaps, not surprising that for insisting on the importance of instinct and intuitions and for probing the irrational in his own being, he was considered eccentric in his own day, even mad.

5.1.2   Poet 1: John Clare (1793–1864)

Two poets   John Clare worked as a hedge-setter and day labourer in Northamptonshire in the English Midlands. In 1837 he became insane and spent the rest of his life in lunatic asylums, where he continued to write.

Poet 2: George Crabbe (1754–1832)

Crabbe's birthplace at Aldeburgh, Suffolk

George Crabbe, a restless, uneasy man, was first a doctor and then for a time curate in his native Aldeburgh on the flat coast of Suffolk in the east of England. After using opium in an attempt to cure vertigo, he became an addict – something he had in common with some other poets of the period.

- Glance at the following poems quickly. Can you guess from the biographical notes above who wrote which?

Poem A

An extract from a long poem. Peter Grimes, a fisherman who has beaten his innocent apprentice to death, is gradually overwhelmed by guilt and madness.

GLOSSARY

neap (l.1): slightly high tide following the first or third quarter of the moon

sultry (l.1): hot and humid

bounding (l.2): surrounding

anchoring (l.5): bringing his boat to a halt by lowering the anchor

slimy (l.7): muddy

eels (l.8): snake-like fish

gaping (l.10): open

mussels (l.10): black shellfish that can be eaten

Slope (l.11): move sideways

trace (l.12): follow the course of

sidelong (l.13): going to one side

scrawl'd (l.13): awkwardly drawn

gull (l.15): mainly white bird that lives on or near the sea

clanging (l.15): making a rough, unpleasant cry

golden-eye (l.15): large-headed diving duck

bittern (l.17): heron-like marsh bird with a loud booming cry

bull-rush (l.17): tall, reed-like plant growing in marshland

bellowing boom (l.18): deep, loud cry

sluice (l.20): floodgate

bound (l.21): limits

When tides were neap, and, in the sultry day,   1
Through the tall bounding mud-banks made their way,
Which on each side rose swelling, and below
The dark warm flood ran silently and slow;
There anchoring, Peter chose from man to hide,   5
There hang his head, and view the lazy tide
In its hot slimy channels slowly glide;
Where the small eels that left the deeper way
For the warm shore, within the shallows play;
Where gaping mussels, left upon the mud,   10
Slope their slow passage to the fallen flood; –
Here dull and hopeless he'd lie down and trace
How sidelong crabs had scrawl'd their crooked race;
Or sadly listen to the tuneless cry
Of fishing gull or clanging golden-eye;   15
What time the sea-birds to the marsh would come,
And the loud bittern from the bull-rush home,
Gave from the salt-ditch side the bellowing boom:
He nursed the feelings these dull scenes produce,
And loved to stop beside the opening sluice;   20
Where the small stream, confined in narrow bound,
Ran with a dull, unvaried, sadd'ning sound;
Where all, presented to the eye or ear,
Oppress'd the soul with misery, grief, and fear.

(from 'Peter Grimes')

Poem B

I am

I am—yet what I am, none cares or knows;   1
  My friends forsake me like a memory lost:
I am the self-consumer of my woes—
  They rise and vanish in oblivions host,
Like shadows in love frenzied stifled throes   5
  And yet I am, and live—like vapours tost

Into the nothingness of scorn and noise,
  Into the living sea of waking dreams,
Where there is neither sense of life or joys,
  But the vast shipwreck of my lifes esteems;   10
Even the dearest that I love the best
  Are strange—nay, rather, stranger than the rest.

I long for scenes where man hath never trod
  A place where woman never smiled or wept
There to abide with my Creator God,   15
  And sleep as I in childhood sweetly slept,
Untroubling and untroubled where I lie
  The grass below, above, the vaulted sky.

GLOSSARY

forsake (l.2): abandon
self-consumer (l.3): only one interested
woes (l.3): sorrows
oblivions host (l.4): a large number of forgetfulnesses
love frenzied stifled throes (l.5): intense love in which pain is suppressed
tost (l.6): tossed (thrown carelessly)
esteems (l.10): things of value (*archaic*)
vaulted (l.18): like a large curved roof

● Check your answers in the Key at the back of the book.

Appreciation   Read the poems again. Write Poem A or B next to as many of these phrases as you can. Some may refer to both poems.

  i) rhyming couplets (heroic couplets)   five beats a line
     mainly alternate end-rhymes   imagery

  ii) sense of isolation and being lost in chaos   realistic descriptions of Nature
      desires a remembered paradise, such as the Garden of Eden   concerned
      to tell a story   rural subject matter   poet is writing about himself

  iii) gloomy   simple and direct   many layers of meaning   powerful

Further information   Poet 1: John Clare

Clare was rarely read until this century, although he had published such works as The *Village Minstrel* (1821) and *The Shepherd's Calendar* (1827). Most of his poems contain quietly intense observations of the rural scene, written from the viewpoint of one who had a sensitive and intimate experience of it and who loved it. Insisting to his publisher he would continue to write in his own language, dialect and idiosyncratic grammar, he avoided artificiality of diction. While Clare's verse is not very profound or subtle it has an attractive unpretentiousness.
The following lines, from a sonnet describing a May morning, are more characteristic of his best poems than those already quoted:

GLOSSARY

hues (l.1): shades of lightness and darkness

gemmed (l.2): made beautiful

gosling broods (l.5): families of young geese

waddle (l.7): walk with short steps, swinging from side to side

The sunshine bathes in clouds of many hues   1
And mornings feet are gemmed with early dews
Warm Daffodils about the garden beds
Peep thro their pale slim leaves their golden heads
Sweet earthly suns of spring–the gosling broods   5
In coats of sunny green about the road
Waddle in extacy.

(from 'May')

Poet 2: George Crabbe

Crabbe's aim was to 'paint the cot/ As Truth will paint it, and as bards will not'. His verse tales, showing nature as it was to the simple and poor, are realistic and precisely observed, very unlike traditional pastoralism (the classical literary tradition which idealised the life of shepherds and herdsmen). His major works were *The Village* (1783), The *Parish Register* (1807) and *The Borough* (1810). They were almost like short stories in their economy, their careful alternation of description and action and their avoidance of direct comment (preferring instead to make a point through careful juxtapositions). Although similar to Augustan poetry (see pages 91–99) in its use of the heroic couplet and in its moral assurance – as well as its concern for man in society and its sense of balance and proportion – Crabbe's verse was unique. It was much admired not only by Dr Johnson but also by Sir Walter Scott (who called him 'the English Juvenal' – the Roman satirical poet ?AD 60–?136), Lord Byron (who described him as 'Nature's sternest painter yet the best'), Jane Austen and, later, Alfred, Lord Tennyson.

5.2 The novel (1) – Jane Austen (1775–1817)

Jane Austen, a clergyman's daughter, wrote about the quiet, prosperous middle-class world of the provinces. Her novels, in their intelligence about the human character, were entirely new. In retrospect, they seem to combine eighteenth-century rationality with a new spirit of adventure. Unusually, the heroines were individuals, able to form their own judgements.

What do these pictures tell you about 'polite society' of the time? How does this society seem to differ from the society in which Crabbe lived?

5.2.1
Pride and Prejudice
(1813)

Extract 1   This is the opening of Jane Austen's novel *Pride and Prejudice*:

> It is a truth universally acknowledged that a single man in pos- 1
> session of a good fortune must be in want of a wife.
>   However little known the feelings or views of such a man may be
> on his first entering a neighbourhood, this truth is so well fixed in
> the minds of the surrounding families, that he is considered as the 5
> rightful property of some one or other of their daughters.

- Is this humorous? Ironic? Does the opening sentence seem to express the author's view?
  Do you think the author's view is the same or different from that of the 'surrounding families'?

Extract 2   Mr Collins, a clergyman, is to be the next heir to the Longbourne estate near London, upon the death of his distant cousin, Mr Bennet. Encouraged by his patroness, Lady Catherine de Bourgh, he is proposing marriage to the lively and spirited Elizabeth Bennet, one of the Bennets' five daughters, to make amends for the fact that he must someday dispossess the family of their estate!

'... You can hardly doubt the purport of my discourse, however your natural delicacy may lead you to dissemble; my attentions have been too marked to be mistaken. Almost as soon as I entered the house I singled you out as the companion of my future life. But before I am run away with by my feelings on this subject, perhaps it will be advisable for me to state my reasons for marrying, and, moreover, for coming into Hertfordshire with the design of selecting a wife, as I certainly did.'

The idea of Mr Collins, with all his solemn composure, being run away with by his feelings, made Elizabeth so near laughing that she could not use the short pause he allowed in any attempt to stop him further, and he continued,–

'My reasons for marrying are, first, that I think it a right thing for every clergyman in easy circumstances (like myself) to set the example of matrimony in his parish; secondly, that I am convinced it will add very greatly to my happiness; and thirdly, which perhaps I ought to have mentioned earlier, that it is the particular advice and recommendation of the very noble lady whom I have the honour of calling patroness. Twice has she condescended to give me her opinion (unasked too!) on this subject; and it was but the very Saturday night before I left Hunsford–between our pools at quadrille, while Mrs Jenkinson was arranging Miss De Bourgh's footstool–that she said, "Mr Collins, you must marry. A clergyman like you must marry. Choose properly, choose a gentlewoman, for *my* sake and for your *own*; let her be an active, useful sort of person, not brought up high, but able to make a small income go a good way. This is my advice. Find such a woman as soon as you can, bring her to Hunsford, and I will visit her." Allow me, by the way, to observe, my fair cousin, that I do not reckon the notice and kindness of Lady Catherine de Bourgh as among the least of the advantages in my power to offer. You will find her manners beyond anything I can describe; and your wit and vivacity, I think, must be acceptable to her, especially when tempered with the silence and respect which her rank will inevitably excite. Thus much for my general intention in favour of matrimony; it remains to be told why my views were directed to Longbourn instead of my own neighbourhood, where, I assure you, there are many amiable young women. But the fact is, that being, as I am, to inherit this estate after

GLOSSARY

purport ... discourse (1.1):
  general purpose of what I had to say
dissemble (1.2): hide your feelings
pools at quadrille (1.20):
  games of quadrille (a card game for four couples)

133

the death of your honoured father (who, however, may live many years longer), I could not satisfy myself without resolving to choose a wife from among his daughters, that the loss to them might be as little as possible when the melancholy event takes place which, however, as I have already said, may not be for several years. This has been my motive, my fair cousin, and I flatter myself it will not sink me in your esteem. And now nothing remains for me but to assure you in the most animated language of the violence of my affection. To fortune I am perfectly indifferent, and shall make no demand of that nature on your father, since I am well aware that it could not be complied with, and that one thousand pounds in the four per cents, which will not be yours till after your mother's decease, is all that you may ever be entitled to. On that head, therefore, I shall be uniformly silent, and you may assure yourself that no ungenerous reproach shall ever pass my lips when we are married.'

It was absolutely necessary to interrupt him now.

'You are too hasty, sir,' she cried. 'You forget that I have made no answer. Let me do it without further loss of time. Accept my thanks for the compliment you are paying me. I am very sensible of the honour of your proposals, but it is impossible for me to do otherwise than decline them.'

'I am not now to learn,' replied Mr Collins, with a formal wave of the hand, 'that it is usual with young ladies to reject the addresses of the man whom they secretly mean to accept, when he first applies for their favour; and that sometimes the refusal is repeated a second or even a third time. I am, therefore, by no means discouraged by what you have just said, and shall hope to lead you to the altar ere long.'

'Upon my word, sir,' cried Elizabeth, 'your hope is rather an extraordinary one after my declaration. I do assure you that I am not one of those young ladies (if such young ladies there are) who are so daring as to risk their happiness on the chance of being asked a second time. I am perfectly serious in my refusal. You could not make *me* happy, and I am convinced that I am the last woman in the world who would make *you* so. Nay, were your friend Lady Catherine to know me, I am persuaded she would find me in every respect ill qualified for the situation.'

Nay (1.74): no (*archaic*)

(from *Pride and Prejudice*)

Understanding and interpretation

i) Which of these does Mr Collins *not* give as a reason for wanting to marry Elizabeth:

to obey his patroness   because he loves her   to make himself happy
to set an example   because he wants the estate to stay in the family

ii) Select *two* adjectives which best describe Mr Collins's manner. Then find lines to illustrate them.

pompous   conceited   stupid   humiliating   insensitive   proud
servile   shallow   obsequious   insulting

iii) Which lines best illustrate Elizabeth's character?

iv) What can we deduce about Lady Catherine's character?

Response
Do you find the scene comic? What does it add to your awareness of the society Jane Austen was writing about?

Language
Find a word in the passage which means:

division of a county with its own church   lowered herself   softened easy and pleasant   uninterested in   speedy   courtship

Critical response
Read what these novelists have said about Jane Austen. How do their views differ?

That young lady had a talent for describing the involvement and feelings and characters of ordinary life which is to me the most wonderful I have ever met with. The Big Bow-wow strain [the tone of a noisy and dramatic epic] I can do myself like any now going, but the exquisite touch which renders ordinary commonplace things and characters interesting from the truth of the description and the sentiment is denied me. (Sir Walter Scott)   1

  5

The Passions are perfectly unknown to her; even to the Feelings she vouchsafes no more than an occasional graceful but distant recognition; too frequent converse with them would but ruffle the elegance of her progress. Her business is not half so much with the human heart as with the human eyes, mouth, hands and feet: what sees keenly, speaks aptly, moves flexibly, it suits her to study, but what throbs fast and full, though hidden, what the blood rushes through, what is the unseen seat of Life, and the sentient target of death – *this* Miss Austen ignores; she no more, with her mind's eye, beholds the heart of her race than each man, with bodily vision, sees the heart in his heaving breast. (Charlotte Brontë)   10

  15

This, again, is the tragedy of social life today. In the old England, the curious blood-connection held the classes together. The squires might be arrogant, violent, bullying and unjust, yet in some ways they were *at one* with the people, part of the same blood-stream. We feel it in Defoe or Fielding. And then, in the mean Jane Austen, it is gone. Already this old maid typifies 'personality' instead of character, the sharp knowing in apartness instead of knowing in togetherness, and she is, to my feeling, thoroughly unpleasant. English in the bad, mean, snobbish sense of the word, just as Fielding is English in the good generous sense. (D.H. Lawrence)   20

  25

GLOSSARY

renders (l.5): causes them to become

vouchsafes (l.9): gives

ruffle (l.10): disturb

aptly (l.13): in a manner suitable for the occasion

throbs (l.14): beats (from the heart)

sentient (l.15): which has feelings and consciousness

beholds (l.17): sees (archaic)

heaving (l.18): rising and falling (with passion)

squires (l.20): main landowners

mean (l.23): ungenerous

5.2.2

***Emma* (1816)**

Setting: A dinner party for the Eltons at the Woodhouses' at Hartfield, a gracious house in the imaginary village of Highbury in Surrey.

Characters: Emma Woodhouse (clever, pretty and self-satisfied young woman – mistress of the Woodhouse household); Miss Jane Fairfax (orphan of an army officer and a penniless recluse – intellectual – secretly engaged to Frank Churchill); Mr John Knightley (lawyer married to Isabella, Mr Woodhouse's eldest daughter – brother to Mr George Knightley, the Woodhouses' bachelor neighbour and owner of a large

house and estate); Mr Woodhouse (Emma's father); Mrs Elton (recently
married to the young vicar); Mrs Weston (Emma's former governess);
Henry and John (Mr John Knightley's young sons).

Previous action: Jane has been to the post office for a letter from her lover;
no one knows this.

The day came, the party were punctually assembled, and Mr John
Knightley seemed early to devote himself to the business of being
agreeable. Instead of drawing his brother off to a window while
they waited for dinner, he was talking to Miss Fairfax. Mrs Elton,
as elegant as lace and pearls could make her, he looked at in silence 5
–wanting only to observe enough for Isabella's information–but
Miss Fairfax was an old acquaintance and a quiet girl, and he could
talk to her. He had met her before breakfast as he was returning
from a walk with his little boys, when it had been just beginning to
rain. It was natural to have some civil hopes on the subject, and he 10
said,

'I hope you did not venture far, Miss Fairfax, this morning, or I
am sure you must have been wet.–*We* scarcely got home in time. I
hope you turned directly.'

'I went only to the post-office,' said she, 'and reached home before 15
the rain was much. It is my daily errand. I always fetch the letters
when I am here. It saves trouble, and is a something to get me out.
A walk before breakfast does me good.'

'Not a walk in the rain, I should imagine.'

'No, but it did not absolutely rain when I set out.' 20

Mr John Knightley smiled, and replied,

'That is to say, you chose to have your walk, for you were not six
yards from your own door when I had the pleasure of meeting you;
and Henry and John had seen more drops than they could count
long before. The post-office has a great charm at one period in our 25
lives. When you have lived to my age, you will begin to think letters
are never worth going through the rain for.'

There was a little blush, and then this answer,

'I must not hope to be ever situated as you are, in the midst of
every dearest connection, and therefore I cannot expect that simply 30
growing older should make me indifferent about letters.'

'Indifferent! Oh! no–I never conceived you could become indifferent. Letters are no matter of indifference; they are generally a
very positive curse.'

'You are speaking of letters of business; mine are letters of 35
friendship.'

'I have often thought them the worst of the two,' replied he coolly.
'Business, you know, may bring money, but friendship hardly ever
does.'

'Ah! you are not serious now. I know Mr John Knightley too well 40
–I am very sure he understands the value of friendship as well as
any body. I can easily believe that letters are very little to you,
much less than to me, but it is not your being ten years older than

myself which makes the difference, it is not age, but situation. You have every body dearest to you always at hand, I, probably, never shall again; and therefore till I have outlived all my affections, a post-office, I think, must always have power to draw me out, in worse weather than to-day.'

'When I talked of your being altered by time, by the progress of years,' said John Knightley, 'I meant to imply the change of situation which time usually brings. I consider one as including the other. Time will generally lessen the interest of every attachment not within the daily circle–but that is not the change I had in view for you. As an old friend, you will allow me to hope, Miss Fairfax, that ten years hence you may have as many concentrated objects as I have.'

It was kindly said, and very far from giving offence. A pleasant 'thank you' seemed meant to laugh it off, but a blush, a quivering lip, a tear in the eye, shewed that it was felt beyond a laugh. Her attention was now claimed by Mr Woodhouse, who being, according to his custom on such occasions, making the circle of his guests, and paying his particular compliments to the ladies, was ending with her–and with all his mildest urbanity, said,

'I am very sorry to hear, Miss Fairfax, of your being out this morning in the rain. Young ladies should take care of themselves. –Young ladies are delicate plants. They should take care of their health and their complexion. My dear, did you change your stockings?'

'Yes, sir, I did indeed; and I am very much obliged by your kind solicitude about me.'

'My dear Miss Fairfax, young ladies are very sure to be cared for. —I hope your good grandmamma and aunt are well. They are some of my very old friends. I wish my health allowed me to be a better neighbour. You do us a great deal of honour to-day, I am sure. My daughter and I are both highly sensible of your goodness, and have the greatest satisfaction in seeing you at Hartfield.'

The kind-hearted, polite old man might then sit down and feel that he had done his duty, and made every fair lady welcome and easy.

By this time the walk in the rain had reached Mrs Elton, and her remonstrances now opened upon Jane.

'My dear Jane, what is this I hear?—Going to the post-office in the rain!—This must not be, I assure you.—You sad girl, how could you do such a thing?—It is a sign I was not there to take care of you.'

Jane very patiently assured her that she had not caught any cold.

'Oh! do not tell *me*. You really are a very sad girl, and do not know how to take care of yourself.—To the post-office indeed! Mrs Weston, did you ever hear the like? You and I must positively exert our authority.'

'My advice,' said Mrs Weston kindly and persuasively, 'I certainly do feel tempted to give. Miss Fairfax, you must not run such risks.—Liable as you have been to severe colds, indeed you ought to be particularly careful, especially at this time of year. The spring I always think requires more than common care. Better wait an hour or two, or even half a day for your letters, than run the risk of bringing on your cough again. Now do not you feel that you had? Yes, I am sure you are much too reasonable. You look as if you would not do such a thing again.'

'Oh! she *shall not* do such a thing again,' eagerly rejoined Mrs Elton. 'We will not allow her to do such a thing again:'—and nodding significantly—'there must be some arrangement made, there must indeed. I shall speak to Mr E. The man who fetches our letters every morning (one of our men, I forget his name) shall inquire for yours too and bring them to you. That will obviate all difficulties, you know; and from *us* I really think, my dear Jane, you can have no scruple to accept such an accommodation.'

'You are extremely kind,' said Jane; 'but I cannot give up my early walk. I am advised to be out of doors as much as I can, I must walk somewhere, and the post-office is an object; and upon my word, I have scarcely ever had a bad morning before.'

'My dear Jane, say no more about it. The thing is determined, that is (laughing affectedly) as far as I can presume to determine any thing without the concurrence of my lord and master. You know, Mrs Weston, you and I must be cautious how we express ourselves. But I do flatter myself, my dear Jane, that my influence is not entirely worn out. If I meet with no insuperable difficulties therefore, consider that point as settled.'

'Excuse me,' said Jane earnestly, 'I cannot by any means consent to such an arrangement, so needlessly troublesome to your servant.

If the errand were not a pleasure to me, it could be done, as it always   120
is when I am not here, by my grandmamma's—'

'Oh! my dear; but so much as Patty has to do!–And it is a kindness
to employ our men.'

Jane looked as if she did not mean to be conquered; but instead
of answering, she began speaking again to Mr John Knightley.   125

'The post-office is a wonderful establishment!' said she.–'The
regularity and dispatch of it! If one thinks of all that it has to do,
and all that it does so well, it is really astonishing!'

'It is certainly very well regulated.'

'So seldom that any negligence or blunder appears! So seldom   130
that a letter, among the thousands that are constantly passing about
the kingdom, is even carried wrong–and not one in a million, I
suppose, actually lost! And when one considers the variety of
hands, and of bad hands too, that are to be deciphered, it increases
the wonder.'   135

'The clerks grow expert from habit.–They must begin with some
quickness of sight and hand, and exercise improves them. If you
want any further explanation,' continued he, smiling, 'they are
paid for it. That is the key to a great deal of capacity. The public
pays and must be served well.'   140

(from *Emma*)

GLOSSARY

errand (l.16): short journey
to get something
quivering (l.58): trembling
Liable (l.92): likely
obviate (l.104): get rid of
scruple (l.106): doubt
concurrence (l.113):
agreement
blunder (l.130): careless
mistake

● Did you enjoy reading this scene? Who did you like? Who irritated you? Why?

Understanding and interpretation

i) Match the two parts of each sentence:

Mr Knightley   is kind-hearted but fussy.
Mrs Elton   is vain and insensitive.
Mr Woodhouse   is kindly and straightforward in manner.

ii) Choose the best alternative:

Jane Fairfax
a) shows no emotion at all;
b) is unrestrained in her behaviour;
c) gives the impression of being trapped.

iii) Find evidence in the text that Mr Knightley

a) is, on the surface, cynical about the ways of the world;
b) is amused by the way Jane deals with Mrs Elton.

iv) What can you deduce from these phrases?

a) 'wanting only to observe enough for Isabella's information' (l.6)
b) 'There was a little blush' (l.28)
c) 'he replied coolly' (l.37)
d) 'you may have as many concentrated objects as I have' (l.55)
e) 'a quivering lip, a tear in the eye' (l.58–59)

Language

In context, what parts of speech (for example, *noun* or *verb*) are the following words? Can you work out their meaning?

'civil' (l.10)   'venture' (l.12)   'urbanity' (l.63)   'remonstrances' (l.81)
'rejoined' (l.99)   'determine' (l.112)   'negligence' (l.130)

Jane Austen   Jane Austen was the sixth child in a family of seven. Outwardly, her life was uneventful; she didn't marry, although she had several suitors, one of whom she accepted one evening, only to change her mind the following morning. Her novels—such as *Sense and Sensibility* (1811), *Pride and Prejudice* (1813), *Mansfield Park* (1814) – were generally well received from publication on, although, recently, one critic has suggested that her books are 'as she meant them to be, read and enjoyed by precisely the sort of people she disliked'. After her death from Addison's disease, *Northanger Abbey* and *Persuasion* were published posthumously in 1818.

5.2.3
Creative writing

Write one of the following:
– a description of a dinner party
– a story which involves a secret correspondence
– a short critical article for a journal on Jane Austen's style

5.2.4
The Gothic novel

By contrast with Jane Austen's works, Gothic novels contained stories which were macabre, fantastic and supernatural, usually set in haunted castles, graveyards, ruins and wild landscapes. They reached the height of their fashion in the 1790s and the early years of the nineteenth century. The first true Gothic novel was *The Castle of Otranto* (1764), by Horace Walpole. Jane Austen, however, satirised the genre in *Northanger Abbey* and Wordsworth disliked its 'gaudy and inane phraseology'. A little later Sir Walter Scott's interest in the Middle Ages gave the genre a new and more realistic lease of life, and many of Byron's heroes (especially in his dramas) were Gothic in spirit.

5.3 Poetry (2): The Lake Poets

The term 'Lake Poets' originated in the *Edinburgh Review* (October 1807) to include William Wordsworth (1770–1850), Samuel Taylor Coleridge (1772–1834) and Robert Southey (1774–1843), who for a time all lived in close association in the mountainous Lake District in the northwest of England. The essayist and critic Thomas de Quincey (1785–1859) also settled in the district though he denied that the poets represented a 'school'.

Warm-up

i) What do you understand by the word 'Romantic'?
ii) Think of as many non-English writers, painters and musical composers as you can who might be called Romantic. What do they have in common? How do they differ?
iii) Have there been Romantic Movements in your country?

5.3.1
William Wordsworth
(1770–1850)

After he graduated from Cambridge University in 1791, Wordsworth made a return visit to France and was fired with enthusiasm for the republican ideals of the French Revolution. He also fell in love with Annette Vallon, a young woman four years older than he, who bore him a daughter. However, he returned to England in 1792 and the Reign of Terror in France (1793–1794) marked the beginning of his disillusionment with radical politics. In 1795 his financial situation was eased when he was left a legacy, and in 1798, in collaboration with Coleridge, the first edition of *Lyrical Ballads* was published anonymously,

William Wordsworth

now considered a landmark of English Romanticism. After a trip to Germany (1798–1799), he and his devoted sister Dorothy settled in Grasmere in the Lake District and he married Mary Hutchinson in 1802. Early critics of his verse regarded his language as too simple and too violent: as De Quincey said, 'up to 1820 the name of Wordsworth was trampled underfoot'. However, in later life he became a patriotic and conservative public man, much to the taste of the Victorians. (A second generation of Romantic poets such as Byron and Shelley regarded him as 'simple' and 'dull'.) In 1843 he was made Poet Laureate.

● Which of the following is correct?
  a) Wordsworth was twenty-two when he first went to France.
  b) Wordsworth became famous as soon as *Lyrical Ballads* was published.
  c) Wordsworth married when he was thirty-two.
  d) Wordsworth was made Poet Laureate six years before his death.

These are some of Wordsworth's views:

On his own poetry:

The principal object ... which I proposed to myself in these poems   1
was to choose incidents and situations from common life, and to
relate or describe them, throughout, as far as was possible, in a
selection of language really used by men; and at the same time, to
throw over them a certain colouring of imagination, whereby ordi-   5
nary things should be presented to the mind in an unusual way;
and, further, and above all, to make these incidents and situations
interesting by tracing in them, truly though not ostentatiously, the

primary laws of our nature: chiefly, as far as regards the manner in which we associate ideas in a state of excitement. Low and rustic life was generally chosen, because in that condition the essential passions of the heart find a better soil in which they can attain their maturity, are less under restraint, and speak a plainer and more emphatic language ... 10

On the poet: 15

The poet ... considers man and nature as essentially adapted to each other, and the mind of man as naturally the mirror of the fairest and most interesting qualities of nature.

The objects of the poet's thoughts are everywhere ... he will follow wheresoever he can find an atmosphere of sensation in which to move his wings. Poetry is the first and last of all knowledge – it is as immortal as the heart of man. 20

On poetic creation:

I have said that poetry is the spontaneous overflow of powerful feelings: it takes its origin from emotion recollected in tranquillity: the emotion is contemplated till by a species of reaction the tranquillity gradually disappears, and an emotion, kindred to that which was before the subject of contemplation, is gradually produced, and does itself actually exist in the mind. In this mood successful composition generally begins, and in a mood similar to this it is carried on; but the emotion, of whatever kind and in whatever degree, from various causes is qualified by various pleasures, so that in describing any passions whatsoever, which are voluntarily described, the mind will upon the whole be in a state of enjoyment. 25 30

GLOSSARY

tracing (l.8): finding the origins (of)

ostentatiously (l.8): in an unnecessarily showy manner

rustic (l.10): typical of the country (as opposed to the town)

attain (l.12): reach

restraint (l.13): control

recollected in tranquility (l.25): remembered in moments of quietness

species (l.26): type

kindred (l.27): related

The Prelude (published 1850)

The Prelude, Wordsworth's long autobiographical poem in blank verse, was originally written 1799–1805 but revised at intervals throughout his

Ullswater

142

life. Wordsworth said it was 'a thing unprecedented in literary history that a man should talk so much about himself'. No version of it was published until his death in 1850 – and then it was a later version. Addressed to Coleridge, the poem describes the mixed joys and terrors of his country childhood as well as his progress in poetry and thought.

In this extract the young Wordsworth is on holiday at Ullswater, one of the large lakes in the Lake District.

One summer evening (led by her) I found   1
A little boat tied to a willow tree
Within a rocky cave, its usual home.
Straight I unloosed her chain, and stepping in
Pushed from the shore. It was an act of stealth   5
And troubled pleasure, nor without the voice
Of mountain-echoes did my boat move on;
Leaving behind her still, on either side,
Small circles glittering idly in the moon,
Until they melted all into one track   10
Of sparkling light. But now, like one who rows,
Proud of his skill, to reach a chosen point
With an unswerving line, I fixed my view
Upon the summit of a craggy ridge,
The horizon's utmost boundary, for above   15
Was nothing but the stars and the grey sky.
She was an elfin pinnace; lustily
I dipped my oars into the silent lake,
And, as I rose upon the stroke, my boat
Went heaving through the water like a swan;   20
When, from behind that craggy steep till then
The horizon's bound, a huge peak, black and huge,
As if with voluntary power instinct
Upreared its head. I struck and struck again,
And growing still in stature the grim shape   25
Towered up between me and the stars, and still,
For so it seemed, with purpose of its own
And measured motion like a living thing,
Strode after me. With trembling oars I turned,
And through the silent water stole my way   30
Back to the covert of the willow tree;
There in her mooring-place I left my bark, –
And through the meadows homeward went, in grave
And serious mood; but after I had seen
That spectacle, for many days, my brain   35
Worked with a dim and undetermined sense
Of unknown modes of being; o'er my thoughts
There hung a darkness, call it solitude
Or blank desertion. No familiar shapes
Remained, no pleasant images of trees,   40
Of sea or sky, no colours of green fields;

GLOSSARY

by her (l.1): (by Nature)
stealth (l.5): secrecy
With . . . line (l.13): without going from side to side
craggy ridge (l.14): rough, steep line of mountain tops
utmost (l.15): furthest
elfin pinnace (l.17): small, lively boat
lustily (l.17): vigorously
heaving (l.20): moving with great effort
As if . . . instinct (l.23): as if of its own accord
Upreared (l.24): lifted up
covert (l.31): hiding place
mooring-place (l.32): place where boats are tied up
bark (l.32): boat (*poetic*)
undetermined (l.36): unclear; unsteady

> But huge and mighty forms, that do not live
> Like living men, moved slowly through the mind
> By day, and were a trouble to my dreams.
>   Wisdom and Spirit of the universe! 45
> Thou Soul that art the eternity of thought,
> That giv'st to forms and images a breath
> And everlasting motion, not in vain
> By day or star-light thus from my first dawn
> Of childhood didst thou intertwine for me 50
> The passions that build up our human soul;
> Not with the mean and vulgar works of man,
> But with high objects, with enduring things –
> With life and Nature, purifying thus
> The elements of feeling and of thought, 55
> And sanctifying, by such discipline,
> Both pain and fear, until we recognize
> A grandeur in the beatings of the heart.

intertwine (l.50): join together

(from *The Prelude*)

Understanding and interpretation

i) These lines indicate changes in the boy's feelings:

'nor without the voice/Of mountain-echoes did my boat move on' (l.6–7)
'I fixed my view/Upon the summit' (l.3–14)
'I struck and struck again' (l.24)
'With trembling oars I turned' (l.29)
'in grave/And serious mood' (l.33–34)
'No familiar shapes/Remained' (l.39)

Match them with the following descriptions:

1. Panic   2. Sombreness   3. Guilty pleasure   4. Fear and remorse
5. Normality disturbed   6. Determination

ii) What do these refer to?

'one track' (l.10); 'that spectacle' (l.35); 'thou' (l.50)

iii) Choose the correct alternatives:

a) He 'fixed his view/Upon the summit' *so he wouldn't get lost/to set his course.*
b) He was frightened by *the huge peak/the summit of the ridge* which *got bigger as he approached it/emerged from behind the line of mountain tops.*
c) In the lines 'Wisdom and Spirit . . . beatings of the heart' (l.45–58) Wordsworth indicates that *natural objects can be both a source of terror and a source of strength and delight/childhood is a time when experience is easily forgotten.*

iv) Explain at least *one* of the following:

'as I rose upon the stroke' (l.19); 'growing still in stature' (l.25); 'There hung a darkness' (l.38); 'Thou Soul that art the eternity of thought' (l.46); 'by such discipline' (l.56)

Language and style

i) With reference to either of the following sections, how does the movement of the verse help to make us feel what is being described?

a) 'lustily . . . like a swan' (l.17–20); b) 'As if with voluntary. . . . struck again' (l.23–24)

144

ii) What is there in this image which intensifies the boy's feelings of fear and guilt?

'the grim shape ... like a living thing/Strode after me.' (l.25–29)

iii) Which lines, if any, could you use to illustrate Wordsworth's phrase 'real language of men'?

iv) John Keats (see pages 160–167) said that both Milton and Wordsworth asserted the individual self of the poet – for which he used the phrase 'egotistical sublime' – whereas Shakespeare seemed to forget his own personality and identify completely with his characters – for which he used the phrase 'negative capability'. However, there are many differences between Milton and Wordsworth. Look back at 3.3.1. Which of the two writers does each of the following phrases refer to?
a) mythical in subject matter
b) uses 'poetic diction' (language used in poetry)
c) direct and ordinary

'A slumber did my spirit seal'

The following poem is one of the poems in the *Lyrical Ballads* written in Germany about 'Lucy', a solitary, unknown girl. Coleridge thought that Wordsworth was trying to imagine the emotional consequences of his sister's death.

'A slumber did my spirit seal'

A slumber did my spirit seal;   1
  I had no human fears:
She seemed a thing that could not feel
  The touch of earthly years.

No motion has she now, no force;   5
  She neither hears nor sees,
Rolled round in earth's diurnal course,
  With rocks, and stones, and trees.

GLOSSARY
slumber (l.1): sleep
seal (l.1): close up
diurnal (l.7): daily

● Discuss the following statements:
  – The first stanza refers to a time when the poet thought the girl would not die; it suggests a sense of sleepy unreality.
  – In the second stanza the poet is very conscious the girl is dead; he is both bitter and calm.
  – The dead girl is now safe and in inanimate community with the natural world.
  – The poem's strong emotions are presented in a very controlled – almost uninvolved and factual – way.

William Wordsworth – an appraisal

Like Plato, Wordsworth in his early verse seemed to imply that God and the natural universe could not be separated. However, for the 1850 version of *The Prelude* – in contrast with the 1805–6 version – Wordsworth tried to eliminate such pantheistic tendencies because they were contrary to his later orthodox Christian beliefs.

Read the following appraisal by William Hazlitt (1788–1830). Hazlitt, the essayist and critic, was the early friend and admirer of Wordsworth and Coleridge, though he later resented what he considered their betrayal of the liberal cause:

Mr Wordsworth's genius is a pure emanation of the Spirit of the Age. Had he lived in any other period of the world, he would never have been heard of. ... His style is vernacular: he delivers household truths. He sees nothing loftier than human hopes, nothing deeper than the human heart. ... He takes the simplest elements of nature and of the human mind, the mere abstract conditions inseparable from our being, and tries to compound a new system of poetry from them; and has perhaps succeeded as well as any one could. ... In a word, his poetry is founded on setting up an opposition (and pushing it to the utmost length) between the natural and the artificial, between the spirit of humanity and the spirit of fashion and of the world.

It is one of the innovations of the time. It partakes of, and is carried along with, the revolutionary movement of our age: the political changes of the day were the model on which he formed and conducted his poetical experiments. His Muse (it cannot be denied, and without this we cannot explain its character at all) is a levelling one. It proceeds on a principle of equality, and strives to reduce all things to the same standard. It is distinguished by a proud humility. It relies upon its own resources, and disdains external show and relief. It takes the commonest events and objects, as a test to prove that nature is always interesting from its inherent truth and beauty, without any of the ornaments of dress or pomp of circumstances to set it off. ...

His popular, inartificial style gets rid (at a blow) of all the trappings of verse, of all the high places of poetry: 'the cloud-capt towers, the solemn temples, the gorgeous palaces,' are swept to the ground, and 'like the baseless fabric of a vision, leave not a wreck behind'. All the traditions of learning, all the superstitions of age, are obliterated and effaced. We begin *de novo* on a *tabula rasa* of poetry. ... He elevates the mean by the strength of his own aspirations; he clothes the naked with beauty and grandeur from the stories of his own recollections. ...

(from 'Mr Wordsworth' in *The Spirit of the Age: or Contemporary Portraits*)

5.4 The Romantic revival

The term 'Romantic revival' was first used in France and Germany to refer to the shift in sensibility in art and literature in the period between 1770 and 1847. In essence, the word 'romantic' was used to highlight the contrast between the freedom of imagination of the 'romances' of the Middle Ages and the restraint and discipline of the 'classical' literature of ancient Greece and Rome. In England, the Romantic writers were individuals with many contrary views. They belonged to no clear movement and the connexions with the more 'classical' eighteenth century were still strong (Wordsworth's *Tintern Abbey* – see Supplement 5 – has been called 'the fine flower of eighteenth-century meditative poetry'; and the 'late-Romantic' poet Lord Byron was a great admirer of the Augustan poet Pope and was in many ways a 'classical' poet himself.) However, most 'Romantics' had some things in common with other 'Romantics'.

- i) Put the phrases in the correct order to make sentences.

  a) for a time / supported / most 'Romantics' / political causes / at least / progressive
  b) felt able / freedom and informality / to use language / with more / than eighteenth-century poets / all of them
  c) to the natural environment / except perhaps Blake / insisted on / responded vividly / most / and / an individual relationship with nature
  d) both / the state of / of the individual human being / to explore / Blake and Wordsworth / childhood / used / the nature

- ii) What makes this painting 'Romantic'?

Snowstorm: Steamboat *by J. M. W. Turner*

5.5 Samuel Taylor Coleridge (1772–1834)

Coleridge's fame as a poet rests on far fewer poems than Wordsworth but as a thinker and a literary critic he was more ambitious. Influenced by the German philosopher Immanuel Kant (1724–1804) and opposed to the limited rationalistic and mechanistic tendencies of eighteenth-century philosophy, Coleridge saw poetic creation and the poet's personality as organically related within a grand metaphysical system. Typically for Coleridge, though, he planned to write more than he actually wrote.

147

5.5.1 In *My first Acquaintance with Poets* (1823) Hazlitt (see pages 145–146) describes his memories of meeting Coleridge as a young man twenty-five years before. He also makes comparisons with Wordsworth.

Warm-up   i) Read the following extracts and put *one* adjective in each space.

Coleridge: .... face; .... eyebrows; .... forehead; .... mouth; .... eyes; .... chin; .... nose; .... hair.

Wordsworth: .... face; .... eyes; .... forehead; .... nose; .... mouth.

ii) Who does each of these words most apply to? *inspirational; steady*.

My father was a Dissenting Minister ... and in the year 1798 ... Mr Coleridge came to Shrewsbury, to succeed Mr Rowe in the spiritual charge of a Unitarian congregation there. He did not come till late on the Saturday afternoon before he was to preach; and Mr Rowe, who himself went down to the coach, in a state of anxiety and expectation, to look for the arrival of his successor, could find no one at all answering the description but a round-faced man, in a short black coat (like a shooting jacket) which hardly seemed to have been made for him, but who seemed to be talking at a great rate to his fellow passengers. Mr Rowe had scarce returned to give an account of his disappointment, when the round-faced man in black entered, and dissipated all doubts on the subject, by beginning to talk. He did not cease while he stayed; nor has he since, that I know of. He held the good town of Shrewsbury in delightful suspense for three weeks that he remained there. [1] [5] [10] [15]

... A sound was in my ears as of a Siren's song; I was stunned, startled with it, as from deep sleep; but I had no notion then that I should ever be able to express my admiration to others in motley imagery or quaint allusion, till the light of his genius shone into my soul, like the sun's rays glittering in the puddles of the road. I was at that time dumb, inarticulate, helpless, like a worm by the wayside, crushed, bleeding, lifeless; but now, bursting from the deadly bands that bound them ... my ideas float on winged words ... [20]

His forehead was broad and high, light as if built of ivory, with large projecting eyebrows, and his eyes rolling beneath them, like a sea with darkened lustre. ... His mouth was gross, voluptuous, open, eloquent; his chin good-humored and round; but his nose, the rudder of the face, the index of the will, was small, feeble, nothing – ... His hair (now; alas! gray) was then black and glossy as the raven's, and fell in smooth masses over his forehead. This long pendulous hair is peculiar to enthusiasts, to those whose minds tend heavenward; and is traditionally inseparable (though of a different colour) from the pictures of Christ. It ought to belong, as a character, to all who preach *Christ crucified*, and Coleridge was at that time one of those! ... [25] [30] [35]

GLOSSARY

Dissenting Minister (l.1): clergyman with the Nonconformist Church, which refused to accept doctrines of the Church of England

Unitarian (l.3): belonging to the denomination which stresses a united world community and liberal social action

dissipated (l.12): caused to disappear

Siren's song (l.16): the song of a partly female creature in Greek mythology that led seamen to their destruction by singing – Hazlitt is referring to Coleridge's conversational powers

stunned (l.16): greatly surprised

in motley ... allusion (l.18–19): in verbal images of different kinds and clever indirect references

wayside (l.22): side of the road

lustre (l.27): shining light

rudder (l.28): the device used for controlling the direction of a boat

index of (l.29): guide to

raven (l.30): large bird with shiny black feathers

pendulous (l.31): hanging down

In digressing, in dilating, in passing from subject to subject, he appeared to me to float in air, to slide on ice. He told me in confidence (going along) that he should have preached two sermons before he accepted the situation at Shrewsbury, one on Infant Baptism, the other on the Lord's Supper, showing that he could not administer either, which would have effectually disqualified him for the object in view. I observed that he continually crossed me on the way by shifting from one side of the footpath to the other. This struck me as an odd movement; but I did not at that time connect it with any instability of purpose or involuntary change of principle, as I have done since. He seemed unable to keep on in a straight line...

[On another occasion the following year, Coleridge] lamented that Wordsworth was not prone enough to believe in the traditional superstitions of the place, and that there was a something corporeal, *a matter-of-fact-ness*, a clinging to the palpable, or often to the petty, in his poetry, in consequence. His genius was not a spirit that descended to him through the air; it sprung out of the ground like a flower, or unfolded itself from a green spray, on which the goldfinch sang. He said, however (if I remember right) that this objection must be confined to his descriptive pieces, that his philosophic poetry had a grand and comprehensive spirit in it, so that his soul seemed to inhabit the universe like a palace, and to discover truth by intuition, rather than by deduction. The next day Wordsworth arrived from Bristol at Coleridge's cottage. I think I see him now. He answered in some degree to his friend's description of him, but was more gaunt and Don Quixote-like. . . .

There was a severe, worn pressure of thought about his temples, a fire in his eye (as if he saw something in objects more than the outward appearance), an intense high narrow forehead, a Roman nose, cheeks furrowed by strong purpose and feeling, and a convulsive inclination to laughter about the mouth, a good deal at variance with the solemn, stately expression of the rest of his face. . . .

He sat down and talked very naturally and freely, with a mixture of clear gushing accents in his voice, a deep guttural intonation, and a strong tincture of the northern *burr*, like the crust on wine. He instantly began to make havoc of the half of a Cheshire cheese on the table, and said triumphantly that 'his marriage with experience had not been so unproductive as Mr Southey's in teaching him a knowledge of the good things of this life.' . . .

Wordsworth, looking out of the low, latticed window, said, 'How beautifully the sun sets on that yellow bank!' I thought within myself, 'With what eyes these poets see nature!' . . .

---

digressing (l.37): leaving the main subject to talk about something else

dilating (l.37): commenting at length

prone (l.50): inclined

the place (l.51): a particular place

corporeal (l.51): physical; unspiritual

spray (l.55): flowering branch

goldfinch (l.55): small red, black and yellow bird

gaunt (l.63): very thin

furrowed (l.67): with lines made

gushing (l.71): flowing freely

guttural (l.71): made in the throat

tincture (l.72): quality

burr (l.72): strong /r/ sound made at the back of the throat

crust (l.72): deposit on inside of an old wine bottle

make havoc of (l.73): eat greedily

latticed (l.77): with crossed strips

Coleridge's manner is more full, animated, and varied; Words- 80
worth's more equable, sustained, and internal. The one might be
termed more *dramatic*, the other more *lyrical*. Coleridge has told
me that he himself liked to compose in walking over uneven ground,
or breaking through the straggling branches of a copse wood;
whereas Wordsworth always wrote (if he could) walking up and 85
down a straight gravel walk, or in some spot where the continuity
of his verse met with no collateral interruption. Returning that
same evening, I got into a metaphysical argument with Wordsworth,
while Coleridge was explaining the different notes of the nightingale
to his sister, in which we neither of us succeeded in making our- 90
selves perfectly clear and intelligible.

straggling (l.84): untidy
copse (l.84): with small
    trees close together
collateral (l.87):
    accompanying

(from *My First Acquaintance with Poets* by William Hazlitt)

● iii) Write at least one sentence on each of the following:
   – Coleridge's criticism of Wordsworth.
   – What the passage reveals about the writer, Hazlitt.

iv) Which of the three characters do you find most attractive Coleridge,
    Wordsworth or Hazlitt? Give reasons.

Samuel Taylor
Coleridge

Thomas Carlyle (1795–1881), the Scottish historian and philosopher, got
to know Coleridge much later, in 1824. At the time Coleridge was
attempting a cure for the opium addiction he had developed after 1800.

GLOSSARY

incurvated (l.1): curved
    inwards
rotund (l.2): rounded
snuffy (l.2): soiled with
    snuff (a preparation of
    scented tobacco inhaled
    through the nose)
animal magnetism (l.4):
    physical attractiveness
cardinal sin (l.5): most
    important weakness
resolution (l.6): the ability
    to be definite
bespeaks (l.6): indicates
shovel (l.7): move
    awkwardly
Brow (l.11): forehead
irresolute (l.12): weak in
    character
hazel (l.13): light brown
corkscrew (l.17): twisting
plaintive snuffle (l.19):
    melancholy sniffing
    sound
Kantean (l.21): typical of
    the work of the
    German philosopher
    Immanuel Kant,
    1724–1804
quaver (l.23): tremble

Coleridge ... Figure a fat, flabby, incurvated personage, at once 1
short, rotund, and relaxed, with a watery mouth, a snuffy nose, a
pair of strange brown, timid, yet earnest-looking eyes ... He is a
kind, good soul, full of religion and affection and poetry and animal magnetism. His cardinal sin is that he lacks *will*. He has no 5
resolution. His very attitude bespeaks this. He never straightens
his knee-joints ... In walking he does not tread, but shovel and
slide ... His eyes have a look of anxious impotence. He *would do*
with all his heart, but he knows he dares not.

The good man, he was now getting old ... and gave you the idea of 10
a life that had been full of sufferings ... Brow and head were round,
and of massive weight, but the face was flabby and irresolute. The
deep eyes, of a light hazel, were as full of sorrow as of inspiration;
confused pain looked mildly from them, as in a kind of mild astonishment ... He hung loosely on his limbs ... and a lady once 15
remarked, he never could fix which side of the garden walk would
suit him best, but continually shifted in corkscrew fashion, and
kept trying both ... His voice, naturally soft and good, had con-
tracted itself into a plaintive snuffle and singsong; he spoke as if
preaching ... I still recollect his 'object' and 'subject', terms of 20
continual recurrence in the Kantean province; and how he sang and
snuffled them into 'om-m-mject' and 'sum-m-mject', with a kind of
solemn shake and quaver, as he rolled along.

(from *Life of John Sterling*)

Samuel Taylor Coleridge in 1814

● i) What do the extracts tell us about how Coleridge has changed?

'Frost at Midnight' The following poem, written during the winter months of 1798, has three main themes:
– the radiant future Coleridge predicts for his two-year-old son Hartley;
– Coleridge's present solitude and the sound of his son asleep beside him;
– Coleridge's lonely, meditative boyhood at Christ's Hospital (his school in London).

● In which order do they appear in the poem? Write line numbers to indicate which part of the poem expresses each theme.

Frost at Midnight

GLOSSARY

ministry (l.1): duty (usually associated with the Church)

owlet (l.2): small owl (night time bird with large head)

hark (l.3): listen closely

inmates (l.4): people who live with me

Abstruser musings (l.6): more complicated thoughts

save (l.6): except

cradled (l.7): in a small child's bed

vexes (l.9): disturbs

The Frost performs its secret ministry,   1
Unhelped by any wind. The owlet's cry
Came loud – and hark, again! loud as before.
The inmates of my cottage, all at rest,
Have left me to that solitude, which suits   5
Abstruser musings: save that at my side
My cradled infant slumbers peacefully.
'Tis calm indeed! so calm, that it disturbs
And vexes meditation, with its strange
And extreme silentness. Sea, hill, and wood,   10
This populous village! Sea, and hill, and wood,
With all the numberless goings-on of life,
Inaudible as dreams! the thin blue flame
Lies on my low-burnt fire, and quivers not;

Only that film, which fluttered on the grate,   15
Still flutters there, the sole unquiet thing.
Methinks, its motion in this hush of nature
Gives it dim sympathies with me who live,
Making it a companionable form,
Whose puny flaps and freaks the idling Spirit   20
By its own moods interprets, every where
Echo or mirror seeking of itself,
And makes a toy of Thought.
                           But O! how oft,
How oft, at school, with most believing mind,   25
Presageful, have I gazed upon the bars,
To watch that fluttering *stranger*! and as oft
With unclosed lids, already had I dreamt
Of my sweet birth-place, and the old church-tower,
Whose bells, the poor man's only music, rang   30
From morn to evening, all the hot Fair-day,
So sweetly, that they stirred and haunted me
With a wild pleasure, falling on mine ear
Most like articulate sounds of things to come!
So gazed I, till the soothing things, I dreamt,   35
Lulled me to sleep, and sleep prolonged my dreams!
And so I brooded all the following morn,
Awed by the stern preceptor's face, mine eye
Fixed with mock study on my swimming book:
Save if the door half-opened, and I snatched   40
A hasty glance, and still my heart leaped up,
For still I hoped to see the *stranger's* face,
Townsman, or aunt, or sister more beloved,
My play-mate when we both were clothed alike!
  Dear Babe, that sleepest cradled by my side,   45
Whose gentle breathings, heard in this deep calm,
Fill up the interspersed vacancies
And momentary pauses of the thought!
My babe so beautiful! it thrills my heart
With tender gladness, thus to look at thee,   50
And think that thou shalt learn far other lore,
And in far other scenes! For I was reared
In the great city, pent 'mid cloisters dim,
And saw nought lovely but the sky and stars.
But *thou*, my babe! shalt wander like a breeze   55
By lakes and sandy shores, beneath the crags
Of ancient mountain, and beneath the clouds,
Which image in their bulk both lakes and shores
And mountain crags: so shalt thou see and hear
The lovely shapes and sounds intelligible   60
Of that eternal language, within thy God
Utters, who from eternity doth teach

populous (l.11):
  with a lot of people in
  it
that film (l.15): (a piece of
  soot fluttering on the
  bar of the grate:
  according to Coleridge,
  called a 'stranger' and
  supposed to be a sign
  of the arrival of an
  absent friend in
  popular superstition)
grate (l.15): metal frame
  (with bars) in the
  fireplace to hold the
  fuel
puny flaps and freaks (l.20):
  weak, pointless to and
  fro movements
Presageful (l.26): full of
  thoughts and feelings
  about the future
brooded (l.37): thought
  long and quietly
Awed (l.38): filled with
  respect and fear
stern preceptor (l.38): hard
  and severe teacher
swimming (l.39):
  (Coleridge was not
  concentrating: the
  words were not clear
  on the page)
*My play-mate . . . alike
(l.44)*: (when Coleridge
  and his sister Ann still
  wore infant clothes)
interspersed vacancies (l.47):
  spaces here and there
lore (l.51): knowledge and
  wisdom
*pent 'mid cloisters dim
(l.53)*: confined in dark
  covered passages
crags (l.56): steep rough
  rocks high up
bulk (l.58): great size

redbreast *(l.68)*: type of bird

tufts *(l.69)*: little piles

nigh thatch *(l.70)*: nearby roof made of straw ('nigh' is *poetic*)

eave-drops *(l.71)*: small amounts of water falling (faintly) from the lower part of the roof (also suggests to eavesdrop – to listen secretly?)

trances of the blast *(l.72)*: semi-conscious states – pauses – during the strong wind

> Himself in all, and all things in himself.
> Great universal Teacher! he shall mould
> Thy spirit, and by giving make it ask.   65
>   Therefore all seasons shall be sweet to thee,
> Whether the summer clothe the general earth
> With greenness, or the redbreast sit and sing
> Betwixt the tufts of snow on the bare branch
> Of mossy apple-tree, while the nigh thatch   70
> Smokes in the sun-thaw; whether the eave-drops fall
> Heard only in the trances of the blast,
> Or if the secret ministry of frost
> Shall hang them up in silent icicles,
> Quietly shining to the quiet Moon.   75

● How would you describe the atmosphere of the poem? Reflective?

Understanding and interpretation

Choose the most suitable answer. Justify your answer with lines from the poem.

i) Why does Coleridge say he is unable to meditate? (*it is too quiet/he is disturbed by the sound of his son sleeping*)

ii) What reminds him of his childhood? (*the piece of soot/the bars of the grate/neither/both*)

iii) What did school mean to him? (*it was a type of prison/it was a place full of strangers*)

iv) What does the 'stranger' represent? (*something mysterious from the outside world/his earlier childhood/neither/both*)

v) What does the baby suggest? (*freedom/great potential/neither/both*)

Language and style

Coleridge was to some extent influenced by William Cowper (1731–1800), a humble, devout man who retired from the world to a life of rustic seclusion and whose verse was attractively simple in contrast with the more formal classical styles of his time.

i) Rearrange the letters to make words in the above poem connected with the natural world (for example, SFTOR = FROST):

TWOLE   ROSHES   STREARBED   SCIELIC

Which in context also suggests a supernatural environment?

ii) In which lines is the baby addressed directly? Indicate at least *one* other feature of the style that gives the impression that the poet is actually speaking as he is writing.

iii) Give an example of at least *one* poetic technique that Coleridge uses to make us *feel* what he is describing.

The Ancient Mariner (written 1797)

The Rime of the Ancient Mariner, first published in *Lyrical Ballads* (1798), is written in traditional English ballad style (a ballad is a narrative composition in rhythmic verse, often with repeated lines). A sailor has inexplicably and cruelly killed an albatross – a bird which traditionally brings good luck to seamen. The following extract brings the second part of the ballad to a close. (There are seven parts.) The themes of the poem as a whole are foolishness, guilt and making amends.

● Read the extract. Who is the narrator?

The fair breeze blew, the white foam flew,   1
The furrow followed free;
We were the first that ever burst
Into that silent sea.

Down dropt the breeze, the sails dropt down,   5
'Twas sad as sad could be;
And we did speak only to break
The silence of the sea!

All in a hot and copper sky,
The bloody Sun, at noon,   10
Right up above the mast did stand,
No bigger than the Moon.

Day after day, day after day,
We stuck, nor breath nor motion;
As idle as a painted ship   15
Upon a painted ocean.

GLOSSARY

furrow (l.2): trench left
   behind the ship in the
   water
that silent sea (l.4): (near
   the Equator in the
   Pacific Ocean)

154

Water, water, every where,
And all the boards did shrink;
Water, water, every where,
Nor any drop to drink.   20

The very deep did rot: O Christ!
That ever this should be!
Yea, slimy things did crawl with legs
Upon the slimy sea.

boards (l.18): wooden
  sides of the ship
deep (l.21): sea
slimy (l.23): unpleasantly
  slippery and sticky
in reel and rout (l.25):
  moving round in a
  disorderly fashion
death-fires (l.26):
  (St Elmo's fires –
  electricity in the
  atmosphere – 'danced'
  at night on the ship's
  mast, suggesting
  disaster)
fathom (l.31): a unit of
  length for measuring
  the depth of water –
  about 1.83 metres
utter drought (l.33): long
  period of total dryness
soot (l.36): black powder
  left by smoke
well a-day (l.37):
  (expression used to
  express resignation)

About, about, in reel and rout   25
The death-fires danced at night;
The water, like a witch's oils,
Burnt green, and blue and white.

And some in dreams assured were
Of the Spirit that plagued us so;   30
Nine fathom deep he had followed us
From the land of mist and snow.

And every tongue, through utter drought,
Was withered at the root;
We could not speak, no more than if   35
We had been choked with soot.

Ah! well a-day! what evil looks
Had I from old and young!
Instead of the cross, the Albatross
About my neck was hung.   40

(from *The Rime of the Ancient Mariner*)

● How is the seaman's foolishness punished? Can you guess how the story
  continues?

Language and style   i) Correct these statements:

  – The rhyme scheme is ABBA.
  – Each line has five beats.

ii) Find an example of:

  a) a word which is repeated
  b) a phrase which is repeated
  c) alliteration

  What is the effect of each in context?

iii) Which of these words most characterise the atmosphere for you?
  magical   mysterious   supernatural   unnatural

  Which of these words characterise the style?

  symbolic   musical   economical   simple

Samuel Taylor Coleridge   Coleridge's best-known poems are *The Ancient Mariner* (1797); *Christabel*
(first part written in 1797, second part in 1800 – published in 1816), an

unfinished narrative about an evil enchantress; 'Kubla Khan' (1797) – see Supplement 5; 'Dejection: An Ode' (1802), about the personal predicament of a poet whose powers are failing and the 'shaping spirit of the Imagination'.

His best-known criticism is *Biographia Literaria* (1817) – see Supplement 5.

Coleridge was one of the first critics to pay close attention to language; he also conceived of artistic creation as a united whole involving the total personality of the artist. Like Wordsworth, Coleridge began as an enthusiastic supporter of the French Revolution but by 1800 he was reacting against it and becoming philosophically conservative.

5.6 The novel (2)

5.6.1
Sir Walter Scott
(1771–1832)

Walter Scott's early wealth and fame was based on his poetry. From 1815, though, he became a highly influential novelist throughout Europe – the first true historical novelist – making Scotland, with its grand rugged scenery, an often idealised romantic country full of adventure.

Warm-up

What do you think Dr Johnson meant by the following remark? 'Depend upon it, Sir, when a man knows he is to be hanged in a fortnight, it concentrates the mind wonderfully.'

Public execution at the Grassmarket, Edinburgh

The Heart of Midlothian (1818)

Read the following extract.

In former times, England had her Tyburn, to which the devoted victims of justice were conducted in solemn procession up what is now called Oxford Road. In Edinburgh, a large open street, or rather oblong square, surrounded by high houses, called the Grassmarket, was used for the same melancholy purpose. It was not ill chosen for such a scene, being of considerable extent, and therefore fit to accommodate a great number of spectators, such as are usually assembled by this melancholy spectacle. On the other hand, few of the houses which surround it were, even in early times, inhabited by persons of fashion; so that those likely to be offended or over deeply affected by such unpleasant exhibitions were not in the way of having their quiet disturbed by them. The houses in the Grassmarket are, generally speaking, of a mean description; yet the place is not without some features of grandeur, being overhung by the southern side of the huge rock on which the castle stands, and by the moss-grown battlements and turreted walls of that ancient fortress.

It was the custom, until within these thirty years, or thereabouts, to use this esplanade for the scene of public executions. The fatal day was announced to the public by the appearance of a huge black gallows-tree towards the eastern end of the Grassmarket. This ill-omened apparition was of great height, with a scaffold surrounding it and a double ladder placed against it, for the ascent of the unhappy criminal and the executioner. As this apparatus was always arranged before dawn, it seemed as if the gallows had grown out of the earth in the course of one night, like the production of some foul demon; and I well remember the fright with which the schoolboys, when I was one of their number, used to regard these ominous signs of deadly preparation. On the night after the execution the gallows again disappeared, and was conveyed in silence and darkness to the place where it was usually deposited, which was one of the vaults under the Parliament House, or courts of justice. This mode of execution is now exchanged for one similar to that in front of Newgate—with what beneficial effect is uncertain. The mental sufferings of the convict are indeed shortened. He no longer stalks between the attendant clergymen, dressed in his graveclothes, through a considerable part of the city, looking like a moving and walking corpse, while yet an inhabitant of this world; but, as the ultimate purpose of punishment has in view the prevention of crimes, it may at least be doubted, whether in abridging the melancholy ceremony, we have not in part diminished that appalling effect upon the spectators which is the useful end of all such inflictions, and in consideration of which alone, unless in very particular cases, capital sentences can be altogether justified.

On the 7th day of September, 1736, these ominous preparations for execution were descried in the place we have described, and at an early hour the space around began to be occupied by several

GLOSSARY

Tyburn (l.1): The site of public executions by hanging until 1783; near the modern Marble Arch in London

devoted (l.1): cut off from society

battlements (l.16): low wall round the flat castle roof with spaces to shoot through

turreted (l.16): with small towers (usually used for defence)

esplanade (l.19): area of clear ground in front of the castle

gallows-tree (l.21): wooden frame from which murderers were hanged

ill-omened (l.21): indicating something bad was going to happen

scaffold (l.22): raised stage on which the gallows were placed

vaults (l.32): underground rooms

Newgate (l.34): prison in London, demolished in 1902

capital sentences (l.44): decisions by the courts in which the criminal is put to death

groups, who gazed on the scaffold and gibbet with a stern and vindicate show of satisfaction very seldom testified by the populace,
whose good-nature, in most cases, forgets the crime of the con-   50
demned person, and dwells only on his misery. But the act of which
the expected culprit had been convicted was of a description calculated nearly and closely to awaken and irritate the resentful feelings
of the multitude. The tale is well known; yet it is necessary to recapitulate its leading circumstances, for the better understanding what   55
is to follow; and the narrative may prove long, but I trust not uninteresting, even to those who have heard its general issue. At any
rate, some detail is necessary, in order to render intelligible the
subsequent events of our narrative.

Contraband trade, though it strikes at the root of legitimate   60
government, by encroaching on its revenues, – though it injures
the fair trader, and debauches the minds of those engaged in it, – is
not usually looked upon, either by the vulgar or by their betters, in
a very heinous point of view. On the contrary, in those counties
where it prevails, the cleverest, boldest, and most intelligent of the   65
peasantry, are uniformly engaged in illicit transactions, and very
often with the sanction of the farmers and inferior gentry. Smuggling was almost universal in Scotland in the reigns of George I.
and II.; for the people, unaccustomed to imposts, and regarding
them as an unjust aggression upon their ancient liberties, made no   70
scruple to elude them whenever it was possible to do so.

(from *The Heart of Midlothian*)

gibbet (l.48): upright post
  with projecting arm
  (part of the gallows)
vindicate (l.48): full of
  vengeance
populace (l.49): members
  of the public
culprit (l.52): guilty person
recapitulate (l.54): repeat
Contraband trade (l.60):
  unlawfully bringing
  goods into or out of a
  country; smuggling
*encroaching on its revenues
  (l.61):* taking away some
  of its income (from taxes)
debauches (l.62): corrupts
heinous (l.64): shameful
sanction (l.67): approval
imposts (l.69): taxes
made no scruple (l.70): had
  no worries
elude (l.71): escape from
  paying

Understanding i) What do the following refer to?

'the same melancholy purpose' (l.5); 'This ill-omened apparition (l.21); 'their
number' (l.28); 'This mode of execution' (l.32); 'in the place we have described'
(l.46)

ii) What do these words mean in context? If you don't know, try to work out the
meaning.

'abridging' (l.40); 'appalling' (l.41); 'descried' (l.46); 'debauches' (l.62);
'vulgar' (l.63); 'gentry' (l.67); 'smuggling' (l.67); 'elude' (l.71)

What helped you decide? Check in a dictionary.

Interpretation Write questions about the passage using the prompts. Start each question
with one of these:

What   Why   How

a) Grassmarket – good place – executions?
b) executions – in Edinburgh – changed?
c) narrator – feel – preparations – schoolboy?
d) narrator – hangings – now?
e) people – condemned criminals?
f) narrator – smuggling?

The above extract is the opening of the novel *The Heart of Midlothian*.
Midlothian is the county in Scotland in which Edinburgh is situated; the title
was the nickname of the old Tolbooth prison in Edinburgh. The story

concerns Jeanie Deans's journey on foot to London to appeal to the Duke of Argyle on behalf of her sister Effie, who has been wrongly charged with child murder.

The extract is followed by a description of the riot in the prison in 1736 (which actually happened) after the reprieve of Captain John Porteous, the commander of the City Guard sentenced to death for firing on the crowd during the hanging of a convicted robber. In the riot, in which Porteous is taken out and hanged by a group of angry citizens, Effie refuses to escape.

Jeanie visiting Effie in prison

Sir Walter Scott

Scott wrote a great many novels at great speed. However, his antiquarian knowledge as well as his interest in the religious and political conflicts of the past – particularly the history of the Jacobites and the drama and tragedy of the Scottish side of the Anglo-Scottish border – enabled him to bring the past to life in a way which avoided the unrealities of the Gothic novel. His characters are an integral part of the society in which they lived. This is more true when Scott wrote in Scottish dialect than when he wrote in English, where he is sometimes heavy and cliché-ridden.

His novels include *Rob Roy* (1817), *Ivanhoe* (1819) and *Quentin Durward* (1823). Politically, Scott was a Tory whose natural conservatism led him to favour the old values of chivalry, honour, courtly manners and loyalty to the king.

5.7 Poetry (3): The later Romantics

The later Romantic poets George Gordon, Lord Byron (1788–1824), Percy Bysshe Shelley (1792–1822) and John Keats (1795–1821) were at the same time influenced by Wordsworth and Coleridge and critical of them.

5.7.1 The ode

An ode is a form of lyric poem often addressed to a particular subject. The form was established by the Greek poet Pindar (fifth century BC) to glorify the winners of the Olympics and other games. It was meant to be chanted by a chorus to the accompaniment of instrumental music and dancing. A later tradition was established by Horace (65–8 BC) whose patriotic odes on Roman politics were both moral and personal. In English, many of the great poets (Spenser, Marvell, Dryden, Gray, Wordsworth and Coleridge) wrote odes. The form is characterised by complex stanza forms, varying line length, and usually a grand style and elevated tone.

5.7.2 John Keats (1795–1821)

John Keats's social background was humbler than Byron's or Shelley's. His father was the manager of a livery stables and died when he was eight. His mother remarried but died of tuberculosis when he was fourteen. Keats had two younger brothers, George and Tom, and a younger sister, Fanny. In 1810 he was apprenticed to an apothecary–surgeon and in 1815 became a student at Guy's Hospital.

In his early poems Keats was also influenced by Spenser and Milton and even more by Shakespeare.

John Keats in his sitting room (1821), painted by Joseph Severn

Keats on his deathbed, by Joseph Severn

'Ode to a Nightingale'

'Ode to a Nightingale', a poem in eight stanzas, begins:

> My heart aches, and a drowsy numbness pains
> My sense, as though of hemlock I had drunk.

('a drowsy numbness' means 'a heavy sleepy lack of feeling'; 'pains My sense' suggests that the narrator is both losing sensation and in pain; 'hemlock' is a poisonous herb)

● What is the nightingale usually noted for? Can you guess what the poem is about?

Stanza 1

GLOSSARY

opiate (l.3): drug from opium inducing dullness and inaction

to the drains (l.3): until it was all gone

Lethe-wards (l.4): towards Lethe, the river in Hades (the underworld in Greek myth), whose waters cause forgetfulness

lot (l.5): fate

Dryad (l.7): tree nymph in Greek mythology

beechen (l.9): from the beech trees

Ode to a Nightingale

My heart aches, and a drowsy numbness pains   1
   My sense, as though of hemlock I had drunk,
Or emptied some dull opiate to the drains
   One minute past, and Lethe-wards had sunk:
'Tis not through envy of thy happy lot,   5
   But being too happy in thy happiness, –
      That thou, light-winged Dryad of the trees,
         In some melodious plot
Of beechen green, and shadows numberless,
   Singest of summer in full-throated ease.   10

● i) Which is more accurate?
   a) I drank hemlock and thought I heard the joyful sound of a nightingale.
   b) I am lost in the nightingale's happy song.

  ii) In which line does the narrator first address the nightingale directly?

Stanza 2

O for a draught of vintage, that hath been
   Cool'd a long age in the deep-delved earth,
Tasting of Flora and the country green,
   Dance, and Provençal song, and sunburnt mirth!
O for a beaker full of the warm South,   15
   Full of the true, the blushful Hippocrene,
      With beaded bubbles winking at the brim,
         And purple-stained mouth;
That I might drink and leave the world unseen,
   And with thee fade away into the forest dim: 20

GLOSSARY

o, for a . . . (l.11): I wish I had . . . *(poetic)*

draught of vintage (l.11): drink of good wine

delved (l.12): dug (in antiquity, a way of keeping wine cool)

Flora (l.13): Roman goddess of flowers

Provençal song (l.14): (Provençal, in southern France, was in the Middle Ages known for its love songs)

beaker (l.15): large drinking cup with wide mouth

Hippocrene (l.16): spring on Mount Helicon in Greece; the waters of inspiration

beaded bubbles (l.17): bubbles of liquid

winking at the brim (l.17): shining at the top (of the cup)

dim (l.20): in which there isn't much light

161

- i) Which is more accurate?
  - a) I wish I could disappear and go with you into the forest.
  - b) I wish I could drink enough to help me forget you.
- ii) In what way would the 'vintage' the narrator desires be unusual? Why does he want it?
- iii) Do you think he wishes to merge his identity with that of the nightingale?
- iv) How does the narrator's mood contrast with his mood in the previous stanza?

Stanza 3

GLOSSARY

fret (l.23): agitation

groan (l.24): make a deep complaining noise

palsy (l.25): uncontrollable trembling

spectre (l.26): like a ghost

lustrous (l.29): shining

pine at (l.30): have a strong desire for (which it is impossible to fulfil)

Fade far away, dissolve, and quite forget
   What thou among the leaves hast never known,
The weariness, the fever, and the fret
   Here, where men sit and hear each other groan;
Where palsy shakes a few, sad, last grey hairs,   25
   Where youth grows pale, and spectre-thin, and dies;
Where but to think is to be full of sorrow
     And leaden-eyed despairs;
Where Beauty cannot keep her lustrous eyes,
   Or new Love pine at them beyond to-morrow.   30

- i) Which is more accurate?
  - a) I wish I too could forget the sorrows and decay of the human world that you have never known.
  - b) There are too many old men who have neither beauty nor love.
- ii) Does the narrator wish to die?
- iii) What is the rhyme scheme of the poem?

Stanza 4

GLOSSARY

Bacchus . . . pards (l.32): (Bacchus, god of wine, was sometimes represented in a chariot drawn by leopards; the line means 'not by getting drunk')

viewless. . . . Poesy (l.33): invisible wings of poetic fancy

perplexes . . . retards (l.34): confuses and slows down

haply (l.36): perhaps (*archaic*)

Queen-Moon (l.36): Artemis (in Greek myth the goddess of the hunt; Diana in Roman myth)

Fays (l.37): fairies; attendants (*poetic*)

verdurous glooms (l.40): darkness made by green leaves

Away! away! for I will fly to thee,
   Not charioted by Bacchus and his pards,
But on the viewless wings of Poesy,
   Though the dull brain perplexes and retards:
Already with thee! tender is the night,   35
   And haply the Queen-Moon is on her throne,
     Cluster'd around by all her starry Fays;
       But here there is no light,
Save what from heaven is with the breezes blown
   Through verdurous glooms and winding mossy ways.   40

- i) Which is more accurate?
   - a) When I read poetry in the night I imagine you going through woods.
   - b) I will reach you through my poetic imagination rather than wine.
- ii) What is the narrator saying in the opening line ('Away! away!' ...)?
- iii) In which line does he 'join' the nightingale?
- iv) Where do you think 'here' is?

Stanza 5

I cannot see what flowers are at my feet,
   Nor what soft incense hangs upon the boughs,
But, in embalmed darkness, guess each sweet
   Wherewith the seasonable month endows
The grass, the thicket, and the fruit-tree wild;   45
   White hawthorn, and the pastoral eglantine;
   Fast-fading violets cover'd up in leaves;
      And mid-May's eldest child,
   The coming musk-rose, full of dewy wine,
      The murmurous haunt of flies on summer eves.   50

GLOSSARY

incense (l.42): pleasing smell

embalmed (l.43): perfumed; preserved after death

sweet (l.43): sweet things, flowers

thicket (l.45): thick growth of bushes and small trees

hawthorn (l.46): type of thorny shrub or tree with red, white or pink flowers

pastoral eglantine (l.46): thorny tree with red, white or pink

violets (l.47): small bluish-purple sweet-smelling flowers

musk-rose (l.49): rambling rose with large, sweet-smelling flowers

dewy wine (l.49): intoxicating juice

murmurous ... flies (l.50): the place where flies go, filled with their soft sounds

- i) Which is more accurate?
   - a) I cannot actually see the beauty of nature, only imagine it.
   - b) The darkness makes it impossible for me to see the beauty of nature; I can only hear the sound of flies.
- ii) What time of the year do you imagine the 'seasonable month' refers to?
- iii) How does the mood of this stanza differ from the previous one?
- iv) What does the phrase 'embalmed darkness' suggest?
- v) How does Keats help us 'hear' the sound of the flies?

Stanza 6

GLOSSARY

Darkling (l.51): in the dark; creature of the dark

easeful (l.52): free from pain

mused rhyme (l.53): meditated poem

requiem (l.60): song for the soul of a dead person

sod (l.60): piece of earth

Darkling I listen; and for many a time
   I have been half in love with easeful Death,
Call'd him soft names in many a mused rhyme,
   To take into the air my quiet breath;
Now more than ever seems it rich to die,   55
   To cease upon the midnight with no pain,
      While thou art pouring forth thy soul abroad
         In such an ecstasy!
   Still wouldst thou sing, and I have ears in vain –
      To thy high requiem become a sod.   60

- i) Which is more accurate?
  - a) Death is sweet but I cannot wish that you would die too.
  - b) It would be lovely to die now lost in your song.
- ii) Who are 'him' (l.53) and 'thou' (l.57)?
- iii) What does the world 'half' (l.52) tell us?
- iv) Explain the last line ('To thy high . . .'). Does the poet still desire death?

Stanza 7

Thou wast not born for death, immortal Bird!
  No hungry generations tread thee down;
The voice I hear this passing night was heard
  In ancient days by emperor and clown:
Perhaps the self-same song that found a path   65
  Through the sad heart of Ruth, when sick for home,
    She stood in tears amid the alien corn;
      The same that oft-times hath
Charm'd magic casements, opening on the foam
  Of perilous seas, in faery lands forlorn.   70

- i) Which is more accurate?
  - a) You'll never die because you are magical and don't really exist.
  - b) Your song is immortal and has charmed rich and poor throughout history.
- ii) What magical effects has the nightingale's voice had?

Stanza 8

Forlorn! the very word is like a bell
  To toll me back from thee to my sole self.
Adieu! the fancy cannot cheat so well
  As she is famed to do, deceiving elf,
Adieu! adieu! thy plaintive anthem fades   75
  Past the near meadows, over the still stream,
    Up the hill-side; and now 'tis buried deep
      In the next valley-glades:
Was it a vision, or a waking dream?
  Fled is that music: – do I wake or sleep?   80

- i) Which is more accurate?
  - a) Your sad song seems to be moving too quickly and I cannot keep up with it; perhaps it was really a dream.
  - b) The imagination is not so powerful; I am coming back to reality and losing the sound of your voice; was I dreaming?
- ii) What purpose does the word 'forlorn' have?
- iii) How does the narrator's mood change?
- iv) In one sentence can you summarise the theme of the whole poem?

John Keats In 1818 Keats' brother, like their mother, died of tuberculosis.

'In the spring of 1819 a nightingale had built her nest near my house. Keats felt a tranquil and continual joy in her song; and one morning he took his chair from the breakfast table to the grass plot under a plum tree, where he sat for two or three hours. When he came into the house, I perceived he had some scraps of paper in his hand ... On inquiry, I found those scraps ... contained his poetic feeling on the song of our nightingale.'
(Charles Brown, with whom Keats was then living in Hampstead, London. In the same house he had met Fanny Brawne, with whom he was in love until his death.)

Most of Keats's great works were written in 1819. In 1820 he too was very ill with tuberculosis. At the invitation of the poet Shelley (see pages 168–171), he took a ship to Italy, where he died the following year.

The Spanish Steps in Rome where Keats stayed shortly before his death

Keats's letters Read the following extracts from Keats's letters. What do they add to your understanding of the poem?

> **I am certain of nothing but of the holiness of the Heart's affections** 1
> **and the truth of Imagination – What the imagination seizes as Beauty**
> **must be truth – whether it existed before or not – for I have the same**
> **Idea of all our Passions as of Love they are all in their sublime,**
> **creative of essential Beauty –** 5

I scarcely remember counting upon any Happiness – I look not for it if it be not in the present hour – nothing startles me beyond the Moment. The setting sun will always set me to rights – or if a Sparrow come before my Window I take part in its existence and pick about the Gravel.

. . . the excellence of every Art is its intensity, capable of making all disagreeables evaporate, from their being in close relationship with Beauty and Truth.

. . . at once it struck me, what quality went to form a Man of Achievement especially in Literature and which Shakespeare posessed so enormously – I mean *Negative Capability*, that is when man is capable of being in uncertainties, Mysteries, doubts, without any irritable reaching after fact and reason –

(1817)

We hate poetry that has a palpable design upon us – and if we do not agree, seems to put its hand in its breeches pocket. Poetry should be great and unobtrusive, a thing which enters into one's soul, and does not startle it or amaze it with itself but with its subject.

. . . if Poetry comes not as naturally as the Leaves to a tree it had better not come at all.

As to the poetical Character itself, (I mean that sort of which, if I am any thing, I am a Member; that sort distinguished from the wordsworthian or egotistical sublime; which is a thing per se and stands alone) it is not itself – it has no self – it is every thing and nothing – It has no character – it enjoys light and shade; it lives in gusto, be it foul or fair, high or low, rich or poor, mean or elevated –

A Poet is the most unpoetical of any thing in existence; because he has no Identity – he is continually in for – and filling some other Body – The Sun, the Moon, the Sea and Men and Women who are creatures of impulse are poetical and have about them an unchangeable attribute – the poet has none; no identity – he is certainly the most unpoetical of all God's Creatures.

It is a wretched thing to confess; but is a very fact that not one word I ever utter can be taken for granted as an opinion growing out of my identical nature – how can it, when I have no nature? When I am in a room with People if I ever am free from speculating on creations of my own brain, then not myself goes home to myself: but the identity of every one in the room begins to press upon me that, I am in a very little time an[ni]hilated – not only among Men; it would be the same in a Nursery of children.

if it be not (l.7): if it isn't (archaic)

startles (l.7): surprises

Gravel (l.10): small stones used for making a path

disagreeables (l.12): unpleasant things

Negative capability (l.16): (see page 145)

irritable (l.18): bad-tempered

palpable design upon us (l.20): obvious intention to influence us

breeches (l.21): trousers

egotistical sublime (l.28): (see page 145)

per se (l.28): by itself (Latin)

in gusto (l.30): vigorously

be it (l.31): whether it is

attribute (l.36): natural quality

annihilated (l.44): put completely out of existence

in the interval (l.47): in the meantime

assay (l.47): try (archaic)

I am ambitious of doing the world some good: if I should be spared that may be the work of maturer years – in the interval I will assay to reach to as high a summit in Poetry as the nerve bestowed upon me will suffer.

(1818)   50

Call the world if you Please. 'The vale of Soul-making' Then you will find out the use of the world (I am speaking now in the highest terms for human nature admitting it to be immortal which I will here take for granted for the purpose of showing a thought which has struck me concerning it) I say *'Soul making'* Soul as distinguished   55 from an Intelligence – There may be intelligences or sparks of the divinity in millions – but they are not Souls till they acquire identities, till each one is personally itself. I[n]telligences are atoms of perception – they know and they see and they are pure, in short they are God – how then are Souls to be made? How then are these   60 sparks which are God to have identity given them – so as ever to possess a bliss peculiar to each ones individual existence? How, but by the medium of a world like this?

(1819)

There is no doubt that an english winter would put an end to me,   65 and do so in a lingering hateful manner, therefore I must either voyage or journey to Italy as a soldier marches up to a battery. My nerves at present are the worst part of me, yet they feel soothed when I think that come what extreme may, I shall not be destined to remain in one spot long enough to take a hatred of any four par-   70 ticular bed-posts.

(1820)

nerve ... suffer (l.48): strength I have been given will allow

Call ... making (l.51): (Keats prefers a notion of the world as a 'vale' – a valley – in which souls are shaped through sorrow, instead of the Christian notion of the world as a 'vale of tears' – a place of sorrow – from which God can rescue the sinner)

bliss (l.62): great happiness

lingering (l.66): slow to finish

battery (l.67): number of guns (lined up against him in battle)

soothed (l.68): calmed

John Keats – critical reputation

Keats has always been regarded as one of the principal Romantic poets and his reputation has grown steadily through all changes of fashion. For example, Alfred Tennyson (1809–1892) regarded him as the greatest poet of the nineteenth century and Matthew Arnold (1822–1888) commended his 'intellectual and spiritual passion' for beauty, noting that 'the thing to be seized is, that Keats had flint and iron in him, that he had character'.

However, the extent of his genius is disputed, Gerard Manley Hopkins (1844–1889) thought his mind had 'the distinctly masculine powers in abundance, his character the manly virtues' but in his poetry, when 'he gave himself up to dreaming and self-indulgence ... they were held in abeyance'. Arthur Symons (1865–1945), a leading critic in the Decadent movement, said, 'Keats, definite in every word, in every image, lacks intellectual structure'. The Cambridge critic F.R. Leavis (1895–1978) disagreed with this but went on to say about the Odes that 'It is as if ... the genius of the major poet were working in the material of the minor poet'. D.H. Lawrence (1885–1930), much influenced by Keats in his youth, in an essay on nightingales mocked the unreality of Keats's nightingale. T.S. Eliot (1888–1965) thought Keats's letters 'certainly the most notable and most important ever written by any English poet'.

5.7.3 Percy Bysshe Shelley (1792–1822)

Hazlitt's view of Shelley was that he was 'not a poet, but a sophist, a theorist, a controversial writer in verse'. J.S. Mill (1806–1873), the philosopher and economist, said Shelley 'had scarcely yet acquired the consecutiveness of thought necessary for a long poem', echoing those who dislike what they refer to as Shelley's vague and emotional rhetoric and self-absorption.

Nevertheless, Shelley has many admirers. Some are hero worshippers in love with the idea of his life: the intellectual revolutionary from an aristocratic background, the lover of the Golden Age of the Classical past, the campaigner against oppression and injustice who hoped for a better world, the young poet who was drowned in a storm on a return trip from visiting Byron at Livorno in Italy. Others praise his poetic skills. Interestingly, even critical opponents of Shelley note a less confident maturity and disenchantment in his last poem, 'The Triumph of Life', and regret his early death.

The Funeral of Shelley *by Fournier*

Extract 1 In his verse drama *Prometheus Unbound* (1819) Shelley expresses his revolutionary idealism. Prometheus, who in Greek myth stole fire from heaven and gave it to mankind, stands for all that is finest in humanity. Asia (or nature) is his bride:

GLOSSARY

cloven (l.1): split in two
Cars (l.2): chariots
steeds (l.2): horses (*poetic*)
trample (l.3): press down with their hooves (feet)
as fiends (l.5): as if evil spirits
clasped (l.10): seized
locks (l.10): hair

ASIA: **The rocks are cloven, and through the purple night**   1
I see Cars drawn by rainbow-winged steeds
Which trample the dim winds – in each there stands
A wild-eyed charioteer, urging their flight.
Some look behind, as fiends pursued them there   5
And yet I see no shapes but the keen stars:
Others with burning eyes lean forth, and drink
With eager lips the wind of their own speed,
As if the thing they loved fled on before,
And now – even now they clasped it; their bright locks   10
Stream like a comet's flashing hair: they all
Sweep onward. –

(from *Prometheus Unbound*)

- Try to put the adjective in the poem into categories, such as 'colour' and 'fire'. Do you think Shelley's use of adjectives is precise or vague? What is their effect?

Extract 2   'Ode to the West Wind' (1819), written in a wood by the River Arno, near Florence in Italy, is an invocation to a wind which is both the seasonal force of renewal in nature, suggesting hope and energy, and an autumnal destroyer. Not an ode in traditional form, the poem is composed in five stanzaic movements, each taking the form of a sonnet, with complex musical patterns of internal rhyme and run-on lines. This is the second movement describing a tempestuous Mediterranean sky:

GLOSSARY

Thou (l.1): (the West Wind)

commotion (l.1): confusion

tangled boughs (l.3): branches disordered and twisted (the higher clouds, formed by air and vapour drawn up from the ocean by the sun)

Angels (l.4): messengers

aëry surge (l.5): the rising and falling movement in the sky (*poetic*)

Maenad (l.7): female worshipper of Dionysus, the Greek god of wine and vegetation, usually represented with streaming hair; frenzied dancer

thou dirge (l.9): hymn of grief (the West Wind)

sepulchre (l.11): burial place

vaulted (l.12): covered over (as in a burial chamber)

congregated might (l.12): collected power

vapours (l.13): clouds (*poetic*)

Thou on whose stream, mid the steep sky's commotion,   1
Loose clouds like earth's decaying leaves are shed,
Shook from the tangled boughs of Heaven and Ocean,

Angels of rain and lightning: there are spread
On the blue surface of thine aëry surge,   5
Like the bright hair uplifted from the head

Of some fierce Maenad, even from the dim verge
Of the horizon to the zenith's height,
The locks of the approaching storm. Thou dirge

Of the dying year, to which this closing night   10
Will be the dome of a vast sepulchre,
Vaulted with all thy congregated might

Of vapours, from whose solid atmosphere
Black rain, and fire, and hail will burst: oh, hear!

(from 'Ode to the West Wind')

- i) What do the following refer to/suggest?
     'loose' (l.2); 'Angels' (l.4); 'blue surface' (l.5); 'zenith's height' (l.8); 'sepulchre' (l.11); 'congregated' (l.12)
  ii) Shelley's imagery in this poem has sometimes been judged to be imprecise. Do you agree?

Extract 3   In 'To a Skylark' (1820) the bird that sings only in flight, usually when too high to be visible, is made the emblem of a non-material spirit of pure unintellectual joy. This is the opening:

> Hail to thee, blithe Spirit! 1
>   Bird thou never wert,
> That from Heaven, or near it,
>   Pourest thy full heart
> In profuse strains of unpremeditated art, 5
>
> Higher still and higher
>   From the earth thou springest
> Like a cloud of fire;
>   The blue deep thou wingest,
>
> In the golden lightning 10
>   Of the sunken sun,
> O'er which clouds are bright'ning,
>   Thou dost float and run;
> Like an unbodied joy whose race is just begun.
>
> (from 'To a Skylark')

- i) What is Shelley saying in the line 'Bird thou never wert' (l.2)?
- ii) What is the image 'Like a cloud of fire' (l.8) meant to suggest?
- iii) Refer back to Keats's 'Ode to a Nightingale' (page 161). Which poet most seems to identify with the bird he is writing about?

Extract 4   *Adonais* (1821), in fifty-five Spenserian stanzas, mourns the death of Keats. It is based on *The Lament for Adonis* by Bion (first century BC). Adonis was a beautiful youth killed by a wild boar. This is stanza forty-nine. Shelley is talking to the reader:

> Go thou to Rome, – at once the Paradise, 1
> The grave, the city, and the wilderness;
> And where its wrecks like shattered mountains rise,
> And flowering weeds, and fragrant copses dress
> The bones of Desolation's nakedness 5
> Pass, till the spirit of the spot shall lead
> Thy footsteps to a slope of green access
> Where, like an infant's smile, over the dead
> A light of laughing flowers along the grass is spread . . .
>
> (from *Adonais*)

- Find nouns/noun phrases which suggest the following: *death, decay, innocence*

Extract 5   *A Defence of Poetry* (1821) was written in Pisa (in Italy) in answer to Shelley's friend Thomas Love Peacock (1785–1866), who argued, humorously, that poetry was an obsolete art. Against a background of classical and European literature, Shelley discusses the nature of poetic thought and inspiration, the problems of translation, the value of erotic writing, the connections between poetry and politics and the essentially moral nature of the imagination. Here is an extract:

Poetry is indeed something divine. It is at once the centre and circumference of knowledge; it is that which comprehends all science, and that to which all science must be referred. It is at the same time the root and blossom of all other systems of thought; it is that from which all spring, and that which adorns all; and that which, if blighted, denies the fruit and the seed, and withholds from the barren world the nourishment and the succession of the scions of the tree of life. It is the perfect and consummate surface and bloom of all things: it is as the odour and the colour of the rose to the texture of the elements which compose it, as the form and splendour of unfaded beauty to the secrets of anatomy and corruption. What were virtue, love, patriotism, friendship – what were the scenery of this beautiful universe which we inhabit; what were our consolations on this side of the grave – and what were our aspirations beyond it, if poetry did not ascend to bring light and fire from those eternal regions where the owl-winged faculty of calculation dare not ever soar? Poetry is not like reasoning, a power to be exerted according to the determination of the will. A man cannot say, 'I will compose poetry.' The greatest poet even cannot say it; for the mind in creation is as a fading coal, which some invisible influence, like an inconstant wind, awakens to transitory brightness; this power arises from within, like the colour of a flower which fades and changes as it is developed, and the conscious portions of our natures are unprophetic either of its approach or its departure. Could this influence be durable in its original purity and force, it is impossible to predict the greatness of the results; but when composition begins, inspiration is already on the decline, and the most glorious poetry that has ever been communicated to the world is probably a feeble shadow of the original conceptions of the poet. I appeal to the greatest poets of the present day, whether it is not an error to assert that the finest passages of poetry are produced by labour and study!

(from *A Defence of Poetry*)

GLOSSARY

circumference (l.1–2): outside circle

comprehends (l.2): includes

blighted (l.6): diseased

withholds (l.6): keeps back

barren (l.7): infertile

scions (l.7): living shoots

consummate (l.8): complete

owl-winged (l.16): careful and heavy

are unprophetic ... of (l.24): don't warn us of

● i) Which of the following does Shelley seem to favour? *spontaneity, science, lack of discipline, reason, will-power, inspiration.*
ii) Try to paraphrase the sentence beginning 'It is the perfect ...' (l.8). Is it difficult? If so, why?
iii) In what sense is the 'mind in creation' 'a fading coal'?
iv) Find an example of: simile, metaphor, repetition, rhetorical question (a question used for emphasis rather than enquiry).

5.7.4
George Gordon,
Lord Byron (1788–1824)

Lord Byron was a rebellious aristocrat who mocked the early Romantics such as Wordsworth and Coleridge and preferred the classicism of Pope and the Augustan virtues of Crabbe. While his own poetic style is often loose, vivid and full of vigour, he established himself as an influential Romantic poet as much for his dramatic personality and eventful life as for his verse.

Warm-up The following words have all been used to describe Lord Byron. Select at least three. Can each be used to describe all of the following: a) a person's behaviour, b) character, c) mood and d) style of writing?

cynical   melancholic   genial   theatrical   bitter   impulsive
moody   derisive   humorous   racy   ironic   cheerful
spontaneous   sardonic   defiant   witty   adventurous   observant
shrewd   indignant   satirical

Do your choices describe you in any way?

Match these topics with the extracts below:
a) The funeral of George III   b) Flirtatiousness   c) Mutability   d) Money
e) The sea's immortality

Extract 1

GLOSSARY *fleets (l.2)*: numbers of ships under one command *ravage (l.6)*: destruction *save (l.6)*: except *unknelled (l.9)*: without a proper funeral	... Roll on, thou deep and dark blue Ocean – roll! 1 Ten thousand fleets sweep over thee in vain; Man marks the earth with ruin – his control Stops with the shore; – upon the watery plain The wrecks are all thy deed, nor doth remain 5 A shadow of man's ravage, save his own, When, for a moment, like a drop of rain, He sinks into thy depths with bubbling groan – Without a grave – unknelled, uncoffined, and unknown, (from *Childe Harold*) 10

Extract 2

GLOSSARY *swell (l.2)*: make the crowd (at the 'show') bigger *pall (l.5)*: cloth which covers the coffin	... Of all 1 The fools who flocked to swell or see the show, Who cared about the corpse? The funeral Made the attraction, and the black the woe. There throbbed not there a thought which pierced the pall; 5 And when the gorgeous coffin was laid low, It seemed the mockery of hell to fold The rottenness of eighty years in gold. (from *The Vision of Judgement*)

Extract 3

GLOSSARY *Young (l.1)*: Edward Young (1683–1765) who published his last poem 'Resignation' when he was more than eighty *ere (l.5)*: before (*poetic*) *Orators (l.7)*: public speakers *Dandies (l.8)*: men with exaggerated dress and manners	'Where is the world?' cries Young, 'at *eighty*' – 'Where 1 The World in which a man was born?' Alas! Where is the world of *eight* years past? '*T was there* – I look for it – 't is gone, a globe of glass! Cracked, shivered, vanished, scarcely gazed on, ere 5 A silent change dissolves the glittering mass. Statesmen, Chiefs, Orators, Queens, Patriots, Kings, And Dandies – all are gone on the Wind's wings. (from *Don Juan*)

Extract 4

> Why call the miser miserable? as   1
>   I said before: the frugal life is his,
> Which in a saint or cynic ever was
>   The theme of praise: a hermit would not miss
> Canonization for the self-same cause,   5
>   And wherefore blame gaunt Wealth's austerities?
> Because, you'll say, nought calls for such a trial; –
> Then there's more merit in his self-denial.

(from *Don Juan*)

Extract 5

> Such is your cold coquette, who can't say 'No',   1
>   And won't say 'Yes', and keeps you on and off-ing
> On a lee-shore, till it begins to blow –
>   Then sees your heart wrecked, with an inward scoffing.
> This works a world of sentimental woe,   5
>   And sends new Werters yearly to their coffin;
> But yet is merely innocent flirtation,
> Not quite adultery, but adulteration.

(from *Don Juan*)

- What is the object of Byron's satire in each of these extracts? How would you describe Byron's writing?

What do the following add to your picture of Byron?

a) 'I rattle on exactly as I'd talk
    With anybody in a ride a walk'
    (*Don Juan*, Canto XV 19, in which Byron describes his style of writing)

b)

GLOSSARY

disputatious (l.3): angrily argumentative

unintelligible (l.3): incomprehensible

altogethery (l.3): everybody spoke at the same time

inarticulate (l.3): full of unclear expression

stumbling (l.5): walking unsteadily

corkscrew (l.7): spiral

fermented liquors (l.8): (such as wine)

accommodate themselves (l.9): fit

Yesterday, I dined out with a large-ish party . . . Like other parties of 1
the kind, it was first silent, then talky, then argumentative, then
disputatious, then unintelligible, then altogethery, then inarticu-
late, and then drunk. When we had reached the last step of this
glorious ladder, it was difficult to get down again without stum- 5
bling; and, to crown all, Kinnaird and I had to conduct Sheridan
down a damned corkscrew staircase, which had certainly been con-
structed before the discovery of fermented liquors, and to which no
legs, however crooked, could possibly accommodate themselves.

(From a letter dated 31 October 1815, describing a party at which, as Byron says, 'all was hiccup and happiness for the last hour or so')

c) 'at *heart* you are the most melancholy of mankind, and often when apparantly gayest'.

(*Detached Thoughts* 73: what Byron's wife said about him)

d) 'The fascination of Byron's personality starts with his personal good looks and charm; it is also bound up with the mysterious scandals surrounding his broken marriage and exile (1816), his alleged love for his half-sister, his latest love affairs, and his close association with the liberation movements of Italy and then of Greece, where he died in 1824. Above all, it arises from his pride, independence of spirit, courage, and vigorous wit . . .'

(Christopher Gillie in the *Longman Companion to English Literature*, Longman 1972)

5.8 Chronology

Events in French history made a great impact on the rest of Europe during this period. Can you match the following events with the dates on the left? One has been done for you.

1789   Napoleon made emperor of France
1793   Battle of Trafalgar: Nelson dies in victory against French and Spanish fleets
1804   Storming of Bastille in Paris begins the French Revolution
1805   Napoleon deposed and banished to Elba
1814   Louis XVI executed
1815   Battle of Waterloo and defeat of Napoleon

1760–1820: The reign of George III. The face of England was changed: mechanisation was achieved by the exploitation of coal, iron and steam; roads were vastly improved and canals were constructed. The population increased from seven to about fourteen million and many agricultural areas were enclosed and modernised. George III, insane for the last ten years of his life, was succeeded by George IV (1820–1830), who disgusted the nation by his immoral conduct with women, and William IV (1830–1837), whose reign was too short to redeem the impression left by his brother.

Industrialisation in the early nineteenth century

Other important events:

1821–1832: Greek Wars of Independence. After several hundred years of Ottoman rule Greece successfully established a constitutional monarchy.
1832: A Reform Act in Britain rationalised the electoral system (to include the redistribution of Members of Parliament so as to correspond to the great centres of population) and made the first step towards real democracy.
1833: Slavery was finally abolished in the British colonies, the abolition movement having begun in the eighteenth century for economic and humanitarian reasons.

5.9 Activities

Critical writing Discuss and compare the Romantic poets. Make notes and write a composition to include quotations.

Creative writing Imagine you are given the opportunity to meet one of the Romantic poets. Write a diary entry the night before your meeting expressing your hopes, your worries and the questions you want to ask.

Quiz Individually, write ten questions about texts (not writers) in this Unit. Ask and answer.

UNIT 6

The Victorian age

6.1 The early and middle period (1837–1870)

In 1846, with the repeal of the Corn Laws, which had protected home-grown corn from competition from abroad, it was officially acknowledged that industrial interests in Britain were now more important than traditional agriculture. The Industrial Revolution was complete and the Great Exhibition in London in 1851 was its high point. Britain had become the 'workshop of the world'.

At the same time there was great urban poverty and social injustice. Between 1837 and 1848 the Chartist Movement signalled the emergence of the working-class movement as a political force. The Chartist Movement was so called because of its Charter of six points, which included the right of all males to vote.

Between 1851 and 1870 discontent subsided and Britain was at the height of her wealth and influence.

The Great Exhibition of 1851

6.2 Victorian literary themes: Childhood

The use of child labour in the coal mines and factories led to the Mines Act (1842), forbidding children of under ten from going underground, and the Factory Act (1847), in which hours of work per day were restricted to ten. During the Victorian age education became universal in England.

Before the Romantic poets, childhood had not been an important literary theme in English literature. To Blake, though, writing less than thirty years after the publication of Rousseau's novel *Emile* (1762), which had advocated the education of children through their natural impulses and interests, the child represented 'innocence'. From then on and throughout the nineteenth century the child was a symbol of the artist's dissatisfaction with an unfeeling, rapidly-changing society. However, as more books were written to please children, so childhood tended to become a symbol of nostalgic retreat for adults unwilling to grow up.

At its best, though, the Victorian artist's interest in children served as an attempt to provide a fundamental criticism of contemporary life. It was accepted that children were not merely the imperfect adults they were regarded as in previous centuries. They had their own kinds of experience and values which could be dramatised in fiction.

6.2.1 Charles Dickens (1812–1870) Charles Dickens began his career as a journalist. In his novels, which were published serially in weekly and monthly periodicals, he attacks the injustice of many social systems (such as education and the law) and the inequalities between the rich and the poor. His titles include *Oliver Twist* (1837–1839), *David Copperfield* (1849–1850) and *Bleak House* (1852–1853).

Warm-up The following extracts are from the early chapters of Dickens's *Great Expectations* (1861). Do you know what the novel is about? Can you guess from the title?

Extract 1 Pip, a young boy and the narrator of the story, has been brought up by his sister and brother-in-law, Joe Gargery, a humble blacksmith. The scene is the marshland between the River Thames and the River Medway in the southeast of England.

Still from the film Great Expectations *by courtesy of The Rank Organisation Plc*

177

GLOSSARY

flaxen (l.10): pale yellow
Hercules (l.14): mythical
  Greek hero famed for
  his strength

My sister, Mrs Joe Gargery, was more than twenty years older than I, and had established a great reputation with herself and the neighbours because she had brought me up 'by hand'. Having at that time to find out for myself what the expression meant, and knowing her to have a hard and heavy hand, and to be much in the habit of laying it upon her husband as well as upon me, I supposed that Joe Gargery and I were both brought up by hand.

She was not a good-looking woman, my sister; and I had a general impression that she must have made Joe Gargery marry her by hand. Joe was a fair man, with curls of flaxen hair on each side of his smooth face, and with eyes of such a very undecided blue that they seemed to have somehow got mixed with their own whites. He was a mild, good-natured, sweet-tempered, easy-going, foolish, dear fellow – a sort of Hercules in strength, and also in weakness.

- Which of these words apply to Joe Gargery, which to Mrs Gargery?
  meek, simple-minded, domineering.
  What are Pip's feelings towards his sister and brother-in-law?

Extract 2 It is Christmas Eve and Pip has been frightened by an escaped convict into stealing some food for him from the Gargery household. At tea, Pip hides his bread and butter down his trousers. Joe thinks he has eaten it quickly.

GLOSSARY

consternation (l.1): great
  shock and worry
on the threshold of (l.1):
  just as he was about
  to
remonstrance (l.7): protest
chawed (l.8): chewed
trifle on (l.11): small bit of
aghast (l.12): shocked
elth (l.12): health
stuck pig (l.19): (old
  expression 'to stare like
  a stuck pig' – a pig
  with its throat cut)

The wonder and consternation with which Joe stopped on the threshold of his bite and stared at me, were too evident to escape my sister's observation.

'What's the matter now?' said she, smartly, as she put down her cup.

'I say, you know!' muttered Joe, shaking his head at me in a very serious remonstrance. 'Pip, old chap! You'll do yourself a mischief. It'll stick somewhere. You can't have chawed it, Pip.'

'What's the matter *now*?' repeated my sister, more sharply than before.

'If you can cough any trifle on it up, Pip, I'd recommend you to do it,' said Joe, all aghast. 'Manners is manners, but still your elth's your elth.'

By this time my sister was quite desperate, so she pounced on Joe, and, taking him by the two whiskers, knocked his head for a little while against the wall behind him: while I sat in the corner, looking guiltily on.

'Now, perhaps you'll mention what's the matter,' said my sister, out of breath, 'you staring great stuck pig.'

Joe looked at her in a helpless way; then took a helpless bite, and looked at me again.

'You know, Pip,' said Joe, solemnly, with his last bite in his cheek, and speaking in a confidential voice, as if we two were quite alone, 'you and me is always friends, and I'd be the last to tell upon you, any time. But such a –' he moved his chair, and looked about the floor between us, and then again at me – 'such a most uncommon bolt as that!'

'Been bolting his food, has he?' cried my sister.

'You know, old chap,' said Joe, looking at me, and not at Mrs Joe, with his bite still in his cheek, 'I Bolted, myself, when I was your age – frequent – and as a boy I've been among a many Bolters; but I never see your bolting equal yet, Pip, and it's a mercy you ain't Bolted dead.'   30

My sister made a dive at me, and fished me up by the hair: saying nothing more than the awful words, 'You come along and be dosed.'   35

Some medical beast had revived Tar-water in those days as a fine medicine, and Mrs Joe always kept a supply of it in the cupboard; having a belief in its virtues correspondent to its nastiness. At the best of times, so much of this elixir was administered to me as a choice restorative, that I was conscious of going about, smelling like a new fence. On this particular evening, the urgency of my case demanded a pint of this mixture, which was poured down my throat, for my greater comfort, while Mrs Joe held my head under her arm, as a boot would be held in a boot-jack. Joe got off with half a pint.   40 45

bolting (l.28): act of eating quickly

dosed (l.35): given your medicine

Tar-water (l.36): mixture of water and tar (a black substance obtained from coal, used to preserve wood)

elixir (l.39): remedy

choice restorative (l.40): high-quality medicine

boot-jack (l.44): device used for pulling off boots

- i) Do you find the passage funny? Which parts?
- ii) Divide the following nouns into those which, in context, have a positive connotation and those which have a negative connotation: *affection, insult, helpfulness, protection, tyranny, domination.* Make them into adjectives. Which describe Joe and which describe Mrs Joe? Support your point of view with examples from the text.
- iii) Find an example of: a) hyperbole used for comic effect; b) simile used for comic effect; c) Dickens enjoying the sound of a word.

Extract 3   Early next morning Pip sets off from home having stolen some bread and cheese, a pork pie and some brandy, which he has taken from a bottle in the kitchen cupboard and replaced with the equivalent amount of water from a jug.

- What do you imagine his feelings are?

It was a rimy morning, and very damp. I had seen the damp lying on the outside of my little window, as if some goblin had been crying there all night, and using the window for a pocket-handkerchief. Now I saw the damp lying on the bare hedges and spare grass, like a coarser sort of spiders' webs; hanging itself from twig to twig and blade to blade. On every rail and gate, wet lay clammy, and the marsh-mist was so thick, that the wooden finger on the post directing people to our village – a direction which they never accepted, for they never came there – was invisible to me until I was quite close under it. Then, as I looked up at it, while it dripped, it seemed to my oppressed conscience like a phantom devoting me to the Hulks. The mist was heavier yet when I got out upon the marshes, so that instead of my running at everything, everything seemed to run at me. This was very disagreeable to a guilty mind. The gates   1 5 10

GLOSSARY

rimy (l.1): frosty

goblin (l.2): evil ugly-looking fairy

spare (l.4): small amount of

clammy (l.6): cold and sticky

Hulks (l.12): large ships used as prisons

and dykes and banks came bursting at me through the mist, as if   15
they cried as plainly as could be, 'A boy with Somebody-else's
pork pie! Stop him!' The cattle came upon me with like suddenness,
staring out of their eyes, and steaming out of their nostrils, 'Holloa,
young thief!' One black ox, with a white cravat on – who even had
to my awakened conscience something of a clerical air – fixed me so   20
obstinately with his eyes, and moved his blunt head round in such
an accusatory manner as I moved round, that I blubbered out to
him, 'I couldn't help it, sir! It wasn't for myself I took it!' Upon
which he put down his head, blew a cloud of smoke out of his
nose, and vanished with a kick-up of his hindlegs and a flourish of   25
his tail.

dykes (l.15): ditches
cravat (l.19): neck scarf
blubbered (l.22): cried
  loudly
hindlegs (l.25): back legs

- i) How are we made aware of Pip's feelings?
  ii) Find an example of personification. What effect does it have?

Extract 4   Pip gives the convict the food and returns home. For Christmas lunch the
Gargery household is joined by Mr Wopsle, a church clerk, Mr Hubble,
a wheelwright (a person who makes wooden carts), Mrs Hubble and
Uncle Pumblechook, Joe's uncle.

GLOSSARY

pantry (l.2): small room
  for keeping food
regaled with (l.5): given
scaly tips (l.6): hard
  bits of skin at the end
drumsticks (l.6): lower
  part of legs of a cooked
  bird such as a chicken
smartingly touched up (l.13):
  stung
goads (l.13): pricks

Among this good company I should have felt myself, even if I hadn't   1
robbed the pantry, in a false position. Not because I was squeezed
in at an acute angle of the table-cloth, with the table in my chest,
and the Pumblechookian elbow in my eye, nor because I was not
allowed to speak (I didn't want to speak), nor because I was regaled   5
with the scaly tips of the drumsticks of the fowls, and with those
obscure corners of pork of which the pig, when living, had had the
least reason to be vain. No; I should not have minded that if they
would only have left me alone. But they wouldn't leave me alone.
They seemed to think the opportunity lost, if they failed to point   10
the conversation at me, every now and then, and stick the point
into me. I might have been an unfortunate little bull in a Spanish
arena, I got so smartingly touched up by these moral goads.

- i) Which of the following alternatives is wrong? He was *given the worst food/
  ignored/forced to be silent/taunted*.
  ii) How does Dickens convey the gap between Pip and the adults?

Extract 5   Mrs Hubble asks Pip's sister if he has been any trouble to her.

- Can you guess what her reaction is?

'Trouble?' echoed my sister, 'trouble?' And then entered on a fear-   1
ful catalogue of all the illnesses I had been guilty of and all the acts
of sleeplessness I had committed, and all the high places I had
tumbled from, and all the low places I had tumbled into, and all
the injuries I had done myself, and all the times she had wished me   5
in my grave and I had contumaciously refused to go there.
    I think the Romans must have aggravated one another very
much, with their noses. Perhaps, they became the restless people

180

they were, in consequence. Anyhow, Mr Wopsle's Roman nose so aggravated me, during the recital of my misdemeanours, that I should have liked to pull it until he howled. But, all I had endured up to this time, was nothing in comparison with the awful feelings that took possession of me when the pause was broken which ensued upon my sister's recital, and in which pause everybody had looked at me (as I felt painfully conscious) with indignation and abhorrence. . . . 10

'Have a little brandy, uncle,' said my sister.

O Heaven, it had come at last! He would find it was weak, he would say it was weak, and I was lost! I held tight to the leg of the table, under the cloth, with both hands, and awaited my fate. 20

My sister went for the stone bottle, came back with the stone bottle, and poured his brandy out: no one else taking any. The wretched man trifled with his glass – took it up, looked at it through the light, put it down – prolonged my misery. All this time Mrs Joe and Joe were briskly clearing the table for the pie and pudding. 25

I couldn't keep my eyes off him. Always holding tight by the leg of the table with my hands and feet, I saw the miserable creature finger his glass playfully, take it up, smile, throw his head back, and drink the brandy off. Instantly afterwards, the company were seized with unspeakable consternation, owing to his springing to 30 his feet, turning round several times in an appalling spasmodic whooping-cough dance, and rushing out at the door; he then became visible through the window, violently plunging and expectorating, making the most hideous faces, and apparently out of his mind. 35

I held on tight, while Mrs Joe and Joe ran to him. I didn't know how I had done it, but I had no doubt I had murdered him somehow. In my dreadful situation, it was a relief when he was brought back, and surveying the company all round as if *they* had disagreed with him, sank down into his chair with the one significant gasp, 40 'Tar!'

(from *Great Expectations*)

GLOSSARY

contumaciously (l.6): stubbornly and disobediently

recital (l.10): detailed account

misdemeanours (l.10): wrongdoings

ensued upon (l.14): immediately followed

abhorrence (l.16): hatred and disgust

trifled (l.23): played idly

consternation (l.30): fear and confusion

spasmodic (l.31): occasionally violent

whooping-cough (l.32): long noisy coughing with desperate breathing in of air

expectorating (l.33): coughing out phlegm

* i) What had Pip done by mistake?
  ii) What do the following phrases refer to: 'all the acts of sleeplessness I had committed' (l.2) and 'it had come at last' (l.18)?
  iii) Why did the adults look at Pip 'with indignation and abhorrence' (l.15)?

Appreciation   Answer at least one of the following:

  i) How is Pip shown in relation to other people? How does Dickens keep us sympathetic to him?
  ii) Comment on Dickens's descriptions of places and people's physical characteristics. What is their role?
  iii) How does Dickens make us laugh?

Charles Dickens   Dickens's father was a government official who liked to live prosperously. His sudden poverty and imprisonment for debt was a great shock to the boy Dickens. Many of the novels contain prison themes and describe the

misery of childhood in the urban, industrial environment of early Victorian England.

The novels also reflect the profound social changes which took place throughout the nineteenth century as new manufacturing towns sprang up around the coal mines and the north of England. Instead of the old village and family stability, we see a new industrialism which brought with it widespread corruption and a lack of concern for the emotional and imaginative lives of individuals, particularly children.

Children working in a factory in the 1840s

Dickens is still the most popular of English novelists. He has an astonishing range of characters of all classes and is a master of many styles of language – notably poetic prose and comic dialogue. His narrative inventiveness is unique and his graphic, tragi-comic vision of the world (which sometimes slips into sentimentality) has great appeal. As a man he was reputed to be full of charm, enthusiasm and exuberance. He had a large family with his wife Catherine, whom he married in 1836 but was separated from in 1858. In 1867–1868 he visited the USA for a second time, for a strenuous reading tour. He died suddenly in 1870, leaving unfinished his last novel *The Mystery of Edwin Drood*. (For Dickens see also Supplement 6)

6.2.2
Queen Victoria
(1819–1901)

Queen Victoria became queen at only seventeen. The following year, on 12 April 1838, Thomas Carlyle, the Scottish essayist, wrote about her in a letter to his mother:

GLOSSARY

troopers (l.3): soldiers on horseback

Windsor (l.3): Windsor Castle, a royal residence outside London

Yesterday, going through one of the Parks, I saw the poor little Queen. She was in an open carriage, preceded by three or four swift red-coated troopers; all off for Windsor just as I happened to pass. Another carriage or carriages followed with maids-of-honour, etc.: the whole drove very fast. It seemed to me the poor little Queen was a bit modest, nice sonsy little lassie; blue eyes, light

1

5

maids-of-honour (l.4): ladies who look after the queen

sonsy (l.6): sweet (*Scottish*)

liveryman (l.9): servant who looks after the horses

bairn (l.10): child (*Scottish*)

Parson (l.11): priest

Greet (l.11): weep

brethren (l.11): brothers

yea verily (l.11): truly

fashion (l.12): way

hair, fine white skin; of extremely small stature: she looked timid, anxious, almost frightened; for the people looked at her in perfect silence; one old liveryman alone touched his hat to her: I was heartily sorry for the poor bairn, – tho' perhaps she might have said as Parson Swan did, '*Greet* not for me brethren; for verily, yea verily, I greet not for mysel'.' It is a strange thing to look at the fashion of this world! 10

Queen Victoria

6.3 Work

In 1842, out of a population of 18 million, 1.5 million were unemployed. Factories were closed, wages were reduced and riots suggested that revolution might be close.

6.3.1 Thomas Carlyle (1795–1881)

'Men are grown mechanical in heart and head,' wrote the historian Thomas Carlyle, deploring the materialism, spiritual mediocrity and moral weakness of his time. Carlyle, the son of a humble Scottish stonemason and dissenting Presbyterian, had no faith in rule by democracy or in the worth of the landed aristocracy. In *Past and Present* (1843), he contrasts the life and vigour of a medieval abbot with contemporary values and calls for heroic leadership.

- The following statements represent the opposite of Carlyle's argument. For each one, select a sentence in the passage which makes Carlyle's view clear.

a) We will always worship money
b) Risking money for high profit is preferable to work.
c) Workers should be kept down.

But it is my firm conviction that the 'Hell of England' will *cease* to be that of 'not making money'; that we shall get a nobler Hell and a nobler Heaven! I anticipate light *in* the Human Chaos, glimmering, shining more and more; under manifold true signals from without That light shall shine. Our deity no longer being Mammon, – O Heavens, each man will then say to himself: 'Why such deadly haste to make money? I shall not go to Hell, even if I do not make money! There is another Hell, I am told!' Competition, at railway-speed, in all branches of commerce and work will then abate: – good felt-hats for the head, in every sense, instead of seven-feet lath-and-plaster hats on wheels, will then be discoverable! Bubble-periods, with their panics and commercial crises, will again become infrequent; steady modest industry will take the place of gambling speculation. To be a noble Master, among noble Workers, will again be the first ambition with some few; to be a rich Master only the second. . . .

Awake, ye noble Workers, warriors in the one true war: all this must be remedied. It is you who are already half-alive, whom I will welcome into life; whom I will conjure in God's name to shake off your enchanted sleep, and live wholly! Cease to count scalps, gold-purses; not in these lies your or our salvation. Even these, if you count only these, will not be left. Let bucaniering be put far from you; alter, speedily abrogate all laws of the bucaniers, if you would gain any victory that shall endure. Let God's justice, let pity, nobleness and manly valour, with more gold-purses or with fewer, testify themselves in this your brief Life-transit to all the Eternities, the Gods and Silences. It is to you I call; for ye are not dead, ye are already half-alive: there is in you a sleepless dauntless energy, the prime-master of all nobleness in man. Honour to you in your kind. It is to you I call: ye know at least this, That the mandate of God to His creature man is: Work! The future Epic of the World rests not with those that are near dead, but with those that are alive, and those that are coming into life.

(from *Past and Present*)

Appreciation

i) Discuss the importance of the following: a) capital letters for such phrases as 'Human Chaos'; b) the 'will' form of the verb; c) the imperative ('Awake', 'Cease'); d) 'ye', the archaic form of 'you'; e) the repetition of the word 'noble'

ii) Can you see any influence of Puritanism or Romanticism in Carlyle's writing?

iii) Do you have any sympathy with his views?

Thomas Carlyle

In his own day, Carlyle was thought of as a wise man and prophet. Although he is nowadays out of fashion – partly because of his eccentric, rather dated style – many of his views are echoed in writers then and since, from the educationist and critic Matthew Arnold (1822–1888) to the novelist D.H. Lawrence (1885–1930). As a philosopher, he supported the anti-scientific emotional, intuitive school of thought, characteristic of German thinkers such as Goethe, rather than the cold logic of the French school.

6.4 Death and grief

● The Victorian age was fond of poems about death. Do you think our attitude to death is different from what it used to be?

6.4.1 Alfred Tennyson (1809–1892)

Like Carlyle, Alfred Tennyson was much disturbed by social and industrial change. Fourth out of twelve children of a Lincolnshire clergyman, he was extremely uneasy about the attacks on traditional religious belief by scientists and evolutionists. In 1833, his close friend at Cambridge University, the brilliant Arthur Henry Hallam, died in Vienna, aged twenty-two, and within a few weeks Tennyson had begun to write the long elegy *In Memoriam A. H. H.* The one hundred and thirty sections of varying length were assembled slowly and published in 1850, eight years after Tennyson had first achieved fame as a poet.

Alfred Lord Tennyson

Extract 1   (Section 2)

GLOSSARY

Yew (l.1): the dark ever-green tree, with small red berries, growing near the clock tower and church where Hallam was to be buried; the yew has been associated with death and funerals since antiquity

graspest (l.1): takes a firm hold of

firstling (l.6): first born

branding (l.11): burning

avail (l.11): are of any use

Old Yew, which graspest at the stones   1
  That name the under-lying dead,
  Thy fibres net the dreamless head,
Thy roots are wrapt about the bones.

The seasons bring the flower again,   5
  And bring the firstling to the flock;
  And in the dusk of thee, the clock
Beats out the little lives of men.

O not for thee the glow, the bloom,
  Who changest not in any gale,   10
  Nor branding summer suns avail
To touch thy thousand years of gloom:

sullen *(l.13)*: dark and
unpleasant
incorporate *(l.16)*: united
(as one body)

> And gazing on thee, sullen tree,
>   Sick for thy stubborn hardihood,
>   I seem to fail from out my blood   15
> And grow incorporate into thee.

- i) What do you imagine the following refer to? 'the stones' (l.1), 'Thy fibres'
  (l.3), 'the bones' (l.4), 'the flock' (l.6), 'dusk of thee' (l.7), 'thy thousand years'
  (l.12), 'thy stubborn hardihood' (l.14).
  ii) Why is the head 'dreamless' (l.3)?
  iii) What is Tennyson saying in the lines 'I seem . . . into thee' (l.15–16)?
  iv) How would you describe his mood?

Extract 2   (Section 7)

> Dark house, by which once more I stand   1
>   Here in the long unlovely street,
>   Doors, where my heart was used to beat
> So quickly, waiting for a hand,
>
> A hand that can be clasp'd no more –   5
>   Behold me, for I cannot sleep,
>   And like a guilty thing I creep
> At earliest morning to the door.
>
> He is not here; but far away
>   The noise of life begins again,   10
>   And ghastly thro' the drizzling rain
> On the bald street breaks the blank day.

GLOSSARY

Dark house *(l.1)*: (the
house on Wimpole
Street, in London,
where Hallam had
lived)
ghastly *(l.11)*: pale;
unpleasant
bald *(l.12)*: without
anything attractive in it
blank *(l.12)*: empty

- i) Describe the scene in your own words.
  ii) How many beats are there in each line? What is the rhyme scheme? What is
  the effect of: a) the stress of 'Doors' at the beginning of l.3; b) the alliteration
  in the last line?

Extract 3   (Part of section 50, addressed to his dead friend)
In this extract, loneliness stimulates thoughts of immortality after death:

GLOSSARY

tingle *(l.3)*: have a
stinging feeling in the
skin
rack'd *(l.6)*: tortured
pangs *(l.6)*: sharp, sudden
feelings of pain
Fury *(l.8)*: goddess in
Greek mythology who
punished crimes
slinging *(l.8)*: throwing
carelessly

> Be near me when my light is low,   1
>   When the blood creeps, and the nerves prick
>   And tingle; and the heart is sick,
> And all the wheels of Being slow.
>
> Be near me when the sensuous frame   5
>   Is rack'd with pangs that conquer trust;
>   And Time, a maniac scattering dust,
> And Life, a Fury slinging flame.
> . . .

Be near me when I fade away,　　　　　10
　　To point the term of human strife,
　　And on the low dark verge of life

term (l.10): end

The twilight of eternal day.

● i) Underline the metaphors for old age. Circle the expressions concerning death.
　 ii) What is the effect of the repeated phrase 'Be near me when...'?

Extract 4 (Section 119)

Despite intense doubts, the poet comes to accept his loss and re-affirm his faith:

Doors, where my heart was used to beat　　　1
　　So quickly, not as one that weeps
　　I come once more; the city sleeps;
I smell the meadow in the street;

I hear a chirp of birds; I see　　　　　5
　　Betwixt the black fronts long-withdrawn
　　A light-blue lane of early dawn,
And think of early days and thee,

GLOSSARY

Betwixt (l.6): between
　(archaic)
bland (l.9): comforting

And bless thee, for thy lips are bland,
　　And bright the friendship of thine eye;　　10
　　And in my thoughts with scarce a sigh
I take the pressure of thine hand.

(from *In Memoriam A. H. H.*)

● What images convey the change of mood?
　 What qualities strike you about Tennyson's verse?

The poem's epilogue is a marriage song for the wedding of Tennyson's sister, Emily, who had been engaged to Hallam.

Tennyson saw the poem as 'rather the cry of the whole human race than mine'. He saw it as a message of hope and an affirmation of faith in God in an age which was growing increasingly sceptical. However, the poet T.S. Eliot (see page 260) commented: 'It is not religious because of the quality of its faith, but because of the quality of its doubt. Its faith is a poor thing, but its doubt is a very intense experience. *In Memoriam* is a poem of despair, but of despair of a religious kind.'

Fond of declaiming his verse to a respectful audience, Tennyson became a representative voice of his age. In 1850 he succeeded Wordsworth as Poet Laureate and wrote such patriotic verse as *The Charge of The Light Brigade* (1854). Nowadays he is more appreciated for the beauty of his early verse (see Supplement 6).

6.4.2
Emily Brontë
(1818–1848)

Emily Brontë was one of the six children (five daughters, one son) of a Yorkshire clergyman of Irish origin. Her mother died in 1821 and all the children died before their father. Emily, a quiet young woman with few friends wrote only one novel, *Wuthering Heights* (1847).

The title *Wuthering Heights* refers to the name of an old house in a remote part of the Yorkshire moors occupied by a farming family, the Earnshaws. The more 'civilised' Linton family – landed gentry – live in Thrushcross Grange in the valley. The Earnshaws adopt a young boy called Heathcliff, who has lived like a wild animal in the slums of Liverpool. The novel concerns Catherine Earnshaw and the effect of Heathcliff on both families.

Warm-up This family tree shows how the families become linked in the novel (note that *m.* means 'married to' and the names in italics are 'outsiders'):

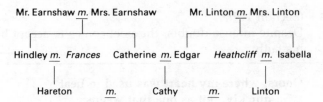

Do Catherine and Heathcliff marry each other? How many times was the younger Cathy married?

The tale is told by more than one narrator in a series of flashbacks and time shifts. In the following extract Catherine Linton has just died in childbirth.

● From the extract, try to work out:

a) the narrator's feelings and character;
b) the relationship between Heathcliff and Catherine;
c) Heathcliff's feelings and character.

GLOSSARY

ventured (l.1): risked

protracted (l.3): long; extended

larches (l.5): type of tree with small cones and light green leaves

budded (l.14): with buds (leaves not yet grown)

ousels (l.16): type of small bird of the thrush family

snivel (l.21): cry in a weak, complaining way

The master looked asleep, and I ventured soon after sunrise to quit the room and steal out to the pure refreshing air. The servants thought me gone to shake off the drowsiness of my protracted watch; in reality, my chief motive was seeing Mr Heathcliff. If he had remained among the larches all night, he would have heard nothing of the stir at the Grange; unless, perhaps, he might catch the gallop of the messenger going to Gimmerton. If he had come nearer, he would probably be aware, from the lights flitting to and fro, and the opening and shutting of the outer doors, that all was not right within. I wished, yet feared, to find him. I felt the terrible news must be told and I longed to get it over; but *how* to do it, I did not know. He was there – at least a few yards further off in the park; leant against an old ash tree, his hat off, and his hair soaked with the dew that had gathered on the budded branches, and fell pattering round him. He had been standing a long time in that position, for I saw a pair of ousels passing and repassing scarcely three feet from him, busy in building their nest, and regarding his proximity no more than that of a piece of timber. They flew off at my approach, and he raised his eyes and spoke –

'She's dead!' he said; 'I've not waited for you to learn that. Put your handkerchief away – don't snivel before me. Damn you all! she wants none of *your* tears!'

1

5

10

15

20

I was weeping as much for him as her; we do sometimes pity creatures that have none of the feeling either for themselves or others. When I first looked into his face, I perceived that he had got intelligence of the catastrophe; and a foolish notion struck me that his heart was quelled and he prayed, because his lips moved and his gaze was bent on the ground.

'Yes, she's dead!' I answered, checking my sobs and drying my cheeks. 'Gone to heaven, I hope; where we may, every one, join her, if we take due warning and leave our evil ways to follow good!'

'Did *she* take due warning, then?' asked Heathcliff, attempting a sneer. 'Did she die like a saint? Come, give me a true history of the event. How did' –

He endeavoured to pronounce the name, but could not manage it; and compressing his mouth he held a silent combat with his inward agony, defying, meanwhile, my sympathy with an unflinching ferocious stare. 'How did she die?' he resumed at last – fain, notwithstanding his hardihood, to have a support behind him; for, after the struggle, he trembled, in spite of himself, to his very finger-ends.

'Poor wretch!' I thought; 'you have a heart and nerves the same as your brother men! Why should you be anxious to conceal them? Your pride cannot blind God! You tempt Him to wring them, till he forces a cry of humiliation.'

'Quietly as a lamb!' I answered aloud. 'She drew a sigh, and stretched herself, like a child reviving, and sinking again to sleep; and five minutes after I felt one little pulse at her heart, and nothing more!'

'And – did she ever mention me?' he asked, hesitating, as if he dreaded the answer to his question would introduce details that he could not bear to hear.

'Her senses never returned; she recognized nobody from the time you left her,' I said. 'She lies with a sweet smile on her face; and her latest ideas wandered back to pleasant early days. Her life closed in a gentle dream – may she wake as kindly in the other world!'

'May she wake in torment!' he cried, with frightful vehemence, stamping his foot, and groaning in a sudden paroxysm of ungovernable passion. 'Why, she's a liar to the end. Where is she? Not *there* – not in heaven – not perished – where? Oh! you said you cared nothing for my sufferings! And I pray one prayer – I repeat it till my tongue stiffens – Catherine Earnshaw, may you not rest as long as I am living! You said I killed you – haunt me, then! The murdered *do* haunt their murderers, I believe. I know that ghosts *have* wandered on earth. Be with me always – take any form – drive me mad! only *do* not leave me in this abyss, where I cannot find you! Oh, God! it is unutterable! I *cannot* live without my life! I *cannot* live without my soul!'

(from *Wuthering Heights*)

quelled (l.27): made quiet
unflinching (l.38): firm
fain ... hardihood (l.40): obliged, despite his strength
wring them (l.45): twist them (your nerves)
dreaded (l.52): greatly feared
paroxysm (l.60): explosive expression

<table>
<tr><td>Understanding and interpretation</td><td>

i) Which alternative is most likely to be true? Give reasons.
  a) The narrator is (*an old manservant who saw Catherine die/the housekeeper who cared for Catherine in her final days*)
  b) Catherine was (*deeply attached to Heathcliff/indifferent to Heathcliff*)

ii) What do these tell you? 'the master' (l.1): 'my protracted watch' (l.3); 'I wished, yet feared' (l.10); 'Damn you all' (l.21); 'his heart was quelled' (l.27); 'could not manage it' (l.36); 'ferocious' (l.39); 'You said I killed you' (l.65)

iii) Can you say anything about the narrator's attitude to Heathcliff?

</td></tr>
</table>

Understanding and interpretation

i) Which alternative is most likely to be true? Give reasons.
  a) The narrator is (*an old manservant who saw Catherine die/the housekeeper who cared for Catherine in her final days*)
  b) Catherine was (*deeply attached to Heathcliff/indifferent to Heathcliff*)

ii) What do these tell you? 'the master' (l.1): 'my protracted watch' (l.3); 'I wished, yet feared' (l.10); 'Damn you all' (l.21); 'his heart was quelled' (l.27); 'could not manage it' (l.36); 'ferocious' (l.39); 'You said I killed you' (l.65)

iii) Can you say anything about the narrator's attitude to Heathcliff?

Appreciation

Emily's sister, Charlotte, said she doubted 'whether it was right or advisable to create beings like Heathcliff'. How are his intense emotions presented to us?

Wuthering Heights

The period of the novel is the end of the eighteenth century. Cathy and Heathcliff had developed a strong bond as children but their relationship was only able to flourish on the moors, away from the family, outside the house. After Mr Earnshaw's death, Heathcliff was maltreated by Hindley, then master of the house. Heathcliff ran away when he realised he would never be able to marry Catherine but returned three years later, a rich man determined to destroy both families.

Despite the powerful presence of Heathcliff, Catherine is in many ways the centre of the novel. Emily Bronte's aim seems to have been to present an image of the deeper feminine personality, which, despite or because of the social constrictions of the time, finds itself attracted to wild and basic energies not understood or accepted by society at large.

| | 6.4.3 | *Either*: |
| **Creative Writing** | | Choose one of the following themes: childhood, death or work. Make a list of ten words you associate with it. Exchange your list with a partner. Choose three words from your partner's list and write a short story to include the chosen words at least once. Exchange stories and see whether your partner's story coincides with your thoughts. |

6.4.3
Creative Writing

Either:
Choose one of the following themes: childhood, death or work. Make a list of ten words you associate with it. Exchange your list with a partner. Choose three words from your partner's list and write a short story to include the chosen words at least once. Exchange stories and see whether your partner's story coincides with your thoughts.

Or:
Imagine you have just read the extracts from *Great Expectations* in 6.2.1. Write a letter to a friend saying why you liked/didn't like them.

6.5 The Victorian novel

One reason for the development of the novel was the desire by the reading public to understand the huge social changes of the time.

- Try to make each of the following into a complete sentence:

  a) Romantic age – poetry – Victorian age – novel
  b) first British public library – Canterbury – 1847 – end of century four hundred libraries
  c) middle class – rise – power and importance; middle class – readers – novels
  d) Victorian novelists – duty – enlighten – stimulate conscience – make society more sensitive
  e) Dickens – city – Emily Brontë – country

Check with your teacher that your statements are correct.

6.6 The Americans

Early American literature was more European in spirit than American (see Supplement 4). Even for some time after the Declaration of Independence in 1776 many American works with distinctively American themes still sounded European. Slowly, though, the break with Europe came about.

6.6.1
The Transcendentalists

In the first half of the century. New England was full of intellectual activity. In 1836, Ralph Waldo Emerson (1803–1882) formed the highly influential Transcendental Club to discuss quasi-mystical philosophical ideas. ('Nature is the incarnation of thought. The world is the mind precipitated.') It rejected both conservative Puritanism and the newer faith of Unitarianism (which in turn rejected the notion of the Trinity of the Father, Son and Holy Spirit in one God), regarding them both as 'negative, cold, lifeless'. Although the Transcendentalists owed much to Coleridge, Wordsworth and Carlyle, in his Harvard Address of 1837 Emerson urged America to assert its intellectual independence ('We have listened too long to the courtly muses of Europe').

6.6.2
Nathaniel Hawthorne
(1804–1864)

Nathaniel Hawthorne was born of a prominent Puritan family. Perhaps because of his family background his writing is generally pessimistic and he became a critic of the Transcendentalists for their failure to deal with doubt, sin and guilt.

The Scarlet Letter (1850) is both a sombre moral fable on the theme of guilt and an exploration of moral isolation. It tells the story of a strong independent woman, Hester Prynne, sent by her husband to set up home in Boston. When he arrives two years later he finds she has an illegitimate child and has been forced by the Puritans to wear the scarlet letter 'A' as a punishment. The baby girl, Pearl, is born, an 'outcast of the infantile world' with 'no right among christened infants', a 'little creature, whose innocent life had sprung, by the inscrutable decree of Providence, a lovely and immortal flower, out of the rank luxuriance of a guilty passion'. After she was born the 'first object of which Pearl seemed to become aware' was not her mother's smile but 'the scarlet letter on Hester's bosom'. Every day, Hester 'looked fearfully into the child's expanding nature; ever dreading to detect some dark and wild peculiarity that should correspond with the guiltiness to which she owed her being'.

*Lillian Gish
as Hester Prynne
in* The Scarlet Letter

● Try to guess the answers to these questions before you read the extract!
a) Does Pearl believe she was born in heaven?
b) What do you imagine Hester's feelings are when Pearl asks about her origin?

Extract 1

GLOSSARY

elf (l.4): small mischievous fairy

clasped (l.6): pressed together

penance (l.7): (need for) self-punishment

wrought out (l.7): made to happen

battery (l.9): persistent attack

In the afternoon of a certain summer's day, after Pearl grew big 1
enough to run about, she amused herself with gathering handfuls
of wild-flowers and flinging them, one by one, at her mother's
bosom, dancing up and down like a little elf whenever she hit the
scarlet letter. Hester's first motion had been to cover her bosom 5
with her clasped hands. But, whether from pride or resignation or
a feeling that her penance might best be wrought out by this un-
utterable pain, she resisted the impulse, and sat erect, pale as death,
looking sadly into little Pearl's wild eyes. Still came the battery of

flowers, almost invariably hitting the mark, and covering the 10
mother's breast with hurts for which she could find no balm in this
world, nor knew how to seek it in another. At last, her shot being
all expended, the child stood still and gazed at Hester with that little, laughing image of a fiend peeping out – or, whether it peeped
or no, her mother so imagined it – from the unsearchable abyss of 15
her black eyes.

'Child, what art thou?' cried the mother.

'O, I am your little Pearl!' answered the child.

But, while she said it, Pearl laughed, and began to dance up and
down, with the humorsome gesticulation of a little imp whose next 20
freak might be to fly up the chimney.

'Art thou my child, in very truth?' asked Hester.

Nor did she put the question altogether idly, but, for the moment,
with a portion of genuine earnestness; for such was Pearl's wonderful intelligence that her mother half doubted whether she were not 25
acquainted with the secret spell of her existence, and might not
now reveal herself.

'Yes; I am little Pearl!' repeated the child, continuing her antics.

'Thou art not my child! Thou art no Pearl of mine!' said the
mother, half playfully; for it was often the case that a sportive 30
impulse came over her, in the midst of her deepest suffering. 'Tell
me, then, what thou art, and who sent thee hither?'

'Tell me, Mother!' said the child seriously, coming up to Hester,
and pressing herself close to her knees. 'Do thou tell me!'

'The Heavenly Father sent thee!' answered Hester Prynne. 35

But she said it with a hesitation that did not escape the acuteness
of the child. Whether moved only by her ordinary freakishness, or
because an evil spirit prompted her, she put up her small forefinger,
and touched the scarlet letter.

'He did not send me!' cried she, positively. 'I have no Heavenly 40
Father!'

'Hush, Pearl, hush! Thou must not talk so!' answered the mother,
suppressing a groan. 'He sent us all into this world. He sent even
me, thy mother. Then, much more, thee! Or, if not, thou strange
and elfish child, whence didst thou come?' 45

'Tell me! Tell me!' repeated Pearl, no longer seriously, but laughing, and capering about the floor. 'It is thou that must tell me!'

But Hester could not resolve the query, being herself in a dismal
labyrinth of doubt. She remembered – betwixt a smile and a shudder – the talk of the neighbouring townspeople, who, seeking 50
vainly elsewhere for the child's paternity, and observing some of
her odd attributes, had given out that poor little Pearl was a demon
offspring; such as, ever since old Catholic times, had occasionally
been seen on earth, through the agency of their mother's sin, and to
promote some foul and wicked purpose. Luther, according to the 55
scandal of his monkish enemies, was a brat of that hellish breed;
nor was Pearl the only child to whom this inauspicious origin was
assigned, among the New England Puritans.

balm (l.11): comfort

expended (l.13): used up

fiend (l.14): devil

abyss (l.15): great dark
hole with no end

gesticulation (l.20):
expressive physical
movements

imp (l.20): little devil

freak (l.21): peculiar action

antics (l.28): playful
behaviour

sportive (l.30): playful

hither (l.32): to this place

freakishness (l.37): peculiar
behaviour

labyrinth (l.49): (her
feelings are complex:
she cannot see her way
out)

betwixt (l.49): between
(archaic)

through the agency of (l.54):
as the result of

Luther (l.55): leader of
the Reformation in
Germany, 1483–1546

brat (l.56): naughty child

inauspicious (l.57):
indicating an unlucky
future

- i) In what way do you think Pearl's actions with the wild flowers are symbolic? What do they represent to Hester?
  ii) Why is the image of Pearl touching the scarlet letter A so powerful?

Extract 2   While in many ways a European novelist, Hawthorne was painfully aware of American attempts to modify the European tradition and escape from its Colonial past.

This is a description from the next chapter of the garden belonging to Governor Bellingham, an Englishman.

GLOSSARY
bow-window (l.1): window built outwards, in a curve
vista (l.2): long view
rude (l.3): primitive
relinquished (l.4): given up
amid (l.6): in the middle of

Pearl ... ran to the bow-window, at the farther end of the hall, and 1
looked along the vista of the garden walk, carpeted with closely
shaven grass, and bordered with some rude and immature attempt
at shrubbery. But the proprietor appeared already to have relin-
quished, as hopeless, the effort to perpetuate on this side of the 5
Atlantic, in a hard soil and amid the close struggle for subsistence,
the native English taste for ornamental gardening. Cabbages grew
in plain sight; and a pumpkin-vine, rooted at some distance, had
run across the intervening space, and deposited one of its gigan-
tic products directly beneath the hall window; as if to warn the 10
Governor that this great lump of vegetable gold was as rich an
ornament as New England would offer him..

(from *The Scarlet Letter*)

- From this passage, what do we learn about the characteristic English garden? What does the pumpkin represent?

Critical response   Henry James (1843–1916), a New York novelist even more conscious of the conflict between the old and new traditions, felt that *The Scarlet Letter* was something that 'might at last be sent to Europe as exquisite in quality as anything that had been received, and the best of it was that the thing was absolutely American ... it came out of the very heart of New England'. Nevertheless, he complained of Hawthorne's 'exaggerated, painful, morbid national consciousness'.

6.6.3
Walt Whitman
(1819–1892)

Whitman, a printer and a wandering schoolteacher with little formal education, described his collection of poems *Leaves of Grass* (first edition 1855) as full of 'the vehemence of pride and audacity of freedom necessary to loosen the mind of still-to-be-form'd America from the folds, the superstitions, and all the long, tenacious and stifling anti-democratic authorities of Asiatic and European past'. Emerson described it as 'the most extraordinary piece of wit and wisdom that America has yet contributed'. Whitman was probably freer of Europe and more optimistic for America than any earlier poet.

Here are three extracts from his verse:

Extract 1

Walt Whitman, a kosmos, of Manhattan the son, 1
Turbulent, fleshy, sensual, eating, drinking and breeding,
No sentimentalist, no stander above men and women or
  apart from them,
No more modest than immodest. 5

Unscrew the locks from the doors!
Unscrew the doors themselves from their jambs!

Whoever degrades another degrades me,
And whatever is done or said returns at last to me.

Through me the afflatus surging and surging, through me 10
  the current and index.

I speak the pass-word primeval, I give the sign of democracy,
By God! I will accept nothing which all cannot have their
  counterpart of on the same terms.
. . . 15

Through me forbidden voices,
Voices of sexes and lusts, voices veil'd and I remove the veil,
Voices indecent by me clarified and transfigur'd.

I do not press my fingers across my mouth,
I keep as delicate around the bowels as around the head and heart, 20
Copulation is no more rank to me than death is.

(from 'Song of Myself' in *Leaves of Grass*)

GLOSSARY

kosmos (l.1): cosmos: an harmonious universe
Turbulent (l.2): restless and uncontrolled
jambs (l.7): side posts
afflatus (l.10): divine inspiration
current and index (l.11): flow and direction
primeval (l.12): from the beginning of time
transfigur'd (l.18): changed and made beautiful
copulation (l.21): sexual intercourse
rank (l.21): bad

Extract 2

Come lovely and soothing death, 1
Undulate round the world, serenely arriving, arriving,
In the day, in the night, to all, to each,
Sooner or later delicate death.

Prais'd be the fathomless universe, 5
For life and joy, and for objects and knowledge curious,
And for love, sweet love – but praise! praise! praise!
For the sure-enwinding arms of cool-enfolding death.

Dark mother always gliding near with soft feet,
Have none chanted for thee a chant of fullest welcome? 10
Then I chant it for thee, I glorify thee above all,
I bring thee a song that when thou must indeed come, come
  unfalteringly.

(from *When lilacs last in the dooryard bloom'd* 1865–1866, a
sixteen-part elegy for Abraham Lincoln, after his assassination)

GLOSSARY

Undulate (l.2): move like waves rising and falling
fathomless (l.5): too deep to be understood and measured
enwinding (l.8): winding around
enfolding (l.8): enclosing
unfalteringly (l.13): without hesitation

Extract 3

A Noiseless Patient Spider

A noiseless patient spider,   1
I mark'd where on a little promontory it stood isolated,
Mark'd how to explore the vacant vast surrounding,
It launch'd forth filament, filament, filament, out of itself,
Ever unreeling them, ever tirelessly speeding them.   5

And you O my soul where you stand,
Surrounded, detached, in measureless oceans of space,
Ceaselessly musing, venturing, throwing, seeking the spheres to connect them,
Till the bridge you will need be form'd, till the ductile anchor hold,   10
Till the gossamer thread you fling catch somewhere, O my soul.

Understanding and interpretation	i) Which of these does Whitman *not* seem to be in favour of? *freedom, democracy, sex, modesty, himself*

ii) Find evidence for:

   a) The poet as the consciousness of the world.

   b) Vigorous support of the life-force.

   c) Extension of the self to include the universe.

iii) What is Whitman's image of himself? In what way does he identify with the spider?

iv) Can we say Whitman's poems are carefully constructed?

Walt Whitman

Whitman believed that reality was a continuous flow without beginning or end. He wrote in 'free verse', without rhyme or stanza pattern and without a regular pattern of stresses and line lengths. Nevertheless, his frequent repetitions of words and syntax and his patterns of description contain a certain song-like musicality. Ironically, it was not until he was recognised in England that Whitman found favour in America.

6.6.4 Emily Dickinson (1830–1886)

During her early years Emily Dickinson was lively, witty and sociable but from her mid-twenties she gradually withdrew from the world. In her forties she refused to leave home and avoided all contact with strangers. Only seven out of her nearly two thousand poems (her 'letter to the world') were published in her lifetime.

Here, in a poem written during the developing crisis in her life in 1861 and 1862, she describes a funeral. Possibly she is imagining a moment of semi-consciousness after her own death; possibly she is referring to to the funeral of a friend of her brother's; possibly she wishes to suggest some kind of spiritual death, as of love or hope or religious belief, within herself.

'I felt a Funeral, in my Brain'

I felt a Funeral, in my Brain,   1
And Mourners to and fro
Kept treading – treading – till it seemed
That Sense was breaking through –

And when they all were seated,   5
A Service, like a Drum –
Kept beating – beating – till I thought
My Mind was going numb –

And then I heard them lift a Box
And creak across my Soul   10
With those same Boots of Lead, again,
Then Space – began to toll,

As all the Heavens were a Bell,
And Being, but an Ear,
And I, and Silence, some strange Race   15
Wrecked, solitary, here –

And then a Plank in Reason, broke,
And I dropped down, and down –
And hit a World, at every plunge,
And Finished knowing – then –   20

GLOSSARY

Mourners (l.2): friends or relatives of dead person at a funeral

creak (l.10): make a noise like a badly oiled door opening

toll (l.12): ring with slow, regular strokes

Plank (l.17): board of wood (planks are laid over the grave and the coffin rests on them during the burial service; they are then removed and the coffin is lowered. Here the plank breaks)

plunge (l.19): violent movement downwards

Appreciation

i) *Stanzas 1/2*: Try to explain the last line of both stanzas. What is the effect of the repetition of the words 'treading' and 'beating'?

ii) *Stanza 3*: What is the 'Box'? The 'Boots of Lead' describe the mourners' heavy boots on a wooden floor as they carry the coffin on their shoulders. What atmosphere does the image suggest? In reality, can 'space' 'toll'?

iii) *Stanza 4*: Does 'As' mean 'as if' or 'because'? In line 14, does 'Being' mean 'conscious existence' (noun) or 'since they were' (verb phrase)? What do 'Silence', 'some strange Race', 'wrecked' and 'solitary' tell you about the narrator at this point?

iv) *Stanza 5*: Try to explain 'then a Plank in Reason, broke'. 'Dropped down' where? What does 'Finished knowing' suggest? What does 'then' suggest?

v) What do you notice about the use of capital letters and punctuation in the poem?

Do you find the poem difficult to understand? If so, why?

Emily Dickinson

Emily Dickinson's poems, written in the metre of the hymns of her childhood church, reflect both her New England Calvinist upbringing and her reading of Emerson. They never seem to refer to major national events like the Civil War. She believed that we should 'move outwards towards limits shrouded in mystery' and her short, almost mystical verses (on such themes as faith, death, immortality, fame and poetic vocation) seem like obscure riddles reflecting a painful inner struggle.

6.7 More Victorian themes: Men and women

Victorian novels frequently tell of the need of individuals, often women, to fulfill themselves in a society offering limited opportunities. Sometimes their predicament is intensified by a situation where the individualism of the Anglo-Saxon Protestant tradition and Latin–Catholic authoritarianism come into conflict with each other. Sometimes the vulnerability of women, in both social and domestic contexts, is seen to be at the mercy of arrogant male attitudes. Love may be personal and passionate and yet marriages, representing the values of society, are often disastrous.

6.7.1
George Eliot
(1819–1880)

George Eliot was the pen name of Mary Ann Evans. Brought up in a strict Evangelical tradition (Evangelicalism was a rather austere movement for Protestant revival in the late eighteenth-century Church which emphasised personal salvation by faith in the death and resurrection of Jesus Christ), she nevertheless became an agnostic in her early twenties and cultivated a wide range of intellectual interests. Her friendship with the philosopher and critic George Henry Lewes (1817–1878) led to an 'illicit' union for more than twenty years (he was already married), a difficult decision in times rigidly opposed to unions not legalised by marriage. *Daniel Deronda* (1876) was George Eliot's last novel.

Henleigh Grandcourt is a rich, aristocratic man of the world. He has had a long-standing affair with Lydia Glasher and had children by her but is to propose marriage to Gwendolen Harleth, a provincial girl from a financially-ruined upper-class family. She has recently been disillusioned about her talents as a singer by Herr Klesmer, a cultured German musician.

• i) The following phrases occur in the extracts you are going to read. They are in the correct order. Try to imagine the situation. What could be the problem? What happens?

'that glimpse of his past'; 'not going to accept Grandcourt; 'the prospect of making all things easy for "poor mamma"'; 'wooed by this silent man'; 'Is there any man who stands between us?'; 'said with something of her former clearness and defiance'; 'liked him to be there'; 'long, narrow, impenetrable eyes met hers';

ii) Do you think Gwendolen accepts his proposal? Make guesses about the characters of Grandcourt and Gwendolen.

iii) Underline the phrases in i) above in the following extracts and find out if your guesses were correct.

Extract 1

> ... the question of love on her own part had occupied her scarcely   1
> at all in relation to Grandcourt. The desirability of marriage for her
> had always seemed due to other feelings than love; and to be
> enamoured was the part of the man, on whom the advances de-
> pended. Gwendolen had found no objection to Grandcourt's way   5
> of being enamoured before she had had that glimpse of his past,
> which she resented as if it had been a deliberate offence against

her. His advances to *her* were deliberate, and she felt a retrospective disgust for them. Perhaps other men's lives were of the same kind – full of secrets which made the ignorant suppositions of the woman they wanted to marry a farce at which they were laughing in their sleeves.

These feelings of disgust and indignation had sunk deep ... it was chiefly their reverberating activity which kept her firm to the understanding with herself, that she was not going to accept Grandcourt. She had never meant to form a new determination; she had only been considering what might be thought or said. If anything could have induced her to change, it would have been the prospect of making all things easy for 'poor mamma'; that, she admitted, was a temptation. But no! she was going to refuse him. Meanwhile, the thought that he was coming to be refused was inspiriting ... there was a new current in her frame ... she was going to exercise her power.

Was this what made her heart palpitate annoyingly when she heard the horse's footsteps on the gravel? – when Miss Merry, who opened the door to Grandcourt, came to tell her that he was in the drawing-room? The hours of preparation and the triumph of the situation were apparently of no use: she might as well have seen Grandcourt coming suddenly on her in the midst of her despondency. While walking into the drawing-room she had to concentrate all her energy in that self-control which made her appear gravely gracious as she gave her hand to him, and answered his hope that she was quite well in a voice as low and languid as his own. A moment afterwards, when they were both of them seated on two of the wreath-painted chairs – Gwendolen upright with downcast eyelids, Grandcourt about two yards distant, leaning one arm over the back of his chair and looking at her, while he held his hat in his left hand – anyone seeing them as a picture would have concluded that they were in some stage of love-making suspense. And certainly the love-making had begun: she already felt herself being wooed by this silent man seated at an agreeable distance, with the subtlest atmosphere of attar of roses and an attention bent wholly on her. And he also considered himself to be wooing: he was not a man to suppose that his presence carried no consequences; and he was exactly the man to feel the utmost piquancy in a girl whom he had not found quite calculable.

GLOSSARY

advances (l.4): efforts to gain love

reverberating activity (l.14): (they kept coming back)

inspiriting (l.22): filled her with spirit

palpitate (l.24): beat rapidly

Miss Merry (l.25): (described as a 'meek', 'elderly' governess)

despondency (l.29): melancholy; loss of hope

languid (l.33): slow-moving

wreath-painted (l.35): with twisted circular patterns (suggesting a circle of flowers placed on a coffin?)

upright (l.35): sitting straight up

attar (l.42): pleasant-smelling essence

piquancy (l.45): pleasantly interesting and exciting nature

calculable (l.46): understandable

Extract 2 Grandcourt expresses his disappointment that he had missed Gwendolen at a fashionable resort. She had left early 'on account of family troubles'.

'... Are you quite reckless about me?'

It was impossible to say 'yes' in a tone that would be taken seriously; equally impossible to say 'no'; but what else could she say? In her difficulty, she turned down her eyelids again and blushed over face and neck. Grandcourt saw her in a new phase,

GLOSSARY

reckless (l.1): careless and unthinking

and believed that she was showing her inclination. But he was determined that she should show it more decidedly.

'Perhaps there is some deeper interest? Some attraction – some engagement – which it would have been only fair to make me aware of? Is there any man who stands between us?'

Inwardly the answer framed itself, 'No; but there is a woman.' Yet how could she utter this? Even if she had not promised that woman to be silent, it would have been impossible for her to enter on the subject with Grandcourt. But how could she arrest this wooing by beginning to make a formal speech – 'I perceive your intention – it is most flattering, &c.'? A fish honestly invited to come and be eaten has a clear course in declining, but how if it finds itself swimming against a net? And apart from the network, would she have dared at once to say anything decisive? Gwendolen had no time to be clear on that point. As it was, she felt compelled to silence, and after a pause, Grandcourt said –

'Am I to understand that some one else is preferred?'

Gwendolen, now impatient of her own embarrassment, determined to rush at the difficulty and free herself. She raised her eyes again and said with something of her former clearness and defiance, 'No' – wishing him to understand, 'What then? I may not be ready to take *you*.' There was nothing that Grandcourt could not understand which he perceived likely to affect his *amour propre*.

'The last thing I would do, is to importune you. I should not hope to win you by making myself a bore. If there were no hope for me, I would ask you to tell me so at once, that I might just ride away to – no matter where.'

Almost to her own astonishment, Gwendolen felt a sudden alarm at the image of Grandcourt finally riding away. What would be left her then? Nothing but the former dreariness. She liked him to be there. She snatched at the subject that would defer any decisive answer.

'I fear you are not aware of what has happened to us. I have lately had to think so much of my mamma's troubles, that other subjects have been quite thrown into the background. She has lost all her fortune, and we are going to leave this place. I must ask you to excuse my seeming preoccupied.'

In eluding a direct appeal Gwendolen recovered some of her self-possession. She spoke with dignity and looked straight at Grandcourt, whose long, narrow, impenetrable eyes met hers, and mysteriously arrested them: mysteriously; for the subtly-varied drama between man and woman is often such as can hardly be rendered in words put together like dominoes, according to obvious fixed marks. The word of all work Love will no more express the myriad modes of mutual attraction, than the word Thought can inform you what is passing through your neighbour's mind. It would be hard to tell on which side – Gwendolen's or Grandcourt's – the influence was more mixed. At that moment his strongest wish was to be completely master of this creature – this piquant com-

arrest (l.14): put a stop to
amour propre (l.28): self-esteem; love of himself (French)
importune (l.29): beg
dreariness (l.35): dullness
eluding (l.43): cleverly avoiding
dominoes (l.48): small pieces of wood/bone with spots, put next to each other in a table game
myriad (l.50): great and varied in number

bination of maidenliness and mischief: that she knew things which   55
had made her start away from him, spurred him to triumph over
that repugnance; and he was believing that he should triumph.
And she – ah, piteous equality in the need to dominate! –she was
overcome like the thirsty one who is drawn towards the seeming
water in the desert, overcome by the suffused sense that here in   60
this man's homage to her lay the rescue from helpless subjection to
an oppressive lot.

All the while they were looking at each other; and Grandcourt
said, slowly and languidly, as if it were of no importance, other
things having been settled –   65

'You will tell me now, I hope, that Mrs Davilow's loss of fortune
will not trouble you further. You will trust me to prevent it from
weighing upon her. You will give me the claim to provide against
that.'

The little pauses and refined drawlings with which this speech   70
was uttered, gave time for Gwendolen to go through the dream of a
life. As the words penetrated her, they had the effect of a draught
of wine, which suddenly makes all things easier, desirable things
not so wrong, and people in general less disagreeable. She had a
momentary phantasmal love for this man who chose his words so   75
well, and who was a mere incarnation of delicate homage. Repugnance, dread, scruples – these were dim as remembered pains, while
she was already tasting relief under the immediate pain of hope-
lessness. She imagined herself already springing to her mother,
and being playful again. Yet when Grandcourt had ceased to speak,   80
there was an instant in which she was conscious of being at the
turning of the ways.

'You are very generous,' she said, not moving her eyes, and
speaking with a gentle intonation.

'You accept what will make such things a matter of course?' said   85
Grandcourt, without any new eagerness. 'You consent to become
my wife?'

This time Gwendolen remained quite pale. Something made her
rise from her seat in spite of herself and walk to a little distance.
Then she turned and with her hands folded before her stood in   90
silence.

Grandcourt immediately rose too, resting his hat on the chair,
but still keeping hold of it. The evident hesitation of this destitute
girl to take his splendid offer stung him into a keenness of interest
such as he had not known for years. None the less because he at-   95
tributed her hesitation entirely to her knowledge about Mrs Glasher.
In that attitude of preparation, he said –

'Do you command me to go?' No familiar spirit could have
suggested to him more effective words.

'No,' said Gwendolen. She could not let him go: that negative   100
was a clutch. She seemed to herself to be, after all, only drifted
towards the tremendous decision: – but drifting depends on something besides the currents, when the sails have been set beforehand.

maidenliness (l.55):
   unmarried girlishness
spurred (l.56): encouraged
repugnance (l.57): feelings
   of strong dislike
ah, piteous ... need (l.58):
   equally with a foolish
   need
suffused (l.60): which
   spread throughout
   her
homage (l.61): flattering
   attention
an oppressive lot (l.62): her
   unhappy situation
Mrs Davilow (l.66):
   (Gwendolen's 'mamma'
   – she never knew her
   father and her step-
   father Captain Davilow
   had died)
drawlings (l.70): slow way
   of speaking
draught (l.72): drink
phantasmal (l.75): unreal
incarnation (l.76): perfect
   example
dread (l.77): great fear and
   anxiety
scruples (l.77): moral
   principles
turning of the ways (l.82):
   point at which a
   change occurs
destitute (l.93): without
   possessions or money
clutch (l.101): something
   which held her tight

'You accept my devotion?' said Grandcourt, holding his hat by his side and looking straight into her eyes, without other movement. Their eyes meeting in that way seemed to allow any length of pause; but wait as long as she would, how could she contradict herself? What had she detained him for? He had shut out any explanation.

'Yes,' came as gravely from Gwendolen's lips as if she had been answering to her name in a court of justice. He received it gravely, and they still looked at each other in the same attitude. Was there ever before such a way of accepting the bliss-giving 'Yes'? Grandcourt liked better to be at that distance from her, and to feel under a ceremony imposed by an indefinable prohibition that breathed from Gwendolen's bearing.

But he did at length lay down his hat and advance to take her hand, just pressing his lips upon it and letting it go again. She thought his behaviour perfect, and gained a sense of freedom which made her almost ready to be mischievous. Her 'Yes' entailed so little at this moment, that there was nothing to screen the reversal of her gloomy prospects . . .

105

110

115

120

(from *Daniel Deronda*)

bliss-giving (l.113):
   happiness-making
bearing (l.116): manner
entailed (l.120): made
   necessary
screen . . . prospects (l.121):
   stop her from having a
   happy future after all

● Who do you feel more sympathy with, Gwendolen or Grandcourt?

Understanding and interpretation

i) Put these in the correct order:
   Gwendolen's hesitation
   Acceptance
   Someone between them?
   Insecurity
   She will not marry him
   Persuasion

   Divide the passage into sections using each as a heading.

ii) What do these tell you?
   The use of the 'had' verb form (Extract 1 l.5–8); 'poor mamma' (Extract 1 l.19); 'blushed' (Extract 2 l.5); 'No; but there is a woman' (Extract 2 l.11); 'former dreariness' (Extract 2 l.35); 'as if she had been answering to her name in a court of justice' (Extract 2 l.110–111)

iii) a) Why had Gwendolen decided to refuse Grandcourt?
    b) Why do you think she accepted?
    c) Which phrases describe Grandcourt's voice and manner? What impression do we get of his character?
    d) How would you describe his wooing 'technique'?

iv) Find at least *two* places where the characters have emotions which they don't expect.

v) In the paragraph beginning 'In eluding' (Extract 2 l.43), which lines/phrases make clear the position of the author as 'omniscient narrator' (the narrator who seems to know everything)?

Language and style

How would you describe George Eliot's style in this extract? Subtle? Complicated?

Daniel Deronda	The novel partly concerns Gwendolen's discovery of her own nature and her moral and intellectual development. In the early chapters she is shown as having led a spoilt and protected life, isolated from the world of greater causes. She is immature, high-spirited, confident and self-centred. After her marriage to a man who turns out to be arrogant, selfish and cold-hearted, she suffers from guilt about Mrs Glasher and from her husband's increasing power over her. He is later drowned at Genoa, in a manner that leaves her feeling partly guilty for his death.
George Eliot	George Eliot's early novels were *Adam Bede* (1859), *The Mill on the Floss* (1860) and *Silas Marner* (1861).

> Up until *Romola* (1863) the novels and tales deal with life in the countryside in which she was brought up; the society is depicted as a strong and stable one, and the novelist combines in an unusual degree sharp, humorous observation and intelligent imaginative sympathy. *Romola* marks a dividing point . . . it seems to have opened the way to the more comprehensive treatment of English society in her last three novels. (Christopher Gillie, *Longman Companion to English Literature*, Longman 1972)

Her last three novels were *Felix Holt* (1866), *Middlemarch* (1872) and *Daniel Deronda* (1874–1876)

6.7.2 **Robert Browning** **(1812–1889)**	Aware that he was writing poetry in an age of technology and prose, Robert Browning delighted in a lively, unconventional approach which contained a lot of surface energy and colloquial language. His contemporary, Gerard Manley Hopkins (1844–1889) said that Browning was like 'a man bouncing up from table with his mouth full of bread and cheese saying that he meant to stand no blasted nonsense'. In this poem, entitled 'Love in a Life', from the collection *Men and Women* (1855), Browning suggests that it is not easy to get close to a lover and that each time we try, we only discover empty spaces.

Love in a Life

I

GLOSSARY

cornice-wreath (l.7): flower-like decoration to hide curtain fixtures or in the plaster of the walls

anew (l.7): in a new and different way

Yon (l.8): that over there (archaic)

looking-glass (l.8): mirror

Room after room,   1
I hunt the house through
We inhabit together.
Heart, fear nothing, for heart, thou shalt find her –
Next time, herself! – not the trouble behind her   5
Left in the curtain, the couch's perfume!
As she brushed it, the cornice-wreath blossomed anew:
Yon looking-glass gleamed at the wave of her feather.

II

Range (l.12): wander round
quest (l.14): search
suites (l.15): sets of rooms
closets (l.16): small private rooms
alcoves (l.16): spaces set into the wall of the room
importune (l.16): beg

Yet the day wears,
And door succeeds door;   10
I try the fresh fortune –
Range the wide house from the wing to the centre.
Still the same chance! she goes out as I enter.
Spend my whole day in the quest, – who cares?
But 't is twilight, you see, – with such suites to explore,   15
Such closets to search, such alcoves to importune!

Understanding and interpretation

Which alternative is probably the most accurate in each of the following?

a) 'We' (l.3) refers to *the narrator and his lover/the narrator and his friend who are both looking for the woman*
b) 'Heart' (l.4) refers to *the narrator's heart/his lover/his friend*
c) The poet's mood at the end of the poem is one of *enjoyment/frustration*
d) 'such alcoves to importune' (l.16) means *so many people I have to ask in each alcove/so many alcoves I have to look into*

Appreciation

i) What is the poem's rhyme scheme?
ii) Find an example of lively, colloquial language.

Robert Browning

Robert Browning (1812–1889) rescued the poet Elizabeth Barrett from ill-health and a possessively tyrannical father. They were married and lived in Italy from 1846 until her death in 1861. During their marriage, his wife was the more famous of the two.

Browning's poems are often dramatic monologues by characters from history intended to show something of their mental characteristics. (In a letter to Elizabeth Barrett in 1845 Browning wrote regretfully: 'You speak out, you, – I only make men and women speak, give you truth broken into prismatic hues, and fear the pure white light, even if it is in me'). Hostile critics complain that despite his allusions to art and history and his frequent linguistic obscurity, Browning's verse is more eccentric than profound. He has, however, influenced many subsequent poets, such as Ezra Pound (see page 256).

6.8 Evolution

Scientific scholarship on biblical texts and contemporary theories concerning the geological development of the earth had already caused some intellectuals to have religious doubts. However, traditional beliefs were more widely shaken by the controversy caused by theories of evolution. To many scientists the evidence was unsound. To clergymen such theories contradicted a literal interpretation of the Bible and showed a lack of faith in the life and immortality of the soul.

6.8.1 Charles Darwin (1809–1882)

At Cambridge University, Charles Darwin studied to be a clergyman. In 1831 he was naturalist on the ship HMS *Beagle* on its voyage to South America. In 1859 *On the Origin of Species by means of Natural Selection* was published.

The following passages are from *The Descent of Man* (1871), in which Darwin discusses sexual selection. He argues that man evolved from the higher primates.

Extract 1

Although we have some positive evidence that birds appreciate bright and beautiful objects, as with the bowerbirds of Australia, and although they certainly appreciate the power of song, yet I fully admit that it is an astonishing fact that the females of many birds and some mammals should be endowed with sufficient taste for what has apparently been effected through sexual selection; and this is even more astonishing in the case of reptiles, fish, and insects. But we really know very little about the minds of the lower animals. It cannot be supposed that male birds of paradise or peacocks, for instance, should take so much pains in erecting, spreading, and vibrating their beautiful plumes before the females for no purpose. We should remember the fact given on excellent authority in a former chapter, namely that several peahens, when debarred from an admired male, remained widows during a whole season rather than pair with another bird.

Nevertheless I know of no fact in natural history more wonderful than that the female argus pheasant should be able to appreciate the exquisite shading of the ball-and-socket ornaments and the elegant patterns on the wing feathers of the male. He who thinks that the male was created as he now exists must admit that the great plumes, which prevent the wings from being used for flight, and which, as well as the primary feathers, are displayed in a manner quite peculiar to this one species during the act of courtship, and at no other time, were given to him as an ornament. If so, he must likewise admit that the female was created and endowed with the capacity of appreciating such ornaments. I differ only in the conviction that the male argus pheasant acquired his beauty gradually, through the females having preferred during many generations the more highly ornamented males; the aesthetic capacity of the females having been advanced through exercise or habit in the same manner as our own taste is gradually improved.

Extract 2

The main conclusion arrived at in this work, namely that man is descended from some lowly-organized form, will, I regret to think, be highly distasteful to many persons. But there can hardly be a doubt that we are descended from barbarians. The astonishment which I felt on first seeing a party of Fuegians on a wild and broken shore will never be forgotten by me, for the reflection at once rushed into my mind – such were our ancestors. These men were absolutely naked and bedaubed with paint, their long hair was tangled, their mouths frothed with excitement, and their expression

frothed (l.9): gave off a
    mass of white bubbles

startled (l.10): very
    surprised

arts (l.10): skills

as soon be (l.15): with
    equal willingness

baboon (l.18): large kind
    of monkey

astonished dogs (l.19):
    incidents described in
    Chapter IV to
    demonstrate that
    animals may have a
    moral sense

infanticide (l.21): the crime
    of killing children

grossest (l.22): most vulgar

organic (l.26): of living
    things

aboriginally (l.27): like the
    first primitive
    inhabitants

debased (l.33): people of
    the lowest status

benevolence (l.33): a wish
    to do good

exalted powers (l.36): noble
    faculties

indelible stamp (l.37):
    unremovable
    impression

lowly origin (l.37): simple
    beginnings on earth

was wild, startled, and distrustful. They possessed hardly any arts, and like wild animals lived on what they could catch; they had no government and were merciless to everyone not of their own small tribe. He who has seen a savage in his native land will not feel much shame, if forced to acknowledge that the blood of some more humble creature flows in his veins. For my own part I would as soon be descended from that heroic little monkey, who braved his dreaded enemy in order to save the life of his keeper; or from that old baboon, who, descending from the mountains, carried away in triumph his young comrade from a crowd of astonished dogs – as from a savage who delights to torture his enemies, offers up bloody sacrifices, practices infanticide without remorse, treats his wives like slaves, knows no decency, and is haunted by the grossest superstitions.

Man may be excused for feeling some pride at having risen, though not through his own exertions, to the very summit of the organic scale; and the fact of his having thus risen, instead of having been aboriginally placed there, may give him hopes for a still higher destiny in the distant future. But we are not here concerned with hopes or fears, only with the truth as far as our reason allows us to discover it. I have given the evidence to the best of my ability; and we must acknowledge, as it seems to me, that man with all his noble qualities, with sympathy which feels for the most debased, with benevolence which extends not only to other men but to the humblest living creature, with his godlike intellect which has penetrated into the movements and constitution of the solar system – with all these exalted powers – Man still bears in his bodily frame the indelible stamp of his lowly origin.

(from *The Descent of Man*)

•   i) Complete the following sentences:
        a) The male argus pheasant has developed its beauty because . . .
        b) Darwin sees it is as no worse to be descended from a monkey than . . .

    ii) One effect of Darwin's essays – which really came out of the eighteenth-century rationalist tradition – was to create the optimistic view that man was subject to a general law of progress. This in turn encouraged an uncritical attitude towards history and society. Can you find a suggestion of this view in the extracts?

    iii) What do you know about theories of evolution? Do you agree we evolved from 'lower' forms of life?

6.9 Chronology

Queen Victoria, the first monarch to live in Buckingham Palace, reigned from 1837 to 1901, the longest of any British sovereign. With her serious-minded and intelligent German husband, Prince Albert (1819–1861) – sometimes distrusted for being a foreigner – she restored the prestige of the monarchy so that when she died it was more popular than ever. Victoria had both natural gaiety and great dignity. Her personal behaviour represented to her subjects moral dignity and devotion to husband and family. However, after Albert's death she lived in seclusion, causing her to lose some popularity, until her Jubilee (the fiftieth anniversary of her reign) in 1887.

6.9.1
Domestic politics

Complete the following by choosing one of the verbs and putting it in the correct form:

Parliamentary politics (*occupy/dominate*) .... by the conflict between Benjamin Disraeli (1804–1881) and William Gladstone (1809–1898). Disraeli, of Italian–Jewish descent, (*make/do*) .... Tory Prime Minister in 1868 and from 1874–1880. 'Dizzy', as he (*regard/know*) .... by Victoria, (*win/conquer*) .... the Queen's confidence and (*contribute/promote*) .... British power abroad. Gladstone, four times Prime Minister for the Liberals (formerly known as the 'Whigs'), (*lack/miss*) .... the charm of his rival but (*have/obtain*) .... great energy and seriousness. He (*support/endure*) .... social reform at home and justice for the weaker nations abroad.

Disraeli recognised that the monarchy was an effective symbolic head of the Empire and in 1877 encouraged Victoria to adopt the title Empress of India.

6.9.2
Fashion

Do the dresses in the second picture tell you anything about the Victorian period?

Women's fashions 1800-1809

Women's fashions 1850-1859

207

6.9.3
The British Empire

To find out about the rise and fall of the British Empire, rewrite the following paragraphs, putting the sentences in the correct order. (The first sentence of each paragraph is in the correct place.)

a) At its height the British Empire covered a quarter of the earth's surface. In the eighteenth and nineteenth centuries it took place particularly in Africa but also Australia, New Zealand and Egypt. To locate its beginnings one would have to go back to the pioneering voyages of discovery by Elizabethan seamen in the sixteenth century. In the seventeenth century expansion was primarily in the Americas, India and Africa.

b) Interestingly, expansion of the Empire was mainly unorganised and carried out bit by bit, with the British Government often being less interested than the trading companies. Perhaps it was inevitable, then, that when its people began to settle abroad in the nineteenth century they should be allowed to make the move towards self-government. Today, those countries which have not broken away from Britain completely form a free association of sovereign states, known as the Commonwealth of Nations, acknowledging the Queen as its

The Illustrated London News
celebrating Queen Victoria's
Jubilee

titular head. In Egypt, for example, although there was British administration for half a century, there was never any actual sovereignty. Another reason for the breakup was that two world wars in the twentieth century helped drain Britain of men and wealth, depriving it of its former strength and power. In fact, the degree of sovereignty the British Government had over a country was never uniform.

Give each paragraph a title.

Although the main motives for expansion were initially conquest and trade, in the eighteenth and nineteenth centuries there were also important strategic and missionary considerations.

6.9.4 The Crimean War (1854–1856)

The following answers relate to the Crimean War. They refer to deaths, participants, location, effect and cause but not in that order. Write the questions:

a) On the Crimean Peninsula, a part of southern Russia.
b) Russia on the one hand; Turkey, Britain, France and Sardinia-Piedmont on the other.
c) Mainly by Russian demands to exercise protection over the Turkish Empire.
d) 250,000 on each side, a large number from disease.
e) Russia lost its dominant position in the East.

The war was poorly managed and commanded on both sides. Because of the electric telegraph, the British people were stirred by up-to-date reports of such incidents as the glorious but useless Charge of the Light Brigade at Balaclava and of the shocking conditions in which the men were forced to live and die. Teams of nurses were sent out under Florence Nightingale, who, despite the hostility of the military authorities, became 'mother to fifty thousand soldiers' through a combination of brilliant organisation and compassion. Her work eventually led to the reform of the nursing profession.

Florence Nightingale tending wounded soldiers in the Crimea

6.10 Activities

Critical writing   John Stuart Mill (1806–1873) wrote the following in *What is Poetry*? (written in 1833 before most of the great Victorian novels):

> Poetry, when it is really such, is truth; and fiction also, if it is good for anything, is truth: but they are different truths. The truth of poetry is to paint the human soul truly: the truth of fiction is to give a true picture of life.

Mill argued that the poet 'describes the inward man' whereas the novelist describes 'outward things', 'actions and events, not feelings'. However, he saw the 'possibility of combining both elements'.

Choose *one* of the novelists in this unit. Describe how 'both elements' are combined (if you agree).

Creative writing   Write a short description, of approximately twenty lines, of something that happened to you as a child.

Who is it?   Take it in turns to think of a writer you have read in this unit (including the Supplement). Explain some things about the writer (for example, 'The writer uses the phrase "..."' or 'The writer was born in ...'). Don't make it too easy. The other students should try to guess the name.

UNIT 7

Into the twentieth century

7.1 The late Victorian period (1870–1901)

After the Civil War the United States began to recover economically. Germany, too, after the defeat of France in 1871, united into one empire under the 'Iron Chancellor', Otto von Bismarck, and emerged as a major military and naval power. During these years Britain lost a lot of its international commerce to both the United States and Germany and ceased to be the 'workshop of the world'. Nevertheless it survived as the world's banker, with the pound sterling considered the international currency. As an imperial power, Britain became more aggressive and suspicious of its rivals. The Boer War (1899–1902), fought against the Dutch Boer settlers in South Africa and eventually won after some humiliating defeats, aroused great bitterness.

7.1.1
Race and colour

Black slaves, mainly from Africa, were brought into Virginia in the Americas as early as 1619. When slavery was abolished in the United States by President Lincoln in 1863, there were over four million blacks. Despite a gradual integration by blacks into white American society racial prejudice has persisted in both the North and South and segregation in public education was not ended until 1954.

Warm-up

Discuss either of these:

i) Are human feelings universal? Imagine you had been born into another race and another colour. How different would your feelings be? What would determine the differences?

ii) Is it possible to say why races feel superior or inferior to each other? What are the causes and the effects of prejudice?

7.1.2
Mark Twain
(1835–1910)

Mark Twain, whose real name was Samuel Langhorne Clemens, was an American Southerner, brought up in Hannibal, Missouri, on the banks of the River Mississippi. After his early successes as a writer, in 1871 he moved to a large mansion in Connecticut, New England, and was deeply affected by the eastern America of the Gilded Age, a term which comes from his satirical novel of that name, published in 1873. (The word 'gilded' means 'covered with gold' and refers to the time under President Grant (1869–1877) in which national expansion and the growth of capitalism was mixed in with uncontrolled greed, unstable values and political corruption.)

Puddenhead Wilson

Puddenhead Wilson (1894), a comic-satiric novel of Twain's darker period, tells the story of Dawson's Landing, a fifty-year-old provincial slaveholding town, 'sleepy, comfortable and contented', 'a snug little collection of modest one- and two-storey frame dwellings', between the years 1830 and 1853.

Mark Twain with a farm worker at his wife's family home in Elmira, New York

The action begins when two similar-looking babies are exchanged in their cradles. One baby – later known as 'Chambers' (the 'Valet de Chambre') – is the son of Percy Driscoll, a prosperous white slave-owner. The other – known as 'Tom' – is the son of Roxy, a nearly-white (but 'black') slave. Because of the exchange, 'Tom' is brought up as white, and 'Chambers' is brought up as black. Later 'Tom' discovers he is really a negro.

● What do you imagine his feelings are when he makes the discovery?

Extract 1

Every now and then, after Tom went to bed, he had sudden wakings out of his sleep, and his first thought was, 'Oh, joy, it was all a dream!' Then he laid himself heavily down again, with a groan and the muttered words, 'A nigger! I am a nigger! Oh, I wish I was dead!' 1

5

He woke at dawn with one more repetition of this horror, and then he resolved to meddle no more with that treacherous sleep. He began to think. Sufficiently bitter thinkings they were. They wandered along something after this fashion:

'Why were niggers *and* whites made? What crime did the un- 10 created first nigger commit that the curse of birth was decreed for him? And why is this awful difference made between white and black? ... How hard the nigger's fate seems, this morning! – yet until last night such a thought never entered my head.'

He sighed and groaned an hour or more away. Then 'Chambers' 15 came humbly in to say that breakfast was nearly ready. 'Tom'

GLOSSARY

nigger (l.4): negro (usually an offensive term when used by whites)

meddle (l.7): interfere

decreed (l.11): officially ordered

212

cringe (l.17): bend down humbly

eyesore (l.20): something one would prefer not to look at

irruption ... Krakatoa (l.23): the volcano, Krakatoa, in Indonesia, had erupted in 1883

tidal waves (l.24): unusually large and dangerous waves, often caused by earthquakes

prairies (l.27): large areas of grassland without trees

sackcloth and ashes (l.31): garment worn as a sign of sorrow and regret for wrongdoing

pumice-stone and sulphur (l.32): volcanic rock and chemicals coming out of a volcano

blushed scarlet to see this aristocratic white youth cringe to him, a nigger, and call him 'Young Marster'. He said roughly:

'Get out of my sight!' and when the youth was gone, he muttered: 'He has done me no harm, poor wretch, but he is an eyesore to me now, for he is Driscoll the young gentleman, and I am a – oh, I wish I was dead!' — 20

A gigantic irruption, like that of Krakatoa a few years ago, with the accompanying earthquakes, tidal waves, and clouds of volcanic dust, changes the face of the surrounding landscape beyond recog- — 25 nition, bringing down the high lands, elevating the low, making fair lakes where deserts had been, and deserts where green prairies had smiled before. The tremendous catastrophe which had befallen Tom had changed his moral landscape in much the same way. Some of his low places he found lifted to ideals, some of his ideals had — 30 sunk to the valleys, and lay there with the sackcloth and ashes of pumice-stone and sulphur on their ruined heads.

i) Why do you think
  – the idea of being a negro horrified Tom (l.4)?
  – Tom assumes the 'uncreated first nigger' must have committed a crime (l.10)?
  – Tom 'blushed scarlet' (l.17)?

ii) What does the Krakatoa image convey?

iii) What makes the sentence 'How hard the nigger's fate ...' (l.13) humorously ironic? What is Mark Twain's purpose?

iv) How do you think his behaviour changes?

Extract 2

GLOSSARY

get his bearings (l.2): understand his new position

limp (l.4): lifeless

abashed (l.6): ashamed

rowdy and loafer (l.9): noisy person and lazy person

idol (l.10): god-like image

dread (l.12): to be feared

shrinking and skulking (l.13): moving about secretly, trying not to be noticed

yonder (l.14): over there

For days he wandered in lonely places, thinking, thinking, thinking — 1 – trying to get his bearings. It was new work. If he met a friend, he found that the habit of a lifetime had in some mysterious way vanished – his arm hung limp, instead of involuntarily extending the hand for a shake. It was the 'nigger' in him asserting its humi- — 5 lity, and he blushed and was abashed. And the 'nigger' in him was surprised when the white friend put out his hand for a shake with him. He found the 'nigger' in him involuntarily giving the road, or the sidewalk, to the white rowdy and loafer. When Rowena, the dearest thing his heart knew, the idol of his secret worship, invited — 10 him in, the 'nigger' in him made an embarrassed excuse and was afraid to enter and sit with the dread white folks on equal terms. The 'nigger' in him went shrinking and skulking here and there and yonder, and fancying it saw suspicion and maybe detection in all faces, tones, and gestures. So strange and uncharacteristic was — 15 Tom's conduct that people noticed it, and turned to look after him when he passed on; and when he glanced back – as he could not help doing, in spite of his best resistance – and caught that puzzled expression in a person's face, it gave him a sick feeling, and he took himself out of view as quickly as he could. He presently came to have a hunted sense and a hunted look, and then he fled away to the hill-tops and the solitudes. He said to himself that the curse of Ham was upon him. 20

He dreaded his meals; the 'nigger' in him was ashamed to sit at the white folks' table, and feared discovery all the time; and once when Judge Driscoll said, 'What's the matter with you? You look as meek as a nigger,' he felt as secret murderers are said to feel when the accuser says, 'Thou art the man!' Tom said he was not well, and left the table. 25

His ostensible 'aunt's' solicitudes and endearments were become a terror to him, and he avoided them. 30

And all the time hatred of his ostensible 'uncle' was steadily growing in his heart; for he said to himself, 'He is white; and I am his chattel, his property, his goods, and he can sell me, just as he could his dog.' 35

i) How is it that 'Tom' can have both a 'meek', 'hunted' look and feel hatred? Despite Tom's bad character (which comes out in the rest of the book) do you have any sympathy for his situation?

ii) How did Tom's behaviour change? Write one sentence for each of the following:

    a) handshakes
    b) encounters in the street
    c) invitations
    d) mealtimes

iii) Do you think it is possible for Tom's character to have changed permanently?

Extract 3

For as much as a week after this Tom imagined that his character had undergone a pretty radical change. But that was because he did not know himself. 1

In several ways his opinions were totally changed, and would never go back to what they were before, but the main structure of his character was not changed and could not be changed. One or two very important features of it were altered, and in time effects would result from this if opportunity offered – effects of a quite serious nature too. Under the influence of a great mental and moral upheaval his character and habits had taken on the appearance of complete change, but after a while, with the subsidence of the storm both began to settle toward their former places. He dropped gradually back into his old frivolous and easy-going ways and conditions of feeling and manner of speech, and no familiar of his could have detected anything in him that differentiated him from the weak and careless Tom of other days. 5 10 15

(from *Puddenhead Wilson*)

Language and style	Twain's narrator writes in a conversational style rather than the style of formal prose. Look at the sentences 'For as much . . . serious nature too' (l.1–9). Find an example of

a) a word used mainly in conversation;
b) a sentence beginning with a connecting word;
c) word-repetition;
d) a place where the rhythm forces the reader to stress important words.

Mark Twain	Twain's early career was as a newspaper correspondent. His most famous novels are *The Adventures of Tom Sawyer* (1876) and *The Adventures of Huckleberry Finn* (1884), humorous satires of adventure with young boys as the main characters. Twain's later pessimism and bitterness were increased by his financial problems, the death of his wife in 1904 and the deaths of two of his three daughters.

Creative writing	Imagine you are a reporter in Dawson's Landing investigating the story of the exchanged babies. Make a list of at least five questions you would ask 'Tom Driscoll' (the boy everyone *thought* was Tom Driscoll) about both his past and his future.

7.2 The path to Aestheticism (1)

The Aesthetic Movement blossomed in England in the 1880s. Its origins can be found in earlier intellectual opposition to materialism and industrialisation.

7.2.1 **John Ruskin**	The art critic John Ruskin (1819–1900) was a friend and public champion of the Romantic painter J.M.W. Turner (see page 147) and a disciple and admirer of the Victorian 'prophet' Thomas Carlyle (see pages 183–184). His early essays explore the relationship between art and society. They assert the morality of great art and were very influential in the Gothic revival in English architecture. In the latter part of his life Ruskin attacked the social philosophies of political economists and attempted to awaken the working classes to their artistic and moral impoverishment, views which were to influence early leaders of the British Labour Party. He also gave the whole of his father's large fortune to charitable and philanthropic causes.

The Stones of Venice (1851–1853) is at once a scholarly study of Renaissance architecture, a description of the contrasting relations between authority and workman in feudal times and Victorian times, and an emotional attempt to reform society.

Extract 1

GLOSSARY

degrees (l.3): units of measurement for angles

cogwheels (l.3): wheels in machines with 'teeth'

compasses (l.4): instruments used for drawing circles

Men were not intended to work with the accuracy of tools, to be 1
precise and perfect in all their actions. If you will have that precision
out of them, and make their fingers measure degrees like cogwheels,
and their arms strike curves like compasses, you must unhumanize
them. All the energy of their spirits must be given to make cogs 5
and compasses of themselves. All their attention and strength must
go to the accomplishment of the mean act. The eye of the soul must

be bent upon the finger point, and the soul's force must fill all the invisible nerves that guide it, ten hours a day, that it may not err from its steely precision, and so soul and sight be worn away, and 10 the whole human being be lost at last – a heap of sawdust, so far as its intellectual work in this world is concerned; saved only by its Heart, which cannot go into the form of cogs and compasses, but expands, after the ten hours are over, into fireside humanity.

bent (l.8): concentrated
err (l.9): wander away from (*archaic*)
sawdust (l.11): very small bits of wood that fall when it is being sawn

- i) What do the following refer to: 'the mean act' (l.7); 'its Heart' (l.12); 'fireside humanity' (l.14)?
  ii) Find an example of a metaphor and comment on its effectiveness.
  iii) Do you agree with Ruskin's argument?

Extract 2   Ruskin refers to the Gothic craftsmen of the Middle Ages:

GLOSSARY
goblins (l.3): imaginary creatures that play tricks on people
anatomiless (l.4): without human proportion
rank (l.6): occupy a position
charters (l.7): written statements giving rights
charities (l.7): acts of generosity

... go forth again to gaze upon the old cathedral front, where you 1 have smiled so often at the fantastic ignorance of the old sculptors: examine once more those ugly goblins, and formless monsters, and stern statues, anatomiless and rigid; but do not mock at them, for they are signs of the life and liberty of every workman who struck 5 the stone; a freedom of thought, and rank in scale of being, such as no laws, no charters, no charities can secure; but which it must be the first aim of all Europe at this day to regain for her children.

- i) What form are the verbs 'go' (l.1), 'examine' (l.3) and 'do not mock' (l.4) in? What does the use of this form show?
  ii) Find an example of alliteration.

Extract 3

GLOSSARY
ill (l.1): badly
verily (l.6): truly (an archaic word much used in the 1611 translation of the Bible)
of old (l.9): in earlier times
precipice (l.11): steep drop
pestilential (l.12): destructive and evil

It is not that men are ill fed, but that they have no pleasure in the 1 work by which they make their bread, and therefore look to wealth as the only means of pleasure. It is not that men are pained by the scorn of the upper classes, but they cannot endure their own; for they feel that the kind of labour to which they are condemned is 5 verily a degrading one, and makes them less than men. Never had the upper classes so much sympathy with the lower, or charity for them, as they have at this day, and yet never were they so much hated by them: for, of old, the separation between the noble and the poor was merely a wall built by law; now it is a veritable dif- 10 ference in level of standing, a precipice between upper and lower grounds in the field of humanity, and there is pestilential air at the bottom of it.

- Find an example of each of the following: *repetition; generalisation; metaphor*. What is their overall effect?

Extract 4

. . . imperfection is in some sort essential to all that we know of life. 1
It is the sign of life in a mortal body, that is to say, of a state of progress and change. Nothing that lives is, or can be, rigidly perfect;
part of it is decaying, part nascent. The foxglove blossom – a third
part bud, a third part past, a third part in full bloom – is a type of 5
the life of this world. And in all things that live there are certain
irregularities and deficiencies which are not only signs of life, but
sources of beauty. No human face is exactly the same in its lines on
each side, no leaf perfect in its lobes, no branch in its symmetry.
All admit irregularity as they imply change; and to banish imper- 10
fection is to destroy expression, to check exertion, to paralyze vitality. All things are literally better, lovelier, and more beloved for
the imperfections which have been divinely appointed, that the
law of human life may be Effort, and the law of human judgment,
Mercy. 15

(from *The Stones of Venice*)

● What is the effect of the words 'no' (l.8) and 'all' (l.10 and l.12)?

Understanding and interpretation

Rewrite the following paragraph, filling in the gaps with as many words as you like to summarise Ruskin's argument. Use your own words as far as possible.

Ruskin argues that when you make man work with the preciseness of machines

.... For Ruskin sculptors in the Middle Ages represent

.... Men are nowadays degraded by .... and

so the gap between the upper and lower classes .... Perfection

....

**7.2.2
The Pre-Raphaelite
Brotherhood**

The Pre-Raphaelite Brotherhood was an essentially anti-Victorian movement of poets and painters which began just before 1850. For them the Italian artist Raphael (1483–1520) represented technical skill at the

A Hireling Shepherd *by William Holman Hunt*

217

expense of spiritual feeling. Echoing Ruskin they looked back to the tender, unmechanical spirit of the Middle Ages, but with more of a spirit of fantasy and nostalgia.

● Make one sentence from each of these groups of words.

a) for its own sake / saw 'being inspired' / as social duties / and were opposed to technique / The Pre-Raphaelites / and creating beauty

b) modern ugliness / In revolt / the Brotherhood / supported beauty and style / against

c) Keats and Tennyson / its poetical inspiration / drew / on the ardour of / for / The movement

d) little connection / having / of the time / The Pre-Raphaelites saw / an autonomous activity / the political and social issues / art as / with

e) The Brotherhood was encouraged by the Oxford Movement / that it was a direct descendant / between post-Reformation Catholicism and Protestantism / which argued that the Church of England should be independent of the state / and so was a middle way / of the medieval Catholic Church / a religious movement

Pre-Raphaelite poetry became more an escape from reality than an illumination of it. It is frequently dreamlike and personal in a way that excludes the reader. Relying on the poetic language and rhythms of previous writers it is mainly highly artificial, lacking in spontaneity, freshness and immediacy.

7.2.3 Dante Gabriel Rossetti (1828–1882)

A colourful and extravagant personality, Dante Gabriel Rossetti (the son of an Italian political refugee) was the founder of the Pre-Raphaelite movement. His sister Christina (1830–1894) was a deeply religious Anglo-Catholic and product of the Oxford Movement, whose verse was simpler and extremely pious.

This is from the sonnet sequence *The House of Life* (1870–1881), an evocation of 'life representative, as associated with aspiration and foreboding, or with ideal art and beauty'. The sequence, regarded by some Victorians as lewd and excessively sensual, has also been seen as an expression of Rossetti's sorrow over his wife's death and a record of his love for the wife of William Morris (see below).

Willowwood – 1

I sat with Love upon a woodside well,   1
    Leaning across the water, I and he;
    Nor ever did he speak nor looked at me,
But touched his lute wherein was audible
The certain secret thing he had to tell.   5
    Only our mirrored eyes met silently
In the low wave; and that sound came to be
The passionate voice I knew; and my tears fell.

GLOSSARY

well (l.1): place in the ground where water comes from, usually with round walls leading down to the water

lute (l.4): an ancient stringed instrument

drouth (l.11): (drought) long period without water

ripples (l.12): very small waves

brimming (l.14): full to the top

And at their fall, his eyes beneath grew hers;
And with his foot and with his wing feathers   10
   He swept the spring that watered my heart's drouth.
Then the dark ripples spread to waving hair,
And as I stooped, her own lips rising there
   Bubbled with brimming kisses at my mouth.

7.2.4 William Morris (1834–1896)

William Morris was a later associate of the Brotherhood, although never actually a member. He was a highly respected painter of his day and is still well known as a designer of textiles and fabrics, a craftsman who rejected the machine in favour of handiwork. Morris, both a Victorian 'prophet' and a man of action, was also one of the founders of the Socialist League (1884) and at the very time the optimistic belief in material progress was declining in England, described a socialist England in 'utopian' terms. For him, poetry was a relaxation and an amusement.

Towards the end of his early 'medieval romance' *The Hollow Land* (1856), Florian and his love Margaret finally reach the 'hollow city in the Hollow Land':

GLOSSARY

fanning (l.2): causing the air to blow

many-coloured banners (l.2): heraldic flags

cloistered (l.5): shut off from the world

din and hubbub (l.6): confused mixture of loud noises

dwelt (l.7): lived

ungolden times (l.7): times of great unhappiness and lack of prosperity and achievement

golden dwellings (l.10): superbly built living places

clasped (l.14): embraced tightly

leafage and tendrils (l.15): leaves and stems

valves (l.16): doors on hinges

winged and garlanded (l.17): decorated with wings and flowers

raiment (l.18): clothes

awe (l.20): a mixture of admiration and fear

Through the golden streets under the purple shadows of the houses   1
we went, and the slow fanning backward and forward of the many-coloured banners cooled us: we two alone; there was no one with us, no soul will ever be able to tell what we said, how we looked.

At last we came to a fair palace, cloistered off in the old time,   5
before the city grew golden from the din and hubbub of traffic; those who dwelt there in the old ungolden times had had their own joys, their own sorrows, apart from the joys and sorrows of the multitude: so, in like manner, was it now cloistered off from the eager leaning and brotherhood of the golden dwellings: so now it   10
had its own gaiety, its own solemnity, apart from theirs; unchanged, unchangeable, were its marble walls, whatever else changed about it.

We stopped before the gates and trembled, and clasped each other closer; for there among the marble leafage and tendrils that were   15
round and under and over the archway that held the golden valves, were wrought two figures of a man and woman, winged and garlanded, whose raiment flashed with stars; and their faces were like faces we had seen or half seen in some dream long and long and long ago, so that we trembled with awe and delight   20

(from *The Hollow Land*)

● In what ways are the extracts from Rossetti and Morris typically Pre-Raphaelite?

7.3 The Labour Movement

*The Socialist League 1884
(William Morris is fourth
from the right in the
second row from the
front)*

In England, the late Victorian period was a time of popular political and social movements.

● i) Punctuate the following. Add capital letters and parentheses where necessary.

In 1868 the Trades Union Congress tuc was started and trade unionism after a stormy history had at last a national organisation in 1871 strikes were legalised and in 1876 unions had a right to exist as corporations the labour party was founded in 1900 as a consequence of a tuc resolution with the support of such socialist groups as the fabians set up in 1884 a society of socialistic intellectuals who believed in piecemeal action through parliamentary reform rather than revolution and were led for a time by george bernard shaw 1856 1950 and beatrice webb 1858 1943 the labour party has always received strong financial support from the unions

ii) Do you know the names of any Labour prime ministers?

7.4 More Victorian Themes: Nature

In the nineteenth century natural science suggested that nature was essentially destructive and indifferent to man. In Tennyson this idea is set against the idea of the love of God.

**7.4.1
Gerard Manley
Hopkins
(1844–1889)**

Gerard Manley Hopkins, however, suggests that nature is delicate and capable of being destroyed. As a poet he manages to recreate in words the living actuality of a natural scene as well as the poet's response to it.

This is a prose paraphrase of the lyric poem 'Binsey Poplars' (1879):

A whole row of aspen trees I loved have been cut down. Their leaves took the heat and light out of the lively sun and made a shadow which looked a bit like a sandal as it moved over the river and meadow. I wish we knew what we were doing when we dig up and cut down the green things of nature! The countryside is delicate and sensitive – just like our eyeball – and can be destroyed by a single careless action. Even when we want to put nature right we kill her. People who come to that very special spot later will never be able to guess the beauty and distinctive life that only ten or twelve cuts have taken away.

Binsey Poplars

My aspens dear, whose airy cages quelled,   1
Quelled or quenched in leaves the leaping sun,
All felled, felled, are all felled;
    Of a fresh and following folded rank
        Not spared, not one   5
        That dandled a sandalled
    Shadow that swam or sank
On meadow and river and wind-wandering weed-winding bank.

O if we but knew what we do
    When we delve or hew –   10
Hack and rack the growing green!
    Since country is so tender
To touch, her being so slender,
That, like this sleek and seeing ball
But a prick will make no eye at all,   15
Where we, even where we mean

        To mend her we end her,
    When we hew or delve:
After-comers cannot guess the beauty been.
Ten or twelve, only ten or twelve   20
    Strokes of havoc unselve
        The sweet especial scene,
Rural scene, a rural scene,
Sweet especial rural scene.

● Which word suggests the sun is like a wild beast?

Appreciation   i) Notice that although there are some rhythmic regularities in this poem there is no single unifying form (as there is in a sonnet). This enables the verse to move in such a way that it can convey the poet's emotions, the life of nature and the actions described.

Find an example of:
a) repetition to convey sadness;
b) part of a long sentence which conveys calmness and gentle movement;
c) sound-repetition to suggest the poet's anger at the violent destruction;
d) sound-repetition to convey a sense of playfulness.

ii) Find at least one example of:

a) alliteration;

b) rhythm which helps us experience the meaning;

c) repeated echoes of one sound over several lines.

What is lost in the prose paraphrase?

Gerard Manley Hopkins

Influenced by the Oxford Movement, Hopkins (see also Supplement 7) gave up poetry in 1868 and joined the Roman Catholic Church. Nine years later he started to write again, although his poems were so unusual they were not published until 1918, after his death. Since 1930 he has been regarded as the outstanding poet of the period, whose energy and seriousness is in contrast with much of the 'literary', derivative work of his contemporaries. Nevertheless, his thought had something in common with Pre-Raphaelite 'philosophy' and he too was influenced by the sensuous immediacy of Keats.

7.5 The path to Aestheticism (2)

Aesthetes such as Oscar Wilde (1854–1900), the Catholic convert Lionel Johnson (1867–1902) and the naturalistic novelist George Moore (1852–1933) owed much to the early nineteenth-century French doctrine of 'L'art pour l'Art' (Art for Art's sake). Influenced by Walter Pater, they rejected Ruskin's moral purpose in art in favour of beauty of form and, at their most extreme, cultivated artificial (if witty) styles of speech and manner and eccentricity of dress. Although they gave the impression of 'fin de siècle', high-society decadence and shocked Victorian society, the Aesthetes nevertheless retained – if not always obviously – a very English concern for moral values.

A satire on the Aesthetic Movement that appeared in Punch *in 1880*

NINCOMPOOPIANA.—THE MUTUAL ADMIRATION SOCIETY.

Our Gallant Colonel (who is not a Member thereof, to Mrs. Cimabue Brown, who is). "AND WHO'S THIS YOUNG HERO THEY'RE ALL SWARMING OVER NOW!"

Mrs. Cimabue Brown. "JELLABY POSTLETHWAITE, THE GREAT POET, YOU KNOW, WHO SAT FOR MAUDLE'S 'DEAD NARCISSUS'! HE HAS JUST DEDICATED HIS *LATTER-DAY SAPPHICS* TO ME. IS NOT HE *BEAUTIFUL*!"

Our Gallant Colonel. "WHY, WHAT'S THERE *BEAUTIFUL* ABOUT HIM!"

Mrs. Cimabue Brown. "OH, LOOK AT HIS GRAND HEAD AND POETIC FACE, WITH THOSE FLOWERLIKE EYES, AND THAT EXQUISITE SAD SMILE! LOOK AT HIS SLENDER WILLOWY FRAME, AS YIELDING AND FRAGILE AS A WOMAN'S! THAT'S YOUNG MAUDLE, STANDING JUST BEHIND HIM—THE GREAT PAINTER, YOU KNOW. HE HAS JUST PAINTED ME AS 'HÉLOÏSE,' AND MY HUSBAND AS 'ABÉLARD.' IS NOT HE *DIVINE*!"

N.B.—Postlethwaite and Maudle are quite unknown to fame. [*The Colonel hooks it.*

Walter Pater, the scholar and critic, insisted that art should be a fusion of psychic and sensuous ecstasy. It should aim only at beauty and not concern itself with moral purpose or social practicalities. In his most famous work, *Studies in the History of the Renaissance* (1873), he tries to convey the 'special unique impression of pleasure' that Renaissance artists, like the then-neglected Botticelli (1444–1510) made on him. Pater's artificially 'beautiful' style, however, has subsequently led to him being ignored by twentieth-century readers.

In the following extract Pater describes Botticelli's *The Birth of Venus*.

● Do you agree with his interpretation?

The Birth of Venus *by Sandro Botticelli*

GLOSSARY

mere (l.1): nothing more than

cloyed you (l.2): given you too much and made it unpleasant

promontory (l.3): point of land sticking out into the sea

slopes down (l.4): goes down

The light is indeed cold – mere sunless dawn; but a later painter   1
would have cloyed you with sunshine; and you can see the better
for that quietness in the morning air each long promontory, as it
slopes down to the water's edge. Men go forth to their labours until
the evening; but she is awake before them, and you might think   5
that the sorrow in her face was at the thought of the whole long day
of love yet to come. An emblematical figure of the wind blows hard
across the grey water, moving forward the dainty-lipped shell on

which she sails, the sea 'showing his teeth' as it moves in thin lines
of foam, and sucking in, one by one, the falling roses, each severe   10
in outline, plucked off short at the stalk, but embrowned a little, as
Botticelli's flowers always are. Botticelli meant all that imagery to
be altogether pleasurable; and it was partly an incompleteness of
resources, inseparable from the art of that time, that subdued and
chilled it; but his predilection for minor tones counts also; and   15
what is unmistakable is the sadness with which he has conceived
the goddess of pleasure, as the depositary of a great power over the
lives of men.

(from *Studies in the History of the Renaissance*)

7.5.2
Algernon Charles Swinburne (1837–1909)

In contrast with novelists such as George Eliot and Dickens, who were
searching for deeper moral experience, the poet and critic Algernon
Charles Swinburne saw his vocation as the pursuit of beauty for its own
sake. He rejected Christianity (as we can see in the lines addressed to
Christ: 'Thou hast conquered, O pale Galilean, the world/has grown grey
with thy breath') and, being something of a dissipated aristocrat, turned
middle-class morality on its head on such matters as sex. ('The lilies and
langours of virtue/The roses and raptures of vice').

Although Swinburne's wordy and literary verse is no longer much
read, Tennyson praised it for 'its wonderful rhythmic invention'.

This is the opening of the choral hymn to Artemis (or, in Roman
mythology, Diana), the huntress and virgin goddess of the moon, at the
beginning of Swinburne's early play *Atalanta in Calydon* (1865):

When the hounds of spring are on winter's traces,   1
   The mother of months in meadow or plain
Fills the shadows and windy places
   With lisp of leaves and ripple of rain;
And the brown bright nightingale amorous   5
Is half assuaged for Itylus,
For the Thracian ships and the foreign faces,
   The tongueless vigil and all the plain.

(from *Atalanta in Calydon*)

GLOSSARY

hounds (l.1): hunting dogs
mother . . . (l.2):
(because the goddess of
the moon affects the
seasons)
lisp (l.4): unclear sound
like the sound of the
tongue on the teeth

nightingale (l.5): (after
Philomela, daughter of
a king of Athens, was
raped by her brother-
in-law, Tereus, and had
her tongue cut out, she
was changed into a
nightingale)
assuaged for (l.6): pacified
(after the death of . . .)

Itylus (l.6): (In revenge for
Philomela's rape, her
sister, Procne, killed
her own son, Itylus,
and fed the child's
body to her husband,
Tereus)
Thracian (l.7): (Thrace is a
region which includes
part of Greece, Bulgaria
and Turkey)

- Critics have used these lines from the poem to make the following critical points:
  - Swinburne's use of rhythm and sounds hypnotises the reader and obscures the
    lack of real meaning.

– Alliteration is used to create no more than pleasing sounds.
– The verse is lacking in visual precision.

Select one. Do you agree? Show why/why not.

**7.5.3
Oscar Wilde
(1854–1900)**

Oscar Wilde

● What can you deduce about Wilde's art and life from the following extracts?

Extract 1
This extract is from the preface to *The Picture of Dorian Gray* (1891), a Gothic novel about a handsome young man in pursuit of sensual pleasure:

> The artist is the creator of beautiful things. 1
> To reveal art and conceal the artist is art's aim.
> The critic is he who can translate into another manner or a new material his impression of beautiful things.
> The highest, as the lowest, form of criticism is a mode of auto- 5 biography.
> Those who find ugly meaning in beautiful things are corrupt without being charming. This is a fault.
> Those who find beautiful meanings in beautiful things are the cultivated. For these there is hope. 10
> They are the elect to whom beautiful things mean only Beauty.
> There is no such thing as a moral or an immoral book.
> Books are well written, or badly written. That is all.
>
> All art is at once surface and symbol.
> Those who go beneath the surface do so at their peril. 15
> Those who read the symbol do so at their peril.

It is the spectator, and not life, that art really mirrors.

Diversity of opinion about a work of art shows that the work is new, complex, and vital.

When critics disagree the artist is in accord with himself. We can forgive a man for making a useful thing as long as he does not admire it. The only excuse for making a useless thing is that one admires it intensely. All art is quite useless. 20

● For Wilde, art is deeply moral. True or false?

Extract 2   This extract is from the novel *The Picture of Dorian Gray*:

The worship of the senses has often, and with much justice, been decried, men feeling a natural instinct of terror about passions and sensations that seem stronger than themselves, and that they are conscious of sharing with the less highly organized forms of existence. But it appeared to Dorian Gray that the true nature of the senses had never been understood, and that they had remained savage and animal merely because the world had sought to starve them into submission or to kill them by pain, instead of aiming at making them elements of a new spirituality, of which a fine instinct for beauty was to be the dominant characteristic. As he looked back upon men moving through History, he was haunted by a feeling of loss. So much had been surrendered! and to such little purpose! . . . 1

5

10

Yes: there was to be a new Hedonism that was to recreate life, and to save it from that harsh, uncomely puritanism that is having, in our own day, its curious revival. . . . Its aim, indeed, was to be experience itself, and not the fruits of experience, sweet or bitter as they might be. Of the asceticism that deadens the senses, as of the vulgar profligacy that dulls them, it was to know nothing. But it was to teach man to concentrate himself upon the moments of a life that is itself but a moment. 15

20

(from *The Picture of Dorian Gray*)

● According to Dorian Gray, sensual passion should be respected. True or false?

Dorian Gray is allowed to remain eternally young while his portrait ages and shows signs of corruption. Seeing his image grow monstrous and ugly, Gray is overcome by guilt and tries to destroy the painting. However, he is the one who dies while his portrait returns to its former beauty.

Extract 3   This extract is from the beginning of the play *The Importance of Being Earnest* (1895), of which Wilde said, 'it has as its philosophy . . . that we should treat all trivial things of life seriously, and all the serious things of life with sincere and studied triviality'.

● Which poet in this unit has the first name Algernon? What can you deduce about the three characters in the extract?

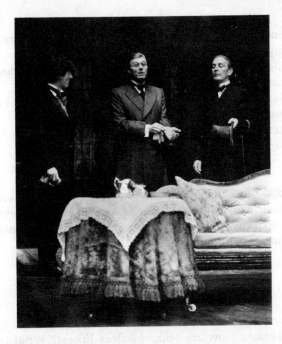

The Importance of Being Earnest
(National Theatre 1982)

Morning-room in Algernon's flat in Half-Moon Street. The room is luxuriously and artistically furnished. The sound of a piano is heard in the adjoining room.

[*LANE is arranging afternoon tea on the table and, after the music has ceased, ALGERNON enters.*]

ALGERNON: Did you hear what I was playing, Lane?

LANE: I didn't think it polite to listen, sir.

ALGERNON: I'm sorry for that, for your sake. I don't play accurately – anyone can play accurately – but I play with wonderful expression. As far as the piano is concerned, sentiment is my forte. I keep science for Life.

LANE: Yes, sir.

ALGERNON: And, speaking of the science of Life, have you got the cucumber sandwiches cut for Lady Bracknell?

LANE: Yes, sir. [*Hands them on a salver*]

ALGERNON [*Inspects them, takes two, and sits down on the sofa*]: Oh! ... by the way, Lane, I see from your book that on Thursday night, when Lord Shoreman and Mr Worthing were dining with me, eight bottles of champagne are entered as having been consumed.

LANE: Yes, sir; eight bottles and a pint.

ALGERNON: Why is it that at a bachelor's establishment the servants invariably drink the champagne? I ask merely for information.

LANE: I attribute it to the superior quality of the wine, sir. I have often observed that in married households the champagne is rarely of a first-rate brand.

ALGERNON: Good heavens! Is marriage so demoralizing as that?

LANE: I believe it *is* a very pleasant state, sir. I have had very little experience of it myself up to the present. I have only been married

GLOSSARY

Half-Moon Street (l.1): once a highly fashionable street in London

adjoining (l.3): next

sentiment (l.10): (playing the piano with) tender feeling

forte (l.10): strong point

salver (l.15): silver tray

your book (l.17): (the 'cellar book' in which records were kept of wines)

brand (l.26): quality

227

once. That was in consequence of a misunderstanding between myself and a young person.

ALGERNON [*languidly*]: I don't know that I am much interested in your family life, Lane.

LANE: No, sir; it is not a very interesting subject. I never think of it myself.

ALGERNON: Very natural, I am sure. That will do, Lane, thank you.

LANE: Thank you, sir.

[*LANE goes out*]

ALGERNON: Lane's views on marriage seem somewhat lax. Really, if the lower orders don't set us a good example, what on earth is the use of them? They seem, as a class, to have absolutely no sense of moral responsibility.

[*Enter LANE*]

LANE: Mr Ernest Worthing.

[*Enter JACK. LANE goes out*]

ALGERNON: How are you, my dear Ernest? What brings you up to town?

JACK: Oh, pleasure, pleasure! What else should bring one anywhere? Eating as usual, I see, Algy!

ALGERNON [*stiffly*]: I believe it is customary in good society to take some slight refreshment at five o'clock. Where have you been since last Thursday?

JACK [*sitting down on the sofa*]: In the country.

ALGERNON: What on earth do you do there?

JACK [*pulling off his gloves*]: When one is in town one amuses oneself. When one is in the country one amuses other people. It is excessively boring.

ALGERNON: And who are the people you amuse?

JACK [*airily*]: Oh, neighbours, neighbours.

ALGERNON: Got nice neighbours in your part of Shropshire?

JACK: Perfectly horrid! Never speak to one of them.

ALGERNON: How immensely you must amuse them!

lax (l.39): unstrict
lower orders (l.40): people from the lower social classes
Shropshire (l.61): a county in the west of England

(from *The Importance of Being Earnest*)

Extract 4   In 1895 Wilde was arrested and sentenced to two years in prison for homosexuality. This extract is from the *Ballad of Reading Gaol* (1898), a poem about a soldier in the cavalry sentenced to death for murdering 'the woman whom he loved':

The Governor was strong upon
  The Regulations Act:
The Doctor said that Death was but
  A scientific fact:
And twice a day the Chaplain called,
  And left a little tract.

And twice a day he smoked his pipe,
  And drank his quart of beer:
His soul was resolute, and held
  No hiding-place for fear;   10
He often said that he was glad
  The hangman's day was near.

But why he said so strange a thing
  No warder dared to ask:
For he to whom a watcher's doom   15
  Is given as his task,
Must set a lock upon his lips
  And make his face a mask.

Or else he might be moved, and try
  To comfort or console: 20
And what should Human Pity do
  Pent up in Murderer's Hole?
What word of grace in such a place
  Could help a brother's soul?   (from *Ballad of Reading Goal*)

● The soldier seems to be looking forward to death. True or false?

Extract 5 These extracts are from *De Profundis* (Wilde's confession, written in prison as a letter to his friend Alfred Douglas and published in 1905):

The gods had given me almost everything. I had a genius, a dis- 1
tinguished name, high social position, brilliancy, intellectual daring.
... I treated art as the supreme reality and life as a mere mode of
fiction. ... But I let myself be lured into long spells of senseless
and sensual ease. ... Tired of being on the heights, I deliberately 5
went to the depths in the search for new sensation. What the
paradox was to me in the sphere of thought, perversity became to
me in the sphere of passion. Desire, at the end, was a malady, or a
madness, or both. I grew careless of the lives of others. I took pleasure where it pleased me, and passed on. I forgot that every little 10
action of the common day makes or unmakes character, and that
therefore what one has done in the secret chamber one has some
day to cry aloud on the house tops. ... I ceased to be lord over myself. I was no longer the captain of my soul, and did not know it. I
allowed pleasure to dominate me. I ended in horrible disgrace! 15
There is only one thing for me now, absolute humility ... something tells me that nothing in the whole world is meaningless, and
suffering least of all.

I am completely penniless, and absolutely homeless. Yet there are 20
worse things in the world than that. I am quite candid when I say
that rather than go out from this prison with bitterness in my heart

against the world, I would gladly and readily beg my bread from door to door. If I got nothing from the house of the rich I would get something at the house of the poor. Those who have much are often greedy; those who have little always share.

Religion does not help me. The faith that others give to what is unseen, I give to what one can touch, and look at. My gods dwell in temples made with hands; and within the circle of actual experience is my creed made perfect and complete: too complete, it may be, for like many or all of those who have placed their heaven in this earth, I have found in it not merely the beauty of heaven, but the horror of hell also.

creed (l.30): set of beliefs

(from *De Profundis*)

Understanding and interpretation

i) Is Wilde still a proud man?
ii) From the previous extracts find at least one example of three of the following:
  a) the philosophy of aestheticism
  b) a belief that desires and instincts should be immediately satisfied
  c) morality and guilt
  d) contempt for others
  e) cynical wit

iii) Try to describe Wilde in your own words. How many of these phrases do you agree with?

complex   weak   extremely sensitive   deliberately shocking for its own sake   upper-class snob   self-centred and self-pitying   intelligent   courageous   vulgar in his opposition to the vulgar

Oscar Wilde

Wilde was the son of an eminent Irish surgeon. On landing at New York for a lecture tour in 1882 he said: 'I have nothing to declare except my genius'. In 1884 he married and had two sons. On release from prison in 1897 he lived in exile in France, under the showy pseudonym of Sebastian Melmoth. His health was poor and he had financial problems. Shortly before his death, he declared: 'I am dying beyond my means.'

7.6 Europeans in Africa

In Africa, European greed for profit and territory led to brutal exploitation of the natives.

7.6.1 Joseph Conrad (1857–1924)

Joseph Conrad, the son of a Polish exile, first went to sea on a French ship in 1874. Ten years later he became a British citizen; twenty years later he gave up the sea because of ill-health and settled in England to write in English, his third language. In 1890 Conrad had made an expedition to the Congo in Central Africa – the voyage which caused his illness and stimulated his desire to write – where he saw the corruption of the European colonialists and the desolation of the natives at first hand. In contrast to the Aesthetes and their belief in Art for Art's sake, for Conrad, life and art were integrated and completely serious.

Heart of Darkness In *Heart of Darkness* (1902) the narrator, Marlow, on board a boat anchored peacefully in the Thames, tells the story of his river journey for a European trading company to the middle of the ivory trade in the depths of Central Africa.

Extract 1 At the beginning of his journey, at the company's Outer Station (the first stopping place on a voyage to the interior), he comes across a slave gang, tied together by chains.

● What state do you imagine they were in?

GLOSSARY

toiling (l.1): walking wearily

clink (l.3): high, sharp sound of metal against metal

loins (l.4): from the waist to the lower part of the hips

waggled (l.4): moved from side to side

bights (l.7): hanging curved parts in the middle

report (l.8): loud explosion (the Europeans were blowing holes in rock to build a railway)

meagre breasts panted (l.13): very thin chests breathed fast

violently . . . quivered (l.14): (their) much larger than usual nostrils were trembling

Six black men advanced in a file, toiling up the path. They walked erect and slow, balancing small baskets full of earth on their heads, and the clink kept time with their footsteps. Black rags were wound round their loins, and the short ends behind waggled to and fro like tails. I could see every rib, the joints of their limbs were like knots in a rope; each had an iron collar on his neck, and all were connected together with a chain whose bights swung between them rhythmically clinking. Another report from the cliff made me think suddenly of that ship of war I had seen firing into a continent. It was the same kind of ominous voice; but these men could by no stretch of imagination be called enemies. They were called criminals, and the outraged law, like the bursting shells, had come to them, an insoluble mystery from the sea. All their meagre breasts panted together, the violently dilated nostrils quivered, the eyes stared stonily up-hill. They passed me within six inches, without a glance, with that complete, death-like indifference of unhappy savages. [1] [5] [10] [15]

Extract 2 Going under some trees to get in the shade Marlow steps 'into the gloomy circle of some Inferno', a place where 'black shapes' had 'withdrawn to die'.

● What do you think his feelings are? What would yours be?

GLOSSARY

recesses (l.4): secret hidden places

time contracts (l.5): arrangements, legal in Europe, for 'employing' slaves

uncongenial (l.5): unnatural; unpleasant

moribund (l.7): dying

gleam (l.8): bright light

flicker (l.13): unsteady shining

orbs (l.13): eyes

They were dying slowly – it was very clear. They were not enemies, they were not criminals, they were nothing earthly now, – nothing but black shadows of disease and starvation, lying confusedly in the greenish gloom. Brought from all the recesses of the coast in all the legality of time contracts, lost in uncongenial surroundings, fed on unfamiliar food, they sickened, became inefficient, and were then allowed to crawl away and rest. These moribund shapes were free as air – and nearly as thin. I began to distinguish the gleam of the eyes under the trees. Then, glancing down, I saw a face near my hand. The black bones reclined at full length with one shoulder against the tree, and slowly the eyelids rose and the sunken eyes looked up at me, enormous and vacant, a kind of blind, white flicker in the depths of the orbs, which died out slowly. The man [1] [5] [10] seemed young – almost a boy – but you know with them it's hard to tell. I found nothing else to do but to offer him one of my good Swede's ship's biscuits I had in my pocket.   15

Understanding and interpretation	i) From which phrases do we know
	  a) what work the natives are doing?
	  b) that they have not been well fed?
	  c) that they are beyond life?
	
	ii) Where do we get a sense of Marlow's detachment? His kindness?
	
	iii) What justification did the traders use for enslaving the natives?

Extract 3	After a 200-mile trek across land to the Central Station to join the steamboat he will command, Marlow's expedition eventually sets off on the two-month river voyage into what he calls the 'patient wilderness'. Their aim is to get to the Inner Station, the company's innermost point, to bring back Mr Kurtz, their most successful agent, who is seriously ill.

A steamboat on an African river

Going up that river was like travelling back to the earliest beginnings of the world, when vegetation rioted on the earth and the big trees were kings. An empty stream, a great silence, an impenetrable forest. The air was warm, thick, heavy, sluggish. There was no joy in the brilliance of sunshine. The long stretches of the waterway   5
ran on, deserted, into the gloom of overshadowed distances. On silvery sandbanks hippos and alligators sunned themselves side by side. The broadening waters flowed through a mob of wooded islands; you lost your way on that river as you would in a desert, and butted all day long against shoals, trying to find the channel,   10
till you thought yourself bewitched and cut off for ever from everything you had known once – somewhere – far away – in another

existence perhaps. There were moments when one's past came
back to one, as it will sometimes when you have not a moment to
spare to yourself; but it came in the shape of an unrestful and noisy   15
dream, remembered with wonder amongst the overwhelming rea-
lities of this strange world of plants, and water, and silence. And
this stillness of life did not in the least resemble a peace. It was the
stillness of an implacable force brooding over an inscrutable intention. It looked at you with a vengeful aspect.   20

Extract 4   In this part of the jungle, the natives are not slaves.

- What sounds do you think Marlow heard and saw in the jungle? Do you think he
felt excited or frightened?

It was very quiet there. At night sometimes the roll of drums behind   1
the curtain of trees would run up the river and remain sustained
faintly, as if hovering in the air high over our heads, till the first
break of day. Whether it meant war, peace, or prayer we could not
tell. The dawns were heralded by the descent of a chill stillness;   5
the wood-cutters slept, their fires burned low; the snapping of a
twig would make you start. We were wanderers on prehistoric
earth, on an earth that wore the aspect of an unknown planet. We
could have fancied ourselves the first of men taking possession of
an accursed inheritance, to be subdued at the cost of profound   10
anguish and of excessive toil. But suddenly, as we struggled round
a bend, there would be a glimpse of rush walls, of peaked grass-
roofs, a burst of yells, a whirl of black limbs, a mass of hands clap-
ping, of feet stamping, of bodies swaying, of eyes rolling, under
the droop of heavy and motionless foliage. The steamer toiled along   15
slowly on the edge of a black and incomprehensible frenzy. The
prehistoric man was cursing us, praying to us, welcoming us – who
could tell? We were cut off from the comprehension of our surroundings; we glided past like phantoms, wondering and secretly
appalled, as sane men would be before an enthusiastic outbreak in   20
a madhouse. We could not understand because we were too far and
could not remember, because we were travelling in the night of first
ages, of those ages that are gone, leaving hardly a sign – and no
memories.

The earth seemed unearthly. We are accustomed to look upon the   25
shackled form of a conquered monster, but there – there you could
look at a thing monstrous and free. It was unearthly, and the men
were – No, they were not inhuman. Well, you know, that was the
worst of it – this suspicion of their not being inhuman. It would
come slowly to one. They howled and leaped, and spun, and made   30
horrid faces; but what thrilled you was just the thought of their
humanity – like yours – the thought of your remote kinship with
this wild and passionate uproar. Ugly. Yes, it was ugly enough; but
if you were man enough you would admit to yourself that there
was in you just the faintest trace of a response to the terrible frank-   35
ness of that noise, a dim suspicion of there being a meaning in it

valour (l.40): strength of mind; bravery

gape (l.42): look in surprise with mouth open

shudder (l.42): shake with fear

without a wink (l.42): without closing his eyes

stuff (l.44): essence

rags (l.46): clothes

which you – you so remote from the night of first ages – could comprehend. And why not? The mind of man is capable of anything – because everything is in it, all the past as well as all the future. What was there after all? Joy, fear, sorrow, devotion, valour, rage – who can tell? – but truth – truth stripped of its cloak of time. Let the fool gape and shudder – the man knows, and can look on without a wink. But he must at least be as much of a man as these on the shore. He must meet that truth with his own true stuff – with his own inborn strength. Principles won't do. Acquisitions, clothes, pretty rags – rags that would fly off at the first good shake. No; you want a deliberate belief. 40

45

(from *Heart of Darkness*)

A trading post in Swaziland

Understanding and interpretation

i) a) Which phrases show you that the jungle is not kind and gentle?
 b) Which words describe: Air, Light, Vegetation, Temperature?
 c) Which lines refer to the jungle's prehistorical aspect?
 d) Which words/phrases/lines suggest Marlow's difficulty in understanding?

ii) What can you deduce from: 'you lost . . . desert' (Extract 3, l.9); 'the snapping . . . start' (Extract 4, l.6).

iii) What impression do the lines 'a burst of . . . rolling' (Extract 4, l.13–14) make?

iv) What is it that connects Marlow, the civilised man, with the 'savages'?

Language and style

The following are features of Conrad's style
– the vocabulary is very rich;
– he adds one powerful adjective on top of another to create an atmosphere of mystery;
– he is attracted to phrases which say that something cannot be expressed;
– his writing is very musical, containing poetic rhythms and sound-echoes;
– he uses colour symbolically.

234

Analyse one or two sentences to illustrate some of these features.

Mr Kurtz once believed that commercial exploitation would bring culture and civilisation to the natives. He has, though, given in to barbaric rites and allowed the natives to worship him as a semi-divine power. He is at the heart of the darkness which Marlow is both disgusted by and recognises a deep kinship with. He also recognises in Kurtz elements of greatness.

Conrad's short novel is also a symbolic journey of the soul towards the heart of man, which he sees as capable of great evil. It can also be interpreted as an expedition to the underworld, through the circles of hell, to a confrontation with Kurtz, the devil himself.

Joseph Conrad   Conrad's other novels include *Typhoon* (1902), *Nostromo* (1904), *The Secret Agent* (1907) and *Under Western Eyes* (1911).

Read what Conrad had to say about art:

> ... art itself may be defined as a single-minded attempt to render the highest kind of justice to the visible universe, by bringing to light the truth, manifold and one, underlying its every aspect. It is an attempt to find in its forms, in its colors, in its light, in its shadows, in the aspects of matter and in the facts of life, what of each is fundamental, what is enduring and essential – their one illuminating and convincing quality – the very truth of their existence ...
>
> ... the artist appeals to that part of our being which is not dependent on wisdom: to that in us which is a gift and not an acquisition – and, therefore, more permanently enduring. He speaks to our capacity for delight and wonder, to the sense of mystery surrounding our lives; to our sense of pity, and beauty, and pain; to the latent feeling of fellowship with all creation – and to the subtle but invincible conviction of solidarity that knits together the loneliness of innumerable hearts, to the solidarity in dreams, in joy, in sorrow, in aspirations, in illusions, in hope, in fear, which binds men to each other, which binds together all humanity – the dead to the living and the living to the unborn.
>
> (from the preface to *The Nigger of the Narcissus*)

7.7 Henry James (1843–1916): Americans in Europe

Henry James was a New Yorker who spent much of his life in England. In novels such as *The Europeans* (1878), Europeans and Americans brought up in Europe are introduced into American New England, a society with its own traditions based on English Puritanism. In novels such as *The Ambassadors* (1903), we see how different American types get on in Europe.

The novels of James's middle period (such as *What Masie Knew*, 1897) mainly concern English society. The novels of his early period (such as *The*

Portrait of a Lady, 1881) and his later period (such as *The Golden Bowl*, 1904) mainly concern the relationship between the two different consciousnesses of America and Europe. Neither culture is regarded as perfect.

Warm-up When critics describe the contrast between Americans and Europeans in James's novels they use many of the following words:

Americans: innocent   crude   simple   energetic   loud   generous vulgar   honest   commercially-minded   extremely confident   sincere

Europeans: lacking in energy   cultured   corrupt   rich in tradition   formal sophisticated   not serious in attitudes to art   mannered   weak   educated

Which of these do you imagine have a positive connotation? Are you able to say whether such a contrast is true today?

7.7.1
The Portrait of a Lady (1881)

In *The Portrait of a Lady* James explores through the thoughts of the characters such themes as possessiveness, the will to dominate and the corruption of innocence.

Setting: Rome, Italy.

Characters (or 'individual centres of consciousness' – which James thought to be a more accurate term):

Isabel Archer: a beautiful, bright, adventurous girl with a newly-acquired fortune, brought over from New England by her aunt; although open, honest and 'free', in Europe she feels herself to be culturally inferior.

Gilbert Osmond: a handsome, forty-year-old American who has lived in Europe for a number of years; artistic and cultured; self-centred and spiteful; cold-hearted and morally trivial; a man who 'had done nothing apart from achieving a style'; to Isabel, though, he is like a prince.

Situation: Despite worthier offers of marriage, Isabel marries Gilbert believing that he has been unjustly deprived of wealth and nobility; in fact he marries her for her money. Slowly, she begins to wake up to what sort of person she has married and the prison she is in ('the shadows had begun to gather; it was as if Osmond deliberately, almost malignantly had put out the lights one by one.').

● What do you imagine her worries are?

She knew of no wrong he had done; he was not violent, he was not cruel: she simply believed he hated her. That was all she accused him of, and the miserable part of it was precisely that it was not a crime, for against a crime she might have found a redress. He had discovered that she was so different, that she was not what he had believed she would prove to be. He had thought at first he could change her, and she had done her best to be what he would like. But she was, after all, herself – she couldn't help that; and now there was no use pretending, wearing a mask or a dress, for he knew her and had made up his mind. ...

She had effaced herself when he first knew her; she had made herself small, pretending there was less of her than there really was. It was because she had been under the extraordinary charm that he,

GLOSSARY
redress (l.4): way of making things right
effaced (l.11): made herself appear unimportant

1

5

10

on his side, had taken pains to put forth. He was not changed; he
had not disguised himself, during the year of his courtship, any
more than she. But she had seen only half his nature then, as one
saw the disk of the moon when it was partly masked by the shadow
of the earth. She saw the full moon now – she saw the whole
man. ...

He was better than any one else. This supreme conviction had filled
her life for months, and enough of it still remained to prove to her
that she could not have done otherwise. The finest – in the sense of
being the subtlest – manly organism she had ever known had become her property, and the recognition of her having but to put out
her hands and take it had been originally a sort of act of devotion.
She had not been mistaken about the beauty of his mind; she knew
that organ perfectly now. She had lived with it, she had lived *in* it
almost – it appeared to have become her habitation. If she had been
captured it had taken a firm hand to seize her; that reflexion perhaps
had some worth. A mind more ingenious, more pliant, more cultivated, more trained to admirable exercises, she had not encoun-
tered; and it was this exquisite instrument she had now to reckon
with. ...

He said to her one day that she had too many ideas and that she
must get rid of them. He had told her that already, before their
marriage; but then she had not noticed it: it had come back to her
only afterwards. This time she might well have noticed it, because
he had really meant it. The words had been nothing superficially;
but when in the light of deepening experience she had looked into
them they had then appeared portentous. He had really meant it –
he would have liked her to have nothing of her own but her pretty
appearance. She had known she had too many ideas; she had more
even than he had supposed, many more than she had expressed to
him when he had asked her to marry him. Yes, she *had* been hypocritical; she had liked him so much. She had too many ideas for
herself; but that was just what one married for, to share them with
some one else. One couldn't pluck them up by the roots, though of
course one might suppress them, be careful not to utter them. It
had not been this, however, his objecting to her opinions; this had
been nothing. She had no opinions – none that she would not have
been eager to sacrifice in the satisfaction of feeling herself loved for
it. What he had meant had been the whole thing – her character, the
way she felt, the way she judged. This was what she had kept in
reserve; this was what he had not known until he had found himself – with the door closed behind, as it were – set down face to face
with it. She had a certain way of looking at life which he took as a
personal offence. ...

Hadn't he assured her that he had no superstitions, no dull limita-
tions, no prejudices that had lost their freshness? Hadn't he all the

his courtship (l.15): when
  he tried to win her
  affections
organism (l.23): living
  being
act of devotion (l.25): action
  of dedicating herself to
  him completely – the
  phrase has a religious
  connotation
ingenious (l.30): clever and
  skilful
pliant (l.30): open to
  suggestion
exquisite (l.32): very clever
  (*archaic*); perfect
portentous (l.40): like a
  threat
hypocritical (l.44): (she
  pretended to be
  something she wasn't)
pluck (l.47): pull

appearance of a man living in the open air of the world, indifferent 60
to small considerations, caring only for truth and knowledge and
believing that two intelligent people ought to look for them together
and, whether they found them or not, find at least some happiness
in the search? He had told her he loved the conventional; but there
was a sense in which this seemed a noble declaration. In that sense, 65
that of the love of harmony and order and decency and of all the
stately offices of life, she went with him freely, and his warning
had contained nothing ominous. But when, as the months had
elapsed, she had followed him further and he had led her into the
mansion of his own habitation, then, *then* she had seen where she 70
really was. ...

Between those four walls she had lived ever since; they were to surround her for the rest of her life. It was the house of darkness, the
house of dumbness, the house of suffocation. Osmond's beautiful
mind gave it neither light nor air; Osmond's beautiful mind indeed 75
seemed to peep down from a small high window and mock at her.
Of course it had not been physical suffering; for physical suffering
there might have been a remedy. She could come and go; she had
her liberty; her husband was perfectly polite. He took himself so
seriously; it was something appalling. Under all his culture, his 80
cleverness, his amenity, under his good-nature, his facility, his
knowledge of life, his egotism lay hidden like a serpent in a bank
of flowers. She had taken him seriously, but she had not taken him
so seriously as that. How could she – especially when she had
known him better? She was to think of him as he thought of him- 85
self – as the first gentleman in Europe. So it was that she had
thought of him at first, and that indeed was the reason she had
married him. But when she began to see what it implied she drew
back; there was more in the bond than she had meant to put her
name to. It implied a sovereign contempt for every one but some 90
three or four very exalted people whom he envied, and for everything in the world but half a dozen ideas of his own. ...

He had his ideal, just as she had tried to have hers; only it was
strange that people should seek for justice in such different quarters.
His ideal was a conception of high prosperity and propriety, of the 95
aristocratic life, which she now saw that he deemed himself always,
in essence at least, to have led. He had never lapsed from it for an
hour; he would never have recovered from the shame of doing
so. ...

Her notion of the aristocratic life was simply the union of great 100
knowledge with great liberty; the knowledge would give one a
sense of duty and the liberty a sense of enjoyment. But for Osmond
it was altogether a thing of forms, a conscious calculated attitude.
He was fond of the old, the consecrated, the transmitted; so was
she, but she pretended to do what she chose with it. He had an 105

stately offices (l.67): noble duties

ominous (l.68): which was a bad sign for the future

peep (l.76): look secretly

amenity (l.81): pleasantness

facility (l.81): ability to do things easily

sovereign contempt (l.90): great lack of respect

exalted (l.91): noble and dignified

propriety (l.95): the conventions and manners of polite society

immense esteem for tradition; he had told her once that the best thing in the world was to have it, but that if one was so unfortunate as not to have it one must immediately proceed to make it. ...

Then it was that her husband's personality, touched as it never had been, stepped forth and stood erect. The things she had said were answered only by his scorn, and she could see he was ineffably ashamed of her. What did he think of her – that she was base, vulgar, ignoble? He at least knew now that she had no traditions! It had not been in his prevision of things that she should reveal such flatness; her sentiments were worthy of a radical newspaper or a Unitarian preacher. The real offence, as she ultimately perceived, was her having a mind of her own at all. Her mind was to be his – attached to his own like a small garden-plot to a deer-park. He would rake the soil gently and water the flowers; he would weed the beds and gather an occasional nosegay. It would be a pretty piece of property for a proprietor already far-reaching. He didn't wish her to be stupid. On the contrary, it was because she was clever that she had pleased him. But he expected her intelligence to operate altogether in his favour, and so far from desiring her mind to be a blank he had flattered himself that it would be richly receptive. He had expected his wife to feel with him and for him, to enter into his opinions, his ambitions, his preferences ...

(from *The Portrait of a Lady*)

110
115
120
125

deemed (l.96): believed

lapsed from it (l.97): failed to live up to his high standards

consecrated (l.104): sacred

transmitted (l.104): things passed down from generation to generation

esteem (l.106): respect

ineffably (l.111): so much so he couldn't express it in words

base (l.112): of humble birth (archaic); inferior

prevision (l.114): what he could see in advance

Unitarian (l.116): a member of a Christian denomination that rejects the doctrine of the Holy Trinity and stresses a united world community

deer-park (l.118): a park attached to a country house

rake (l.119): make the ground in the garden smooth

nosegay (l.120): small bunch of flowers

● How do you think their relationship will develop?

Understanding and interpretation

i) Which of the following, according to Isabel's thoughts, are true of earlier attitudes?

a) Gilbert thought he could change her.

b) She never tried to hide what she was.

c) She was charmed by him.

d) She felt she could dominate him.

e) He only wanted her to be pretty and not to have a mind of her own.

f) He appeared to love only truth and knowledge.

ii) Which of these, according to her thoughts, do we know to be true of present attitudes?

a) He likes her to have a mind which is separate and independent.

b) He is physically violent with her.

c) He feels contempt for her.

d) She still believes him to be a cultured person.

e) He hates her.

iii) Find one phrase which best suggests:

a) Isabel's 'imprisonment'

b) the European consciousness

c) the American consciousness

iv) Discuss the following:

a) Gilbert's 'egotism lay hidden like a serpent in a bank of flowers' (l.82). What does the 'bank of flowers' represent?

b) Why is the phrase 'exquisite instrument' (l.32) ironical?

c) Isabel wanted Gilbert's 'manly organism' to become 'her property' (l.23)? Can we say that she too is egotistic?

Language and style

i) Find one sentence which contains the past perfect tense. What is its purpose?

ii) Find examples of two 'stylistic devices' (for example imagery, repetition, rhythm) and comment on their effect.

iii) The vocabulary of these extracts is probably 'easier' than Conrad's, yet James's style is often regarded as difficult. What do you think it is that makes it difficult?

iv) Unlike Dickens, whose characters come from all parts of society, James mainly writes about the middle or upper-middle classes. Can you make other observations which contrast him with novelists you have read (for example with George Eliot, of whom he was a great admirer)?

7.8 Rupert Brooke (1887–1915) and Georgian poetry

● Find answers to these questions in the passage below:

i) How is Georgian poetry different from the poetry which came immediately before it?

ii) What does the death of Rupert Brooke symbolise?

Between 1912 and 1922, during the reign of George V, there appeared a series of verse anthologies entitled *Georgian Poetry*, edited by Edward Marsh (1872–1953), a classical scholar and distinguished civil servant. Some contributors, such as Robert Graves (1895–1985), objected to being labelled 'Georgian', and the strong-minded, highly-original poetry of T.S. Eliot (1888–1965) and Ezra Pound (1885–1972) which was starting to come out during this period quickly made the movement seem unexciting and conventional. Nevertheless, the volumes had a freshness of vision, a colloquialism and a meditative note that was missing from the decadent romanticism of the latter part of the previous century. While the subject matter was sometimes the exotic and the magical, it was often the quiet pleasures of the English countryside.

Many contributors, such as D.H. Lawrence (1885–1930) and Isaac Rosenberg (1890–1918), now have a high reputation not limited by the term 'Georgian'. Perhaps the most representative voice is that of Rupert Brooke, a young poet of great promise and physical beauty whose verse seems to suggest that he lived in a prosperous and talented world of liberal culture. Brooke's early death is seen as symbolic of the death of a whole generation, whose early idealistic, patriotic attitudes never survived the horrors of the First World War.

This is the opening of his sonnet 'The Soldier' (1914):

> If I should die, think only this of me, 1
> That there's some corner of a foreign field
> That is forever England. There shall be
> In that rich earth a richer dust concealed,
> A dust whom England bore, shaped, made aware, 5
> Gave, once, her flowers to love, her ways to roam,
> A body of England's, breathing English air,
> Washed by the rivers, blest by suns of home.
>
> (from 'The Soldier')

Having served as a soldier in Belgium, Brooke was sent to the Dardanelles – a narrow passage of water separating European and Asian Turkey – but died of blood poisoning on the way.

7.9 War

**7.9.1
The American Civil
War (1861–1865)**

The Civil war was the great trauma of mid-nineteenth-century America. The Southern states, with their large plantations and the institution of slavery, came into conflict with the free industrial and commercial North and tried to break away.

*Federal troops in the
American Civil War*

**7.9.2
Stephen Crane
(1871–1900)**

The Red Badge of Courage (1895) is set in the American Civil War. It tells the story of Henry Fleming, an inexperienced soldier who goes off to war enthusiastically but runs away during his first battle. After being accidentally butted by a rifle he pretends to his colleagues that he has been shot and that the bloody bandage around his head is a 'red badge of courage'. The novel concerns Fleming's reactions to the meaningless confusion around him.

A still from the film The Red Badge of Courage

● Try to imagine the scene the morning after Fleming's accident.

When the youth awoke it seemed to him that he had been asleep for a thousand years, and he felt sure that he opened his eyes upon an unexpected world. Gray mists were slowly shifting before the first efforts of the sun's rays. An impending splendor could be seen in the eastern sky. An icy dew had chilled his face, and immediately upon arousing he curled farther down into his blanket. He stared for a while at the leaves overhead, moving in a heraldic wind of the day.

The distance was splintering and blaring with the noise of fighting. There was in the sound an expression of a deadly persistency, as if it had not begun and was not to cease.

About him were the rows and groups of men that he had dimly seen the previous night. They were getting a last draught of sleep before the awakening. The gaunt, careworn features and dusty figures were made plain by this quaint light at the dawning, but it dressed the skin of the men in corpselike hues and made the tangled limbs appear pulseless and dead. The youth started up with a little cry when his eyes first swept over this motionless mass of men, thick-spread upon the ground, pallid, and in strange postures. His disordered mind interpreted the hall of the forest as a charnel place. He believed for an instant that he was in the house of the dead, and he did not dare to move lest these corpses start up, squalling and

1

5

10

15

20

squalling and squawking
(l.22): screaming and shouting

prophecy (l.25): image of the future

pottering (l.27): moving about from job to job

bugle (l.30): brass musical instrument used by armies as a signal

brazen gamecocks (l.32): shamelessly defiant male game birds

rustled (l.34): made a gentle, light sound

bass (l.36): deep-toned sound

grumbling oaths (l.36): complaining curses

correct (l.37): destroy the strength of the horrors of

peremptory tenor (l.38): quick high voice expecting to be obeyed

unraveled (l.39): separated from each other

corpse-hued (l.40): with the colour of dead bodies

eye-sockets (l.41): the places in the head where the eyes fit

squawking. In a second, however, he achieved his proper mind. He swore a complicated oath at himself. He saw that this somber picture was not a fact of the present, but a mere prophecy. 25

He heard then the noise of a fire crackling briskly in the cold air, and, turning his head, he saw his friend pottering busily about a small blaze. A few other figures moved in the fog, and he heard the hard cracking of axe blows.

Suddenly there was a hollow rumble of drums. A distant bugle 30 sang faintly. Similar sounds, varying in strength, came from near and far over the forest. The bugles called to each other like brazen gamecocks. The near thunder of the regimental drums rolled.

The body of men in the wood rustled. There was a general up-lifting of heads. A murmuring of voices broke upon the air. In it 35 there was much bass of grumbling oaths. Strange gods were addressed in condemnation of the early hours necessary to correct war. An officer's peremptory tenor rang out and quickened the stiffened movement of the men. The tangled limbs unraveled. The corpse-hued faces were hidden behind fists that twisted slowly in 40 the eye sockets.

(from *The Red Badge of Courage*)

- What effect do the drums and bugles have on the men?

Appreciation Crane's poetic style was described by Conrad as 'impressionistic' (it reminded him of the late nineteenth-century French painters who produced effects by light and colour rather than by realistic details of form).

i) Find words/phrases in the extract which relate to each of these: colour, light, noise, movement

ii) Which lines are the most dreamlike?

iii) Find examples of where the sounds of words echo each other. What is the general effect?

Crane was more concerned to express a personal vision of war through an individual experience than to give an accurate account of it or to give it a political and economic dimension.

i) Fleming has a vision of the men as corpses. What does it suggest?

ii) Do you get a sense of Fleming's detachment?

iii) Nature is personified in the passage (it is made into a person, as in 'it dressed the skin of the men . . .', l.15). What is its effect?

iv) How does the spirit of the extract contrast with the spirit of the Brooke poem in 7.8?

Stephen Crane The American Civil War finished six years before Crane's birth. Although he never took part in military action, he became an overseas war reporter for a news syndicate. Crane came to England and became a friend of Henry James and Joseph Conrad. He wrote several short stories and two volumes of 'free verse'. He died of tuberculosis in Baden-Baden.

7.9.3
The First World War
(1914–1918)

What do you know about World War 1? Where was it fought? Who was it between?

Approximately 8,700,000 lives were lost and 21 million people were wounded, although there was no single decisive battle in the whole war. For three years the battle line, which stretched from the Belgian coast to the Swiss border (the 'Western Front'), moved only a few miles. Both sides inhabited trenches in the ground, often half-filled with water and infested with rats, about 180 metres apart from each other. Having made repeated, costly and generally useless attempts to advance, they felt that what seemed like a living hell would go on for ever.

Attending to the wounded in the trenches during the First World War

After almost a whole generation of young men was destroyed, Europe was left with a sense that the bases of civilisation and the traditional values that went with them had disappeared.

Until the Battle of the Somme in 1916, poems written by the soldiers and officers were mainly heroic and patriotic. After that the mood darkened, and some of them made powerful poetry out of their terrible experiences. The effort gave new life to literature.

The following poem is called 'Break of Day in the Trenches'.

It includes these words/phrases:
'rat' 'poppy' 'this English hand' 'the same to a German'

● Can you guess the theme of the poem?

Break of Day in the Trenches

GLOSSARY

crumbles away (l.1): breaks up and disappears

druid (l.2): the druids were a Celtic religious order found in ancient Gaul, Britain and Ireland

queer (l.4): strange

sardonic (l.4): mocking

parapet (l.5): wall protecting the trench

Droll (l.7): strange and amusing

antipathies (l.9): feelings of strong dislike

haughty (l.15): arrogant

less . . . life (l.16): less likely than you to live

Bonds (l.17): ties

whims (l.17): sudden and unexpected desires

Sprawled in the bowels (l.18): spread out in the depths

shrieking (l.21): wild high noise of

Hurled (l.22): thrown violently

quaver (l.23): trembling

aghast (l.23): full of fear

The darkness crumbles away –   1
It is the same old druid Time as ever.
Only a live thing leaps my hand –
A queer sardonic rat –
As I pull the parapet's poppy   5
To stick behind my ear.
Droll rat, they would shoot you if they knew
Your cosmopolitan sympathies
(And God knows what antipathies).
Now you have touched this English hand   10
You will do the same to a German –
Soon, no doubt, if it be your pleasure
To cross the sleeping green between.
It seems you inwardly grin as you pass
Strong eyes, fine limbs, haughty athletes   15
Less chanced than you for life,
Bonds to the whims of murder,
Sprawled in the bowels of the earth,
The torn fields of France.
What do you see in our eyes   20
At the shrieking iron and flame
Hurled through still heavens?
What quaver – what heart aghast?
Poppies whose roots are in man's veins
Drop, and are ever dropping;   25
But mine in my ear is safe,
Just a little white with the dust.

● Do you feel you are sharing the poet's experience in any way?

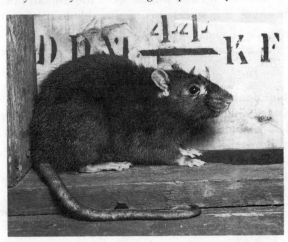

The Common or Brown Rat

i) How does the rat first come to the poet's attention?
ii) In which line does he start talking to it?
iii) In what sense is it 'cosmopolitan'?
iv) Why does it seem to 'inwardly grin'?
v) Is there meant to be an answer to the question 'What do you see ...? (l.20)?

Field poppy

Appreciation

i) What does the poppy symbolise? Can the poet save the symbolic poppies?
ii) Rosenberg's verse has been praised for its new rhythms, imagery and dramatic effects; economic use of language; controlled conversational tone; rich vocabulary; realism. Select two or three lines and illustrate at least one of these points.
iii) What does the theme of the poem have in common with the Crane extract?

Isaac Rosenberg

Rosenberg's humble Jewish parents were emigrés from western Russia. In 1911 another Jewish family paid for him to study art. Defying his family's pacifist views, Rosenberg served as a private in the trenches and was killed in action.

In 1916 Rosenberg, sometimes thought of as obscure, wrote, 'I will not leave a corner of my consciousness covered up but saturate myself with the strange and extraordinary new conditions of this life, and it will refine itself into poetry later on.'

**7.9.5
Wilfred Owen
(1893–1918)**

Poison gas was first used in the second battle of Ypres in 1915.

The following poem, written in 1917, is called '*Dulce et Decorum Est Pro Patria Mori*', a Latin phrase from the Roman poet Horace (65–8 BC), meaning 'It is sweet and honourable to die for your country.'

● What do you imagine the poet's attitude towards war is?

GLOSSARY

Knock-kneed (l.2): having knees which turn inwards and knock together
hags (l.2): ugly, old witches
sludge (l.2): thick mud
haunting (l.3): appearing and re-appearing; staying in the memory

Dulce et Decorum Est Pro Patria Mori

Bent double, like old beggars under sacks,   1
Knock-kneed, coughing like hags, we cursed through sludge,
Till on the haunting flares we turned our backs
And towards our distant rest began to trudge.
Men marched asleep. Many had lost their boots   5
But limped on, blood-shod. All went lame; all blind;
Drunk with fatigue; deaf even to the hoots
Of tired, outstripped Five-Nines that dropped behind.

flares (l.3): light signals shot into the sky

trudge (l.4): walk heavily and slowly

limped (l.6): walked with uneven steps

blood-shod (l.6): with feet covered with blood

hoots (l.7): long whistling cries

outstripped (l.8): (which the men had gone out of reach of)

Five-nines (l.8): shells containing poison gas

fumbling (l.9): feeling about nervously

flound'ring (l.12): making desperate efforts not to lose control

lime (l.12): sticky substance used to catch birds

panes (l.13): sheets of glass

plunges at (l.16): falls towards

guttering (l.16): dying

smothering (l.17): suffocating

writhing (l.19): twisting in pain

jolt (l.21): sudden shake

gargling (l.22): blowing from the throat

cud (l.23): swallowed food

zest (l.24): eager excitement

Gas! Gas! Quick, boys! – An ecstasy of fumbling,
Fitting the clumsy helmets just in time;   10
But someone still was yelling out and stumbling
And flound'ring like a man in fire or lime . . .
Dim, through the misty panes and thick green light,
As under a green sea, I saw him drowning.
In all my dreams, before my helpless sight,   15
He plunges at me, guttering, choking, drowning.

If in some smothering dreams you too could pace
Behind the wagon that we flung him in,
And watch the white eyes writhing in his face,
His hanging face, like a devil's sick of sin;   20
If you could hear, at every jolt, the blood
Come gargling from the froth-corrupted lungs,
Obscene as cancer, bitter as the cud
Of vile, incurable sores on innocent tongues, –
My friend, you would not tell with such high zest   25
To children ardent for some desperate glory,
The old Lie: Dulce et decorum est
Pro patria mori.

- How would you describe the poet's mood?

Understanding and interpretation
i) Which adjectives describe the state of the men as they march?
ii) What happened to the 'someone' (l.11)?
iii) Why do you think Owen makes his description of the dead man so horrible?

Appreciation
i) What is the rhyme scheme of the poem?
ii) How many beats do the first two lines have? Why does Owen make the second line heavier and slower? How does he achieve this?

Wilfred Owen
Owen distrusted all the traditional ideologies that kept the war going and yet he served as an infantry officer, was wounded in 1917, won the Military Cross and was killed a week before the Armistice. Most of his poems were written during a creative burst between the summer of 1917 and the autumn of the next year. Only five were published in his lifetime.

This is what Owen wrote about his poetry:

> Above all I am not concerned with poetry. My subject is war, and the pity of war. The poetry is in the pity. Yet these elegies are to this generation in no sense consolatory. They may be to the next. All the poet can do is warn. That is why true poets must be truthful.

247

This is what *Siegfried Sassoon (1886–1967)*, who also wrote war poetry from the trenches, said of Owen's poetry:

> There was a slowness and sobriety in his method, which was, I think, nondramatic and elegiac rather than leapingly lyrical . . . Stately and processional, it has the rhythm of emotional depth and directness and the verbal resonance of one who felt in glowing primary colours and wrote with solemn melodies in his mind . . .

7.9.6
Robert Graves
(1895–1985)

Until the truth of what was happening was spread by returning soldiers, the horrors of the war were kept from the ordinary people of England, still caught up in patriotic fervour.

This is what Robert Graves, the poet and novelist, wrote in his autobiography *Goodbye to All That* (1929):

> **I had wired my parents that I should be arriving at Waterloo** 1
> **Station the next morning. The roadway from the hospital**
> **train to a row of waiting ambulances had been roped off; as**
> **each stretcher case was lifted from the train, a huge hysterical**
> **crowd surged up to the barrier and uttered a new roar. Flags** 5
> **were being waved. The Somme battle seemed to be regarded**
> **at home as the beginning of the end of the war. As I looked**
> **idly at the crowd, one figure detached itself: to my embarrass-**
> **ment – I recognised my father, hopping about on one leg,**
> **waving an umbrella, and cheering with the best of them . . .** 10
>
> **England looked strange to us returned soldiers. We could not**
> **understand the war-madness that ran wild everywhere, look-**
> **ing for a pseudo-military outlet. The civilians talked a foreign**
> **language; and it was newspaper language. I found serious**
> **conversation with my parents all but impossible . . .** 15

7.10 Chronology

In the twentieth century, in Britain and America, the reading of serious literature has declined. Why do think this is so? Is it a bad thing, do you think?

7.10.1
Town and country

Choose from these prepositions to fill the gaps:

    of   with   from   on   by

i) After the agricultural depression .... 1870–1902 there were 150,000 fewer agricultural labourers, a decrease .... just over forty per cent. It was the end of rural England .... any significant scale; even countrymen became urbanised. The movement towards the towns, and the creation of a lower middle class, was aided .... a 'Free Trade' economic policy.

ii) Although most literary themes became urbanised, many writers such as Thomas Hardy (1840–1928) and Edward Thomas (1878–1917) mourned the loss .... a way of life. George Sturt (1863–1927) wrote eloquently .... the various types of satisfaction that country craftsmen and labourers had derived .... their work, and critics such as F.R. Leavis (1895–1978) have contrasted the organic nature .... the older rural society .... the disharmony and spiritual impoverishment .... a modern technological society.

7.10.2 Beliefs

Victorian family life – Many Happy Returns by *W. P. Frith*

The destruction of many traditional beliefs and assumptions was accelerated at the beginning of the twentieth century. Authority – strict fathers, dominant husbands, powerful politicians – was something to be suspicious of; at the same time there was a decline in the Victorian sense of individual responsibility.

● Which one of the following do you think may have contributed most to the breakdown?

i) The Women's Suffrage Movement pursued mildly violent action to secure political rights for women before and during the First World War. Militants such as Christabel Pankhurst (the daughter of Mrs Emmeline Pankhurst, the founder of the Women's Social and Political Union) were known as 'suffragettes'. In Britain the movement ended in 1918 when votes were given to women of thirty and over; in America, voting rights were given the following year.

ii) Humanity was considered – for example by the German socialist philosopher Karl Marx (1818–1883) – much more in economic and social terms than in religious terms.

iii) Humanity was now seen as part of the natural world and was investigated in a sceptical scientific spirit. Psychologists, in particular Sigmund Freud (1856–1939), showed that a person's actions could be motivated by unconscious and irrational forces in the human personality.

249

iv) The First World War showed the incompetence of the older generation – its politicians and generals.

v) In 1857 desertion was also made grounds for divorce (as well as adultery and cruelty), and proceedings were taken out of the hands of the Church courts.

The First World War is often regarded as the point dividing the 'old' world from the modern world. In the novel *Kangaroo* (1923), D.H. Lawrence wrote:

> It was in 1915 the old world ended. In the winter 1915–16 the spirit of the old London collapsed; the city, in some way, perished, perished from being the heart of the world, and became a vortex of broken passions, lusts, hopes, fears, and horrors. The integrity of London collapsed and the genuine debasement began, the unspeakable baseness of the press and the public voice . . .

7.10.3 The monarchy

Edward VII (reign 1901–1910), Victoria's sixty-year-old son, had had little political experience. His influence was less than Victoria's, although his visit to Paris in 1903 helped cement the 'Entente Cordiale', an informal agreement in 1904 for peace between Britain and France.

George V (reign 1910–1936), Edward's youngest son, won popularity for the work he did during the First World War. He also gave up all German titles and in 1917, in deference to British hostility to Germany, the House of Hanover became the House of Windsor.

7.10.4 British political changes

Which of these phrases fits all of the following gaps?

    made way for   led to

1870: An Education Act .... much greater literacy.

1902: An Education Act .... local authorities administering schooling.

1903: An agreement between middle-class and working-class radicals .... twenty-six Labour victories in the 1906 election (in which the Liberals won a landslide victory) and much reform in the years 1906–1914.

1909: The 'People's Budget' .... the taxation of the wealthy. After its rejection by the House of Lords a Parliament Bill (1910) effectively removed the Lords' right of veto and .... the further decline of the aristocracy. The Reform Act of 1918 .... an increase in the number of those able to vote from a pre-war level of eight million to twenty-one million. The number of MPs was also increased.

1913: The Irish were granted self-government.

During this period further government assistance was given to old age pensions as well as unemployment and health insurance.

7.11 Activities

Creative Writing

Choose one:

– Imagine you are in the trenches during the First World War resting between battles. Write a letter home.

– Imagine you are in the American Civil War. You are just waking up as Henry Fleming looks around him. Write an entry in your diary.

– Write a detailed appreciation of one of the texts in Supplement 7.

Anagrams   Solve the following anagrams. They are all surnames of writers in this and earlier units. The ringed letters form another surname.

E L A W O M R   _ _ _ _ _ ◯ _

H P E K S A A E E S R ◯ _ _ _ _ _ _ _ _ _ _

D I E W L   ◯ _ _ _ _

R T E S E N   _ ◯ _ _ _ _

E L A M V R L   ◯ _ _ _ _ _ _

S M J E A   _ ◯ _ _ _

N O O N H J S   _ _ _ _ _ ◯ _

UNIT 8

Modern times

8.1 New poetry

An exhausted post-1918 world was suspicious of all manifestations of authority. In general, the period of the twenties was anti-heroic and a time of revolt against notions of assertion and will.

8.1.1
W(illiam) B(utler)
Yeats (1865–1939)

W.B. Yeats, an Irish Protestant, shared with the Pre-Raphaelites a hostility to urban and industrial ugliness and the materialism of contemporary English life. Until 1899 he was a leading member of the Aesthetic Movement and wrote dreamy poetry in the tradition of Spenser and Shelley. However, from 1919 until his death he wrote some of the finest poetry in English: vigorous, symbolic and harsh, his sharp contemplation of actuality making him a profoundly modern poet.

W. B. Yeats (left)

Yeats in his later years (right)

'The Second Coming'

The title of Yeats's poem 'The Second Coming' (1919) refers to the Christian belief that Jesus Christ will one day come back into the world. The word 'gyre' (literally a circular or spiral turn) is used in the poem to suggest a cycle of history which is continually turning, dragging behind it a succession of consequences. Yeats believed that human history can be charted on a 'Great Wheel', with each turning of the wheel marking a 2000-year period. In the poem Yeats imagines the end of our 'scientific democratic fact-finding heterogeneous civilisation' and the beginning of the next 2000-year cycle.

Warm-up What do these lines tell you about the poem?

> Things fall apart; the centre cannot hold;
> Mere anarchy is loosed upon the world . . .

> The best lack all conviction, while the worst
> Are full of passionate intensity.

GLOSSARY

falcon (l.2): bird trained to hunt and kill animals

anarchy (l.4): lawlessness and social disorder

revelation (l.9): making known (of the truth – possibly from God)

Spiritus Mundi (l.12): spirit of the world (*Latin*) (the 'Great Memory', the universal unconscious from which poets draw symbolic images)

Reel (l.17): go round and round

indignant (l.17): angry and contemptuous

twenty centuries (l.19): before Christ was born. (Yeats saw the birth of Christ as bringing to an end the cycle from the 'Babylonian mathematical starlight' – 2000 BC – to the dissolution of Greco-Roman culture)

vexed (l.20): shaken (into noisy confusion – archaic)

a rocking cradle (l.20): (the cradle of the infant Christ in Bethlehem)

Slouches (l.22): moves in a tired and lazy way

The Second Coming

crist

Turning and turning in the widening gyre   1
The falcon cannot hear the falconer;
Things fall apart; the centre cannot hold;
Mere anarchy is loosed upon the world,
The blood-dimmed tide is loosed, and everywhere   5
The ceremony of innocence is drowned;
The best lack all conviction, while the worst
Are full of passionate intensity.

Surely some revelation is at hand;
Surely the Second Coming is at hand.   10
The Second Coming! Hardly are those words out
When a vast image out of Spiritus Mundi
Troubles my sight: somewhere in sands of the desert
A shape with lion body and the head of a man,
A gaze blank and pitiless as the sun,   15
Is moving its slow thighs, while all about it
Reel shadows of the indignant desert birds.
The darkness drops again; but now I know
That twenty centuries of stony sleep
Were vexed to nightmare by a rocking cradle,   20
And what rough beast, its hour come round at last,
Slouches towards Bethlehem to be born?

Understanding and interpretation

i) The poem is divided into two parts. How does the second differ from the first in subject and tone?

ii) The poem was written just after the 1914–1918 war, the Russian Revolution (1917) and the Irish troubles of 1916 and 1919–1921. Choose one phrase which best suggests:
   a) a loss of order
   b) the positive value of ritual

iii) Explain the images of the 'falcon' (l.2), the 'tide' (l.5) and the 'darkness' (l.18).

iv) In the Bible (Matthew 24), Christ describes the Second Coming as 'coming in the clouds of heaven with power and great glory. And he shall send his angels with a great sound of a trumpet . . .'. How does this contrast with Yeats's vision?

253

What effect do the following have?

a) repetition of the words 'turning' (l.1), 'loosed' (l.4, l.5) and 'Surely' (l.9, l.10)
b) the word 'Slouches' (l.22)

W.B. Yeats

Yeats believed in the occult. During a magical experience he had an image of 'a desert, and a black Titan [a mythical giant that once ruled the earth] raising himself up by his hands from the middle of a heap of ancient ruins'; 'at my left side just out of the range of sight, a brazen winged beast that I associated with laughing destruction'. He declared that 'we may be about to accept the most implacable authority the world has known'. Later he accepted that the poem 'The Second Coming' might also have been an unconscious prophecy of the rise of Fascism.

In common with other Irish poets, Yeats the nationalist looked to ancient Celtic myth and to Irish peasant folk traditions. In his early years he was very much the poet of the *Celtic Twilight* (the title of his 1893 collection of stories illustrating an Irish belief in the supernatural) and dreamed of legendary heroisms of kings and queens, of fairies, of misty mountains and lakes. Yeats was dissatisfied, though, that he was not expressing his deeper self. For ten years, from 1899, he built up the Irish National Theatre, in the Abbey Theatre, Dublin. As its manager he attempted to make the theatre the voice of a distinctively Irish culture and wrote plays mainly based on Irish myth. Eventually, though, he became disillusioned with Irish politics and in 1911 and 1913 turned away from Ireland until the Easter Rebellion in 1916. Each collection of poems moved further away from the elaborate Pre-Raphaelite style of the 1890s and became sharper in focus, the diction more severe with fewer adjectives and much stronger rhythms. His collections of poems include *The Wild Swans at Coole* (1917) and *The Tower* (1928). (See also Supplement 8.)

● In which of the following extracts from his essays does Yeats

a) appear dissatisfied with life and determined to discover his true self?
b) show confident literary judgement?
c) show his hatred of vulgarity and his sympathy with the aristocracy?

Extract 1

GLOSSARY

vex (l.4): disturb

startle (l.4): surprise; shock

marmorean Muse (l.7): marble-like goddess of poetic inspiration

quiver (l.11): shake (from fear)

bayonet (l.11): soldier's knife at the end of a gun

When I come home after meeting men who are strange to me, and 1
sometimes even after talking to women, I go over all I have said in
gloom and disappointment. Perhaps I have overstated everything
from a desire to vex or startle, from hostility that is but fear; or all
my natural thoughts have been drowned by an undisciplined 5
sympathy. . . . But when I shut my door and light the candle, I invite
a marmorean Muse, an art where no thought or emotion has come
to mind because another man has thought or felt something differ-
ent, for now there must be no reaction, action only, and the world
must move my heart but to the heart's discovery of itself, and I 10
begin to dream of eyelids that do not quiver before the bayonet: all
my thoughts have ease and joy, I am all virtue and confidence.
When I come to put in rhyme what I have found, it will be a hard
toil, but for a moment I believe I have found myself and not my
anti-self. 15

(from *Anima Hominis, 1917*)

Extract 2

All exploitation of the life of the wealthy, for the eye and the ear of   1
the poor and half-poor, in plays, in popular novels, in musical
comedy, in fashion papers, at the cinema, in *Daily Mirror* photo-
graphs, is a travesty of the life of the rich; and if it were not would
all but justify some Red Terror; and it impoverishes and vulgarises   5
the imagination, seeming to hold up for envy and to commend a
life where all is display and hurry, passion without emotion,
emotion without intellect, and where there is nothing stern and
solitary.

All this exploitation is a rankness that has grown up recently   10
among us and has come out of an historical necessity that has made
the furniture and the clothes and the brains, of all but the leisured
and the lettered, copies and travesties.

(from *A People's Theatre*, 1919)

GLOSSARY

travesty (l.4): ridiculously false description

Red Terror (l.5): the term used for the violent communist campaign in Russia in 1918 in which the opposition was murdered and executed

rankness (l.10): great unpleasantness

Extract 3

[T.S.] Eliot has produced his great effect upon his generation   1
because he has described men and women that get out of bed or
into it from mere habit; in describing this life that has lost heart his
own art seems grey, cold, dry. He is an Alexander Pope, working
without apparent imagination, producing his effects by a rejection   5
of all rhythms and metaphors used by the more popular romantics . . .
Not until *The Hollow Men* and *Ash-Wednesday*, where he is helped
by the short lines, and in the dramatic poems where his remarkable
sense of actor, chanter, scene, sweeps him away, is there rhythmical
animation. Two or three of my friends attribute the change to an   10
emotional enrichment from religion, but his religion . . . lacks all
strong emotion; a New England Protestant by descent, there is little
self-surrender in his personal relation to God and the soul.

Ezra Pound has made flux his theme; plot, characterisation, logical
discourse, seem to him abstractions unsuitable to a man of his   15
generation. . . . When I consider his work as a whole I find more
style than form; at moments more style, more deliberate nobility
and the means to convey it than in any contemporary poet known
to me, but it is constantly interrupted, broken, twisted into nothing
by its direct opposite, nervous obsession, nightmare, stammering   20
confusion; he is an economist, poet, politician, raging at malignants
with inexplicable characters and motives, grotesque figures out of
a child's book of beasts. This loss of self-control, common among
uneducated revolutionists, is rare – Shelley had it in some degree –
among men of Ezra Pound's culture and erudition. Style and its   25
opposite can alternate, but form must be full, sphere-like, single.

GLOSSARY

chanter (l.9): singer

animation (l.10): liveliness

flux (l.14): continuous changes; never being settled in one particular time and period

stammering (l.20): with sudden stops and repetitions

raging (l.21): expressing passionate anger

malignants (l.21): diseases; bad people

grotesque (l.22): strange and unnatural

erudition (l.25): great learning

unbridged transitions (l.28):
changes from one thing
to another without any
connections

ejaculations (l.29): sudden,
short utterances

unintelligible (l.29):
impossible to
understand

Even where there is no interruption he is often content, if certain verses and lines have style, to leave unbridged transitions, unexplained ejaculations, that make his meaning unintelligible. He has great influence, more perhaps than any contemporary except Eliot . . . 30

(from the introduction to the *Oxford Book of Verse*, 1938)

● In 1907, Yeats wrote dreamily of beauty and feeling. What can you infer about his development from the above passages?

8.1.2 Imagism

Imagism was a British and American poetic movement founded in England in 1912. Led by Ezra Pound, an American, it reacted against the 'Romanticism' of poets like Swinburne, whose words, the Imagists felt, obscured emotion rather than clarified it.

They agreed upon the following principles:

To use common speech with exactness.
To try new musical rhythms and create new moods.
To have freedom of subject.
To avoid vagueness in imagery: to be 'hard', clear and direct.
To be economical in their use of language.

8.1.3 Ezra Pound (1885–1972)

Ezra Pound was a controversial American poet who made his home in Europe. He was concerned with trying to conserve what was best in European culture.

GLOSSARY

poppy-cock (l.3): foolish
nonsense (*informal*)

nearer to the bone (l.3):
reduced to the essential

granite (l.4): very hard
rock

forcible (l.6): powerful

rhetorical din (l.7): noisy,
pompous language

luxurious riot (l.7): with
a lot of ornamentation

painted (l.7): (for
decoration only)

impeding (l.8): interfering
with

stroke (l.8): sudden blow

austere (l.9): plain and
severe

slither (l.9): slippery
polish

As to Twentieth century poetry, and the poetry which I expect to 1
see written during the next decade or so, it will, I think, move
against poppy-cock, it will be harder and saner, it will be . . . 'nearer
to the bone'. It will be as much like granite as it can be, its force
will lie in its truth, its interpretative power (of course, poetic force 5
does always rest there); I mean it will not try to seem forcible by
rhetorical din, and luxurious riot. We will have fewer painted ad-
jectives impeding the shock and stroke of it. At least for myself, I
want it so, austere, direct, free from emotional slither.

(from *Retrospect*, 1918)

Pound separated from the Imagist movement in 1914.
In this poem, 'A Girl' (1912), the girl 'becomes' a tree:

A Girl

The tree has entered my hands,   1
The sap has ascended my arms,
The tree has grown in my breast –
Downward,
The branches grow out of me, like arms.   5

Tree you are,
Moss you are,
You are violets with wind above them.
A child – *so* high – you are,
And all this is folly to the world.   10

GLOSSARY

sap (l.2): liquid in a
plant; essential life

folly (l.10): foolishness

i) Who is speaking to whom in the last five lines? What does the poem suggest
to you?

ii) In what sense is the poem Imagist? Is the central image clear?

In this poem, 'Commission' (1916), Pound gives 'instructions' to his songs
(his poems).

Commission

Go, my songs, to the lonely and the unsatisfied,   1
Go also to the nerve-racked, go to the enslaved-by-convention,
Bear to them my contempt for their oppressors.
Go as a great wave of cool water,
Bear my contempt of oppressors.   5

Speak against unconscious oppression,
Speak against the tyranny of the unimaginative,
Speak against bonds.
Go to the bourgeoise who is dying of her ennuis,
Go to the women in suburbs.   10
Go to the hideously wedded,
Go to them whose failure is concealed,
Go to the unluckily mated,
Go to the bought wife,
Go to the woman entailed.   15

Go to those who have delicate lust,
Go to those whose delicate desires are thwarted,
Go like a blight upon the dullness of the world;
Go with your edge against this,
Strengthen the subtle cords,   20
Bring confidence upon the algae and the tentacles of the soul.

GLOSSARY

the nerve-racked (l.2): those
that are unable to do
things calmly

bourgeoise (l.9): middle-
class

ennuis (l.9): tiredness
and lack of interest

entailed (l.15): fixed in a
particular state

thwarted (l.17): prevented
from being fulfilled

blight (l.18): disease
things calmly

Go in a friendly manner,
Go with an open speech.
Be eager to find new evils and new good,
Be against all forms of oppression.
Go to those who are thickened with middle age,   25
To those who have lost their interest.

algae and tentacles (l.21):
growths on top of, and
the things that reach out
of

Go to the adolescents who are smothered in family –
Oh how hideous it is
To see three generations of one house gathered together!   30
It is like an old tree with shoots,
And with some branches rotted and falling.

vegetable . . . blood (l.34):
the roots and
connected families
have made slaves of
them all

mortmain (l.35): enforced
association (the system
whereby bequeathed
property may not be
given or sold to anyone
else, from the French,
meaning 'dead hand')

Go out and defy opinion,
Go against this vegetable bondage of the blood.
Be against all sorts of mortmain.   35

• How would you summarise the effect the poet hopes his poems will have? Where in the poem does he seem to be trying to shock?
Are Pound's poems 'hard and sane' (the phrase he used in *Retrospect*) ? Is the diction that of everyday speech or is it 'poetic'?

*Ezra Pound
in the garden
of his Paris studio*

Ezra Pound   To find out more about Ezra Pound, choose from these prepositions to complete the gaps in the following notes:

of   on   for   in   from   with   at

a) **1908–1920**: Pound made London his home; a great influence .... English poetry and .... his fellow American T.S. Eliot, who described him as 'more responsible for the XXth Century revolution in poetry than any other individual'; moved away .... the constraints of Imagism, finding freedom .... translations .... Anglo-Saxon and Chinese verse.

b) **1920–1924**: Lived .... Paris with his English wife; part .... a new literary scene with expatriate Americans Gertrude Stein (1874–1946) and Ernest Hemingway (1899–1961); continued to work .... his *Cantos* the long poem which he worked on for much .... the rest of his life – a rich, multi-cultural work full .... literary allusions (final *Drafts and Fragments of Cantos CX to XCVII*) did not appear until 1970).

c) **1925–1972**: Settled permanently .... Rapallo, Italy; became increasingly preoccupied .... economic theories and believed that credit capitalism lay .... the root of all social and spiritual evils; led into anti-Semitism and sympathy with the Fascists; his broadcasts .... Italian radio led, in 1945, to his arrest .... treason by the American military authorities; taken back to Washington; 1946–1958 in mental institution; returned to Italy until his death.

Ezra Pound offered many fresh insights into the French and Italian poetry of the Middle Ages as well as the Latin and Greek classics. As T.S. Eliot remarked, Pound suffered from being seen as 'objectionably modern' and 'objectionably antiquarian' at the same time. He was both a great master of traditional verse forms and the man who regenerated the poetic tradition of his day.

8.1.4
Two literary terms

i) Modernism

'Modernism' is a term used to distinguish early experimental twentieth-century writing from the narrative, descriptive and rational frameworks and conventions of nineteenth-century writing (we are now sometimes said to be in a 'post-modernist' phase). The Spanish critic and philosopher José Ortega y Gasset (1883–1955) felt that 'modernism' took us towards chaos and dehumanisation, away from the 'all too human elements predominant in romantic and naturalistic production'.

● Think of an example of contemporary culture – from literature, music or the cinema. How would you describe it? 'Modernist', romantic, traditional or merely commercial?

ii) Free Verse

Free verse (*vers libre*) is a way of writing poetry with broken-up lines of variable length, without use of rhyme, stanza pattern or metre. It is, however, often very rhythmical, with patches of metrical regularity. The method was practised in the first thirty years of this century, in an attempt to escape from the rather mechanical use of rhyme and metre by the late Romantics.

Whitman pioneered a form of free verse in America (see page 194), D.H. Lawrence wrote much of his poetry in it but T.S. Eliot attacked the concept on the grounds that it could only be defined by negatives, and that the best verse has at least some relationship with poetic form:

<table>
<tr>
<td>

GLOSSARY

approximating to (l.4): getting near to

</td>
<td>

... the most interesting verse which has yet been written in our language has been done either by taking a very simple form, like the iambic pentameter, and constantly withdrawing from it, or taking no form all, and constantly approximating to a very simple one.

(from T. S. Eliot *Reflections on Vers Libre*. 1917)

</td>
<td>1</td>
</tr>
</table>

Ezra Pound was more generous.

<table>
<tr>
<td>

GLOSSARY

marked (l.1): noticeable
hackneyed (l.2): used so much that it has become boring

</td>
<td>

At times I can find a marked metre in 'vers libres', as stale and hackneyed as any pseudo-Swinburnian, at times the writers seem to follow no musical structure whatever. But it is, on the whole, good that the field should have been ploughed. Perhaps a few good poems have come from the new method, and if so it is justified.

(from Ezra Pound *Retrospect, 1918*)

</td>
<td>1

5</td>
</tr>
</table>

- Do you prefer poetry to have an obvious poetic form?

8.1.5
T(homas) S(tearns)
Eliot (1888–1965)

From 1917–1919 T.S. Eliot was assistant editor of *The Egoist*, the magazine which advocated Imagism, and his own early poems were in many ways like montages of cinematic images. His major works, in particular *The Waste Land* (1922) and the *Four Quartets* (1935–1942), have given new poetic expression to the modern consciousness. Eliot also wrote plays (for example *Murder in the Cathedral*, 1935) and has been an influential literary critic.

In 1915, influenced by French writers such as Charles Baudelaire (1821–1867), Eliot published four poems called *Preludes*.

Warm-up

i) Look at these words from one of the Preludes. What visual images do they suggest?

morning   beer   street   muddy   coffee-stands   dingy

ii) The following words appear in another of the Preludes. Can you guess what it is about?

city-block   trampled   conscience   images   suffering

Prelude 2 (1910)

The morning comes to consciousness   1
Of faint stale smells of beer
From the sawdust-trampled street
With all its muddy feet that press
To early coffee-stands.   5
With the other masquerades
That time resumes,
One thinks of all the hands
That are raising dingy shades
In a thousand furnished rooms.   10

●   What do the following suggest?
    a) the lines 'The morning ... smells of beer' (l.1–2)
    b) the phrase 'furnished rooms' (l.10)

Prelude 4 (1912)

His soul stretched tight across the skies   1
That fade behind a city block,
Or trampled by insistent feet
At four and five and six o'clock;
And short square fingers stuffing pipes,   5
And evening newspapers, and eyes
Assured of certain certainties,
The conscience of a blackened street
Impatient to assume the world.

I am moved by fancies that are curled   10
Around these images, and cling:
The notion of some infinitely gentle
Infinitely suffering thing.

Wipe your hand across your mouth, and laugh;
The worlds revolve like ancient women   15
Gathering fuel in vacant lots.

●   i) What do these refer to? 'fade' (l.2), 'trampled' (l.3)
   ii) What do these tell us? 'curled'/'cling' (l.10/l.11); 'suffering thing' (l.3); 'ancient
      women' (l.16)
   iii) What similarities/differences are there between the two Preludes in:
      a) the time of day?
      b) how people are described?
      c) the atmosphere?

Appreciation   For Eliot, Baudelaire 'gave new possibilities to poetry in a new stock of
images from contemporary life'. As a result, the new poetry of 1910–1920
looked to the big city for its images rather than the countryside. It
nevertheless rejected the values of the commercial middle class.

Give an example from the *Preludes* of one image and one phrase that you cannot
imagine occurring in the poetry of previous centuries. Can you say anything
about the rhythm and rhyme of these poems?

'The Journey of the Magi' (1927)

Where did the men in this picture (called Magi) come from? What are they doing? (The Story is told in Matthew 2:1–12 in the Bible.)

In Eliot's poem 'The Journey of the Magi' one of the Magi is recalling in old age the meaning of the experience.

GLOSSARY

Magi: (The three wise men from the East who brought gifts to the infant Jesus)

A cold . . . winter (l.1–5): (these lines are adapted from a Nativity sermon by Bishop Lancelot Andrews, Christmas Day 1622)

galled (l.6): tired and sore

refractory (l.6): difficult to manage

regretted (l.8): mourned the absence of

sherbet (l.10): an oriental cold drink of sweetened and diluted fruit juice

in snatches (l.18): short periods of time

temperate (l.21): neither too hot nor too cold

three trees (l.24): (suggesting the three crosses with Christ crucified in the centre)

The Journey of the Magi

'A cold coming we had of it,   1
Just the worst time of the year
For a journey, and such a long journey:
The ways deep and the weather sharp,
The very dead of winter.'   5

And the camels galled, sore-footed, refractory,
Lying down in the melting snow.
There were times we regretted
The summer palaces on slopes, the terraces,
And the silken girls bringing sherbet.   10
Then the camel men cursing and grumbling
And running away, and wanting their liquor and women,
And the night-fires going out, and the lack of shelters,
And the cities hostile and the towns unfriendly
And the villages dirty and charging high prices: 15
A hard time we had of it.
At the end we preferred to travel all night,
Sleeping in snatches,
With the voices singing in our ears, saying
That this was all folly.   20

Then at dawn we came down to a temperate valley,
Wet, below the snow line, smelling of vegetation;
With a running stream and a water-mill beating the darkness,
And three trees on the low sky,
And an old white horse galloped away in the meadow.   25
Then we came to a tavern with vine-leaves over the lintel,
Six hands at an open door dicing for pieces of silver,
And feet kicking the empty wine-skins.
But there was no information, and so we continued
And arrived at evening, not a moment too soon   30
Finding the place; it was (you may say) satisfactory.

All this was a long time ago, I remember,
And I would do it again, but set down
This set down
This: were we led all that way for   35
Birth or Death? There was a Birth, certainly,
We had evidence and no doubt. I had seen birth and death,
But had thought they were different; this Birth was
Hard and bitter agony for us, like Death, our death.
We returned to our places, these Kingdoms,   40
But no longer at ease here, in the old dispensation,
With an alien people clutching their gods.
I should be glad of another death.

white horse (l.25): (in the Book of Revelation in the Bible, Christ the conqueror rides on a white horse)

lintel (l.26): top part of the door frame

six hands ... (l.27): (In *The Use of Poetry and the Use of Criticism*, 1933, Eliot recalls an image of 'six ruffians seen through an open window playing cards at night at a small French railway junction where there was a water mill'.)

dicing ... silver (l.27): (suggesting the soldiers gambling for Christ's garments and Judas's betrayal of him for thirty pieces of silver)

wine-skins (l.28): bags made from animal skins for holding wine

old dispensation (l.41): (before Christianity)

● What do you think the last line means?

Understanding and interpretation

i) Match the following descriptions with parts of the poem:
  a) The Magus describes images which suggest death.
  b) The Magus is reflecting on the meaning of the experience.
  c) The difficulties of the journey.
  d) Images of birth, springtime and renewal.
  e) The feelings of the Magi on their return to their countries.
  f) Arrival in Bethlehem.
  g) The Magus tells his listener to record his uncertainties about what the experience meant.
  h) What the Magi missed about their countries.

ii) What do you think the following refer to?

  'it' (l.1); 'we' (l.8); 'the camel men' (l.11); 'the place' (l.32); 'do it' (l.34); 'our places' (l.41); 'alien people' (l.43)

iii) How does the mood of the Magus's story change with the words 'Then at dawn ...' (l.21)?

Appreciation

i) Find evidence in the poem for either of these statements:

  The poem is built on a series of contrasts.
  The rhythm of the poem reinforces the sense.

ii) What is the effect of the repetition of the word 'and' (l.10–15)?

T.S. Eliot: critical essays

In 1927 (the year he wrote 'The Journey of the Magi') Eliot became a British subject and a member of the Anglican Church. As a critic he was outstanding in reviving admiration for the seventeenth century Metaphysical Poets (see pages 58–64) and reducing the relative status of Spenser and Milton. At the same time he was a believer in tradition, hierarchy and community, seeing himself as 'classical in literature, royalist in politics, and Anglo-Saxon in religion.'

● Read the following extracts from Eliot's critical essays.

Extract 1 On poetry and personality:

It is not in his personal emotions, the emotions provoked by particular events in his life, that the poet is in any way remarkable or interesting. His particular emotions may be simple, or crude, or flat. The emotion in his poetry will be a very complex thing, but not with the complexity of the emotions of people who have very complex or unusual emotions in life. One error, in fact, of eccentricity in poetry is to seek for new human emotions to express; and in this search for novelty in the wrong place it discovers the perverse. The business of the poet is not to find new emotions, but to use the ordinary ones and, in working them up into poetry, to express feelings which are not in actual emotions at all. And emotions which he has never experienced will serve his turn as well as those familiar to him. Consequently, we must believe that 'emotion recollected in tranquillity' is an inexact formula. For it is neither emotion, nor recollection, nor, without distortion of meaning, tranquillity. It is a concentration, and a new thing resulting from the concentration, of a very great number of experiences which to the practical and active person would not seem to be experiences at all; it is a concentration which does not happen consciously or of deliberation. These experiences are not 'recollected,' and they finally unite in an atmosphere which is 'tranquil' only in that it is a passive attending upon the event. Of course this is not quite the whole story. There is a great deal, in the writing of poetry, which must be conscious and deliberate. In fact, the bad poet is usually unconscious where he ought to be conscious, and conscious where he ought to be unconscious. Both errors tend to make him 'personal.' Poetry is not a turning loose of emotion, but an escape from emotion; it is not the expression of personality, but an escape from personality. But, of course, only those who have personality and emotions know what it means to want to escape from these things.

(from *Tradition and the Individual Talent*, 1917)

● What does Eliot mean when he says that poetry is an 'Escape from emotion'?

264

Extract 2:   On tradition:

The existing monuments form an ideal order among themselves,   1
which is modified by the introduction of the new (the really new)
work of art among them. The existing order is complete before the
new work arrives; for order to persist after the supervention of
novelty, the *whole* existing order must be, if ever so slightly, altered;   5
and so the relations, proportions, values of each work of art toward
the whole are readjusted; and this is conformity between the old
and the new.

(from *Tradition and the Individual Talent, 1917*)

● For Eliot, is tradition something dead?

Extract 3:   On criticism:

Criticism, on the other hand, must always profess an end in view,   1
which, roughly speaking, appears to be the elucidation of works of
art and the correction of taste . . .

. . . the larger part of the labour of an author in composing his
work is critical labour; the labour of sifting, combining, con-   5
structing, expunging, correcting, testing: this frightful toil is as
much critical as creative . . .

If so large a part of creation is really criticism, is not a large part of
what is called 'critical writing' really creative? If so, is there not
creative criticism in the ordinary sense? The answer seems to be,   10
that there is no equation. I have assumed as axiomatic that a creation, a work of art, is autotelic; and that criticism, by definition, is
about something other than itself. Hence you cannot fuse creation
with criticism as you can fuse criticism with creation. The critical
activity finds its highest, its true fulfilment in a kind of union with   15
creation in the labour of the artist.

(from *Function of Criticism, 1923*)

● According to Eliot, how do criticism and 'creative writing' differ? Do you agree?

Two critical expressions were invented by Eliot in two of his essays and have been much used by critics ever since:

Objective correlative ('Hamlet', 1919): 'The only way of expressing emotion in the form of art is by finding an "objective correlative"; in other words, a set of objects, a situation, a chain of events which shall be the formula of that *particular* emotion; such that when the external facts . . . are given, the emotion is immediately evoked.'

Dissociation of sensibility, ('The Metaphysical Poets', 1921): 'Tennyson and Browning are poets, and they think; but they do not feel their thought as the odour of a rose. A thought to Donne was an experience: it modified his sensibility . . . The poets of the seventeeth century . . . possessed a mechanism of sensibility which would devour any kind of experience . . . in the seventeenth century a dissociation of sensibility set in, from which we have never recovered . . .' After that date, 'while the language became more refined, the feeling became more crude'.

8.2 Fiction: Two trends

Popular novels – by, for example, Arnold Bennett (1867–1931) and John Galsworthy (1867–1933) – in which the characters seem to have been wholly shaped by the social environment. According to Virginia Woolf, these novelists were 'materialists . . . who spend immense skill and immense industry making the trivial and transitory appear the true and enduring'; D.H. Lawrence felt their characters 'seem to us to have lost caste as human beings, and to have sunk to the level of the social being'.

Novels which explore the interrelation between the individual self, the social self and nature – in particular those of D.H. Lawrence (1885–1930), who explored the psychic ills of contemporary society through the inner experience of individuals and their relationships and who looked for more instinctive vitality than could be found in most contemporary society. However, of *The Rainbow* (see below), John Galsworthy, who had little sympathy with its picture of sexual creativity, said: 'I much prefer a frankly pornographic book to one like this.'

Warm-up Can you make word-association chains from these words?

a) Farm animals (for example: cows–udders–milk)
b) Plants (for example: crops–wheat–harvest–grain)

8.2.1
D(avid) H(erbert)
Lawrence (1885–1930)

Lawrence (see also page 6) was the first major novelist to have truly working-class origins. In *The Rainbow* (1915), suppressed for a time on grounds of immorality, he tells the story of the lives of three generations in a farming family in the East Midlands, the Brangwens, who work the land near an expanding industrial area.

Extract 1 This is a description of the first generation of Brangwens at the beginning of the novel.

GLOSSARY
necessity (l.1): poverty
thriftless (l.3): careless
  with money

So the Brangwens came and went without fear of necessity, working hard because of the life that was in them, not for want of the money. Neither were they thriftless. They were aware of the last halfpenny, 1

and instinct made them not waste the peeling of their apple, for it
would help to feed the cattle. But heaven and earth was teeming
around them, and how should this cease? They felt the rush of the
sap in spring, they knew the wave which cannot halt, but every
year throws forward the seed to begetting, and, falling back, leaves
the young-born on the earth. They knew the intercourse between
heaven and earth, sunshine drawn into the breast and bowels, the
rain sucked up in the daytime, nakedness that comes under the
wind in autumn, showing the birds' nests no longer worth hiding.
Their life and interrelations were such; feeling the pulse and body
of the soil, that opened to their furrow for the grain, and became
smooth and supple after their ploughing, and clung to their feet
with a weight that pulled like desire, lying hard and unresponsive
when the crops were to be shorn away. The young corn waved and
was silken, and the lustre slid along the limbs of the men who saw
it. They took the udder of the cows, the cows yielded milk and
pulse against the hands of the men, the pulse of the blood of the
teats of the cows beat into the pulse of the hands of the men. They
mounted their horses, and held life between the grip of their knees,
they harnessed their horses at the wagon, and, with hand on the
bridle-rings, drew the heaving of the horses after their will.

i) Make a sentence in your own words for each of these:

  a) Brangwens – money
  b) autumn – wind

ii) The passage describes the interrelation between man and nature. Which
   phrases are particularly sensual?

iii) Find three verbs and three nouns which suggest energy and movement.

Extract 2   Later in the year:

In autumn the partridges whirred up, birds in flocks blew like
spray across the fallow, rooks appeared on the grey, watery heavens,
and flew cawing into the winter. Then the men sat by the fire in the
house where the women moved about with surety, and the limbs
and the body of the men were impregnated with the day, cattle and
earth and vegetation and the sky, the men sat by the fire and their
brains were inert, as their blood flowed heavy with the accumulation from the living day.

i) Why do you think the women moved about the house with surety?
ii) Find examples of figurative language.

Extract 3 But the harmony was not total:

The women were different. On them too was the drowse of blood-intimacy, calves sucking and hens running together in droves, and young geese palpitating in the hand while the food was pushed down their throttle. But the women looked out from the heated, blind intercourse of farm-life, to the spoken world beyond. They were aware of the lips and the mind of the world speaking and giving utterance, they heard the sound in the distance, and they strained to listen.

It was enough for the men, that the earth heaved and opened its furrows to them, that the wind blew to dry the wet wheat, and set the young ears of corn wheeling freshly round about; it was enough that they helped the cow in labour, or ferreted the rats from under the barn, or broke the back of a rabbit with a sharp knock of the hand. So much warmth and generating and pain and death did they know in their blood, earth and sky and beast and green plants, so much exchange and interchange they had with these, that they lived full and surcharged, their senses full fed, their faces always turned to the heat of the blood, staring into the sun, dazed with looking towards the source of generation, unable to turn round.

But the woman wanted another form of life than this, something that was not blood-intimacy. Her house faced out from the farm-buildings and fields, looked out to the road and the village with church and Hall and the world beyond. She stood to see the far-off world of cities and governments and the active scope of man, the magic land to her, where secrets were made known and desires fulfilled. She faced outwards to where men moved dominant and creative, having turned their back on the pulsing heat of creation, and with this behind them, were set out to discover what was beyond, to enlarge their own scope and range and freedom; whereas the Brangwen men faced inwards to the teeming life of creation, which poured unresolved into their veins.

GLOSSARY

drowse (l.1): light sleepy state

blood-intimacy (l.1): the women's natures had warm and deep connections with animal life

in droves (l.2): in large numbers

palpitating (l.3): with their hearts beating rapidly and strongly

throttle (l.4): windpipe

wheeling (l.11): revolving

ferreted (l.12): tried to get out

barn (l.13): large farm building for the animals and corn

surcharged (l.17): excessively filled

Hall (l.23): the large manor house of the landowner

unresolved (l.31): without making real harmony

- i) Complete the following sentences:
  The difference between the men and the women was …………………………
- ii) What is the effect of the second 'so much' in the sentence beginning 'So much warmth …' (l.14)?
- iii) Imagine you were doing a painting which tried to convey the sense of this scene. What would it look like?

Extract 4 Later in the novel, Tom Brangwen's wife, a Polish woman with a daughter from a previous marriage, is about to give birth to Brangwen's first child:

One afternoon, the pains began, Mrs Brangwen was put to bed, the midwife came. Night fell, the shutters were closed, Brangwen came in to tea, to the loaf and the pewter teapot, the child, silent and quivering, playing with the glass beads, the house, empty, it seemed, or exposed to the winter night, as if it had no walls.

Sometimes there sounded, long and remote in the house, vibrating through everything, the moaning cry of a woman in labour. Brangwen, sitting downstairs, was divided. His lower, deeper self was with her, bound to her, suffering. But the big shell of his body remembered the sound of owls that used to fly round the farmstead when he was a boy. He was back in his youth, a boy, haunted by the sound of the owls, waking up his brother to speak to him. And his mind drifted away to the birds, their solemn, dignified faces, their flight so soft and broad-winged. And then to the birds his brother had shot, fluffy, dustcoloured, dead heaps of softness with faces absurdly asleep. It was a queer thing, a dead owl.

He lifted his cup to his lips, he watched the child with the beads. But his mind was occupied with owls, and the atmosphere of his boyhood, with his brothers and sisters. Elsewhere, fundamental, he was with his wife in labour, the child was being brought forth out of their one flesh. He and she, one flesh, out of which life must be put forth. The rent was not in his body, but it was of his body. On her the blows fell, but the quiver ran through to him, to his last fibre. She must be torn asunder for life to come forth, yet still they were one flesh, and still, from further back, the life came out of him to her, and still he was the unbroken that has the broken rock in its arms, their flesh was one rock from which the life gushed, out of her who was smitten and rent, from him who quivered and yielded.

He went upstairs to her. As he came to the bedside she spoke to him in Polish.

'Is it very bad?' he asked.

She looked at him, and oh, the weariness to her of the effort to understand another language, the weariness of hearing him, attending to him, making out who he was, as he stood there fair-bearded and alien, looking at her. She knew something of him, of his eyes. But she could not grasp him. She closed her eyes.

He turned away, white to the gills.

'It's not so very bad,' said the midwife.

(from *The Rainbow*)

GLOSSARY

midwife (l.2): person who helps a woman give birth

pewter (l.3): greyish metal made by mixing lead and tin

in labour (l.7): suffering the pains of childbirth

rent (l.22): tearing

quiver (l.23): slight trembling

asunder (l.24): into pieces

smitten (l.28): dealt a severe blow

white to the gills (l.38): with a completely white face

- i) Complete the following sentence:
  Tom Brangwen is divided between ....
- ii) Why do you think he is so divided?
- iii) What details in the description help to make the scene vivid?

Critical opinion In the letter quoted in 8.2, John Galsworthy also said of *The Rainbow*:

Frankly – I think it's aesthetically detestable. Its perfervid futuristic style revolts me. Its reiterations bore me to death. And – worse than all – at the back of its amazing fecundity – what is there? What real discovery, what of the spirit, what that is touching, or even true? There is a spurious creativeness about it all, as of countless bodies made with tremendous gusto, and not an ounce of soul within them, in spite of incredible assertions and pretence of sounding life to its core. It's a kind of portent; a paean of the undisciplined shallow fervour that passes with the young in these days for art. It has no time-resisting quality whatever. Brittle as glass, and with something of its brilliance.

By contrast, the critic F.R. Leavis (1895–1978) (see page 451) felt that Lawrence's writing had great power because of his attention to the link between the individual and life as a whole:

That the intuition of the oneness of life conveyed with such power at the beginning of *The Rainbow* is characteristic of Lawrence's genius doesn't need emphasizing; it is a commonplace. What perhaps may still be attested with some insistence is the other aspect of the given truth: the intensity of that intuition expresses itself in an intensity of preoccupation with the individual. No one could have been more profoundly possessed by the perception that life is a matter of individual lives, and that except in individual lives there is no life to be interested in or reverent about, and no life to be served.

In a famous letter to Edward Garnett in 1914 Lawrence himself said that his exploration of the individual in *The Rainbow* was intended to be below the level of the ego and the social personality:

I don't so much care about what the woman *feels* – in the ordinary usage of the word. That presumes an *ego* to feel with. I only care about what the woman *is* – what she IS – inhumanly, physiologically, materially . . . You mustn't look in my novel for the old stable *ego* of the character. There is another *ego*, according to whose action the individual is unrecognizable, and passes through, as it were, allotropic states which it needs a deeper sense than any we've been used to exercise, to discover are states of the same single radically unchanged element. (Like as diamond and coal are the same pure single element of carbon. The ordinary novel would trace the history of the diamond – but I say, 'Diamond, what! This is carbon.' And my diamond might be coal or soot, and my theme is carbon.)

allotropic (l.7): existing in different forms with different physical properties

soot (l.12): black powder left by smoke

D.H. Lawrence

Lawrence's reputation has grown so that he is now probably the most widely read writer of his times. He was an outstanding novelist, his better-known novels include *Sons and Lovers* (1913) *Women in Love* (1920) and *Lady Chatterley's Lover* (1928) which in Britain was banned in its entirety until 1959 for its detailed descriptions of sexual union. He was also a fine short-story writer, essayist and critic, a distinctive poet and even a quite original (and at the time scandalous) painter. His hatred of the First World War, together with the German origins of his wife, with whom he had previously eloped to Italy, caused them great unhappiness. They subsequently travelled the world, visiting such places as Austria and New Mexico. One of Lawrence's most influential beliefs was that modern man was perverting his nature by the divorce of his consciousness from spontaneous feelings.

8.2.2.
James Joyce
(1882–1941)

James Joyce (see also Supplement 8), Irish author of *Ulysses* (1914–1921) and *Finnegans Wake* (1939) was educated in Dublin but after 1902 lived on the Continent, returning to Ireland only briefly.

The Portrait of the Artist as a Young Man (1916) is the largely autobiographical story of a middle-class Irish boy, Stephen Dedalus, from his infancy in the strongly Catholic, intensely nationalistic environment of Dublin in the 1880s to his departure from Ireland, having realised that in order to fulfill his destiny as an artist he must rise above the vulgarity of his environment and live apart from others.

Despite guilt about his sexual desires, Stephen has been tempted to enter the priesthood. In the following extract, walking by the seashore, he sees his friends, a group of Christian Brothers, swimming in the water. They call out his name in Greek, which causes him great excitement. He feels he is flying like that 'hawk-like man', Daedalus – in Greek myth, an artist of wonderful powers who escaped from Crete by making wings for himself and his son Icarus and flying across the sea. He rejects 'the inhuman voice that had called him to the pale service of the altar' and decides instead to become a poet. Nervously, 'his cheeks aflame and his throat throbbing with song', 'a lust of wandering in his feet that burned to set out for the ends of the earth', Stephen enters the grey water whose coldness and sub-human smell he hates so much.

In a few moments he was barefoot, his stockings folded in his pockets and his canvas shoes dangling by their knotted laces over his shoulders and, picking a pointed salteaten stick out of the jetsam among the rocks, he clambered down the slope of the breakwater.

There was a long rivulet in the strand and, as he waded slowly up its course, he wondered at the endless drift of seaweed. Emerald and black and russet and olive, it moved beneath the current, swaying and turning. The water of the rivulet was dark with endless drift and mirrored the highdrifting clouds. The clouds were drifting above him silently, and silently the seatangle was drifting below him and the grey warm air was still and a new wild life was singing in his veins.

Where was his boyhood now? Where was the soul that had hung back from her destiny, to brood alone upon the shame of her wounds and in her house of squalor and subterfuge to queen it in faded cerements and in wreaths that withered at the touch? Or where was he?

He was alone. He was unheeded, happy and near to the wild heart of life. He was alone and young and wilful and wildhearted, alone amid a waste of wild air and brackish waters and the seaharvest of shells and tangle and veiled grey sunlight and gayclad, lightclad figures of children and girls and voices childish and girlish in the air.

A girl stood before him in midstream, alone and still, gazing out to sea. She seemed like one whom magic had changed into the likeness of a strange and beautiful seabird. Her long slender bare legs were delicate as a crane's and pure save where an emerald trail of seaweed had fashioned itself as a sign upon the flesh. Her thighs, fuller and softhued as ivory, were bared almost to the hips, where the white fringes of her drawers were like feathering of soft white down. Her slateblue skirts were kilted boldly about her waist and dovetailed behind her. Her bosom was as a bird's, soft and slight, slight and soft as the breast of some darkplumaged dove. But her long fair hair was girlish: and girlish, and touched with the wonder of mortal beauty, her face.

She was alone and still, gazing out to sea; and when she felt his presence and the worship of his eyes, her eyes turned to him in quiet sufferance of his gaze, without shame or wantonness. Long, long she suffered his gaze and then quietly withdrew her eyes from his and bent them towards the stream, gently stirring the water with her foot hither and thither. The first faint noise of faintly moving water broke the silence, low and faint and whispering, faint as the bells of sleep; hither and thither, hither and thither; and a faint flame trembled on her cheek.

Heavenly God! cried Stephen's soul, in an outburst of profane joy.

slateblue (l.31): greenish grey blue

kilted (l.31): folded up

dovetailed (l.32): tied

darkplumaged (l.33): with dark feathers

wantonness (l.38): sexual mischief

hither and thither (l.41): in all directions

profane (l.45): unholy

aglow (l.48): bright with excitement

strode (l.49): walked with long steps

advent (l.50): arrival

He turned away from her suddenly and set off across the strand. His cheeks were aflame; his body was aglow; his limbs were trembling; on and on and on he strode, far out over the sands, singing wildly to the sea, crying to greet the advent of the life that had cried to him.

(from *The Portrait of the Artist as a Young Man*)

Understanding and interpretation

Joyce used the word 'epiphany' to describe an intense flash of understanding which illuminates the most commonplace of objects. Entering the sea was like a baptism for Stephen. He is rewarded with a vision of the girl as both a bird and an angel, without the desire either to possess or convert her. He feels the joy of an artist in the presence of her reality.

Find evidence for the following:
a) Stephen felt he had reached a new stage of his life.
b) Stephen no longer wished to bury himself in religious observance.
c) Stephen has a very vivid imagination.

'Stream of consciousness'

This term was first used by the American philosopher, William James (brother of Henry – see page 235) in 1890 to describe the flow of thoughts of the waking mind. Now it is also widely used to describe a narrative method consisting of the characters' unspoken thoughts and feelings, as they pass by often without logical sequence or syntax. A related term, 'interior monologue', is used to describe the inner movement of consciousness in a character's mind without the obvious intervention of the author. Most writers who used these techniques saw themselves as probing the unconscious mind objectively, not giving themselves up to it as a Romantic might have done. In *Portrait of the Artist* Joyce tried to present the hero's experience, as well as his mood and character, through language which is characteristic of the stage of life he is speaking from.

- i) Find examples in the extract above which could be described as either 'stream of consciousness' or 'interior monologue'.
  ii) How does Joyce convey the feeling of ecstasy in the paragraph beginning 'He was alone ... ' (l.18)?

8.2.3
Virginia Woolf
(1882–1941)
Warm-up

Virginia Woolf has been regarded as one of the principal exponents of Modernism.

Imagine you are entering a deserted house, somewhere in the country, for the first time. Is there any furniture? Is the garden overgrown? Are you frightened? Write one sentence which expresses your feelings.

To the Lighthouse

To the Lighthouse (1927) is set in a holiday house in the Hebrides – islands off the western coast of Scotland. The story, told through the 'stream' of thoughts and feelings running through the characters, has no plot in the conventional sense and is dominated by two symbols: a lighthouse out at sea (representing in part the search for values in the harsh reality of the world) and a painting of the house by a female painter (representing in part the struggle and cost of female creativity).

In the middle section, called 'Time Passes', we see the empty house, subject to the changes of time during the period of the First World War. Mrs McNab, the old cleaning woman, represents the easily-broken but untiring spirit which, despite her complaints that the family have abandoned her and the house, manages to keep memories of happier, earlier days alive.

GLOSSARY

trifling (l.3): insignificant

nibbling (l.3): which ate away at it bit by bit

clammy (l.4): damp

fumbling (l.4): which felt about awkwardly

shawl (l.6): a piece of material worn round a woman's shoulders

thistle (l.6): wild plant with sharp-pointed leaves

thrust (l.7): pushed

larder (l.7): room in which food is kept

shovelfuls (l.9): large amounts

rafters (l.9): wooden beams which hold up the roof

gnaw (l.10): eat away at

wainscots (l.10): wooden coverings on the lower half of the walls

Tortoise-shell (l.10): type of butterfly with orange, yellow, brown and black colours

chrysalis (l.11): hard outer form (of the butterflies in their inactive stage)

The house was left; the house was deserted. It was left like a shell on a sandhill to fill with dry salt grains now that life had left it. The long night seemed to have set in; the trifling airs, nibbling, the clammy breaths, fumbling, seemed to have triumphed. The saucepan had rusted and the mat decayed. Toads had nosed their way in. Idly, aimlessly, the swaying shawl swung to and fro. A thistle thrust itself between the tiles in the larder. The swallows nested in the drawing-room; the floor was strewn with straw; the plaster fell in shovelfuls; rafters were laid bare; rats carried off this and that to gnaw behind the wainscots. Tortoise-shell butterflies burst from the chrysalis and pattered their life out on the window-pane. Poppies sowed themselves among the dahlias; the lawn waved with long grass; giant artichokes towered among roses; a fringed carnation flowered among the cabbages; while the gentle tapping of a weed at the window had become, on winters' nights, a drumming from sturdy trees and thorned briars which made the whole room green in summer.

What power could now prevent the fertility, the insensibility of nature? Mrs McNab's dream of a lady, of a child, of a plate of milk soup? It had wavered over the walls like a spot of sunlight and vanished. She had locked the door; she had gone. It was beyond the strength of one woman, she said. They never sent. They never wrote. There were things up there rotting in the drawers – it was a shame to leave them so, she said. The place was gone to rack and ruin. Only the Lighthouse beam entered the rooms for a moment, sent its sudden stare over bed and wall in the darkness of winter, looked with equanimity at the thistle and the swallow, the rat and the straw. Nothing now withstood them; nothing said no to them.

pattered (l.11): made a soft hitting sound

dahlias (l.12): big, brightly-coloured garden flowers

sturdy (l.16): strong and firm

briars (l.16): prickly bushes

wavered (l.20): made an unsteady movement

sent (l.22): communicated

was gone to rack and ruin (l.24): was now in a ruined state

with equanimity (l.27): calmly

seed itself (l.29): drop its seeds in the ground

chintz (l.32): flowery patterned cloth

alight in (l.35): come down on to

pitched (l.37): fallen

ward off (l.41): keep out

hemlocks (l.42): poisonous plants with white flowers

blotted out (l.42): covered completely

lustily (l.43): vigorously

mound (l.43): pile of earth

trespasser (l.44): person who enters without permission

red-hot poker (l.44): tall cultivated plant with a spike of yellow flowers changing to red at the top

Let the wind blow; let the poppy seed itself and the carnation mate with the cabbage. Let the swallow build in the drawing-room, and the thistle thrust aside the tiles, and the butterfly sun itself on the faded chintz of the arm-chairs. Let the broken glass and the china lie out on the lawn and be tangled over with grass and wild berries.

For now had come that moment, that hesitation when dawn trembles and night pauses, when if a feather alight in the scale it will be weighed down. One feather, and the house, sinking, falling, would have turned and pitched downwards to the depths of darkness. In the ruined room, picnickers would have lit their kettles; lovers sought shelter there, lying on the bare boards; and the shepherd stored his dinner on the bricks, and the tramp slept with his coat round him to ward off the cold. Then the roof would have fallen; briars and hemlocks would have blotted out path, step, and window; would have grown, unequally but lustily over the mound, until some trespasser, losing his way, could have told only by red-hot poker among the nettles, or a scrap of china in the hemlock, that here once some one had lived; there had been a house.

(from _To the Lighthouse_)

30

35

40

45

● Did you find the passage evocative?

Understanding and interpretation

i) Make separate lists of the animals, plants, birds and insects mentioned in the passage. Use a dictionary if necessary.
ii) Why had Mrs McNab left?
iii) What was in danger of happening to the house?
iv) In the paragraph beginning 'What power . . .' (l.18), which lines do you think are Mrs McNab's words?

Language and style

i) What does the 'darkness' (l.26 and l.38) represent?
ii) Find at least two repetitions of phrases. What is the effect of each?

Virginia Woolf

Virginia Woolf was admired by T.S. Eliot (he said of _Jacob's Room_, 1922, 'you have freed yourself from any compromise between the traditional novel and your original gift') and attacked by F.R. Leavis ('In _The Waves_ there is a fatal falsification between what her impressions actually are and what they are supposed to signify'). As time went on her novels became increasingly experimental. As well as *The Waves* (1931) titles include *Mrs Dalloway* (1925) and *Between the Acts* (1941).

In 1904, after the death of her father, who was the literary critic Leslie Stephen, Virginia Woolf's house in the Bloomsbury district of London became the centre of the Bloomsbury group of intellectuals – a group which strongly emphasised the value of personal relations and the cultivation of the sensibility (the capacity to feel). Through her technique Woolf tried to capture what she saw as the essence of the sensibility.

8.2.4
Creative Writing

Either:
Imagine you are the girl Stephen Dedalus sees in the water. Retell the incident from your point of view. Make it as amusing as possible.
Or:
Imagine you are a radio reporter interviewing one of the early Brangwens about their life on the farm. Write out (and, if possible, record) the dialogue using information from the beginning of *The Rainbow*.

8.3 The Twenties in Britain

. . . the spirit of the time was calling all traditions – social, moral, religious, philosophical, psychological – in question, and thinking men were no longer sure of what it means to call oneself a human being. Even less were they certain of human values, or how to evaluate human experience. If novels were still to be what they always had been, images of life as it is lived from day to day, then some novelists considered that such images should take new forms, and these forms varied according to their personal conceptions of how experiences are received, or how they ought to be received, or how they can be made significant.

(From Christopher Gillie *Longman Companion to English Literature*, 1972)

GLOSSARY

pretentious bunglers (l.2):
people who pretend to be important but in fact do their job badly

rendering character (l.6):
making the characters in her novels come to life through words

[Except for Joyce and Woolf] 'all the other so-called innovators are (if not pretentious bunglers) merely innovators in subject matter and the praise we give them is of the kind we should accord to scientists . . . But they do not advance the novelist's art. Virginia Woolf has already done that a little, and if she succeeds in her problem of rendering character, she will advance it enormously.'

(the novelist E.M. Forster in 1925)

1

5

8.4 The USA after the First World War

Although the USA emerged from the First World War prosperous, the experience of the war had had a powerful disillusioning effect. Despite President Harding's election slogan in 1920 of 'back to normalcy', a cynical, materialistic, and emancipated youth appeared. For them money was easy to come by and the frivolity of the 'Roaring Twenties' began. 'The uncertainties of 1919 were over – there seemed little doubt about what was going to happen – America was going on the greatest, gaudiest spree in history.' (F. Scott Fitzgerald)

8.4.1
F(rancis) Scott (Key)
Fitzgerald (1896–1940)

After the success of *This Side of Paradise* (1920), his first novel, F. Scott Fitzgerald (see also Supplement 8) married the glamorous Zelda Sayre. Together they led a life of high living, big spending and all-night party-going. They saw themselves as representatives of the 'Jazz Age'. Nevertheless, Fitzgerald felt that the twenties would end badly for both himself and America, and so 'All the stories that came into my head had a touch of disaster in them.'

Warm-up

If you were a millionaire, what sort of house would you live in? Describe one room in detail.

Extract 1

In the story *The Diamond as Big as the Ritz*, John T. Unger, a Southern boy at school in Boston, is invited by a wealthy schoolfriend, Percy Washington, to spend the summer with him. This is the morning after his arrival:

GLOSSARY
drowsily (l.1): sleepily
ebony (l.2): made of a hard black wood

Morning. As he awoke he perceived drowsily that the room had at the same moment become dense with sunlight. The ebony panels of one wall had slid aside on a sort of track, leaving his chamber half open to the day. A large Negro in a white uniform stood beside his bed. 1

5

277

'Good evening,' muttered John, summoning his brains from the wild places.

'Good morning, sir. Are you ready for your bath, sir? Oh, don't get up – I'll put you in, if you'll just unbutton your pyjamas – there. Thank you, sir.'

John lay quietly as his pyjamas were removed – he was amused and delighted; he expected to be lifted like a child by this black Gargantua who was tending him, but nothing of the sort happened; instead he felt the bed tilt up slowly on its side – he began to roll, startled at first, in the direction of the wall, but when he reached the wall its drapery gave way, and sliding two yards farther down a fleecy incline he plumped gently into water the same temperature as his body.

He looked about him. The runway or rollway on which he had arrived had folded gently back into place. He had been projected into another chamber and was sitting in a sunken bath with his head just above the level of the floor. All about him, lining the walls of the room and the sides and bottom of the bath itself, was a blue aquarium, and gazing through the crystal surface on which he sat, he could see fish swimming among amber lights and even gliding without curiosity past his outstretched toes, which were separated from them only by the thickness of the crystal. From overhead, sunlight came down through sea-green glass.

'I suppose, sir, that you'd like hot rosewater and soapsuds this morning, sir – and perhaps cold salt water to finish.'

The Negro was standing beside him.

'Yes,' agreed John, smiling inanely, 'as you please.' Any idea of ordering this bath according to his own meagre standards of living would have been priggish and not a little wicked.

The Negro pressed a button and a warm rain began to fall, apparently from overhead, but really, so John discovered after a moment, from a fountain arrangement near by. The water turned to a pale rose colour and jets of liquid soap spurted into it from four miniature walrus heads at the corners of the bath. In a moment a dozen little paddle-wheels, fixed to the sides, had churned the mixture into a radiant rainbow of pink foam which enveloped him softly with its delicious lightness, and burst in shining, rosy bubbles here and there about him.

'Shall I turn on the moving-picture machine, sir?' suggested the Negro deferentially. 'There's a good one-reel comedy in this machine today, or I can put in a serious piece in a moment, if you prefer it.'

'No, thanks,' answered John, politely but firmly. He was enjoying his bath too much to desire any distraction. But distraction came. In a moment he was listening intently to the sound of flutes from just outside, flutes dripping a melody that was like a waterfall, cool and green as the room itself, accompanying a frothy piccolo, in play more fragile than the lace of suds that covered and charmed him.

Gargantua (l.13): gigantic person (name of the gigantic king in the novel *Gargantua* by the French satirist François Rabelais, ?1494–?1553)

tilt up (l.14): rise up on one side

drapery (l.16): curtains

fleecy (l.17): soft and woolly

incline (l.17): slope

plumped (l.17): suddenly dropped

amber (l.25): yellowish brown

rosewater (l.29): mixture of rose oils and water used as a scent

inanely (l.32): sillily

meagre (l.33): relatively poor

priggish (l.34): (because he was pleased with his moral superiority)

paddle-wheels (l.40): power-driven wheels with wide blades (as on a steamboat)

deferentially (l.45): respectfully

one-reel comedy (l.45): short comedy film

frothy piccolo (l.52): small woodwind instrument making a light and amusing sound

lace of suds (l.53): decorative covering of soapy bubbles

After a cold salt-water bracer and a cold fresh finish, he stepped
out and into a fleecy robe, and upon a couch covered with the same
material he was rubbed with oil, alcohol, and spice. Later he sat in
a voluptuous chair while he was shaved and his hair was trimmed.

'Mr Percy is waiting in your sitting-room,' said the Negro, when
these operations were finished. 'My name is Gygsum, Mr Unger,
sir. I am to see Mr Unger every morning.'

bracer (l.55): shower to strengthen him
voluptuous (l.58): sensually pleasurable

55

60

● Did John enjoy the experience? Does it seem real or a fantasy? What seems to be
Fitzgerald's purpose?

Understanding and interpretation

What is wrong with the following description?:

When John woke up, a large Negro servant took the boy's pyjamas off and threw
him into a fish tank of cold water. Instantly he was sprayed with a cold shower
from above which turned the water green. The servant put on the video and said
he would have nothing more to do with him.

Language and style

i) What do the following tell you? 'the wild places' (l.7); 'starled at first' (l.15);
'smiling inanely' (l.32)

ii) What do the words 'delicious' (l.42) and 'voluptuous' (l.58) tell you?

iii) Which words describe a) colour, b) temperature? What is their effect?

Extract 2

Percy's father, Braddock Washington, made his money from a diamond
mine. Later in the story the mine begins to collapse after an earthquake.
John sees Braddock at the top of a mountain:

Braddock Washington was standing there motionless, silhouetted
against the grey sky without sound or sign of life. As the dawn
came up out of the east, lending a cold green colour to the earth, it
brought the solitary figure into insignificant contrast with the new
day.

While John watched, his host remained for a few moments absorbed in some inscrutable contemplation; then he signalled to the
two Negroes who crouched at his feet to lift the burden which lay
between them. As they struggled upright, the first yellow beam of
the sun struck through the innumerable prisms of an immense and
exquisitely chiselled diamond – and a white radiance was kindled
that glowed upon the air like a fragment of the morning star. The
bearers staggered beneath its weight for a moment – then their
rippling muscles caught and hardened under the wet shine of the
skins and the three figures were again motionless in their defiant
impotency before the heavens.

After a while the white man lifted his head and slowly raised his
arms in a gesture of attention, as one who would call a great crowd
to hear – but there was no crowd, only the vast silence of the mountain and the sky, broken by faint bird voices down among the trees.
The figure on the saddle of rock began to speak ponderously and
with an inextinguishable pride.

'You out there –' he cried in a trembling voice. 'You – there –!' He

1

5

10

15

20

GLOSSARY
inscrutable (l.7): mysterious
prisms (l.10): sides
exquisitely chiselled (l.11): beautifully cut
was kindled (l.11): lit up
rippling (l.14): which move like waves
impotency (l.16): inability to have any effect
saddle of rock (l.21): large rock with two peaks
ponderously (l.21): slowly and heavily

paused, his arms still uplifted, his head held attentively as though
he were expecting an answer. John strained his eyes to see whether   25
there might be men coming down the mountain, but the mountain
was bare of human life. There was only sky and a mocking flute of
wind along the tree-tops. Could Washington be praying? For a
moment John wondered. Then the illusion passed – there was
something in the man's whole attitude antithetical to prayer.   30
   'Oh, you above there!'
The voice was become strong and confident. This was no forlorn
supplication. If anything, there was in it a quality of monstrous
condescension.
   'You there –'   35
Words, too quickly uttered to be understood, flowing one into
the other . . . John listened breathlessly, catching a phrase here and
there, while the voice broke off, resumed, broke off again – now
strong and argumentative, now coloured with a slow, puzzled
impatience. Then a conviction commenced to dawn on the single   40
listener, and as realization crept over him a spray of quick blood
rushed through his arteries. Braddock Washington was offering a
bribe to God!

antithetical (l.30): which
   was completely
   opposed
forlorn supplication (l.32):
   unhappy pleading
condescension (l.34):
   superiority
a spray (l.41): fine jet

(from *The Diamond as Big as the Ritz*)

● Do you think this is meant to be funny or horrifying?

F. Scott Fitzgerald   Fitzgerald's novels include *The Beautiful and Damned* (1922), *The Great
Gatsby* (1925), *Tender is the Night* (1934) – a novel about the moral decline
of a young American psychiatrist as he pursues wealth, not well received
in the depression era of the thirties – and *The Last Tycoon*, an unfinished
novel about Hollywood.

   Fitzgerald's observations on the wealthy are frequently penetrating, but
how far was he able to distinguish fantasy from reality? Did he really
condemn the corrupting influence of money and have a strong sense of
moral value (as he seemed to think he had) or was he too much in love
with the high life himself?

8.4.2   i) To find out more about this period, put the verbs in the correct form:
The twenties
The capitalist economy of the USA (transform) .... as technological
innovations (increase) .... production and the trade unions
(weaken) .... Huge secondary markets (create) .... in
South America after the Europeans (leave) .... and the powerful
political influence of the USA (continue) .... to extend. In the
1920s the USA (produce) .... nearly 40 per cent of the world's coal
and over half the world's manufactured goods. Partly in reaction to the First
World War, there was a trend in the USA towards nationalism and isolationism.

ii) Gertrude Stein described as the 'Lost Generation' those American
intellectuals that, in Fitzgerald's words, had 'grown up to find all gods
dead, all wars fought, all faiths in man shaken'. Many of these writers
became expatriates in Europe, attracted by the relative lack of puritanism
and the greater artistic sophistication. They felt alienated from the

general American public and free to experiment. It was a very
innovative period artistically.

The verse of e.e. cummings (as Cummings always wrote his name; see
also Supplement 8) was influenced by Gertrude Stein, Ezra Pound,
Cubism (an art movement developed by Pablo Picasso and Georges
Braque, in which forms were broken down into geometric shapes) and
Dada (the nihilistic art and literature movement founded in Zurich and
New York in 1916). It is now mainly known for its technical
experimentation. Particularly noticeable are the split words and unusual
grammar arrangements, the odd punctuation and the mixing of
established poetic forms with free verse.

In the title of the poem 'my sweet old etcetera', 'my sweet old' is (we
assume) meant to be a cliché and 'etcetera' is the latin for 'and so on'.

---

my sweet old etcetera

```
my sweet old etcetera                              1
aunt lucy during the recent

war could and what
is more did tell you just
what everybody was fighting                        5

for,
my sister

isabel created hundreds
(and
hundreds)of socks not to                          10
mention shirts fleaproof earwarmers

etcetera wristers etcetera, my
mother hoped that

i would die etcetera
bravely of course my father used                  15
to become hoarse talking about how it was
a privilege and if only he
could meanwhile my

self etcetera lay quietly
in the deep mud et                                20

cetera
(dreaming,
et
    cetera, of
Your smile                                        25
eyes knees and of your Etcetera)
```

GLOSSARY

hoarse (l.16): rough-
  sounding from talking
  too much

Cummings hated 'unman', whom he saw as living without heart and soul, in an 'unworld' of empty patriotic gestures. In 1916 Cummings volunteered for the American Ambulance Corps in France and in 1917 was confined for three months in a detention camp falsely charged with spying.

- i) What is the poet's attitude towards his 'family'?
- ii) Who do you think 'Your smile' (l.25) refers to?
- iii) What do you notice about the typography and punctuation?

8.4.4
Ernest Hemingway
(1899–1961)

Ernest Hemingway served for a time in an ambulance unit in France before transferring to the Italian infantry until the close of the First World War. After working as an overseas correspondent for a Canadian newspaper Hemingway settled in Paris as an expatriate writer.

The following lines are from the novel which made his name, *The Sun Also Rises* (1926), a portrait of young Americans living in Paris:

> You're an expatriate. You've lost touch with the soil. Fake
> European standards have ruined you. You drink yourself
> to death. You become obsessed by sex. You spend all
> your time talking, not working. You are an expatriate,
> see? You hang around cafés.

In *A Farewell to Arms* (1929), Frederic Henry, an American lieutenant in the Italian ambulance service in the First World War, falls in love with Catherine Barkley, an English nurse. He is wounded and she nurses him. She becomes pregnant but refuses to marry him. After returning to his post Frederic deserts and joins Catherine in Stresa.

That night at the hotel, in our room with the long empty hall outside and our shoes outside the door, a thick carpet on the floor of the room, outside the windows the rain falling and in the room light and pleasant and cheerful, then the light out and it exciting with smooth sheets and the bed comfortable, feeling that we had come home, feeling no longer alone, waking in the night to find the other one there, and not gone away; all other things were unreal. We slept when we were tired and if we woke the other one woke too so one was not alone. Often a man wishes to be alone and a girl wishes to be alone too and if they love each other they are jealous of that in each other, but I can truly say we never felt that. We could feel alone when we were together, alone against the others. It has only happened to me like that once. I have been alone while I was with many girls and that is the way that you can be most lonely. But we were never lonely and never afraid when we were together. I know that the night is not the same as the day: that all things are different, that the things of the night cannot be explained in the day, because they do not then exist, and the night can be a dreadful time for lonely people once their loneliness has started. But with Catherine there was almost no difference in the night except that it was an even better time. If people bring so much courage to this world the world has to kill them to break them, so of course it kills them. The world breaks everyone and afterward many are strong at the broken places. But those that will not break it kills. It kills the very good and the very gentle and the very brave impartially. If you are none of these you can be sure it will kill you too but there will be no special hurry.

I remember waking in the morning. Catherine was asleep and the sunlight was coming in through the window. The rain had stopped and I stepped out of bed and across the floor to the window. Down below were the gardens, bare now but beautifully regular, the gravel paths, the trees, the stone wall by the lake and the lake in the sunlight with the mountains beyond. I stood at the window looking out and when I turned away I saw Catherine was awake and watching me.

(from *A Farewell to Arms*)

● How are we given a sense of the lovers' world being cut off from the rest of the world?

Appreciation   Discuss at least one of the following with reference to the text:

a) The language is simpler, more direct and less inflated than the language in the F. Scott Fitzgerald extracts.

b) Hemingway is experimenting with 'stream of consciousness' techniques, such as the 'interior monologue' and a disregard of grammatical logic.

c) Although Hemingway usually keeps emotion at a distance, recording only the bare details and emphasising points through understatement, in this extract he is almost sentimental.

Creative writing   Rewrite the passage from Catherine's point of view.

Ernest Hemingway   Most of Hemingway's stories are about 'tough' people whose essential courage and honesty are implicitly contrasted with the brutality of civilised society. *Death in the Afternoon* (1932) celebrates bullfighting, *The Green Hills of Africa* (1935) celebrates big-game hunting, *For Whom the Bell Tolls* (1940) is set against the background of the Spanish Civil War (1936–1939) and *The Old Man and the Sea* (1952), a parable of man against nature, concerns a deep-sea fisherman. In his later years, Hemingway lived in Cuba. He shot himself in 1961, having been seriously ill for some time.

8.5 The Depression

From 1929–1934 there was a major slump in the world economy, partly caused by the dependence of the world economy on the USA. Prosperity was wiped out overnight and gay cynicism turned to resentful bitter pessimism. In 1932, the worst year, the index for industrial production was only just above half what it had been in 1929 and the national income fell by 38 per cent. Although they had less far to fall than the rich, the poorer sections of society suffered the most.

●   i) What does this picture tell you of the effect of the Depression in the USA?

A migrant worker and family leaving Oklahoma in the Depression

ii) Re-order the following groups of words to make sentences about the causes of the Depression in the USA:
   a) poor distribution / There was / in agriculture / and / overproduction
   b) from Europe / A falsely prosperous stock-market / and general panic / collapsed on 24 October 1929 / after a fever of speculation / the calling back of American loans
   c) which in turn led / there was a fall / and / and exports / Because of a shortage of capital / mass unemployment / in internal consumption / to reduced industrial production

iii) Put the verbs in the correct form to make sentences about the effect of the Depression.
   a) Immigration (restrict) .... : from 1820 to 1929, over thirty-two million immigrants (arrive) .... from Europe.
   b) Attempts at economic nationalism and self-sufficiency (make) .... more intense through the imposition of import taxes.
   c) There was a feeling that in recent years liberal civilisation (lose) .... its power to control events. This (encourage) .... the establishment of totalitarian regimes and political nationalist movements, such as the German Nazis.

8.6 A new Naturalism

In the USA, among the intellectuals, there was a swing to the left politically and a greater sense of social responsibility. Writers turned away from twenties materialism and were less concerned to conduct literary experiments simply for their own sake.

8.6.1.
John Steinbeck
(1902–1968)

The novels of John Steinbeck attempt to combine realism and romance and portray, through the lives of individuals, the national spirit. His settings are often rural areas, where people live most happily when close to nature, but where malevolent forces, such as drought or capitalism or human greed, destroy this vital relationship.

Warm-up

Either:
In pairs, tell each other your most vivid memories of a rainstorm.
Or:
Stand in groups. Imagine it is a sunny day. Then great clouds gather. At first it rains gently, but then harder and harder. You have to find shelter. You are getting soaked. Then slowly the rain stops. Mime the scene. Be as expressive as you can.

The Grapes of Wrath

The Grapes of Wrath (1940) tells the story of the Joads, a farming family who leave the Oklahoma Dust Bowl in their broken-down automobile after terrible winds have destroyed their land. They migrate to California, which they believe is the land of plenty. Once there, they are haunted by starvation, troubled by sheriffs and experience the violence and injustice of Californian landowners.

285

Extract 1

GLOSSARY

gusty (l.1): with a
sudden strong rush of
wind

freshets (l.9): overflowing
streams

The rain began with gusty showers, pauses and downpours; and
then gradually it settled to a single tempo, small drops and a steady
beat, rain that was grey to see through, rain that cut midday light to
evening. And at first the dry earth sucked the moisture down and
blackened. For two days the earth drank the rain, until the earth
was full. Then puddles formed, and in the low places little lakes
formed in the fields. The muddy lakes rose higher, and the steady
rain whipped the shining water. At last the mountains were full,
and the hillsides spilled into the streams, built them to freshets,
and sent them roaring down the canyons into the valleys.

1

5

10

- Which words and phrases most suggest sounds?

Extract 2

GLOSSARY

huddled (l.1): pressed
close together

shovels (l.5): (like spades
but with a broad square
blade)

dykes (l.5): walls of earth

canvas (l.6): strong,
rough cloth used for
tents

fouled the ignition (l.11):
prevented the engines
from starting

*fouled the carburettors
(l.12)*: got into the part
of the engines that
mixes petrol and air
and prevented it from
working

were shorted (l.14): had a
faulty connection and
wouldn't work

engulfed (l.15): surrounded
and swallowed up
completely

waded (l.15): walked
through water

barn (l.18): farm building
used for storage

relief offices (l.20): places
where financial
assistance was
supposed to be given

pneumonia (l.29): a serious
lung illness

measles (l.29): a disease
which causes a fever
and small red spots

mastoids (l.30): parts of
the bone behind the ear

culverts (l.32): pipes under
the road from the
drains

When the first rain started, the migrant people huddled in their
tents, saying: It'll soon be over, and asking: How long's it likely to
go on?

And when the puddles formed, the men went out in the rain
with shovels and built little dykes around the tents. The beating
rain worked at the canvas until it penetrated and sent streams
down. And then the little dykes washed out and the water came
inside, and the streams wet the beds and the blankets. The people
sat in wet clothes. They set up boxes and put planks on the boxes.
Then, day and night, they sat on the planks.

Beside the tents the old cars stood, and water fouled the ignition
wires and water fouled the carburettors. The little grey tents stood
in lakes. And at last the people had to move. Then the cars wouldn't
start because the wires were shorted; and if the engines would run,
deep mud engulfed the wheels. And the people waded away,
carrying their wet blankets in their arms. They splashed along,
carrying the children, carrying the very old, in their arms. And if a
barn stood on high ground, it was filled with people, shivering and
hopeless.

Then some went to the relief offices, and they came sadly back to
their own people.

They's rules – you got to be here a year before you can git relief.
They say the gov'ment is gonna help. They don' know when.

And gradually the greatest terror of all came along.

They ain't gonna be no kinda work for three months.

In the barns the people sat huddled together; and the terror came
over them, and their faces were grey with terror. The children cried
with hunger, and there was no food.

Then the sickness came, pneumonia, and measles that went to
the eyes and to the mastoids.

And the rain fell steadily, and the water flowed over the high-
ways, for the culverts could not carry the water.

Then from the tents, from the crowded barns, groups of sodden

1

5

10

15

20

25

30

sodden (l.33): completely wet

slopping (l.34): messy and wet; noisy when they move

pulp (l.34): liquid mass

cringe (l.36): behave like a servant without self-respect

smoulder (l.38): exist without being known or seen

swore in deputies (l.41): appointed people and gave them power to help him

in droves (l.41): in large numbers

rifles (l.41): guns (fired from the shoulder)

tear gas (l.42): a gas that causes watering of the eyes, used in crowd control

men went out, their clothes slopping rags, their shoes muddy pulp. They splashed out through the water, to the towns, to the country stores, to the relief offices, to beg for food, to cringe and beg for food, to beg for relief, to try to steal, to lie. And under the begging, and under the cringing, a hopeless anger began to smoulder. And in the little towns pity for the sodden men changed to anger, and anger at the hungry people changed to fear of them. Then sheriffs swore in deputies in droves, and orders were rushed for rifles, for tear gas, for ammunition. Then the hungry men crowded the alleys behind the stores to beg for bread, to beg for rotting vegetables, to steal when they could. 35 40

(from *The Grapes of Wrath*)

● What do you think could have been done for the migrants? Do you like 'naturalistic' writing of this sort?

Understanding and interpretation

i) Choose the most suitable alternative.

a) At first the rain was *heavy/intermittent/light*; then it was *continuous/showery/ light*.

b) The streams *became puddles/overflowed/went underground*.

c) The migrants couldn't get financial relief because *the government couldn't get the money through/they had been there too long/they weren't entitled to it*.

ii) Complete the following sentences:

a) The migrants tried to stop the water flowing into their tents by ....

b) Inside the tents the migrants tried to keep dry by ....

c) The townspeople were afraid and ....

Language

Find a word in the passage for each of the following: a) surrounded and swallowed up; b) burn slowly.

Appreciation

Compare the style and content of this extract with either the Hemingway extract (page 283) or the F. Scott Fitzgerald extract (page 277).

8.7 Anti-Utopianism and fear

At the beginning of the century in Britain, the plays of Bernard Shaw (see page 439) had behind them, in part, a belief that socialism would make for a more socially just society. Even more 'Utopian' were the early scientific fantasies of H.G. Wells (see page 432): Wells held to a belief in the inevitable progress of mankind which would result from the rapid development of science and technology. (In the first 'Utopian' work in English – *Utopia* (1516) by Sir Thomas More – an imaginary country was used as a model by which to judge earthly societies.)

With the economic depression of the thirties and the consequent threat of totalitarianism from both Fascism and Communism, popular works of the time were more 'dystopian', showing a society in the future with all our fears realised. Mass culture was seen to be manipulated, through technology, for political or commercial reasons.

8.7.1 Aldous Huxley (1894–1963)

Aldous Huxley was the grandson of the nineteenth-century agnostic biologist, Thomas Huxley. Sceptical of Christian religion as a solution to the spiritual problems of the twentieth century, in the 1930s he turned to eastern religions such as Buddhism. His novels include *Point Counter Point* (1928) and *Ape and Essence* (1948).

Brave New World (1932) is a comic–satirical 'novel of ideas' (it is more concerned to give points of view than establish characters). It is meant to show, in Huxley's words, 'the horror of the Wellsian Utopia and a revolt against it'. In a society which has become dominated by technology and lost all its life and culture there are no deep human emotions, no past and no art. Life is trivial, sterile and spiritually empty.

Extract 1

The action takes place at an imaginary time, in the seventh century AF (after Ford: Henry Ford was the American industrialist who declared that 'All history is bunk!'). In the highly controlled society which is depicted, human beings are ranked. The highest intellectuals are known as Alpha-Pluses; the lowest manual workers are known as Epsilons. Babies are hatched in incubators like fish and poultry and brought up in communal nurseries. Natural birth is an obscenity and forbidden by law.

GLOSSARY

tiptoeing (l.1): walking quietly on the tips of their toes

shuttered (l.3): with the light cut out by door-like covers

cots (l.3): beds for children

Class Consciousness (l.10): (lessons which make them aware of their position in society)

D.H.C. (l.13): the Director of Hatcheries and Conditioning

trumpet (l.16): instrument for making the sounds louder

khaki (l.20): yellowish-brown cloth

beastly (l.23): nasty

Fifty yards of tiptoeing brought them to a door which the Director   1
cautiously opened. They stepped over the threshold into the twilight
of a shuttered dormitory. Eighty cots stood in a row against the
wall. There was a sound of light regular breathing and a continuous
murmur, as of very faint voices remotely whispering.   5

A nurse rose as they entered and came to attention before the
Director.

'What's the lesson this afternoon?' he asked.

'We had Elementary Sex for the first forty minutes,' she answered.
'But now it's switched over to Elementary Class Consciousness.'   10

The Director walked slowly down the long line of cots. Rosy and
relaxed with sleep, eighty little boys and girls lay softly breathing.
There was a whisper under every pillow. The D.H.C. halted and,
bending over one of the little beds, listened attentively.

'Elementary Class Consciousness, did you say? Let's have it   15
repeated a little louder by the trumpet.'

At the end of the room a loud-speaker projected from the wall.
The Director walked up to it and pressed a switch.

'. . . all wear green,' said a soft but very distinct voice, beginning
in the middle of a sentence, 'and Delta children wear khaki. Oh no,   20
I don't want to play with Delta children. And Epsilons are still
worse. They're too stupid to be able to read or write. Besides, they
wear black, which is such a beastly colour. I'm *so* glad I'm a Beta.'

• What does the phrase 'a whisper under every pillow' (l.13) tell you? Can you guess which rank wears green?

Extract 2 Children are introduced early to the need for instant pleasure:

GLOSSARY

shrill (l.3): high, sharp

shrubs (l.4): low bushes

soliloquized (l.5): sang to themselves

boskage (l.5): group of small trees and shrubs

cuckoo (l.6): grey bird with a call that sounds like its name

drowsy (l.7): sleepy

Centrifugal Bumble-puppy (l.9): (a name invented by Huxley for a type of children's game.)

chrome-steel (l.10): made of a mixture of steel and chromium

apertures (l.13): holes

cylindrical (l.13): tube-shaped

Our Ford's day (l.16): (in the old days, when Ford was alive)

apparatus (l.17): equipment

netting (l.18): string made into a net

folly (l.18): foolishness

bay (l.25): area enclosed by a curve

heather (l.26): small bush with pink/purple flowers

gravely (l.27): seriously

rudimentary (l.29): simple

patronizing (l.32): (as though the D.H.C. were less clever than they were)

Outside, in the garden, it was playtime. Naked in the warm June sunshine, six or seven hundred little boys and girls were running with shrill yells over the lawns, or playing ball games, or squatting silently in twos and threes among the flowering shrubs. The roses were in bloom, two nightingales soliloquized in the boskage, a cuckoo was just going out of tune among the lime trees. The air was drowsy with the murmur of bees and helicopters. [5]

The Director and his students stood for a short time watching a game of Centrifugal Bumble-puppy. Twenty children were grouped in a circle round a chrome-steel tower. A ball thrown up so as to land on the platform at the top of the tower rolled down into the interior, fell on a rapidly revolving disk, was hurled through one or other of the numerous apertures pierced in the cylindrical casing, and had to be caught. [10]

'Strange,' mused the Director, as they turned away, 'strange to think that even in Our Ford's day most games were played without more apparatus than a ball or two and a few sticks and perhaps a bit of netting. Imagine the folly of allowing people to play elaborate games which do nothing whatever to increase consumption. It's madness. Nowadays the Controllers won't approve of any new game unless it can be shown that it requires at least as much apparatus as the most complicated of existing games.' He interrupted himself. [15] [20]

'That's a charming little group,' he said, pointing.

In a little grassy bay between tall clumps of Mediterranean heather, two children, a little boy of about seven and a little girl who might have been a year older, were playing, very gravely and with all the focussed attention of scientists intent on a labour of discovery, a rudimentary sexual game. [25]

'Charming, charming!' the D.H.C. repeated sentimentally. [30]

'Charming,' the boys politely agreed. But their smile was rather patronizing. They had put aside similar childish amusements too recently to be able to watch them now without a touch of contempt. Charming? but it was just a pair of kids fooling about; that was all. Just kids. [35]

• Indicate at least three points of detail which make the atmosphere odd.

Extract 3 A disease-free world of comfort and mass-produced happiness, in which sexual partners must be changed regularly, contrasts with the 'world before Ford', a world before families were abolished. In this extract, Huxley puts a description of Lenina, a nurse, getting out of a bath, next to an image conjured up by Mustapha Mond, the world controller, of the 'horrors' of the earlier period:

Lenina got out of the bath, towelled herself dry, took hold of a long flexible tube plugged into the wall, presented the nozzle to her breast, as though she meant to commit suicide, pressed down the trigger. A blast of warmed air dusted her with the finest talcum powder. Eight different scents and eau-de-Cologne were laid on in the little taps over the wash-basin. She turned on the third from the left, dabbled herself with chypre and, carrying her shoes and stockings in her hand, went out to see if one of the vibro-vacuum machines were free.

And home was as squalid psychically as physically. Psychically, it was a rabbit hole, a midden, hot with the frictions of tightly packed life, reeking with emotion. What suffocating intimacies, what dangerous, insane, obscene relationships between the members of the family group! Maniacally, the mother brooded over her children (*her* children) ... brooded over them like a cat over its kittens; but a cat that could talk, a cat that could say, 'My baby, my baby,' over and over again. 'My baby, and oh, oh, at my breast, the little hands, the hunger, and that unspeakable agonizing pleasure! Till at last my baby sleeps, my baby sleeps with a bubble of white milk at the corner of his mouth. My little baby sleeps ...'

'Yes,' said Mustapha Mond, nodding his head, 'you may well shudder.'

(from *Brave New World*)

GLOSSARY

nozzle (l.2): short tube fitted to the end
trigger (l.4): the device for turning it on
dabbled (l.7): wet
chypre (l.7): a type of heavy perfume
vibro-vacuum machines (l.8): massage machines
squalid (l.10): dirty and unpleasant
midden (l.2): pile of rubbish
reeking (l.3): smelling strongly
brooded over (l.14): hung over (in an excessively maternal fashion)
shudder (l.22): make an uncontrollable movement (showing your disgust)

● Which words show the hostility of the Controller to families?

This 'brave new world' has no aggression or violence. Its controllers are highly intelligent, detached and disillusioned, not mad or sadistic. But there is no freedom or individuality; the world is planned the way they believe is best.

● Is there anything in the extracts which seems to you true of today's world?

8.7.2 George Orwell (1903–1950)

George Orwell, who disliked and rejected his real name Eric Blair, thought of himself as being on the political left even though he never joined a political party. After an upper-class education at Eton, he worked for the Burma Police (1922–1927), resigning 'to escape not merely from imperialism but from every form of man's dominion over man'. During the Depression, to appease his sense of guilt about his upbringing, he lived for eighteen months in destitution. In 1937 he fought for the Republicans in the Spanish Civil War. From then on he worked as a journalist and novelist. His novels include *Homage to Catalonia* (1938), about his experiences in Spain, and *Animal Farm* (1945), a satirical fable about Stalin's Russia.

Orwell's *1984* (written in 1948) presents a gloomy world under a Stalinist-style dictatorship. The following three extracts are from the opening of the novel:

It was a bright cold day in April, and the clocks were striking thir- teen. Winston Smith, his chin nuzzled into his breast in an effort to escape the vile wind, slipped quickly through the glass doors of Victory Mansions, though not quickly enough to prevent a swirl of gritty dust from entering along with him.

The hallway smelt of boiled cabbage and old rag mats. At one end of it a coloured poster, too large for indoor display, had been tacked to the wall. It depicted simply an enormous face, more than a metre wide: the face of a man of about forty-five, with a heavy black moustache and ruggedly handsome features. Winston made for the stairs. It was no use trying the lift. Even at the best of times it was seldom working, and at present the electric current was cut off during daylight hours. It was part of the economy drive in preparation for Hate Week. The flat was seven flights up, and Winston, who was thirty-nine and had a varicose ulcer above his right ankle, went slowly, resting several times on the way. On each landing, opposite the lift-shaft, the poster with the enormous face gazed from the wall. It was one of those pictures which are so con- trived that the eyes follow you about when you move. BIG BROTHER IS WATCHING YOU, the caption beneath it ran.

Outside, even through the shut window-pane, the world looked cold. Down in the street little eddies of wind were whirling dust and torn paper into spirals, and though the sun was shining and the sky a harsh blue, there seemed to be no colour in anything, except the posters that were plastered everywhere. The black- moustachio'd face gazed down from every commanding corner. There was one on the house-front immediately opposite. BIG BROTHER IS WATCHING YOU, the caption said, while the dark eyes looked deep into Winston's own. Down at street level another poster, torn at one corner, flapped fitfully in the wind, alternately covering and uncovering the single word INGSOC. In the far distance a helicopter skimmed down between the roofs, hovered for an instant like a bluebottle, and darted away again with a curving flight. It was the police patrol, snooping into people's windows. The patrols did not matter, however. Only the Thought Police mattered.

Winston kept his back turned to the telescreen. It was safer; though, as he well knew, even a back can be revealing. A kilometre away the Ministry of Truth, his place of work, towered vast and white above the grimy landscape. This, he thought with a sort of vague distaste – this was London, chief city of Airstrip One, itself the third most populous of the provinces of Oceania. He tried to squeeze out some childhood memory that should tell him whether London had always been quite like this. Were there always these vistas of rotting nineteenth-century houses, their sides shored up with baulks of timber, their windows patched with cardboard and their roofs with corrugated iron, their crazy garden walls sagging in all directions?

willow-herb (l.49): tall
plant with long spikes
of pinkish, purple
flowers
straggled (l.49): spread
around untidily
rubble (l.49): broken
stones and bricks
tableaux (l.53): (like scenes
on a stage)

And the bombed sites where the plaster dust swirled in the air and the willow-herb straggled over the heaps of rubble; and the places where the bombs had cleared a larger patch and there had sprung up sordid colonies of wooden dwellings like chicken-houses? But it was no use, he could not remember; nothing remained of his childhood except a series of bright-lit tableaux occurring against no background and mostly unintelligible.

50

(from 1984)

i) What seems to be the purpose of the opening sentence?
ii) Which phrases describe the weather? What is the effect?
iii) Identify at least three other phrases which suggest a) a hostile environment; b) a devastated environment.

In *Brave New World Revisited* (1958), Aldous Huxley wrote:

GLOSSARY

magnified projection (l.1):
enlarged, imaginary
throwing forward
Stalinism (l.2): the rigid
principles and policies
associated with the
Soviet leader Joseph
Stalin, 1879–1953
tyrant (l.5): cruel,
unjust ruler
got ... stride (l.5): started
to work with full power
brutal (l.8): cruel
*gruesome verisimilitude
(l.13)*: appearance of
horrible truth
Great Powers (l.15):
The Soviet Union and
the USA
refrain (l.15): stop
themselves

George Orwell's *1984* was a magnified projection into the future of a present that contained Stalinism and an immediate past that had witnessed the flowering of Nazism. *Brave New World* was written before the rise of Hitler to supreme power in Germany and when the Russian tyrant had not yet got into his stride. In 1931 systematic terrorism was not the obsessive contemporary fact which it had become in 1948, and the future dictatorship of my imaginary world was a good deal less brutal than the future dictatorship so brilliantly portrayed by Orwell. In the context of 1948, *1984* seemed dreadfully convincing. But tyrants, after all, are mortal and circumstances change. Recent developments in Russia, and recent advances in science and technology, have robbed Orwell's book of some of its gruesome verisimilitude. A nuclear war will, of course, make nonsense of everybody's predictions. But, assuming for the moment that the Great Powers can somehow refrain from destroying us, we can say that it now looks as though the odds were, more in favour of something like *Brave New World* than of something like *1984*.

1

5

10

15

(from 'Brave New World Revisited')

Although both *Animal Farm* and *1984* touched the nerve of the wider public in Britain and the USA, it has been suggested that Orwell put his own personal fears and his self-hatred into a vision of the world around him.

Here is the opening of Orwell's essay 'England Your England', written in 1941 during the Second World War:

> **As I write, highly civilized human beings are flying overhead, trying to kill me.** 1
>
> **They do not feel any enmity against me as an individual, nor I against them. They are 'only doing their duty', as the saying goes. Most of them, I have no doubt, are kind-hearted law-abiding men** 5 **who would never dream of committing murder in private life. On the other hand, if one of them succeeds in blowing me to pieces with a well-placed bomb, he will never sleep any the worse for it. He is serving his country, which has the power to absolve him from evil.** 10
>
> **One cannot see the modern world as it is unless one recognizes the overwhelming strength of patriotism, national loyalty. In certain circumstances it can break down, at certain levels of civilization it does not exist, but as a *positive* force there is nothing to set beside it. Christianity and international Socialism are as weak as straw in** 15 **comparison with it. Hitler and Mussolini rose to power in their own countries very largely because they could grasp this fact and their opponents could not.**
>
> (from 'England Your England')

GLOSSARY
enmity against (l.3): hatred of
law-abiding (l.5): who habitually obey the law
absolve (l.9): free
overwhelming (l.12): too great to oppose
straw (l.15): dried stalks of wheat

● From these extracts, can you say how Orwell's and Huxley's writings differ in tone and content?

8.7.3 Topicality in verse	W.H. Auden, the son of a devout Anglo-Catholic mother, was recognised as the leader of a group of left-wing writers such as the poets Cecil Day-Lewis (1904–1972), Louis MacNeice (1907–1963) and the novelist Christopher Isherwood (1904–1986). Their social observations were immediate, topical (i.e. they were of general interest at time) and in the main limited in aim.

8.7.4 W(ystan) H(ugh) Auden (1907–1973)	In 1937 W.H. Auden visited Spain for two months to support the Republicans in the Spanish Civil War. In January 1939 he and Isherwood left Europe for America, to live, as he saw it, where the crises of modern civilisation were at their most intense, away from the traditionalism of English life. He became a US citizen in 1946. Later in his life, though, he became rather an isolated figure and spent much of his time back in Oxford, where he had been at university.
Warm-up	Auden saw the painting overleaf, *Landscape with the fall of Icarus* by Brueghel, in the Musée des Beaux Arts in Brussels in December 1983. To many in Europe at that time it was clear that another massive war was not far away.

● Where is Icarus in the picture? What else is happening?

Musée des Beaux Arts

About suffering they were never wrong,   1
The Old Masters: how well they understood
Its human position; how it takes place
While someone else is eating or opening a window or just
walking dully along;   5
How, when the aged are reverently, passionately waiting
For the miraculous birth, there always must be
Children who did not specially want it to happen, skating
On a pond at the edge of the wood:
They never forgot   10
That even the dreadful martyrdom must run its course
Anyhow in a corner, some untidy spot
Where the dogs go on with their doggy life and the torturer's
horse

294

Scratches its innocent behind on a tree.   15
In Brueghel's Icarus, for instance; how everything turns away
Quite leisurely from the disaster; the ploughman may
Have heard the splash, the forsaken cry,
But for him it was not an important failure; the sun shone
As it had to on the white legs disappearing into the green   20
Water; and the expensive delicate ship that must have seen
Something amazing, a boy falling out of the sky,
Had somewhere to get to and sailed calmly on.

behind (l.15): buttocks
forsaken (l.18): (of someone who has been deserted)

Understanding and interpretation	i) Which of the following alternatives best summarises the narrator's argument? Great artists of the past realised that
	  a) powerful individual human experiences can exist while life goes on as normal nearby.
	  b) human suffering occurs while miraculous events are experienced elsewhere.
	ii) What do you think the following refer to?
	  'it' (l.3); 'miraculous birth' (l.7); 'They' (l.10); 'the dreadful martyrdom' (l.11)

Appreciation	i) What effect do these words/phrases create in context: 'just' (l.4); 'forsaken' (l.18); 'As it had to' (l.20)? ii) Think of two or three phrases or words that summarise the tone of the poem (the narrator's mood and manner). iii) List some of the contrasts in the poem (for example, 'the aged' (l.6) 'children' (l.8). What is their overall effect? iv) How does Auden create an effect of directness and immediacy?
Language and style	i) Rewrite the lines 'About suffering . . . Masters' (l.1–l.2) using standard English syntax. What do they lose in comparison with the original? ii) A distinctive feature of Auden's verse is his use of plural nouns (for example, 'The Old Masters' (l.2) for the purposes of generalisation. How many can you find in this poem?
W.H. Auden	Auden's verse is noted for its strong didactic tendency and its tone of moral responsibility. Its reputation rests partly on its great technical virtuosity and its range of poetic styles; it is also noted for the poet's ability to reconcile traditional verse patterns with a fresh and easy contemporary language.

8.8 The Second World War and after

- Find out as much as you can about the Second World War. Write an account using these notes to help you.

1939: 1st September Germany invades Poland: 3rd September France and Britain declare war on Germany.

1940: Germany invades and defeats Holland, Belgium and France but fails to win air superiority over Britain; Italy joins with Germany.

1941: Germany invades Yugoslavia, Greece and Russia; Japan attacks British and American bases; Germany and Italy declare war on USA.

1942: British troops break through Italian and German troops in North Africa; Germans begin to be thrown back in Russia.

1943: US troops land in Morocco; Russia breaks through German front in Stalingrad; Allied troops invade Sicily and Italy; Italy makes separate peace.

1944: Paris liberated.

1945: Allied troops link up with Russians; Germans surrender; Japanese surrender after the dropping of two atomic bombs.

The following excerpt is from one of the speeches of the British Prime Minister Winston Churchill in 1940, made after 200,000 British troops and 120,000 French troops had been evacuated from Dunkirk, a port in Northern France:

The evacuation of Dunkirk, June 1940

The British Empire and the French Republic, linked together in their cause and in their need, will defend to the death their native soil, aiding each other like good comrades to the utmost of their strength. Even though large tracts of Europe and many old and famous States have fallen or may fall into the grip of the Gestapo and all the odious apparatus of Nazi rule, we shall not flag or fail. We shall go on to the end, we shall fight in France, we shall fight on the seas and oceans, we shall fight with growing confidence and growing strength in the air, we shall defend our Island, whatever the cost may be, we shall fight on the beaches, we shall fight on the landing grounds, we shall fight in the fields and in the streets, we shall fight in the hills; we shall never surrender, and even if, which I do not for a moment believe, this Island or a large part of it were subjugated and starving, then our Empire beyond the seas, armed and guarded by the British Fleet, would carry on the struggle, until, in God's good time, the New World, with all its power and might, steps forth to the rescue and the liberation of the Old.

- What seems to be the purpose of the speech? What are some of the rhetorical devices Churchill uses?

The following are accounts of Britain after the Second World War. Punctuate, adding capital letters where necessary. In some cases there is more than one possibility.

i) *The Welfare State*

in 1945 after the war the conservatives under churchill lost the general election in their place the first majority labour government ever introduced a system of social security financed by payments made by most members of the adult community as a consequence the state became largely responsible for the health and education of the nation the concept was the opposite of nineteenth-century laissez faire policies which allowed society to develop freely according to economic forces and without government control to the dismay of many however the security of the welfare state did nothing to stop in fact some say it encouraged a steep rise in crime.

ii) *The affluent society*

the fifties was a time of almost full employment great american influence and a rapid increase in consumerism it was the period when teenager wealth became a major economic influence and encouraged the power of advertising and television in 1956 the screening of the film rock around the clock had a tremendous impact it coincided with the abandonment of many traditional values and the growth of more materialistic attitudes until 1962 and the commonwealth immigrants act a large number of immigrants from the commonwealth came to settle in britain attracted by the relatively high standard of living for a variety of reasons the population grew considerably unemployment reared its head again in the late fifties and idealistic protests were made by the middle class young

iii) *The sixties*

in 1957 a home office committee under sir john wolfenden recommended that homosexual acts in private between consenting male adults should no longer be a crime in 1959 penguin books won the right to publish d h lawrences lady chatterleys lover which had been prosecuted under the obscene publications act both these events signalled the beginning of the permissive hedonistic more cosmopolitan society of the late 1960s in which protest against the vietnam war merged with an outpouring of frivolous and fashionable creativity a lack of sexual restraint and the so called drug culture it was the time of the beatles the hugely influential pop group from liverpool

8.9 Disillusion and the 'Angry Young Men'

In the mid-fifties it was becoming clear that the new world promised in 1945 would not materialise. Despite the reduced importance Britain had in the world after the war, the 'establishment' (the traditional institutions of the state) seemed incapable of change and to have no sense of direction. The dissatisfaction and alienation felt by many of the young led to a reaction against middle-class values and a release of working-class energies.

The term 'Angry Young Men' was a journalistic phrase widely applied for about ten years to writers of the time who vigorously expressed their disillusion without having many positive values to put in the place of those they opposed.

Plays: *Look Back in Anger* (1956) by John Osborne (b. 1929), *A Taste of Honey* (1958) by Shelagh Delaney (b. 1939) and *Chicken Soup with Barley* (1958) by Arnold Wesker (b. 1932). These were termed 'kitchen sink dramas' because of their portrayal of working-class middle-class life and their emphasis on domestic realism.

Other works: Novels such as *Lucky Jim* (1954) by Kingsley Amis (b. 1922), *Saturday Night and Sunday Morning* (1958) by Alan Sillitoe (b. 1928), and *The Outsider* (1956) by Colin Wilson (b. 1931), a study of the alienation of the man of genius.

8.9.1
John Osborne (b.1929)

John Osborne's plays include *The Entertainer* (1954), *Luther* (1961) and *Inadmissable Evidence* (1964). At their most positive his plays praise the qualities of loyalty, tolerance and friendship.

8.9.2
Look Back in Anger

In part written as a reaction against the drawing-room comedies and middle-class dramas of Noël Coward (1899–1973) and Sir Terence Rattigan (1911–1977), *Look Back in Anger* was a landmark in the history of the theatre. Although not generally thought of as a great play in itself, it nevertheless manages to convey the sense of restlessness and dissatisfaction of the time with intensity and vigour, in the idiom of the actual speech of the young. After its first production in 1956 the theatre in Britain opened up to a whole range of influences and became livelier than at any time for more than 250 years.

The action of the play takes place in a one-roomed flat in the Midlands. It centres on the marital conflicts of Jimmy and Alison Porter. To Jimmy, Alison and her upper-class family (including her brother Nigel) personify the 'establishment'. Cliff is their lodger.

Warm-up

In his attack, Jimmy makes use of the words 'sycophantic', 'phlegmatic' and 'pusillanimous'. Do you know what they mean? If not, look them up in a dictionary.

JIMMY: ... **Have you ever seen her brother? Brother Nigel? The straight-backed, chinless wonder from Sandhurst? I only met him once myself. He asked me to step outside when I told his mother she was evil minded.**   1

CLIFF: **And did you?**   5

JIMMY: **Certainly not. He's a big chap. Well, you've never heard so many well-bred commonplaces come from beneath the same bowler hat. The Platitude from Outer Space – that's brother Nigel. He'll end up in the Cabinet one day, make no mistake. But somewhere at the back of that mind is the**   10 **vague knowledge that he and his pals have been plundering and fooling everybody for generations. [*Going upstage, and turning.*] Now Nigel is just about as vague as you can get without being actually invisible. And invisible politicians aren't much use to anyone – not even to *his* supporters!**   15 **And nothing is more vague about Nigel than his knowledge. His knowledge of life and ordinary human beings is so** hazy, he really deserves some sort of decoration for it – a medal inscribed 'For Vaguery in the Field'. But it wouldn't do for him to be troubled by any stabs of conscience, how- 20 ever vague. [*Moving down again.*] Besides, he's a patriot and an Englishman, and he doesn't like the idea that he may have been selling out his countryman all these years, so what does he do? The only thing he *can* do – seek sanctuary in his own stupidity. The only way to keep things as much 25 like they always have been as possible, is to make any alter- native too much for your poor, tiny brain to grasp. It takes some doing nowadays. It really does. But they knew all about character building at Nigel's school, and he'll make it all right. Don't you worry, he'll make it. And, what's more, 30 he'll do it better than anybody else!

There is no sound, only the plod of Alison's iron. Her eyes are fixed on what she is doing. Cliff stares at the floor. His cheer- fulness has deserted him for the moment. Jimmy is rather shakily triumphant. He cannot allow himself to look at either 35 of them to catch their response to his rhetoric, so he moves across to the window, to recover himself, and look out.

It's started to rain. That's all it needs. This room and the rain.

He's been cheated out of his response, but he's got to draw 40 blood somehow.

[*conversationally*] Yes, that's the little woman's family. You know Mummy and Daddy, of course. And don't let the Marquess of Queensberry manner fool you. They'll kick you in the groin while you're handing your hat to the maid. 45 As for Nigel and Alison – [*In a reverent, Stuart Hibberd voice.*] Nigel and Alison. They're what they sound like: sycophantic, phlegmatic and pusillanimous.

CLIFF: I'll bet that concert's started by now. Shall I put it on?
JIMMY: I looked up that word the other day. It's one of those words 50 I've never been quite sure of, but always thought I knew.
CLIFF: What was that?
JIMMY: I told you – pusillanimous. Do you know what it means?
Cliff shakes his head.
Neither did I really. All this time, I have been married to 55 this woman, this monument to non-attachment, and sud- denly I discover that there is actually a word that sums her up. Not just an adjective in the English language to describe her with – it's her name! Pusillanimous! It sounds like some fleshy Roman matron, doesn't it? The Lady Pusillanimous 60 seen here with her husband Sextus, on their way to the Games.
Cliff looks troubled, and glances uneasily at Alison.

(from *Look Back in Anger*)

GLOSSARY

chinless wonder (l.2): weak and foolish man from the upper classes

Sandhurst (l.2): military academy for army officers

step outside (l.3): (Nigel challenged Jimmy to a fight)

well-bred (l.7): refined

commonplaces (l.7): uninteresting remarks

bowler hat (l.8): black round hat formerly worn by London business men and civil servants

Platitude (l.8): true, but uninteresting remark

Cabinet (l.9): the group of most important government ministers

pals (l.11): friends

plundering (l.11): taking (things) by force

upstage (l.12): towards the back of the stage

hazy (l.18): vague

in the field (l.19): (in life)

selling out (l.23): betraying

sanctuary (l.24): place where he can be safe

plod (l.32): slow falling movement

rhetoric (l.36): impressive- sounding language (said for effect; a bit artificial)

Marquess of Queensberry manner (l.44):(which makes it seem as if he's looking for a fair fight)

groin (l.45): crotch

Stuart Hibberd voice (l.46): (with an upper-class accent like that of an old-style BBC announcer)

● What do you think of Jimmy?

299

Understanding and interpretation

i) In 'caricature', human characteristics are exaggerated and distorted, usually for the purposes of satire. Nigel is a caricature of his class. Where are the following referred to?
   a) the type of school Nigel went to
   b) the type of professional training he has had
   c) the type of job he has

ii) Where does Jimmy seem to be saying the following?
   a) the upper classes have exploited the country
   b) the upper classes are polite on the surface but cruel underneath

iii) This is John Osborne's description of Jimmy in the stage directions:

He is a disconcerting mixture of sincerity and cheerful malice, of 1
tenderness and freebooting cruelty; restless, importunate, full of
pride, a combination which alienates the sensitive and insensitive
alike. Blistering honesty, or apparent honesty, like his, makes few
friends. To many he may seem sensitive to the point of vulgarity. 5
To others, he is simply a loudmouth. To be as vehement as he is is
to be almost non-committal.

Which phrases in Osborne's description can be applied to these places in the extract?
   a) 'I told his mother she was evil minded' (l.4)
   b) '– it's her name! Pusillanimous!' (l.59)

Appreciation

Do you agree with the following?

   a) Jimmy enjoys the sound of his own rhetoric
   b) Jimmy's attack on society could be a cover for his resentment of Alison

8.10 America and its search for itself

The 'naturalism' of American literature of the early thirties – characterised by its descriptions of poor people trapped by society and driven by forces within themselves – frequently had behind it ideological commitment and social protest. The 'naturalistic' novels about the Second World War, while broadly 'anti-war', preferred to examine in a more detached way, with great attention to authenticity and accuracy of detail, the effects of war on both soldiers and ordinary people. Nevertheless, *The Naked and the Dead* (1948) by Norman Mailer (b. 1923), based on the author's army experiences in the Pacific, not only evokes in realistic manner a strong sense of place and action, it also presents a lively conflict of ideas.

After the War, America entered an 'Age of Anxiety', obsessed with the 'threat' of Communism and the possibility of a nuclear attack from Russia.

American writers became more obsessed with their own selves and began to explore their cultural, racial and personal backgrounds. For example, the dramatist Tennessee Williams (1911–1983) – see Supplement 8 – powerfully portrays in rather heavy poetic prose, the loneliness and violence of the South where he was born; and the Jewish-American novelist Saul Bellow (b. 1915) – also see Supplement 8 – in *Herzog* (1964) reveals the intense inner life of a Jewish intellectual driven to the verge of breakdown by his second wife's adultery with his close friend.

<table>
<tr><td>

8.10.1
The 'Beat' Generation

</td><td>

In America, the mid-fifties discontent against 'square' (conventional) society was centred in San Francisco and New York. The 'Beats' looked towards 'beatitude' (a state of great happiness) and expressed themselves in a fashionable 'street' language. Influenced by both jazz and Oriental philosophy, the 'Beat' intellectuals were, paradoxically, anti-intellectual and placed great emphasis on spontaneity, improvisation and living in the present. Among their obsessions were drugs, alcohol, sex and fast, intense conversation.

</td></tr>
<tr><td>

8.10.2
Jack Kerouac
(1922–1969)

</td><td>

Jack Kerouac, sometimes thought of as the spokesperson for the Beat generation, came from a French-Canadian family in Massachusetts. His novels – rather loose in style and structure – include *Doctor Sax* (1959), a fictional re-creation of the author's youth, *Maggie Cassidy* (1959), about an adolescent search for identity, and *Big Sur* (1962), which tells the story of the crack up of a leader of the 'Beats'.

</td></tr>
<tr><td>

Warm-up

</td><td>

Tell each other about a frightening car journey you have made.

</td></tr>
<tr><td>

On the Road

</td><td>

On the Road (1957) by Jack Kerouac is a fast-moving, episodic semi-autobiographical novel. It describes the frantic wanderings across America of the narrator Sal Paradise – a young writer – and his friend and hero, Dean Moriarty, in search of freedom and excitement.

</td></tr>
</table>

GLOSSARY

flinch (l.2): make sudden movements (from fear)

rammed (l.4): forced them by pushing

teased their bumpers (l.4): got close to hitting the cars in front

eased (l.5): moved slowly, carefully into a different position

craned (l.5): stretched his neck

filed by (l.7): advanced

shuddered (l.8): suddenly shook from fear

Nebraska, Iowa (l.9): midwestern states

straightaway (l.9): straight road

'Dean, don't drive so fast in the daytime.'   1
'Don't worry, man, I know what I'm doing.' I began to flinch.
Dean came up on lines of cars like the Angel of Terror. He almost
rammed them along as he looked for an opening. He teased their
bumpers, he eased and pushed and craned around to see the curve,   5
then the huge car leaped to his touch and passed, and always by a
hair we made it back to our side as other lines filed by in the opposite direction and I shuddered. I couldn't take it any more. It is
only seldom that you find a long Nebraskan straightaway in Iowa,
and when we finally hit one Dean made his usual 110 and I saw   10
flashing by outside several scenes that I remembered from 1947 – a
long stretch where Eddie and I had been stranded two hours. All
that old road of the past unreeling dizzily as if the cup of life had
been overturned and everything gone mad. My eyes ached in nightmare day.   15
  'Ah hell, Dean, I'm going in the back seat, I can't stand it any
more, I can't look.'
  'Hee-hee-hee!' tittered Dean and he passed a car on a narrow

_110 (l.10):_ 110 miles –
177 km – per hour

flashing (l.11): moving
quickly

stranded (l.12): left without
transport

unreeling (l.13): unwinding

dizzily (l.13): as if
everything were turning
round

cup of life (l.13): from where
the spirit of normal life
comes

tittered (l.18): laughed sillily

swerved (l.19): changed
direction suddenly

shell (l.24): outer structure

unfurling (l.26): unrolling

Ahab (l.27): the mad captain
who hunted the white
whale in Melville's novel
Moby Dick (1851)

vibrating (l.29): moving
rapidly backwards and
forwards

Des Moines (l.32): city in
Iowa

snarled (l.33): caught up

sedan (l.35): saloon car

boil (l.40): infected swelling
(under the skin)

upshot (l.41): result

floppy (l.44): loose

bridge and swerved in dust and roared on. I jumped in the back
seat and curled up to sleep. One of the boys jumped in front for the 20
fun. Great horrors that we were going to crash this very morning
took hold of me and I got down on the floor and closed my eyes
and tried to go to sleep. As a seaman I used to think of the waves
rushing beneath the shell of the ship and the bottomless deeps
thereunder – now I could feel the road some twenty inches beneath 25
me, unfurling and flying and hissing at incredible speeds across
the groaning continent with that mad Ahab at the wheel. When I
closed my eyes all I could see was the road unwinding into me.
When I opened them I saw flashing shadows of trees vibrating on
the floor of the car. There was no escaping it. I resigned myself to 30
all. And still Dean drove, he had no thought of sleeping till we got
to Chicago. In the afternoon we crossed old Des Moines again.
Here of course we got snarled in traffic and had to go slow and I got
back in the front seat. A strange pathetic accident took place. A fat
coloured man was driving with his entire family in a sedan in front 35
of us; on the rear bumper hung one of those canvas desert waterbags
they sell tourists in the desert. He pulled up sharp. Dean was
talking to the boys in the back and didn't notice, and we rammed
him at five miles an hour smack on the waterbag, which burst like a
boil and squirted water in the air. No other damage except a bent 40
bumper. Dean and I got out to talk to him. The upshot of it was an
exchange of addresses and some talk, and Dean not taking his eyes
off the man's wife whose beautiful brown breasts were barely
concealed inside a floppy cotton blouse.

(from _On The Road_)

Understanding and interpretation

i) Give the extract a title.

ii) Find at least two verbs and two nouns which show Sal's fear.

iii) In which lines is Sal reminded of the past?

iv) What can you infer from these phrases: 'leapt to his touch' (l.6), 'always by
a hair' (l.6); 'finally hit one' (l.10); 'curled up to sleep' (l.20); 'not taking his
eyes off the man's wife' (l.42).

Appreciation

Which of the following 'Beat' characteristics can be found in the passage?
fashionable street language; the search for pleasure; the need for intense
excitement; the challenge to conventional society. Find an example for each.

**8.10.3
The 'Hippy' movement**

In the mid-sixties, the 'Beat' movement merged into the much bigger
'Hippy' movement. Both urged a 'revolution in consciousness' through
drugs and Oriental religions, and opposed 'traditional', consumer values.
The Hippy movement, though, coincided with a whole wave of political
dissent, both in the USA and throughout most of Western Europe. One
of its intellectual 'gurus' was the German–American political thinker,
Herbert Marcuse (1898–1979).

- To find out more about the period, match the two halves of the sentences.

a) At this time the USA ...

i) ... at home and anti-Americanism around the world.

b) President Kennedy had been assassinated in 1963; and his brother Bobby ...

ii) ... and the Black Civil Rights leader Martin Luther King were assassinated in 1968.

c) Also 'the most powerful nation on earth' was unable to win ...

iii) ... was a deeply troubled nation and losing its sense of omnipotence.

d) It faced massive opposition and unpatriotic attitudes ...

iv) ... demanding their place in American society.

e) Vigorous protest came, too, from militant blacks, homosexuals and women's liberationists ...

v) ... an unpopular, long-drawn-out war in Vietnam.

Against such a background, the Hippy movement developed a pacifist cult of peace and love ('flower power'). Instead of jazz (which the 'Beats' favoured) pop music was thought of as one of the main mediums of expression; clothes became brightly coloured and hair was worn very long. In time, though, after some violent incidents, a sense of despair set in and the movement lost its energy, whereupon the design and 'pop' music industries absorbed its fashions into the consumer economy so that instead of opposing society it became a part of society.

Warm-up Imagine you are in a conservative American bar in 1966 and a group of long-haired hippies come in.
Write at least two phrases which describe the customers' reactions.

8.10.4
Allen Ginsberg
(b. 1926)

The early verse of Allen Ginsberg (b. 1926) – in particular the long poem *Howl* (1956) – was a major focus for the 'Beat' generation. Later, Ginsberg's poetic attacks on modern corruption and authoritarianism, his public homosexuality and his belief in Zen Buddhism made him a cult figure of the hippies. Very much influenced by Whitman (see page 194), Ginsberg's 'free verse' is often passionate but it is sometimes repetitive and careless.

In this poem, 'Uptown' (1966) Ginsberg is in a New York bar with a group of young musicians:

Uptown : residential
  district of a city
  (*American*)

Budweiser (l.1): an
  American beer

bartender (l.2): barman
  (*American*)

thru (l.3): through
  (*informal American*)

Adamic (l.3): like Adam
  (suggesting 'original
  sin')

Montana (l.4): state in
  the northwest USA

Manhattan (l.4): borough
  of New York

antique booth (l.5): old-
  fashioned type of
  enclosure in a bar (for
  privacy)

literary salon (l.6):
  gathering place for
  writers

Amsterdam Avenue (l.10): a
  New York street

decades later (l.10): a long
  time later (*hyperbole*)

snarled (l.11): said angrily

dapper (l.13): neatly-
  dressed

Uptown

Yellow-lit Budweiser signs over oaken bars,   1
'I've seen everything' – the bartender handing me change of $10,
I stared at him amiably eyes thru an obvious Adamic beard –
with Montana musicians homeless in Manhattan, teen age
curly hair themselves – we sat at the antique booth & gossiped,   5
Madame Grady's literary salon a curious value in New York –
'If I had my way I'd cut off your hair and send you to Vietnam' –
'Bless you then' I replied to a hatted thin citizen hurrying to the
    barroom door
upon wet dark Amsterdam Avenue decades later –   10
'And if I couldn't do that I'd cut your throat' he snarled farewell,
and 'Bless you sir' I added as he went to his fate in the rain,
    dapper Irishman.

Understanding and interpretation

i) Choose the correct alternative: The expression 'I've seen everything' means the barman *is bored and tired with life/is telling the writer about his travels/is expressing his disapproval and shock at the way the writer looks.*

ii) Who in the poem is a) well-dressed? b) hairy?

iii) Which words/phrases bring out the contrasting attitudes? How would you describe the contrast?

8.10.5
Black literature

Warm-up

i) How much of the following paragraph can you complete?
Black slaves were first brought into Virginia from .... in .... Slavery was abolished by .... in .... The first industrial school for blacks was opened by the black educator .... in 1881. During World War I blacks emigrated from the South to .... In the 1920s, ..., a largely black area of New York, became known for its black musical productions. In ....,

segregation in education was abolished. A movement for integration led by Martin Luther King based on passive resistance came to an end when he was assassinated in .... This marked the beginning of 'Black Power', a black separatist movement. In 1980 blacks formed .... of the population of the USA.

ii) Do you know how, in general, American blacks have been portrayed in literature and film during this century?

 iii) Now listen to the history of black America on tape and correct your answers. The tapescript is printed in the Key at the back of the book. You will also find in the Key a list of some of the major works of black literature.

8.10.6
W(illiam) E(dward)
B(urghardt) Du Bois
(1868–1963)

The following is an extract from the *The Souls of Black Folk* (1903):

GLOSSARY

veil (l.1): cover (over him) which he can see through

second-sight (l.2): ability to see things others (whites) can't see

revelation (l.4): seeing and knowing

tape (l.7): (measuring tape)

unreconciled strivings (l.9): struggles without final harmony

strife (l.10): conflict

longing to attain (l.11): strong desire to reach

bleach (l.15): make white

The Negro is a sort of seventh son, born with a veil, and gifted with second-sight in this American world – a world which yields him no true self-consciousness, but only lets him see himself through the revelation of the other world. It is a peculiar sensation, this double-consciousness, the sense of always looking at one's self through the eyes of others, of measuring one's soul by the tape of a world that looks on in amused contempt and pity. One ever feels his twoness – an American, a Negro; two souls, two thoughts, two unreconciled strivings. . . . 5

The history of the American Negro is the history of this strife – this longing to attain self-conscious manhood, to merge his double self into a better and truer self. In this merging he wishes neither of the older selves to be lost. He would not Africanise America, for America has too much to teach the world and Africa. He would not bleach his Negro soul in a flood of white Americanism, for he knows that Negro blood has a message for the world. He simply wishes to make it possible to be both a Negro and an American. 10 15

8.10.7
Martin Luther King,
Jr (1929–1968)

From a speech given at the Lincoln Memorial, Washington, D.C. during a civil rights demonstration in 1963:

GLOSSARY

whirlwinds (l.2): destructive confusion

creed (l.9): set of beliefs

'We hold . . .' (l.9): (from the *Declaration of Independence*, 1776 – see page 369)

There will be neither rest nor tranquillity in America until the Negro is granted his citizenship rights. The whirlwinds of revolt will continue to shake the foundations of our nation until the bright day of justice emerges. 1

I say to you today, my friends, that in spite of the difficulties and frustrations of the moment I still have a dream. It is a dream deeply rooted in the American dream. 5

I have a dream that one day this nation will rise up and live out the true meaning of its creed: 'We hold these truths to be self-evident; that all men are created equal.' 10

I have a dream that one day on the red hills of Georgia the sons of former slaves and the sons of former slaveowners will be able to sit down together at the table of brotherhood.

I have a dream that one day even the state of Mississippi, a desert state sweltering with the heat of injustice and oppression, will be transformed into an oasis of freedom and justice. 15

I have a dream that my four little children will one day live in a nation where they will not be judged by the color of their skin but by the content of their character.

I have a dream today. 20

I have a dream that one day the state of Alabama whose governor's lips are presently dripping with the words of interposition and nullification, will be transformed into a situation where little black boys and black girls will be able to join hands with little white boys and white girls and walk together as sisters and brothers. 25

I have a dream today.

I have a dream that one day every valley shall be exalted, every hill and mountain shall be made low, the rough places will be made plains, and the crooked places will be made straight, and the glory of the Lord shall be revealed, and all flesh shall see it together.... 30

Georgia (l.11): a state in the southeast

sweltering (l.15): unpleasantly hot

oasis (l.16): pleasant place (by contrast)

governor's (l.21): (Governor George Wallace of the southeastern state of Alabama)

presently (l.22): at present

interposition and nullification (l.22): separation (of the races) and making (integration) legally invalid

exalted (l.27): praised

8.10.8
Claude Brown
(b. 1937)

In *Manchild in the Promised Land* (1965) Claude Brown remembers a conversation he had in 1956 with a friend, Alley Bush, who had become a Muslim in prison. Alley tried to convert Brown (whose nickname is Sonny)·

'If you're not mad, I feel sorry for you, Sonny, because you're crazy, and you're lost, man. So there, black man, you've got to be mad, brother.'

'Alley, man, you can get mad about this shit, but if you can't do anything about it, it's gon fuck with your mind, you know? Unless you stop being mad because you realize you have to stop, for your own good.'

'How the hell are you gon stop bein' mad when you've got a foot up in your ass?'

I said, 'Look, man, if you're going to live, you got to try and take the foot out of your ass. There's some things, man, that anger doesn't mean a damn thing to. You can get mad if you want to, but why bother if nobody's going to pay any attention to you? Alley, the way I feel about it is that we – you, me, the cats we came up with, probably all the cats that were in jail with you – we were angry all our lives. That's what that shit was all about. We were having our revolution. The revolution that you're talking about, Alley, I've had it. I've had that revolution since I was six years old. And I fought it every day – in the streets of Harlem, in the streets of Brooklyn, in the streets of the Bronx and Lower Manhattan, all over – when I was there stealing, raising hell out there, playing hookey. I rebelled against school because the teachers were white. And I went downtown and robbed the stores because the store owners were white. I ran through the subways because the cats in the charge booths were white.

'I was rebelling every time I went to someplace like the Children's Center, like the Youth House, like Wiltwyck, like Warwick. I was rebelling, man. And all I met in there were other young, rebellious cats who couldn't take it either.

'But nobody was winning. That revolution was hopeless. The cats who had something on the ball and they could dig it in time, they stopped. They stopped. They didn't stop being angry. They just stopped cutting their own throats, you know?'

(from *Manchild in the Promised Land*)

GLOSSARY

mad (l.1): angry (*American English*)

shit (l.4): rubbish (*vulgar*)

gon ... mind (l.5): going to ruin you (*vulgar*)

a foot up in your ass (l.8): the pain of someone pressing you down (*vulgar American English*)

take ... ass (l.10): get rid of the pain (*vulgar American*)

cats we came up with (l.14): men we came to prison with (*cats = slang*)

charge booths (l.25): the places where tickets were issued

Children's Center ... Warwick (l.26–27): (reform school or prison)

something ... ball (l.31): knew what they were doing

dig (l.31): understand

Understanding and interpretation

i) Is the writer for or against the following for black America?

Du Bois: Having the same identity as white America.
King: Equality with white America.
Brown: Revolution against white America.

ii) Which sentence in each extract best illustrates the writer's point of view?

Appreciation

Which extract is meant to be read as an essay?
Which contains most rhetorical techniques?
Which most uses the language of the streets?
Which most uses the language of the church sermon?

The black writer Ralph Ellison has been a visiting professor of creative writing, black culture and humanities at various American universities.

● Ellison called his novel, published in 1952, *The Invisible Man*. It is now regarded as a classic. Can you guess what point he is trying to make in the title?

It goes a long way back, some twenty years. All my life I had been looking for something, and everywhere I turned someone tried to tell me what it was. I accepted their answers too, though they were often in contradiction and even self-contradictory. I was naïve. I was looking for myself and asking everyone except myself questions which I, and only I, could answer. It took me a long time and much painful boomeranging of my expectations to achieve a realization everyone else appears to have been born with: That I am nobody but myself. But first I had to discover that I am an invisible man!

And yet I am no freak of nature, nor of history. I was in the cards, other things having been equal (or unequal) eighty-five years ago. I am not ashamed of my grandparents for having been slaves. I am only ashamed of myself for having at one time been ashamed. About eighty-five years ago they were told that they were free, united with others of our country in everything pertaining to the common good, and, in everything social, separate like the fingers of the hand. And they believed it. They exulted in it. They stayed in their place, worked hard, and brought up my father to do the same. But my grandfather is the one. He was an odd old guy, my grandfather, and I am told I take after him. It was he who caused the trouble. On his deathbed he called my father to him and said, 'Son, after I'm gone I want you to keep up the good fight. I never told you, but our life is a war and I have been a traitor all my born days, a spy in the enemy's country ever since I give up my gun back in the Reconstruction. Live with your head in the lion's mouth. I want you to overcome 'em with yeses, undermine 'em with grins, agree 'em to death and destruction, let 'em swoller you till they vomit or bust wide open.' They thought the old man had gone out of his mind. He had been the meekest of men. The younger children were rushed from the room, the shades drawn and the flame of the lamp turned so low that it sputtered on the wick like the old man's breathing. 'Learn it to the younguns,' he whispered fiercely; then he died.

(from *The Invisible Man*)

GLOSSARY

naïve (l.4): innocent and simple

boomeranging (l.7): (I was disappointed; they came back and did me harm)

freak (l.11): something physically abnormal

in the cards (l.11): a probability

pertaining to (l.16): connected with

exulted (l.18): showed great delight

Reconstruction (l.26): (see page (308)

swoller (l.28): swallow

meekest (l.30): most uncomplaining

shades (l.31): window blinds (*American*)

sputtered on the wick (l.32): made a popping sound

younguns (l.33): young children

Understanding and interpretation

i) Explain fully what 'it' refers to in the following sentences:
   a) 'It goes a long way back, some twenty years' (l.1)
   b) ' "Learn it to the younguns," he whispered fiercely' (l.33)

ii) What do these mean in context? 'I am nobody but myself' (l.9); 'Live with your head in the lion's mouth' (l.26)

iii) Why were grandfather's final pronouncements so shocking?

8.11 Feminism

Feminism, the reform movement in England and the USA which aimed at the social, educational and political equality of women with men began in the late eighteenth century. In the 1960s, however, it achieved in the US a new dynamic with the National Organization for Women (NOW) and the change of the term 'feminism' to 'Women's Liberation'. The best-known expositions of the movement at that time were, in America, *The Feminine Mystique* (1963) by Betty Friedan and *Sexual Politics* (1970) by Kate Millett, and in England *The Female Eunuch* (1970) by Germaine Greer, who was born in Australia.

**8.11.1
Feminist criticism**

Feminist literary criticism is a critical approach which acquired a distinct identity in the late 1960s and 1970s. It seeks to re-examine women's literature of the past and present from a feminist point of view, looking closely at such things as female and male stereotypes in literature and the socio-economic situation of women authors. Both in Britain and the USA Women's Studies as a separate subject has grown in popularity and several feminist publishing houses have been founded.

**8.11.2
Alice Walker
(b. 1944)**

Alice Walker, the black feminist writer, was born in Georgia. Her novels include *Meridian* (1976), about a black woman torn between the revolutionary Civil Rights movements of the 1960s in the North and her affection for the unsophisticated blacks of the South. Her poems include 'Once' (1968), dealing with both the Civil Rights movement and her experiences of living in Africa.

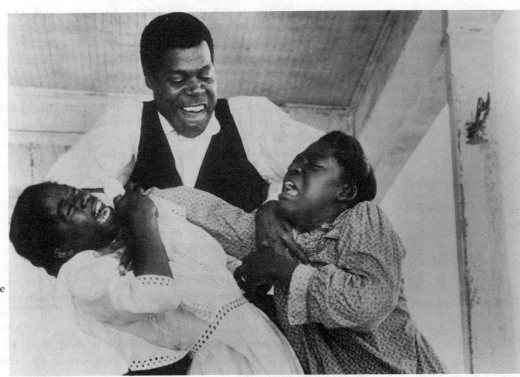

From the film
The Color Purple

The Color Purple (1983)

Set in the Deep South between the First and Second World Wars, *The Color Purple* concerns two devoted black sisters, Celie and Nettie. Celie has been sexually assaulted by the man she calls father, her two children have been taken away from her, and she has been forced into an ugly marriage with Albert. She has no one to talk to but God. Nettie has gone to live in Africa. However, through Shug Avery, a singer and magic woman, she discovers the love and support of women. The novel is epistolary in form (told through a series of letters from Celie and from Nettie), although its language is the rich spoken language of the America South and therefore different from standard written English.

Dear God,

Now that I know Albert hiding Nettie's letters, I know exactly where they is. They in his trunk. Everything that mean something to Albert go in his trunk. He keep it locked up tight, but Shug can git the key.

One night when Mr _____ and Grady gone, us open the trunk. Us find a lot of Shug's underclothes, some nasty picture postcards, and way down under his tobacco, Nettie's letters. Bunches and bunches of them. Some fat, some thin. Some open, some not.

How us gon do this? I ast Shug.

She say, Simple. We take the letters out of the envelopes, leave the envelopes just like they is. I don't think he look in this corner of the trunk much, she say.

I heated the stove, put on the kettle. Us steam and steam the envelopes until we had all the letters laying on the table. Then us put the envelopes back inside the trunk.

I'm gonna put them in some kind of order for you, say Shug.

Yeah, I say, but don't let's do it in here, let's go in you and Grady room.

So she got up and us went into they little room. Shug sat in a chair by the bed with all Nettie letters spread round her, I got on the bed with the pillows behind my back.

These the first ones, say Shug. They postmark right here.

Dear Celie, *the first letter say.*

You've got to fight and get away from Albert. He ain't no good.

When I left you all's house, walking, he followed me on his horse. When we was well out of sight of the house he caught up with me and started trying to talk. You know how he do, You sure is looking fine, Miss Nettie, and stuff like that. I tried to ignore him and walk faster, but my bundles was heavy and the sun was hot. After while I had to rest, and that's when he got down from his horse and started to try to kiss me, and drag me back in the woods.

Well, I started to fight him, and with God's help, I hurt him bad enough to make him let me alone. But he was some mad. He said because of what I'd done I'd never hear from you again, and you would never hear from me.

GLOSSARY

trunk (l.3): large box for storage

bundles (l.31): clothes and possessions tied together

mad (l.35): angry (*American English*)

310

I was so mad myself I was shaking.

Anyhow, I got a ride into town on somebody's wagon. And that same somebody pointed me in the direction of the Reverend Mr _____'s place. And what was my surprise when a little girl opened the door and she had your eyes set in your face.

40

love,

Nettie

(from The Color Purple)

● What feelings do the letters arouse in you?

Understanding and interpretation

Complete the following sentence:

i) Albert has probably hidden Nettie's letters because ....

ii) What do these tell us about Albert? 'nasty picture postcards' (l.7); 'started to try to kiss me' (l.33)

Language and style

List some of the ways in which the narrator's language differs from standard English.

8.12 Recent years

Much recent literature has behind it a political, social or racial 'cause'. In Britain and the USA many writers without such commitment have revealed undercurrents of cynicism and nihilism, and a loss of faith in contemporary man.

8.12.1 Existential uncertainty

Existentialism is a term used to describe some loosely connected philosophical ideas which assert the unique and the particular in human experience and the ability of the individual to be what he or she chooses to be. Existentialists such as the French philosopher Jean-Paul Sartre (1905–1980) believed we cannot escape responsibility for our character and actions by referring to external standards beyond our control (for example, human nature).

8.12.2 Tom Stoppard (b. 1937)

Tom Stoppard was born in Czechoslovakia of a Czechoslovakian family. In 1939 they all moved to Singapore to avoid the German invasion, where his father was killed during the Japanese occupation. He left school at seventeen and worked as a journalist until 1963 when his first play, *A Walk on the Water*, was televised. His work consistently poses ethical problems with wit and a strong sense of theatre.

The influential play *Waiting for Godot* (first published in French in 1952) by the Irish playwright Samuel Beckett (b. 1906) interprets the human condition, humorously and wittily, as one of delusion and paralysis, with flashes of sympathy and hope. A questioning of Existentialist ideas which lies behind the play leads to a belief in man's solitude and his essential lack of mastery over his own life. Tom Stoppard continues in this vein in his play *Rosencrantz and Guildenstern are Dead* (1966). Stoppard has made it clear that Existentialism is not, in his own words, 'a philosophy I find either attractive or plausible'. He adds: 'there is very often no single, clear statement in my plays'.

Rosencrantz and Guildenstern are two characters from Shakespeare's *Hamlet*, set in Denmark. In Stoppard's play they appear to be bewildered witnesses and predestined victims of a pattern of events happening somewhere else. Do you know what role they play in Shakespeare?

Rosencrantz and
Guildenstern are Dead

Rosencrantz and Guildenstern have realised that although they are supposed to be spying on Hamlet for his uncle Claudius, Hamlet has discovered more about them than they have about him.

ROS: [*Licks his finger and holds it up – facing audience.*] Is that southerly? (*They stare at audience.*)   1

GUIL: It doesn't *look* southerly. What made you think so?

ROS: I didn't *say* I think so. It could be northerly for all I know.

GUIL: I wouldn't have thought so.   5

ROS: Well, if you're going to be dogmatic.

GUIL: Wait a minute – we came from roughly south according to a rough map.

ROS: I see. Well, which way did we come in? [GUIL *looks round vaguely.*] Roughly.   10

GUIL: [*clears his throat*]: In the morning the sun would be easterly. I think we can assume that.

ROS: That it's morning?

GUIL: If it is, and the sun is over *there* [*his right as he faces the audience*] for instance, *that* [*front*] would be northerly. On the   15 other hand, if it is not morning and the sun is over *there* [*his left*] . . . that . . . [*lamely*] would *still* be northerly. [*picking up*]. To put it another way, if we came from down there [*front*] and it is morning, the sun would be up there [*his left*], and if it is actually over *there* [*his right*] and it's still morning, we   20 must have come from up *there* [*behind him*], and if *that* is southerly [*his left*] and the sun is really over *there* [*front*], then it's the afternoon. However, if none of these is the case —

ROS: Why don't you go and have a look?

GUIL: Pragmatism?! – is that all you have to offer? You seem to have   25 no conception of where we stand! You won't find the answer written down for you in the bowl of a compass – I can tell you that. [*Pause.*] Besides, you can never tell this far north – it's probably dark out there.

ROS: I merely suggest that the position of the sun, if it is out,   30 would give you a rough idea of the time; alternatively, the clock, if it is going, would give you a rough idea of the position of the sun. I forget which you're trying to establish.

GUIL: I'm trying to establish the direction of the wind.

ROS: There isn't any wind. *Draught*, yes.   35

GUIL: In that case, the origin. Trace it to its source and it might give us a rough idea of the way we came in – which might give us a rough idea of south, for further reference.

ROS: It's coming up through the floor. [*He studies the floor.*] That can't be south, can it?   40

GLOSSARY

be dogmatic (l.6): expect me to accept your ideas without question

lamely (l.17): weakly

Pragmatism (l.25): a practical approach to problems (also: American philosophical movement which asserted that the truth of a concept depends on its practical consequences)

bowl of a compass (l.27): deep round container holding instrument to show direction

this far north (l.28): (Elsinore, on the northeastern tip of the Danish island of Zealand)

Draught (l.35): current of cold air flowing through a room

GUIL: **That's not a direction. Lick your toe and wave it around a bit.**
  [ROS *considers the distance of his foot.*]
ROS: **No, I think you'd have to lick it for me.**
  [*Pause.*]
GUIL: **I'm prepared to let the whole matter drop.**   45
ROS: **Or I could lick yours, of course.**

(from *Rosencrantz and Guildenstern are Dead*)

Understanding and interpretation

i) Which of the following describes what Rosencrantz and Guildenstern seem to be trying to do?

a) They are trying to find their bearings, both physically and metaphysically.
b) They are trying to find the road out of Denmark.

ii) Which of each of these alternatives seems to be more at the heart of this extract?

a) action/inaction; b) freedom/lack of freedom; c) isolation/belonging;
d) futility/meaningfulness

iii) Write R (for Rosencrantz), G (for Guildenstern) or RG (for both) next to each of these:

dominant ....; practical ....; intellectual ....; stupid ....;
pompous ....

What else distinguishes their characters?

Appreciation   Which parts of the extract (if any) do you find humorous? Why?

Extension   Either act out the scene, or write a description of the scene as witnessed by an imaginary onlooker.

8.12.3
Philip Larkin
(1922–1985)

In the sixties and seventies one of the dominant voices in British poetry was that of Philip Larkin.

Philip Larkin was one of a group of poets and novelists known in the fifties as the 'Movement'. They believed that honesty meant expressing self-doubt in an anti-romantic, witty, ironic tone.

In Larkin's poem 'Love Songs in Age', an older woman discovers some printed love songs from her youth:

Love Songs in Age

GLOSSARY
in Age (title): in old age
songs (l.1): (the printed words and music, which often have pictures of a singer on the cover)
bleached (l.3): turned white
tidy fit (l.5): short, strong desire to tidy up

She kept her songs, they took so little space,   1
** The covers pleased her:**
One bleached from lying in a sunny place,
One marked in circles by a vase of water,
One mended, when a tidy fit had seized her,   5
** And coloured, by her daughter –**
So they had waited, till in widowhood
She found them, looking for something else, and stood

frank submissive chord (l.9):
set of musical notes,
sounded together, that
openly suggested
willingness to obey
someone

ushered in (l.10): showed
the way for

sprawling (l.11): very
spread out

spring-woken (l.13): which
has come alive in spring

glare (l.17): hard, bright
lights

incipience (l.19): suggestion
that things are about to
begin

lamely (l.23): weakly

Relearning how each frank submissive chord
 Had ushered in   10
Word after sprawling hyphenated word,
And the unfailing sense of being young
Spread out like a spring-woken tree, wherein
 That hidden freshness sung,
That certainty of time laid up in store   15
As when she played them first. But, even more,

That glare of that much-mentioned brilliance, love,
 Broke out, to show
Its bright incipience sailing above,
Still promising to solve, and satisfy,   20
And set unchangeably in order. So
 To pile them back, to cry,
Was hard, without lamely admitting how
It had not done so then, and could not now.

- i) What do we know about the woman and her life?
- ii) What does the image of the tree suggest (l.13)? In what way is it ironic?
- iii) Which of these phrases, used by Larkin's critics about his poems, are true of this poem? 'conversational'; 'lacking in dignity'; 'offhand'; 'mocking of emotion'.

For Further extracts from modern literature, see Supplement 8.

8.13 Chronology

Many of the important events of this period have already been mentioned. Here are ten more:

1927: American Charles Lindbergh flies first non-stop solo flight across the Atlantic, from New York to Paris.

1936: Edward VIII is uncrowned monarch of the UK from January to December but because of his love for a divorced American woman, Mrs Simpson, abdicates in favour of his brother George VI. On George's death in 1952, Elizabeth II becomes queen.

1947: India is divided into two countries, Hindu India and Muslim Pakistan, after it is given independence from British rule in 1947, Mahatma Gandhi is assassinated by a Hindu fanatic in 1948.

1949: General Mao Tse-Tung proclaims the People's Republic of China.

1958: The first American satellite, Explorer 1, is launched, following the Russian satellite success the previous year.

1960: John F. Kennedy is elected President of the USA.

1962: There is major Cold War confrontation between the USA and the Soviet Union over the building of Russian missile sites in Cuba.

1967: Israel wins a six-day war against the Arab nations.

1969: The USA lands the first man on the moon.

1974: President Nixon resigns over the Watergate scandal.

- Can you add in other important dates from this unit? What other events do you know about?

8.14 Activities

Writing

Choose one of the following:
- Imagine you are a journalist interviewing one of the writers in this unit. Write out the interview.
- Write an appreciation of one of the texts in Supplement 8.
- Write an essay summarising some of the trends in twentieth-century literature.

Literary terminology

Match these definitions with terms in the Index. Quote or name at least one example from the book.

a) story where a more general, less literal meaning can be understood to lie behind the surface narrative
b) line of poetry in which the sentence continues into the next line
c) figure of speech in which one thing is said to be like another using 'as' or 'like'
d) saying one thing while meaning another
e) five metrical feet, each with an unstressed syllable followed by a stressed syllable
f) repetition of initial consonant in successive words of stressed syllables
g) figure of speech in which things or ideas are treated as if they were human
h) lyric poem usually of 14 lines, divided into a mixture of octave (8 lines) and sestet (6 lines) or three quatrains (of 4 lines each) and a couplet (2 lines)
i) figure of speech which makes an emphasis through exaggeration
j) break or pause in a line of poetry, most commonly in the middle of a line

How have you got on?

i) Which units in this book have you found most/least interesting? Which exercises have you found most/least useful? Give reasons.
ii) Choose a text in Supplement 8. Ask yourself some of the questions in the Prologue Part A (page 4). Do you notice any improvements?

Supplement 1

Beowulf
(?8th century)

Beowulf is the oldest known Anglo-Saxon epic narrative poem. The first part tells the story of Beowulf, the hero of the Geats (a south Scandinavian tribe), and his killing of Grendel, an evil monster who has been attacking the house of the Danish king. Grendel's mother – doomed to live in icy waters since Cain killed his brother (a story told in the Bible) – tries to avenge the death of her son.

In this extract from a modern English translation, Beowulf confronts Grendel's mother in her home at the bottom of the sea.

Then he seized Grendel's mother by the hair – the man of the War-Geats was not afraid of the fight. Hardened from battle and now full of anger, he pulled his deadly enemy so that she fell to the floor. Quickly in her turn she repaid him with her cruel claws and grasped out towards him: then weary-hearted, the strongest of warriors, of foot-soldiers, stumbled so that he fell. Then she sat upon the hall-guest and pulled out her knife, broad and bright-edged. She would avenge her child, her only son. The woven breast-armour lay on his shoulder: that protected his life, withstood entry of point or of edge. 1

Then the son of Ecgtheow, the hero of the Geats, would have found death under the wide waters if the battle-shirt – the hard war-net – had not helped him and if holy God had not achieved victory in war; the wise Lord, Ruler of the Heavens, brought about the right result – easily – when Beowulf stood up again. Then he saw among the armour a victory-blessed weapon, an old sword made by the giants, strong-edged, the glory of warriors: it was the best of weapons, except that it was larger than any other man might carry to the sport of war, trusty and beautifully decorated, the work of giants. The hero of the Scyldings [the Danes], angered and grim in battle, seized the belted handle, drew the ring-marked sword, despairing of life; he struck furiously so that it gripped her hard against the neck, breaking the bone-rings [vertebrae]. The blade went straight through the doomed body. She fell to the floor, the sword was bloody, the man rejoiced in his work. 5 10 15 20 25

(from *Beowulf*)

● This is the original Old English version. Can you recognise any of the phrases?

Gefēng þā be feaxe   (nālas for fǣhðe mearn) 1
Gūðgēata lēod   Grendles mōdor;
brægd þā beadwe heard,   þa hē gebolgen wæs,

feorhgeniðlan,   þæt hēo on flet gebēah.

Hēo hi eft hraþe   andlēan forgeald   5
grimman grāpum   and him tōgēanes fēng:
oferwearp þā wērigmōd   wigena strengest,
fēþecempa,   þæt hē on fylle wearð.
Ofsæt þā þone selegyst   and hyre seax getēah,
brād [ond] brūnecg,   wolde hire bearn wrecan,   10
āngan eaferan.   Him on eaxle læg
brēostnet brōden;   þæt gebearh fēore,
wið ord and wið ecge   ingang forstōd.

   Hæfde ðā forsiðod   sunu Ecgþēowes
under gynne grund,   Gēata cempa,   15
nemne him heaðobyrne   helpe gefremede,
herenet hearde,   and hālig God
gewēold wigsigor,   wītig Drihten;
rodera Rǣdend   hit on ryht gescēd
ȳðelīce,   syþðan hē eft āstōd.   20
Geseah ðā on searwum   sigeēadig bil,
eald sweord eotenisc   ecgum þyhtig,
wigena weorðmynd: þæt [wæs] wǣpna cyst,
būton hit wæs māre   ðonne ǣnig mon ōðer
tō beadulāce   ætberan meahte,   25
gōd and geatolic   gīganta geweorc.
Hē gefēng þā fetelhilt,   freca Scyldinga,
hrēoh and heorogrim   hringmǣl gebrǣgd,
aldres orwēna   yrringa slōh,
þæt hire wið halse   heard grāpode,   30
bānhringas brǣc;   bil eal ðurhwōd
fǣgne flǣschoman;   hēo on flet gecrong;
sweord wæs swātig;   secg weorce gefeh.

The poem is sometimes seen both as a conflict between good and evil, in
some ways similar to the stories in the Christian Old Testament, as well
as a pagan story with a monster and a hero.

   Like *Battle of Maldon*, the manuscript dates from about the tenth century,
although the poem was probably composed two and a half centuries
before that. The narrative refers to events which are supposed to have
taken place in the late fifth and early sixth centuries, although many of
the folk-tale elements had probably been passed down orally from
generation to generation through poems and songs. From the pagan
tradition the poem took a love of war and the virtues of courage; from the
Christian tradition it took morality, obedience to God and avoidance of
pride.

Lyrics Lyrics are short, personal poems, usually sung or recited. Those from the
Middle English period are both secular and religious in their subject
matter. Although often rather stylised, closely paralleling thirteenth-
century French lyrics, they are, even to the modern ear, fresh, unself-
conscious and direct.

This thirteenth-century lyric, 'How Death Comes', is both humorous and lively:

How Death Comes

Wanne mine eyhnen misten,   1
And mine heren sissen,
And my nose coldet,
And my tunge foldet,
And my rude slaket,   5
And mine lippes blaken,
And my muth grennet,
And my spotel rennet,
And mine her riset,
And mine herte griset,   10
And mine honden bivien,
And mine fet stivien –
Al to late! al to late!
Wanne the bere is ate gate.

Thanne I schel flutte   15
From bedde to flore,
From flore to here,
From here to bere,
From bere to putte,
And te putt fordut.   20
Thanne lyd mine hus uppe mine nose.
Of al this world ne give I it a pese!

This is a prose version in modern English:

GLOSSARY

slack (l.2): loose

spittle (l.3): saliva; watery liquid produced in the mouth

bier (l.5): vehicle on which a dead body is taken to be buried

shroud (l.6): cloth put round a dead person

When my eyes get misty, and my ears are full of hissing, and my   1
nose gets cold, and my tongue folds, and my face goes slack, and
my lips go black, and my mouth grins, and my spittle runs, and my
hair falls out, and my heart trembles, and my hands shake, and my
feet get stiff – all too late! when the bier is at the gate. Then I shall   5
pass from bed to floor, from floor to shroud, from shroud to bier,
from bier to grave, and the grave will be closed up. Then my house
rests on my nose. I don't give a damn for the whole world!

● What is the poet's attitude towards death?

William Langland (?1330–?1386)

In literature, an allegory is a symbolic story that represents thought, experience and human truths through characters, actions and images. *Piers Plowman* is a Christian moral allegory by William Langland. Through a series of dreams, it tells of the spiritual journey of Piers – the dramatic hero of the poem who seems to represent the essential goodness of English rural life – as he passes through the pride, greed and ostentation of his day in search of ultimate truth.

319

In this extract, the dreamer meets Nature (Kynde) and is shown all the wonders of creation:

And slepynge I seigh al this; and sithen cam Kynde   1
And nempned me by my name, and bad me nymen hede,
And thorugh the wondres of this world wit for to take.
And on a mountaigne that Myddelerthe highte, as me tho thoughte,
I was fet forth by ensaumples to knowe,   5
Thorugh ech a creature, Kynde my creatour to lovye.
    I seigh the sonne and the see and the sond after,
And where that briddes and beestes by hir make thei yeden,
Wilde wormes in wodes, and wonderful foweles
With fleckede fetheres and of fele colours.   10
Man and his make I myghte se bothe;
Poverte and plentee, bothe pees and werre,
Blisse and bale – bothe I seigh at ones,
And how men token Mede and Mercy refused.
    Reson I seigh soothly sewen alle beestes   15
In etynge, in drynkynge and in engendrynge of kynde.
And after cours of concepcion noon took kepe of oother
As whan thei hadde ryde in rotey tyme; anoonright therafter
Males drowen hem to males amornynge by hemselve,
And [femelles to femelles ferded and drowe].   20
Ther ne was cow ne cowkynde that conceyved hadde
That wolde belwe after bole, ne boor after sowe.
Bothe hors and houndes and alle othere beestes
Medled noght with hir makes that (mid) fole were.
    Briddes I biheld that in buskes made nestes;   25
Hadde nevere wye wit to werche the leeste.
I hadde wonder at whom and wher the pye
Lerned to legge the stikkes in which she leyeth and bredeth.
Ther nys wrighte, as I wene, sholde werche hir nest to paye;
If any mason made a molde therto, muche wonder it were.   30
    And yet me merveilled moore: many othere briddes
Hidden and hileden hir egges ful derne
In mareys and moores for men sholde hem noght fynde,
And hidden hir egges whan thei therfro wente,
For fere of othere foweles and for wilde beestes.   35

(Passus XI 320–354)

(from *Piers Plowman*)

This is a modern English translation:

I saw all these things in my sleep. Then Nature came towards me, calling me by my name; and he told me to pay attention, and obtain wisdom from all the wonders of the world. And I dreamt that he led me out on to a mountain called Middle-Earth, so that I might learn from all kinds of creatures to love my Creator. And I saw the   5

coupled (l.15): united sexually

bellow (l.18): make a loud, deep sound (typical of a bull)

boar (l.18): male pig (sometimes kept for breeding)

grunt (l.19): make short, deep, rough sounds (typical of a pig)

sow (l.19): fully grown female pig

magpie (l.23): bird with black and white feathers

mason (l.25): worker who builds with stone

mould (l.26): container in to which hot liquid is poured to cool into a particular shape

moors (l.28): open land covered with rough grass

marshlands (l.28): soft, wet lowlands

birds of prey (l.30): birds which kill and eat other animals

sun and the sea, and the sandy shores, and the places where birds and beasts go out with their mates – wild snakes in the woods, and wonderful birds whose feathers were flecked with many colours. And I could also see man and his mate, in poverty and plenty, in peace and war; and I saw how men lived in happiness and misery at the same time, and how they took money, and refused mercy.

And I noticed how surely Reason followed all the beasts, in their eating and drinking and procreation of their kind. For when their mating-time was over, they no longer cared for each other as they did when they had coupled together; but soon, all the males drew apart together, and both by morning and evening they left the females alone. And having once conceived, no cow or creature like her would bellow after the bull. And the boar would no longer grunt for the sow, neither would horse nor hound, nor any other beast couple with its mate if she were heavy with young.

And I saw the birds in the bushes building their nests, which no man, with all his intelligence, could ever make. And I marvelled to know who taught the magpie to place the sticks in which to lay her eggs and to breed her young; for no craftsman could make such a nest hold together, and it would be a wonderful mason who could construct a mould for it!

And yet I wondered still more at other birds – how they concealed and covered their eggs secretly on moors and marshlands, so that men should never find them; and how they hid them more carefully still when they went away, for fear of the birds of prey and of wild beasts.

10

15

20

25

30

'And slepynge I seigh al this…'

However, Piers turns against Reason. Later he is identified with Christ himself.

Not much is known about Langland. Perhaps he was a rural parish priest. *Piers Plowman* was immensely popular for about a hundred years after his death. There are three versions (A, B and C), which Langland seems to have worked on for the last twenty years of his life. The above extract is from the B version.

Langland's verse is remembered for its immediacy, its vitality, its clear visual qualities and its ability to suggest strong personal emotion. Formally, it more or less follows the Anglo-Saxon alliterative line with a break in the middle (see page 20). However, the rhythm is guided not by the mechanical counting of syllables but by the placing of stress on the words that convey most meaning.

● Examine, for example, the following line:

Wilde wormes in wodes, and wonderful foweles (l.9)

Geoffrey Chaucer   The *Prologue* by Geoffrey Chaucer is the poem which introduces *The Canterbury Tales* (see page 21). It is written in ten-syllable couplets and is eight hundred and fifty-eight lines long. Here at the beginning there is a sense of harmony between man and nature. The stirrings of spring in nature are associated with the impulse among people to go on pilgrimages:

Extract 1

GLOSSARY

shoures soote (l.1): sweet showers of rain

droghte (l.2): drought

perced (l.2): pierced; penetrated

veyne ... licour (l.3): vein with such juice

Of ... flour (l.4): from which power the flower is born

Zephirus (l.5): the west wind

holt and heeth (l.6): wood and heathland

Ram (l.8): (Aries, a group of stars in the sky)

halve ... yronne (l.8): (the sun has run only half way through its course in Aries)

foweles (l.9): birds

ye (l.10): eye

So ... corages (l.11): so nature forces them according to their disposition

Whan that Aprill with his shoures soote   1
The droghte of March hath perced to the roote,
And bathed every veyne in swich licour
Of which vertu engendred is the flour;
Whan Zephirus eek with his sweete breeth   5
Inspired hath in every holt and heeth
The tendre croppes, and the yonge sonne
Hath in the Ram his halve cours yronne,
And smale foweles maken melodye,
That slepen al the nyght with open ye   10
(So priketh hem nature in hir corages);
Thanne longen folk to goon on pilgrimages ...

The portraits of the pilgrims in the *Prologue* are lively and sometimes satirical, with a generous sympathy for the springs of vitality in each individual character, whether righteous or sinful. Here is the Summoner, an official in a bishop's court:

Extract 2

A SOMONOUR was ther with us in that place,   1
That hadde a fyr-reed cherubynnes face,
For saucefleem he was, with eyen narwe.
As hoot he was and lecherous as a sparwe,
With scalled browes blake and piled berd.   5
Of his visage children were aferd.
Ther nas quyk-silver, lytarge, ne brymstoon,
Boras, ceruce, ne oille of tartre noon;
Ne oynement that wolde clense and byte,
That hym myghte helpen of his whelkes white,   10
Nor of the knobbes sittynge on his chekes.
Wel loved he garleek, oynons, and eek lekes,
And for to drynken strong wyn, reed as blood;
Thanne wolde he speke and crie as he were wood.
And whan that he wel dronken hadde the wyn,   15
Thanne wolde he speke no word but Latyn.

(from *The Canterbury Tales*)

● The Summoner is one of the most unpleasant characters in *The Canterbury Tales*. What makes him so unattractive to look at? What do we know about his character?

Sir Gawain and the Green Knight (?1375)

Sir Gawain and the Green Knight, an alliterative poem in the northwest Midlands dialect, was written at much the same time as *Piers Plowman*. It combines folk myth and religion in a subtle poetic drama about man's duty as a knight, a lover and a Christian.

The story opens with King Arthur's Knights at Camelot during a New Year's feast. They are challenged by a huge green man with an axe and a branch of holly (a bush with red berries and sharp-pointed leaves which is green all the year). He says any knight can cut off his head, provided that the man who does so comes to the Green Chapel next Christmas Eve and submits to similar execution. Gawain accepts the challenge and beheads him; the green knight picks up his head and rides away. Nearly a year later Gawain sets off to keep his side of the bargain and stops at a beautiful castle where he is graciously received. The lord of the castle makes an agreement with Gawain: at the end of each day he will give Gawain whatever he gets from his hunting and Gawain will give him whatever he gets while he remains in the castle at ease.

These extracts come from an exciting passage concerning the hunt and an amorous approach to Gawain from the lady of the castle. The modern English translation is given first, followed by the original.

323

Extract 1   Very early in the morning the hunters get ready:

In the faint light before dawn folk were stirring;   1
Guests who had to go gave orders to their grooms,
Who busied themselves briskly with the beasts, saddling,
Trimming their tackle and tying on their luggage.
Arrayed for riding in the richest style,   5
Guests leaped on their mounts lightly, took hold of their bridles,
And each rider rode out on his own chosen way.

Ful erly bifore the day   the folk uprisen,
Gestes that go wolde   hor gromes thay calden,
And thay busken up bilive   blonkkes to sadel,   10
Tyffen her takles,   trussen her males,
Richen hem the richest,   to ride alle arayde,
Lepen up lightly,   lachen her brideles,
Eche wighe on his way   wher him wel liked.

Extract 2   The hunt begins:

At the first cry wild creatures quivered with dread.   1
The deer in distraction darted down to the dales
Or up to the high ground, but eagerly they were
Driven back by the beaters, who bellowed lustily.
They let the harts with high-branching heads have their freedom,   5
And the brave bucks, too, with their broad antlers,
For the noble prince had expressly prohibited
Meddling with male deer in the months of close season.
But the hinds were held back with a 'Hey' and a 'Whoa!'
And does driven with much din to the deep valleys.   10

At the first quethe of the quest   quaked the wylde;
Der drof in the dale,   doted for drede,
Highed to the highe,   bot heterly thay were
Restayed with the stabile,   that stoutly ascried.
Thay let the herttes haf the gate,   with the highe hedes,   15
The breme bukkes also,   with hor brode paumes;
For the fre lorde hade defende   in fermisoun time
That ther shulde no mon meve   to the male dere.
The hindes were halden in   with *Hay!* and *War!*
The does driven with gret din   to the depe slades;   20

Extract 3   Meanwhile, Gawain is in bed in the castle:

Thus by the forest borders the brave lord sported,   1
And the good man Gawain, on his gay bed lying,
Lay hidden till the light of day gleamed on the walls,

Covered with fair canopy, the curtains closed,
And as in slumber he slept on, there slipped into his mind   5
A slight, suspicious sound, and the door stealthily opened.
He raised up his head out of the bedclothes,
Caught up the corner of the curtain a little
And watched warily towards it, to see what it was.
It was the lady, loveliest to look upon,   10
Who secretly and silently secured the door,
Then bore towards his bed: the brave knight, embarrassed,
Lay flat with fine adroitness and feigned sleep.
Silently she stepped on, stole to his bed,
Caught up the curtain, crept within,   15
And seated herself softly on the side of the bed.
There she watched a long while, waiting for him to wake.

Thus laykes this lorde   by linde-wodes eves,
And Gawayne the god mon   in gay bed liges,
Lurkkes whil the daylight   lemed on the wowes,   20
Under covertour ful clere,   cortined aboute;
And as in slomering he slode,   sleyly he herde
A littel din at his dor,   and derfly upon:
And he heves up his hed   out of the clothes,
A corner of the cortin   he caght up a littel,   25
And waites warly thiderwarde   what hit be might.
Hit was the ladi,   lofliest to beholde,

325

That drow the dor after hir ful dernly and stille,
And bowed towarde the bed; and the burne shammed,
And layde him down listily, and let as he slepte. 30
And ho stepped stilly and stel to his bedde,

Kest up the cortin and creped withinne,
And set hir ful softly on the bed-side,
And lenged there selly longe, to loke when he wakened. 35

Extract 4 Eventually, Gawain decides to show the lady he is awake:

'Good morning, Sir Gawain,' the gay one murmured, 1
'How unsafely you sleep, that one may slip in here!
Now you are taken in a trice. Unless a truce come between us,
I shall bind you to your bed – of that be sure.'
The lady uttered laughingly those playful words. 5
'Good morning, gay lady,' Gawain blithely greeted her.
'Do with me as you will: that well pleases me.
For I surrender speedily and sue for grace,
Which, to my mind, since I must, is much the best course.'

'God moroun, Sir Gawayne,' saide that gay lady, 10
'Ye ar a sleper unslye, that mon may slide hider;
Now ar ye tan astit! Pot true us may shape,
I shal binde you in your bedde, that be ye trayst!'
Al laghande the lady lanced tho bourdes.
'Goud moroun, gay,' quoth Gawayne the blythe, 15
'Me shal worthe at your wille, and that me wel likes,
For I yelde me yederly, and yeye after grace,
And that is the best be my dome, for me bihoves nede'.

(from *Sir Gawain and the Green Knight*)

GLOSSARY

in a trice (l.3): in an instant (*informal*)
truce (l.3): agreement
blithely (l.6): happily, without signs of worry
sue for grace (l.8): ask for mercy

They play and joke, but Sir Gawain survives this test of his virtue, a test not only of his chastity and his loyalty to his host, but of his courtesy, which demands that he should not offend the lady. As a result, the Green Knight, who is the lord of the castle in another form, spares his life.

● What details help to make the story vivid and realistic?

The beginnings of dramatic art

The Morality Plays are moral allegories dating from about the fifteenth century. They dramatise human life by personifying the forces of good and evil. The most famous, *Everyman* (?1509–1519), translated from the Dutch, tells the story of Everyman's life when Death calls him away from the world. Among the 'characters' in the play are Beauty, Knowledge and Strength. Morality Plays later developed into what were called Interludes and influenced the development of Elizabethan drama (see, for example, Marlowe's *Dr Faustus*, page 335). Such plays were probably encouraged by

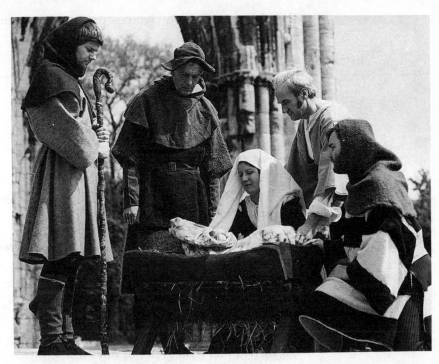

Nativity scene from the York Mystery Plays

churchmen because they thought them to be more edifying entertainment than many of the other plays of the period.

The Mystery Plays (or Miracle Plays), on the other hand, are not allegories but collections of dramas, with recognisable human characters, based on incidents from the Bible and from the lives of the saints. Each was written as part of a 'cycle'. Although their origins may be in the religious plays which were performed in church in Latin, they are full of secular humour and energy and contain much which derived from pre-Christian dramatic ritual. The names of their authors, however, are unknown. From the fourteenth to the sixteenth centuries, on feast days – days which celebrate a joyful religious event – these splendid pageants were performed in both streets and churchyards by various trade guilds (associations of merchants and craftsmen).

They were, however, disapproved of by the Reformation movement (the movement which led to the setting up of the Protestant Church in Northern Europe) and only four cycles survive: from York (48 episodes); from Wakefield (32 episodes); from Chester (25 episodes); and from Coventry (42 episodes). A typical cycle would begin with the Creation of Man, continue with the Fall, proceed through the most significant events of the Old Testament (such as the Flood), go on to the New Testament – to include the Nativity and the Crucifixion – and finish with the Last Judgement.

The *Secunda Pastorum* (*The Second Shepherd's Play*), from the Wakefield cycle, tells the story of three shepherds who follow the star to Bethlehem (and the infant Jesus). Before the explicitly Christian part of the story – which nevertheless fuses the Biblical story with older preoccupations of spiritual rebirth – there is a lively, comic incident portraying the theft of a sheep.

327

The play opens with a vigorous protest by the First Shepherd at the winter weather:

Extract 1

Lord, what these weders ar cold, and   1
   I am ylle happyd;
I am nere-hande dold, so long have I nappyd;
My legys thay fold, my fyngers ar chappyd,
It is not as I wold, for I am al lappyd   5
   In sorow.

Lord, how cold this weather is, and how badly covered I am;
I am nearly dead, I've been asleep so long;
My legs give way, my fingers are chapped,
Things are not as I would like them, for I am all covered in sorow.   10

GLOSSARY
chapped (l.9): sore because of the cold

● What is lost from the rhythm and rhyme in the modern translation?

Extract 2 The shepherd also complains at the oppressions suffered by the poor:

For may he gett a paynt slefe or a broche now on dayes,   1
Wo is hym that hym grefe, or onys agane says,
Dar no man hym reprefe, what mastry he mays,
And yit may no man lefe oone word that he says,
   No letter.   5

If a man gets a decorated sleeve or a brooch nowadays,
Unhappy is the man who complains or tells him he is wrong;
No one dares find fault with him no matter what force he uses.
And yet no one can believe one word he says,
Not a letter.   10

GLOSSARY
decorated sleeve (l.6): a sign of authority

Extract 3 He is joined in his protest by another two shepherds. To cheer themselves up they are singing a song, when Mak, the sheep-stealer, enters, pretending to be a nobleman. They are not fooled and, fearing he will steal one of their sheep, force him to sleep between them. However, he works a spell on them, steals a sheep and takes it home to his wife, Gylle (Gill):

MAK: Good wyff, open the hek. Seys thou not what I bryng?   1
GYLLE: I may thole the dray the snek. A, com in, my swetyng.
MAK: Yee, thou thar not rek of my long standing.
GYLLE: By the nakyd nek art thou lyke for to hyng.
MAK: Do way: 5
   I am worthy my mete,
   For in a strate can I gett
   More then thay that swynke and swette
     All the long day.
Thus it felle to my lotte, Gylle, I had sich grace.   10

GYLLE: It were a fowlle blot to be hanged for the case.
MAK: I have skapyd, Jelott, oft as hard a glase.

MAK: Good wife, open the door. Can't you see what I bring?
GILL: I may let you lift the latch. Ah! Come in, my sweet!   15
MAK: Yes, you don't care about leaving me standing a long time.
GILL: By your naked neck you are likely to hang.
MAK: Get away!
    I earn my meat,
    For in bad times I can get   20
    More than they that work and sweat
    All day long.
    It was just good fortune, Gill, I had such grace.
GILL: It would be a terrible blot to be hanged for the case.
MAK: I've escaped before, Gill, just as hard a misfortune.   25

Extract 4   To cover the crime, they put the sheep in a cradle, suggesting the sleeping Christ. Although Mak returns by the time the shepherds wake up from their sleep, they soon suspect him and go to search his house. Mak and Gill pretend that they have just had another child and the shepherds find nothing. They walk away, when suddenly:

PRIMUS PASTOR: Gaf ye the chyld any thyng?   1
SECUNDUS PASTOR: I trow not oone farthyng.
TERCIUS PASTOR: Fast agayne wille I flyng,
    Abyde ye me there.
  Mak, take it no grefe, if I com to thi barne.   5
MAK: Nay, thou dos me greatt reprefe, and fowlle has
    thou farne.
TERCIUS PASTOR: The child wille it not grefe, that
    lytylle day starne.
  Mak, with youre leyfe, let me gyf youre barne   10
    Bot vj pence.
MAK: Nay, do way: he slepys.
TERCIUS PASTOR: Me thynk he pepys.
MAK: When he wakyns he wepys.
  I pray you go hence.   15
TERCIUS PASTOR: Gyf me lefe hym to kys, and lyft up
    the clowtt.
  What the dewille is this? he has a long snowte
PRIMUS PASTOR: He is merkyd amys. We wate ille abowte.
SECUNDUS PASTOR: Ille spon weft, i-wis, ay commys foulle owte.   20
    Ay so?
  He is lyke to oure shepe.
TERCIUS PASTOR: How, Gyb! May I pepe?
PRIMUS PASTOR: I trow, kynde wille crepe
    Where it may not go.   25

SECUNDUS PASTOR: This was a qwantt gawde and a far cast.
    It was a hee frawde.
TERCIUS PASTOR: Yee, sirs, wast.
    Lett bren this bawde and bynd hir fast.
A! fals skawde, hang at the last   30
    So shalle thou.
    Wylle ye se how thay swedylle
    His foure feytt in the medylle?
    Sagh I never in a credylle   35
      A hornyd lad or now.

FIRST SHEPHERD:	Did you give the child anything?	
SECOND SHEPHERD:	I swear not one farthing!	
THIRD SHEPHERD:	I'll dash back again	40
	You wait for me here.	
	(*He returns to Mak's door*)	
	Mak, don't be angry: I come to your baby.	
MAK:	No, you do me great shame; you have behaved badly.	45
THIRD SHEPHERD:	Your child, that little day star, must not suffer loss.	
	Mak, with your permission, let me give your baby	
	Just sixpence.	50
MAK:	No! Go away! He's asleep!	
THIRD SHEPHERD:	I think his eyes are open.	
MAK:	When he wakes up he cries.	
	Please go away!	
THIRD SHEPHERD:	Let me kiss him and lift up the cover.	55
	What the devil is this? He has a long snout!	
FIRST SHEPHERD:	Something's wrong. Let's not wait about.	
SECOND SHEPHERD:	Badly spun webs, indeed, always come out badly.	
	Ah, I thought so.	60
	He is like our sheep.	
THIRD SHEPHERD:	What do you mean, Gib! Let's have a look.	
FIRST SHEPHERD:	Only a parent could love this child.	
SECOND SHEPHERD:	This was a strange trick and a fine plot.	
	It was a really clever fraud.	65
THIRD SHEPHERD:	Yes, sirs, that it was!	
	Let's burn this woman and tie her up tight.	
	Rotten people hang in the end	
	Just like you will.	
	Look how they wrap	70
	His four feet in the middle!	
	I never saw in a cradle	
	A horned lad until now.	

(from *Secunda Pastorum* (Wakefield Cycle))

GLOSSARY

farthing (l.39): an old British coin worth a quarter of a penny

little day star (l.46): (the phrase used later in the play to describe the Christ child)

sixpence (l.50): six pennies

snout (l.56): nose (of a sheep)

webs (l.58): cloth

horned lad (l.73): boy with horns (suggesting either Christ, 'the Lamb of God', or a child of the devil)

Mak insists that it is his child, but of course they don't believe him. Instead of killing him, though, they show mercy and, in a kind of mock-death, toss him in a blanket. They are rewarded by an invitation to visit the Christ child, the embodiment of charity. After the bleak opening, the play finishes on a note of reverent joy and wonder as the shepherds sing 'Gloria in excelsis'.

The play (?1385) is a mixture of jolly clowning and the most serious poetry, reminding us that we are all equal in the sight of God. In the deeply symbolic story, the Christian and pagan traditions seem to merge harmoniously.

Supplement 2

John Skelton (?1460–1529)

John Skelton was a tutor to Prince Henry (later to become Henry VIII). He was also a priest and a classical scholar, even though his poetry is chiefly comic and satirical. One of his books *Colin Clout* (1519), was a satire on the vices of the clergy, in particular Cardinal Wolsey, the powerful statesman and churchman in the courts of Henry VII and Henry VIII. Skelton's verse is personal and lively, and frequently mixes both high and low styles. In retrospect, though, it seems more to look back to the poetry of the Middle Ages than forward to the Renaissance. In this lyric – not a satire – in praise of Mistress Margaret Hussey (published 1523), we hear the distinctive character of his 'music':

GLOSSARY

Gentle (l.3): refined and well-mannered

falcon (l.3): small bird trained to hunt other birds – pun on 'falcon-gentle' = term applied to female and young

hawk . . . tower (l.4): high-flying bird that sails high in the air before it comes down to kill small animals (suggesting lightness, beauty and nobility)

solace (l.5): comfort

mirth (l.6): amusement

demeaning (l.11): behaving

passing . . . endite (l.13–14): surpassing anything I can write

suffice (l.15): it's enough

Isaphill (l.22): Hypsipyle, queen of Lemnos, famous for her devotion to her father and children

To Mistress Margaret Hussey

Merry Margaret,   1
    As midsummer flower,
Gentle as falcon
Or hawk of the tower;
With solace and gladness,   5
Much mirth and no madness,
All good and no badness;
    So joyously,
    So maidenly,
    So womanly   10
    Her demeaning
    In every thing,
    Far, far passing
    That I can endite,
    Or suffice to write   15
Of merry Margaret
    As midsummer flower,
Gentle as falcon
Or hawk of the tower.

| | As patient and as still | 20 |
| | And as full of good will | |

Colyander (l.23): coriander
(sweet-smelling herb
supposed to soothe
pain)

pomander (l.24): ball of
sweet-smelling herbs
used as a guard against
infection and unpleasant
smells

Cassander (l.25): beautiful
daughter of Priam of
Troy, whose accurate
prophesies no one
believed

Steadfast (l.26): firm

wrought (l.27): shaped

Ere (l.29): before (*poetic*)

As fair Isaphill;
Colyander,
Sweet pomander,
Good Cassander;   25
Steadfast of thought,
Well made, well wrought,
Far may be sought
Ere that ye can find
So courteous, so kind   30
As merry Margaret,
This midsummer flower,
Gentle as falcon
Or hawk of the tower.

● i) What impression do we get of Margaret?
  ii) How would you describe the rhythm of the verse? Can you find a pattern in
  the stress and the rhymes?

Sir Thomas Wyatt and the sonnet

Wyatt is usually credited with introducing the sonnet form into England.
Wyatt's sonnets concluded with a rhyming couplet, a practice followed by
Shakespeare but not found in Italian or French sonnets. The most common
rhyme scheme in Wyatt's sonnets is **abba abba cddc ee**.

'Whoso list to hount, I knowe where is an hynde' – an adaptation of a
Petrarch sonnet – is normally thought to refer to Anne Boleyn, whom
Wyatt 'lost' to Henry VIII. In the poem, Wyatt, perhaps rather cynically,
describes the pursuit of an inaccessible lady as a waste of time – a very
different sentiment from Petrarch's! (Spelling and punctuation have been
slightly modernised).

GLOSSARY

Whoso (l.1): whoever
(*archaic*)

list (l.1): wishes

hind (l.1): female deer

vain travail (l.3): useless
effort

sore (l.3): greatly

farthest (l.4): at the
greatest distance away

Draw (l.6): withdraw (he
can't stop thinking
about her)

graven (l.11): engraved
(*archaic*)

*Noli me tangere, for Caesar's
I am (l.13)*: Don't touch
me, for I am Caesar's
(inscribed on the collars
of Caesar's hinds to
protect them from
hunters)

'Whoso list to hunt'

Whoso list to hunt, I know where is an hind,   1
But as for me, alas, I may no more.
The vain travail hath wearied me so sore
I am of them that farthest cometh behind.
Yet may I, by no means, by wearied mind   5
Draw from the deer, but as she fleeth afore,
Fainting I follow. I leave off therefore,
Since in a net I seek to hold the wind.
Who list her hunt, I put him out of doubt,
As well as I, may spend his time in vain.   10
And graven with diamonds in letters plain
There is written, her fair neck round about,
'*Noli me tangere*, for Caesar's I am,
And wild for to hold, though I seem tame.'

i) In what sense is the narrator's love difficult?

ii) In terms of form, what makes this a sonnet? (Count the number of syllables per line and the number of lines. What is the rhyme scheme? – Remember Wyatt seems not to have been too interested in making his verse smooth!)

Edmund Spenser (?1552–1599)

Nowadays, Edmund Spenser is rather unfashionable but in his day he was thought to be the greatest English poet since Chaucer and equal of the great classical epic poets. A great admirer of Sidney, his aim in poetry was to 'fashion a gentleman or noble person in virtuous and gentle discipline'. Spenser's great poems include *The Shepherd's Calender* (1579), verse dialogues in a rural setting in the manner of Virgil (a mixture of nature songs, satires, laments and praise of Queen Elizabeth); *The Faerie Queene* (1589–1596), an unfinished allegorical romance combining the medieval Arthurian legend with religious and Platonic idealism and political commentary (usually regarded as Spenser's masterpiece); and *Amoretti* (1595), love sonnets in honour of his bride, Elizabeth Boyle. Spenser had a tremendous influence on subsequent poets, in particular Milton, Gray, Shelley and Keats. This is Sonnet 70 from *Amoretti*:

GLOSSARY

herald (l.1): sign of what is to come

cote armour (l.2): coat of armour

arrayd (l.4): decorated

bowre (l.6): bower: i) shelter ii) lady's private apartment

staid (l.7): stayed, kept back

forelock (l.8): hair

crew (l.10): group of armed men

make (l.11): mate (lover)

by . . . dew (l.12): be given suitable punishment

Make hast (l.13): move quickly

prime (l.13): early morning

'Fresh spring the herald of loves mighty king'

Fresh spring the herald of loves mighty king,   1
  In whose cote armour richly are displayd
  all sorts of flowers the which on earth do spring
  in goodly colours gloriously arrayd.
Goe to my love, where she is careless layd,   5
  yet in her winters bowre not well awake:
  tell her the joyous time will not be staid
  unless she doe him by the forelock take.
Bid her therefore her selfe soone ready make,
  to wayt on love amongst his lovely crew: 10
  where every one that misseth then her make,
  shall be by him amearst with penance dew.
Make hast therefore sweet love, whilest it is prime,
  for none can call againe the passed time.

i) What is the urgency Spenser is expressing?

ii) What similarities/differences of form are there with the sonnets of Wyatt (page 36) and Sidney (page 38)?

John Lyly (?1554–1606)

John Lyly is best known for the prose romance *Euphues* (1578–1580) and his plays, such as *Endimion* (1591), written – unlike the plays of Marlowe and Shakespeare – for a refined, aristocratic audience and performed by boy actors in private theatres. His style is highly elaborate and sophisticated.

Cupid, son of Venus (the Roman goddess of love and beauty), was the mischievous boy god of love. He is always represented with wings, and with bow and arrows, which he shoots through the heart of victims. In this lyric from the play *Campaspe* (1584), he is playing cards with Campaspe, the beautiful Theban mistress of Alexander the Great.

Cupid and my Campaspe play'd 1
At cards for kisses; Cupid paid:
He stakes his quiver, bow, and arrows,
His mother's doves, and team of sparrows;
Loses them too; then down he throws 5
The coral of his lip, the rose
Growing on 's cheek (but none knows how);
With these, the crystal of his brow;
And then the dimple on his chin;
All these did my Campaspe win. 10
At last he set her both his eyes:
She won, and Cupid blind did rise.
O Love, has she done this to thee?
What shall, alas, become of me?

(from *Campaspe*)

● i) Who does 'his mother' (l.4) refer to? Who does 'she' (l.12 and l.13) refer to?
ii) Who 'says' the last two lines (l.13 and l.14) to whom? The poet to Cupid? Venus to Cupid?
iii) What is the emotion behind the last line?
iv) Which words/phrases describe a card game? What do they tell us about the relationship?

Christopher Marlowe (1564–1593)

Despite his classical learning, Christopher Marlowe is thought to have been a man of violent, and at times, criminal temperament. In fact he lost his life in a quarrel over a bill in a tavern. According to the testimony of his fellow dramatist, Thomas Kyd (1558–1594), he was also an atheist and given to blasphemy. Marlowe's musical handling of the unrhymed ten-syllable line (blank verse) was learned from Spenser and showed the way for Milton and Shakespeare. His plays are powerful, intense and frequently lyrical.

Marlowe's play *Edward II* (?1592) much influenced Shakespeare's play *Richard II*. It tells the story of the execution of the king's favourite, Piers Gaveston, and the subsequent murder of Edward II after his abdication. The play is full of pathos (a quality which arouses pity and sorrow in the audience) and horror but has fewer of the broader historical and political implications of a Shakespeare play. Nevertheless, it is a fine early historical drama. In this scene, Arundel brings Edward II the news of Gaveston's death at the hands of rebellious barons (nobles of the lowest rank):

Enter ARUNDEL

EDWARD: What, Lord Arundel, dost thou come alone?
ARUNDEL: Yea, my good lord, for Gaveston is dead.
EDWARD: Ah, traitors! have they put my friend to death?
Tell me, Arundel, died he ere thou cam'st,

Or didst thou see my friend to take his death? 5

ARUNDEL: Neither, my lord; for as he was surprised,
Begirt with weapons and with enemies round,
I did your highness' message to them all;
Demanding him of them, entreating rather,
And said, upon the honour of my name, 10
That I would undertake to carry him
Unto your highness, and to bring him back.

EDWARD: And tell me, would the rebels deny me that?

YOUNG SPENCER: Proud recreants!

EDWARD: Yea, Spencer, traitors all. 15

ARUNDEL: I found them at first inexorable;
The Earl of Warwick would not bide the hearing.
Mortimer hardly, Pembroke and Lancaster
Spake least: and when they flatly had denied,
Refusing to receive me pledge for him, 20
The Earl of Pembroke mildly thus bespake;
'My lords, because our sovereign sends for him,
And promiseth he shall be safe returned,
I will this undertake to have him hence.
And see him re-delivered to your hands.' 25

EDWARD: Well, and how fortunes [it] that he came not?

YOUNG SPENCER: Some treason, or some villainy was the cause.

ARUNDEL: The Earl of Warwick seized him on his way;
For being delivered unto Pembroke's men,
Their lord rode home thinking his prisoner safe; 30
But ere he came, Warwick in ambush lay,
And bare him to his death; and in a trench
Strake off his head, and marched unto the camp.

YOUNG SPENCER: A bloody part, flatly 'gainst law of arms.

EDWARD: O shall I speak, or shall I sigh and die! 35

YOUNG SPENCER: My lord, refer your vengeance to the sword.
Upon these barons; hearten up your men;
Let them not unrevenged murder your friends!
Advance your standard, Edward, in the field,
And march to fire them from their starting holes.   [EDWARD *kneels*] 40

EDWARD: By earth, the common mother of us all!
By heaven, and all the moving orbs thereof!
By this right hand! and by my father's sword!
And all the honours 'longing to my crown!
I will have heads, and lives for him, as many 45
As I have manors, castles, towns, and towers.   [*Rises*]

(from *Edward II*)

GLOSSARY

Begirt (l.7): surrounded (*poetic*)

entreating (l.9): asking with deep feeling

recreants (l.14): traitors

inexorable (l.16): not prepared to change their mind

bide the hearing (l.17): take any notice of what I had to say (*archaic*)

receive ... him (l.20): accept my guarantee that I would bring him back

Strake (l.33): cut

standard (l.39): royal flag

fire ... holes (l.40): drive them out of their holes in the ground (like rabbits)

orbs (l.42): planets

● i) How would you describe Edward's mood at the end of the extract?
   ii) What atmosphere does Marlowe create?

Marlowe's *Dr Faustus* (?1588 – published 1604), is a tragedy in blank verse with some comic episodes in prose. In many aspects it resembles a medieval Morality Play, in that Faustus sacrifices his soul to the devil

(Mephistopheles) in return for twenty-four years of life and unlimited power. In this speech he calls up Helen of Troy, revealing his tormented mind as the time draws near to surrender his soul:

[*Enter* HELEN *passing over between two* CUPIDS]   1
FAUST: **Was this the face that launched a thousand ships**
And burnt the topless towers of Ilium?
Sweet Helen, make me immortal with a kiss.
Her lips sucks forth my soul – see where it flies!   5
Come, Helen, come, give me my soul again.
Here will I dwell, for heaven is in these lips
And all is dross that is not Helena.

(from *Dr Faustus*)

GLOSSARY

topless (l.3): so high they seemed to have no tops
Ilium (l.3): another name for the city of Troy
dross (l.8): impure waste

William Shakespeare

Richard III
(1592–1593)

Richard III was the last king of England in the House of York, which seized the throne from the House of Lancaster in 1461. Shakespeare portrays Richard as a deformed, cruel and cold-blooded man with a magnetic personality. He has energy and wit and wins the throne by constant treachery.

This is the opening of the play.

GLOSSARY

solus: used in stage directions: alone (*Latin*)
sun (l.3): (pun): i) sun: emblem of King Edward ii) son
loured upon (l.4): were dark and threatening over
monuments (l.7): souvenirs
alarums (l.8): calls to arms
measures (l.9): dances
Grim-visaged (l.10): unpleasant and serious-looking (*archaic/poetic*)
front (l.11): forehead (*poetic*)
mounting barbed steeds (l.12): getting on armoured horses
capers nimbly (l.14): plays lightly
lascivious (l.15): encouraging sexual desire
court . . . glass (l.17): admire myself in a mirror
rudely stamped (l.18): made deformed

ACT I

Scene I. [*London. A street.*]

Enter RICHARD, *Duke of Gloucester, solus.*   1
RICHARD: **Now is the winter of our discontent**
Made glorious summer by this sun of York;
And all the clouds that loured upon our house
In the deep bosom of the ocean buried.   5
Now are our brows bound with victorious wreaths,
Our bruised arms hung up for monuments,
Our stern alarums changed to merry meetings,
Our dreadful marches to delightful measures.
Grim-visaged War hath smoothed his wrinkled   10
    front,
And now, instead of mounting barbed steeds
To fright the souls of fearful adversaries,
He capers nimbly in a lady's chamber
To the lascivious pleasing of a lute.   15
But I, that am not shaped for sportive tricks
Nor made to court an amorous looking glass;
I, that am rudely stamped, and want love's
    majesty
To strut before a wanton ambling nymph;   20
I, that am curtailed of this fair proportion,
Cheated of feature by dissembling Nature,
Deformed, unfinished, sent before my time

want (l.18): lack

strut ... nymph (l.20): walk in a self-important way in front of a seductive girl walking casually

am curtailed ... proportion (l.21): denied any beauty in my shape

feature (l.22): good shape

dissembling (l.22): false

scarce (l.24): almost not (*archaic*)

halt (l.26): limp

piping time (l.27): time when people prefer musical entertainment to the manly pursuit of warfare

descant (l.30): comment

entertain (l.32): pass in an interesting way

well-spoken (l.32): courteous

prove (l.33): show myself to be

Into this breathing world scarce half made up,
And that so lamely and unfashionable   25
That dogs bark at me as I halt by them;
Why, I, in this weak piping time of peace,
Have no delight to pass away the time,
Unless to spy my shadow in the sun
And descant on mine own deformity.   30
And therefore, since I cannot prove a lover
To entertain these fair well-spoken days,
I am determined to prove a villain
And hate the idle pleasures of these days.

(from *Richard III*)

- i) What do you imagine Richard looks like?
  ii) In which lines does he show his obsession with his deformity?
  iii) In which lines are peace and war contrasted?

**The Sonnets
(1595–1599)**   Shakespeare's collection of 154 sonnets was first printed in 1609. Numbers 1–126 are addressed to a man (126 is in fact a twelve-line poem, not a sonnet) and the remainder are addressed to a woman – the so-called 'dark lady of the sonnets' because she is dark in hair and complexion. This is sonnet 65:

Since ... power (l.1–2): since the power of all of these things is destroyed by death

How ... plea (l.3): how can beauty survive?

action (l.4): case (in law)

hold out (l.5): last

wrackful siege (l.6): destructive attack

impregnable (l.7): indestructible

stout (l.7): strong

Nor ... decays (l.8): and there are no steel gates which Time doesn't destroy

fearful meditation (l.9): terrible thought

alack (l.9): (a cry of regret) (*archaic*)

from ... hid (l.10): hide to prevent itself from being shut in Time's strong box

spoil ... forbid (l.12): can prevent his destruction of beauty

might (l.13): power

in ... ink (l.14): through my words in poems

love (l.14): beloved

Since brass, nor stone, nor earth, nor boundless sea,   1
But sad mortality o'erswways their power,
How with this rage shall beauty hold a plea,
Whose action is no stronger than a flower?
O how shall summer's honey breath hold out   5
Against the wrackful siege of battering days,
When rocks impregnable are not so stout
Nor gates of steel so strong, but Time decays?
O fearful meditation! where alack
Shall Time's best jewel from Time's chest lie hid?   10
Or what strong hand can hold his swift foot back?
Or who his spoil of beauty can forbid?
O none, unless this miracle have might,
That in black ink my love may still shine bright.

- i) Time is a cruel destroyer: a theme which has its roots in the 'classical' poetry of Greece and Rome. In Elizabethan poetry the theme is expressed frequently and powerfully. Does this suggest to you anything about the period in which Shakespeare lived?
  ii) What can you say about the rhyme and rhythm of the sonnet?

Measure for Measure
(1604–1605)

Vincentio, duke of Vienna, on the pretext of a journey abroad, hands over the government to Angelo, a man of austere life and rigid principle. Enforcing forgotten laws against sexual licence, Angelo sentences Claudio to death for seducing his betrothed before marriage. The duke, in disguise as a friar, makes a visit of spiritual comfort to Claudio in prison. However, as we can see from this speech to his sister Isabella, Claudio is not consoled:

GLOSSARY

Ay (l.3): yes (*archaic*)

obstruction (l.4): suffocating earth

This sensible warm motion (l.5): this warm movement of the blood and the feelings/ sensations

kneaded clod (l.6): lump of compressed earth

delighted (l.6): beloved (possibly 'dilated')

thrilling region (l.8): purgatory; thrilling = vibrating (*archaic*)

viewless (l.9): invisible

pendent (l.11): hanging in space

lawless (l.12): outside the 'law' of Christ's teaching

those ... howling (l.12–13): the dubious fantasies of poets

ache (l.15): pain

penury (l.15): poverty

CLAUDIO:	**Death is a fearful thing.** 1
ISABELLA:	**And shamed life a hateful.**
CLAUDIO:	**Ay, but to die, and go we know not where;**
	To lie in cold obstruction, and to rot;
	This sensible warm motion to become 5
	A kneaded clod; and the delighted spirit
	To bath in fiery floods, or to reside
	In thrilling region of thick-ribbed ice;
	To be imprison'd in the viewless winds
	And blown with restless violence round about 10
	The pendent world: or to be worse than worst
	Of those that lawless and incertain thought
	Imagine howling, – 'tis too horrible.
	The weariest and most loathed wordly life
	That age, ache, penury and imprisonment 15
	Can lay on nature, is a paradise
	To what we fear of death.

(from *Measure for Measure*)

- Obviously, Claudio doesn't want to die. In which lines is he thinking of the body after death? In which lines the spirit?

Macbeth
(1605–1606)

Macbeth, Scotland's heroic warrior, has been told that he will be king of Scotland. Spurred on by evil ambition – and by his wife – Macbeth is persuaded to murder the present king, Duncan, while he is a guest in Macbeth's castle. But Macbeth's conscience is nevertheless strongly against the terrible deed:

GLOSSARY

He's ... trust (l.1): there are two reasons for our loyalty

Strong both (l.3): both strong arguments

He's here in double trust: 1
First, as I am his kinsman and his subject,
Strong both against the deed; then, as his host,
Who should against his murderer shut the door,
Not bear the knife myself. Besides, this Duncan 5

---

faculties so meek (l.6): kingly powers so gently

clear . . . office (l.7): faultless in his duties

trumpet-tongued (l.8): sounding as loud as trumpets

taking-off (l.9): murder

Striding the blast (l.11): riding on the great wind

cherubin, horsed (l.11): cherubs riding the wild horses of the sky

sightless couriers (l.12): invisible fast horses (the winds)

That (l.14): so that

Hath borne his faculties so meek hath been
So clear in his great office, that his virtues
Will plead like angels, trumpet-tongued, against
The deep damnation of his taking-off;
And pity, like a naked new-born babe,   10
Striding the blast, or heaven's cherubin, horsed
Upon the sightless couriers of the air,
Shall blow the horrid deed in every eye,
That tears shall drown the wind.

(from *Macbeth*)

● i) What picture is created in your mind's eye by the image personifying pity (l.10–l.14)?
ii) Macbeth nevertheless commits the murder. What do you imagine causes him to make up his mind?

King Lear
(1605–1606)

King Lear has divided his kingdom between his two wicked daughters, Goneril and Regan. His third daughter, Cordelia, truly loves her father but she refuses to flatter him and gets nothing. Without power the king is treated cruelly by Goneril and Regan. On a wild heath, in a storm, Lear begins to go mad. Nevertheless, this egotistic man has new moments of pity for others – and, perhaps for the first time in his life, a sense of justice. He addresses the poor and then the rich:

GLOSSARY

bide (l.2): endure

pelting (l.2): heavy rain

looped and windowed (l.4): full of holes

Take physic, pomp (l.7): take this medicine to cure yourself, you who live in a world of luxury and ceremony

wretches (l.8): unfortunate people

shake the superflux to them (l.9): give them everything over and above what you need

Poor naked wretches, wheresoe'er you are,   1
That bide the pelting of this pitiless storm,
How shall your houseless heads and unfed sides,
Your looped and windowed raggedness, defend
     you   5
From seasons such as these? O, I have ta'en
Too little care of this! Take physic, pomp,
Expose thyself to feel what wretches feel,
That thou mayst shake the superflux to them,
And show the heavens more just.   10

(from *King Lear*)

● Where does Lear begin to address the rich?
What do you think the words 'I have ta'en . . . this' (l.6–7) refer to?

The Tempest
(1611–1612)

Prospero, duke of Milan, and his daughter Miranda have lived on a lonely island for many years served only by the brutish savage Caliban and the fairy Ariel. Through his magical powers, Prospero has contrived the shipwreck on the island of his enemies. Two of the servants and Caliban attempt to rob Prospero of his instruments of magic. In the background, they can hear Ariel playing a tune:

afeard (l.1): afraid

twangling (l.3): with musical echoing sounds (Shakespeare invented the word)

methought (l.7): I thought *(archaic)*

I cried . . . again (l.9): the dream was so pleasant that I cried, hoping I could dream it again

CALIBAN: **Be not afeard; the isle is full of noises,**   1
Sounds and sweet airs, that give delight, and hurt not.
Sometimes a thousand twangling instruments
Will hum about mine ears; and sometime voices,
That, if I then had waked after long sleep,   5
Will make me sleep again; and then, in dreaming,
The clouds methought would open, and show riches
Ready to drop upon me; that, when I waked,
I cried to dream again.

(from *The Tempest*)

● i) What image do you get of the island? Is it realistic?
ii) What effect does it have that these lines are spoken by an ugly brute?

Francis Bacon   One of the most prophetic voices of modern scientific rationalism (as
(1561–1626)   distinct from poetic and imaginative expression) was Francis Bacon. For
him the purpose of knowledge was 'the benefit and use of man' and the
method proposed was a 'laborious and sober inquiry of truth', 'ascending
from experiments to the invention of causes, and descending from causes
to the invention of new experiments'. He notes that 'the root of all error'
is 'too untimely a departure and too remote a recess from particulars'.
Most of his philosophy was written in Latin – in the belief that it would
remain the language of international learning forever – but his essays,
written in an aphoristic style (a style which expresses wise sayings in a
few words), were written in English. Bacon's most famous work is *The
Advancement of Learning*, published in 1605 in English and addressed to
King James I. Nowadays, it is noted for the early distinction it makes
between the rational and imaginative faculties, which was later to become
a basic belief in the 'Age of Reason' (beginning 1660). Bacon was trained
as a barrister and entered Parliament in 1584. The rise in his career was
very rapid, but although he advocated truth and virtue, his public life
came to an end after he was charged with taking bribes when he was a
judge! Although the following essay exhibits all the virtues of Bacon's
style – such as a sense of confidence and logic – he manages to reduce
the complex area of human relations to a neat, schematic generalisation.
At the same time there is much which is rhetorical (language intended to
persuade) in his writing:

He that hath wife and children hath given hostages to fortune; for   1
they are impediments to great enterprises, either of virtue or mis-
chief. Certainly the best works, and of greatest merit for the public,
have proceeded from the unmarried or childless men, which both
in affection and means have married and endowed the public. Yet   5
it were great reason that those that have children should have
greatest care of future times, unto which they know they must
transmit their dearest pledges. Some there are who, though they
lead a single life, yet their thoughts do end with themselves, and
account future times impertinences. Nay, there are some other that   10

account wife and children but as bills of charges. Nay more, there are some foolish rich covetous men that take a pride in having no children, because they may be thought so much the richer. ... Unmarried men are best friends, best masters, best servants, but not always best subjects, for they are light to run away, and almost all fugitives are of that condition. A single life doth well with churchmen, for charity will hardly water the ground where it must first fill a pool. It is indifferent for judges and magistrates, for if they be facile and corrupt, you shall have a servant five times worse than a wife. For soldiers, I find the generals commonly in their hortatives put men in mind of their wives and children; and I think the despising of marriage amongst the Turks maketh the vulgar soldier more base. Certainly wife and children are a kind of discipline of humanity; and single men, though they be many times more charitable, because their means are less exhaust, yet, on the other side, they are more cruel and hard-hearted (good to make severe inquisitors), because their tenderness is not so oft called upon. ... Chaste women are often proud and froward, as presuming upon the merit of their chastity. It is one of the best bonds, both of chastity and obedience, in the wife if she think her husband wise, which she will never do if she find him jealous. Wives are young men's mistresses, companions for middle age, and old men's nurses, so as a man may have a quarrel to marry when he will. But yet he was reputed one of the wise men that made answer to the question when a man should marry: 'A young man not yet, an elder man not at all.' It is often seen that bad husbands have very good wives; whether it be that it raiseth the price of their husbands' kindness when it comes, or that the wives take a pride in their patience. But this never fails, if the bad husbands were of their own choosing, against their friends' consent; for then they will be sure to make good their own folly.

(from *Of Marriage and Single Life*)

● Which phrases show Bacon's confidence and definiteness? What do you think of his point of view?

Supplement 3

John Webster (?1578–?1632)

The plays of John Webster have been more frequently revived in the twentieth century than those of any playwright of the period other than Shakespeare. His plays are mainly in the 'revenge' tradition (dating from Seneca (?4 BC–AD 65) and very popular in the Jacobean theatre). In these the hero is usually concerned with the problem of avenging the murder of a relative or someone close. Often characterised by violence and horror, pitiless intrigue and perverse passions, 'revenge tragedy' has sometimes been called 'the tragedy of blood' (Shakespeare's *Hamlet* was related to this tradition). Conventionally, many of the plays were set in the bedrooms, dungeons and graveyards of the courts of Renaissance Spain and Italy.

The Duchess of Malfi (?1613), based on a tale by the Italian writer Matteo Bandello, concerns the revenge taken upon a young, widowed duchess for secretly marrying her steward, Antonio, a man of lower status, behind the backs of her brothers.

In this scene near the beginning of the play, the high-spirited duchess woos Antonio. In an atmosphere of secrecy Cariola, the woman who serves her and who knows the duchess's intention, has been sent to listen behind an arras (a tapestry hanging on the wall):

[*Enter* ANTONIO.]   1

          I sent for you: sit down;
Take pen and ink, and write. Are you ready?
ANTONIO: Yes.
DUCHESS: What did I say?   5
ANTONIO: That I should write somewhat.
DUCHESS: Oh, I remember.
After these triumphs and this large expense,
It's fit, like thrifty husbands, we inquire
What's laid up for tomorrow.   10
ANTONIO: So please your beauteous excellence.
DUCHESS: Beauteous?
Indeed, I thank you: I look young for your sake;
You have ta'en my cares upon you.
ANTONIO: I'll fetch your grace   15
The particulars of your revenue and expense.
DUCHESS: Oh, you are an upright treasurer: but you mistook;
For when I said I meant to make inquiry
What's laid up for tomorrow, I did mean
What's laid up yonder for me.   20
ANTONIO: Where?
DUCHESS: In heaven.
I am making my will (as 'tis fit princes should,
In perfect memory), and I pray sir, tell me,
Were not one better make it smiling thus   25

342

Than in deep groans and terrible ghastly looks.
As if the gifts we parted with procured
That violent distraction?

ANTONIO: O, much better.

DUCHESS: If I had a husband now, this care were quit: 30
But I intend to make you overseer.
What good deed shall we first remember? Say.

ANTONIO: Begin with that first good deed begun i' th' world
After man's creation, the sacrament of marriage:
I'd have you first provide for a good husband;   35
Give him all.

DUCHESS: All?

ANTONIO: Yes, your excellent self.

DUCHESS: In a winding-sheet?

ANTONIO: In a couple.   40

DUCHESS: Saint Winfred, that were a strange will!

ANTONIO: 'Twere stranger if there were no will in you
To marry again.

DUCHESS: What do you think of marriage?

ANTONIO: I take't, as those that deny purgatory;   45
It locally contains or heaven or hell;
There's no third place in 't.

DUCHESS: How do you affect it?

ANTONIO: My banishment, feeding my melancholy,
Would often reason thus –   50

DUCHESS: Pray, let's hear it.

ANTONIO: Say a man never marry, nor have children,
What takes that from him? Only the bare name
Of being a father, or the weak delight
To see the little wanton ride a-cock-horse   55
Upon a painted stick, or hear him chatter
Like a taught starling.

DUCHESS: Fie, fie, what's all this?
One of your eyes is bloodshot; use my ring to 't.
They say 'tis very sovereign. 'Twas my wedding-ring,   60
And I did vow never to part with it
But to my second husband.

ANTONIO: You have parted with it now.

DUCHESS: Yes, to help your eyesight.

ANTONIO: You have made me stark blind.   65

DUCHESS: How?

ANTONIO: There is a saucy and ambitious devil
Is dancing in this circle.

DUCHESS: Remove him.

ANTONIO: How?   70

DUCHESS: There needs small conjuration, when your finger
May do it: thus; is it fit?

         [She puts the ring upon his finger; he kneels.]

(from *The Duchess of Malfi*)

---

ghastly (l.26): pale

procured (l.27): brought on

were quit (l.30): I would be free of (*archaic*)

overseer (l.31): executor (of my will)

sacrament (l.34): solemn promise

In a winding-sheet (l.39): in a sheet in which a corpse is wrapped for burial (as her husband is dead)

Saint Winfred (l.41): a Welsh martyr – and virgin

strange will (l.41): ('Will' also suggested carnal desire)

purgatory (l.45): a place in which the soul of a dead person must be made pure by suffering before entering Heaven

affect it (l.48): feel about it

little ... horse (l.55): child playing on a toy horse

starling (l.57): a type of bird

Fie, fie (l.58): expression of complaint (*archaic*)

bloodshot (l.59): reddened with blood

use my ring (l.59): rub your eye with my ring

sovereign (l.60): has healing powers; royal

vow (l.61): solemnly promise

stark (l.65): completely

saucy (l.67): disrespectfully bold

in this circle (l.68): (a necromancer – a magician in touch with the dead – first draws a charmed circle on the ground; like the duchess's ring)

needs ... conjuration (l.71): is little need for magic spells

- i) What impression do you get of Antonio's character from this scene?
- ii) Find an example of a line where it is clear Antonio is a steward.
- iii) How would you describe the tone and atmosphere of the scene?
- iv) Does the duchess succeed in her purpose by the end?

**Ben Jonson
(1572 – 1637)**

During the reign of James I, the theatre began to move into the court, a change which was to lead to the type of theatre that came into being after the Restoration of the Monarchy in 1660 (see page 116).

By contrast with the 'revenge' tradition, Ben Jonson was mainly known for his 'comedies of humours' (social satires where 'humours' – distorted human qualities such as foolishness, egotism and greed – are made into people). From 1605 Jonson also produced masques at court (masques were dramatic entertainments with dance and music). A learned man and in some ways a traditionalist, Jonson admired and assimilated Latin literature, and yet, sharply observant of the London he lived in and the fashions of the day, his language is poetic, energetic and slangy. Not born into aristocratic circles – he had been a bricklayer, actor and soldier, who had killed men both on and off the battlefield! – he maintained a proud and independent attitude to his noble patrons.

In *The Alchemist* (1610) we are invited to laugh at, and express strong moral disapproval of, the exhibition of folly and corruption of the main characters, whose fantasies and passions are exaggerated and made ridiculous. Set in a house during an outbreak of the plague, Subtle (a fake alchemist – a person who tries to turn all metals into gold), Face (the servant of the absent house-owner, Lovewit) and Dol Common (a prostitute) set about cheating a variety of victims. To Sir Epicure Mammon, a sensual knight, these characters promise the 'philosopher's stone' by which all metals may be turned to gold. Sir Epicure dreams of limitless luxury and the satisfaction of his lust; Surly, his friend, however, is sceptical:

Extract 1   Sir Epicure and Surly first enter Lovewit's house:

MAMMON: Come on, sir. Now you set your foot on shore   1
In *novo orbe*; here's the rich Peru,
And there within, sir, are the golden mines,
Great Solomon's Ophir! He was sailing to't
Three years, but we have reached it in ten months.   5
This is the day wherein to all my friends,
I will pronounce the happy word, 'Be rich'.
This day you shall be *spectatissimi*.
You shall no more deal with the hollow die
Or the frail card . . .   10

This night I'll change
All that is metal in my house to gold,
And early in the morning will I send
To all the plumbers and the pewterers
And buy their tin and lead up; and to Lothbury,   15
For all the copper.

plumbers and pewterers (l.14): people who work in lead or pewter (a metal made by mixing lead and tin)	

SURLY: What, and turn that too?

MAMMON: **Yes, and I'll purchase Devonshire and Cornwall,**
And make them perfect Indies! You admire now?

SURLY: **No, faith.**   20

MAMMON: **But when you see the effects of the great medicine,**
Of which one part projected on a hundred
Of Mercury, or Venus, or the Moon,
Shall turn it to as many of the Sun,
Nay, to a thousand, so *ad infinitum*,   25
You will believe me.

SURLY: **Yes, when I see't, I will.**
But if my eyes do cozen me so, and I
Giving 'em no occasion, sure, I'll have
A whore shall piss 'em out next day.   30

MAMMON: **Ha! Why?**
Do you think I fable with you? I assure you,
He that has once the flower of the sun,
The perfect ruby, which we call elixir,
Not only can do that, but by its virtue,   35
Can confer honour, love, respect, long life,
Give safety, valour, yea, and victory,
To whom he will. In eight and twenty days,
I'll make an old man of fourscore a child.

SURLY: **No doubt he's that already.**   40

Glossary (left column):

plumbers and pewterers (l.14): people who work in lead or pewter (a metal made by mixing lead and tin)

Lothbury (l.15): a street where copper was cast

Devonshire and Cornwall (l.18): counties with tin and copper mines

perfect Indies (l.19): (they will produce gold)

admire (l.19): are amazed

great medicine (l.21): the 'elixir' (the imaginary substance which changed metal into gold)

projected on (l.22): thrown onto (the twelfth and last stage of alchemy)

Mercury . . . Sun (l.23–24): (Mercury=quicksilver; Venus=copper; Moon=silver; Sun=gold)

ad infinitum (l.25): and so on for ever (*Latin*)

cozen (l.28): deceive

whore (l.30): prostitute

piss (l.30): urinate

fable with you (l.32): am inventing all this

ruby (l.34): (the deep red colour reached when the metal is transformed)

elixir (l.34): (the imaginary substance – see above; substance supposed to make life last forever)

confer (l.36): give

fourscore (l.39): eighty

Extract 2   In the next scene Face has promised that the alchemy will be complete in three hours:

MAMMON: **I will have all my beds blown up, not stuffed;**   1
Down is too hard. And then, mine oval room
Filled with such pictures as Tiberius took
From Elephantis, and dull Aretine
But coldly imitated. Then, my glasses   5
Cut in more subtle angles, to disperse
And multiply the figures, as I walk
Naked between my *succubae*. My mists
I'll have of perfume, vapoured 'bout the room
To lose ourselves in; and my baths like pits   10
To fall into; from whence we will come forth
And roll us dry in gossamer and roses.

(Is it arrived at ruby?) – Where I spy
A wealthy citizen or rich lawyer
Have a sublimed pure wife, unto that fellow
I'll send a thousand pound to be my cuckold.

15

(from *The Alchemist*)

GLOSSARY

Down (l.2): soft feathers used for filling mattresses and pillows

oval (l.2): egg-shaped

Tiberius (l.3): Roman emperor, 42 BC–AD 37

Elephantis (l.4): erotic writer

Aretine (l.4): Italian satirist, 1492–1556 – both he and Elephantis wrote poems accompanied by

pornographic pictures

But (l.5): only

glasses (l.5): mirrors

succubae (l.8): mistresses (Latin)

mists (l.8): (perfumed mists – like the Roman Emperor Nero, AD 36–88, arranged to have sprinkled over his guests)

vapoured (l.9): sprayed; sprinkled

lose (l.10): (also = behave freely)

gossamer (l.12): very fine cloth

ruby (l.13): (see Extract 1)

sublimed (l.15): of the highest quality; (converted from a solid to a vapour)

to . . . cuckold (l.16): to allow me to have sex with his wife

i) What is being satirised here?

ii) Where do we see Surly's scepticism?

iii) What is the effect of Mammon's exotic language?

iv) Do you like the mixture of the scholarly and the vulgar?

Jonson also wrote a wide variety of poems, ranging from satire to lyrics. 'On My First Son' is a lament to his first son Benjamin, who died of the plague at the age of seven in 1603. In it, strength of character, grace and emotion are combined:

GLOSSARY

child . . . hand (l.1): (a Hebrew translation of the name Benjamin; implies 'clever with the hands', 'fortunate' and 'favourite')

Exacted (l.4): demanded to pay back

just day (l.4): Day of Judgement (in Christianity, the day when God will judge all people)

could . . . father (l.5): shake off all paternal feelings

poetry (l.10): in Greek *poesis* = creation

all . . . much (l.11–12) (obscure: possibly, from now on he promises that he will never be too pleased with himself for loving; or, that the object of his love will not return the feeling; or that he shouldn't love too much)

On My First Son

Farewell, thou child of my right hand, and joy;   1
My sin was too much hope of thee, loved boy:
Seven years thou wert lent to me, and I thee pay,
Exacted by thy fate, on the just day.
O could I lose all father now! for why   5
Will man lament the state he should envy,
To have so soon 'scaped world's and flesh's rage,
And, if no other misery, yet age?
Rest in soft peace, and asked, say, 'Here doth lie
Ben Jonson his best piece of poetry.'   10
For whose sake henceforth all his vows be such
As what he loves may never like too much.

i) What is the 'state he should envy' (l.6)?

ii) Who does 'his' refer to in l.11? The poet (Ben) or his son (Benjamin)? Both?

iii) What effect do the Christian allusions have?

**Thomas Hobbes
(1588–1679)**

Thomas Hobbes was described by his friend, John Aubrey as good-natured and witty. He was a man who played tennis at seventy-five, got drunk a hundred times in his long life, was timid by nature, and liked to shut himself up and sing.

As a philosopher, Hobbes was narrowly rationalistic. He believed man's life was 'solitary, poore, nasty, brutish and short' and, left to itself, anarchic. He therefore advocated a strong, centralised state under a single sovereign, views which, at the time, found disfavour with both Royalists and Parliamentarians. Unlike Francis Bacon, for whom he once worked as a secretary, he regarded science as essentially deductive (which means he believed that scientific conclusions can be reached logically by reasoning from general laws to a particular case). For him, the basis of all knowledge was sensation, and motion was the one universal principle. Our appetites are our reactions to external motions and serve self-preservation. Human beings are therefore essentially selfish. Hobbes has also been described as a nominalist, owing to the importance he attached to the definition of terms. This can be seen in the extracts below.

In the nineteenth century, Hobbes's sceptical (but superficial?) clear-sightedness and his direct economical prose (which included a sustained use of irony and metaphor) influenced the Utilitarian school of thinkers in their practical, materialistic attempts to devise efficient state and social machinery.

These extracts are from *Leviathan* (written at the end of the second stage of the Civil War in 1651). For Hobbes, the leviathan, a huge sea animal, is a metaphor for his ideal Commonwealth, his 'one assembly of men' in which men 'must confer all their power and strength upon one man' (a single sovereign). Notice Hobbes's contempt for the imagination and by implication most of the other writers in this unit:

When a body is once in motion, it moveth, unless something else   1
hinder it eternally; and whatsoever hindereth it cannot in an instant,
but in time and by degrees, quite extinguish it; and as we see in the
water, though the wind cease, the waves give not over rolling for a
long time after: so also it happeneth in that motion which is made   5
in the internal parts of a man, then when he sees, dreams, etc. For
after the object is removed, or the eye shut, we still retain an image
of the thing seen, though more obscure than when we see it. And
this is it, the Latins call *imagination*, from the image made in seeing;
and apply the same, though improperly, to all the other senses. But   10
the Greeks call it *fancy*; which signifies appearance, and is as proper
to one sense, as to another. Imagination therefore is nothing but
decaying sense; and is found in men, and many other living creatures, as well sleeping as waking.

Much memory, or memory of many things, is called *experience*.   15
Again, imagination being only of those things which have been

formerly perceived by sense, either all at once or by parts at several times; the former, which is the imagining the whole object as it was presented to the sense, is *simple* imagination, as when one imagineth a man, or horse, which he hath seen before. The other is *compounded*; as when, from the sight of a man at one time and of a horse at another, we conceive in our mind a centaur. So when a man compoundeth the image of his own person with the image of the actions of another man, as when a man imagines himself a Hercules or an Alexander, which happeneth often to them that are much taken with reading of romances, it is a compound imagination, and properly but a fiction of the mind. There be also other imaginations that rise in men, though waking, from the great impression made in sense: as from gazing upon the sun, the impression leaves an image of the sun before our eyes a long time after; and from being long and vehemently attent upon geometrical figures, a man shall in the dark, though awake, have the images of lines and angles before his eyes; which kind of fancy hath no particular name, as being a thing that doth not commonly fall into men's discourse.

The imaginations of them that sleep are those we call *dreams*.

The most difficult discerning of a man's dream from his waking thoughts is, then, when by some accident we observe not that we have slept: which is easy to happen to a man full of fearful thoughts, and whose conscience is much troubled; and that sleepeth, without the circumstances of going to bed or putting off his clothes, as one that noddeth in a chair. For he that taketh pains, and industriously lays himself to sleep, in case any uncouth and exorbitant fancy come unto him, cannot easily think it other than a dream. We read of Marcus Brutus (one that had his life given him by Julius Caesar, and was also his favourite, and notwithstanding murdered him), how at Philippi, the night before he gave battle to Augustus Caesar, he saw a fearful apparition, which is commonly related by historians as a vision; but considering the circumstances, one may easily judge to have been but a short dream. For sitting in his tent, pensive and troubled with the horror of his rash act, it was not hard for him, slumbering in the cold, to dream of that which most affrighted him; which fear, as by degrees it made him wake, so also it must needs make the apparition by degrees to vanish; and having no assurance that he slept, he could have no cause to think it a dream, or anything but a vision. And this is no very rare accident; for even they that be perfectly awake, if they be timorous and superstitious, possessed with fearful tales, and alone in the dark, are subject to the like fancies, and believe they see spirits and dead men's ghosts walking in churchyards; whereas it is either their fancy only, or else the knavery of such persons as make use of such superstitious fear, to pass disguised in the night to places they would not be known to haunt.

(from *Leviathan*)

GLOSSARY

hinder (l.2): get in the way of

compounded (l.20): consisting of more than one thing

centaur (l.22): half man and half horse

Hercules (l.25): mythical Greek hero famed for his strength

Alexander (l.25): Alexander the Great, 356–323 BC, the king of Macedonia and a legendary military leader

vehemently (l.31): forcefully

discourse (l.34): conversation

discerning (l.37): (time to be able to separate)

uncouth and exorbitant (l.43): rough and excessive

Marcus Brutus (l.45): Roman politician, ?85–42 BC

Julius Caesar (l.45): Roman general and statesman, 100–44 BC

Augustus Caesar (l.47): nephew of Julius and adopted son, who defeated his uncle's assassins to become the first Emperor of Rome. His reign, the 'Augustan age', was contemporary with the best period of Latin literature

apparition (l.48): ghost

pensive (l.51): deep in thought

rash act (l.51): the murder of Julius Caesar

slumbering (l.52): sleeping

affrighted (l.52): frightened

timorous (l.57): timid

knavery (l.61): deceitful behaviour

- i) In what way can we interpret Hobbes's style as a reaction against the conflict of the Civil Wars and the extreme emotions it generated?
- ii) Hobbes's style is measured and scientific-sounding – more like twentieth-century academic writing than earlier prose writers. Can you point to one or two places where these characteristics are most apparent?
- iii) What else do you notice about his style?

**Robert Herrick
(1591–1674)**

Robert Herrick, the son of a wealthy goldsmith, left London and his literary friends to be a country parson in rural Devonshire, a decision he at first regretted. Nevertheless, he developed a feeling for local folk customs and festivals, which the Puritans had tried to suppress. Herrick was also an ardent Royalist and made friends among the country gentry, writing poems to their daughters. A great admirer of the lyrical style of Ben Jonson, his poems are often both cheerful and graceful but rarely profound. However, they make an immediate appeal and, until relatively recently, were immensely popular. In 1647, under Parliamentary and Puritan rule, Herrick lost his position in the Church and returned to London. The following year his religious and secular poems were printed together in one volume, the only publication of his life.

GLOSSARY

confines (l.1): borders

drooping West (l.1): (Devon – 'drooping' because the sun sets in the west, and because by contrast with London the county was sleepy and depressing)

pregnant East (l.2): (London – full of life and meaning)

Ravished (l.3): overcome with emotion

blest place ... nativity (l.4): (he honours it greatly because he was born there)

hallowed (l.5): greatly respectful; holy

bestowest (l.7): gives as a gift

framed (l.9): designed

kindreds (l.10)): related individuals

Roman (l.11): (a Roman born in the city was though to be 'free' of it, that is, entitled to his liberties)

irksome (l.14): tedious

henceforward (l.15): from this time on

repossessed (l.16): taken back again

urn (l.18): pot for the ashes of the dead

relics (l.20): the remains of his dead body (sacred because he was a priest)

His Return to London

From the dull confines of the drooping West,   1
To see the day spring from the pregnant East,
Ravished in spirit, I come, nay more, I fly
To thee, blest place of my nativity!
Thus, thus with hallowed foot I touch the ground   5
With thousand blessings by thy fortune crowned.
O fruitful genius! that bestowest here
An everlasting plenty, year by year;
O place! O people! Manners framed to please
All nations, customs, kindreds, languages!   10
I am a free-born Roman; suffer then
That I amongst you live a citizen.
London my home is: though by hard fate sent
Into a long and irksome banishment;
Yet since called back; henceforward let me be,   15
O native country, repossessed by thee!
For, rather than I'll to the West return,
I'll beg of thee first here to have mine urn.
Weak I am grown, and must in short time fall;
Give thou my sacred relics burial.   20

- Describe in your own words what London meant to Herrick at this point in his life.

349

The Bible   The first real translation of the Bible was the Greek Old Testament, made from the original Hebrew in Alexandria about the third century BC. (The New Testament was originally written in Greek.) In the Middle Ages the version which the Church based itself on was the Vulgate (so called because it made the word of God common to all) prepared in Latin by St Jerome between AD 383 and AD 405.

Parts of the Bible were translated into Old English from the late seventh century but for centuries the Church opposed attempts to replace the Vulgate with versions in English, arguing that people needed guidance and commentary from religious authorities. Reformers, later known as Protestants, believed that the Church was only trying to retain its power and that no other source than the Bible was needed for religious belief.

It was not until the time of John Wyclif (?1330–1384), the Oxford theologian and religious reformer, that the whole Bible was translated from Latin into English. William Tyndale (?1492–1536), a convinced Protestant, was the first to translate the New Testament into English (1525) from the original Greek text and was burned for heresy in Holland. Later versions were the Great Bible of 1537, prepared by Miles Coverdale (1488–1569); the Geneva Bible prepared by Puritan exiles in 1560; the Bishop's Bible prepared by the Anglicans in 1568; and the Douai-Rheims Bible (1582–1610), prepared from the Vulgate by English Catholic exiles.

In 1611 the Authorised Version was printed with the approval of James I. Instructed to follow the Bishop's Bible as far as possible, a team of forty-seven scholars and theologians set out to revise old translations rather than produce a new translation. Essentially, the Authorised Version is Tyndale's version mixed with some Wyclif, and the language frequently belongs more to the sixteenth century than the seventeenth century.

The social and literary influence of this version has been enormous. Until very recently, when it became replaced in Protestant churches by much less poetic versions of the New Testament (1961) and the Old Testament (1970), it was the version most widely used. In the seventeenth and eighteenth centuries it was the most commonly read book and one can hear the musical cadences of its prose in such diverse writers as John Bunyan (1628–1688), D.H. Lawrence (1885–1930) and T.F. Powys (1875–1953).

This extract is from St Paul's first epistle to the Corinthians, Chapter 13, first from the Authorised Version and then from three earlier versions.

Version 1:   Authorised Version, 1873 edition

> **Though I speak with the tongues of men and of angels, and have** 1
> **not charity, I am become as sounding brass, or a tinkling cymbal.**
> **And though I have the gift of prophecy, and understand all mys-**
> **teries, and all knowledge; and though I have all faith, so that I**
> **could remove mountains, and have no charity, I am nothing. And** 5
> **though I bestow all my goods to feed the poor, and though I give**
> **my body to be burned, and have not charity, it profiteth me nothing.**

When I was a child, I spake as a child, I understood as a child, I thought as a child: but when I became a man, I put away childish things. For now we see through a glass, darkly; but then face to face: now I know in part; but then shall I know even as also I am known. And now abideth faith, hope, charity, these three; but the greatest of these is charity.

10

Version 2:   The Bishop's Bible

Though I speake with the tongues of men, and of Angels, and have not charitie, I am as sounding brasse, or as a tinckling cymbal. And though I have prophecie, and understand all secrets, and all knowledge: yea, if I have all faith, so that I can remoove mountaines, and have not charitie, I am nothing. And though I bestow all my goods to feed the poore, and though I give my body that I should be burned, and have not charitie, it profiteth me nothing.

1

5

When I was a childe, I spake as a childe, I understood as a childe, I imagined as a childe: but assoone as I was a man, I put away childishnes. Now wee see in a glasse, even in a darke speaking: but then shall we see face to face. Now I know unperfectly: but then shall I know, even as I am knowen. Now abideth faith, hope, and charitie, these three: but the chiefe of these is charitie.

10

Version 3:   Tyndale's translation

Though I spake with the tonges of men and angels, and yet had no love, I were even as soundynge brasse: or as a tynklynge cymball. And though I coulde prophesy, and understode all secretes, and all knowledge: yee, yf I had all fayth, so that I coulde move mountayns oute of ther places, and yet had no love, I were nothinge. And though I bestowed all my gooddes to fede the poore, and though I gave my body even that I burned, and yet had no love, it profeteth me nothinge.

1

5

When I was a chylde, I spake as a chylde, I understode as a chylde, I ymagened as a chylde. But assone as I was a man, I put away chyldeshnes. Now we se in a glasse, even in a darke speakynge: but then shall we se face to face. Now I knowe unparfectly: but then shall I knowe even as I am knowen. Now abydeth fayth, hope, and love, even these thre: but the chefe of these is love.

10

Version 4:   Wyclif's version

> If I speke with tungis of men and of aungels, and I have not charite, [1]
> I am maad as bras sownynge, or a cymbal tynklynge. And if I have
> prophecie, and knowe alle mysteries, and al kunnynge, and if I
> have al feith, so that I meve hillis fro her place, and I have not
> charite, I am nought. And if I departe alle my goodis in to the metis [5]
> of pore men, and if I bitake my bodi, so that I brenne, and if I have
> not charite, it profitith to me no thing.
>
> Whanne I was a litil child, I spak as a litil child, I undurstood as a
> litil child, I thoughte as a litil child; but whanne I was maad a man,
> I avoidide tho thingis that weren of a litil child. And we seen now [10]
> bi a myrour in derknesse, but thanne face to face; now I knowe of
> parti, but thanne I schal knowe, as I am knowun. And now dwellen
> feith, hope, and charite, these thre; but the most of these is charite.

- i) Are you able to interpret the sentence beginning 'For now we see . . .' (l.10) in the Authorised Version?
- ii) Which of the four versions is the most unlike the others? What are the main differences?

The following extract is Psalm 137 (136 in the Vulgate), a powerful and moving chant of protest by a group of exiled Israelites who refuse to sing their native songs for the amusement of their captors. Their hanging the harp on the trees is a gesture of that refusal:

GLOSSARY

Babylon (l.1): the ancient city of Babylonia, an ancient country in Asia noted for its materialism and pursuit of sensual pleasure

yea (l.1): yes (*archaic*)

willows (l.3): type of tree that grows near water

midst thereof (l.3): middle of them

wasted (l.5): destroyed

required . . . mirth (l.5): wanted us to entertain them

Zion (l.6): the homeland of the Jews

cunning (l.8): skill (at playing the harp)

my tongue . . . mouth (l.9): me not be able to sing

Edom (l.11): a place south of the Dead Sea, inhabited by Semites

Rase (l.12): demolish

dasheth (l.15): smashes

> By the rivers of Babylon, there we sat down, yea, we wept, when [1]
> we remembered Zion.
> We hanged our harps upon the willows in the midst thereof.
> For there they that carried us away captive required of us a song;
> and they that wasted us required of us mirth, saying, Sing us one [5]
> of the songs of Zion.
> How shall we sing the Lord's song in a strange land?
> If I forget thee, O Jerusalem, let my right hand forget her cunning.
> If I do not remember thee, let my tongue cleave to the roof of my
> mouth; If I prefer not Jerusalem above my chief joy. [10]
> Remember, O Lord, the children of Edom in the day of Jerusalem;
> who said Rase it, rase it, even to the foundation thereof.
> O daughter of Babylon, who art to be destroyed; happy *shall he
> be*, that rewardeth thee as thou hast served us.
> Happy *shall he be*, that taketh and dasheth thy little ones against [15]
> the stones.

(Authorised Version)

The psalm was translated by many different poets for more than a century, including Francis Bacon (1561–1626), Thomas Carew (1594–1640), Richard Crashaw (1612–1649) and Sir John Denham (1615–1669). Here is a version by Thomas Campion (1567–1620).

As by the streams of Babylon   1
Far from our native soil we sat,
Sweet Zion, thee we thought upon,
And every thought a tear begat.

Aloft the trees that spring up there   5
Our silent harps we pensive hung.
Said they that captived us: 'Let's hear
Some song which you in Zion sung.'

Is then the song of our God fit
To be profaned in foreign land?   10
O Salem, thee when I forget,
Forget his skill may my right hand.

Fast to the roof may cleave my tongue
If mindless I of thee be found,
Or if, when all my joys are sung,   15
Jerusalem be not the ground.

John Bunyan (1628–1688)

John Bunyan, of humble origins, fought for the Parliamentarians. In 1653 he preached for a Nonconformist church in Bedford, and in 1660 was put in Bedford prison for preaching without a licence. Released in 1672, he was appointed pastor of his church but in 1676 was again put in prison for a short period, when he probably finished the first part of his hugely successful allegory *The Pilgrim's Progress* (published in its entirety in 1678). After his release Bunyan preached in many parts of the country but was not further troubled.

The main source of Bunyan's inspiration was the Bible. He also worked within the Puritan tradition of self-examination and argument and the allegorising tradition of the village sermon. However, the depth of his experience and the breadth of his imagination (as well as his courage and honesty) make him more than a mere sectarian writer. His writing is beautiful and simple and contains vivid, humorous characterisations.

The allegory takes the form of a dream by the author in which Christian flees from the City of Destruction (having failed to persuade his wife and children to accompany him) and sets out on a pilgrimage through the River of Death to the Celestial City (heaven). Part II of the story relates how his wife, moved by a vision, follows with her children on the same pilgrimage.

In this extract Christian, joined by a fellow pilgrim called Faithful, comes to Vanity Fair (probably based upon the annual fair at Stourbridge, near Cambridge). 'Vanity' here means something empty or worthless, like the cheap goods often sold at fairs:

Southwark Fair

Then I saw in my dream that when they were got out of the wilderness, they presently saw a town before them, and the name of that Town is Vanity; and at the town there is a fair kept called Vanity Fair. It is kept all the year long; it beareth the name of Vanity Fair, because the town where 'tis kept is lighter than vantiy, and also because all that is there sold or that cometh thither is Vanity. As is the saying of the wise, 'All that cometh is vanity.'

This fair is no new erected business, but a thing of ancient standing; I will show you the original of it.

Almost five thousand years agone, there were pilgrims walking to the Celestial City, as these two honest persons are; and Beelzebub, Apollyon, and Legion, with their companions, perceiving by the path that the pilgrims made that their way to the city lay through this town of Vanity, they contrived here to set up a fair, a fair wherein should be sold of all sorts of vanity and that it should last all the year long. Therefore at this fair are all such merchandise

GLOSSARY

they (l.1): (Christian and Faithful)

agone (l.10): ago (*archaic*)

Beelzebub ... Legion (l.11–12): (unclean spirits, devils)

honours (l.17): symbols of distinction

preferments (l.17): promotions to political and ecclesiastical positions bawds (l.19): women who run brothels

juggling (l.22): keeping several objects in the air at the same time (for entertainment)

knaves and rogues (l.23): dishonest people

false swearers (l.26): people who break formal promises

of less moment (l.27): which are less important

vended (l.29): sold

viz (l.30): that is to say

commodity (l.33): article of trade

merchandise (l.35): (the behaviour and power of the Roman Catholic Church)

thereat (l.36): to that happening

lusty (l.38): merry; relating to excessive desire

must needs (l.39): has to

behold (l.41): look! (archaic)

hubbub (l.43): noisy confusion

raiment (l.44): clothing

diverse (l.45): different

bedlams (l.47): madmen

outlandish men (l.47): foreigners

language of Canaan (l.51): language of truly religious people (reference to Isaiah 19:18 in the Bible: 'In that day shall five cities in the land of Egypt speak the language of Canaan, and swear to the Lord of hosts')

barbarians (l.53): inferior foreigners

merchandisers (l.54): people who bought and sold

set very light by (l.55): didn't care very much about

carriages (l.60): manner in which they behaved (archaic)

taunting (l.63): making disrespectful remarks to try to hurt their feelings

smite (l.64): strike

---

sold, as houses, lands, trades, places, honours, preferments, titles, countries, kingdoms, lusts, pleasures, and delights of all sorts, as whores, bawds, wives, husbands, children, masters, servants, lives, blood, bodies, souls, silver, gold, pearls, precious stones, and what not. 20

And, moreover, at this fair there is at all times to be seen jugglings, cheats, games, plays, fools, apes, knaves, and rogues, and that of all sorts.

Here are to be seen, too, and that for nothing, thefts, murders, 25 adulteries, false swearers, and that of a blood-red colour.

And as in other fairs of less moment, there are the several rows and streets under their proper names, where such and such wares are vended. So here likewise, you have the proper places, rows, streets (viz. countries and kingdoms), where the wares of this fair are 30 soonest to be found. Here is the Britain Row, the French Row, the Italian Row, the Spanish Row, the German Row, where several sorts of vanities are to be sold. But as in other fairs, some one commodity is as the chief of all the fair, so the ware of Rome and her merchandise is greatly promoted in this fair. Only our English 35 nation, with some others, have taken a dislike thereat.

Now, as I said, the way to the Celestial City lies just through this town, where this lusty fair is kept, and he that will go to the city, and yet not go through this town, must needs go out of the world. ...

Now these pilgrims, as I said, must needs go through this fair. 40 Well, so they did, but behold, even as they entered into the fair, all the people in the fair were moved and the town itself as it were in a hubbub about them, and that for several reasons; for,

First, the pilgrims were clothed with such kind of raiment as was diverse from the raiment of any that traded in that fair. The people 45 therefore of the fair made a great gazing upon them. Some said they were fools, some they were bedlams, and some they are outlandish men.

Secondly, and as they wondered at their apparel, so they did likewise at their speech, for few could understand what they said. 50 They naturally spoke the language of Canaan, but they that kept the fair were the men of this world. So that from one end of the fair to the other, they seemed barbarians each to the other.

Thirdly, but that which did not a little amuse the merchandisers was that these pilgrims set very light by all their wares; they cared 55 not so much as to look upon them, and if they called upon them to buy, they would put their fingers in their ears and cry, 'Turn away mine eyes from beholding vanity,' and look upwards, signifying that their trade and traffic was in heaven.

One chanced mockingly, beholding the carriages of the men, to 60 say unto them, 'What will ye buy?' But they, looking gravely upon him, said, 'We buy the truth.' At that, there was an occasion taken to despise the men the more; some mocking, some taunting, some speaking reproachfully, and some calling upon others to smite

confounded (l.66): destroyed (archaic)
deputed (l.68): gave power to
overturned (l.69): destroyed

them. At last things came to an hubbub, and great stir in the fair, insomuch that all order was confounded. Now was word presently brought to the great one of the fair, who quickly came down and deputed some of his most trusty friends to take these men into examination, about whom the fair was almost overturned. ...

65

(from *The Pilgrim's Progress*)

- i) What picture of Bunyan's times do you get from these extracts?
- ii) Can you find examples of his humour?

Supplement 4

Thomas Sprat (1635–1713)

The Royal Society of London for Improving Natural Knowledge (see also page 65), gained royal patronage in 1662. As it concerned itself with scientific experiments and observations, many of the clergy felt that such work would lead to a neglect of God. In defence, Thomas Sprat, a clergyman, published the Society's 'history' in 1667, in which he defended (among other things) a plain English prose style, and in so doing conceived of language as a utilitarian instrument.

GLOSSARY

solicitous (l.2): careful
the manner of their discourse (l.2): how they express their ideas
keep in due temper (l.3): remain moderate
superfluity (l.5): more than is needed
forbear recanting (l.8): stop myself taking back
bewitching (l.18): too harmful an influence
just (l.19): morally right and proper
look so big (l.21): make ourselves look important

... there is one thing ... about which the Society has been most solicitous, and that is the manner of their discourse; which, unless they had been very watchful to keep in due temper, the whole spirit and vigour of their design had been soon eaten out by the luxury and redundance of speech. The ill effects of this superfluity of talking have already overwhelmed most other arts and professions, insomuch that when I consider the means of happy living and the causes of their corruption, I can hardly forbear recanting what I said before, and concluding that eloquence ought to be banished out of all civil societies as a thing fatal to peace and good manners. ... They [the ornaments of speech] were at first, no doubt, an admirable instrument in the hands of wise men, when they were only employed to describe goodness, honesty, obedience in larger, fairer, and more moving images.... But now they are generally changed to worse ones ... they are in open defiance against reason, professing not to hold much correspondence with that, but with its slaves, the passions; they give the mind a motion too changeable and bewitching to consist with right practice. ... For now I am warmed with this just anger, I cannot withhold myself from betraying the shallowness of all these seeming mysteries upon which we writers and speakers look so big. And, in few words, I dare say that of all the studies of men, nothing may be sooner obtained than this vicious abundance of phrase, this trick of metaphors, this volubility of tongue, which makes so great a noise

1

5

10

15

20

in the world. But I spend words in vain, for the evil is now so 25
inveterate that it is hard to know whom to blame or where to begin
reform. We all value one another so much on this beautiful deceit,
and labour so long after it in the years of our education, that we
cannot but ever after think kinder of it than it deserves. ... It will
suffice my present purpose to point out what has been done by the 30
Royal Society toward the correcting of its excesses [the use of
ornamental language] in natural philosophy, to which it is, of all
others, a most professed enemy.

They have therefore been most rigorous in putting in execution
the only remedy that can be found for this extravagance: and that 35
has been a constant resolution to reject all the amplifications, digressions, and swellings of style, to return back to the primitive
purity and shortness, when men delivered so many things almost
in an equal number of words. They have exacted from all their
members a close, naked, natural way of speaking; positive ex- 40
pressions, clear senses, a native easiness bringing all things as near
the mathematical plainness as they can; and preferring the language
of artisans, countrymen, and merchants before that of wits or
scholars.

(from *History of the Royal Society*)

volubility (l.24):
 talkativeness
inveterate (l.26): deeply
 settled
rigorous (l.34): strict
putting in execution (l.34):
 providing
amplifications/swellings
 (l.36, 37): expansions/
 enlargements
digressions (l.36): not
 sticking to the point
exacted (l.39): required;
 demanded
artisans (l.43): skilled
 workmen
wits (l.43): thinkers with
 superior intellects

● Sprat argues against 'amplifications, digressions, and swellings of style'. How
plainly expressed is his own argument? Illustrate from the text.

The Tatler (1709–1711)
and The Spectator
(1711–1712 and 1714)

The Tatler was a popular periodical
which appeared three times a week,
edited and largely written by
Richard Steele (1672–1729); its
successor *The Spectator* appeared
daily and was edited by Steele and
Joseph Addison (1672–1719). Both
contained influential essays on the
manners and social conduct of the
time, examining, for example, the
ideal of a gentleman. The aim of the
journals was 'to enliven morality
with wit, and to temper wit with
morality'. Or, to express the purpose
in social terms, to bridge the
distance between the narrow
morality of the large Puritan middle
class and the elegant wit and
fashionable enlightenment of the
London aristocracy. Their tone was
moderate and lightly ironic,
alternating smoothly between
lightness and seriousness over a
wide variety of subjects. Steele's

THE   Syn.5.71.5

SPECTATOR.

VOL. I.

LONDON:

Printed for S. *Buckley*, at the *Dolphin* in *Little-*
Britain; and J. *Tonson*, at *Shakespear's-Head*
over-against *Catherine-street* in the *Strand*. 1712.

contributions were often informal, intimate and entertaining – and sometimes sentimental; Addison's were full of keen observation, graceful expression and were written in clear prose. Particularly famous is the account of the daily life and opinions of a country gentleman, Sir Roger de Coverley. The essays represent the beginnings of the novel as practised later by Fielding and Richardson.

Extract 1 Steele describing a gentleman in *The Tatler*, No. 21, Saturday 28 May 1709:

It is generally thought that warmth of imagination, quick relish of pleasure, and a manner of becoming it, are the most essential qualities for forming this sort of man. But anyone that is much in company will observe that the height of good breeding is shown rather in never giving offence, than in doing obliging things. Thus, he that never shocks you, though he is seldom entertaining, is more likely to keep your favour than he who often entertains, and sometimes displeases you. The most necessary talent therefore in a man of conversation, which is what we ordinarily intend by a fine gentleman, is a good judgment. He that has this in perfection is master of his companion, without letting him see it; and has the same advantage over men of any other qualifications whatsoever, as one that can see would have over a blind man of ten times his strength.

Extract 2 Addison in *The Spectator*, No. 69, Saturday 19 May 1711:

There is no place in the town which I so much love to frequent as the Royal Exchange. It gives me a secret satisfaction, and, in some measure, gratifies my vanity, as I am an Englishman, to see so rich an assembly of countrymen and foreigners consulting together upon the private business of mankind, and making this metropolis a kind of emporium for the whole earth. I must confess I look upon high-change to be a great council, in which all considerable nations have their representatives. Factors in the trading world are what ambassadors are in the politic world; they negotiate affairs, conclude treaties, and maintain a good correspondence between those wealthy societies of men that are divided from one another by seas and oceans, or live on the different extremities of a continent. I have often been pleased to hear disputes adjusted between an inhabitant of Japan and an alderman of London, or to see a subject of the Great Mogul entering into a league with one of the Czar of Muscovy. I am infinitely delighted in mixing with these several ministers of commerce, as they are distinguished by their different walks and different languages; sometimes I am justled among a body of Armenians; sometimes I am lost in a crowd of Jews; and

The Royal Exchange in 1804

sometimes make one in a group of Dutchmen. I am a Dane, Swede, or Frenchman at different times; or rather fancy myself like the old philosopher, who upon being asked what countryman he was, replied, that he was a citizen of the world.

This grand scene of business gives me an infinite variety of solid and substantial entertainments. As I am a great lover of mankind, my heart naturally overflows with pleasure at the sight of a prosperous and happy multitude, insomuch that at many public solemnities I cannot forbear expressing my joy with tears that have stolen down my cheeks. For this reason I am wonderfully delighted to see such a body of men thriving in their own private fortunes, and at the same time promoting the public stock; or in other words, raising estates for their own families, by bringing into their country whatever is wanting, and carrying out of it whatever is superfluous.

20

25

30

Extract 3   Addison in *The Spectator*, No. 112, Monday 9 July 1711:

I am always very well pleased with a country Sunday, and think, if keeping holy the seventh day were only a human institution, it would be the best method that could have been thought of for the polishing and civilizing of mankind. It is certain the country people would soon degenerate into a kind of savages and barbarians were there not such frequent returns of a stated time, in which the whole village meet together with their best faces, and in their cleanliest habits, to converse with one another upon indifferent subjects, hear their duties explained to them, and join together in adoration of the Supreme Being. Sunday clears away the rust of the whole week,

1

5

10

359

citizen ... Change (l.15): a
  ciizen of London (a
  merchant) does on the
  Royal Exchange
after sermon ... rings
  (l.16–17): after or before
  the church service

not only as it refreshes in their minds the notions of religion, but as it puts both the sexes upon appearing in their most agreeable forms, and exerting all such qualities are apt to give them a figure in the eye of the village. A country fellow distinguishes himself as much in the churchyard as a citizen does upon the 'Change, the whole parish politics being generally discussed in that place either after sermon or before the bell rings.

15

Extract 4 Steele on a journey through London in *The Spectator*, No. 454, Saturday 11 August 1712:

An eighteenth-century view of the City of London

GLOSSARY
hacks (l.2): common
  horses
were mingled (l.2): came
  together
equipages (l.2): elegant
  horse-drawn carriages
  with servants
ballad-singers (l.5):
  singers of short, simple
  songs in colloquial
  language
detains (l.5): delays
throws ... expense (l.6):
  costs me money
ragged rascal (l.8):
  dishonest person in
  torn clothes

The day of people of fashion began now to break, and carts and hacks were mingled with equipages of show and vanity; when I resolved to walk it out of cheapness; but my unhappy curiosity is such that I find it always my interest to take coach, for some odd adventure among beggars, ballad-singers, or the like, detains and throws me into expense. It happened so immediately; for at the corner of Warwick Street, as I was listening to a new ballad, a ragged rascal, a beggar who knew me, came up to me, and began to turn the eyes of the good company upon me by telling me he was extreme poor, and should die in the streets for want of drink, except I immediately would have the charity to give him sixpence to go into the next alehouse and save his life. He urged, with a melancholy face, that all his family had died of thirst. All the mob have humour, and two or three began to take the jest; by which Mr

1

5

10

Glossary (left column, top):

sixpence (l.11): a sum of money

alehouse (l.12): pub

take the jest (l.14): enjoy the joke

by which ... coach (l.14–15): at which time a strong, worthy man got out his sword and let me get away to a coach

chequered (l.17): full of contrasts

Richmond (l.17): a place west of London, from where Steele started his journey

children of a new hour (l.18): a different kind/age of child

well-disposed (l.19): with a friendly atmosphere

Sturdy carried his point, and let me sneak off to a coach. As I drove along, it was a pleasing reflection to see the world so prettily chequered since I left Richmond, and the scene still filling with children of a new hour. This satisfaction increased as I moved towards the City; and gay signs, well-disposed streets, magnificent public structures, and wealthy shops, adorned with contented faces, made the joy still rising till we came into the centre of the City, and centre of the world of trade, the Exchange of London.

15

20

- i) What impression of the times do you get from these extracts?
- ii) Can you point to examples of satiric irony in the writing?
- iii) Would you have liked to have lived then? Give reasons for your answer.

Samuel Richardson (1689–1761)

Pamela (1740–1741), a novel in epistolary form by Samuel Richardson (see page 108), had, according to the author, the strict moral purpose of showing young ladies how they should behave. It is about a young servant girl isolated from her parents in the power of her employer, Mr B, a country gentleman. Mr B is in love with her and does everything he can to seduce her before finally deciding to marry her. Although she refuses to become a mere object to serve his lusts, Pamela is nevertheless attracted to Mr B. When Mrs Jewkes (a cruel, older servant who 'looks after' Pamela for Mr B) is out on a visit, Pamela thinks she ought to run away. But she fails to act decisively, partly because she is afraid of being seen, partly because she is frightened of something she thinks is a bull (a symbol of sexual aggression) in a neighbouring field, and partly because she doesn't want to escape at all:

GLOSSARY

out ... purposes (l.1–2): into not doing what I intended

ventured (l.9): dared

a grazing (l.11): eating grass

made ... about (l.12): caused all this confusion

Well, here I am, come back again! frightened, like a fool, out of all my purposes! O how terrible every thing appears to me! I had got twice as far again, as I was before, out of the back-door: and I looked and saw the bull, as I thought, between me and the door; and another bull coming towards me the other way: Well, thought I, here is double witchcraft, to be sure! Here is the spirit of my master in one bull, and Mrs Jewkes's in the other. And now I am gone, to be sure! O help! cried I, like a fool, and ran back to the door, as swift as if I flew. When I had got the door in my hand, I ventured to look back, to see if these supposed bulls were coming; and I saw they were only two poor cows, a grazing in distant places, that my fears had made all this rout about. But as every thing is so frightful to me, I find I am not fit to think of my escape: for I shall be as much frightened at the first strange man that I meet with: and I am

1

5

10

persuaded, that fear brings one into more dangers, than the caution, that goes along with it, delivers one from.

I then locked the door, and put the key in my pocket, and was in a sad quandary; but I was soon determined; for the maid Nan came in sight, and asked, if any thing was the matter, that I was so often up and down stairs? God forgive me, (but I had a sad lie at my tongue's end,) said I; Though Mrs Jewkes is sometimes a little hard upon me, yet I know not where I am without her: I go up, and I come down to walk in the garden; and, not having her, know scarcely what to do with myself. Ay, said the idiot, she is main good company, madam, no wonder you miss her.

in a sad quandary (l.17): unfortunately couldn't make up my mind

idiot (l.24): stupid person (Nan)

(from *Pamela*)

- i) How are Pamela's confused and conflicting feelings revealed?
- ii) Does her state of mind strike you as true to life?
- iii) Does Richardson's intended moral purpose (see the introduction) come out in this extract? If so, where?

Thomas Gray (1716–1771)

Thomas Gray was a shy and reserved scholar who lived in Cambridge most of his life. In his slow-moving and wonderfully evocative meditation 'Elegy in a Country Churchyard' (1750) he addresses the powerful ruling class of the day ('ye proud') on the lack of worldly opportunities for the shepherds and the poor country folk. (At that time England was an expanding world power and its society competitive and aggressive.)

Although Gray was in many ways unique, in superficial ways at least he suggests both the Romantic poets of the end of the eighteenth century (see page 140), particularly in his sensitive response to nature and in his exaltation of humble people, and earlier poets such as Milton, particularly in his use of more conventional poetic diction and imagery. At a deeper level, though, he has more in common with the later Augustan poets, who believed that sentiment should be controlled by the classical ideals of order, restraint, correctness and clarity.

The elegy (an elegy is a poetic lament for the dead) combines images of the rural scene with moral content, and details of everyday life with elevated generalisations. It was an immediate success and is now one of the most quoted poems in English.

This is the well-known part, the first two-thirds:

The curfew tolls the knell of parting day,
  The lowing herd wind slowly o'er the lea,
The plowman homeward plods his weary way,
  And leaves the world to darkness and to me.

Now fades the glimmering landscape on the sight,
  And all the air a solemn stillness holds,
Save where the beetle wheels his droning flight,
  And drowsy tinklings lull the distant folds;

Save that from yonder ivy-mantled tower
   The moping owl does to the moon complain   10
Of such, as wandering near her secret bower,
   Molest her ancient solitary reign.

Beneath those rugged elms, that yew tree's shade,
   Where heaves the turf in many a moldering heap,
Each in his narrow cell forever laid,   15
   The rude forefathers of the hamlet sleep.

The breezy call of incense-breathing Morn,
   The swallow twittering from the straw-built shed,
The cock's shrill clarion, or the echoing horn,
   No more shall rouse them from their lowly bed.   20

For them no more the blazing hearth shall burn,
   Or busy housewife ply her evening care;
No children run to lisp their sire's return,
   Or climb his knees the envied kiss to share.

Oft did the harvest to their sickle yield,   25
   Their furrow oft the stubborn glebe has broke;
How jocund did they drive their team afield!
   How bowed the woods beneath their sturdy stroke!

Let not Ambition mock their useful toil,
   Their homely joys, and destiny obscure;   30
Nor Grandeur hear with a disdainful smile
   The short and simple annals of the poor.

The boast of heraldry, the pomp of power,
   And all that beauty, all that wealth e'er gave,
Awaits alike the inevitable hour.   35
   The paths of glory lead but to the grave.

Nor you, ye proud, impute to these the fault,
   If Memory o'er their tomb no trophies raise,
Where through the long-drawn aisle and fretted vault
   The pealing anthem swells the note of praise.   40

Can storied urn or animated bust
   Back to its mansion call the fleeting breath?
Can Honor's voice provoke the silent dust,
   Or Flattery soothe the dull cold ear of Death?

Perhaps in this neglected spot is laid   45
   Some heart once pregnant with celestial fire;
Hands that the rod of empire might have swayed,
   Or waked to ecstasy the living lyre.

But Knowledge to their eyes her ample page
   Rich with the spoils of time did ne'er unroll;
Chill Penury repressed their noble rage,
   And froze the genial current of the soul.

Full many a gem of purest ray serene,
   The dark unfathomed caves of ocean bear:
Full many a flower is born to blush unseen,
   And waste its sweetness on the desert air.

Some village Hampden, that with dauntless breast
   The little tyrant of his fields withstood;
Some mute inglorious Milton here may rest,
   Some Cromwell guiltless of his country's blood.

The applause of listening senates to command,
   The threats of pain and ruin to despise,
To scatter plenty o'er a smiling land,
   And read their history in a nation's eyes.

Their lot forbade: nor circumscribed alone
   Their growing virtues, but their crimes confined;
Forbade to wade through slaughter to a throne.
   And shut the gates of mercy on mankind.

The struggling pangs of conscious truth to hide,
   To quench the blushes of ingenuous shame,
Or heap the shrine of Luxury and Pride
   With incense kindled at the Muse's flame.

Far from the madding crowd's ignoble strife,
   Their sober wishes never learned to stray;
Along the cool sequestered vale of life
   They kept the noiseless tenor of their way.

Yet even these bones from insult to protect
   Some frail memorial still erected nigh,
With uncouth rhymes and shapeless sculpture decked,
   Implores the passing tribute of a sigh.

Their name, their years, spelt by the unlettered Muse,
   The place of fame and elegy supply;
And many a holy text around she strews,
   That teach the rustic moralist to die.

(from *Elegy in a Country Churchyard*)

curfew . . . knell of (l.1): the sound of the bell signals the (suggesting death)

lowing . . . lea (l.2): mooing cows wander slowly across the fields

plods (l.3): walks heavily

glimmering (l.5): weakly shining

Save (l.7)): except

wheels . . . flight (l.7): flies in circles buzzing

drowsy . . . folds (l.8): light sounds of bells calm the sheep in faraway enclosures

ivy-mantled (l.9): covered in ivy

moping (l.10): sad

bower (l.11): shelter

Molest (l.12): disturb

rugged (l.13): rough

elms (l.13): large, tall tree

yew trees (l.13): evergreen tree often found in churchyards

heaves . . . heap (l.14): grass rises in crumbling piles over the graves)

cell (l.15): grave

rude forefathers (l.16): humble ancestors

hamlet (l.16): small village

breezy . . . Morn (l.17): lively smells on light morning winds

twittering (l.18): making its high, irregular sound

shrill clarion (l.19): piercing early-morning call

echoing horn (l.19): (of the hunters)

lowly (l.20): humble

ply . . . care (l.22): look after them in the evening

lisp . . . return (l.23): announce in an unsteady voice their father's return

Oft . . . yield (l.25): they often cut the corn

Their . . . broke (l.26): they have often ploughed difficult fields

jocund . . . afield (l.27): joyfully they drove their horses across the field

homely (l.30): simple

annals (l.32): year-by-year records

boast of heraldry (l.33): pride of being born noble

pomp (l.33): rich display

impute (l.37): blame

Memory . . . raise (l.38): no one has put a carved memorial over their tomb

Where . . . anthem (l.39–40): where through the long

church aisles and decorated arches the ringing hymn (the 'proud', unlike the poor, are often buried in the church and have a tomb with a plaque over it)

storied (l.41): with an epitaph/a story on it

animated (l.41): lifelike

Back . . . breath (l.42): bring back life

provoke (l.43): arouse

pregnant . . . fire (l.46): full of divine inspiration

rod . . . swayed (l.47): might have influenced the empire

waked . . . lyre (l.48): written wonderful poetry (lyre: Ancient Greek harp to accompany songs)

ample (l.49): large

spoils (l.50): everything that has been learnt

Chill . . . rage (l.51): their noble and vigorous feelings were cooled by poverty

genial current (l.52): creative energies

serene (l.53): clear and bright

Hampden (l.57): John Hampden, 1594–1643, an MP who defended the rights of the people against Charles I

with dauntless breast (l.57): without fear

mute (l.59): who never wrote anything

senates (l.61): governing councils

nor . . . alone (l.65): not only restricted

wade . . . slaughter (l.67): get by killing people

The . . . hide (l.69): to hide the 'attacks' of truth that fight their way into the mind

quench (l.70): put an end to

ingenuous (l.70): natural

Muse (l.72): goddess (of greed?)

Far . . . strife (l.73): a long way from the shameful conflict of the excited crowd

sequestered vale (l.75): secluded valley

noiseless . . . way (l.76): quiet course

frail memorial (l.78): simple tombstone (in contrast with the monumental tombs in the church)

nigh (l.78): near (*poetic*)

uncouth (l.79): awkward

decked (l.79): decorated

Implores (l.80): demands

unlettered (l.81): uneducated

strews (l.83): scatters

rustic (l.84): country

Stoke Poges church

i) Do you find the poem impressive? Give reasons for your answer.

ii) What is Gray's attitude to power and the 'proud'? How do you know?

iii) Match groups of stanzas with the following headings: 'The Churchyard Scene'; 'Death Comes Even to the Rich and Powerful'; 'Unfulfilled Ambition'; 'Memorials for the Poor'.

Early American literature

American literature began with Englishmen describing the colonisation of the New World at the end of the sixteenth century. For the next one hundred and fifty years or so the most notable literature – mainly histories and poetry – came from the Puritan settlers in New England (along the Atlantic coast) who felt they had arrived in the 'Promised Land' of the Bible.

In the eighteenth century, the most memorable literature was the mainly political prose written by the Founding Fathers, the men who led the revolution of 1775–1783 against Britain and who wrote the Constitution of 1789. These men were still essentially European in the sense that they shared many of the philosophic, scientific and rationalistic beliefs common to the 'Age of Reason'. Their aim was to produce in America a just and free society. Man's nature, which they believed was essentially good, should be guided by reason and there should be greater religious tolerance than there had been with their Puritan forefathers.

Benjamin Franklin
(1706–1790)

When he was only twenty-two and on his way to becoming a prosperous printer of books and newspapers, Benjamin Franklin wrote *Poor Richard's*

Benjamin Franklin conducting electrical experiments with a kite in a thunderstorm

Almanac, a mixture of practical information, aphorisms (short, witty sayings), proverbs (short sayings, containing advice) and guidelines on how to lead a useful and virtuous life.

Believing that man should serve God by doing good, Franklin initiated many practical social projects (such as the establishment of a police force, the lighting of city streets and the founding of a hospital) and conducted what became well-known scientific experiments. Later he helped draft the *Declaration of Independence* (see page 369).

In his *Autobiography* (begun in 1771), Franklin's style, detailed, 'plain' and unspiritual, is in some ways reminiscent of Defoe.

Here he describes his arrival in Philadelphia as a young man:

Philadelphia

I have been the more particular in this description of my journey, and shall be so of my first entry into that city, that you may in your mind compare such unlikely beginnings with the figure I have since made there. I was in my working dress, my best clothes being to come round by sea. I was dirty from my journey; my pockets were stuffed out with shirts and stockings, and I knew no soul, nor where to look for lodging. I was fatigued with travelling, rowing, and want of rest, I was very hungry; and my whole stock of cash consisted of a Dutch dollar, and about a shilling in copper. The latter I gave the people of the boat for my passage, who first refused it, on account of my rowing; but I insisted on their taking it. A man being sometimes more generous when he has little money than when he has plenty, perhaps through fear of being thought to have but little.

Then I walked up the street, gazing about till near the market- 15
house I met a boy with bread. I had made many a meal on bread,
and, inquiring where he got it, I went immediately to the baker's
he directed me to in Second Street, and asked for biscuits, intending such as we had in Boston; they, it seems, were not made in
Philadelphia. I then asked for a threepenny loaf, and was told they 20
had none such. So not considering or knowing the difference of
money and the great cheapness nor the names of his bread, I bad
him give me threepenny-worth of any sort. He gave me, accordingly,
three great puffy rolls. I was surprised at the quantity, but took it,
and, having no room in my pockets, walked off with a roll under 25
each arm, and eating the other. Thus I went up Market Street as far
as Fourth Street, passing by the door of Mr Read, my future wife's
father; when she, standing at the door, saw me, and thought I made,
as I certainly did, a most awkward, ridiculous appearance. Then I
turned, and went down Chestnut Street and part of Walnut Street, 30
eating my roll all the way; and, coming round, found myself again
at Market Street wharf, near the boat I came in, to which I went for
a draught of the river water; and, being filled with one of my rolls,
gave the other two to a woman and her child that came down the
river in the boat with us, and were waiting to go farther. 35

Thus refreshed, I walked again up the street, which, by this time,
had many clean-dressed people in it, who were all walking the
same way. I joined them, and thereby was led into the great meeting-
house of the Quakers, near the market. I sat down among them,
and after looking round a while, and hearing nothing said, being 40
very drowsy through labour and want of rest the preceding night, I
fell fast asleep, and continued so till the meeting broke up, when
some one was kind enough to rouse me. This was, therefore, the
first house I was in, or slept in, in Philadelphia.

● Do you think Franklin has an excessive sense of his own importance? How would
you describe his manner?

In his *Studies in Classic American Literature* (1923), D.H. Lawrence mocked
the Franklin who was fond of moralising. This is an extract.

It seems to me just funny, professors and Benjamins fixing the 1
functions of the soul. Why, the soul of man is a vast forest, and all
Benjamin intended was a neat back garden. And we've all got to fit
into his kitchen garden scheme of things. Hail Columbia!

Who knows what will come out of the soul of man? The soul of 5
man is a dark vast forest, with wild life in it. Think of Benjamin
fencing it off!

Oh, but Benjamin fenced a little tract that he called the soul of
man, and proceeded to get it into cultivation. Providence forsooth!
And they think that bit of barbed wire is going to keep us in pound 10

for ever? More fools they.

This is Benjamin's barbed wire fence. He made himself a list of virtues, which he trotted inside like a grey nag in a paddock.

1
TEMPERANCE
Eat not to fulness; drink not to elevation.

15

2
SILENCE
Speak not but what may benefit others or yourself; avoid trifling conversation.

20

3
ORDER
Let all your things have their places; let each part of your business have its time.

4
RESOLUTION
Resolve to perform what you ought; perform without fail what you resolve.

25

5
FRUGALITY
Make no expense but to do good to others or yourself – i.e., waste nothing.

30

(from *Studies in Classic American Literature*)

GLOSSARY
Hail Columbia! (l.4): I salute you America!
tract (l.8): stretch of land
Providence forsooth! (l.9): divine guidance indeed!
barbed wire (l.10): wire with short, sharp points used for fences
in pound (l.10): confined
More fools they (l.11): they are foolish for thinking so
nag ... paddock (l.13): old horse in a small, enclosed field
Temperance (l.15): moderation
to elevation (l.16): until you are drunk
trifling (l.19): unimportant
Frugality (l.30): not being wasteful

● Do you have any sympathy with Lawrence's point of view?

The *Declaration of Independence* (signed 1776)

Perhaps the greatest writers of the period were Thomas Paine (1737–1809), an Englishman who went to America in 1774 and whose pamphlet *Common Sense* (1776) quickly set the colonists openly on the road to independence, and Thomas Jefferson (1743–1826), the chief author of the *Declaration of Independence* and later the third President of the United States. This is the opening of the *Declaration*:

GLOSSARY
station (l.4): position in society
entitle them (l.5): give them a right to
impel (l.6): force

When in the Course of Human Events it becomes necessary for one people to dissolve the political bands which have connected them with another, and to assume among the Powers of the earth, the separate and equal station to which the Laws of Nature and of Nature's God entitle them, a decent respect to the opinions of mankind requires that they should declare the causes which impel them to separation.

1

5

We hold these truths to be self-evident, that all men are created equal, that they are endowed by their Creator with certain unalienable Rights, that among these are Life, Liberty and the pursuit of Happiness.

That to secure these rights, Governments are instituted among Men, deriving their just powers from the consent of the governed, That whenever any Form of Government becomes destructive of these ends, it is the Right of the People to alter or to abolish it, and to institute a new Government, laying its foundation on such principles, and organizing its powers in such form, as to them shall seem most likely to effect their Safety and Happiness.

(from *The Declaration of Independence*)

10

15

hold (l.8): believe
self-evident (l.8): obvious
endowed (l.9): given at birth
unalienable (l.9): which cannot be taken away
instituted (l.12): established
deriving (l.13): obtaining
just (l.13): rightful
effect (l.18): bring about

● i) In no more than fifteen words, paraphrase the first sentence.
ii) Why, according to the second and third paragraphs, did the colonists feel independence to be so necessary?
iii) Is the style of the *Declaration* cool and logical or passionate and angry?

The Declaration of Independence, *1776*

Michael Siberry as Charles Surface in A School for Scandal, 1982

Richard Brinsley Sheridan (1751–1816)

Like most dramatists of note writing in English during the eighteenth and nineteenth centuries, Richard Brinsley Sheridan was of Irish extraction. *The School for Scandal* (1777) shows a revival of the 'Comedy of Manners' which had been dominant at the beginning of the century. Many of Sheridan's characters love scandal and gossip so much that they 'strike a character dead at every word'! In the following scene Charles Surface, a good-natured man who spends money without thinking, reveals his love for Maria:

CHARLES S: 'Fore Heaven, 'tis true! – there's the great degeneracy of the age. Many of our acquaintance have taste, spirit, and politeness; but, plague on't, they won't drink.

CARELESS: It is so indeed, Charles! they give in to all the substantial luxuries of the table, and abstain from nothing but wine and wit. Oh, certainly society suffers by it intolerably; for now, instead of the social spirit of raillery that used to mantle over a glass of bright Burgundy, their conversation is become just like the Spa water they drink, which has all the pertness and flatulence of Champaigne, without the spirit or flavour.

FIRST GENT: But what are they to do who love play better than wine?

CARELESS: True: there's Sir Harry diets himself for gaming, and is now under a hazard regimen.

CHARLES S: Then he'll have the worst of it. What! you wouldn't train a horse for the course by keeping him from corn? For my part, egad, I am never so successful as when I am a little merry: let me

1

5

10

15

gaming (l.13): gambling

under ... regimen (l.14): on a dangerous diet ('hazard' means 'dangerous' and is also the name of a game of chance played with dice)

egad (l.17): (a mild oath like 'my God')

throw ... Champaigne (l.18): throw the dice after I have drunk a bottle of champagne

abjurer (l.22): someone who has given up

Fill ... you (l.23–24): fill twelve glasses to the top with wine each one for a beautiful woman – and the woman you remember after you have drunk them all is the woman who has most charmed you

toast (l.28): raise my glass and drink

round of her peers (l.28): round of toasts to her equals

canonized vestals (l.30): saints, priestesses

heathen (l.30): not Christian

I warrant (l.31): I'm sure

rogues (l.32): wicked men (*playful use*)

Love's calendar (l.36): a list of the people one loves

superlative (l.37): which is greater than all others

though ... eye (l.39): even if your mistress has only got one eye

a song ... you (l.40): a song which will make us forgive you

Here's to (l.44): good health to

bashful (l.44): shy

flaunting (1.46): who parades herself

thrifty (l.47): careful with her money

lass (l.50): girl

dimples (l.52): small hollows in the cheeks (signs of beauty)

nymph (l.55): beautiful young woman

woe (l.59): unhappiness

throw on a bottle of Champaigne, and I never lose – at least, I never feel my losses, which is exactly the same thing.

SEC. GENT: Aye, that I believe.

CHARLES S: And then, what man can pretend to be a believer in love, who is an abjurer of wine? 'Tis the test by which the lover knows his own heart. Fill a dozen bumpers to a dozen beauties, and she that floats atop is the maid that has bewitched you.

CARELESS: Now then, Charles, be honest, and give us your real favourite.

CHARLES S: Why, I have withheld her only in compassion to you. If I toast her, you must give a round of her peers, which is impossible – on earth.

CARELESS: Oh! then we'll find some canonized vestals or heathen goddesses that will do, I warrant!

CHARLES S: Here then, bumpers, you rogues! bumpers! Maria! Maria –

SIR HARRY BUMPER: Maria who?

CHARLES S: Oh, damn the surname – 'tis too formal to be registered in Love's calendar; but now, Sir Harry, beware, we must have beauty superlative.

CARELESS: Nay, never study, Sir Harry, we'll stand to the toast, though your mistress should want an eye, and you know you have a song will excuse you.

SIR HARRY B: Egad, so I have! and I'll give him the song instead of the lady.

SONG:

Here's to the maiden of bashful fifteen;
    Here's to the widow of fifty;
Here's to the flaunting extravagant queen,
    And here's to the housewife that's thrifty.

Chorus:

    Let the toast pass, –
    Drink to the lass,
I'll warrant she'll prove an excuse for the glass.

Here's to the charmer whose dimples we prize;
    Now to the maid who has none, sir:
Here's to the girl with a pair of blue eyes,
    And here's to the nymph with but *one*, sir:
    Chorus: Let the toast pass, etc.

Here's to the maid with a bosom of snow;
Now to her that's as brown as a berry
Here's to the wife with a face full of woe,
    And now to the girl that is merry.
    Chorus: Let the toast pass, etc.

20

25

30

35

40

45

50

55

60

For let 'em be clumsy, or let 'em be slim,
    Young or ancient, I care not a feather;
So fill a pint bumper quite up to the brim,
    And let us e'en toast them together.   65
        Chorus: Let the toast pass, etc.
    ALL: **Bravo! bravo!**

clumsy (l.62): awkward in movement
brim (l.64): top

(from *The School for Scandal*)

● i) What has this extract got in common with *Love for Love*, written 82 years earlier (see page 118)?

ii) Is the humour respectful or disrespectful to women?

Dr Samuel Johnson (1709–1784)

Dr Samuel Johnson was the most eminent literary figure of the later Augustan age and a devout Anglican. His works include poems (for example, 'London', 1738), a tragic play (*Irene*, 1736), critical biography (such as the *Lives of the Poets*, 1779–1781) and an edition of Shakespeare (1765) which became a model for later editions. He also wrote essays (for example, for *The Rambler*, a periodical almost entirely written by Johnson, 1750–1752), a philosophical romance (*Rasselas*, 1759), a travel book (*The Journey to the Western Islands of Scotland*, 1775) and his *Dictionary of the English Language* (1755), the first great work of its kind in English. For many, though, Johnson is remembered as a brilliant conversationalist and the eccentric hero of the most noted biography in English the *Life of Johnson* (1791) by his friend, James Boswell (1740–1795).

The son of a country bookseller, Johnson began his life in poverty and with many physical disadvantages, including poor eyesight and a tendency to severe depression. Yet by the age of fifty he had achieved a great reputation by the force of his intellect, the depth of his moral feeling, and by the weightiness of his generalising style, which gave the impression of a confident and independent (if sometimes rather conservative and metropolitan) voice, expressing what was best and strongest in the civilisation of the time.

Here are some of his views on some of the writers in this book:

Shakespeare:

GLOSSARY

transient (l.6): lasting only a short time
progeny (l.7): children

Shakespeare is, above all writers, at least above all modern writers,   1
the poet of nature; the poet that holds up to his readers a faithful
mirror of manners and of life. His characters are not modified by
the customs of particular places, unpractised by the rest of the
world; by the peculiarities of studies or professions, which can   5
operate but upon small numbers; or by the accidents of transient
fashions or temporary opinions: they are the genuine progeny of
common humanity, such as the world will always supply, and
observation will always find. His persons act and speak by the
influence of those general passions and principles by which all   10

minds are agitated, and the whole system of life is continued in motion. In the writings of other poets a character is too often an individual: in those of Shakespeare it is commonly a species.

(from *The Preface to Shakespeare*)

Milton:

The appearances of nature and the occurrences of life did not satiate his appetite of greatness. To paint things as they are requires a minute attention, and employs the memory rather than the fancy. Milton's delight was to sport in the wide regions of possibility; reality was a scene too narrow for his mind. He sent his faculties out upon discovery, into worlds where only imagination can travel, and delighted to form new modes of existence, and furnish sentiment and action to superior beings, to trace the counsels of hell, or accompany the choirs of heaven.

(from *The Lives of the English Poets*)

Congreve:

Congreve has merit of the highest kind: he is an original writer, who borrowed neither the models of his plot nor the manner of his dialogue. Of his plays I cannot speak distinctly, for since I inspected them many years have passed; but what remains upon my memory is that his characters are commonly fictitious and artificial, with very little of nature, and not much of life. He formed a peculiar idea of comic excellence, which he supposed to consist in gay remarks and unexpected answers; but that which he endeavoured, he seldom failed of performing. His scenes exhibit not much of humour, imagery, or passion; his personages are a kind of intellectual gladiators; every sentence is to ward or strike; the contest of smartness is never intermitted; his wit is a meteor playing to and fro with alternate coruscations. His comedies have therefore, in some degree, the operation of tragedies: they surprise rather than divert, and raise admiration oftener than merriment. But they are the works of a mind replete with images, and quick in combination.

(from *The Lives of the English Poets*)

Addison:

GLOSSARY

grave (l.1): serious

groveling (l.2): too low

scrupulosity (l.2): trying to be too concerned with detail

elaboration (l.3): excessive complexity

equable (l.3): calm

pointed (l.4): excessively sharp

snatch a grace (l.5): display some stylistic ornament

hazardous innovations (l.6): risky new inventions

luminous (l.7): full of light

His prose is the model of the middle style; on grave subjects not formal, on light occasions not groveling; pure without scrupulosity, and exact without apparent elaboration; always equable, and always easy, without glowing words or pointed sentences. Addison never deviates from his track to snatch a grace; he seeks no ambitious ornaments, and tries no hazardous innovations. His page is always luminous, but never blazes in unexpected splendour.

(from *The Lives of the English Poets*)

Gray:

GLOSSARY

character (l.1): essential nature

concur (l.1): agree

refinements of subtilty (l.3): clever delicacy (of scholarship)

dogmatism (l.3): fixed beliefs

abounds with (l.5): is full of

had been vain (l.10): would have been foolish (archaic)

In the character of his *Elegy* I rejoice to concur with the common reader; for by the common sense of readers uncorrupted with literary prejudices, after all the refinements of subtilty and the dogmatism of learning, must be finally decided all claim to poetical honours. The *Churchyard* abounds with images which find a mirror in every mind, and with sentiments to which every bosom returns an echo. The four stanzas beginning 'Yet even these bones' are to me original: I have never seen the notions in any other place; yet he that reads them here persuades himself that he has always felt them. Had Gray written often thus it had been vain to blame, and useless to praise him.

(from *The Lives of the English Poets*)

● i) Do you disagree with any of these judgements?
ii) How would you describe Johnson's tone of voice?

Robert Burns (1759–1796) Robert Burns wrote most of his liveliest and most spontaneous verse in Lowland Scots. A comic poet, with a keen but compassionate eye for human follies and vices, Burns wrote about the lives of the poor and the uneducated. This poem, written in the last year of his life, is a fine example of his good humour and his ability to express thoughts which are both serious and funny in a colloquial style. Notice how flat and awkward the prose 'translation' below sounds by comparison:

Poem on Life
Addressed to Colonel de Peyster, Dumfries, 1796

My honour'd Colonel, deep I feel   1
Your interest in the Poet's weal;
Ah! now sma' heart hae I to speel
      The steep Parnassus,
Surrounded thus by bolus pill,   5
      And potion glasses.

O what a canty warld were it,
Would pain, and care, and sickness spare it;
And fortune favour worth and merit,
      As they deserve: 10
(And aye a rowth, roast beef and claret:
      Syne wha wad starve?)

Dame Life, tho' fiction out may trick her,
And in paste gems and fripp'ry deck her,
Oh! flick'ring, feeble and unsicker   15
      I've found her still,
Aye wav'ring like the willow wicker,
'Tween good and ill.

Then that curst carmagnole, auld Satan,
Watches, like baudrons by a rattan,   20
Our sinfu' saul to get a claut on
      Wi' felon ire;
Syne, whip! his tail ye'll ne'er cast saut on,
      He's off like fire.

Ah Nick! ah Nick! it isna fair,   25
First shewing us the tempting ware,
Bright wines and bonie lasses rare,
      To put us daft;
Syne weave, unseen, thy spider snare
      O' hell's damn'd waft.   30

Poor man, the flie, aft bizzies by,
And aft as chance he comes thee nigh,
Thy auld damn'd elbow yeuks wi'joy,
      And hellish pleasure;
Already in thy fancy's eye,   35
      Thy sicker treasure.

Soon heels-o'er-gowdie! in he gangs,
And like a sheep-head on a tangs,
Thy girning laugh enjoys his pangs
      And murd'ring wrestle,
As, dangling in the wind, he hangs   40
      A gibbet's tassel.

But lest you think I am uncivil,
To plague you with this draunting drivel,
Abjuring a' intentions evil,   45
       I quat my pen:
The Lord preserve us frae the Devil!
       Amen! amen!

My honoured Colonel, I feel deeply your interest in the poet's wel-   1
fare. Ah! now feeble heart I have to climb the steep mountain
Parnassus [the mountain in Greece sacred to Apollo, the God of
poetry] surrounded by a large pill and glasses of medicine.

Oh! what a jolly world it would be if there were no pain, un-   5
happiness and sickness and those worthy of good fortune actually
received it (and who would starve if there were always an abundance of roast beef and claret?)

Though one can deceive Life by making up stories and decorating
her with false jewellery and cheap ornaments, I've always found   10
her unsteady, weak and unsure, wavering like a small willow tree
between good and evil.

Then that bad-tempered rebel, old Satan, is on the lookout, like a
cat next to a rat, so that he can make a grab at our sinful soul with
cruel anger. Then he's off like fire so that you'll never be able to   15
put salt on his tail.

Oh, Nick! Oh, Nick! [you devil] it isn't fair. First you show us
tempting goods, such as rare clear wines and beautiful girls, to
make us mad, then you weave your spider's trap of hell's damned
web.   20

A fly, a poor man, often buzzes by and often by chance comes near
to you so that your old damned elbow itches with joy and hellish
pleasure. Already you imagine you have secured your treasure.

Soon head over heels and in he goes. He is like a sheep's head between tongs and your grinning laugh takes pleasure in his pain and   25
the struggle he makes as he is murdered. He hangs dangling from
the gallows in the wind.

But in case you think I am impolite to bother you with this long-
drawn-out rubbish saying I'm going to give up all evil intentions I
leave my pen. The Lord preserve us from the devil. Amen! Amen!   30

- i) In which stanzas does Burn address the Colonel and which the devil?
  ii) How would you describe the mood of the poem? Defiant? Light-hearted?

377

Supplement 5

The Little Boy found

The little boy lost in the lonely fen.
Led by the wand'ring light.
Began to cry, but God ever nigh.
Appeard like his father in white.

He kissed the child & by the hand led
And to his mother brought.
Who in sorrow pale, thro' the lonely dale
Her little boy weeping sought.

**William Blake
(1757–1827)**

The *Songs of Innocence* (1789) (see also page 128) can be represented as expressing the innocent hopes generated by the French Revolution and the *Songs of Experience* (1794) as expressing the disillusionment which set in as France suffered a reign of terror (1793–1794) under Robespierre.

> The viewpoint in *Innocence* insists on the qualities in human nature that are the source of love – compassion and sympathy – and expresses the reaching out to life of the child, confident in the protective devotion of loving parents. *Experience* shows the ruthlessness in nature and injustice in society, expounds the subtle contrivances of human selfishness, and expresses the inevitability of suffering. (Christopher Gillie *Longman Companion to English Literature*, 1972)

In the following two poems from *Innocence* the child represents the human spirit lost in the 'mire' of the material world and seeking God, the Father.

The Little Boy Lost

'Father! father! where are you going?   1
'O do not walk so fast.
'Speak, father, speak to your little boy,
'Or else I shall be lost.'

The night was dark, no father was there;   5
The child was wet with dew;
The mire was deep, and the child did weep,
And away the vapour flew.

GLOSSARY
mire (l.7): marshy land
vapour (l.8): the vision of
    the 'Father'

378

The Little Boy Found

The little boy lost in the lonely fen,   1
Led by the wand'ring light,
Began to cry; but God, ever nigh,
Appear'd like his father in white.

He kissed the child and by the hand led   5
And to his mother brought,
Who in sorrow pale, thro' the lonely dale,
Her little boy weeping sought.

fen (l.1): low wet land
nigh (l.3): near
dale (l.7): valley

In this poem from *Experience* Blake says that a new church has brought a
life-denying morality to a place of innocent happiness.

The Garden of Love

I went to the Garden of Love,   1
And saw what I never had seen:
A Chapel was built in the midst,
Where I used to play on the green.

And the gates of this Chapel were shut,   5
And 'Thou shalt not' writ over the door;
So I turn'd to the Garden of Love
That so many sweet flowers bore;

And I saw it was filled with graves,
And tomb-stones where flowers should be;   10
And Priests in black gowns were walking their rounds,
And binding with briars my joys and desires.

GLOSSARY

midst (l.3): middle

'Thou shalt not' (l.6): the formulation used for the Ten Commandments in the Bible

writ (l.6): written

briars (l.12): tough stems with thorns on them

● How do the themes of the poems complement each other?

William Wordsworth (1770–1850) In 1798, Wordsworth (see also page 140) returned to the Wye valley and the ruins of Tintern Abbey in Monmouthshire which he had first visited on a walking tour in 1793. In the first part of the poem 'Lines Composed a Few Miles Above Tintern Abbey' (much of which he composed in his head while returning by boat to Bristol), he describes himself back in the natural beauty of that scene. Then he reflects:

<pre>
                          These beauteous forms,   1
              Through a long absence, have not been to me
              As is a landscape to a blind man's eye;
              But oft, in lonely rooms, and 'mid the din
              Of towns and cities, I have owed to them,   5
              In hours of weariness, sensations sweet,
              Felt in the blood, and felt along the heart;
              And passing even into my purer mind,
              With tranquil restoration – feelings too
              Of unremembered pleasure; such, perhaps,   10
              As have no slight or trivial influence
              On that best portion of a good man's life,
              His little, nameless, unremembered, acts
              Of kindness and of love. Nor less, I trust,
              To them I may have owed another gift,   15
              Of aspect more sublime; that blessed mood,
              In which the burthen of the mystery,
              In which the heavy and the weary weight
              Of all this unintelligible world,
              Is lightened – that serene and blessed mood,   20
              In which the affections gently lead us on –
              Until, the breath of this corporeal frame
              And even the motion of our human blood
              Almost suspended, we are laid asleep
              In body, and become a living soul;   25
              While with an eye made quiet by the power
              Of harmony, and the deep power of joy,
              We see into the life of things.
                                          If this
              Be but a vain belief, yet, oh! how oft –   30
              In darkness and amid the many shapes
              Of joyless daylight: when the fretful stir
              Unprofitable, and the fever of the world
              Have hung upon the beatings of my heart –
              How oft, in spirit, have I turned to thee,   35
              O sylvan Wye! thou wanderer through the woods,
              How often has my spirit turned to thee!
</pre>

(from Lines Composed a Few Miles Above
Tintern Abbey)

GLOSSARY

beauteous forms (l.1):
  beautiful images

oft (l.4): often

'mid the din (l.4): in the
  middle of the noise

restoration (l.9): return
  (to health and strength)

of aspect more sublime (l.16):
  which is more noble

burthen (l.17): burden,
  heavy load

serene (l.20): calm;
  untroubled

corporeal frame (l.22):
  human body

suspended (l.24): come to
  a stop

fretful stir (l.32): worried
  movement

sylvan (l.36): wooded

- i) Notice how the rhythms of 'the burthen … world' (1.17–19) are made less
     heavy with the word 'lightened' (1.20).
  ii) Which phrases in the poem describe the contemporary world?

  In the last part of the poem Wordsworth describes the three stages of his
  growing up in terms of his evolving relationship with the natural world.

The Wye Valley

In the following sonnet (1807), Wordsworth complains that in the contemporary world we have lost our imaginative connection with nature.

'The world is too much with us'

GLOSSARY

sordid boon (l.4): unpleasant and shameful act of giving

Pagan . . . outworn (l.10): pre-Christian primitive man brought up on a belief which no longer exists

lea (l.11): open grassland

Proteus (l.13): a sea-god of ancient Greece

Triton (l.14): a Greek sea-god who calmed the waters by blowing on a spiral shell

wreathed (l.14): with a coiled structure

The world is too much with us; late and soon,   1
Getting and spending, we lay waste our powers;
Little we see in Nature that is ours;
We have given our hearts away, a sordid boon!
This Sea that bares her bosom to the moon,   5
The winds that will be howling at all hours,
And are up-gathered now like sleeping flowers,
For this, for everything, we are out of tune;
It moves us not. – Great God! I'd rather be
A Pagan suckled in a creed outworn;   10
So might I, standing on this pleasant lea,
Have glimpses that would make me less forlorn;
Have sight of Proteus rising from the sea;
Or hear old Triton blow his wreathed horn.

● What does this poem have in common with the extract from 'Tintern Abbey'?

381

Dorothy Wordsworth (1771–1855)

Dorothy Wordsworth lived with her brother from 1795 until his death. In their walks, Coleridge referred to them as 'three persons with one soul'. She kept several journals which were not published until after her death.

Friday May 14th 1802. **A very cold morning – hail and snow showers all day. We went to Brothers wood, intending to get plants and to go along the shore of the lake to the foot. We did go a part of the way, but there was no pleasure in stepping along that difficult sauntering Road in this ungenial weather. We turned again and walked backwards and forwards in Brothers wood. William teased himself with seeking an epithet for the Cuckoo. I sat a while upon my last summer's seat the mossy stone – William's unemployed beside me, and the space between where Coleridge has so often lain. The oak trees are just putting forth yellow knots of leaves. The ashes with their flowers passing away and leaves coming out ... After dinner I worked bread then came and mended stockings beside William. He fell asleep. After tea I walked to Rydale for Letters. It was a strange night. The hills were covered over with a slight covering of hail or snow, just so as to give them a hoary winter look with the black Rocks underneath. The woods looked miserable, the coppices green as grass which looked quite unnatural and they seemed half shrivelled up as if they shrunk from the air. O thought I! what a beautiful thing God has made winter to be by stripping the trees and letting us see their shapes and forms. What a freedom does it seem to give to the storms!**

1

5

10

15

20

(from *The Grasmere Journals*)

● What impression do you get of Dorothy?

Samuel Taylor Coleridge (1772–1834)

'Kubla Khan' (1797) came to Coleridge as he lay asleep after reading an old book of travels. He was interrupted after 54 lines, and the poem was never completed:

Kubla Khan

In Xanadu did Kubla Khan
A stately pleasure-dome decree:
Where Alph, the sacred river, ran
Through caverns measureless to man
  Down to a sunless sea.
So twice five miles of fertile ground
With walls and towers were girdled round:
And there were gardens bright with sinuous rills,
Where blossomed many an incense-bearing tree;
And here were forests ancient as the hills,
Enfolding sunny spots of greenery.

1

5

10

But oh! that deep romantic chasm which slanted
Down the green hill athwart a cedarn cover!
A savage place! as holy and enchanted
As e'er beneath a waning moon was haunted   15
By woman wailing for her demon-lover!
And from this chasm, with ceaseless turmoil seething,
As if this earth in fast thick pants were breathing,
A mighty fountain momently was forced:
Amid whose swift half-intermitted burst   20
Huge fragments vaulted like rebounding hail,
Or chaffy grain beneath the thresher's flail:
And 'mid these dancing rocks at once and ever
If flung up momently the sacred river.
Five miles meandering with a mazy motion   25
Through wood and dale the sacred river ran,
Then reached the caverns measureless to man,
And sank in tumult to a lifeless ocean:
And 'mid this tumult Kubla heard from far
Ancestral voices prophesying war!   30
 The shadow of the dome of pleasure
 Floated midway on the waves;
 Where was heard the mingled measure
 From the fountain and the caves.
It was a miracle of rare device,   35
A sunny pleasure-dome with caves of ice!

 A damsel with a dulcimer
 In a vision once I saw:
 It was an Abyssinian maid,
 And on her dulcimer she played,   40
 Singing of Mount Abora.
 Could I revive within me
 Her symphony and song,
 To such a deep delight 'twould win me,
That with music loud and long,   45
I would build that dome in air,
That sunny dome! those caves of ice!
And all who heard should see them there,
And all should cry, Beware! Beware!
His flashing eyes, his floating hair!   50
Weave a circle round him thrice,
And close your eyes with holy dread,
For he on honey-dew hath fed,
And drunk the milk of Paradise.

i) Although difficult to understand, does this poem appeal to you? Give reasons for your answer.

ii) One critic described the poem as having 'much connotation but no denotation' (it suggests more than it describes). In l.1–l.16 ('In Xanadu . . . demon-lover') identify the nouns and the adjectives. Do you agree they do not give a concrete picture?

In 1815 Coleridge wrote *Biographia Literaria*, a work of philosophical autobiography and literary criticism, not published until two years later. The philosophy tries to establish a philosophical and psychological basis for literary criticism and the criticism is mainly devoted to Wordsworth's poetry. The work is sometimes thought to mark the beginning of modern criticism.

Extract 1   Coleridge is describing his education:

GLOSSARY
abstracted (l.1): took away
aphorisms (l.1): wise sayings
deeming (l.1): thinking
diminution (l.6): making smaller
vicious (l.8): full of faults
subordination of its faculties (l.9): making its natural functions subservient one to the other
fuses (l.12): mixes together completely
synthetic (l.12): combining many different elements
appropriated (l.13): taken and given

I abstracted two critical aphorisms, deeming them to comprise the conditions and criteria of poetic style: first, that not the poem which we have *read*, but that to which we *return* with the greatest pleasure, possesses the genuine power and claims the name of *essential* poetry. Second, that whatever lines can be translated into other words of the same language without diminution of their significance, either in sense of association or in any worthy feeling, are so far vicious in their diction . . . The poet, described in *ideal* perfection, brings the whole soul of man into activity, with the subordination of its faculties to each other, according to their relative worth and dignity. He diffuses a tone and spirit of unity that blends and (as it were) *fuses*, each into each, by that synthetic and magical power to which we have exclusively appropriated the name of imagination.
[lines 1, 5, 10]

Extract 2

GLOSSARY
recitation (l.3): reading aloud
diction (l.5): choice of words
bedimmed all the lustre (l.15): caused them to lose much of their brightness

I was in my twenty-fourth year when I had the happiness of knowing Mr Wordsworth personally; and, while memory lasts, I shall hardly forget the sudden effect produced on my mind by his recitation of a manuscript poem which still remains unpublished . . . There was here no mark of strained thought or forced diction, no crowd or turbulence of imagery, and . . . manly reflection and human associations had given both variety and an additional interest to natural objects which in the passion and appetite of the first love they had seemed to him neither to need or permit . . . It was the union of deep feeling with profound thought; the fine balance of truth in observing with the imaginative faculty in modifying the objects observed; and above all the original gift of spreading the tone, the *atmosphere*, and with it the depth and height of the ideal world, around forms, incidents, and situations of which, for the common view, custom had bedimmed all the lustre, had dried up the sparkle and the dew-drops.
[lines 1, 5, 10, 15]

Extract 3   When he and Wordsworth planned the *Lyrical Ballads*:

... it was agreed that my endeavours should be directed to persons
and characters supernatural, or at least romantic; yet so as to transfer
from our inward nature a human interest and a semblance of truth
sufficient to procure for these shadows of imagination that willing
suspension of disbelief for the moment, which constitutes poetic
faith. Mr Wordsworth, on the other hand, was to propose to himself
as his object to give the charm of novelty to things of every day,
and to excite a feeling analogous to the supernatural, by awakening
the mind's attention from the lethargy of custom and directing it to
the loveliness and the wonders of the world before us; an inexhaustible treasure, but for which, in consequence of the film of familiarity
and selfish solicitude, we have eyes yet see not, ears that hear not,
and hearts that neither feel nor understand.

Extract 4   In the following extract, Coleridge expresses his reservations about
Wordsworth's reasons for using in his poetry 'the language really used by
men' from 'humble and rustic life'.

As little can I agree with the assertion that from the objects with
which the rustic hourly communicates the best part of language is
formed. For first, if to communicate with an object implies such an
acquaintance with it, as renders it capable of being discriminately
reflected on; the distinct knowledge of an uneducated rustic would
furnish a very scanty vocabulary. The few things, and modes of
action, requisite for his bodily conveniences, would alone be
individualized; while all the rest of nature would be expressed by a
small number of confused general terms. Secondly, I deny that the
words and combinations of words derived from the objects, with
which the rustic is familiar, whether with distinct or confused
knowledge, can be justly said to form the *best* part of language. It
is more than probable that many classes of the brute creation possess discriminating sounds, by which they can convey to each other
notices of such objects as concern their food, shelter, or safety. Yet
we hesitate to call the aggregate of such sounds a language, otherwise than metaphorically...

I object, in the very first instance, to an equivocation in the use of
the word 'real'. Every man's language varies according to the extent
of his knowledge, the activity of his faculties and the depth or
quickness of his feelings. Every man's language has, first, its
individualities; secondly, the common properties of the *class* to
which he belongs; and thirdly, words and phrases of *universal* use.

For 'real' therefore we must substitute *ordinary*, or *lingua communis*.
And this, we have proved, is no more to be found in the phraseology
of low and rustic life than in that of any other class.

(from *Biographia Literaria*)

- i) Give a heading to each extract.
- ii) What first impressed Coleridge about Wordsworth?
- iii) How could you summarise his later reservations?
- iv) Do you agree/disagree with any of his arguments?

**John Keats
(1795–1821)**

In 'Ode on a Grecian Urn' (1819), Keats (see also page 160) contemplates the sculptured reliefs on an imaginary urn, made up of various details from a number of urns Keats had seen. Moments of vivid life have been given static permanence by the artist, something which seems to have been desired by Keats himself.

Ode on a Grecian Urn

GLOSSARY

Thou (l.1): you, the urn

unravish'd (l.1): undamaged; pure

foster-child (l.2): adopted child

Sylvan (l.3): of woodland scenes (*poetic*)

What ... shape (l.5): what story is told on your surface (which has a leafed border)

deities (l.6): gods and goddesses

Tempe ... Arcady (l.7): beautiful valleys in ancient Greece

loth (l.8): reluctant (to be pursued by boys and gods)

timbrels (l.10): tambourines (small hand drums)

sensual ear (l.13): ear of sense (as opposed to the spirit)

more endear'd (l.13): what is more important

ditties ... tone (l.14): silent tunes

boughs (l.21): branches (of a tree)

shed (l.21): let fall

bid ... adieu (l.22): say goodbye to the spring ('adieu' is *poetic*)

panting (l.27): making short, sharp breaths (from love)

cloy'd (l.29): filled to excess; feeling blocked up

parching (l.30): hot and dry

Thou still unravish'd bride of quietness!   1
  Thou foster-child of Silence and slow Time,
Sylvan historian, who canst thus express
  A flowery tale more sweetly than our rhyme:
What leaf-fringed legend haunts about thy shape   5
  Of deities or mortals, or of both,
    In Tempe or the dales of Arcady?
  What men or gods are these? What maidens loth?
What mad pursuit? What struggle to escape?
  What pipes and timbrels? What wild ecstasy?   10

Heard melodies are sweet, but those unheard
  Are sweeter: therefore, ye soft pipes, play on;
Not to the sensual ear, but, more endear'd,
  Pipe to the spirit ditties of no tone:
Fair youth, beneath the trees, thou canst not leave   15
  Thy song, nor ever can those trees be bare;
    Bold Lover, never, never canst thou kiss,
Though winning near the goal – yet, do not grieve;
  She cannot fade, though thou hast not thy bliss,
For ever wilt thou love, and she be fair!   20

Ah, happy, happy boughs! that cannot shed
  Your leaves, nor ever bid the Spring adieu;
And, happy melodist, unwearied,
  For ever piping songs for ever new;
More happy love! more happy, happy love!   25
  For ever warm and still to be enjoy'd,
    For ever panting and for ever young;
All breathing human passion far above,
  That leaves a heart high sorrowful and cloy'd,
    A burning forehead, and a parching tongue.   30

heifer lowering (l.33): young cow mooing	Who are these coming to the sacrifice?
silken . . . drest (l.34): silk-like sides decorated with circles of flowers and leaves	To what green altar, O mysterious priest,

heifer lowering (l.33): young cow mooing

silken . . . drest (l.34): silk-like sides decorated with circles of flowers and leaves

citadel (l.36): fort

desolate (l.40): empty of inhabitants

pious (l.37): sacred

Attic (l.41): Greek (particularly characteristic of Athens; simple and delicate)

Fair attitude (l.41): how well things have been positioned on it; how well it stands

brede (l.41): interwoven pattern (*poetic*)

overwrought (l.42): decorated; overexcited

Cold Pastoral (l.45): scene of simple country life without life or feeling

woe (l.47): unhappiness

'Beauty . . . beauty' (l.49): ('said' by the urn – critics are uncertain whether the remainder is also 'said' by the urn)

Who are these coming to the sacrifice?
    To what green altar, O mysterious priest,
Lead'st thou that heifer lowering at the skies,
    And all her silken flanks with garlands drest?
What little town by river or sea-shore,   35
    Or mountain-built with peaceful citadel,
        Is emptied of its folk, this pious morn?
And, little town, thy streets for evermore
    Will silent be; and not a soul to tell
        Why thou art desolate, can e'er return.   40

O Attic shape! Fair attitude! with brede
    Of marble men and maidens overwrought,
With forest branches and the trodden weed;
    Thou, silent form, dost tease us out of thought
As doth eternity: Cold Pastoral!   45
    When old age shall this generation waste,
        Thou shalt remain, in midst of other woe
Than ours, a friend to man, to whom thou say'st,
'Beauty is truth, truth beauty, – that is all
    Ye know on earth, and all ye need to know.'   50

●   i) To what do the following refer: 'our rhyme' (l.4); 'those unheard' (l.11); 'happy melodist' (l.23); 'thou' (l.40)?

ii) Describe the picture on the urn in your own words.

iii) In the light of the previous stanzas, what do you think the last two lines mean?

Percy Bysshe Shelley (1792–1822)   In the poem, 'Mutability' (1816), Shelley (see also page 168) complains that nothing in human nature is permanent.

GLOSSARY

veil (l.1): cover

gleam (l.2): give off a soft light

quiver (l.2): tremble slightly

Streaking . . . radiantly (l.3): making the darkness shine with thin bands (of clouds)

lyres (l.5): harps – a kind used by the Greeks to accompany songs; a symbol of lyric poetry

dissonant (l.5): which lack harmony

blast (l.6): movement of air

frail (l.7): not strongly made

Mutability

We are as clouds that veil the midnight moon;   1.
    How restlessly they speed, and gleam, and quiver,
Streaking the darkness radiantly! – yet soon
    Night closes round, and they are lost for ever:

Or like forgotten lyres, whose dissonant strings   5
    Give various response to each varying blast,
To whose frail frame no second motion brings
    One mood or modulation like the last.

We rest. – A dream has power to poison sleep;
    We rise. – One wandering thought pollutes the day;   10
We feel, conceive or reason, laugh or weep;
    Embrace fond woe, or cast our cares away:

modulation (l.8): change
(of tone; of sound)

conceive (l.11): form ideas

fond woe (l.12): foolish
misery ('fond' is *archaic*
in this sense)

Nought (l.16): nothing
(*poetic*)

Mutability (l.16): the fact
that everything changes

It is the same! – For, be it joy or sorrow,
    The path of its departure still is free:
Man's yesterday may ne'er be like his morrow;
    Nought may endure but Mutability.   15

●   i) Paraphrase the lines 'For . . . is free' (1.13–14).

    ii) Comment on the imagery in the poem.

Mary Shelley
(1797–1851)

Mary Shelley, Percy Shelley's second wife, was the daughter of William Godwin (1756–1836), the philosopher and novelist, and Mary Wollstonecraft (1759–1797), the feminist author of *A Vindication of the Rights of Women* (1792). She and Shelley fell in love in 1814 while Shelley was still married to Harriet Westbrook, with whom he had eloped in 1811 when she was only sixteen.

Frankenstein and his monster

In June 1816, Percy, Mary and Mary's step-sister, Claire, joined Lord Byron at a villa in Switzerland, by Lake Geneva. During the visit they all agreed to write ghost stories. The idea for *Frankenstein*, a Gothic tale of terror, came to Mary in a half-waking nightmare. She was also inspired by a visit to Mont Blanc, the highest of the mountains in the Alps. Published in 1818, *Frankenstein* was the only story in the group to be completed.

Through the letters of Captain Walton, an English explorer in the Arctic, the tale tells the story of Victor Frankenstein, an idealistic Genevan student of natural philosophy, who has discovered the secret of giving back life to dead tissue. He collects bones and builds something resembling a human being, which has supernatural strength and size and is terrible in appearance. Often thought of as the origin of modern science fiction, the tale is also a version of the noble savage myth, in which a nature essentially good is corrupted by ill treatment.

Extract 1   Here the monster is brought to life:

It was on a dreary night of November that I beheld the accomplishment of my toils. With an anxiety that almost amounted to agony, I collected the instruments of life around me, that I might infuse a spark of being into the lifeless thing that lay at my feet. It was already one in the morning; the rain pattered dismally against the panes, and my candle was nearly burnt out, when, by the glimmer of the half-extinguished light, I saw the dull yellow eye of the creature open; it breathed hard, and a convulsive motion agitated its limbs.

How can I describe my emotions at this catastrophe, or how delineate the wretch whom with such infinite pains and care I had endeavoured to form? His limbs were in proportion, and I had selected his features as beautiful. Beautiful! – Great God! His yellow skin scarcely covered the work of muscles and arteries beneath; his hair was of a lustrous black, and flowing; his teeth of a pearly whiteness; but these luxuriances only formed a more horrid contrast with his watery eyes, that seemed almost of the same colour as the dun white sockets in which they were set, his shrivelled complexion and straight black lips.

The different accidents of life are not so changeable as the feelings of human nature. I had worked hard for nearly two years, for the sole purpose of infusing life into an inanimate body. For this I had deprived myself of rest and health. I had desired it with an ardour that far exceeded moderation; but now that I had finished, the beauty of the dream vanished, and breathless horror and disgust filled my heart.

1

5

10

15

20

25

Extract 2 That night Victor dreams he comes across Elizabeth, his adopted sister.

Delighted and surprised, I embraced her; but as I imprinted the first kiss on her lips, they became livid with the hue of death; her features appeared to change, and I thought that I held the corpse of my dead mother in my arms; a shroud enveloped her form, and I saw the grave-worms crawling in the folds of the flannel. I started from my sleep with horror; a cold dew covered my forehead, my teeth chattered, and every limb became convulsed: when, by the dim and yellow light of the moon, as it forced its way through the window shutters, I beheld the wretch – the miserable monster whom I had created. He held up the curtain of the bed; and his eyes, if eyes they may be called, were fixed on me. His jaws opened, and he muttered some inarticulate sounds, while a grin wrinkled his cheeks. He might have spoken, but I did not hear; one hand was stretched out, seemingly to detain me, but I escaped, and rushed down stairs.

(from Frankenstein)

● Have you seen any film versions of this story? How was this scene portrayed?

Thomas Love Peacock (1785–1866)

Thomas Love Peacock, the comic satirist, essayist and poet, was a friend of Shelley's. His sceptical essay on the decline of poetry ('The Four Ages of Poetry' – 1820) provoked Shelley's essay 'A Defence of Poetry' (see page 170). Peacock's prose satires, such as *Melincourt* (1817) and *Nightmare Abbey* (1818), are discussion novels with very little plot. They aim to survey the contemporary political and cultural scene from a Radical viewpoint (from the point of view of someone who believes in the need for fundamental political reform). As in Plato's *Symposium* (?371 BC), friendly arguments take place over a dinner table. Peacock's point of view, which emphasises common sense and proportion, is generally more eighteenth-century than Romantic.

In this extract from *Crotchet Castle* (1831), the Rev Dr Folliott, a cheerful and conservative clergyman, is discussing food and drink with Mr Crotchet, a frivolous eccentric, and Mr MacQuedy, a progressive and excessively rationalistic Scots economist:

(THE REV DR FOLLIOTT:) . . ., salmon in May is the king of fish.

MR CROTCHET: That salmon before you, doctor, was caught in the Thames this morning.

THE REV DR FOLLIOTT: Παπαπαῖ! Rarity of rarities! A Thames salmon caught this morning. Now, Mr MacQuedy, even in fish your Modern Athens must yield. *Cedite Graii.*

MR MACQUEDY: Eh! sir, on its own ground, your Thames salmon has two virtues over all others: first, that it is fresh; and, second, that it is rare; for I understand you do not take half-a-dozen in a year.

THE REV DR FOLLIOTT: In some years, sir, not one. Mud, filth, gas-dregs, lock-weirs, and the march of mind, developed in the form of poaching, have ruined the fishery. But when do we catch a salmon, happy the man to whom he falls.

MR MACQUEDY: I confess, sir, this is excellent; but I cannot see 15
why it should be better than a Tweed salmon at Kelso.

THE REV DR FOLLIOTT: Sir, I will take a glass of Hock with you.

MR MACQUEDY: With all my heart, sir. There are several varieties of the salmon genus: but the common salmon, the *salmo salar*, is only one species, one and the same everywhere, just like the human 20
mind. Locality and education make all the difference.

THE REV DR FOLLIOTT: Education! Well, sir, I have no doubt schools for all are just as fit for the species *salmo salar* as for the genus *homo*. But you must allow, that the specimen before us has finished his education in a manner that does honour to his college. However, 25
I doubt that the *salmo salar* is only one species, that is to say, pre-cisely alike in all localities. I hold that every river has its own breed, with essential differences; in flavour especially. And as for the human mind, I deny that it is the same in all men. I hold that there is every variety of natural capacity from the idiot to Newton and 30
Shakespeare; the mass of mankind, midway between these ex-tremes, being blockheads of different degrees: education leaving them pretty nearly as it found them, with this single difference, that it gives a fixed direction to their stupidity, a sort of incurable wry-neck to the thing they call their understanding. 35

(from *Crotchet Castle*)

- i) How do we know from this that MacQuedy is a believer in the power of logic and reason?
- ii) Can you find an example of the Rev Folliott making fun of MacQuedy's arrogance?

**William Cobbett
(1763–1835)**

William Cobbett, the son of a peasant farmer, was a journalist and a political leader of the rural labourer. In *Rural Rides* (1820–1830), he gives an outspoken account, in clear lively English, of his tours through England on horseback, reporting on rural conditions for the enlightenment of a working-class public.

Here he shows his son the spot where he received what he called the 'rudiments of his education':

There is a little hop-garden in which I used to work when from 1
eight to ten years old; from which I have scores of times run to fol-low the hounds, leaving the hoe to do the best that it could to destroy the weeds; but the most interesting thing was a sandhill which goes from a part of the heath down to the rivulet. As a due 5
mixture of pleasure with toil, I, with two brothers, used occasionally to disport ourselves, as the lawyers call it, at this sandhill. Our diversion was this: we used to go to the top of the hill, which was

steeper than the roof of a house; one used to draw his arms out of the sleeves of his smock-frock, and lay himself down with his arms by his sides; and the others, one at the head, and the other at the feet, sent him rolling down the hill like a barrel or a log of wood. By the time he got to the bottom, his hair, eyes, ears, nose, and mouth were all full of this loose sand; then the others took their turn, and at every roll there was a monstrous spell of laughter. I had often told my sons of this while they were very little, and I now took one of them to see the spot. But, that was not all. This was the spot where I was receiving my education; and this was the sort of education; and I am perfectly satisfied that if I had not received such an education, or something very much like it – that, if I had been brought up a milksop, with a nursery-maid everlastingly at my heels, I should have been at this day as great a fool, as inefficient a mortal, as any of those frivolous idiots that are turned out from Winchester and Westminster School, or from any of those dens of dunces called Colleges and Universities. It is impossible to say how much I owe to that sandhill...

(from *Rural Rides*)

● Have you any similar memories? Do you agree that what one learns naturally as a child is more important than what one learns at school?

Thomas De Quincey (1785–1859)

Thomas De Quincey was an early admirer of Coleridge and Wordsworth. In 1809 he moved into Dove Cottage in Grasmere, formerly occupied by the Wordsworths. However, while still at Worcester College, Oxford, this shy and courteous man (who walked out during the final examination and never got a degree!) had begun to take opium to ease rheumatic pain. By 1812 he was an addict. In *Confessions of an Opium Eater* (1822; revised and expanded in 1856), De Quincey displays intimate insights into the non-rational world of memory and dreams. Although, in common with the later Romantic poets, he has a sense of restlessness and isolation, he was nevertheless conservative by nature, a Tory in politics, a moralist and a supporter of the Church of England.

If De Quincey's musical–poetic prose suggests some seventeenth-century writers like Thomas Browne (1605–1682), his sympathy for the suffering of children and his intimate psychologising look forward to the nineteenth-century novel.

Extract 1

In this extract from the 1822 *Confessions* De Quincey deals with an early experience. After running away from school at seventeen and taking refuge in London, he sleeps in an unoccupied rat-infested house. Here he describes his friendship with a sixteen-year-old prostitute, Ann.

– One night, when we were pacing slowly along Oxford Street, and after a day when I had felt more than usually ill and faint, I requested her to turn off with me into Soho Square: thither we went; and we sat down on the steps of a house, which, to this hour, I never

pass without a pang of grief, and an inner act of homage to the spirit
of that unhappy girl, in memory of the noble action which she
there performed. Suddenly, as we sat, I grew much worse: I had

pang (l.5): sudden painful feeling

homage (l.5): respectful tribute

port wine (l.19): strong sweet wine from Portugal

without a murmur (l.22): without complaining

wherewithal (l.23): money

bare necessaries of life (l.24): basic essentials, like food and clothes

reimburse her (l.25): pay her back

benefactress (l.26): woman who gives help

curse (l.29): angry set of words calling for punishment

even so (l.31): in such a way

benediction (l.31): blessing

like prerogative (l.32): similar special right

waylay (l.33): stop unexpectedly (refers to line 10 of Wordsworth's poem 'She was a Phantom of Delight')

brothel (l.34): house of prostitutes

authentic (l.35): genuine

reconciliation (l.36): return to friendship and harmony

pass without a pang of grief, and an inner act of homage to the spirit
of that unhappy girl, in memory of the noble action which she
there performed. Suddenly, as we sat, I grew much worse: I had
been leaning my head against her bosom; and all at once I sank
from her arms and fell backwards on the steps. From the sensations
I then had, I felt an inner conviction of the liveliest kind that without some powerful and reviving stimulus, I should either have
died on the spot – or should at least have sunk to a point of exhaustion from which all re-ascent under my friendless circumstances
would soon have become hopeless. Then it was, at this crisis of my
fate, that my poor orphan companion – who had herself met with
little but injuries in this world – stretched out a saving hand to me.
Uttering a cry of terror, but without a moment's delay, she ran off
into Oxford Street, and in less time than could be imagined, returned to me with a glass of port wine and spices, that acted upon
my empty stomach (which at that time would have rejected all solid
food) with an instantaneous power of restoration: and for this glass
the generous girl without a murmur paid out of her own humble
purse at a time – be it remembered! – when she had scarcely wherewithal to purchase the bare necessaries of life, and when she could
have no reason to expect that I should ever be able to reimburse
her. – Oh! youthful benefactress! how often in succeeding years,
standing in solitary places, and thinking of thee with grief of heart
and perfect love, how often have I wished that, as in ancient times
the curse of a father was believed to have a supernatural power,
and to pursue its object with a fatal necessity of self-fulfillment, –
even so the benediction of a heart oppressed with gratitude, might
have a like prerogative; might have power given to it from above to
chase – to haunt – to waylay – to overtake – to pursue thee into the
central darkness of a London brothel, or (if it were possible) into
the darkness of the grave – there to awaken them with an authentic
message of peace and forgiveness, and of final reconciliation!

Extract 2   Seventeen years later, in June 1819, he has the following dream:

GLOSSARY

commanded (l.4): seen

exalted (l.5): intensified and made glorious

interspace (l.8): space (between)

forest lawns (l.9): open spaces between woods (archaic)

reposing (l.11): lying resting

verdant (l.11): fresh and green

whom I had tenderly loved (l.12): (Wordsworth's daughter, Catherine, who died at the age of four)

I thought that it was a Sunday morning in May, that it was Easter
Sunday, and as yet very early in the morning. I was standing, as it
seemed to me, at the door of my own cottage. Right before me lay
the very scene which could really be commanded from that situation, but exalted, as was usual, and solemnized by the power of
dreams. There were the same mountains, and the same lovely valley
at their feet; but the mountains were raised to more than Alpine
height, and there was interspace far larger between them of meadows
and forest lawns; the hedges were rich with white roses; and no
living creature was to be seen, excepting that in the green churchyard there were cattle tranquilly reposing upon the verdant graves,
and particularly round about the grave of a child whom I had tenderly loved, just as I had really beheld them, a little before sunrise

in the same summer, when that child died. I gazed upon the well-known scene, and I said aloud (as I thought) to myself, 'It yet wants much of sunrise; and it is Easter Sunday; and that is the day on which they celebrate the first-fruits of resurrection. I will walk abroad; old griefs shall be forgotten today; for the air is cool and still, and the hills are high, and stretch away to heaven; and the forest-glades are as quiet as the churchyard; and, with the dew, I can wash the fever from my forehead, and then I shall be unhappy no longer.' And I turned, as if to open my garden gate; and immediately I saw upon the left a scene far different; but which yet the power of dreams had reconciled into harmony with the other. The scene was an Oriental one; and there also it was Easter Sunday, and very early in the morning. And at a vast distance were visible, as a stain upon the horizon, the domes and cupolas of a great city – an image or faint abstraction, caught perhaps in childhood from some picture of Jerusalem. And not a bow-shot from me, upon a stone, and shaded by Judean palms, there sat a woman; and I looked; and it was – Ann! She fixed her eyes upon me earnestly; and I said to her at length: 'So then I have found you at last.' I waited: but she answered me not a word. Her face was the same as when I saw it last, and yet again how different! Seventeen years ago, when the lamplight fell upon her face, as for the last time I kissed her lips (lips, Ann, that to me were not polluted), her eyes were streaming with tears: the tears were now wiped away; she seemed more beautiful than she was at that time, but in all other points the same, and not older. Her looks were tranquil, but with unusual solemnity of expression; and I now gazed upon her with some awe, but suddenly her countenance grew dim, and, turning to the mountains, I perceived vapors rolling between us; in a moment, all had vanished; thick darkness came on; and, in the twinkling of an eye, I was far away from mountains, and by lamplight in Oxford Street, walking again with Ann – just as we walked seventeen years before, when we were both children.

(from *Confessions*)

beheld (l.13): seen (*poetic*)

wants much of (l.15): is far from complete

first . . . resurrection (l.17): (as Christ was the first to rise to a new life from the dead, he was referred to in the Bible as the 'first fruits' – the first 'positive result' – of the dead)

abroad (l.18): out of doors (*archaic*)

glades (l.20): open spaces

dew (l.20): moisture that forms during the night

reconciled (l.24): brought

cupolas (l.27): small domes forming (part of) a roof

abstraction (l.28): vision

not a bow-shot (l.29): not far away

Judean (l.30): of Judea, the land of the ancient Hebrews

awe (l.40): great wonder and respect

countenance (l.41): face

vapors (l.42): mists

in the . . . eye (l.43): in an instant

● What do you imagine the significance of Easter Sunday was in the dream?

Lord Byron (1788–1824) In 1823 Lord Byron (see also pages 171–174) set out for Greece to join the revolutionary forces fighting for independence from Turkey. Although he gave them large sums of money and great inspiration he died after a series of feverish attacks before he saw any serious military action.

In the following poem, written in 1820, Byron is ironical about such gestures:

'When a man hath no freedom to fight for at home'

When a man hath no freedom to fight for at home,   1
   Let him combat for that of his neighbours
Let him think of the glories of Greece and of Rome,
   And get knocked on his head for his labours.

To do good to mankind is the chivalrous plan,   5
   And is always as nobly requited;
Then battle for freedom wherever you can,
   And, if not shot or hanged, you'll get knighted.

- i) Which two lines are most noticeably ironic? What makes them so?
- ii) Comment on the rhythm of the poem.

Charles Lamb (1775–1834)

Charles Lamb, the essayist and critic, a lifelong friend of Coleridge, is reputed to have been a man of great charm. With his sister, Mary, he wrote the *Tales from Shakespeare* (1807) in order to make Shakespeare's stories familiar to children. His best-known work *Essays of Elia* (1823 and 1833), originally published in *The London Magazine*, contains many witty observations and characterisations of his times.

'A clear fire, a clean hearth, and the rigour of the game.' This was   1
the celebrated *wish* of old Sarah Battle (now with God), who, next
to her devotions, loved a good game of whist. She was none of your
lukewarm gamesters, your half-and-half players, who have no
objection to take a hand, if you want one to make up a rubber; who   5
affirm that they have no pleasure in winning; that they like to win
one game and lose another; that they can while away an hour very
agreeably at a card-table, but are indifferent whether they play or
no; and will desire an adversary, who has slipt a wrong card, to
take it up and play another. These insufferable triflers are the curse   10
of a table. One of these flies will spoil a whole pot. Of such it may
be said that they do not play at cards, but only play at playing at
them.

   Sarah Battle was none of that breed. She detested them, as I do,
from her heart and soul, and would not, save upon a striking emer-   15
gency, willingly seat herself at the same table with them. She loved
a thorough-paced partner, a determined enemy. She took, and
gave, no concessions. She hated favours. She never made a revoke,
nor ever passed it over in her adversary without exacting the utmost
forfeiture. She fought a good fight: cut and thrust ... She sate bolt   20
upright, and neither showed you her cards, nor desired to see yours.
All people have their blind side – their superstitions; and I have
heard her declare ... that Hearts was her favourite suit.

   I never in my life – and I knew Sarah Battle many of the best
years of it – saw her take out her snuff-box when it was her turn to   25

revoke (l.18): fail to follow suit in a card game when able to do so

passed it over (l.19): ignored it

exacting ... forfeiture (l.19): punishing them as much as possible

cut and thrust (l.20): with spirited and determined action

snuff-box (l.25): small ornate box for carrying around scented tobacco (snuff) inhaled through the nostrils

snuff a candle (l.26): put out the flame of a candle

connived at (l.27): took part in somebody else's

play; or snuff a candle in the middle of a game; or ring for a servant, till it was fairly over. She never introduced, or connived at, miscellaneous conversation during its process. As she emphatically observed, cards were cards...

(from *Essays of Elia*)

● What impression do we get of Sarah Battle? Is there any irony in the description?

James Fenimore Cooper (1789–1851)

To his irritation, James Fenimore Cooper was often known in Europe as the American Sir Walter Scott. Full of dramatic and romantic incidents, many of his thirty novels are historical adventures, containing conflicts between society and the individual, settlements and the wilderness, civil law and natural rights (particularly those of the American Indians).

The Last of the Mohicans (1826) – subtitled 'A Narrative of 1757' – is the second of Cooper's 'Leatherstocking' tales, so-called because of the deerskin leggings of their hero, Natty Bumppo (Hawk-eye), a typical but sympathetic figure of the frontier (the edge of the territory settled in by the white pioneers, bordering on hostile Indian territory). Hawk-eye is a hunter and a scout (someone who goes out to get information about the enemy) – a man who loves the forest and hates the feeling of restriction in the settlements. Unlike many of his race, he has a great understanding of the Indians.

Hawkeye leading the search for Alice and Cora Munro

Extract 1   Alice and Cora Munro have been captured by Indians. Looking for them are their father (an English commander), Major Duncan Heyward (Alice's fiancé), Hawk-eye, old chief Chingachgook (Hawk-eye's best friend) and his son Uncas (the only survivors of the Mohican 'aristocracy', which had died out in the white pioneers' push westwards):

... the canoe glided over several miles of water. Just as the day dawned, they entered the narrows of the lake, and stole swiftly and cautiously among their numberless little islands. It was by this road that Montcalm had retired with his army, and the adventurers knew not but he had left some of his Indians in ambush, to protect the rear of his forces, and collect the stragglers. They, therefore, approached the passage with the customary silence of their guarded habits.

Chingachgook laid aside his paddle; while Uncas and the scout urged the light vessel through crooked and intricate channels, where every foot that they advanced exposed them to the danger of some sudden rising on their progress. The eyes of the Sagamore moved warily from islet to islet, and copse to copse, as the canoe proceeded; and when a clearer sheet of water permitted, his keen vision was bent along the bald rocks and impending forests that frowned upon the narrow strait.

Extract 2   They realise the French troops or the Indians may be waiting ahead of them. Hawk-eye is explaining their options as they get to a point where the 'entire view of the northern shore of the island' might be seen:

The well-known crack of a rifle, whose ball came skipping along the placid surface of the strait, and a shrill yell from the island, interrupted his speech and announced that their passage was discovered. In another instant several savages were seen rushing into the canoes, which were soon dancing over the water in pursuit. These fearful precursors of a coming struggle produced no change in the countenances and movements of his three guides, so far as Duncan could discover, except that the strokes of their paddles were longer and more in unison, and caused the little bark to spring forward like a creature possessing life and volition.

'Hold them there, Sagamore,' said Hawk-eye, looking coolly backward over his left shoulder, while he still plied his paddle. 'Keep them just there. Them Hurons have never a piece in their nation that will execute at this distance; but 'Kill-deer' has a barrel on which a man may calculate.'

The glossary in the left margin reads:

volition (l.10): the power of independent movement

plied (l.12): moved it backwards and forwards firmly

piece (l.13): gun

execute (l.14): kill anyone

Kill-deer (l.14): type of bird which Hawk-eye uses as a name for his gun

barrel (l.14): the long tube-shaped part of a gun

calculate (l.15): rely

ascertained (l.16): made certain

sufficient of themselves (l.16): able

requisite (l.17): necessary

report (l.20): sound of its shot

nigher (l.21): nearer

fastidious (l.22): very careful

elevating (l.23): raising

muzzle (l.23): front end of the barrel

bow (l.24): front part of the boat

darting (l.29): moving suddenly and quickly

imminently perilous (l.30): going to be (too) dangerous

inclined (l.32): directed

exulting (l.36): extremely joyful

---

nation that will execute at this distance; but 'Kill-deer' has a barrel on which a man may calculate.'

The scout having ascertained that the Mohicans were sufficient of themselves to maintain the requisite distance, deliberately laid aside his paddle and raised the fatal rifle. Three several times he brought the piece to his shoulder, and when his companions were expecting its report, he as often lowered it to request the Indians would permit their enemies to approach a little nigher. At length his accurate and fastidious eye seemed satisfied, and throwing out his left arm on the barrel, he was slowly elevating the muzzle, when an exclamation from Uncas, who sat in the bow, once more caused him to suspend the shot.

'What now, lad?' demanded Hawk-eye. 'You saved a Huron from the death shriek by that word; have you reason for what you do?'

Uncas pointed toward the rocky shore a little in their front, whence another war canoe was darting directly across their course. It was too obvious now that their situation was imminently perilous to need the aid of language to confirm it. The scout laid aside his rifle, and resumed the paddle, while Chingachgook inclined the bows of the canoe a little toward the western shore, in order to increase the distance between them and this new enemy. In the meantime they were reminded of the presence of those who pressed upon their rear, by wild and exulting shouts.

15

20

25

30

35

Extract 3   They try to escape from their enemies:

GLOSSARY

it will be ... mark (l.4): the target they will try to shoot at will be smaller

ill (l.7): bad

dodge (l.7): try to get out of the way

deliberate (l.12): have a serious discussion

a cover (l.12): protection

scrimmage (l.12): disorderly fight

an open ... good (l.12–13): a body without protection will get you killed

'They are preparing for a shot,' said Heyward; 'and as we are in a line with them, it can scarcely fail.'

'Get you then into the bottom of the canoe,' returned the scout; 'you and the colonel; it will be so much taken from the size of the mark.'

Heyward smiled, as he answered:

'It would be but an ill example for the highest in rank to dodge, while the warriors were under fire!'

'Lord! Lord! That is now a white man's courage!' exclaimed the scout: 'and like too many of his notions, not to be maintained by reason. Do you think the Sagamore, or Uncas, or even I ... would deliberate about finding a cover in the scrimmage, when an open body would do no good? For what have the Frenchers reared up their Quebec, if fighting is always to be done in the clearings?'

1

5

10

For what ... clearings
(l.13–14): why have
the French bothered to
establish their own
province of Quebec if
all wars have to be
fought in the open
spaces?
volley (l.17): number of
gunshots
discourse (l.17):
conversation
Notwithstanding (l.19): in
spite of
compelled (l.22): persuaded
encounter (l.23): face; meet
exposure (l.23): lack of
protection

'All that you say is very true, my friend,' replied Heyward. 'Still,   15
our customs must prevent us from doing as you wish.'

A volley from the Hurons interrupted the discourse, and as the
bullets whistled about them, Duncan saw the head of Uncas turned,
looking back at himself and Munro. Notwithstanding the nearness
of the enemy, and his own great personal danger, the countenance   20
of the young warrior expressed no other emotion, as the former was
compelled to think, than amazement at finding men willing to
encounter so useless an exposure. Chingachgook was probably
better acquainted with the notions of white men, for he did not
even cast a glance aside...   25

(from *The Last of the Mohicans*)

● i) Summarise the action in your own words.
   ii) Do you find Cooper's style of writing rather formal, despite the excitement of
       the action? If so, where is this formality used for comic effect?

Supplement 6

**Charles Dickens
(1812–1870)**

In this scene from *Our Mutual Friend* (1864–1865), Dickens's last complete
novel (see page 177), Mr Podsnap, an arrogant, self-satisfied rich London
businessman ('Mr Podsnap was well to do, and stood very high in
Mr Podsnap's opinion') is hosting a dinner party at his house. Here he is
making 'polite' conversation with an 'unfortunately-born foreigner':

'How Do You Like London?' Mr Podsnap now inquired from his   1
station of host, as if he were administering something in the nature
of a powder or potion to the deaf child; 'London, Londres, London?'
The foreign gentleman admired it.
'You find it Very Large?' said Mr Podsnap, spaciously.   5
The foreign gentleman found it very large.
'And Very Rich?'
The foreign gentleman found it, without doubt, enormément
riche.
'Enormously Rich, We say,' returned Mr Podsnap, in a conde-   10
scending manner. 'Our English adverbs do Not terminate in Mong,
and We Pronounce the "ch" as if there were a "t" before it. We say
Ritch.'

'Reetch,' remarked the foreign gentleman.

'And Do You Find, Sir,' pursued Mr Podsnap, with dignity,   15
'Many Evidences that Strike You, of our British Constitution in the
Streets Of The World's Metropolis, London, Londres, London?'

GLOSSARY

his station of (l.1): his
   position as
spaciously (l.5): in an
   expansive manner

The foreign gentleman begged to be pardoned, but did not altogether understand.

'The Constitution Britannique,' Mr Podsnap explained, as if he were teaching in an infant school. 'We Say British, But You Say Britannique, You Know' (forgivingly, as if that were not his fault). 'The Constitution, Sir.' ⟶ 20

The foreign gentleman said, 'Mais, yees; I know eem.'

'I Was Inquiring,' said Mr Podsnap, resuming the thread of his discourse, 'Whether You Have Observed in our Streets as We should say, Upon our Pavvy as You would say, any Tokens –' ⟶ 25

The foreign gentleman, with patient courtesy entreated pardon; 'But what was tokenz?'

'Marks,' said Mr Podsnap; 'Signs, you know, Appearances – Traces.' ⟶ 30

'Ah! Of a Orse?' inquired the foreign gentleman.

'We call it Horse,' said Mr Podsnap, with forbearance. 'In England, Angleterre, England, We Aspirate the "H," and We Say "Horse." Only our Lower Classes Say "Orse!" ' ⟶ 35

'Pardon,' said the foreign gentleman; 'I am alwiz wrong!'

'Our Language,' said Mr Podsnap, with a gracious consciousness of being always right, 'is Difficult. Ours is a Copious Language, and Trying to Strangers. I will not Pursue my Question.'

'It merely referred,' Mr Podsnap explained, with a sense of meritorious proprietorship, 'to Our Constitution, Sir. We Englishmen are Very Proud of our Constitution, Sir. It Was Bestowed Upon Us By Providence. No Other Country is so Favoured as This Country.' ⟶ 40

'And ozer countries? –' the foreign gentleman was beginning, when Mr Podsnap put him right again.

'We do not say Ozer; we say Other: the letters are "T" and "H;" You say Tay and Aish, You Know; (still with clemency). The sound is "th" – "th!" ' ⟶ 45

'And *other* countries,' said the foreign gentleman. 'They do how?' ⟶ 50

'They do, Sir,' returned Mr Podsnap, gravely shaking his head; 'they do – I am sorry to be obliged to say it – *as* they do.'

'It was a little particular of Providence,' said the foreign gentleman, laughing; 'for the frontier is not large.'

'Undoubtedly,' assented Mr Podsnap; 'But So it is. It was the Charter of the Land. This Island was Blest, Sir, to the Direct Exclusion of such Other Countries as – as there may happen to be. And if we were all Englishmen present, I would say,' added Mr Podsnap, looking round upon his compatriots, and sounding solemnly with his theme, 'that there is in the Englishman a combination of qualities, a modesty, an independence, a responsibility, a repose, combined with an absence of everything calculated to call a blush into the cheek of a young person, which one would seek in vain among the Nations of the Earth.' ⟶ 55 ⟶ 60

resuming ... discourse (l.25): carrying on his theme from where he left off

Pavvy (l.27): in French, 'street' is 'rue'; 'pavement' is 'pave'

entreated pardon (l.28): apologised

forbearance (l.33): patience

Aspirate (l.34): pronounce (with the sound of the letter 'H')

Copious (l.38): with a great many words

Trying (l.39): difficult; worrying

meritorious proprietorship (l.40): as though he deserved to be congratulated for owning it

Bestowed Upon us (l.42): given to us

Providence (l.43): God

with clemency (l.47): prepared not to punish him for his mistake

gravely (l.51): seriously and solemnly

particular (l.53): unusual; strange (for Providence to single out England)

Charter (l.56): special privilege

Blest (l.56): made holy and given good fortune

blush (l.63): sudden reddening (because of modesty)

Having delivered this little summary, Mr Podsnap's face flushed, as he thought of the remote possibility of its being at all qualified by any prejudiced citizen of any other country; and, with his favourite right-arm flourish, he put the rest of Europe and the whole of Asia, Africa, and America nowhere.

(from *Our Mutual Friend*)

- i) What is Dickens satirising?
- ii) What do you think of Mr Podsnap? Does his type still exist?
- iii) What makes the scene comic?

Edgar Allan Poe (1809–1849)

Although born in Boston in the North of the U.S., Edgar Allan Poe was brought up by a tobacco exporter in Virginia (in the South) and went to school in England for five years. After a largely unhappy life with little success he died an alcoholic.

Poe's sense of professional dedication to art and his love of beauty (in particular the beauty of melancholy) were to have a great influence over the French symbolists – for example, Arthur Rimbaud (1854–1891) – and the English writers such as Oscar Wilde (1854–1900) who believed in Art for Art's sake (that art need serve no moral or political purpose). However, Emerson dismissed Poe the poet as 'the jingle man' because he seemed more interested in what the poems sounded like than what they meant, and D.H. Lawrence diagnosed his short stories as showing a 'great dead soul . . . writhing in the mystery of his own undoing'.

Poe's interest in feelings of terror and guilt led him to write stories which were often pathological in their content and macabre in their atmosphere. This is the opening of *The Tell-Tale Heart* (1843):

True! – nervous – very, very dreadfully nervous I had been and am; but why *will* you say that I am mad? The disease had sharpened my senses – not destroyed – not dulled them. Above all was the sense of hearing acute. I heard all things in the heaven and in the earth. I heard many things in hell. How, then, am I mad? Hearken! and observe how healthily – how calmly I can tell you the whole story.

It is impossible to say how first the idea entered my brain; but once conceived, it haunted me day and night. Object there was none. Passion there was none. I loved the old man. He had never wronged me. He had never given me insult. For his gold I had no desire. I think it was his eye! yes, it was this! He had the eye of a vulture – a pale blue eye, with a film over it. Whenever it fell upon me, my blood ran cold; and so by degrees – very gradually – I made up my mind to take the life of the old man, and thus rid myself of the eye for ever.

Now this is the point. You fancy me mad. Madmen know nothing. But you should have seen *me*. You should have seen how wisely I proceeded – with what caution – with what foresight – with what dissimulation I went to work! I was never kinder to the old man than during the whole week before I killed him. And every night,

about midnight, I turned the latch of his door and opened it – oh so gently! And then, when I had made an opening sufficient for my head, I put in a dark lantern, all closed, closed, so that no light shone out, and then I thrust in my head. Oh, you would have laughed to see how cunningly I thrust it in! I moved it slowly – very, very slowly, so that I might not disturb the old man's sleep. It took me an hour to place my whole head within the opening so far that I could see him as he lay upon his bed. Ha! – would a madman have been so wise as this? And then, when my head was well in the room, I undid the lantern cautiously – oh, so cautiously – cautiously (for the hinges creaked) – I undid it just so much that a single thin ray fell upon the vulture eye. And this I did for seven long nights – every night just at midnight – but I found the eye always closed; and so it was impossible to do the work; for it was not the old man who vexed me, but his Evil Eye. And every morning, when the day broke, I went boldly into the chamber, and spoke courageously to him, calling him by name in a hearty tone, and inquiring how he had passed the night. So you see he would have been a very profound old man, indeed, to suspect that every night, just at twelve, I looked in upon him while he slept.

Upon the eighth night I was more than usually cautious in open-

25

30

35

40

ing the door. A watch's minute hand moves more quickly than did mine. Never before that night, had I *felt* the extent of my own powers – of my sagacity. I could scarcely contain my feelings of triumph. To think that there I was, opening the door, little by little, 45 and he not even to dream of my secret deeds or thoughts. I fairly chuckled at the idea; and perhaps he heard me; for he moved on the bed suddenly, as if startled. Now you may think that I drew back – but no. His room was as black as pitch with the thick darkness (for the shutters were close fastened, through fear of robbers), and so I 50 knew that he could not see the opening of the door, and I kept pushing it on steadily, steadily.

sagacity (l.44): sharp awareness of all my senses (*archaic* use)

deeds (l.46): actions

fairly chuckled (l.46): had a good laugh

startled (l.48): he had been surprised

pitch (l.49): black substance made from coal-tar

(from *The Tell-Tale Heart*)

i) What do we know about the man the narrator has decided to kill? Is it clear why he has decided to kill him?

ii) The story takes place inside the narrator's mind. How would you describe the state of his mind?

iii) How is the narrator's intensity shown in the style of writing?

William Makepeace Thackeray (1811–1863)

The satirical novels of William Makepeace Thackeray show the upper classes of his day to be dominated by materialistic interests. Like Dickens, Thackeray was opposed to utilitarian beliefs and deplored the absence of spontaneous affection in daily life. He was, however, more resistant to Romantic influence than Dickens and looked for support in an eighteenth-century sense of proportion and elegance. His novels include *The Luck of Barry Lyndon* (1844), a parody of the contemporary fashion in fiction for the hero as a loveable rogue and criminal, and *Esmond* (1852), an historical novel set in the reign of Queen Anne.

Vanity Fair, subtitled 'A Novel without a Hero', was published in serial form and completed in 1848. The title refers to the town in which Christian and Faithful are tempted in Bunyan's *The Pilgrim's Progress* (see pages 353–356).

Becky Sharp, the orphan daughter of a penniless artist and a French opera dancer, is an ingenious adventuress, well able to manipulate the heartlessness and snobbery of those around her. Although married to Rawdon Crawley, a cavalry officer – gallant, ignorant and dissolute – she pursues her social ambitions by becoming the mistress of the aristocratic and degenerate Lord Steyne.

In the following extract, Crawley arrives home unexpectedly.

Steyne was hanging over the sofa on which Becky sate. The wretched 1 woman was in a brilliant full toilette, her arms and all her fingers sparkling with bracelets and rings; and the brilliants on her breast which Steyne had given her. He had her hand in his, and was bowing over it to kiss it, when Becky started up with a faint scream 5 as she caught sight of Rawdon's white face. At the next instant she tried a smile, a horrid smile, as if to welcome her husband: and Steyne rose up, grinding his teeth, pale, and with fury in his looks.

He, too, attempted a laugh – and came forward holding out his hand. 'What, come back! How d'ye do, Crawley?' he said, the nerves of his mouth twitching as he tried to grin at the intruder.

There was that in Rawdon's face which caused Becky to fling herself before him. 'I am innocent, Rawdon,' she said; 'before God, I am innocent.' She clung hold of his coat, of his hands; her own were all covered with serpents, and rings, and baubles. 'I am innocent. – Say I am innocent,' she said to Lord Steyne.

He thought a trap had been laid for him, and was as furious with the wife as with the husband. 'You innocent! Damn you,' he screamed out. 'You innocent! Why, every trinket you have on your body is paid for by me. I have given you thousands of pounds which this fellow has spent, and for which he has sold you. Innocent, by ———! You're as innocent as your mother, the ballet-girl, and your husband the bully. Don't think to frighten me as you have done others. Make way, sir, and let me pass;' and Lord Steyne seized up his hat, and, with flame in his eyes, and looking his enemy fiercely in the face, marched upon him, never for a moment doubting that the other would give way.

But Rawdon Crawley springing out, seized him by the neckcloth, until Steyne, almost strangled, writhed, and bent under his arm. 'You lie, you dog!' said Rawdon. 'You lie, you coward and villain!' And he struck the Peer twice over the face with his open hand, and flung him bleeding to the ground. It was all done before Rebecca could interpose. She stood there trembling before him. She admired her husband, strong, brave, and victorious.

'Come here,' he said. – She came up at once.

'Take off those things.' – She began, trembling, pulling the jewels from her arms, and the rings from her shaking fingers, and held them all in a heap, quivering and looking up at him. 'Throw them down,' he said, and she dropped them. He tore the diamond ornament out of her breast, and flung it at Lord Steyne. It cut him on his bald forehead. Steyne wore the scar to his dying day.

'Come upstairs,' Rawdon said to his wife. 'Don't kill me, Rawdon,' she said. He laughed savagely. 'I want to see if that man lies about the money as he has about me. Has he given you any?'

'No,' said Rebecca, 'that is ———'

'Give me your keys,' Rawdon answered, and they went out together.

Rebecca gave him all the keys but one; and she was in hopes that he would not have remarked the absence of that. It belonged to the little desk which Amelia had given her in early days, and which she kept in a secret place. But Rawdon flung open boxes and wardrobes, throwing the multifarious trumpery of their contents here and there, and at last he found the desk. The woman was forced to open it. It contained papers, love-letters many years old – all sorts of small trinkets and woman's memoranda. And it contained a pocket-book with bank-notes. Some of these were dated ten years back, too, and one was quite a fresh one – a note for a thousand pounds which Lord Steyne had given her.

'Did he give you this?' Rawdon said.

'Yes,' Rebecca answered.

(from *Vanity Fair*)

- i) Which phrases make clear the feelings of the three characters? Why is Steyne angry with Becky?
- ii) Find two phrases which show the narrator's disapproval of Becky's attraction to riches.
- iii) Who do you have sympathy with in this scene? Why?

Elizabeth Barrett Browning (1806–1861)

Elizabeth Barrett Browning was the eldest of twelve children and was tutored at home in Greek and classical philosophy. Forbidden by her father to marry, she corresponded with Robert Browning before marrying him in secret and leaving for Italy where she lived for the rest of her life. During her married life her passions included an interest in the cause of Italian unity and spiritualism. She impressed her contemporaries with her vivid intelligence and quiet sympathetic manner.

The sequence of 44 sonnets entitled *Sonnets from the Portuguese* (1850) describes the growth of her love for Browning, at first hesitating to involve him in her invalid life (she had been seriously ill as a result of a broken blood vessel), finally giving way to acceptance and rapturous happiness. The title of the sequence is an attempt to disguise their personal nature by giving the impression they were translations. (Browning's nickname for his wife was 'the Portuguese'!)

This is one of the sonnets in the sequence.

'When our two souls stand up erect and strong'

When our two souls stand up erect and strong,   1
Face to face, silent, drawing nigh and nigher,
Until the lengthening wings break into fire
At either curved point – what bitter wrong
Can the earth do to us, that we should not long   5
Be here contented? Think. In mounting higher,
The angels would press on us and aspire
To drop some golden orb of perfect song
Into our deep, dear silence. Let us stay
Rather on earth, Beloved – where the unfit   10
Contrarious moods of men recoil away
And isolate pure spirits, and permit
A place to stand and love in for a day,
With darkness and the death-hour rounding it.

GLOSSARY

nigh (l.2): near (*poetic*)
wings (l.3): (of our souls – like angels)
orb (l.8): ball
unfit (l.10): useless
Contrarious (l.11): opposing
recoil (l.11): draw back
rounding (l.14): surrounding (*archaic*)

- What is the narrator urging her 'Beloved' to accept?

Elizabeth Gaskell (1810–1865)

Elizabeth Gaskell was brought up in a Unitarian household in Manchester. She is known now mainly for her novel *Cranford* (1851–1853) and the biography of her friend Charlotte Brontë (1857). A devoted wife and mother, her first novel *Mary Barton* (1848) was written at a time of distress over the death of her infant son during the 'hungry forties' (so called because of the severe economic depression and widespread unemployment). It tells the story of John Barton, a sober and intelligent workman angered by acute poverty and injustice, and his daughter Mary. In effect the novel is a plea for a better understanding between employers and workers. Admired by Carlyle and Dickens, it was much attacked by the Manchester mill owners (and the Tory press) as being biased against employers.

The children clamoured again for bread; but this time Barton took a piece first to the poor, helpless, hopeless woman, who still sat by the side of her husband, listening to his anxious miserable mutterings. She took the bread, when it was put into her hand, and broke a bit, but could not eat. She was past hunger. She fell down on the floor with a heavy unresisting bang. The men looked puzzled. 'She's well-nigh clemmed.' said Barton. 'Folk do say one mustn't give clemmed people much to eat; but, bless us, she'll eat nought.' 5

'I'll tell yo what I'll do,' said Wilson. 'I'll take these two big lads, as does nought but fight, home to my missis for tonight, and I'll get a jug o' tea. Them women always does best with tea, and such-like slop.' 10

So Barton was now left alone with a little child, crying (when it had done eating) for mammy; with a fainting, dead-like woman: and with the sick man, whose mutterings were rising up to screams and shrieks of agonised anxiety. He carried the woman to the fire, and chafed her hands. He looked around for something to raise her head. There was literally nothing but some loose bricks. However, these he got; and taking off his coat he covered them with it as well as he could. He pulled her feet to the fire, which now began to emit some faint heat. He looked round for water, but the poor woman had been too weak to drag herself out to the distant pump, and water there was none. He snatched the child, and ran up the area-steps to the room above, and borrowed their only saucepan with some water in it. Then he began, with the useful skill of a working-man, to make some gruel; and when it was hastily made, he seized a battered iron tablespoon (kept when many other little things had been sold in a lot, in order to feed the baby), and with it he forced one or two drops between her clenched teeth. The mouth opened mechanically to receive more, and gradually she revived. She sat up and looked round; and recollecting all, fell down again in weak and passive despair. Her little child crawled to her, and wiped with its fingers the thick-coming tears which she now had strength to weep. It was now high time to attend to the man. He lay on straw, so damp and mouldy, no dog would have chosen it in preference to flags; over it was a piece of sacking, coming next to his worn skeleton of a body; above him was mustered every article of clothing 15 that could be spared by mother or children this bitter weather; and in addition to his own, these might have given as much warmth as one blanket, could they have been kept on him; but as he restlessly tossed to and fro, they fell off and left him shivering in spite of the burning heat of his skin. Every now and then he started up in his naked madness, looking like the prophet of woe in the fearful plague-picture; but he soon fell again in exhaustion, and Barton found he must be closely watched, lest in these falls he should injure himself against the hard brick floor. 40 45

GLOSSARY (margin):
tossed (l.41): moved about (in a feverish state)
started up (l.42): jumped up suddenly
prophet (l.43): person who tells about the future
woe (l.43): misery
lest (l.45): for fear that

(from *Mary Barton*)

● i) Which phrases show Barton's kindness?
ii) How does poverty like this compare with poverty in the world today?

Alfred Tennyson (1809–1892)

The first three books of Tennyson's own poems, published in 1830, 1832 and 1842, (see also page 185) include what is now considered his best work: for example, 'Mariana', 'The Lady of Shalott', 'Ulysses', 'Morte d'Arthur' and 'The Lotus Eaters'.

This is the opening of the poem 'Tithonus' (written 1832–1833). It concerns an aged Trojan prince, whom the goddess of the dawn has enabled to live forever. Although Tithonus has been cut off from the normal cycle of birth and death, he does not have the gift of everlasting youth.

GLOSSARY (margin):
vapours (l.2): mists
burthen (l.2): burden, rain
tills (l.3): ploughs
swan (l.4): (some species of swan live for more than fifty years)
thine arms (l.6): (of Eos, or Aurora, the goddess of the dawn)
roaming (l.8): travelling about (without purpose)
morn (l.10): morning; dawn

The woods decay, the woods decay and fall, 1
The vapours weep their burthen to the ground,
Man comes and tills the field and lies beneath,
And after many a summer dies the swan.
Me only cruel immortality 5
Consumes: I wither slowly in thine arms,
Here at the quiet limit of the world,
A white-hair'd shadow roaming like a dream
The ever-silent spaces of the East,
Far-folded mists, and gleaming halls of morn. 10

(from 'Tithonus')

● In what sense is immortality cruel?

This is the opening of the poem 'Ulysses' (written in 1873). An aged Greek hero and restless warrior has returned home to Ithaca. However, he has decided to set out on a final journey of exploration to the west.

GLOSSARY (margin):
hearth (l.2): fireplace; home
barren crags (l.2): bare rocks
mete . . . laws (l.3–4): measure out inadequate rewards and punishments

It little profits that an idle king, 1
By this still hearth, among these barren crags,
Match'd with an aged wife, I mete and dole
Unequal laws unto a savage race,
That hoard, and sleep, and feed, and know not me. 5
I cannot rest from travel: I will drink
Life to the lees: all times I have enjoy'd

Ulysses

hoard (l.5): save for the future

to the lees (l.7): until it has all gone

scudding drifts (l.10): driving showers of spray and rain

Hyades (l.10): group of stars whose appearance was assumed to be followed by rain

Vext (l.11): angered

roaming (l.12): travelling about (without purpose)

peers (l.16): companions; equals

ringing (l.17): full of sound

margin (l.20): horizon

Greatly, have suffer'd greatly, both with those
That loved me, and alone; on shore, and when
Thro' scudding drifts the rainy Hyades   10
Vext the dim sea: I am become a name;
For always roaming with a hungry heart
Much have I seen and known; cities of men
And manners, climates, councils, governments,
Myself not least, but honour'd of them all;   15
And drunk delight of battle with my peers,
Far on the ringing plains of windy Troy.
I am a part of all that I have met;
Yet all experience is an arch wherethro'
Gleams that untravell'd world, whose margin fades   20
For ever and for ever when I move.

(from 'Ulysses')

Tennyson is said to have identified with his narrator, expressing what he called his own 'need of going forward and braving the struggle of life' after the death of his friend, Hallam.

- i) Can you see any self-dramatisation in these lines?
- ii) Comment on either of the following: a) sentence length/enjambment; b) rhythm

Emily Brontë (1818–1848)

Here are three extracts from the scene in Wuthering Heights (see page 187) in which Heathcliff realises Catherine will never marry him.

Extract 1 After a violent scene involving Hindley, Catherine tells the housekeeper, Nelly Dean, she has accepted Edgar's proposal of marriage. Heathcliff overhears but only Nelly knows he is there.

'I accepted him, Nelly. Be quick, and say whether I was wrong!' 1
'You accepted him! then what good is it discussing the matter?
You have pledged your word, and cannot retract.'
'But, say whether I should have done so – do!' she exclaimed in
an irritated tone; chafing her hands together, and frowning. 5
'There are many things to be considered before that question can
be answered properly,' I said sententiously. 'First and foremost, do
you love Mr Edgar?'
'Who can help it? Of course I do,' she answered.
Then I put her through the following catechism: for a girl of 10
twenty-two it was not injudicious.
'Why do you love him, Miss Cathy?'
'Nonsense, I do – that's sufficient.'
'By no means; you must say why.'
'Well, because he is handsome, and pleasant to be with.' 15
'Bad!' was my commentary.
'And because he is young and cheerful.'
'Bad, still.'
'And because he loves me.'
'Indifferent, coming there.' 20
'And he will be rich, and I shall like to be the greatest woman of
the neighbourhood, and I shall be proud of having such a husband.'
'Worst of all. And now, say how you love him?'
'As everybody loves – you're silly, Nelly.'
'Not at all – answer.' 25
'I love the ground under his feet, and the air over his head, and
everything he touches, and every word he says. I love all his looks,
and all his actions, and him entirely and altogether. There now!'
'And why?'
'Nay; you are making a jest of it; it is exceedingly ill-natured. It's 30
no jest to me!' said the young lady, scowling, and turning her face
to the fire.

Extract 2   However, Catherine is not happy. She admits to Nelly that something in
her soul and heart tells her that she is wrong:

'. . . I've no more business to marry Edgar Linton than I have to be 1
in heaven; and if the wicked man in there had not brought Heathcliff
so low, I shouldn't have thought of it. It would degrade me to marry
Heathcliff now; so he shall never know how I love him: and that,
not because he's handsome, Nelly, but because he's more myself 5
than I am. Whatever our souls are made of, his and mine are the
same; and Linton's is as different as a moonbeam from lightning,
or frost from fire.'
Ere this speech ended, I became sensible of Heathcliff's presence.
Having noticed a slight movement, I turned my head, and saw him 10
rise from the bench, and steal out noiselessly. He had listened till
he heard Catherine say it would degrade her to marry him, and
then he stayed to hear no further.

Nelly points out how Heathcliff will react to the news:

GLOSSARY

he loses (l.1): Heathcliff loses

Milo (l.7): an athlete in ancient Greece who was trapped in a half-split tree and devoured by wolves

forsake (l.9): leave (forever)

antipathy (l.12): strong dislike and opposition

'... As soon as you become Mrs Linton, he loses friend, and love, and all! Have you considered how you'll bear the separation, and how he'll bear to be quite deserted in the world? Because, Miss Catherine —'

'He quite deserted! We separated!' she exclaimed, with an accent of indignation. 'Who is to separate us, pray? They'll meet the fate of Milo! Not as long as I live, Ellen: for no mortal creature. Every Linton on the face of the earth might melt into nothing, before I could consent to forsake Heathcliff. Oh, that's not what I intend – that's not what I mean! I shouldn't be Mrs Linton were such a price demanded! He'll be as much to me as he has been all his lifetime. Edgar must shake off his antipathy, and tolerate him, at least. He will, when he learns my true feelings towards him. Nelly, I see now, you think me a selfish wretch; but did it never strike you that if Heathcliff and I married, we should be beggars? Whereas, if I marry Linton, I can aid Heathcliff to rise, and place him out of my brother's power.'

(from *Wuthering Heights*)

- i) Can it be said that Catherine 'loves' Edgar?
- ii) Why doesn't she marry Heathcliff?
- iii) What impression do you get of Catherine and Nelly from these extracts?

Charlotte Brontë (1816–1855)

Charlotte Brontë, two years older than her sister Emily, is best known for *Jane Eyre* (1847). *Villette* (1853), Charlotte's last novel, based on her teaching experiences in Brussels, capital of Belgium, was regarded by George Eliot as 'still more wonderful' than *Jane Eyre* with 'almost something preternatural in its power'.

Extract 1

Poor, plain Lucy Snowe, an orphan, first becomes governess and then teacher in Madame Beck's school in the foreign city of Villette. Madame Beck's cousin, the bad-tempered but kind-hearted Paul Emanuel, 'professor of literature', is clearly attracted to her but says nothing. In this extract, everyone in the class except Lucy has presented Monsieur Paul with a bouquet of flowers on his 'fête' day – the day in the year (the first of March) when the school honours him as Madame Beck's relative and advisor. Having suppressed his feelings about Lucy's 'failure', Paul, in front of a map of the world, is coming to the end of his customary 'discours' (speech) to the class, but Lucy isn't listening:

GLOSSARY

thimble (l.2): metal cap for the end of the finger when sewing

stooping (l.2): bending down

crown (l.2): top

Owing to some little accidental movement – I think I dropped my thimble on the floor, and in stooping to regain it, hit the crown of my head against the sharp corner of my desk; which casualties (exasperating to me, by rights, if to anybody) naturally made a slight bustle – M. Paul became irritated, and dismissing his forced equanimity, and casting to the winds that dignity and self-control with which he never cared long to encumber himself, he broke

exasperating (l.4): annoying

slight bustle (l.5): small disturbance

equanimity (l.6): calmness

casting to the wind (l.6): throwing away

encumber himself (l.7): load down with

strain (l.8): way of speaking

contrived (l.9): managed

cynical (l.12): contemptuous

scathed (l.13): made a cruel judgement

'les Anglaises' (l.14): English women (*French*)

handled (l.15): dealt with

stature (l.18): height

slovenly (l.19): untidy

pedantic (l.19): unimaginative and too book-based

impious scepticism (l.19): lack of faith and respect for religion

insufferable (l.20): unbearable

pretentious (l.20): which they claim too much merit for

ground his teeth (l.21): pressed his teeth together noisily

malignantly (l.21): with hatred

singular (l.22): strange and extraordinary

acrid (l.22): bitter

venomous (l.24): full of poison

harass (l.24): worry

you shall ... to me (l.26): I will not care about you

shabbiest ... pyramid (l.26): meanest flowers in your arrangement

grieve (l.28): am unhappy

resolution (l.28): decision

stolid (l.30): unexcited

stoically (l.30): with self-control

cockatrice (l.31): serpent with a look that could kill

sullying ... mud (l.33–34): (being very disrespectful to Britain)

stung (l.34): insulted

'Vive ... Faquins' (l.36–37): Long live England, history and heros. Down with France, fiction and cads (*French*)

forth into the strain best calculated to give him ease.

I don't know how, in the progress of his 'discours,' he had contrived to cross the Channel and land on British ground; but there I found him when I began to listen.

Casting a quick cynical glance round the room – a glance which scathed, or was intended to scathe, as it crossed me – he fell with fury upon 'les Anglaises'.

Never have I heard English women handled as M. Paul that morning handled them: he spared nothing – neither their minds, morals, manners, nor personal appearance. I specially remember his abuse of their tall stature, their long necks, their thin arms, their slovenly dress, their pedantic education, their impious scepticism (!) their insufferable pride, their pretentious virtue: over which he ground his teeth malignantly, and looked as if, had he dared, he would have said singular things. Oh! he was spiteful, acrid, savage; and, as a natural consequence, detestably ugly.

'Little wicked venomous man!' thought I; 'am I going to harass myself with fears of displeasing *you*, or hurting *your* feelings? No, indeed; you shall be indifferent to me, as the shabbiest bouquet in your pyramid.'

I grieve to say I could not quite carry out this resolution. For some time the abuse of England and the English found and left me stolid: I bore it some fifteen minutes stoically enough; but this hissing cockatrice was determined to sting, and he said such things at last – fastening not only upon our women, but upon our greatest names and best men; sullying the shield of Britannia, and dabbling the Union Jack in mud – that I *was* stung. . . . I struck a sharp stroke on my desk, opened my lips, and let loose this cry –

'Vive l'Angleterre, l'Histoire et les Héros! A bas la France, la Fiction et les Faquins!'

- i) Can you imagine the reactions of both the class and Monsieur Paul?
- ii) Why do you think Paul fell 'with fury upon *'les Anglaises'*'?

Extract 2　In the afternoon, the school is empty and Lucy discovers Monsieur Paul going through her desk:

Now, as he sat bending above the desk, he was stirring up its contents; but with gentle and careful hand; disarranging indeed, but not harming. My heart smote me: as I bent over him, as he sat unconscious, doing me what good he could, and I daresay not feeling towards me unkindly, my morning's anger quite melted: I did not dislike Professor Emanuel.

I think he heard me breathe. He turned suddenly: his temperament was nervous, yet he never started, and seldom changed colour; there was something hardy about him.

'I thought you were gone into town with the other teachers,' said he, taking a grim gripe of his self-possession, which half-escaped him – 'It is as well you are not. Do you think I care for being caught? Not I. I often visit your desk.'

'Monsieur, I know it.'

'You find a brochure or tome now and then; but you don't read them, because they have passed under this?' – touching his cigar.

'They have, and are no better for the process; but I read them.'

'Without pleasure?'

'Monsieur must not be contradicted.'

'Do you like them, or any of them? – are they acceptable?'

'Monsieur has seen me reading them a hundred times, and knows I have not so many recreations as to undervalue those he provides.'

'I mean well; and, if you see that I mean well, and derive some little amusement from my efforts, why can we not be friends?'

'A fatalist would say – because we cannot.'

'This morning,' he continued, 'I awoke in a bright mood, and came into class happy; you spoiled my day.'

'No, Monsieur, only an hour or two of it, and that unintentionally.'

'Unintentionally! No. It was my fête-day; everybody wished me happiness but you. The little children of the third division gave each her knot of violets, lisped each her congratulation: you – nothing. Not a bud, leaf, whisper – not a glance. Was this unintentional?'

'I meant no harm.'

(from *Villette*)

GLOSSARY

My heart smote me (l.3): I felt a sudden and strong attraction for him

started (l.8): jumped

hardy (l.9): strong and courageous

grim gripe (l.11): determined hold

brochure or tome (l.15): small or large book

fatalist (l.25): someone who believes that everything is decided by fate

knot of violets (l.31): little bunch of purple flowers

lisped (l.31): spoke in a childish way

bud (l.32): unopened flower

● i) What are the real feelings of the characters at the following points? a) 'Not I.' (l.13); b) 'Monsieur must not be contradicted' (l.19)
ii) How does the characters' mood change in the last part of this extract (from 'I mean well. . .', l.23)?
iii) How would you describe Lucy's personality?

Lucy, the Protestant Anglo-Saxon girl, comes to accept Monsieur Paul, a Latin and a Catholic man. Finally their feelings turn to love. The process is one of self-discovery for both of them.

Henry Wadsworth Longfellow (1807–1882) In the English-speaking world of his time, Henry Wadsworth Longfellow, the American descendant of a colonial family, was second only to Tennyson in popularity.

Hiawatha wooing Minnehaha

The Song of Hiawatha (1855) is a narrative in unrhymed trochaic tetrameter (consisting of lines of four feet, each foot consisting of a strongly stressed syllable followed by a weakly stressed syllable). It tells the story of the life and death of the American Indian Hiawatha, reared by his grandmother, Nokomis, on the shores of Lake Superior, largest of the lakes in North America. In this extract Hiawatha is about to bid farewell to Nokomis and leave on his final journey to the Isles of the Blest to rule the kingdom of the Northwest Wind.

By the shore of Gitche Gumee,   1
By the shining Big-Sea-Water,
At the doorway of his wigwam,
In the pleasant Summer morning,
Hiawatha stood and waited.   5
All the air was full of freshness,
All the earth was bright and joyous,
And before him, through the sunshine,
Westward toward the neighboring forest
Passed in golden swarms the Ahmo,   10
Passed the bees, the honey-makers,
Burning, singing in the sunshine.
   Bright above him shone the heavens,
Level spread the lake before him;
From its bosom leaped the sturgeon,   15
Sparkling, flashing in the sunshine;
On its margin the great forest
Stood reflected in the water,
Every tree-top had its shadow,

Motionless beneath the water.   20
  From the brow of Hiawatha
Gone was every trace of sorrow,
As the fog from off the water,
As the mist from off the meadow.
With a smile of joy and triumph,   25
With a look of exultation,
As of one who in a vision
Sees what is to be, but is not,
Stood and waited Hiawatha.
  Toward the sun his hands were lifted,   30
Both the palms spread out against it,
And between the parted fingers
Fell the sunshine on his features,
Flecked with light his naked shoulders,
As it falls and flecks an oak-tree   35
Through the rifted leaves and branches.

brow (l.21): face (*poetic*)
exultation (l.26): great joy
Flecked (l.34): marked with
  small patches
rifted (l.36): (the gaps
  between)

(from *The Song of Hiawatha*)

Nowadays, Longfellow is regarded as a very conventional figure. His gentle and sweet verse, much influenced by the German Romantics, is said to be lacking in passion.

●   i) Do you agree with the above view?
     ii) Are the lines quoted here memorable and moving?
     iii) Do you think the rhythm of the verse sounds like Indian drums?

**Anthony Trollope
(1815–1882)**

The novels of Anthony Trollope, famed for their characterisations, are quiet and workmanlike and convey a sense of solid Victorian ordinariness. Critical of the commercial arrogance of the upper middle class, Trollope believed in the more traditional virtues and values of the privileged gentry.

> Trollope novels . . . precisely suit my taste, solid and substantial, written on the strength of beef and through the inspiration of ale, and just as real as if some giant had hewn up a great lump of earth, and put it under a glass dome, with all its inhabitants going about their daily business, and not suspecting that they were being made a show of.
> (Nathaniel Hawthorne)

Barchester Towers (1857), the second in the Barsetshire series of novels, records a power struggle among the churchmen of Barchester, an imaginary place based on the town of Winchester in the south of England. The ineffectual Dr Proudie has been made bishop. In the contest between Mr Slope, the bishop's self-seeking and hypocritical chaplain, and the powerfully dominating Mrs Proudie over who is to be warden of a hospital, Dr Proudie has uncharacteristically resisted his wife in favour of Mr Slope.

mutiny (l.1): revolt

her high behests (l.2): Mrs Proudie's commands

carried ... high hand (l.2): behaved arrogantly

slavery (l.3): doing everything his wife told him to

milk ... honey (l.5–6): (in the Bible, Palestine was a land of milk and honey – a land of plenty)

quaff (l.6): drink

tantalise (l.6): raise hopes that cannot be realised

every ... bishop (l.8): a real bishop in every way

cowed (l.9): weakened

'Ce ... coûte' (l.11): all that counts is the first step (French)

magnanimously (l.12): nobly and courageously

ruffle (l.15): disturb

trifling (l.17): unimportant

projected (l.17): planned

bided her time (1.22): waited for the right moment

chimney-piece (l.26): shelf above the fireplace

stilly (l.26): calm and quiet

ghost ... (l.28): (ghosts were thought to be able to wander over the earth until daybreak)

serf (l.31): slave

betook himself (l.33): went

sherry (l.35): a strong wine from Spain

Far ... us (l.35): we shouldn't

thither (l.36): in that direction

attenuated (l.41): thin and weak

emaciated (l.41): very thin

grizzled locks (l.42): grey hair

palpably (l.42): noticeably

materially (l.44): noticeably

florid (l.48): healthy

nipping frost (l.49): (something which damages the health)

On that memorable day, memorable for his mutiny and rebellion against her high behests, he had carried his way with a high hand, and had really begun to think it possible that the days of his slavery were counted. He had begun to hope that he was now about to enter into a free land, a land delicious with milk which he himself might quaff, and honey which would not tantalise him by being only honey to the eye. When Mrs Proudie banged the door, as she left his room, he felt himself every inch a bishop. To be sure his spirit had been a little cowed by his chaplain's subsequent lecture; but on the whole he was highly pleased with himself, and flattered himself that the worst was over. 'Ce n'est que le premier pas qui coûte,' he reflected; and now that the first step had been so magnanimously taken, all the rest would follow easily.

He met his wife as a matter of course at dinner, where little or nothing was said that could ruffle the bishop's happiness. His daughters and the servants were present and protected him.

He made one or two trifling remarks on the subject of his projected visit to the archbishop, in order to show to all concerned that he intended to have his own way; and the very servants perceiving the change transferred a little of their reverence from their mistress to their master. All which the master perceived; and so also did the mistress. But Mrs Proudie bided her time.

After dinner he returned to his study where Mr Slope soon found him, and there they had tea together and planned many things. For some few minutes the bishop was really happy; but as the clock on the chimney-piece warned him that the stilly hours of night were drawing on, as he looked at his chamber candlestick and knew that he must use it, his heart sank within him again. He was as a ghost, all whose power of wandering free through these upper regions ceases at cock-crow; or rather he was the opposite of a ghost, for till cock-crow he must again be a serf. And would that be all? Could he trust himself to come down to breakfast a free man in the morning?

He was nearly an hour later than usual, when he betook himself to his rest. Rest! what rest? However, he took a couple of glasses of sherry, and mounted the stairs. Far be it from us to follow him thither. There are some things which no novelist, no historian should attempt; some few scenes in life's drama which even no poet should dare to paint. Let that which passed between Dr Proudie and his wife on this night be understood to be among them.

He came down the following morning a sad and thoughtful man. He was attenuated in appearance; one might almost say emaciated. I doubt whether his now grizzled locks had not palpably become more gray than on the preceding evening. At any rate he had aged materially. Years do not make a man old gradually and at an even pace. Look through the world and see if this is not so always, except in those rare cases in which the human being lives and dies without joys and without sorrows, like a vegetable. A man shall be possessed of florid youthful blooming health till, it matters not what age. Thirty – forty – fifty, then comes some nipping frost, some period

1

5

10

15

20

25

30

35

40

45

of agony, that robs the fibres of the body of their succulence, and   50
the hale and hearty man is counted among the old.

He came down and breakfasted alone; Mrs Proudie being indisposed took her coffee in her bed-room, and her daughters waited upon her there. He ate his breakfast alone, and then, hardly knowing what he did, he betook himself to his usual seat in his study.   55

(from *Barchester Towers*)

i) What is the difference between Dr Proudie at the beginning of the scene and Dr Proudie at the end? What do we assume happened overnight?

ii) What can we infer from the following phrases: 'memorable day' (l.1); 'daughters and the servants ... protected him' (l.16); 'transferred ... master' (l.20–21); 'he took a couple of glasses of sherry' (l.34)?

iii) Do you feel sorry for Dr Proudie?

**Herman Melville
(1819–1891)**

Herman Melville was born in New York City. Nowadays he is best known for his great symbolic epic *Moby Dick* (1851), but when it was published it was the novel that caused him to lose popularity and drove him further within himself.

Some of Melville's shorter stories are attacks on commercialism and selfishness. They also show a separation from society and an uncertainty about how to integrate with other people. In *Bartleby the Scrivener* (1856), a Wall Street lawyer (the narrator) hires a curious, corpse-like figure (Bartleby) to copy legal documents. However, Bartleby refuses to mix with the other employees and when asked to do anything other than copy documents, always says 'I would prefer not to.'

GLOSSARY

insolence (l.2): rudeness

his aspect ... involuntary (l.2–3): the expression on his face shows that he can't help his odd behaviour

willfulness (l.8): determination not to do as he is told

lay up (l.9): store

morsel (l.9): something small and pleasing

invariable (l.10): unchanging

goaded (l.12): urged

essayed ... soap (l.14–15): tried to light a fire by hitting soap (it was impossible)

impulse (l.15): desire to act without thinking about the consequences

compare (l.17): examine

mulish vagary (l.20): obstinate behaviour

Poor fellow! thought I, he means no mischief; it is plain he intends   1
no insolence; his aspect sufficiently evinces that his eccentricities are involuntary. He is useful to me. I can get along with him. If I turn him away, the chances are he will fall in with some less-indulgent employer, and then he will be rudely treated, and perhaps driven forth miserably to starve. Yes. Here I can cheaply   5
purchase a delicious self-approval. To befriend Bartleby; to humor him in his strange willfulness, will cost me little or nothing, while I lay up in my soul what will eventually prove a sweet morsel for my conscience. But this mood was not invariable with me. The   10
passiveness of Bartleby sometimes irritated me. I felt strangely goaded on to encounter him in new opposition – to elicit some angry spark from him answerable to my own. But, indeed, I might as well have essayed to strike fire with my knuckles against a bit of Windsor soap. But one afternoon the evil impulse in me mastered   15
me, and the following little scene ensued:

'Bartleby,' said I, 'when those papers are all copied, I will compare them with you.'

'I would prefer not to.'

'How? Surely you do not mean to persist in that mulish vagary?'   20
No answer.

I threw open the folding-doors near by, and, turning upon Turkey and Nippers, exclaimed:

'Bartleby a second time says, he won't examine his papers. What do you think of it, Turkey?'   25

It was afternoon, be it remembered. Turkey sat glowing like a brass boiler; his bald head steaming; his hands reeling among his blotted papers.

'Think of it?' roared Turkey; 'I think I'll just step behind his screen, and black his eyes for him!'   30

So saying, Turkey rose to his feet and threw his arms into a pugilistic position. He was hurrying away to make good his promise, when I detained him, alarmed at the effect of incautiously rousing Turkey's combativeness after dinner.

'Sit down, Turkey,' said I, 'and hear what Nippers has to say.   35
What do you think of it, Nippers? Would I not be justified in immediately dismissing Bartleby?'

'Excuse me, that is for you to decide, sir. I think his conduct quite unusual, and, indeed, unjust, as regards Turkey and myself. But it may only be a passing whim.'   40

'Ah,' exclaimed I, 'you have strangely changed your mind, then – you speak very gently of him now.'

'All beer,' cried Turkey; 'gentleness is effects of beer – Nippers and I dined together to-day. You see how gentle *I* am, sir. Shall I go and black his eyes?'   45

'You refer to Bartleby, I suppose. No, not to-day, Turkey,' I replied; 'pray, put up your fists.'

I closed the doors, and again advanced towards Bartleby. I felt additional incentives tempting me to my fate. I burned to be rebelled against again. I remembered that Bartleby never left the office.   50

'Bartleby,' said I, 'Ginger Nut is away; just step around to the Post Office, won't you? (it was but a three minutes' walk), and see if there is anything for me.'

'I would prefer not to.'

'You *will* not?'   55

'I *prefer* not.'

I staggered to my desk, and sat there in a deep study. My blind inveteracy returned. Was there any other thing in which I could procure myself to be ignominiously repulsed by this lean, penniless wight? – my hired clerk? What added thing is there, perfectly rea-   60
sonable, that he will be sure to refuse to do?

(from *Bartleby the Scrivener*)

Turkey and Nippers (l.22): both copyists. Turkey was nearly 60, an Englishman whose face was always very red after lunch. Nippers was about 25, very ambitious, had whiskers and looked like a pirate

glowing ... boiler (l.26): (very red and hot)

reeling (l.27): moving around

blotted (l.28): which had been dried with absorbent paper

screen (l.30): upright frame separating him from the others

pugilistic (l.31): like a boxer

make good (l.32): keep

incautiously ... combativeness (l.33–34): unwisely stirring Turkey up to fight

whim (l.40): strange idea (personal to him, that will soon pass)

gentleness ... beer (l.43): the beer he had for lunch has made him soft

pray (l.47): please (*archaic*)

incentives (l.49): things urging

Ginger Nut (l.51): the office boy

inveteracy (l.58): obstinate feelings

procure ... wight (l.59–60): get this poor, thin person to do which would also be rejected and hurt my pride

● i) What does the narrator say his reasons are for not dismissing Bartleby? What do you think his real reasons are?

ii) How would you describe his mood at the end of the extract?

iii) What would you have done?

Wilkie Collins (1824–1889)

Detective fiction, in which a detective solves a mysterious crime through deduction, originated in the scientific ethos of Victorian culture. The genre began with Edgar Allan Poe's stories about the detective Dupin (for example, *The Murders of the Rue Morgue*, 1841) and achieved its greatest popularity with the Sherlock Holmes novels of Arthur Conan Doyle (1859–1930).

Wilkie Collins, a Londoner and a friend of Dickens, was a great believer in a good story but used suspense and crime for more artistic purposes than most of his successors. In *The Woman in White* (1860) Collins experimented with describing the whole action through the eyes of different characters placed, as he put it, 'in different positions along the chain of events'.

Extract 1

The plot is complicated, beginning with a midnight encounter on a lonely road between Walter Hartright, an artist, and a mysterious and agitated woman dressed entirely in white.

... in one moment, every drop of blood in my body was brought to a stop by the touch of a hand laid lightly and suddenly on my shoulder from behind me.

I turned on the instant, with my fingers tightening round the handle of my stick.

There, in the middle of the broad, bright high-road – there, as if it had that moment sprung out of the earth or dropped from the heaven – stood the figure of a solitary Woman, dressed from head to foot in white garments, her face bent in grave inquiry on mine, her hand pointing to the dark cloud over London, as I faced her.

I was far too seriously startled by the suddenness with which this extraordinary apparition stood before me, in the dead of night and in that lonely place, to ask what she wanted. The strange woman spoke first.

'Is that the road to London?' she said.

I looked attentively at her, as she put that singular question to me. It was then nearly one o'clock. All I could discern distinctly by the moonlight was a colourless, youthful face, meagre and sharp to look at about the cheeks and chin; large, grave, wistfully attentive eyes; nervous, uncertain lips; and light hair of a pale, brownish-yellow hue. There was nothing wild, nothing immodest in her manner: it was quiet and self-controlled, a little melancholy and a little touched by suspicion; not exactly the manner of a lady, and, at the same time, not the manner of a woman in the humblest rank of life. The voice, little as I had yet heard of it, had something curiously still and mechanical in its tones, and the utterance was remarkably rapid. She held a small bag in her hand: and her dress – bonnet, shawl, and gown all of white – was, so far as I could guess, certainly not composed of very delicate or very expensive materials. Her figure was slight, and rather above the average height – her gait and actions free from the slightest approach to extravagance. This was all that I could observe of her in the dim light and under the perplexingly strange circumstances of our meeting. What sort of a

grossest (l.36): most vulgar
and common
misconstrue (l.37): take
wrongly
fretfulnes (l.40): show of
dissatisfaction

woman she was, and how she came to be out alone in the high-road, an hour after midnight, I altogether failed to guess. The one thing of which I felt certain was, that the grossest of mankind could not have misconstrued her motive in speaking, even at that suspiciously late hour and in that suspiciously lonely place.   35

'Did you hear me?' she said, still quietly and rapidly, and without the least fretfulness or impatience. 'I asked if that was the way to London.'   40

'Yes,' I replied, 'that is the way...'

● Which words/phrases describe the woman's appearance? Which describe her manner?

Extract 2   Later in the novel, Walter sees her again, by the grave of Mrs Fairlie – the woman in white's benefactress and the mother of a woman in love with Walter.

... I saw the woman in the cloak approach close to the grave, and stand looking at it for a little while. She then glanced all round her, and taking a white linen cloth or handkerchief from under her cloak, turned aside towards the brook. The little stream ran into the churchyard under a tiny archway in the bottom of the wall, and ran out again, after a winding course of a few dozen yards, under a similar opening. She dipped the cloth in the water, and returned to the grave. I saw her kiss the white cross, then kneel down before the inscription, and apply her wet cloth to the cleansing of it.   1

     5

After considering how I could show myself with the least possible chance of frightening her, I resolved to cross the wall before me, to skirt round it outside, and to enter the churchyard again by the stile near the grave, in order that she might see me as I approached. She was so absorbed over her employment that she did not hear me coming until I had stepped over the stile. Then she looked up, started to her feet with a faint cry, and stood facing me in speechless and motionless terror.   10

     15

'Don't be frightened,' I said. 'Surely you remember me?'

I stopped while I spoke – then advanced a few steps gently – then stopped again – and so approached by little and little till I was close to her. If there had been any doubt still left in my mind, it must have been now set at rest. There, speaking affrightedly for itself – there was the same face confronting me over Mrs Fairlie's grave which had first looked into mine on the high-road by night.   20

'You remember me?' I said. 'We met very late, and I helped you to find the way to London. Surely you have not forgotten that?'   25

(from *The Woman in White*)

GLOSSARY
brook (l.4): small stream
inscription (l.9): what was
written on it
skirt round (l.12): go
round (the outside)
stile (l.12): step (for
climbing over the wall)
affrightedly (l.22): in a
frightened manner
(*archaic*)

● i) Can you describe the woman in your own words? What guesses can you make about her?

ii) How does Collins make the atmosphere suspenseful?

**John Stuart Mill
(1806–1873)**

Until the second half of the nineteenth century unmarried women in Britain had few career prospects and little chance of an intellectual education. However, in 1848, Queen's College was founded in London for the higher education of women and in 1869 Girton College was founded in Cambridge. The Married Women's Property Act (1882) for the first time gave wives rights to their property, although it was not until the twentieth century that political rights were fully won.

● What important changes of status have taken place in your country in relation to women's rights? When/How did they occur?

There were many great women in the nineteenth century. Elizabeth Fry (1780–1845) was a distinguished social worker and prison reformer, Florence Nightingale (1820–1910) reformed the nursing profession and Beatrice Webb (1858–1943) was a pioneer in education. There were also a number of great novelists, notably Jane Austen, the Brontë sisters and George Eliot.

The campaign to give women the right to vote in political elections began in 1866 when a group of women presented a petition to the highly influential writer and emancipationist John Stuart Mill. However, his attempt to get the Reform Act of 1867 (which gave the vote to all working-class men in the towns) amended to include women was defeated.

In his essay 'The Subjection of Women' (1869) Mill stated that 'the principle which regulates the existing social relations between the two sexes – the legal subordination of one sex to the other – is wrong in itself, and now one of the chief hindrances to human improvement; . . . it ought to be replaced by a principle of perfect equality, admitting no power or privilege on the one side, nor disability on the other'.

● Look back to the extract from *The Taming of the Shrew* (pages 11–15). How far do you think Shakespeare would have sympathised with the views Mill expresses in the following passage?

GLOSSARY

sentiments (l.2): thoughts and feelings

brutish (l.2): cruel and unthinking

submission (l.12): acceptance of (male) authority

sentimentalities (l.14): weak and foolish ideas

abnegation (l.15): self-sacrifice

indefeasible (l.19): unbreakable

polar star (l.27): guiding principle

Men do not want solely the obedience of women, they want their sentiments. All men, except the most brutish, desire to have, in the woman most nearly connected with them, not a forced slave but a willing one, not a slave merely, but a favourite. They have therefore put everything in practice to enslave their minds. The masters of all other slaves rely, for maintaining obedience, on fear; either fear of themselves, or religious fears. The masters of women wanted more than simple obedience, and they turned the whole force of education to effect their purpose. All women are brought up from the very earliest years in the belief that their ideal of character is the very opposite to that of men; not self-will, and government by self-control, but submission, and yielding to the control of others. All the moralities tell them that it is the duty of women, and all the current sentimentalities that it is their nature, to live for others; to make complete abnegation of themselves, and to have no life but in their affections. And by their affections are meant the only ones they are allowed to have – those to the men with whom they are

1

5

10

15

420

connected, or to the children who constitute an additional and indefeasible tie between them and a man. When we put together three things – first, the natural attraction between opposite sexes; secondly, the wife's entire dependence on the husband, every privilege or pleasure she has being either his gift, or depending entirely on his will; and lastly, that the principal object of human pursuit, consideration, and all objects of social ambition, can in general be sought or obtained by her only through him, it would be a miracle if the object of being attractive to men had not become the polar star of feminine education and formation of character.

20

25

(from 'The Subjection of Women')

Nowadays, Mill's reputation is largely of someone who reasserted the needs of the imagination and emotions in the face of the more extreme forms of Utilitarianism, a philosophy deriving from eighteenth-century rationalism. In his *Autobiography* (1873), Mill outlines how he recovered from a spiritual crisis, partly through the 'greatly increased interest in the common feelings and common destiny of human beings' that Wordsworth's poetry brought him. Wordsworth's poems, he wrote,

> . . . expressed not mere outward beauty, but states of feeling, and of thought coloured by feeling, under the excitement of beauty. They seemed to be the very culture of feelings which I was in quest of. In them I seemed to draw from a source of inward joy, of sympathetic and imaginative pleasure, which could be shared in by all human beings.

Mill's essays on 'the two great seminal minds of England in this age', Jeremy Bentham (1748–1832), the founder of Utilitarianism and an associate of Mill's father, and Coleridge (see page 147), are still read today.

● Do you regard poetry as a source of strength and pleasure? If so, which poems in particular have this power for you?

Supplement 7

Matthew Arnold
(1822–1888)

Matthew Arnold served as a school inspector for thirty-five years, travelling extensively throughout England. He wrote elevated, melancholic poetry (for example, the epic narrative *Sohrab and Rustum*, 1853 and the short lyric 'Dover Beach', 1867) which was, in tone, fairly representative of his time. However, it is as a critic that Arnold is most remembered. His thought had a great influence on such critics as I.A. Richards (1893–1979), T.S. Eliot, F.R. Leavis, and R. Williams (1921–1988), who saw it as deeply relevant to twentieth-century problems.

Arnold was critical of English life for such things as its provincialism (that is, its limited ideas and its lack of intellectual curiosity); middle-class 'Philistinism' (a word he introduced into English, meaning lack of real culture); its sectarianism (that is, the narrow beliefs held by different minority groups); and the kind of utilitarian materialism criticised by many of his near-contemporaries (for example, Carlyle). He argued vigorously in favour of the critic and his endeavour to 'see the object as in itself it really is'.

Extract 1　In this extract from the essay 'The Function of Criticism at the Present Time' in *Essays in Criticism* (1865), Arnold makes clear what he expects of the English literary critic:

English criticism should clearly discern what rule for its course . . . 1
it ought to take. The rule may be summed up in one word – *dis-*
interestedness. **And how is criticism to show disinterestedness? By**
keeping aloof from what is called 'the practical view of things'; by
resolutely following the law of its own nature, which is to be a free 5
play of the mind on all subjects which it touches. By steadily
refusing to lend itself to any of those ulterior, political, practical
considerations about ideas, which plenty of people will be sure to
attach to them, which perhaps ought often to be attached to them,
which in this country at any rate are certain to be attached to them 10
quite sufficiently, but which criticism has really nothing to do
with. Its business is, as I have said, simply to know the best that is
known and thought in the world, and by in its turn making this
known, to create a current of true and fresh ideas.

By the very nature of things, as England is not all the world, much 15
of the best that is known and thought in the world cannot be of
English growth, must be foreign; by the nature of things, again, it
is just this that we are least likely to know, while English thought
is streaming in upon us from all sides, and takes excellent care that
we shall not be ignorant of its existence. The English critic of litera- 20
ture, therefore, must dwell much on foreign thought, and with
particular heed on any part of it, which, while significant and fruit-
ful in itself, is for any reason specially likely to escape him. Again
judging is often spoken of as the critic's one business, and so in
some sense it is; but the judgement which almost insensibly forms 25
itself in a fair and clear mind, along with fresh knowledge, is the
valuable one; and thus knowledge, and ever fresh knowledge,
must be the critic's great concern for himself.

(from 'The Function of Criticism at the Present Time')

GLOSSARY

disinterestedness (l.2): independence and objectivity of mind

aloof (l.4): apart; distant

resolutely (l.5): firmly

ulterior (l.7): below the surface

insensibly (l.25): unconsciously

Extract 2　The following extract is from *Culture and Anarchy* (1869), a collection of essays written after the Reform Bill of 1867, which gave the vote to many who, Arnold thought, were not well educated enough to use it properly.

422

More and more . . . because of our want of light to enable us to look beyond machinery to the end for which machinery is valuable, this and that man, and this and that body of men, all over the country, are beginning to assert and put in practice an Englishman's right to do what he likes; his right to march where he likes, meet where he likes, enter where he likes, hoot as he likes, threaten as he likes, smash as he likes. All this, I say, tends to anarchy; and though a number of excellent people, and particularly my friends of the Liberal or progressive party, as they call themselves, are kind enough to reassure us by saying that these are trifles, that a few transient outbreaks of rowdyism signify nothing, our system of liberty is one which itself cures all the evils which it works, that the educated and intelligent classes stand in overwhelming strength and majestic repose, ready, like our military force in riots, to act at a moment's notice, – yet one finds that one's Liberal friends generally say this because they have such faith in themselves and their nostrums, when they shall return, as the public welfare requires, to place and power.

. . . one finds . . . that the outbreaks of rowdyism tend to become less and less of trifles, to become more frequent rather than less frequent; and that meanwhile our educated and intelligent classes remain in their majestic repose, and somehow or other, whatever happens, their overwhelming strength, like our military force in riots, never does act.

(from *Culture and Anarchy*)

GLOSSARY

want (l.1): need

end (l.2): purpose

hoot (l.6): shout and laugh in a disrespectful fashion

anarchy (l.7): the collapse of government and order in society

trifles (l.10): unimportant things

transient (l.11): lasting only a short time

rowdyism (l.11): noisy, rough behaviour

majestic repose (l.14): in a calm and grand manner

nostrums (l.17): favourite remedies for political and social unrest

Extract 3 In the following two extracts Arnold expresses his views on poetry. This is from an essay which introduced his selection of Wordsworth's poems (1879):

It is important, therefore, to hold fast to this: that poetry is at bottom a criticism of life; that the greatness of a poet lies in his powerful and beautiful application of ideas to life – to the question: How to live. Morals are often treated in a narrow and false fashion; they are bound up with systems of thought and belief which have had their day; they are fallen into the hands of pedants and professional dealers; they grow tiresome to some of us. We find attraction, at times, even in a poetry of revolt against them. . . . Or we find attractions in a poetry indifferent to them: in a poetry where the contents may be what they will, but where the form is studied and exquisite. We delude ourselves in either case; and the best cure for our delusion is to let our minds rest upon that great and inexhaustible word *life*, until we learn to enter into its meaning. A poetry of revolt against moral ideas is a poetry of revolt against life; a poetry of indifference towards moral ideas is a poetry of indifference towards *life*.

GLOSSARY

pedants (l.6): people who pay too much attention to unimportant details

studied and exquisite (l.10): carefully and beautifully constructed

Extract 4   This is from his essay 'The Study of Poetry' (1888):

> The future of poetry is immense, because in poetry, where it is   1
> worthy of its high destinies, our race, as time goes on, will find an
> ever surer and surer stay. There is not a creed which is not shaken,
> not an accredited dogma which is not shown to be questionable,
> not a received tradition which does not threaten to dissolve. Our   5
> religion has materialized itself in the fact, in the supposed fact; it
> has attached its emotion to the fact, and now the fact is failing it.
> But for poetry the idea is everything; the rest is a world of illusion,
> of divine illusion. Poetry attaches its emotion to the idea; the idea
> *is* the fact. The strongest part of our religion today is its unconscious   10
> poetry.
>
> More and more mankind will discover that we have to turn to poetry
> to interpret life for us, to console us, to sustain us. Without poetry,
> our science will appear incomplete; and most of what now passes
> with us for religion and philosophy will be replaced by poetry.   15
> Science, I say, will appear incomplete without it.
>
> But for supreme poetical success more is required than the powerful
> application of ideas to life; it must be an application under the
> conditions fixed by the laws of poetic truth and poetic beauty.
> Those laws fix as an essential condition, in the poet's treatment of   20
> such matters as are here in question, high seriousness; the high
> seriousness which comes from absolute sincerity.

GLOSSARY
console (l.13): comfort

(from 'The Study of Poetry')

- i) In context, which of these have a positive connotation? 'disinterestedness' (Extract 1 l.2); 'foreign thought' (Extract 1 l.21); 'fresh knowledge' (Extract 1 l.26); 'machinery' (Extract 2 l.2); 'our educated and intelligent classes' (Extract 2 l.21); 'professional dealers' (Extract 3 l.6); 'a poetry of revolt against moral ideas' (Extract 3 l.13); 'high seriousness' (Extract 4 l.21)
- ii) Could you describe Arnold as an Aesthete (see page 222)? Give reasons for your answer.
- iii) Find one idea in these extracts you either agree with or disagree with. Give reasons.
- iv) Make at least one statement about Arnold's style.

Edward Lear (1812–1888): Comic literature   Despite its later reputation as an age of solemnity, the Victorian age produced a remarkable amount of humorous prose and verse: for example, Dickens's *Pickwick Papers* (1837); the children's book *Alice's Adventures in Wonderland* (1865) by Lewis Carroll (Charles Lutwidge Dodgson, 1832–1898); and comic operas such as *The Pirates of Penzance* (1879) by Sir W.S. Gilbert (1836–1911) and Sir A. Sullivan (1842–1900).

Limericks (a form of comic verse epigram) were popularised by Edward Lear:

424

> **There was a Young Lady whose Nose**   1
> **Continually prospers and grows;**
> **When it grew out of sight,**
> **She exclaimed in a fright:**
> **'Oh! Farewell to the end of my Nose!'**   5

Notice that the form consists of five lines with the first, second and fifth lines rhyming (each has three metrical 'feet') and the third and fourth lines rhyming (each has two metrical 'feet').

Lear, by profession a landscape painter, was also a great writer of 'Nonsense Literature', a literature which deliberately defies common sense and creates an upside-down world of absurdity, puzzle and fantasy. Its aim was to amuse children, but looking back we can see a mental unease and a tendency to melancholia characteristic of, for example, Arnold and Tennyson.

This is from Lear's poem 'The Jumblies' (1871):

> **They went to sea in a sieve, they did;**   1
> **In a sieve they went to sea;**
> **In spite of all their friends could say,**
> **On a winter's morn, on a stormy day,**
> **In a sieve they went to sea.**   5
> **And when the sieve turned round and round,**
> **And everyone cried, 'You'll be drowned!'**
> **They called aloud, 'Our sieve ain't big,**
> **But we don't care a button; we don't care a fig –**
> **In a sieve we'll go to sea!'**   10
> **Far and few, far and few,**
> **Are the lands where the Jumblies live.**
> **Their heads are green, and their hands are blue;**
> **And they went to sea in a sieve.**

GLOSSARY
sieve (l.1): wire net used for separating large and small solids (or solids from liquids)
ain't (l.8): isn't (*not standard English*)
We don't care . . . fig (l.9): we don't care at all

They sailed away in a sieve, they did,   15
  In a sieve they sailed so fast,
With only a beautiful pea-green veil
Tied with a ribbon, by way of a sail,
  To a small tobacco-pipe mast.
And everyone said who saw them go,   20
'Oh! won't they be soon upset, you know,
For the sky is dark, and the voyage is long;
And, happen what may, it's extremely wrong
  In a sieve to sail so fast.'

(from 'The Jumblies')

pea-green veil (l.17): light
  yellowish-green piece
  of cloth
mast (l.19): upright post
  for the sail
upset (l.21): overturned

● i) What makes the sieve so unlikely a boat?
  ii) What rhythmic pattern has the verse got?

George Meredith
(1828–1909)

Goerge Meredith had a high reputation as a poet and a novelist well into this century. Oscar Wilde regarded his fiction as excellent philosophy: 'incomparable novelist ... His people not merely live, but they live in thought.' In recent years, though, he has been much less highly regarded. Virginia Woolf said of his style, 'now he twists himself into iron knots, now he lies as flat as a pancake'; F.R. Leavis described him as the 'flashy product of unusual but vulgar cleverness' and Ezra Pound dismissed him as 'chiefly a stink'.

Meredith was partly educated in Germany and his novels show the influence of the ideas about comedy of the German Jean Paul Richter (1763–1825) and the eigthteenth-century French 'Philosophes', a group of writers united by their faith in reason and their dislike of repressive traditions. However, Meredith resembles many of his British Victorian contemporaries. Like Carlyle he was hostile to the mechanistic qualities of his age and like Browning he was interested in psychological exploration. Meredith's early poems include the volume *Modern Love* (1862), fifty verses spoken by a narrator who discovers how unreal and idealistic are his ideas of women. His best-known novel is *The Egoist* (1879), the story of the courting of a woman by a rich and fashionable 'egoist' and her fight for independence. (According to Meredith, if man's task in life was to contribute to the forward movement of humanity, as the evolutionists believed, 'egoism', man's primitive drive to assert his own selfish desires, must be kept in check. This could be done with the help of what he called the 'Comic Spirit'.)

The Tale of Chloe (1879) is a short novel about a generous woman called Chloe in love with the unprincipled Caseldy. Caseldy seduces a young ex-dairymaid called Susan, married to an old duke. Chloe is heartbroken and determined to 'save' Susan by preventing her from eloping with Caseldy. In this extract Susan is about to leave:

**Chloe was asleep, at peace by this time, she thought; and how she   1
envied Chloe! 'She might be as happy if she pleased. Why not? But
what kind of happiness was it?' She likened it to that of the corpse**

underground, and shrank distastefully.

Susan stood at her glass to have a look at the creature, about 5
whom there was all this disturbance, and she threw up her arms
high for a languid, not unlovely yawn, that closed in blissful
shuddering with the sensation of her lover's arms having wormed
round her waist and taken her while she was defenceless. For surely
they would. She took a jewelled ring, his gift, from her purse, and 10
kissed it, and drew it on and off her finger, leaving it on. Now she
might wear it without fear of inquiries and virtuous eyebrows. O
heavenly now – if only it were an hour hence, and going behind
galloping horses!

The clock was at the terrible moment. She hesitated internally 15
and hastened; once her feet stuck fast, and firmly she said, 'No;'
but the clock was her lord. The clock was her lover and her lord;
and obeying it, she managed to get into the sitting-room, on the
pretext that she merely wished to see through the front window
whether daylight was coming. 20

How well she knew that half-light of the ebb of the wave of
darkness.

Strange enough it was to see it showing houses regaining their
solidity of the foregone day, instead of still fields, black hedges,
familiar shapes of trees. The houses had no wakefulness, they 25
were but seen to stand, and the light was a revelation of emptiness.
Susan's heart was cunning to reproach her duke for the difference
of the scene she beheld from that of the innocent open-breasted
land. Yes, it was dawn in a wicked place that she should never
have been allowed to visit. But where was he whom she looked 30
for? There! The cloaked figure of a man was at the corner of the
street. It was he. Her heart froze; but her limbs were strung to throw
off the house, and reach air, breathe, and (as her thoughts ran)
swoon, well-protected. To her senses the house was a house on fire,
and crying to her to escape. 35

Yet she stepped deliberately, to be sure-footed in a dusky room;
she touched along the wall and came to the door, where a foot-stool
nearly tipped her. Here her touch was at fault, for though she knew
she must be close by the door, she was met by an obstruction unlike
wood, and the door seemed neither shut nor open. She could not 40
find the handle; something hung over it. Thinking coolly, she fancied the thing must be a gown or dressing-gown; it hung heavily.
Her fingers were sensible of the touch of silk; she distinguished a
depending bulk, and she felt at it very carefully and mechanically,
saying within herself, in her anxiety to pass it without noise, 'If I 45
should awake poor Chloe, of all people!' Her alarm was that the
door might creak. Before any other alarm had struck her brain, the
hand she felt with was in a palsy, her mouth gaped, her throat
thickened, the dustball rose in her throat, and the effort to swallow
it down and get breath kept her from acute speculation while she 50
felt again, pinched, plucked at the thing, ready to laugh, ready to
shriek. Above her head, all on one side, the thing had a round white

top. **Could it be a hand that her touch had slid across? An arm too!
this was an arm! She clutched it, imagining that it clung to her. She
pulled it to release herself from it, desperately she pulled, and a
lump descended, and a flash of all the torn nerves of her body told
her that a dead human body was upon her.** 55

lump (l.56): solid mass

(from The Tale of Chloe)

- i) What can you deduce from the following? 'For surely they would.' (l.9);
'behind galloping horses' (l.13); 'as her thoughts ran' (l.33); 'the touch of silk
(l.43)
- ii) Whose body do you think it was? (The answer is in the Key.)
- iii) Were you made to feel you were in Susan's mind?

Gerard Manley Hopkins (1844–1889)

Much of the poetry of Gerard Manley Hopkins (see page 220) is a religious
celebration of the natural world. It has the rhythmical freedom of the
spoken language and contains, in a spirit of joy, many new words and
new word compounds. Hopkins was interested in what he called 'inscape'
(the qualities that give an object its individual reality) and 'instress' (the
energy from these qualities as it flows into the mind of the observer). At
a technical level the appearance of originality his verse has is also helped
by the use of a 'sprung rhythm' (a combination of regular stress patterns
with a varying number of syllables).

However, in poems written between 1885 and 1889 (his 'terrible sonnets')
there is a powerful sense of exile and frustration. The following sonnet
was written three months before his death. Like the early seventeeth-
century devotional poets John Donne and George Herbert, the narrator
addresses God directly:

GLOSSARY

Justus quidem . . . (title):
(Jeremiah 12:1:
Righteous are thou, O
Lord, when I plead
with thee: yet let me
talk with thee of thy
judgements: Wherefore
does the way of the
wicked prosper – *Latin*)
contend (l.1): dispute
Wert thou (l.5): if you
were . . . (*archaic*)
thwart (l.7): frustrate
sots and thralls of (l.7):
foolish slaves to
banks and brakes (l.9):
clumps of fern
fretty chervil (l.11): chervil,
a type of wild parsley,
with interlaced patterns
Time's eunuch (l.13):
deprived of vitality
through old age
Mine (l.14): (my roots?
my God?)

*Justus quidem tu es, Domine, si disputem tecum: verumtamen
    justa loquar ad te: Quare via impiorum prosperatur?*

Thou art indeed just, Lord, if I contend 1
With thee; but, sir, so what I plead is just.
Why do sinners' ways prosper? and why must
Disappointment all I endeavour end?
**   Wert thou my enemy, O thou my friend,** 5
How wouldst thou worse, I wonder, than thou dost
Defeat, thwart me? Oh, the sots and thralls of lust
Do in spare hours more thrive than I that spend,
Sir, life upon thy cause. See, banks and brakes
Now, leaved how thick! laced they are again 10
With fretty chervil, look, and fresh wind shakes
Them; birds build – but not I build; no, but strain,
Time's eunuch, and not breed one work that wakes.
Mine, O thou lord of life, send my roots rain.

i) Explain the phrase 'birds build – but not I build' (l.12).

ii) What do you think 'one work' (l.13) refers to?

Rudyard Kipling
(1865–1936)

Rudyard Kipling, the poet, short story writer and novelist, was born in Bombay in India but settled in England in 1889. His works include the novel *Kim* (1901), based on his childhood in India, and the children's stories *The Jungle Books* (1894–1895) and *Puck of Pook's Hill* (1906). While Kipling was able to identify with the humble soldier (or the Indian peasant) he nevertheless admired action, power and efficiency, and, from time to time, tended to crude chauvinism. Kipling's collection of verses about British soldiers was collected in *Barrack Room Ballads* (1892), for forty years the most popular book of verse in the English-speaking world.

Oscar Wilde said that Kipling made him feel 'as if one were seated under a palm tree reading life by superb flashes of vulgarity', and Henry James wrote that Kipling 'never arranges or glosses or falsifies, but goes straight for the common and the characteristic'.

A traditional ballad is a narrative poem or song in colloquial language, expressing popular feelings about actual events. 'Danny Deever' which T.S. Eliot described as 'technically remarkable' and having 'the intensity of poetry', is a Cockney ballad (that is, it is spoken in the idiom of a native Londoner) whose structure is based on a rude song entitled 'Barnacle Bill the Sailor'. It concerns the hanging of a British soldier in India for shooting a colleague in his sleep. Although public executions were discontinued in England in 1868, they were carried out in India a few years longer.

GLOSSARY

bugles (l.1): brass instruments used in armies for giving signals

Files-on-Parade (l.1): an army private (the lowest rank)

Colour-Sergeant (l.2): high-ranking non-commissioned officer

regiment (l.7): large military group

'ollow square (l.7): ceremonial formation with the troops lining four sides of a parade square, facing inwards

stripes (l.8): Danny was degraded before execution by having his regimental buttons and the strips of his rank torn off

rear-rank (l.10): back row

swing ... hound (l.17): he's soon going to hang for being a nasty, murdering dog

Danny Deever

'What are the bugles blowin' for?' said Files-on-Parade.   1
'To turn you out, to turn you out,' the Colour-Sergeant said.
'What makes you look so white, so white?' said Files-on-Parade.
'I'm dreadin' what I've got to watch,' the Colour-Sergeant said.
    For they're hanging' Danny Deever, you can hear the Dead   5
      March play,
    The regiment's in 'ollow square – they're hangin' him to-day;
    They've taken of his buttons off an' cut his stripes away,
    An' they're hangin' Danny Deever in the mornin'.

'What makes the rear-rank breathe so 'ard?' said Files-on-Parade.   10
'It's bitter cold, it's bitter cold,' the Colour-Sergeant said.
'What makes that front-rank man fall down?' say Files-on-Parade.
'A touch o' sun, a touch o' sun,' the Colour-Sergeant said.
    They are hangin' Danny Deever, they are marchin' of 'im
      round,   15
    They 'ave 'alted Danny Deever by 'is coffin on the ground;
    An' 'e'll swing in 'arf a minute for a sneakin' shootin' hound –
    O they're hangin' Danny Deever in the mornin'!

' 'Is cot was right-'and cot to mine,' said Files-on-Parade.
' 'E's sleepin' out an' far tonight,' the Colour-Sergeant said.   20
'I've drunk 'is beer a score o' times,' said Files-on-Parade.
' 'E's drinkin' bitter beer alone,' the Colour-Sergeant said.
   They are hangin' Danny Deever, you must mark 'im to 'is
     place,
   For 'e shot a comrade sleepin' – you must look 'im in the face;   25
   Nine 'undred of 'is county an' the regiment's disgrace,
   While they're hangin' Danny Deever in the mornin'.

'What's that so black agin the sun?' said Files-on-Parade.
'It's Danny fightin' 'ard for life,' the Colour-Sergeant said.
'What's that that whimpers over'ead?' said Files-on-Parade.
'It's Danny's soul that's passin' now,' the Colour-Sergeant said.   30
   For they're done with Danny Deever, you can 'ear the
     quickstep play,
   The regiment's in column, an' they're marchin' us away;
   Ho! the young recruits are shakin', an' they'll want their   35
     beer today,
   After hangin' Danny Deever in the mornin'.

right-'and cot (l.19): on the right of my bed

score 'o (l.21): many

bitter (l.22): type of sharp, unsweet English beer (it also suggests Danny's suffering)

mark ... place (l.23): watch him go to the place where he will be hanged

county (l.26): regiment, usually carrying the name of the county from which most of its men have been recruited

agin (l.28): against

whimpers (l.30): making a protesting sound

quickstep (l.33): spirited march tune

- i) How would you describe the 'Files-on-Parade'?
  ii) What is the attitude of the 'Colour-Sergeant'?
  iii) What is the reaction of the men?
  iv) Can you describe the action?

British soldiers in India

430

Thomas Hardy (1840–1928)

Thomas Hardy is sometimes thought of as the last of the Victorians and the first of the moderns. The son of a builder in Dorset, his novels and poems are full of accurately observed country details, providing a record of the rapid disintegration of small town and village life.

Like many Victorian intellectuals, Hardy suffered from a loss of religious faith. He developed a gloomy and sombre philosophy of human destiny, showing human beings to be the victims of indifferent forces. At its worst, this side of his writing can be heavy and melodramatic and unnaturally full of coincidence. At its best, it can be very moving.

Tess of the D'Urbervilles: A Pure Woman (1891) concerns the intelligent, sensitive daughter of a poor family, driven to murder by a series of ironic events and unfortunate circumstances. The publication of the novel caused violent reactions, most reviewers considering it immoral and pessimistic ('What has Providence done to Mr Hardy that he should rise up in the arable land of Wessex and shake his fist at his creator?' – Edmund Gosse). Henry James felt the novel was 'chockful of faults and falsity'.

Near the beginning of the novel, Jack Durbeyfield, Tess's father, celebrates the discovery that he is descended from the ancient aristocratic family of D'Urberville. The next morning he is not sober enough to take a consignment of beehives to the nearby town of Casterbridge. Tess goes instead, with her younger brother Abraham. He is asleep and she is unable to keep awake at the reins of the cart.

A sudden jerk shook her in her seat, and Tess awoke from the sleep into which she, too, had fallen. [1]

They were a long way further on than when she had lost consciousness, and the waggon had stopped. A hollow groan, unlike anything she had ever heard in her life, came from the front, followed by a shout of 'Hoi there!' [5]

The lantern hanging at her waggon had gone out, but another was shining in her face – much brighter than her own had been. Something terrible had happened. The harness was entangled with an object which blocked the way. [10]

In consternation Tess jumped down, and discovered the dreadful truth. The groan had proceeded from her father's poor horse Prince. The morning mail-cart, with its two noiseless wheels, speeding along these lanes like an arrow, as it always did, had driven into her slow and unlighted equipage. The pointed shaft of the cart had [15] entered the breast of the unhappy Prince like a sword, and from the wound his life's blood was spouting in a stream, and falling with a hiss into the road.

In her despair Tess sprang forward and put her hand upon the hole, with the only result that she became splashed from face to [20] skirt with the crimson drops. Then she stood helplessly looking on. Prince also stood firm and motionless as long as he could; till he suddenly sank down in a heap.

By this time the mail-cart man had joined her, and began dragging and unharnessing the hot form of Prince. But he was already dead, [25] and, seeing that nothing more could be done immediately, the mail-cart man returned to his own animal, which was uninjured.

'You was on the wrong side,' he said. 'I am bound to go on with the mail-bags, so that the best thing for you to do is to bide here with your load. I'll send somebody to help you as soon as I can. It is getting daylight, and you have nothing to fear.' 30

He mounted and sped on his way; while Tess stood and waited. The atmosphere turned pale, the birds shook themselves in the hedges, arose, and twittered; the lane showed all its white features, and Tess showed hers, still whiter. The huge pool of blood in front 35 of her was already assuming the iridescence of coagulation; and when the sun rose a hundred prismatic hues were reflected from it. Prince lay alongside still and stark; his eyes half open, the hole in his chest looking scarcely large enough to have let out all that had animated him. 40

' 'Tis all my doing – all mine!' the girl cried, gazing at the spectacle. 'No excuse for me – none. What will mother and father live on now? Aby, Aby!' She shook the child, who had slept soundly through the whole disaster. 'We can't go on with our load – Prince is killed!' 45

(from *Tess of the D'Urbervilles*)

● What do you think this scene is meant to show us about Tess's future?

H(erbert) G(eorge) Wells (1866–1946)

The History of Mr Polly (1910) by H.G. Wells has the vigorous humour and sharp characterisation of early Dickens. However, Wells also believed in the urgent need to enlighten mankind and, ignoring the values of traditional culture and art, became fascinated by the prospects that science offered. (Joseph Conrad said to him: 'You don't really care for people, but you think they can be improved; I do, but I know they can't.')

In *The First Men in The Moon* (1901) two men, Cavor and the narrator, have landed on the moon's surface in a 'sphere'. From the inside they watch the sunrise:

Clutching at one another we spun about, pitched this way and that, 1 our bale of packages leaping at us, pounding at us. We collided, we gripped, we were torn asunder – our heads met, and the whole universe burst into fiery darts and stars! On the earth we should have smashed one another a dozen times, but on the moon, luckily 5 for us, our weight was only one-sixth of what it is terrestrially, and we fell very mercifully. I recall a sensation of utter sickness, a feeling as if my brain were upside down within my skull, and then –

Something was at work upon my face, some thin feelers worried my ears. Then I discovered the brilliance of the landscape about me 10 was mitigated by blue spectacles. Cavor bent over me, and I saw his face upside down, his eyes also protected by tinted goggles. His breath came irregularly, and his lip was bleeding from a bruise. 'Better?' he said, wiping the blood with the back of his hand.

Everything seemed swaying for a space, but that was simply my giddiness. I perceived that he had closed some of the shutters in the outer sphere to save me from the direct blaze of the sun. I was aware that everything about us was very brilliant.

He assisted me into a sitting position, and I could see with my own eyes.

The harsh emphasis, the pitiless black and white of the scenery had altogether disappeared. The glare of the sun had taken upon itself a faint tinge of amber; the shadows upon the cliff of the crater wall were deeply purple. To the eastward a dark bank of fog still crouched and sheltered from the sunrise, but to the westward the sky was blue and clear.

We were no longer in a void. An atmosphere had arisen about us. The outline of things had gained in character, had grown acute and varied; save for a shadowed space of white substance here and there, white substance that was no longer air but snow, the arctic appearance had gone altogether. Everywhere broad rusty brown spaces of bare and tumbled earth spread to the blaze of the sun. Here and there at the edge of the snowdrifts were transient little pools and eddies of water, the only things stirring in that expanse of barrenness.

15

20

25

30

35

(from *The First Men in The Moon*)

mitigated (l.11): made less severe
tinted goggles (l.12): slightly coloured glasses used to protect the eyes
space (l.15): time
giddiness (l.16): feeling that everything was turning round
amber (l.23): yellowish-brown colour
crater (l.23): round hole in the ground
void (l.27): empty space
save for (l.29): except for
transient (l.33): short-lived
eddies of (l.34): moving in circles

● i) Which verbs express violent motion?
 ii) Men first landed on the moon in 1969. Does Wells's imaginary description appear accurate to you?

*From the film of
The First Men in the Moon*

Jack London
(1876–1916)

Jack London, the American novelist, was much influenced by Darwin's ideas about 'the survival of the fittest'. He had a number of legal and illegal jobs and took part in the Klondike gold rush of 1897. He was also a socialist who vigorously attacked capitalism and exploitation.

The Call of the Wild (1903) tells the story of a dog, Buck, who is taken from his easy life in California and brought to the cold and primitive world of Alaska.

... the call ... sounding in the depths of the forest ... filled him with a great unrest and strange desires. It caused him to feel a vague, sweet gladness, and he was aware of wild yearnings and stirrings for he knew not what. Sometimes he pursued the call into the forest, looking for it as though it were a tangible thing, barking softly or defiantly, as the mood might dictate. He would thrust his nose into the cool wood moss, or into the black soil where the long grasses grew, and snort with joy at the fat earth smells; or he would crouch for hours, as if in concealment, behind fungus-covered trunks of fallen trees, wide-eyed and wide-eared to all that moved and sounded about him. It might be, lying thus, that he hoped to surprise this call he could not understand. But he did not know why he did these various things. He was impelled to do them, and did not reason about them at all.

One night he sprang from sleep with a start, eager-eyed, nostrils quivering and scenting, his mane bristling in recurrent waves. From the forest came the call (or one note of it, for the call was many-noted), distinct and definite as never before – a long-drawn howl, like, yet unlike, any noise made by husky dog. And he knew it, in the old familiar way, as a sound heard before. He sprang through the sleeping camp and in swift silence dashed through the woods. As he drew closer to the cry he went more slowly, with caution in every movement, till he came to an open place among the trees, and looking out saw, erect on haunches, with nose pointed to the sky, a long, lean, timber wolf.

He had made no noise, yet it ceased from its howling and tried to sense his presence. Buck stalked into the open half-crouching, body gathered compactly together, tail straight and stiff, feet falling with unwonted care. Every movement advertised commingled threatening and overture of friendliness. It was the menacing truce that marks the meeting of wild beasts that prey. But the wolf fled at sight of him. He followed, with wild leapings, in a frenzy to over-take. He ran him into a blind channel, in the bed of the creek, where a timber jam barred the way. The wolf whirled about, pivoting on his hind legs after the fashion of ... all cornered husky dogs, snarl-ing and bristling, clipping his teeth together in a continuous and rapid succession of snaps.

Buck did not attack, but circled him about and hedged him in with friendly advances. The wolf was suspicious and afraid; for Buck made three of him in weight, while his head barely reached Buck's shoulder. Watching his chance, he darted away, and the

even ... flank (l.44–45):
  parallel with his side
whirl (l.45): move quickly
  (around)
at bay (l.45): forced to face
  Buck with defiance
pertinacity (l.47): holding
  on with determination
coy (l.50): shy
belie (l.50): hide

chase was resumed. Time and again he was cornered, and the thing repeated, though he was in poor condition, or Buck could not so easily have overtaken him. He would run till Buck's head was even with his flank, when he would whirl around at bay, only to dash away again at the first opportunity.   45

But in the end Buck's pertinacity was rewarded; for the wolf, finding no harm was intended, finally sniffed noses with him. Then they became friendly, and played about in the nervous, half-coy way with which fierce beasts belie their fierceness.   50

(from *The Call of the Wild*)

- i) Which verb phrases describe Buck's actions?
- ii) Which noun phrases describe his attraction to 'the Wild'?
- iii) Which adjectives describe the wolf's feelings?
- iv) Find at least one place in which London is concerned to show us how the animals differ from humans.

Later in the novel Buck leads a wolf pack.

George Gissing (1857–1903)

George Gissing, a self-absorbed secretive man, was twice unhappily married to working-class women. As his friend H.G. Wells said, 'He felt that to make love to any woman he could regard as a social equal would be too elaborate ... so he flung himself at a social inferior whom he expected to be eager and grateful.'

Gissing's best-known novel is *New Grub Street* (1891), a study of the jealousies and intrigues of literary life in late nineteenth-century London. In a vision that was serious and powerfully sombre, Gissing opposed the spread of a commercialised culture as hostile to the interests of the artist and a healthy civilisation.

The *Private Papers of Henry Ryecroft* (1903) is the imaginary but largely autobiographical journal of a scholarly recluse who, having received a legacy, finds contented release from poverty and worry in books, memories and reflections. As Gissing says in the preface, Ryecroft was a man 'of independent and rather scornful outlook', who, although he had 'suffered much from defeated ambition' was 'not a broken spirit, but a mind and temper ... sternly disciplined.' This is an extract from the journal.

GLOSSARY
tenor (l.1): character
shrink aloof (l.3): become
  distant and superior
abhorrence (l.4): deep
  ·dislike
Demos (l.6): the common
  people – as in an
  ancient Greek state
temper (l.7): characteristic
  state of feeling
disposition for (l.12):
  inclination towards

I am no friend of the people. As a force, by which the tenor of the   1
time is conditioned, they inspire me with distrust, with fear; as a
visible multitude, they make me shrink aloof, and often move me
to abhorrence. ...
Every instinct of my being is anti-democratic, and I dread to think   5
of what our England may become when Demos rules irresistibly.

Right or wrong, this is my temper. But he who should argue
from it that I am intolerant of all persons belonging to a lower social
rank than my own would go far astray. Nothing is more rooted in
my mind than the vast distinction between the individual and the   10
class. Take a man by himself, and there is generally some reason to
be found in him, some disposition for good; mass him with his

fellows in the social organism, and ten to one he becomes a blatant creature, without a thought of his own, ready for any evil to which contagion prompts him. It is because nations tend to stupidity and baseness that mankind moves so slowly; it is because individuals have a capacity for better things that it moves at all.

It has occurred to me that one might define Art as: an expression, satisfying and abiding, of the zest of life.

In this high summertide, I remember with a strange feeling that there are people who, of their free choice, spend day and night in cities, who throng to the gabble of drawing-rooms, make festival in public eating-houses, sweat in the glare of the theatre. They call it life; they call it enjoyment. Why, so it is, for them; they are so made. The folly is mine, to wonder that they fulfil their destiny.

But with what deep and quiet thanksgiving do I remind myself that never shall I mingle with that well-millinered and tailored herd! Happily, I never saw much of them. Certain occasions I recall when a supposed necessity took me into their dismal precincts; a sick buzzing in the brain, a languor as of exhausted limbs, comes upon me with the memory. The relief with which I stepped out into the street again, when all was over! Dear to me then was poverty, which for the moment seemed to make me a free man. Dear to me was the labour at my desk, which, by comparison, enabled me to respect myself.

Never again shall I shake hands with man or woman who is not in truth my friend. Never again shall I go to see acquaintances with whom I have no acquaintance. All men my brothers? Nay, thank Heaven, that they are not! I will do harm, if I can help it, to no one; I will wish good to all; but I will make no pretence of personal kindliness where, in the nature of things, it cannot be felt. I have grimaced a smile and pattered unmeaning words to many a person whom I despised or from whom in heart I shrank; I did so because I had not courage to do otherwise. For a man conscious of such weakness, the best is to live apart from the world.

(from *Private Papers of Henry Ryecroft*)

organism (l.13): system made up of different but interrelated parts

blatant (l.13): noisy and vulgar

contagion (l.15): corrupting influence

baseness (l.16): meanness and degradation

abiding (l.19): lasting (for a long time)

zest (l.19): interesting and exciting quality

In this high summertide (l.20): in the middle of this summer

throng (l.22): crowd

gabble (l.22): foolish talk

glare (l.23): hard bright light; cheap splendour

folly (l.25): foolishness

to wonder ... destiny (l.25): to be surprised they are only doing what they are fated to do

mingle (l.27): mix

well-millinered and tailored (l.27): in elegant hats and dress

dismal precincts (l.29): gloomy neighbourhoods

languor (l.30): lack of energy

pretence (l.40): false claim

grimaced (l.42): forced myself to make

pattered (l.42): spoke quickly

- i) Despite the opening paragraph – which has echoes from Matthew Arnold (see page 421) – what evidence is there that Ryecroft is not misanthropic?
- ii) Which rhetorical techniques can you identify in the paragraph beginning 'Never again shall I . . .' (l.36)? What is their overall effect?
- iii) Do you share Ryecroft's feelings?

Walter de la Mare (1873–1956)

The poems of Walter de la Mare seem unaffected by the fashions of the times in which he lived. They are skilfully crafted, unassuming, and delicate in their technique. Their tone is one of quiet intensity, with an undercurrent of melancholy. They express a dreamworld of nostalgia and fantasy and create an atmosphere of mystery. Much of de la Mare's writing was addressed to children. This poem, 'The Ghost', is about love and loss:

GLOSSARY

restore (l.2): bring back into existence

thorn (l.3): woody plant with sharp spines

hither (l.3): come to this place

lurks . . . fair (l.7–8): lies waiting by the waters ready to take notice of what I have to say, then I say nice things about you

Lone (l.10): isolated

yearned (l.11): strongly desired

thine (l.12): yours (*archaic*)

Brake (l.14): broke

groped (l.15): made its way by feeling

chaos of vacancy (l.18): like a deep hole of emptiness, as before the creation of the universe and distinct forms

Nought (l.19): nothing

sweet cheat (l.20): (it is all an illusion; the phrase comes from the title of one of the volumes of Proust's *Remembrance of Things Past*)

The Ghost

'Who knocks?' 'I, who was beautiful,   1
  Beyond all dreams to restore,
I, from the roots of the dark thorn am hither,
  And knock on the door.'

'Who speaks?' 'I – once was my speech   5
  Sweet as the bird's on the air,
When echo lurks by the waters to heed;
  'Tis I speak thee fair.'

'Dark is the hour!' 'Ay, and cold.'
  'Lone is my house.' 'Ah, but mine?'   10
'Sight, touch, lips, eyes yearned in vain.'
  'Long dead these to thine . . .'

Silence. Still faint on the porch
  Brake the flames of the stars.
In gloom groped a hope-wearied hand   15
  Over keys, bolts, and bars.

A face peered. All the grey night
  In chaos of vacancy shone;
Nought but vast sorrow was there –
  The sweet cheat gone.   20

i) In the first three stanzas which parts are uttered by the narrator, which by the 'ghost'?

ii) Comment on the response 'Ah, but mine' (l.10).

iii) What does 'these' refer to (l.12)?

iv) What thoughts and feelings does the poem arouse in you?

Supplement 8

James Joyce
(1882–1941)

Ulysses (published in Paris, 1922) was banned in England until 1936 for its alleged obscenity. The story shows, in immense detail, twenty-four hours (16 June 1904) in the life of Leopold Bloom, a lonely Jew of Hungarian origin, living in Dublin, Ireland – a man with numerous casual acquaintances and a wife whose fidelity he distrusts. (Another important character in the novel is Stephen Dedalus, the hero of *A Portrait of the Artist as a Young Man* – see page 271). Joyce attempts to show, through the 'stream of consciousness' technique (see page 273), a 'whole individual', made representative of the history of Europe by being set against the background of Homer's early Greek epic *The Odyssey*.

In the following extract (slightly abridged) Bloom is at the funeral of Paddy Dignam, a jolly drunkard. As it expresses Bloom's sometimes interrupted, sometimes unexplained thoughts and feelings in broken sentences, it is not always easy to know what is being referred to.

Mr Bloom stood far back, his hat in his hand, counting the bared heads. Twelve. I'm thirteen. No. The chap in the macintosh is thirteen. Death's number. Where the deuce did he pop out of? He wasn't in the chapel, that I'll swear. Silly superstition that about thirteen. 5

Nice soft tweed Ned Lambert has in that suit. Tinge of purple. I had one like that when we lived in Lombard street west. Dressy fellow he was once. Used to change three suits in the day. . . .

The coffin dived out of sight, eased down by the men straddled on the gravetrestles. They struggled up and out: and all uncovered. 10
Twenty.

Pause.

If we were all suddenly somebody else.

Far away a donkey brayed. Rain. No such ass. Never see a dead one, they say. Shame of death. They hide. Also poor papa went 15
away

Gentle sweet air blew round the bared heads in a whisper. Whisper. The boy by the gravehead held his wreath with both hands staring quietly in the black open space. Mr Bloom moved behind the portly kindly caretaker. Well cut frockcoat. Weighing 20
them up perhaps to see which will go next. Well it is a long rest. Feel no more. It's the moment you feel. Must be damned unpleasant. Can't believe it at first. Mistake must be: someone else. Try the house opposite. Wait, I wanted to. I haven't yet. Then darkened deathchamber. Light they want. Whispering around you. Would 25
you like to see a priest? Then rambling and wandering. Delirium all you hid all your life. The death struggle. His sleep is not natural. Press his lower eyelid. Watching is his nose pointed is his jaw sinking are the soles of his feet yellow. Pull the pillow away and finish it off on the floor since he's doomed. . . . 30

The gravediggers took up their spades and flung heavy clods of clay in on the coffin. Mr Bloom turned his face. And if he was alive all the time? Whew! By Jingo, that would be awful! No, no: he is dead, of course. Of course he is dead. Monday he died. They ought to have some law to pierce the heart and make sure or an electric 35
clock or a telephone in the coffin and some kind of a canvas airhole. Flag of distress. Three days. Rather long to keep them in summer. Just as well to get shut of them as soon as you are sure there's no.

The clay fell softer. Begin to be forgotten. Out of sight, out of mind. 40

(from *Ulysses*)

GLOSSARY

the deuce (l.3): the devil (used to add force to the question)

pop out of (l.3): come from (unexpectedly)

tweed (l.6): type of thick woollen cloth

Tinge (l.6): small amount

Dressy (l.7): fashionably dressed

straddled on the gravetrestles (l.9): with their legs on either side of the frame of the grave

uncovered (l.10): without hats on

brayed (l.14): made its natural cry

ass (l.14): donkey

wreath (l.18): ring of flowers as a sign of respect

portly (l.20): rather fat and heavy

frockcoat (l.20): knee-length coat for men

Weighing . . . next (l.20–21): (perhaps trying to work out from looking at them who will die next)

Delirium (l.26): an excited dreamy state

clods (l.31): lumps

By Jingo (l.33): (mild oath)

get shut of (l.38): get rid of

● i) Can you separate the narrator's descriptions from Mr Bloom's thoughts?
ii) Do you find this type of writing attractive?

George Bernard Shaw (1856–1950)

George Bernard Shaw was born in Dublin. Between 1879 and 1883 he wrote five novels but his first success was as a music and drama critic. Shaw was notorious as a 'freethinker' who liked to shock conventional society; he was also a supporter of women's rights and an advocate of equality of income and the abolition of private property. From 1885–1911 he served on the executive committee of the Fabian Society (see page 220). His other major belief was in what he called the 'Life Force', the power of the human will in characters of genius which enables humanity to make progress. Shaw's plays are conflicts of ideas rather than of physical passion, and his characters tend to make a lot of witty speeches. At the same time they contain many clever theatrical effects.

Saint Joan (1924) shows many of Shaw's strengths and weaknesses. Its discussions of political motives and class antagonisms are lively but its efforts to move us emotionally are often less convincing.

In the fifteenth century, Jeanne d'Arc, a French country girl, helped to lead an army to drive the English out of France. Later, she was burned as a witch. Although Shaw saw her simply as a fine heroic woman, Joan had been made a Roman Catholic saint in 1920. In this lively scene we meet her for the first time. Captain Robert de Baudricourt is, in Shaw's words in the stage directions, ' a military squire, handsome and physically energetic, but with no will of his own ... disguising that effect in his usual fashion by storming terribly at his Steward, a trodden worm'.

Joan of Arc

[JOAN *appears in the turret doorway. She is an able-bodied country*   1
girl of seventeen or eighteen, respectably dressed in red with an
uncommon face: eyes very wide apart and bulging as they often

do in very imaginative people, a long, well-shaped nose with 5
wide nostrils, a short upper lip, resolute but full-lipped mouth
and handsome fighting chin. She comes eagerly to the table,
delighted at having penetrated to BAUDRICOURT'S *presence at*
last, and full hope as to the result. His scowl does not check or
frighten her in the least. Her voice is normally a hearty, coaxing
voice, very confident, very appealing, very hard to resist.] 10

JOAN: [*bobbing a curtsey*]: Good morning, captain squire. Captain, you are to give me a horse and armor and some soldiers, and send me to the Dauphin. Those are your orders from my Lord.

ROBERT: [*outraged*]: Orders from *your* lord! And who the devil may your lord be? Go back to him, and tell him that I am neither duke 15 nor peer at his orders: I am squire of Baudricourt; and I take no orders except from the king.

JOAN: [*reassuringly*]: Yes, squire: that is all right. My Lord is the King of Heaven.

ROBERT: Why, the girl's mad. [*To the steward*] Why didnt you tell 20 me so, you blockhead?

STEWARD: Sir: do not anger her; give her what she wants.

JOAN: [*impatient but friendly*]: They all say I am mad until I talk to them, squire. But you see that it is the will of God that you are to do what He has put into my mind. 25

ROBERT: It is the will of God that I will send you back to your father with orders to put you under lock and key and thrash the madness out of you. What have you to say to that?

JOAN: You think you will, squire; but you will find it all coming quite different. You said you would not see me; but here I am. 30

STEWARD: [*appealing*]: Yes, sir, You see, sir.

ROBERT: Hold your tongue, you.

STEWARD: [*abjectly*]: Yes, sir.

ROBERT: [*to Joan, with a sour loss of confidence*]: So you are presuming on my seeing you, are you? 35

JOAN: [*sweetly*]: Yes, squire.

ROBERT: [*feeling that he has lost ground, brings down his two fists squarely on the table, and inflates his chest imposingly to cure the unwelcome and only too familiar sensation*]: Now, listen to me. I am going to assert myself. 40

JOAN: [*busily*]: Please do, squire. The horse will cost sixteen francs. It is a good deal of money; but I can save it on the armor. I can find a soldier's armor that will fit me well enough: I am very hardy: and I do not need beautiful armor made to my measure like you wear. I shall not want many soldiers: the Dauphin will 45 give me all I need to raise the siege of Orleans!

ROBERT: [*flabbergasted*]: To raise the siege of Orleans!

JOAN: [*simply*]: Yes, squire: that is what God is sending me to do. Three men will be enough for you to send with me if they are good men and gentle to me. 50

(from *Saint Joan*)

GLOSSARY

turret (l.1): small tower in a castle

able-bodied (l.1): physically strong

bulging (l.3): curving outwards

resolute (l.5): showing determination

scowl (l.8): angry frown

check (l.8): hold back

coaxing (l.9): persuading

squire (l.11): gentleman-at-arms: a man who defends the king

Dauphin (l.13): the eldest son of a king of France

peer (l.16): noble person

blockhead (l.21): stupid person

thrash (l.27): beat

Hold your tongue (l.32): be quiet

abjectly (l.33): in a cowardly manner

squarely (l.38): directly

imposingly (l.38): in a grand, impressive manner

assert myself (l.40): show my authority

hardy (l.44): strong and able to endure suffering

raise the siege of Orleans (l.46): to end the British attack on the French town of Orleans

flabbergasted (l.47): astonished

● i) Do you find any parts of this funny?

ii) Where do we most see Joan's confidence and Robert's weakness?

iii) What indications are there that Shaw expects his plays to be read as well as performed?

E(dward) M(organ) Forster (1879–1970)

In 1897, after an unhappy time at a public school in Tonbridge, E.M. Forster went to King's College, Cambridge, where he found congenial friends and an atmosphere of free intellectual discussion. He travelled in Europe, lived for a time in Egypt, and visited India (1912–1913 and 1921–1922). In 1946 he returned to King's and lived there as an honorary fellow for the rest of his life. Forster's novels include *A Room with a View* (1908) and *Howard's End* (1910).

In *A Passage to India* (1922–1924), two visitors to India, Mrs Moore and Adela Quested, are enthusiastically invited by Aziz (a young Muslim doctor) to visit the local Marabar Caves, which have a strong significance for Hindus. The following episode (slightly abridged) represents a turning point in the novel and causes an outbreak of antagonism between the English and the Indians. Professor Godbole is a rather detached but saintly Brahmin, a Hindu of the highest rank.

GLOSSARY

inlaid ... colours (l.9): with lovely colours set in it

interpose (l.10): come between them

nebulae (l.10): mass of gas and dust among the stars, appearing as a bright cloud

evanescent (l.12): quick to disappear

granite (l.12): hard, grey stone

voluptuous (l.15): physically pleasurable

retinue (l.22): helpers and followers

Crammed (l.23): filled too full

stench (l.29): very strong unpleasant smell

They are dark caves. Even when they open towards the sun, very little light penetrates down the entrance tunnel into the circular chamber. There is little to see, and no eye to see it, until the visitor arrives for his five minutes, and strikes a match. Immediately another flame rises in the depths of the rock and moves towards the surface like an imprisoned spirit: the walls of the circular chamber have been most marvellously polished. The two flames approach and strive to unite, but cannot, because one of them breathes air, the other stone. A mirror inlaid with lovely colours divides the lovers, delicate stars of pink and grey interpose, exquisite nebulæ, shadings fainter than the tail of a comet or the midday moon, all the evanescent life of the granite, only here visible. Fists and fingers thrust above the advancing soil – here at last is their skin, finer than any covering acquired by the animals, smoother than windless water, more voluptuous than love. The radiance increases, the flames touch one another, kiss, expire. The cave is dark again, like all the caves. [1] [5] [10] [15]

A Marabar cave had been horrid as far as Mrs Moore was concerned, for she had nearly fainted in it, and had some difficulty in preventing herself from saying so as soon as she got into the air again. It was natural enough: she had always suffered from faintness, and the cave had become too full, because all their retinue followed them. Crammed with villagers and servants, the circular chamber began to smell. She lost Aziz and Adela in the dark, didn't know who touched her, couldn't breathe, and some vile naked thing struck her face and settled on her mouth like a pad. She tried to regain the entrance tunnel, but an influx of villagers swept her back. She hit her head. For an instant she went mad, hitting and gasping like a fanatic. For not only did the crush and stench alarm her; there was also a terrifying echo. [20] [25] [30]

Professor Godbole had never mentioned an echo; it never impressed him, perhaps. There are some exquisite echoes in India; there is the whisper round the dome at Bijapur; there are the long, solid sentences that voyage through the air at Mandu, and return unbroken to their creator. The echo in a Marabar cave is not like these, it is entirely devoid of distinction. Whatever is said, the same monotonous noise replies, and quivers up and down the walls until it is absorbed into the roof. 'Boum' is the sound as far as the human alphabet can express it, or 'bou-oum', or 'ou-boum' – utterly dull. Hope, politeness, the blowing of a nose, the squeak of a boot, all produce 'boum'. Even the striking of a match starts a little worm coiling, which is too small to complete a circle, but is eternally watchful. And if several people talk at once, an overlapping howling noise begins, echoes generate echoes, and the cave is stuffed with a snake composed of small snakes, which writhe independently.

After Mrs Moore all the others poured out. She had given the signal for the reflux. Aziz and Adela both emerged smiling and she did not want him to think his treat was a failure, so smiled too. As each person emerged she looked for a villain, but none was there, and she realized that she had been among the mildest individuals, whose only desire was to honour her, and that the naked pad was a poor little baby, astride its mother's hip. Nothing evil had been in the cave, but she had not enjoyed herself; no, she had not enjoyed herself, and she decided not to visit a second one.

(from *A Passage to India*)

devoid of (l.36): without
quivers (l.37): makes a slight trembling movement
coiling (l.42): twisting round
overlapping (l.43): with louder sounds going over the top of the others
writhe (l.45): twist and turn
reflux (l.48): flowing out

- i) Who or what are the 'lovers' (l.10)?
  ii) What atmosphere does Forster try to create?
  iii) What insights are we given about British-Indian relations?

W.B. Yeats

Byzantium (modern Istanbul) was for W.B. Yeats (see page 252) the symbol of art and eternal man-made creation, as opposed to the natural and sensual world of growth and decay. In the poem 'Sailing to Byzantium' (1927) critics have pointed to a feeling of tension in Yeats's love of the very thing he wishes to leave behind.

GLOSSARY

That . . . (l.1): (Ireland)

salmon-falls (l.4): where a great number of salmon – a large fish with silvery skin – fall down a steep drop in the river, like a waterfall

mackerel (l.4): type of striped sea-fish found in the North Atlantic

commend (l.5): show how worthy

begotten (l.6): caused to be born

sensual (l.7): related pleasurably to the senses

paltry (l.9): small and worthless

tattered (l.10): torn

sages (l.17): wise men; saints

gold mosaic (l.18): (like the mosaic figures in the Church of Hagia Sophia in Byzantium)

perne in a gyre (l.19): going round and round (he asks the saints on the wall to descend in this spinning motion – symbolic of the spinning of fate – to help him enter their eternal state)

artifice (l.24): man-made creation

such . . . awake (l.27–29): ('I have read somewhere that in the Emperor's palace at Byzantium was a tree made of gold and silver, and artificial birds that sang' – Yeats; 'gold enameling' is a golden substance used for decoration)

drowsy (l.29): sleepy

Sailing to Byzantium

That is no country for old men. The young   1
In one another's arms, birds in the trees
– Those dying generations – at their song,
The salmon-falls, the mackerel-crowded seas,
Fish, flesh, or fowl, commend all summer long   5
Whatever is begotten, born, and dies.
Caught in that sensual music all neglect
Monuments of unaging intellect.

An aged man is but a paltry thing,
A tattered coat upon a stick, unless   10
Soul clap its hands and sing, and louder sing
For every tatter in its mortal dress,
Nor is there singing school but studying
Monuments of its own magnificence;
And therefore I have sailed the seas and come   15
To the holy city of Byzantium.

O sages standing in God's holy fire
As in the gold mosaic of a wall,
Come from the holy fire, perne in a gyre,
And be the singing-masters of my soul.   20
Consume my heart away; sick with desire
And fastened to a dying animal
It knows not what it is; and gather me
Into the artifice of eternity.

Once out of nature I shall never take   25
My bodily form from any natural thing,
But such a form as Grecian goldsmiths make
Of hammered gold and gold enameling
To keep a drowsy Emperor awake;
Or set upon a golden bough to sing   30
To lords and ladies of Byzantium
Of what is past, or passing, or to come.

● What does each of these phrases tell us? 'mackerel-crowded seas' (l.4); 'sensual music' (l.7); 'tattered coat upon a stick' (l.10); 'Once out of nature' (l.25)

F. Scott Fitzgerald   For thirteen years from January 1920 the manufacture and sale of alcohol was prohibited in the USA. *The Great Gatsby* (1925) by F. Scott Fitzgerald (see page 277) tells the story of the mysterious Jay Gatsby, whose mansion and fabulous entertainments are financed by the illegal production of alcohol. The narrator is Nick, Gatsby's neighbour.

There was music from my neighbour's house through the summer 1
nights. In his blue gardens men and girls came and went like
moths among the whisperings and the champagne and the stars. At
high tide in the afternoon I watched his guests diving from the
tower of his raft, or taking the sun on the hot sand of his beach 5
while his two motor-boats slit the waters of the Sound, drawing
aquaplanes over cataracts of foam. On weekends his Rolls-Royce
became an omnibus, bearing parties to and from the city between
nine in the morning and long past midnight, while his station
wagon scampered like a brisk yellow bug to meet all trains. And on 10
Mondays eight servants, including an extra gardener, toiled all day
with mops and scrubbing-brushes and hammers and garden-shears,
repairing the ravages of the night before.

Every Friday five crates of oranges and lemons arrived from a
fruiterer in New York – every Monday these same oranges and 15
lemons left his back door in a pyramid of pulpless halves. There
was a machine in the kitchen which could extract the juice of two
hundred oranges in half an hour if a little button was pressed two
hundred times by a butler's thumb.

(from *The Great Gatsby*)

- i) What impression do you have of Gatsby's world?
- ii) What does each of the following phrases suggest? 'like moths' (l.2) 'blue gardens' (l.2)?
- iii) The writer's focus is activity rather than people as individuals. What effect does this have?
- iv) Comment on the literary style.

e.e. cummings

Although e.e. cummings (see page 281) made adventurous experiments with form, the themes of his poetry are more traditional. His 'transcendental' faith in individuality and the freedom of self-reliant man is close to Emerson and Whitman, and his joyful love of nature and hatred of science is reminiscent of the English Romantics.

'O sweet spontaneous'

O sweet spontaneous 1
earth how often have
the
doting

    fingers of 5
prurient philosophers pinched
and
poked

thee
, has the naughty thumb 10
of science prodded
thy

    beauty   .how
often have religions taken
thee upon their scraggy knees 15
squeezing and

buffeting thee that thou mightest conceive
gods
    (but
true 20

to the incomparable
couch of death thy
rhythmic
lover

               25
    thou answerest

them only with
      spring)

GLOSSARY

doting (l.4): which show too much affection and are foolish

prurient (l.6): with an unhealthily strong interest in sex

scraggy (.15): thin and rough

buffeting (l.17): knock sharply and unkindly

couch of death (l.22): secret place for sleep; death-bed

---

   i) What do the words 'prurient' and 'scraggy' tell you of Cummings's views of philosophers and religions?

   ii) Why is 'earth' superior?

   iii) Who (or what) do you think is 'thy rhythmic lover'?

William Carlos Williams (1883–1963)

Willam Carlos Williams was for many years a pediatrician in his home town of Rutherford, New Jersey. In his early days he was a friend of Ezra Pound (see page 256) and his poems were Imagist (page 256) in style. Later, he was critical of so-called 'free verse' and moved to what he called 'Objectivism', writing simple scenes of ordinary American life in warm, casual, everyday language. Each poem expects the reader to concentrate on the significance of the created poem itself and the 'very form it assumes' rather than the poet – who should be 'invisible' – and the occasion which created it. Williams is now sometimes seen as a master of 'Modernism' (see page 259).

The following poem, 'This is Just to Say' (1934), is one of Williams's best-known:

This Is Just to Say

I have eaten   1
the plums
that were in
the icebox

and which   5
you were probably
saving
for breakfast

Forgive me
they were delicious   10
so sweet
and so cold

- i) Can you guess who might be speaking to whom?
  ii) In what way is the poem 'Objectivist'?

William Faulkner (1897–1962)

William Faulkner spent most of his life in what he called his own 'little postage stamp of soil' in Mississippi and wrote powerfully, in an intense, highly rhetorical style, about the decline of the old South into racism and psychological sickness. He frequently experimented with narrative chronology in an attempt to represent time as it is experienced. His novels include *The Sound and the Fury* (1929), the unhappy story of the Compson family, representatives of the old South, told from four different points of view each with its own separate view of reality; *As I Lay Dying* (1930) and *Absalom, Absalom!* (1936). The principal setting of Faulkner's novels is Jefferson, a composite picture of several Mississippi towns. This is the (slightly abridged) opening of the short story 'Dry September' (1931):

Through the bloody September twilight, aftermath of sixty-two rainless days, it had gone like a fire in dry grass – the rumor, the story, whatever it was. Something about Miss Minnie Cooper and a Negro. Attacked, insulted, frightened; none of them, gathered in the barber shop on that Saturday evening where the ceiling fan stirred, without freshening it, the vitiated air, sending back upon them, in recurrent surges of stale pomade and lotion, their own stale breath and odors, knew exactly what had happened.

'Except it wasn't Will Mayes,' a barber said. He was a man of middle age; a thin, sand-colored man with a mild face, who was shaving a client. 'I know Will Mayes. He's a good nigger. And I know Miss Minnie Cooper, too.'

'What do you know about her?' a second barber said.

'Who is she?' the client said. 'A young girl?'

'No,' the barber said. 'She's about forty, I reckon. She aint married. That's why I dont believe –'

'Believe, hell!' a hulking youth in a sweat-stained silk shirt said. 'Wont you take a white woman's word before a nigger's?'

'I dont believe Will Mayes did it,' the barber said. 'I know Will Mayes.'

'Maybe you know who did it, then. Maybe you already got him out of town, you damn niggerlover.'

'I dont believe anybody did anything. I dont believe anything happened. I leave it to you fellows if them ladies that get old without getting married dont have notions that a man cant –'

'Then you are a hell of a white man,' the client said. He moved under the cloth. The youth had sprung to his feet.

'You dont?' he said. 'Do you accuse a white woman of lying?'

The barber held the razor poised above the half-risen client. He did not look around.

'It's this durn weather,' another said. 'It's enough to make a man do anything. Even to her.'

Nobody laughed.

The screen door crashed open. A man stood in the floor, his feet apart and his heavy-set body poised easily. His white shirt was open at the throat; he wore a felt hat. His hot, bold glance swept the group. His name was McLendon. He had commanded troops at the front in France and had been decorated for valor.

'Well.' he said, 'are you going to sit there and let a black son rape a white woman on the streets of Jefferson?'

Butch sprang up again. The silk of his shirt clung flat to his heavy shoulders. At each armpit was a dark halfmoon. 'That's what I been telling them! That's what I –'

'Did it really happen?' a third said. 'This aint the first scare she

1

5

10

15

20

25

30

35

40

GLOSSARY

aftermath (l.1): the result of

vitiated (l.6): weakened

surges (l.7): powerful waves

pomade (l.7): hair-oil

hulking (l.17): big and heavy

durn (l.31): damn (American)

screen door (l.34): an inner door made of net which allows air into the room but keeps insects out

felt (l.36): thick firm cloth made of wool.

decorated (l.38): given an official mark of honour (perhaps a medal)

ever had, like Hawkshaw says. Wasn't there something about a   45
man on the kitchen roof, watching her undress, about a year ago?'

'What?' the client said. 'What's that?' The barber had been slowly
forcing him back into the chair; he arrested himself reclining, his
head lifted, the barber still pressing him down.

McLendon whirled on the third speaker. 'What the hell difference   50
does it make? Are you going to let the black sons get away with it
until one really does it?'

(from *Dry September*)

i) In this passage, what illogicalities do the more extreme racial attitudes expose?
What emotions do they stir in you?

ii) What atmosphere does Faulkner create in the opening paragraph? How does
he achieve it?

Tennessee Williams
(1911–1983)

Tennessee Williams was also born in Mississippi and with Arthur Miller
(b. 1915) brought new life to the American theatre. His first play *The Glass
Menagerie* (1945) is a semi-autobiographical family drama set in St Louis.
Typically, Williams's characters are lonely, guilty and passionate.
Through them we see a brutal world of irrationality and sexual desire – as
well as a sad, defeated past. They are often larger-than-life, dream-like and
unreal, and express their feelings in the vivid poetic rhythms of colloquial
Southern speech.

A Streetcar Named Desire (1947) is set in New Orleans. Blanche Dubois
has fantasies of refinement and grandeur. She is both repelled and
attracted by the animal nature of Stanley Kowalski, married to her gentle
and delicately beautiful sister Stella, five years younger than herself.

BLANCHE: ... A man like that is someone to go out with – once –   1
twice – three times when the devil is in you. But live with? Have
a child by?

STELLA: I have told you I love him.

BLANCHE: Then I *tremble* for you! I just – *tremble* for you. ...   5

STELLA: I can't help your trembling if you insist on trembling!
[*There is a pause.*]

BLANCHE: May I – speak – plainly?

STELLA: Yes, do. Go ahead. As plainly as you want to.

[*Outside, a train approaches. They are silent till the noise subsides.*   10
They are both in the bedroom. Under cover of the train's noise
STANLEY *enters from outside. He stands unseen by the women, holding*
some packages in his arms, and overhears their following conver-
sation. He wears an under-shirt and grease-stained seersucker
pants.]   15

BLANCHE: Well – if you'll forgive me – he's *common*!

STELLA: Why, yes, I suppose he is.

BLANCHE: Suppose! You can't have forgotten that much of our bringing up, Stella, that you just *suppose* that any part of a gentleman's
in his nature! *Not one particle, no!* Oh, if he was just – *ordinary*!   20

Just *plain* – but good and wholesome, but – *no*. There's something downright – *bestial* – about him! You're hating me saying this, aren't you?

STELLA: [*coldly*] Go on and say it all, Blanche.

BLANCHE: He acts like an animal, has an animal's habits! Eats like one, moves like one, talks like one! There's even something – sub-human – something not quite to the stage of humanity yet! Yes, something – ape-like about him, like one of those pictures I've seen in – anthropological studies! Thousands and thousands of years have passed him right by, and there he is – Stanley Kowalski – survivor of the Stone Age! Bearing the raw meat home from the kill in the jungle! And you – *you* here – *waiting* for him! Maybe he'll strike you or maybe grunt and kiss you! That is, if kisses have been discovered yet! Night falls and the other apes gather! There in the front of the cave, all grunting like him, and swilling and gnawing and hulking! His poker night! you call it – this party of apes! Somebody growls – some creature snatches at something – the fight is on! *God!* Maybe we are a long way from being made in God's image, but Stella – my sister – there has been *some* progress since then! Such things as art – as poetry and music – such kinds of new light have come into the world since then! In some kinds of people some tenderer feelings have had some little beginning! That we have got to make *grow*! And *cling* to, and hold as our flag! In this dark march toward whatever it is we're approaching. . . . *Don't* – *don't hang back with the brutes!*

[*Another train passes outside.* STANLEY *hesitates, licking his lips. Then suddenly he turns stealthily about and withdraws through the front door. The women are still unaware of his presence.*]

(from *A Streetcar Named Desire*)

25

30

35

40

45

GLOSSARY

seersucker pants (l.14): light cotton trousers

common (l.16): rough and from a low social class

particle (l.20): little bit

downright (l.22): completely

bestial (l.22): like an animal

anthropological (l.29): relating to the development of the human race

swilling and gnawing and hulking (l.35): drinking, chewing their food, moving heavily and awkwardly

His poker night (l.36): the night he plays the card game poker with his friends

stealthily (l.47): secretly and unseen

- i) What can we assume about Stella's 'bringing up' (l.18)?
- ii) How could you describe Blanche's outburst? What effect does it have on us knowing that Stanley is listening?

Saul Bellow (b. 1915)   Saul Bellow was born in Canada of Russian-Jewish parents but has lived in Chicago – where he was educated – since 1962. His novels focus on lonely, alienated characters in large cities, frequently people of European Jewish descent. Titles include *Henderson the Rain King* (1959), *Mr Sammler's Planet* (1969) and *Humboldt's Gift* (1974). In 1976 Bellow was awarded a Nobel Prize.

Herzog (1964) is about a crisis in the life of Moses Herzog, a professor of history in New York. Herzog's wife has divorced him and gone to live with his best friend. Hearing that they are neglecting his daughter, June, Herzog leaves for Chicago where they live. In the following extract, father and daughter have just visited the Museum of Science and decide to go for lunch.

GLOSSARY

parking lot (l.1): car park (American)

circumspect (l.2): very careful

his Falcon (l.2): (his car)

reckoned with (l.3): taken into account

truck (l.5): lorry (American)

rammed it (l.8): pushed it hard

utility pole (l.8): pole used to support telephone and electrical wires (American)

clutched at (l.9): took hold of

kid (l.10): young person (American slang); (June)

radically (l.13): extremely

losing ground to (l.13): failing to make progress against

numbness (l.14): a feeling of deadness

passing out (l.15): fainting

locomotive (l.17): train

Illinois Central (l.18): (the train-line; Chicago is in the state of Illinois)

blundering (l.19): moving unsteadily

Drive (l.19): street

blots (l.20): spots

dwindled presently (l.20): now grew smaller

iridescent specks (l.20): very small spots of changing colour

pants (l.21): trousers (American)

chill (l.22): cold feeling

Czarist roubles (l.25): money that was used in Russia before 1917 and the collapse of the Tsars

pistol (l.25): hand gun

gotten (l.27): got (American)

Stretched limp (l.33): lying out flat, loosely without strength

cops (l.34): police (slang)

stiff (l.35): rigid

pricking (l.36): feeling of light sharp pain

come to himself (l.38): recover

squad car (l.38): police car (American)

grackles (l.40): type of dark American song bird

flexibly (l.41): in an easy changing movement

Field Museum (l.42): (natural history museum in Chicago)

mummy (l.43): preserved dead body (as in Ancient Egypt)

cellar (l.43): place where things are stored (usually underground)

They left the parking lot carefully enough, Herzog later thought. He was a circumspect driver. But getting his Falcon into the main stream of traffic he should perhaps have reckoned with the long curve from the north on which the cars picked up speed. A little Volkswagen truck was on his tail. He touched the brakes, meaning to slow up and let the other driver pass. But the brakes were all too new and responsive. The Falcon stopped short and the small truck struck it from behind and rammed it into a utility pole. June screamed and clutched at his shoulders as he was thrown forward, against the steering wheel. The kid! he thought; but it was not the kid he had to worry about. He knew from her scream that she was not hurt, only frightened. He lay over the wheel, feeling weak, radically weak; his eyes grew dark; he felt that he was losing ground to nausea and numbness. He listened to June's screams but could not turn to her. He notified himself that he was passing out, and he fainted away.

They spread him out on the grass. He heard a locomotive very close – the Illinois Central. And then it seemed somewhat farther off, blundering in the weeds across the Drive. His vision at first was bothered by large blots, but these dwindled presently to iridescent specks. His pants had worked themselves up. He felt a chill in his legs.

'Where's June? Where's my daughter?' He raised himself and saw her between two Negro policemen, looking at him. They had his wallet, the Czarist roubles and the pistol, of course. There it was. He closed his eyes again. He felt the nausea return as he considered what he had gotten himself into. 'Is she all right?'

'She's okay.'

'Come here, Junie.' He leaned forward and she walked into his arms. As he felt her, kissed her scared face, he had a sharp pain in his ribs. 'Papa lay down for a minute. It's nothing.' But she had seen him lying on this grass. Just pass the new building beyond the Museum. Stretched limp, looking dead, probably, while the cops went through his pockets. His face felt bloodless, hollow, stiff, its sensations intensely reduced, and this frightened him. From the pricking of his hair at the roots he thought it must be turning white all at once. The police were giving him a few minutes to come to himself. The blue light of the squad car flashed, revolving. The driver of the small truck was staring at him, angry. A little beyond, the grackles were walking, feeding, the usual circle of lights working flexibly back and forth about their black necks. Over his shoulder Herzog was aware of the Field Museum. If only I were a mummy in that cellar! he thought.

(from Herzog)

450

i) Whose fault do you think the accident was? Give a reason.
ii) What sort of person do you imagine Herzog to be?
iii) What do the following tell us: 'the Czarist roubles and the pistol' (l.25); 'If only I were a mummy in that cellar' (l.42)?
iv) Where and how does Bellow make us feel that we are 'inside' Herzog and that the 'outside' world is remote?

F(rank) R(aymond) Leavis (1895–1978)

The literary critical tradition of Matthew Arnold (see page 421) concerned itself with the existence of literature in an industrialised society. This tradition was maintained first by T.S. Eliot (see page 260) and then more vehemently by F.R. Leavis, whose personal intensity seemed to stem partly from his feeling that intelligent literary criticism at such a time of cultural crisis was almost impossible. Their criticism focused both on the work of literature itself and, since they regarded literature as the 'consciousness of the age', also on the culture which produced it.

From 1932–1953, the literary review *Scrutiny*, based in Cambridge, was attacked as a renegade enterprise – or ignored – by the university system and the cultural elites on which it frequently declared war. Yet, with the help of Leavis's provocative personality, the review was to exert a powerful influence in education in both Britain and America. Although it emphasised the need for discussion between the various university 'disciplines' (between, for example, specialists in English Literature and History), it was mainly in the sphere of English studies, with its insistence on rigorous, discriminating reading, that the review had its effect.

Extract 1   In this extract from his long essay 'Education and the University' (1943), Leavis examines what he saw as the contemporary cultural 'disease':

GLOSSARY
drift (l.2): tendency
intricacies (l.7): complicated details
ends (l.8): (their purpose)
debility (l.12): weakening
naïve (l.16): inexperienced and too ready to believe
technocratic (l.18): tendency to allow organisations to be controlled by scientific and technical specialists.

American conditions are the conditions of modern civilization, [1]
even if the 'drift' has gone further on the other side of the Atlantic
than on this. On the one hand there is the enormous technical
complexity of civilization, a complexity that could be dealt with
only by an answering efficiency of co-ordination – a co-operative [5]
concentration of knowledge, understanding and will (and 'under-
standing' means not merely a grasp of intricacies, but a perceptive
wisdom about ends). On the other hand, the social and cultural dis-
integration that has accompanied the development of the inhumanly
complex machinery is destroying what should have controlled the [10]
working. It is as if society, in so complicating and extending the
machinery of organization, had incurred a progressive debility of
consciousness and of the powers of co-ordination and control – lost
intelligence, memory and moral purpose. ... The inadequacy to
their function of statesmen and labour-leaders is notorious, de- [15]
pressing and inevitable, and in our time only the very naïve have
been able to be exhilarated by the hopes of revolutionaries. The
complexities being what they are, the general drift has been tech-
nocratic, and the effective conception of the human ends to be
served that accompanies a preoccupation with the smooth running [20]
of the machinery tends to be a drastically simplified one.

(from 'Education and the University')

Extract 2   Here, in their Preface to the book *Dickens the Novelist* (1970), Leavis and his wife, the critic Q.D. Leavis, attack the scholarship industry.

GLOSSARY

ineptness (l.1): silly incompetence

consort (l.2): go together

misrepresentation (l.3): giving a false account (of a writer)

bias (l.5): tendency to be in favour (or against)

insinuating (l.5): making suggestions indirectly

pretentious (l.10): self-important

inward (l.13): close to the mind and spirit

The ineptness of scholars as literary critics is a notorious fact. 1
Essential ignorance can consort with a great deal of scholarly in-
dustry in assembling irrelevant data, and misrepresentation with
interpreting that so-called 'factual matter', owing to a more or less
unconscious bias, and with insinuating, through critical stupidity, 5
false assumptions about the subject's art, character, personality
and history: the subject often becoming a victim. In these respects
the older biographers are much the safest, and even, surprisingly,
the most useful still, for they shared and understood the age of
which they wrote. They are also less pretentious as critics, have no 10
modern psychological jargon, and were more really knowledgeable
in presenting their subjects, as well as more truly respectful and
essentially more inward with them.

(from *Dickens the Novelist*)

●   i) What are some of the things Leavis is 'for' and 'against'?
    ii) How many of his arguments do you agree with?
    iii) His style is sometimes difficult to read. Can you think of any advantages to such a style?

From criticism to critical theory

Another critical approach which advocated close textual criticism was put forward by I.A. Richards (1893–1979) in *Practical Criticism* (1929). Richards aimed to study poetry without being influenced by the author of the poem and his or her reputation. His methods were more obviously philosophic, linguistic and psychological than those of Leavis (who opposed most of the systems of belief coming from such university 'disciplines'). His theory and practice were also more overtly 'scientific' and utilitarian (asking what is 'the use' of poetry). Richards paid great attention to semantics (a branch of linguistics concerned with meaning). He had a great influence on many academics, particularly in the USA, who labelled his approach 'New Criticism'.

With the exception of Coleridge (see page 147), the English have until recently been too pragmatic to be attracted by many critical theories. However, with the decline of the kind of humanist criticism associated with Dr Johnson (see page 373) and Matthew Arnold (see page 421) and indeed with the further reduction in the educated reading public, literary academics have come under the influence of the continental European theorists, particularly with regard to the following ideas:

1. *Structuralism*: deriving from Ferdinand de Saussure (1857–1913) and more recently Roland Barthes (1915–1980). The theory sees literature as a 'system of signification', a structure of signs, the elements of which only have meaning in relation to each other. Consequently, works of literature have no real and independent existence of their own but only obtain significance from their place within the system. As such, the theory challenges the humanist assumption that literature reflects a given reality and is the individual expression of a creative writer.

2. *Deconstruction*: a 'post-structuralist' theory deriving from Jacques Derrida (b. 1930) which aims to show that all texts undermine their own claims to absolute meaning, emphasising that the reader plays an essential part in the production of meaning. Derrida believes all language only has meaning in relation to all other possible meanings in its surrounding system of language. He asks us to 'deconstruct' the literature of the past and reveal the essential paradox at the heart of language. The theory stresses that absolute meaning is an illusion. As such it undermines the whole basis of Western thought and has met with a lot of hostility.

There are also influential advocates of Feminist and Marxist literary criticism.

Harold Pinter (b. 1930) The dramatist Harold Pinter is most noted for his ability to turn the nuances of colloquial speech into 'absurdist' ritual. (The 'theatre of the absurd' is a label used to describe the plays of such writers as Eugene Ionesco, b. 1912, who tried to represent through very odd situations the 'absurdity' of human existence in a meaningless universe.) In Pinter's plays there is often a threatening but comic–erotic atmosphere of mistrust and fear. His characters search for personal identity in a world where betrayal is common and non-communication more significant than communication. Typically, Pinter's dialogue includes cross-talk, silences, repetitions and inconsistencies. His plays include *The Birthday Party* (1958), *The Caretaker* (1960) and *No Man's Land* (1975).

The Homecoming (1965) is a black, Freudian drama. Teddy, an academic working in the USA, has returned with his wife to his North London home. Lenny is one of his brothers; Sam is an uncle.

LENNY: 1
Where's my cheese-roll?

Pause.

**Someone's taken my cheese-roll. I left it there. [*To* SAM.]
You been thieving?**   5
TEDDY: **I took your cheese-roll, Lenny.**

Silence.
SAM *looks at them, picks up his hat and goes out of the front door.*
Silence.

LENNY: **You took my cheese roll?**   10
TEDDY: **Yes.**
LENNY: **I made that roll myself. I cut it and put the butter on. I sliced
a piece of cheese and put it in between. I put it on a plate and I
put it in the sideboard. I did all that before I went out. Now I
come back and you've eaten it.**   15
TEDDY: **Well, what are you going to do about it?**
LENNY: **I'm waiting for you to apologize.**
TEDDY: **But I took it deliberately, Lenny.**

LENNY: You mean you didn't stumble on it by mistake?

TEDDY: No, I saw you put it there. I was hungry, so I ate it.   20

Pause.

LENNY: Barefaced audacity.

Pause.

What led you to be so . . . vindictive against your own brother? I'm
bowled over.   25

Pause.

Well, Ted, I would say this is something approaching the naked
truth, isn't it? It's a real cards on the table stunt. I mean, we're in
the land of no holds barred now. Well, how else can you interpret
it? To pinch your younger brother's specially made cheese roll   30
when he's out doing a spot of work, that's not equivocal, it's
unequivocal.

Pause.

Mind you, I will say you do seem to have grown a bit sulky during
the last six years. A bit sulky. A bit inner. A bit less forthcoming.   35
It's funny, because I'd have thought that in the United States of
America, I mean with the sun and all that, the open spaces, on
the old campus, in your position, lecturing, in the centre of all
the intellectual life out there, on the old campus, all the social
whirl, all the stimulation of it all, all your kids and all that, to   40
have fun with, down by the pool, the Greyhound buses and all
that, tons of iced water, all the comfort of those Bermuda shorts
and all that, on the old campus, no time of the day or night you
can't get a cup of coffee or a Dutch gin, I'd have thought you'd
have grown more forthcoming, not less. Because I want you to   45
know that you set a standard for us, Teddy. Your family looks up
to you, boy, and you know what it does? It does its best to follow
the example you set. Because you're a great source of pride to us.
That's why we were so glad to see you come back, to welcome
you back to your birthplace. That's why.   50

Pause.

No, listen, Ted, there's no question that we live a less rich life
here than you do over there. We live a closer life. We're busy, of
course. Joey's busy with his boxing, I'm busy with my occupation,
Dad still plays a good game of poker, and he does the cooking as   55
well, well up to his old standard, and Uncle Sam's the best chauffeur in the firm. But nevertheless we do make up a unit, Teddy,
and you're an integral part of it. When we all sit round the back-
yard having a quiet gander at the night sky, there's always an
empty chair standing in the circle, which is in fact yours. And so   60
when you at length return to us, we do expect a bit of grace, a bit
of je ne sais quoi, a bit of generosity of mind, a bit of liberality of

GLOSSARY

roll (l.2): small quantity
of bread baked in the
shape of a ball

sideboard (l.14): piece of
furniture, with drawers
and cupboards, kept in
the dining room

stumble on it (l.19): discover
it accidentally

Barefaced audacity: (l.22):
daring in a way which
is rude and shows no
respect

vindictive (l.24): showing
the desire to harm
(when I haven't harmed
you)

bowled over (l.25): very
surprised

cards . . . stunt (l.28):
declaring of your
position

no holds barred (l.29): being
able to say anything
without holding back

pinch (l.30): take without
permission

*not equivocal, it's
unequivocal (l.31):* it can
only be interpreted in
one way, not in different
ways

sulky (l.34): silent and
bad-tempered

inner (l.35): inclined to
think a lot

forthcoming (l.35): ready to
talk

social whirl (l.39): fast and
active social life

Bermuda shorts (l.42):
knee-length short
trousers

poker (l.55): type of card
game

chauffeur (l.56): (Uncle
Sam works as a car
driver)

*you're an integral part of it
(l.58):* you can't be left
out

gander (l.59): look (*informal*)

je ne sais quoi (l.62): (French
expression meaning 'I
don't know what'; used
to suggest something
refined)

spirit, to reassure us. We do expect that. But do we get it? Have we got it? Is that what you've given us?

Pause. 65

TEDDY: Yes.

(from *The Homecoming*)

- i) Typically, Pinter turns an incident as insignificant' as the 'pinching' of a cheese-roll into a crisis full of meaning and menace. What does the incident seem to signify to the two characters?
- ii) Many of the allusions are, in context, rich in connotation. What, for example, are these meant to suggest? 'younger brother's' (l.30); 'empty chair' (l.60)
- iii) How does Pinter create a sense of tension?

Ted Hughes (b. 1930) Ted Hughes's verse is more energetic, less restrained and more self-consciously virile than that of his contemporary, Philip Larkin (see page 313). His poems are frequently set in a mythological, elemental universe rather than a domestic, urban environment. Their subjects are often animals – represented both physically and metaphysically – whose instincts are opposed to civilised human consciousness but close to subrational human behaviour.

In this poem, 'The Harvest Moon', Hughes creates an atmosphere of strangeness and wonder:

The Harvest Moon

The flame-red moon, the harvest moon, 1
Rolls along the hills, gently bouncing,
A vast balloon,
Till it takes off, and sinks upward
To lie in the bottom of the sky, like a gold doubloon. 5

The harvest moon has come,
Booming softly through heaven, like a bassoon.
And earth replies all night, like a deep drum.

So people can't sleep,
So they go out where elms and oak trees keep 10
A kneeling vigil, in a religious hush.
The harvest moon has come!

And all the moonlit cows and all the sheep
Stare up at her petrified, while she swells
Filling heaven, as if red hot, and sailing 15
Closer and closer like the end of the world.

Till the gold fields of stiff wheat
Cry 'We are ripe, reap us!' and the rivers
Sweat from the melting hills.

GLOSSARY

Harvest Moon (title): full moon in autumn when day and night are of equal length

vast (l.3): very large

doubloon (l.5): Spanish gold coin

Booming (l.7): making a deep hollow sound

bassoon (l.7): large woodwind instrument

elms (l.10): large tall trees

vigil (l.11): staying awake at night, as a religious duty

hush (l.11): calmness and silence

petrified (l.14): greatly frightened

swells (l.14): gets bigger

stiff (l.17): rigid

reap (l.18): cut and gather

- i) Which images make the scene seem strange and unusual? Analyse at least two: what makes them unusual?
- ii) Do you like the poem? Why/Why not?

The future At present, most of the well-known British poets avoid big issues and universal generalisations. Their characteristic poetry describes a rather narrow experience in great detail with technical skill, in a detached way without much emotion. Nevertheless, some interesting poems are being written, often by less well-known writers.

This poem, 'Several excuses for having stayed', is from a collection called *Settlement in a School of Whales* (1983) by Roger Nash (b. 1942). Nash was born in Britain but now works in Canada as a teacher of philosophy.

Several excuses for having stayed

I knew I just shouldn't stay. But the butter 1
in her eyes melted over my shoes
when I started to walk away. Then the gate
fumbled free from under my hand
and went to earth in the rockery. 5

I knew I shouldn't step in. The empty
sofa creaked like a snare. There was a flash
of gunshots from her hair as the light
ricocheted around it; and geese
in the print on the wall took faded flight. 10

I knew I shouldn't sit down. But each pear
on the table stuttered its speckles of brown,
anxious for conversation. Her smile
laced my shoes together, while the sun
pulled me up the glint on a chair. 15

I knew I shouldn't sit near. But the guitar
on the radio borrowed my hand to steer
glittering chords through her hair. Light
wouldn't let us out of its sight.
Each beam brought pans on the wall 20

to brass crescendos. The kitchen was caught
in the fevered throat of a constricted trumpet.
Its sides gleamed in and flared us together.
We knew we just shouldn't stay. But the sun
wouldn't stop to let us get away. 25

GLOSSARY

fumbled free (l.4): fell down and I failed to stop it

went to earth (l.5): landed

rockery (l.5): rocks laid out in a garden with plants growing between them

snare (l.7): animal trap

richocheted (l.9): made sharp changes of direction

stuttered (l.12): moved unevenly; had difficulty in speaking

speckles (l.12): small irregular marks

laced (l.14): fastened

glint (l.15): flash of reflected light

steer (l.17): direct

chords (l.18): sets of musical notes sounded together

crescendos (l.21): passages (of music) which get increasingly loud

constricted (l.22): which made a tight, narrow sound

flared us (l.23): burnt us brightly

- i) Who do you imagine 'her' is (l.2)?
- ii) How would you describe the narrator's images? Give an example. How does it create its effect?

456

This poem 'Greeting the Ice-Cold Day', is by Peter Abbs, from his collection *For Man and Islands* (1978):

Greeting the Ice-Cold Day

Last night as we lay undressed   1
Wind-locked
              like half-fallen tress pressed
Together, cold
Winter came and boldly   5
Hugged and caressed this beautiful and
Ancient body of Wales.

Today I wander in the garden
Dazed. How
              she has changed!   10
Her tips white. Her curls white – and
Over her bare thighs, her
Dishevelled dress, such a slender
Cobweb of shadows,
Such tender patches of shade!   15

And, as if there was invisible accord
Between us,
I greet this ice-cold day.

GLOSSARY

Wind-locked (l.2): held together by the wind
Dishevelled (l.13): network
accord (l.16): agreement

- i) Who do you think 'she' (l.10) refers to?
- ii) What scene is evoked?
- iii) Which of the last two poems do you prefer? Why?

Key

1.1.4   Greenland; Iceland; Faeroe Islands; Shetland Islands; Newfoundland; Orkney Islands

1.3.2   In Malory's *Morte D'Arthur*, companionship is symbolised by the Round Table. When seated round it all the knights were equal, although a special place was reserved for the knight who found the Holy Grail (the cup used by Christ before his death). The Wars of the Roses, and the resulting misery and confusion, destroyed this harmony and, in effect, marked the end of medieval England, even though Malory managed to keep such reality at a distance by a kind of aristocratic remoteness and a tone of romantic fantasy.

The Wars of the Roses were civil wars between the Houses of York and Lancaster, two junior branches of the Plantagenets, the great medieval royal family. They took place between 1455 and 1485. The name of the wars came from the emblems the families chose: the Lancastrians chose the red rose, the Yorkists the white rose. The immediate cause of the wars was to do with who should be King of England. Although the Lancastrian Henry IV was on the throne, having seized it from his cousin Richard II, the Yorkists thought they had the better claim. The disagreement broke into open war after the drop in Lancastrian prestige when England was finally defeated in France in 1453 at the end of the Hundred Years War. At this point social causes become important: power in England was in the hands of rich, self-interested nobles, whose energies were no longer taken up by the war abroad and who tried instead to dominate the government at home. Also a mass of unemployed soldiers was suddenly let loose upon England. The towns tended to be Yorkist and the rural areas Lancastrian. The Wars of the Roses were felt to be both useless and evil by the majority of the nation. They were finally brought to an end by the House of Tudor bringing its members great respect. Reconciliation was symbolised by the Tudor emblem of the combined red and white rose and the marriage of Henry Tudor on the Lancastrian side (Henry VII) with Elizabeth York, daughter of Edward IV.

After the Wars, the medieval nobility was much weakened and discredited, thus bringing to an end an era of feudalism. Under the Tudor sovereigns, men of lesser family rose to the nobility and it is from them that most of the aristocratic families of modern England, such as the Cecils and the Russells, are descended. The reign of the Tudor queen Elizabeth I (1558–1603) was haunted by the fear that the civil wars might return since she, like Richard II, had no direct heirs.

1.6   **A:** i) Excalibur   ii) a division in a line of poetry, in which there is usually a stressed syllable and a number of unstressed syllables   iii) the Tabard   iv) in a fire   v) 1066
B: i) Geoffrey and Thomas   ii) Boccaccio   iii) AD 991   iv) he seized King Arthur's kingdom   v) a tribe of Germanic origin who conquered southeast Britain

2.7   1 gown   2 Cromwell   3 Lepidus   4 Tottell   5 Timon   6 Boleyn   7 Actium   8 Erasmus   9 awry   10 Grey

3.5   fable; simile; allegory; elegy; sonnet; couplet; metaphor; enjambment; assonance; rhythm; lyric; hyperbole; verse; epic; essay; alliteration; irony

4.9   Samuel; 1666; houses were blown up to make gaps thus preventing the fire from spreading; Oliver Goldsmith; Dryden died a Catholic; the 'machinery' were supernatural agents; an heroic couplet is a pair of rhymed lines of verse with ten syllables and five stresses in each line; the Baron cut off the lock of hair with a pair of scissors; Swift was Dean of Dublin Cathedral; John Locke was a 'natural philosopher'; a picaresque novel contains a series of episodes in which the often daring hero is forced to seek his fortune outside of stable society; Squire Allworthy or Squire Western; Charles Lamb; Jeremy is Valentine's servant; the 'humours' were phlegm, blood, choler and black bile; the Petitioners were later called 'Whigs'; Charles Stuart (Bonnie Prince Charlie) was the Young Pretender

5.1.2   Poem A is by George Crabbe, Poem B by John Clare.

5.8   1789: Storming of the Bastille; 1793: Louis XVI executed; 1804: Napoleon made emperor; 1805: Battle of Trafalgar; 1814: Napoleon deposed; 1815: Battle of Waterloo

7.11   Marlowe; Shakespeare; Wilde; Sterne; Marvell; James; Johnson. The other surname is Whitman.

8.10.5   **Tapescript**: Black slaves were originally brought into Virginia as early as 1619. From then on they came in increasing numbers. Although some were brought in the early days from the West Indies, most came directly from Africa. In 1863, during the Civil War, President Abraham Lincoln ended slavery, freeing more than four million blacks. From 1865–1877, during the period of re-adjustment following the war, known as the Reconstruction, blacks were theoretically able to compete with whites for a place in American society. However, particularly in the South, where they were mainly located on tobacco and cotton plantations, violent attempts were made to keep blacks from political, social or economic equality.

White educational centres were unofficially closed to blacks. However, in 1881 Booker T. Washington, a black educator, was chosen to organise an industrial black school, emphasising industrial training as a means to self-respect and economic independence. This idea was attacked by the black civil rights leader W. E. B. Du Bois for being too conciliatory and an attempt to conform to white society.

Considerable emigration from the South did not occur until World War I when there was increased demand for black labour in northern factories. A growing population outside the South tended to congregate in cities, particularly in New York, where there grew up the black centre of Harlem, which in the 'Jazz Age' of the 1920s became famous for its musical reviews containing negro performers. During the Depression, in their poverty, blacks found a new militancy and made common cause with their white fellows in the trade union movement.

In 1954, a Supreme Court decision against segregation in education led to a stronger and more effective struggle for civil rights and economic advancement. In the fifties and sixties, a black Protestant Minister, Martin Luther King, led a movement based on passive resistance and tried to unite with the white progressive parties. His assassination in 1968 marked the beginning of 'Black Power', a black separatist movement which opposed whites through violent uprisings in the big-city ghettos. Although in 1980 blacks formed 11.7 per cent of the population of the U.S.A, racial prejudice has not disappeared.

In 19th century American literature, the Negro was mainly a humorous, pathetic figure, associated with the Southern plantations. In contemporary literature, blacks are highly active, often aggressive and sometimes violent, and are usually based in the urban north. Much black literature, however, shows the duality of blacks wanting to assimilate themselves into American society, but at the same time determined to preserve their distinctive culture, the colourful slang of urban street life and the rhythms of the blues and the spirituals.

Major Works in Black Literature

1903: *The Souls of Black Folk* by W. E. B. Du Bois (1868–1963), a sociological description of the effects of white American prejudice on the minds of the blacks.

Du Bois uses the idea of the single 'nation' of blacks; in the thirties he becomes interested in Africa as the spiritual home of blacks.

1922: *Dream Variations* (1922), a collection of poems by the Harlem writer, Langston Hughes, inspired by jazz and the blues. They helped to give voice to the 'Negro Renaissance' (a flowering of black literature in the twenties) and bring a new honesty to black literature.

1923: *Cane* by Jean Toomer (1894–1967) combines poems and short stories. It is noted in part for its twenties-style verbal experimentation.

1925: *Yet Do I Marvel* by Countee Cullen (1903–1925), a collection of poems expressing the wish to be more than just a black poet, more a poet for mankind.

1938: *Uncle Tom's Children* by Richard Wright (1908–1960) gives a naturalistic, but angry, description of the violence of Southern whites towards blacks.

1952: *Invisible Man* by Ralph Ellison (b. 1914), the most famous novel of black American literature (see p. 308)

1953: *Go Tell It on the Mountain* by James Baldwin (1924–1987) a vividly autobiographical story about a fifteen-year-old boy's search for religious salvation, set in Harlem. Much of Baldwin's later writing in the sixties reflects black anger.

1964: *Dutchman* by LeRoi Jones, a symbolic play about a black man and a white woman. In his poems Jones demands 'poems that kill'. In the fifties he was close to the 'Beat' movement.

1965: *Autobiography of Malcolm X* by Alex Haley (b. 1921), a description of the spiritual growth of Malcolm X, the black revolutionary leader.

1968: *Malcolm X* by Gwendolyn Brooks (b. 1917), a poem which uses sexual images to describe the man.

1983: *The Color Purple*, a novel by Alice Walker (b. 1944), the feminist poet and novelist, now made into a film (see p. 310).

8.14   i) Allegory: *Pilgrim's Progress*;

ii) Enjambment: 'I am fire and air; my other elements
I give to baser life...' *Antony and Cleopatra*

iii) Simile: 'The barge she sat in like a burnished throne' *Antony and Cleopatra*

iv) Irony: the opening sentence of *Pride and Prejudice* (see p. 132)

v) Iambic pentameter; 'Was this the face that launched a thousand ships'
Dr Faustus

vi) Alliteration: 'A slumber did my spirit seal' (Wordsworth)

vii) Personification: 'Purple the sails, and so perfumed that
The winds were love-sick with them.' *Antony and Cleopatra*

viii) Sonnet: 'Since brass, nor stone, nor earth, nor boundless sea' (see p. 337)

ix) Hyperbole: 'The crown o' th' earth doth melt' *Antony and Cleopatra*

x) Caesura: 'Within a rock cave, / its usual home' (Wordsworth's *Prelude*)

Supplement 7:   Meredith: It was Chloe's body.

Index of Authors/Titles

463

Index of Terms *for primary references/definitions*

Topic Index

Topic Map

Prologue
B: Mother and child (Parents, Birth)
C: Loneliness (Old Age); Love
D: Men and Women
Getting ready: Winter

UNIT 1

1.1.1   Fighting (Heroism) (War and Peace)
1.1.3   Character Description; Fables (Tricks)
1.3.1   Dreams; Legends (Death)

UNIT 2

2.1.1   Desertion
2.1.2   Love
2.2.1   Suicide (Death)
2.2.5   Love (Death)
2.4.2   Language (Education); Teaching (Education)

UNIT 3

3.1.1   Farewells; Religion (Sin)
3.1.3   Peace
3.2.1   Character Description
3.2.2   Character Description
3.3.1   Character Description
3.3.5   Religion (Nature)
3.3.7   Freedom

UNIT 4

4.1.1   Disasters (London)
4.2.1   Satire
4.4.1   Satire (Vanity)
4.5.1   Satire
4.6.1   Isolation
4.6.2   Disputes (Drinking); Gallantry (Sex, Desire)
4.6.3   Birth
4.7.1   Comedy (Money)

UNIT 5

5.1.1   Society (Freedom)
5.1.2   A: Nature; B: Identity (Misery)
5.2.1   Marriage (Comedy)
5.2.2   Love (Secrets)
5.3.1   Childhood (Fear); Literary Criticism; Death
5.5.1   Character Description; The Future (Childhood); The Sea (Sin)
5.6.1   Executions; Forgiveness (Family)
5.7.2   Permanence (Identity, Imagination, Animals and Birds) Belief
5.7.3   Imagination; Nature; Nature (Animals and Birds); Death (Heroism); Literary Criticism (Poetry)

5.7.4   Death (The Sea); Death; Change; Money (Generosity)

UNIT 6

6.2.1   Character Description; Secrets; Nature (Guilt); Secrets (Childhood)
6.2.2   Character Description
6.3.1   Work
6.4.1   Death (Misery)
6.4.2   Death (Love)
6.6.2   Guilt (Sin)
6.6.3   Freedom (Individuality; Character Description); Death; Identity
6.6.4   Death
6.7.1   Marriage (Men and Women)
6.7.2   Love
6.8.1   Evolution

UNIT 7

7.1.2   Race (Childhood); Race; Race (Character Description)
7.2.1   Work (Art)
7.2.3   Love (Fantasy)
7.2.4   Fantasy
7.4.1   Nature
7.5.1   Art
7.5.3   Art; Pleasure; Class (Comedy); Crime; Character Description
7.6.1   Colonialism (Race); Race (Poverty); Nature; Race
7.7.1   Marriage
7.8   War and Peace; Death
7.9.2   War and Peace
7.9.4   War and Peace
7.9.5   War and Peace; Death

UNIT 8

8.1.1   The Future
8.1.3   Youth; Poetry
8.1.5   Cities; Birth; Poetry; Tradition; Literary Criticism
8.2.1   Time (Nature); Animals and Birds; Men and Women; Birth
8.2.2   Visions
8.2.3   Houses
8.4.1   Luxury (Wealth); Wealth
8.4.3   Patriotism (Family)
8.4.4   Rain (Love)
8.6.1   Rain (Poverty)
8.7.1   The Future (Science Fiction); The Future (Science Fiction; Childhood); The Future (Family)
8.7.2   The Future (Science Fiction)
8.7.4   Suffering
8.8   War and Peace (Patriotism)

468

Acknowledgements

We are grateful to the following for permission to reproduce copyright material;

the author, Peter Abbs for his poem 'Greeting the Ice Cold Day' from *For Man & Islands* (Tern Press, 1978); Edward Arnold for extracts from *A Passage to India* by E M Forster; the author's agent for an extract from *Herzog* by Saul Bellow (Weidenfield & Nicolson Ltd); The Bodley head on behalf of the author's Estate & Charles Scribner's Sons, an imprint of Macmillan Publishing Co, for extracts from 'The Diamond as Big as the Ritz' by F Scott Fitzgerald in *The Bodley Head F Scott Fitzgerald & Tales of the Jazz Age*. US copyright 1922 by Charles Scribner's Sons, renewed copyright 1950 by Frances Scott Fitzgerald Lanahan; Jonathan Cape Ltd on behalf of the author's Estate & Henry Holt & Co, Inc for the poem 'Stopping by Woods on a Snowy Evening' by Robert Frost from *The Poetry of Robert Frost* edited by Edward Connery Lathem, US copyright 1923 by Holt, Rinehart & Winston, renewed 1951 by Robert Frost; Jonathan Cape Ltd on behalf of the Executors of the author's Estate & The Society of Authors as literary representative of the author's Estate for an extract from *Portrait of the Artist as a Young Man* by James Joyce; Carcanet Press Ltd for the poem 'This Is Just To Say' by William Carlos Williams from *Collected Poems 1909–1939* edited by A Walton Litz & C MacGowan; Chatto & Windus on behalf of Mrs Laura Huxley for extracts from *Brave new World* by Aldous Huxley; Joan Daves for an extract from 'I Have A Dream' speech by Martin Luther King, Jr. Copyright (c) 1963 by Martin Luther King, Jr; Faber & Faber Ltd for the poem 'Musee de Beaux Arts' from *Collected Poems* by W H Auden, extracts from 'Tradition & the Individual Talent' & 'Hamlet', abridged extracts from 'The Metaphysical Poets' & 'The Function of Criticism' from *Selected Essays* by T S Eliot, an extract from 'Reflections on Vers Libre' from *To Criticize the Critic* by T S Eliot, the poems 'Prelude 2', 'Prelude 4' & 'Journey of the Magi' from *Collected Poems 1909–1962* by T S Eliot, a slightly adapted extract from 'The Battle of Maldon' from *A Choice of Anglo-Saxon Verse* translated by Richard Hamer, the poem 'Love Songs in Age' from *The Whitsun Weddings* by Philip Larkin, an extract from *Look Back In Anger* by John Osborne & the poems 'A Girl' & 'Commission' from *Collected Shorter Poems* by Ezra Pound; Faber & Faber Ltd & Viking Penguin, Inc, a division of Penguin Books USA, Inc for the poem 'The Harvest Moon' from *Season Songs* by Ted Hughes, text copyright (c) 1968, 1973, 1975 by Ted Hughes; Grafton Books, a division of the Collins Publishing Group, & Liveright Publishing Corporation for the poems 'O sweet spontaneous' from *Complete Poems 1913–1962* by E E Cummings & *Tulips & Chimneys* by E E Cummings, edited by George James Firmage. Copyright 1923, 1925 & renewed 1951, 1953 by E E Cummings. Copyright (c) 1973, 1976 by the Trustees for the E E Cummings Trust. Copyright (c) 1973, 1976 by George James Firmage & 'my sweet old etcetera' in *Complete Poems 1913–1962* by E E Cummings & *IS 5* poems by E E Cummings, edited by George James Firmage. Copyright (c) 1985 by E E Cummings Trust. Copyright (c) 1926 by Horace Liveright. Copyright (c) 1954 by E E Cummings. Copyright (c) 1985 by George James Firmage; William Heinemann Ltd for extracts from *The Grapes of Wrath* by John Steinbeck; The Hogarth Press on behalf of the Executors of the author's Estate for an extract from *To The Lighthouse* by Virginia Woolf; the author's agent for the poem 'One Flesh' from *Collected Poems* by Elizabeth Jennings; Longman Group UK Ltd for an abridged extract from *Longman Companion to English Literature* by Christopher Gillie (1972); Methuen & Co Ltd, London, for an extract from *The Homecoming* by Harold Pinter; the author, Roger Nash for his poem 'Several Excuses for Having Stayed' from *Settlement in a School of Whales* (Brynmill Press Ltd/Fiddlehead Press); New Directions Publishing Corporation for an extract from *A Streetcar Named Desire* by Tennesse Williams, copyright 1947 by Tennessee Williams; W W Norton & Co, Inc for extracts from *The Norton Anthology of English Literature* (W W Norton, 1979); the author's agent on behalf of the Estate of the late Sonia Brownwell Orwell for extracts from *Nineteen Eighty Four* by George Orwell (Martin Secker & Warburg Ltd) & 'England Your England' from *Selected Essays* by George Orwell (Penguin Books Ltd, 1957); Penguin Books Ltd for a slightly adapted extract from *The Pelican Guide to English Literature: The Age of Chaucer* edited by Boris Ford (Penguin Books Ltd, 1954, 1959, 1969, 1982), copyright (c) Boris Ford & John Spiers, 1954, 1959, 1969, 1982; Penguin Books Ltd & the author. Allen Ginsberg for the poem 'Uptown' from *Collected Poems 1947–1980* by Allen Ginsberg (Viking, 1985), copyright (c) Allen Ginsberg, 1984; The Society of Authors as the representative of the Literary Trustees of Walter de la Mare for the poem 'The Ghost' by Walter de la Mare; The Society of Authors on behalf of the Bernard Shaw Estate for an extract from *Saint Joan* by George Bernard Shaw; the author's